THE ATHEIST VIEWPOINT

THE ATHEIST VIEWPOINT

Advisory Editor:
Madalyn Murray O'Hair

Fifty Years of Freethought

BY GEORGE E. MACDONALD

[Volumes I & II]

ARNO PRESS & THE NEW YORK TIMES
New York / 1972

Reprint Edition 1972 by Arno Press Inc.

LC#   76-161334
ISBN 0-405-03793-7

The Atheist Viewpoint
ISBN for complete set: 0-405-03620-5
See last pages of this volume for titles.

Manufactured in the United States of America

Fifty Years of
Freethought

EDWARD TUCK, 1931.

Fifty Years of Freethought

BEING THE STORY OF *THE TRUTH SEEKER*, WITH THE NATURAL HISTORY OF ITS THIRD EDITOR

BY GEORGE E. MACDONALD

VOLUME I

Parts First and Second

NEW YORK:

THE TRUTH SEEKER COMPANY

1929

To the Readers

of

The Truth Seeker.

Not adventitious therefore will the wise man regard the faith which is in him. The highest truth he sees he will fearlessly utter; knowing that, let what may come of it, he is thus playing his right part in the world. . . .

—HERBERT SPENCER (*First Principles, Par.* 34).

PREFACE

THIS is the book of George Macdonald, hand, head and heart. It tells of his life and activities, first as a farm boy, later as a laborer in the vineyard of Freethought. For upwards of fifty years he has been a part of that movement, at once the oldest and the newest, which seeks to make clear the truth that the melioration of man's condition—progress of any kind, in any degree—lies in reliance upon his own powers of reason and initiative, in nowise upon dispensation and authority.

George E. Macdonald's own life peculiarly exemplifies this. Scarcely anybody ever gave him anything, except an opportunity to work. From his earliest years there has always been something for George to do. How well he has done it shows in the vigorous survival of the paper upon which he has been engaged for half a century, a period during which journals of opinion have fallen leaf-like in shriveled hosts.

The Truth Seeker, like its editor, is hale and hearty. Subscribers stoutly and repeatedly assure the one that the other is "better than ever." This, perhaps, is what accounts for the slight flush always to be found upon his cheeks and which beams forth again as the rays of a genial sun. The humor of The Truth Seeker is proverbial and has as much to do with its popularity as its more solid qualities.

The chapters which follow appeared serially in The Truth Seeker during 1928 and 1929. The paper's files for fifty years back record the history of Freethought in detail, a moving pageant in which its three editors take active and prominent parts. The present editor's life is so inextricably bound up with this journal's history as not to be separated from it without damage to the account. This circumstance only has moved him to include in the story of The Truth Seeker somewhat of him hitherto known as "We."

This work is intended to afford a reliable surview of the Rationalist movement in the United States for fifty years onward from 1875. That was the author's chief purpose in undertaking it. Its production has occupied all of the editor's spare time for nearly two years. For foundation he applied himself to the rereading of the fifty-five bound volumes of The Truth Seeker, light calisthenics for a man in his eighth decade. An equally valuable repository has been his mortmain memory, unassisted by diary or notes. A considerable correspondence, carried on without secretarial aid, was a third source. The subsigned, privileged to be his amanuensis in the preparation of the book, can certify that into it went enthusiasm and application, both unflagging, in equal parts.   B. R.

PART FIRST
THE MINORITY OF ONE

CONTENTS

CHAPTER I—Sullivan, N. H.—A Soldier's Son—Quaker and Scriptural Antecedents—My Mother—A Recruit for Lincoln............................ 11

CHAPTER II—Surry—Echoes from the Schoolroom—Girl Invaders—My Life's One Scandal............ 27

CHAPTER III—My Uncle Clem—Books and Minstrelsy—I Go Out to Work—A Woman of Simple Speech—Surry South End........................ 46

CHAPTER IV—The Traveler's Ghost—Moving On—I Am Oppressed—East Westmoreland—Pat Advises Me About Churches............................... 65

CHAPTER V—The Deacon and I—Albert Chickering—Remarks on Bundling—Brother of the Ox—My Station Rises 83

CHAPTER VI—The Girl Intrudes—Rural New Hampshire—The Puritans—"New Morals for Old"—Language—Christmas Not Observed.................... 105

CHAPTER VII—I Take Leave of the Invisibles—How I Came to New York—The Truth Seeker and D. M. Bennett.................................... 131

CHAPTER VIII—Amongst the Idealists—An Adventure of Which I Am the Mid-Victorian Hero—Milady Agatha—Through with Women............. 150

CHAPTER IX—Bennett's Wealth of Words—I First Behold Ingersoll—The Paine Habit Formed—Grant's Message to Congress............................ 167

CHAPTER X—Life in The Truth Seeker Office—Arrest Comes to Mr. Bennett—Doris—Through with Women—Friends 185

CHAPTER XI—Guests at 308 Third Avenue—Hilda—Catholic and Freethinking Girls—Anyhow, I Was Through with Women—The Bennett Prosecutions—Split in the Liberal League—Who Was Who in 1878?. 206

CHAPTER XII—The Jailing of D. M. Bennett—In Albany Penitentiary—What the Cat Brought In—"New England and the People Up There".......... 243

CHAPTER XIII—Organizing a Political Party—State Gatherings—Bennett Liberated—The Character of A. Comstock 264

CHAPTER XIV—Putnam Coming Forward—The Inspired Assassin of Garfield—I Join the Nonpareils.. 292

CHAPTER XV—Religions on Trial with Guiteau—Ingersoll's Memorial Day Address—Herndon and Lincoln—Bennett Around the World and Home—Death and a Monument................................... 306

CHAPTER XVI—I Am Assistant Editor—Man with the Badgepin—Monsignor Capel—The Truth Seeker Company 332

CHAPTER XVII—Life in Third Avenue—Spiritualists as Secularists—Chainey Converted—Blaine and Burchard 352

CHAPTER XVIII — Giordano Bruno — Feminists—Amrita Lal Roy—The Dynamiters—Death Among the Veterans—I Interview Ingersoll—The Haymarket Bomb—Henry George's Canvass..................... 371

CHAPTER XIX—Economic and Labor Situation—Dr. McGlynn—Liberal, Mo.—The Lucifer Match—Death of S. P. Andrews................................... 393

CHAPTER XX—Lecturers in the Field—Chicago Anarchists Hanged—Reynolds Blasphemy Trial—Mrs. Slenker's Arrest—A "Globe" Story.................. 415

CHAPTER XXI—San Francisco—A Historic Printing Office—Getting Married—Death of Courtlandt Palmer—A Temblor 435

CHAPTER XXII—San Francisco Continued—Organization and Lectures—Advent of Bellamy—Topolobampo—Death of Horace Seaver.................... 470

CHAPTER XXIII—Local Meetings— Observations on the State—Henry Replogle—A Lick Incident—The Chinese Press—Prophecies of Disaster—An Infant Son 496

CHAPTER XXIV—Putnam in Sacramento—James Barry of The Star—Deaths: Bradlaugh, James Parton, J. R. Monroe—Freethought Suspends.......... 524

FIFTY YEARS OF
FREETHOUGHT

CHAPTER I.

1—I APPEAR.

W ITH the consent of the reader, my story
shall begin where and when I did, which
was in Gardiner, Maine, April 11, 1857.
It was the year they discovered the Neanderthal

CONTEMPORARIES

man. My father, (Patrick) Henry Macdonald (b.
Oct. 14, 1825), was known to all his acquaintances
and to the check-list as Henry, since early in life he
had dropped the Patrick—though remembering

"Give me liberty or give me death"—as calculated to furnish a wrong clue to his ancestry, which was Scotch, and to his religion, which was not Catholic. As to personality, his comrades in war and other scrapes told me that although not a big man, he was "able"; that, in fact, few men of his inches, unless "scienced," had any business to stand before him. Through this heredity, I early became seized of a deep respect for ability and science. A mechanic and millwright was Henry, and when I first learned to recognize him he was running a sawmill for Lanmon Nims on a small stream in East Sullivan, N. H., where he had lately come, with his wife and two boys, from Maine.

Sullivan is among the least of towns, difficult to find or to recognize as a town when discovered; but she has a mighty history—on paper. One of her sons, the Rev. Josiah Lafayette Seward, D. D., wrote that history in two weighty volumes comprising 1619 octavo pages, capacious enough to contain a fair history of the civilized world ancient and modern. Everybody who lived in Sullivan from 1777 to 1917 is named in those tomes. My father, a resident of Sullivan at the breaking out of the Civil War, enlisting in Company E. 6th regiment, New Hampshire volunteers, moved to Keene, the county seat, for convenience to the fair grounds where the troops were drilled. He went to the front in December, 1861, and fell in the second battle of Bull Run the following August. I possess as relics of him a leather wallet with a strap that goes all the way around it, and through loops; a letter (undated) in a fair round hand, sent from the front to my brother, in which "we" is consistently spelled with two *e's;* and a glazed earthenware container for liquids made in the shape of a book but with a mouth and stopper (for the bottle was contraband in Maine as early as 1850). I have put a book label on it and marked it a best seller. (In his spelling of "wee" he merely may have been old-fashioned. His fathers spelled it that way before him.) I know little else about my father, except that his mother's name was Rebecca. My brother once met that old lady, whom I suppose to have been Scotch, and reported her speech to be so different from any he had ever heard that he could hardly understand her. He called the peculiarity of accent a "brogue"; it was probably a "burr." The name Macdonald was pronounced in our family as though the first syllable were spelled muck and the second one dough. The war records have it that Henry was a native of Palermo, Me., and that his father is unknown.

2—A SOLDIER'S LETTER.

In 1887, when I took a vacation in New Hampshire, my cousin's wife, Addie Chickering Clement, handed me a letter, found among his father's papers, which she thought I should have if it interested me. Thus the writing ran:

"An account of the death of Henry Macdonald, who enlisted in Company E, 6th Regiment, New Hampshire Volunteers, and fell at the second Battle of Bull Run (Virginia), August the 28th, 1862, in the War of the Great Rebellion. He was 36 years of age, having been born October the 14th, 1825.

"*By a Comrade.*

"FRIEND CLEMENT: You have probably heard various

accounts of our battle in the woods, where we suffered so severely; so I will attempt no description except of Macdonald's death. I was by his side; or, rather, we were facing each other, he with his left side to the enemy. We had fired, and were loading. We had reserved our fire somewhat, trying to see a good mark to sight. He fired first. After firing I stepped back close to him. He said, 'Did you see him?' I answered, 'Yes.' Said he, 'So did I.' The words were scarcely spoken, when Almon Nutting, who was forward, was struck on the head by a ball, inflicting a serious wound. At the same instant Macdonald was hit just forward of the top of the ear, the ball passing squarely through the head, and coming out on the other side at the spot opposite. He fell on his back, his eyes set. He did not speak or recognize me. The wound bled very fast. He suffered none, and passed away feeling not the pains of death, nor its fears. He was as cool, and spoke as calmly, as though we had been shooting squirrels. I think it was the ball which wounded Nutting that killed him, as both were struck at the same moment.

"After speaking to Nutting, I was obliged to leave, the regiment having moved forward and left us behind. I had no time to save Macdonald's money, or the clothing upon him. Indeed, the chance of my coming out myself was so small I did not think to do it. When we returned, it was by a different route, and on the double-quick, so he fell into the hands of the enemy, who were careful to carry away everything except the clothes. The shoes they took, if good. He was probably buried by our men, who went back for that purpose with a flag of truce. There will be no means of identifying the spot. His knapsack, with contents, was left behind.   H. Towne."

The letter, which bore no date, appears to have been written soon after the "battle in the woods" (second Bull Run), August 28-29, 1862. The writer was Hosea Towne, afterwards appointed postmaster at Marlow, N. H.

This my father's picture is drawn from a painting executed about 1880 by Madam Gherardi, sister of the admiral of that name. It was done out of her affection for soldiers. For "copy" Madam Gherardi had an 1861 tintype, now lost; and tintypes are like a reflection in a mirror, an offset, which faces the subject the other way. That is why this soldier is shown in an improper position for one standing at parade-rest, with his right hand next the muzzle of his piece and the right foot advanced.

He was of that whiskered generation raised up before the Civil War and enduring so long after its close that we discover facial foliage on the earlier professional baseball players. Gradual modification by way of chin shaving, leaving only sidewhiskers and moustache, produced the clean-shaven soldier of the World war.

3—"THE UNRETURNING BRAVE."

Sullivan's memorial to her "unreturning brave," as described in a pamphlet "printed at the New Hampshire Sentinel Job Office, 1867," is "of the best Italian marble, and is very beautiful in design and finish. It stands near the meeting-house, on a spot fitted up with much labor and expense. The mound on which it stands is elevated eight feet above the level of the common, and the monument rises fifteen feet above the mound. The base is a three and a half feet square."

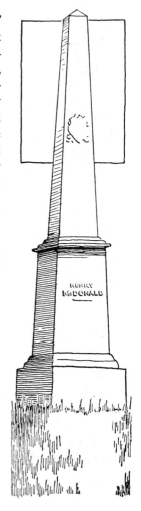

The name of Henry Macdonald, spelled McDonald, is at the top of the list on the front of the shaft. He may, then, have been the first of the unreturning brave of the Civil War whose name was thus preserved on a town monument.

The history of Sullivan in the Chesire County Gazetteer, 1736-1885, says of its soldiers who died: "All were honest, respectable, industrious, and reliable young men. There was no exception to this statement." Father lived only half the span the Bible allots to man, while I have been living on borrowed time ever since I began this history of the True Macdonald. But he missed the worse half, for one accumulates his pleasant memories in his first thirty-six years and regrets them in the next three or four decades. When an old man is heard talking to himself, he is muttering maledictions on remembered follies which he committed before he was thirty-six. An enfeebled memory allows him to forget the later ones.

The people of the town of Sullivan were uncommonly worked up over the war. They hanged in effigy a local "Copperhead," a poisonous sympathizer with the South and the institution of slavery: my mother writing his sentence, found pinned to the figure, judicially imposing the extreme penalty. The residents of this hamlet are said to have preceded all others in moving to erect a soldiers' monument.

4—HURRAH, AND GOODBY.

The Sixth New Hampshire regiment entrained for the front at Keene, December 25, 1861. I was at the depot to see the men file aboard and the train go out. In his blue overcoat with a cape to it, father looked the ideal soldier. Twenty-eight years had passed when I contributed the following to Memorial Day verse:

I see them bringing their flowers today
To the spot where the heroes sleep,

And I think of an unmarked soldier's grave
　Where Virginia's breezes sweep.
And I wonder if someone plucks a flower
　By the rivulet of Bull Run,
And lays it above the dust of him
　Who made me a soldier's son.

The days that are gone I live once more
　As I close my eyes and think,
And the chain of memory stretches back
　And I follow it link by link.
And spanning eight and a score of years
　I return to a Christmas day
When the streets are filled with marching men,
　And the air with their banners gay.

But I have sight that sees but one,
　A man with a bearded face
And a kindly eye and a stalwart tread,
　Who walks in a forward place.
I watch the train move out of town,
　With its smoke and its clanging bell,
And the smoke takes form of clouds of war,
　And the clang is a funeral knell.

He wore the blue as a soldier should,
　Was tender and true and brave:
He gave his life for a nation's life,
　And his pay was a soldier's grave.
A random shot, and above his corpse
　Sweeps forward the battle's tide;
And when the stars shine out that night
　They bury him where he died.

So I watch them strewing their flowers today
　On the spot where the heroes sleep,
And I think of an unmarked soldier's grave
　Where Virginia's willows weep.

And I wonder if someone plucks a flower
  By the rivulet of Bull Run,
And drops it above the dust of him
  Who made me a soldier's son.

The verses have been heard in Sons of Veterans camps. When they had been written twenty years, I discovered that Capt. George Clymer of Glen Ridge, N. J., Grand Army Instructor in Patriotism, recited them to pupils in the public schools that he visited.

5—QUAKER AND SCRIPTURAL ANTECEDENTS.

My mother was born in Unity, Maine, in June, 1830, the daughter of Esther Chase and Stephen Hussey, who named her Asenath. There were enough biblical names in my ancestry—Rebecca, Esther, Asenath, and Stephen—to produce a prophet. The Chases were Quakers. I was but five years old when, being taken down to Maine by my mother on a visit to her relatives in Unity, I attended a Quaker meeting and spent a week in the family of her Quaker cousin, Uncle John Chase. This short period was so dreary that I have been under the depression of it ever since.

There is a certain risk in publishing the fact that one is a Chase by ancestry. Somebody is sure to offer you a book for a dollar containing your genealogy. The Macdonald family can be traced, through Scott's Tales of a Grandfather, to a gang of Highland cattle-thieves, who were all but ex-terminated by outraged neighbors whom they had

plundered. In that direction "mine ancient but
ignoble blood hath run through scoundrels since the
flood," but the Chases are all respectable, being
elders or ministers or Quakers. The Husseys I
suspect of being Puritans. Three brothers of them,
from England, came to New England among the
early arrivals. They were Stephen, Batchelder, and
Sylvanus. Each of them made a practice of naming
his sons after their uncles, and the three names
came down to the last generation. I had an uncle
Batchelder, and an uncle Sylvanus, a cousin Sylvanus, and a cousin Stephen. Passing through the
town of Houlton, Maine, forty years ago, I saw
the name of Hussey everywhere—on the signboards
of doctors, lawyers, merchants, and—I did not examine the police record for the other class. My
parents bestowed upon me the name of George
Everett Hussey—George for Washington, Everett
for Edward Everett, and Hussey as a matter of
course. I dropped the third one out at an early
age, but the Testament I won by learning many
verses of the seventh of Matthew has on its fly-leaf
this inscription: "Presented to George E. H. Macdonald by his Sabbath School Teacher, Keene, N.
H., Jan. 21st, 1863." George E. H. sounds plebeian
alongside my brother's name, which was Eugene
Montague. I lower a hook into the well of memory
to catch that teacher's name. It brings up "Miss
Dunbar." If there is an old resident of Keene who
ever went to Sunday school he may be able to correct or confirm my guess. Yet more likely that
oldtimer, when found, will say there used to be a
man named Dunbar that owned a horse he thought

could trot. And drove him onto the track at the
fair grounds hitched to a sulky, and got run into and
dished a wheel. Deaf man, he was; couldn't hear
a dam' sound. His daughter maybe.

6—THE SMART ONE OF THE FAMILY.

Asenath, my mother, coming at about the middle
of ten or eleven children, was the only one of them
who ever entertained "views." At thirteen she was
teaching a school that had an algebra class in it,
and on her way to her daily task waded through
deep snow minus leg-garments worn by girls of a
later day but now discarded largely, I perceive, as
individual entities. She afterwards left home to
learn a trade, that of stitching men's coats. The
death of Henry, after their few years of married
life, found her working in a peg-shop, making pegs
for shoes, in Keene, N. H., and supporting two
boys, 7 and 5 years of age. Our family doctor was
named Twichell. On an occasion when an elderly
woman patient (say Mrs. Carter) wanted a nurse,
Dr. Twichell recommended mother. She proved so
competent that the doctor advised her to prepare
herself for nursing as a profession. There was then
an advanced medical practitioner and reformer,
named Dio Lewis, conducting a training school for
nurses in Massachusetts, to whom she was recommended. Dio Lewis dressed his pupils in "gym"
clothes and gave them physical training; and I remember that when my mother, home on a vacation,
told my aunt, with whom we were living, about this
innovation in women's dress, my aunt replied that

the less said about it the better, especially in the presence of her daughter Ella, who was but 15 and wore skirts down to her instep.

I have no likeness of mother. The last time I was in New Hampshire I asked this niece, Mrs. Ella Clement Priest, if there was any picture of her in the family. She replied: "No; I don't believe Aunt 'Sene ever kept still long enough to have one taken."

As a trained nurse, and one of the first of that profession, Asenath commanded a wage larger than local patients would pay. She therefore looked abroad. She became nurse and companion to Mrs. Bierstadt, wife of the artist whose great picture of the Rocky Mountains won fame in those days. I received letters from her afterwards written on the stationery of the yacht Resolute, belonging to Banker Hatch, with a summer home at Navesink. Mrs. Hatch was her patient. Because I heard few other names, and little of anything else at that period, I am able to remember those of her employers, Minturn, Wingate, and so on. Her pay was good and employment steady, so that with her widow's pension, and something extra on account of children, the problem of maintenance for her boys was solved. She also contributed to the support of her sister's family and helped them buy the farm. As one of the earliest trained and professional nurses, she was in at the close of the era when persons in moderate circumstances could be sick within their means.

On my return to Keene, late in 1864, from a

stay with an uncle in Maine, who, having no boy of
his own, proposed to adopt me and take me with
him into the Aroostook (to which mother would
not consent), we lived with this same sister's family
a mile out of the town of Keene, on Marlborough
street. Here I first began to understand what I
heard my elders read from the newspapers. We
took The Banner of Light, a Spiritualist paper that
by a coincidence began publication in Boston on
the day I was born, its first number being dated
April 11, 1857. I have long survived my journalistic twin. Mother and aunt read it aloud by turns,
and I lay in bed and heard them. In spite of Spiritualism in the family, the children went to the Unitarian Sunday school in Keene. The minister of
this church, on the east side of Main street, was
known as Priest White. The orthodox church
stood at the head of the square. They called its
minister Parson Barstow.

7—A RECRUIT FOR LINCOLN.

Among the things the child of 5 or 6 does not
comprehend is the fact of death. Accustomed to
the absence of my father from the house during his
ten hours a day as a mechanic, I had learned not to
miss his presence. I now supposed he was just away.
The tale of his death meant nothing to me, although
I had seen my mother's burst of weeping, her head
falling on her crossed arms at the bench where she
worked in the peg-shop, when I accompanied the
bearer to her of the news that father had fallen in
battle. So, persuaded that he must be somewhere,

and that people were mistaken in saying I should not see him again, day after day I watched the road, which I could command for some distance each way, and all the men who passed underwent inspection. This house on Marlborough street, where we lived with my mother's sister Louisa, who had married Benjamin Franklin Clement of Montville, Maine, was later made over and occupied by Frank Cole, son of a neighbor—a baby when we moved away. We were there in the fall of 1864, and in the Lincoln canvass of that year I fought the Irish, who were trying to make the world safe for democracy by campaigning for McClellan. Surely they were times of terror for a non-pugnacious Lincoln boy. In those precincts he met the Irish boys in small gangs and was interrogated: "Be you an Irish feller?" "Be you for McClellan?" No. The fight opened with aggressions on the part of the gang.

One with a snub nose not readily caused to bleed, and with an underpinning patterned after the forelegs of an ox, for such was I, endured long without being put out or overthrown; and he was fired with a mighty cause. The reelection of Lincoln caused a general belief to pass from parents to children that the country was saved. Months later, when the news of his assassination reached my aunt, I saw the color leave her face. She gasped "What will become of us?" as though we had been passengers on a ship with a mutinous element in the crew, the captain overboard, and no one left who understood navigation.

8—BACK TO THE LAND.

While we were in the Marlborough street house my uncle Clement came back from the war. Thence in the fall of 1865 we moved to a farm in Surry, which I was to think of when homesick for the next ensuing ten years. And those ten years are

The Place I Was Homesick For.

crowded with so many distinct memories they seem to cover the principal part of my life. The days were interminably long. Our family must have been classed as poor, though we never were needy, and together the breadwinners had purchased an equity in the house that they now traded for the farm.

The war had made living expensive—butter fifty cents a pound, flour ten dollars a barrel. Women wore "print," or calico, and men wore shoddy. I heard my aunt murmur:

"Butter and cheese is fifty cents a pound,
      An' everything else is accordin',
    Before next spring we'll all be on the town
      Or landed on the other side of Jordan."

We came upon the farm late in the fall. There was no fruit to pick, and butter was short because of one farrow cow. Pork and potatoes, pork and beans, and pork fat for the enrichment of salt codfish mixed with potato; pork fat on slices of brownbread, pork fat and Porto Rico molasses (with slivers of cane in it) on hot biscuits—that was the diet on which I throve. Without butter, a condition my aunt took pains to conceal, we could carry no bread for our school luncheons, lest its unbuttered state should provoke comment. My aunt therefore, made great sheets of gingerbread wherefrom she filled our dinner pails. Sometimes it froze on the two-and-a-half-mile carry and thawing in the warm school room turned glutinous when masticated, dropping into the stomach "kerlunker," as we said. The next season, with apples to stew and dry, berries to can and a cow come in, brought better fare. Hardship is like romance—always in the past. While being undergone it is unrecognized. Life was happy despite zero weather, drifts half-way to the roof, clothes that let in the snow to melt against the flesh, and a ration not scientifically balanced.

CHAPTER II.

SURRY (pop. 350) lies a little west of the geographical center of Chesire county, toward the southwest corner of the state. Over the southern boundary of the county you are in Massachusetts; over the western line, which is the Connecticut river, you are in Vermont. According to the way you view Surry, with its twenty square miles of territory, it is a valley town or a hill town, or both. It has hills east and west. The hills at one time met near the north end; but the Ashuelot river broke through and ran south along the foot of Surry mountain, on the east, which is fifteen hundred feet high and steep. That mountain guards the eastern side of the town. On the top of it there is a mysterious pond, said to be fathomless, but white lilies float on its surface near the margin defended by tangled tree trunks, and can be gathered by swimming for them in the dark waters.

The Ashuelot in its meanderings from immemorial time has created a valley half a mile wide, with a plateau for the village of a dozen houses, town hall, school, and church to be built upon. To the west the ground continues to rise until it reaches the summit of Surry Hill and the borders of the adjoin-

27

ing towns on that side. Surry once belonged to
the towns lying east and west of it, but being inaccessible from those directions on account of the
height of land, it was allowed to take a name and
"go it alone," as they say there. The smooth way
to get into Surry is from the south, where the river
has leveled the country and there are fewer ups and
downs.

The farm I called my home (1865-'75) lies two
miles and a half southwest of the village, and is
reached from there by a road which rises all the
way. By a happy freak of nature, the ground the
road runs on for half a mile in one direction from
the house and a mile in the other, is level, but there
is a half-mile hill at each end of this, the only level
stretch on that so-called Old Walpole Road for
eight miles. The arable acres of the farm, that
have been cultivated for the past one hundred and
twenty-five years, cover a long knoll, with the
buildings at the south and sunny end. Men born
and reared in Surry return when aged and prosperous and make show-places of the old homesteads.
One could find no location there so well situated for
the purpose as this one, which has even a spring and
a pond on it. The hill back of the house rises by
an abrupt acclivity to near a level with the top of
Surry mountain, and looks it in the face two miles
away. At the very peak of the hill there crops out
a ledge, and on that ledge the last glacier to come
through left standing, balanced on its smaller end,
a rock fifteen feet high, of a formation not native to
those parts. As a barefooted boy I often climbed

it by inserting my toes into its fissures and crevices, and once at the top could see all the country from there to Mount Monadnock, fifteen miles south, including the city of Keene. I spent hours on that

VIEWING THE LANDSCAPE O'ER.

rock, viewing the landscape, while the address of William Tell to his native mountains ran in my mind. The last time I stood at the base of the big boulder, its summit appeared inaccessible except by means of an elevator; and I had then forgotten what William Tell said.

How plainly voices from the road below carried up the side of that hill, especially the bell-like accents of our not-distant neighbor, Mr. Reed, who sometimes drove by. One standing on its brow heard a woman in her doorway inquire after the health of Mr. Reed's family, and his reply: "Wal, not so very good. You see my boy Charlie stepped on a scythe and cut his heel; my boy George is suffering from a boil on his hindermost sitdown; my wife has just had a baby; and I have been troubled with b-a-a-d Di-Or-Re-Or." My selection is not happy, but it is authentic; and this is a true book.

Perhaps once a year, in the fall, a drover going south to Boston went through that road with a hundred head of cattle, gathered from all the way north to the Canadian line, or beyond—a boy and a dog footing it and a man riding in a buggy. When night overtook him, the drover paid for the privilege of turning his cattle into fields where there was fall feed. He furnished a topic of conversation for a week. Another notable to go by there once was Max Shinburn, the bank robber, on his way to commit a robbery in Walpole. Other days, hardly a team would pass. A team was any rig, single or double. Such as went that way were from further up the road, going to Keene. These were such regular passersby that they were known before they came in sight by the familiar rhythm of the horses's feet beating on the ground, or by the peculiar rattle of the wagon or the "chuck" of the wheels on the axle. The horse could be recognized though a stranger might be driving it. In Keene, where we had lived, the street traffic, of considerable volume, was negligible as a spectacle; here, one left his work, if need be, so as not to miss anything moving past, man or animal. In Keene we ran only to "see the cars go by." Here we might catch the sound of a freight engine a mile or two off puffing on the upgrade to the Summit, but we saw no trains. The sound of an axe falling on a tree would carry half a mile, and the chopper might have struck the next blow and the next before it got to us. If the man was working in sight, it seemed as if the axe made the noise when it was above his head. The silence, when you stopped to listen to it, was as distinctly audible as the roar of a city.

The hill capped by the big rock was the cow pasture, covering eighty acres, with twenty of them wooded. The best feed for the cows grew farthest from the barn and around a waterhole. That was a terrible land for me, when I got there after sundown to drive the cows home; for, looking about me, I could see all of creation except the cows. Sheep would be plentiful, if you were not hunting for them, and the colts were either there or visible at a distance. The kine might have started for the barn by another route than the one I had taken in reaching the spot. If so, I must follow them down an old sled-road through the woods, where, pausing anon to hark for that cow bell, I should hear myself discussed by the birds and insects that become garrulous and conversational as the shadows fall; or I might meet a questing hedgehog on his way to the cornfield for his grub. I might even, so my fears told me, encounter the bobcat or the bear lately reported in that neighborhood. A tree-toad would start his evensong almost at my ear. Perhaps I should scare up a partridge whose sudden whirr would for a second or two paralyze me with fright. The partridge's flight is always unexpected. He seems to start from between your feet, and he is the bird that set the airplane an example in making a noise when taking off. But in the open the boy who stood still, listening for the bell, heard nothing but his own vital organs working, his heart thumping like a hydraulic pump, his ears "singing." He was a small speck in a big universe. This "chore" of combing eighty acres to find a few cows was all in the day's work. A girl might say she was afraid to go after the cows at night, but a boy wouldn't. A quarter of a century later than this experience of mine, I heard an elderly lady from Providence, R. I., ask a small boy, her "grand"-nephew, if he would not like to live with her in the city. He objected long, but finally came to terms. "I might go and live with you for a while," he said, "but I wouldn't go after the cows, by Jesus." Yet

THERE WAS ALWAYS WOOD TO SAW

hunting cows at night was only one pest of farm life. Weeds had to be pulled in summer days and the woodsaw pushed in winter. It seemed to me that all the disagreeable duties fell to the youngest.

2—WHILE SCHOOL KEPT IT WAS VACATION.

Schooldays came as a furlough. The cartoonists who comically portray the reluctance of the small boy at going back to school were never farmers' boys in my circumstances, nor was Shakespeare one either. I knew of at least one who took an early start and then crept not like a snail but ran. He did what looked most like creeping on the home stretch. To me the eight to sixteen weeks of school in the course of a year meant ease and playtime. They were my vacation.

As regards my education, which was fragmentary, a dozen district schools contributed to it. To the first of these, in East Sullivan, I was conducted by Amanda Dunn—later my aunt by marriage but then only a big girl—with my mother's consent, not mine. As I was in my fourth year, I might have forgotten about that school by now, except that I took recess with a parcel of fresh girls, who, moved only by what I regarded as an unworthy curiosity, gathered about me at a time when all a man wanted was to be let alone. Followed Public School No. 2 in Keene, where I nearly got my head knocked off by the crank of a chain pump that reversed itself. I know no more than this about that school, for I was only 4, save that there I made the acquaintance of Ed. Kimball (he had a share of the stock when The Truth Seeker Company was organized) and Charlie and Jennie Sanger, who as residents of Boston turned out a dozen years later to be the grandchildren of Edmund Woodward of Surry, the farmer that had me then for "hired man." Ed. Kimball's father Horatio served as mayor of Keene for a number of terms. Another Keene school, perhaps No. 1, for the street it stood on was named School Street, claimed me for a pupil. There the scholars sang Civil War songs when they were the latest successes. Then, at 5, I went to school in Unity, Maine, again attended by a large girl, one Amelia Webb. The teacher caused me to answer her with scorn by asking if I knew my letters, whereas I could read. The Marlborough street school in Keene enrolled me the next year. The teacher, Miss Willard, had the odd front name of Bial. By the time I was out of school at 8 I knew Colburn's Mental Arithmetic, including the penultimate example about the farmer who, if he had as many geese and half as many more and two geese and a half, would have had a hundred.

My schooling was continued at the Four Corners, half way between Keene and Surry Hill. My brother and cousin Stephen with me made the three-mile descent from the hill in the morning and climbed that grade again at night. I first noticed, then, the reading of the Bible in school. A large boy, having searched the scriptures, wrote biblical references on slips of paper and passed them to the girls. The countenance of a high-spirited girl, Sarah Darling by name, blazed with indignation when he lured her into looking up Romans iv, 19. I knew the Bible was inspired, because so informed by Sunday school teachers; yet at that I wondered why an inspired work should contain so large an excess of suspended mud; for this industrious youth had been obliging enough to mark the low spots in most of the Bibles used in that school.

Straight east from our Surry Hill house, across a mile and a half of rugged pasture land and wooded territory, the South End school invited. For a winter's term the three of us took it in, breaking our own path and wading depths of snow. Again, a mile off to the northwest of our home stood the Surry Hill schoolhouse, in a district once fairly populous. It opened for me during one term, the scholars numbering four. At this school we first had geographies that contained pictures of prehistoric men and monsters, and possibly an outline of evolution. When snow made the schoolhouse inaccessible we stayed home, the teacher being a boarder, and held the school in our "other room," which suited us and was convenient for the neighbors' children. Now the schoolhouse has come down from the hill and set itself alongside the farmhouse. Two of these schools, namely the South End and Surry Village, were exceptional: I attended each more than one term. Going to whatever locality the farmer might happen to be in who wanted a boy, I in these instances returned to a district where I had been before. There are four more to be named. From the first place where I lived as hired boy I attended the Walpole Hill school, and also the school in Christian Holler (Walpole). When I changed again to a school new to me, I found myself in the London district, East Westmoreland. My scholastic training ended in Westmoreland village. Such learning as these dozen schools diffused, afforded me all I have ever needed of mathematics, made me a successful contender at spelling-schools, and grounded me safely in grammar. Even though at 18 I could have had a good-sized school to teach if I would take it, my ignorance on general subjects was profound. Knowledge has its limits, but ignorance is measureless. Mine was total except for the look-in I had on a few subjects. It was all look-in; I had no outlook.

3—ECHOES FROM THE SCHOOL ROOM.

The one-room district schools had advantages missed by separated pupils in graded schools. In them the attentive scholar could learn his own lessons and the lessons of all the classes ahead of him by hearing them recite. Thus listening in, I learned the contents of books I had never possessed or opened. There was a large variety in these, for textbooks changed as often as I went from one district to another. A worn copy of the Weld & Quackenbos grammar book to which I clung in all my shifting about, would sometimes put me in a grammar class by myself.

My mind not being chargeable with resistance to the intrusion of knowledge, I was apt at committing words and recitations to memory. My contemporaries will remember the appended fragments from readings and declamations. I heard them in the voices of large scholars when I was a small one:

> "Sir Ralph the Rover tore his hair,
> And cursed himself in his despair;

> But the waves rush in on every side
> And the vessel sinks beneath the tide."

"A verb used to denote an action or feeling by a subject or agent that passes over from the subject or agent to and terminates upon some person or thing as its object is a transitive verb."

> "And heralds shouted in his ear,
>   'Bow down, ye slave, bow down.' "

> " 'Make way for liberty !' he cried;
> Made way for liberty and died."

> "I will go to my tent and lie down in despair;
> I will paint me in black and sever my hair.
> I will sit on the shore when the hurricane blows,
> And reveal to the god of the tempest my woes."

"Lords of creation indeed, and can't even take care of an umbrella. . . . . "

"Pizzaro—How now, Gomez, what bringest thou?

"Gomez—In yonder camp we have surprised an old Peruvian. Escape us by flight he could not, and we took him without resistance."

"Not many years ago where you now stand, surrounded by all that exalts and embellishes civilized life, the rank thistle nodded in the wind, and the wild fox dug his hole unscared. . . . Here too lived and loved another race of beings. . . . dipped his paddle in yon sedgy lake . . . . beneath the same moon that smiles for you the Indian lover wooed his dusky mate."

"The mounds of the western prairies are among the most interesting features of the country. They are so regular in form that they are generally supposed to have been work of human hands, but by whom they were reared or for what purpose is unknown."

"The voyagers said we will wait until the line gales have done with their equinoctial fury. . . . Death was the pilot that stood at the helm, but no one knew it . . . the ill-omened Vesta dealt her death stroke to the Arctic."

I am obliged to suspend.   My notes made with
a view to citing these and other quotations number forty-one, and I desist.   Having deleted thirty-
odd reëchoing ones, I retain the last of the ten remaining because it started me on a line of inquiry
that took me into skepticism.   The excerpt, with
errors and omissions, is from a sermon by Henry
Ward Beecher on the Loss of the Arctic; but what
was "equinoctial fury"?   My aunt said that when
the sun crosses the equator a storm is kicked up
called the line gale, or the "equinoctial."   If I would
notice, there was always a storm when the sun
crossed the line.   Why?   Because it makes the
days and the nights of the same length, March 21
and September 23.   I heard mention of the line
gale all the days of my youth, but the gale never
arrived on schedule time.   Any storm within a fortnight answered for the name.   The Weather Bureau
has exploded the myth of the "equinoctial."   The
remains may be laid away with the ground hog and
St. Swithin as weather breeders.

Now, then, I believe I left myself some pages
back, hunting cows on the summit of Surry Hill,
with all creation (except the cows) in view just
beyond the horizon.   That landscape, the town of
Surry, its village and its farms, lies spread before
me still like a map, or better than any map, since
I can see them all, every square acre of them, almost, without looking.   The old-growth pines that
then were landmarks, a hundred feet high or more,
went to the sawmill long ago, but they are still
in this picture of mine that was never photographed.

4—SCANDALOUS DOINGS

And Surry village! I never can forget that hamlet,
for was it not the scene of the only scandal that
has enriched my life? That scandal came early.
I was no more than ten years old; and probably
was but nine. From the farm on the Hill I went

THE SURRY VILLAGE SCHOOL HOUSE.
This is a late and defective picture. It does not show
Sam Poole's blacksmith shop that stood at right.

to the school house in the village, near the river
and mountain, by walking the two and a half miles
of lonesome road that lay between, with only one
house on it. The school "kept" in summer for
children too small to do farm work. That is how
I know I was under eleven. I guess that the teacher
that summer was Charlotte Ellis—destined years
later to become the wife of J. R. Holman of Hinsdale, who took The Truth Seeker. Did Mr. Holman
indulge in any spacious remarks on the editorial

knowledge displayed in this paper, Charlotte could reply: "Your editor! I taught that boy all he knows."* Not more than twenty scholars came, mostly girls. Inside the schoolhouse the sexes were divided; outside they mingled and played the same games. In our young minds I doubt the disstinctions between us were recognized as sexual. Girls were only an inferior variety of boy, wearing different clothes and longer hair; they could run fast, but couldn't throw a stone, and were spiteful in a scuffle. Yet for all these serious disabilities, they were tolerated and admitted to games they could play, squat-tag and "high-spy" and maybe others. And then one day the boys deserted them —disappeared without trace. To one of these bright lads it had occurred that we could dam the little brook in the hollow back of the schoolhouse and make a place to go in swimming. The erecting of the dam with small stones and pieces of sod consumed more than one noon hour. The second day saw the feat of engineering accomplished; on the third the swimming began; we stripped and went in. The expanse of water was all of ten feet long and nearly that wide; maximum depth 20 inches. One could swim three or four strokes before grounding. And how about the girls we left behind us? On the fourth day, when playing by themselves had lost its edge, a half dozen of

*The thought is not original with me but adapted. When an old sailor under whom as a boy Morgan Robertson served an apprenticeship on the Great Lakes heard of him as an author, he exclaimed: "That feller writin' books! Hell, I learnt Morg Robertson all he ever knew."

them followed us to the pond, the size and depth of which quite astonished them. The squeals they emitted, expressive of admiration, gratified our pride as builders, but when they took for granted their right to enter the water, they were sternly for-

THE FEMALE PERIL.

bidden and ordered to find a wading-place further upstream. They retreated to where the alders, meeting over the brook at the head of our pond, hid them from our view. They were noisy creatures, with their screaming and laughing, but what they found to excite them we were not interested to inquire. We learned soon enough anyhow. The water from our dam backed up beyond the alders and spread there into a fine place to wade. And that was not quite all they had to exclaim and giggle over, for they were taking off their dresses and leaving them ashore to keep the skirts dry.

One of them came into view promenading the bank with no dress on. She thereby rose in the estimation of a boy, for when a girl stepped out of her skirt in those days she revealed a garment that had the promise and possibilities of pants. I only record the feeling of gratification experienced at seeing this near approach of a girl to the human form. She was all right. So were the rest of them, who could now wade and wet no clothes. Yet those girls were not contented to let well enough alone. When we came out to dress we observed that they had progressed to complete immersion and were resuming underthings, as after a swim. They had kept quiet about it. The boys felt it was none of their business and said nothing. The girls, when picking up their clothes, politely faced the spectator. If they must turn the back they modestly covered the lower part with a garment. The idyllic scenes were repeated with no interference or trespass on either side until a later day, when consternation fell upon us to see the alders parted and one girl and then another come striding down the brook between them. They moved forward with arms extended and feet far apart to keep their balance. The boys who saw stood paralyzed by the spectacle—the cheek of those girls wanting to use the boys' pond when they had one of their own! The brother of the leading girl angrily ordered her back. She shamelessly stood her ground and said, "I won't." He swung back his hand, threatening. "Out of this or I'll splash you," and he struck the surface of the water, throwing a "wave" in her face. He

was joined by others, who went to it desperately,
splashing and scooping water over the invaders—all
of whom most unexpectedly and successfully threw
it back. Certain of their forces, unable to come
through, had left the stream and deployed around
the alders, entering the water behind us and making
a rear attack. What was the use? They were too
many for us. Our arms were weary. A truce followed. The bathing became established as mixed.
Laughter and the spirit of play and comradeship prevailed. A man grown cannot quite get back to the
reaction of the small boy toward the small girl. It
is part wonder and part his dislike for what he cannot understand. He dismisses the subject from his
mind lest his attitude toward her change to one of
sympathy, which is girlish. There was among them
a little freckle-face with long red curls or ringlets
who pulled me by the hand and made me run along
the bank and around about to dry. That girl had
me gentled. In winter, when the game was playing
horse, and the boys were lined up facing the school
house for a "stable," and stood there pawing and
whickering till the girls put on the reins and drove
them away, I always knew whose horsey I was going
to be. I heard from her forty years later, when she
sent word that she "remembered." Remembered
what? If Freckle Face lives still, her ringlets are
either bobbed or gray. She was a year older than I.

5—THE SCANDAL BREAKS

But the scandal! The boys and girls went to
their different dressing-places, and returned to
school clothed and in their right minds. Drouth or

rain or change of temperature put an end in time
to the bathing season. When it was all over and
forgotten by the children, the scandal exploded
among their elders. Girls were heard asking one
another with grave faces what their mothers had
said to them. I caught a ride part of the way home
in the hind end of an open buggy driven by a
woman. We were stopped by another woman, who
came out of her house with an apron wound about
her arms, and they discussed the matter in "blind"
language that I understood perfectly. Both tried
to look horrified. Each was afraid that the other
would think she condoned such goings on, and I
believe that both chuckled over it when alone. The
woman in the buggy sighed: "Well, I suppose the
less said the soonest mended." The woman with
her arms in the apron said: "Yes, the more it is
stirred the worse it will stink." I thought of the
bright little girl, white and clean as a pond-lily, who
led her mates between the alders and into the water
where the boys were, and decided the mother should
not have chosen that malodorous word.

Later that village had a real scandal. A girl of
fifteen, who virtuously would have switched her
little sister for going in swimming with boys, experienced religion and joined the church. In less
than a year something happened. Nobody told me
just what. Those things are hidden from babes
and revealed unto the wise and prudent; and I was
only twelve. The officers of the church took action
to expel the girl from the fold and turn her back
again to "the world." I happened to hear the judg-

ment of "the world" on that proceeding. In the village store when I was there on an errand for Aunt Polly Abbott, who had me in her employ that winter, three of the most enlightened men of the town were met. There were William H. Porter, M.D., the village doctor; Holland Stevens, the village Spiritualist; and George K. Harvey, later a state senator. They took up the matter of the girl thrown back upon the world by the church, and inquired if such things could be. Harvey questioned whether the church might land a damaged member on the world without the world's consent. Dr. Porter proposed that the three there present appoint themselves a committee on behalf of the world to take the affair under consideration. Holland Stevens contended ably that when anything lawfully in the possession of the world was taken from it by the unworldly, the world had a clear right to insist that, if returned, the article should be in as good order as before. "For instance," he said, to illustrate, "if I get a piece of goods from Marsh Britton here" (Marshall Britton kept the store), "and keep it awhile and then carry it to him all mussed up, Marsh ain't under any obligation to take it back." George Harvey voted Aye to that, and Dr. Porter said: "Holland, I deputize you, then, as representing this Committee of the World, to wait on these church people and tell them the world declines to receive this girl except with the guarantee that she is in as good condition in all respects as when they took her in, damn 'em."

CHAPTER III.

IN this account of my childhood I have said
that when mother was widowed and her two
boys orphaned (1862), she placed my brother
Eugene and me in the care of her sister, Louisa,
Mrs. Benjamin Clement, and went out to service
as a nurse. I suspect my uncle, Ben Clement, of
distaste for sustained labor. I certainly heard
neighbors and others call him shiftless—judgments
that were perhaps unfair, since he shortly drew a
pension as a veteran disabled by heart disease contracted during the war in the performance of duty
at the front. But one member of his regiment, being
drunk, declared in my hearing that "Clem" never
got to the front and was never in any action of the
war. The attacks of heart disease came on as the
regiment approached the scene of conflict and Clem
fell out of the ranks. So, although he was in the
same company, he was not in the fight at Bull Run
where my father fell, but was lying under an ambulance or other wagon suffering from palpitation of
the heart. Army life irked my uncle. He told me
plainly that when they brought to him the news
that Henry (my father) had fallen, he repined that
he was not in Henry's restful place under the sod

46

and the dew. I am sure I shared his regrets if it meant my own father's survival in his place. On demobilization he joined the Invalid Corps and spent a term at Gallops Island.

By trade my uncle was a carpenter and joiner, also called a mechanic. The tools of a carpenter then required a lumber wagon to move them. They included planes from eight inches to four feet long, a raft of them for smoothing, matching, joining, beading, grooving; chisels of all measurements, including one that rode in the bottom of the chest and reached from end to end. The big plane was a long jointer; the chisel a jimmyslick. With the smaller chisels he could mortise a window sash; with the larger ones great beams for the frame of a barn. There were gimlets and bits, augers and pod-augers; files flat, half round and round, and three cornered; a battery of saws running from large dimensions down to keyhole size. He could make window frames, doors and trim, and cut his own beads and moldings. The carpenter might lay a stone foundation, build the house on it, and lath, plaster and paint, for all which operations he carried the tools in his chest. Today carpenters are seen going to their jobs bearing only a hand tool-chest smaller than a portable typewriter case, with saw and steel square protruding. But though Clem could do these things, he worked discontinuously; perhaps it was his health, perhaps a dull labor market.

It was merely my bad luck that my uncle looked upon "flogging" and "the rod" as essential to a boy's deportment; therefore he presented me with whippings on the same principle that my aunt administered sulphur and molasses, for treatment and precaution.   Aunt had a kind heart that disapproved of the horsewhip for boys. She would not let him touch her own boy Stephen except over her body. I heard her plead with him on a day I was to be thrashed, and still thank her for her futile "O Benjamin, don't," though he thrust her back through the doorway into the house. He was whaling me at the moment for going in swimming all summer without his consent. An eccentric if not crazy character in the neighborhood named Bill Mason, reputed to possess extraordinary strength, warned my uncle that if he ever whipped me again he would cut some withes and twist them and give him a trimming. His heart attacks never seized him when duty called him to wallop me. A friendly chap, Riley Kenney by name, who lived back over the hill, hearing that I was "stented" to pick up a half acre of potatoes in a day or take a flogging at sundown, came to help me, if needed, in the middle of the afternoon. By wasting no time straightening my back or looking at the sun, which is the farmer's clock, I had gathered the potatoes into baskets and borne them to a cart.

Yet my uncle was a tolerably kind man when not bound by the dictum of Solomon on the virtues of the rod of correction. He had no understanding of boys. He believed they should learn to work with poor tools, dull axes and saws. "The bad workman complains of his tools," he said. When I murmured he quoted: "If the iron be blunt, and he do not whet the edge, then must he put to more strength." I aspired to grow up and return one of his thrashings, but on a Fourth of July, the annual

THE OLD BRIDGE STILL STANDS.

It is over the Ashuelot on the River road from Keene to Surry. I squared my uncle with myself by taking his boy, who could not swim, out of the deep water.

go-in-swimming day, I saved his son from drowning and called the account square. Although it was a rule for a boy to remain on the home farm as long as the old man could lick him, my deportment passed from his control in 1870, when I was 13.

Eugene, being more than two years my senior, had already tried for two seasons the life of a farmer's hired boy. The hire was board, school, and washing. Although an advanced scholar always, in build he was slight; in childhood he was rather

pindling. I passed him in bulk when I was five and
he seven, and he never caught up. He looked for
lighter work than farm labor. People say that a
boy raised on a farm sets out in life with a good
constitution. He does. He has a good constitution if he survives. Mother took Eugene to a New
York printer for a time, thus fitting him for a few
years' work on a Keene newspaper. But he was
back in New York at 19, printer on The Truth
Seeker for five years, running the paper in the
proprietor's absence for three years, ('79-82), then
editor for a quarter of a century.

2—BOOKS AND MINSTRELSY.

I will say in behalf of our Surry home that it
sheltered the only bookish or reading family for
miles around. It established connection with a
library that provided us with the books of the day,
which my aunt read aloud to the other members
gathered around the table. The shaded kerosene
lamp stood between her eyes and the pages of the
book. The authors were Trowbridge, Farjeon,
Capt. Mayne Reid, and whoever wrote the Life of
Isaac Tatem Hopper (grandfather of DeWolf).
Add to these "The Man with the Broken Ear," by
Edmond About, and "The Dove in the Eagle's
Nest," by Charlotte M. Yonge. The New England
Farmer brought a story every week for her to read
to us. This paper also carried the advertisement of a
merchant who expressed himself through the medi-
um of poetry. He soared to lofty heights:

"The planets as they roll around
   In the vast realms of space,
Will all be found, if traced with care,
   Fixed in their proper place."

And then came down to business:

"The proper place to buy boys' clothes—
   Hats, caps, pants, coat and shoes complete—
Is at the store of George Fenno's,
   Corner of Beech and Washington Streets."

Josh Billings and the Danbury News Man were writing; so was Petroleum V. Nasby. The "Rollo" books were dated for me in my sixth year. Give me now one of Beadle's Dime Novels and let me read of Old Rube the Trailer. Better it were for a boy to read Beadle's Dime Novels than not to read at all. Farmers called at each other's houses winter evenings for no purpose but to talk. They kept their hats on. Nor were we without minstrelsy. Uncle Billy Wright went from house to house, arriving preferably at meal time, carrying his fiddle in a green bag, and scraping it while he sang. His songs had stories in them, or they celebrated historical events, like this:

"The tenth of September let us all remember
   As long as this globe on its axis rolls round.
Our tars and marines on Lake Erie were seen
   To pull the proud flag of Great Britain come down."

He knew all of George Washington's **preference,** "The Darby Ram," the last line being **very daring.** One of his songs contained the splendid **stanza:**

> "Then on to the table Jack he **rolled**
> Five hundred guineas in bright **gold.**
> Said he: 'I am your lover bold,
> For I am Jack the Sailor'."

Jack had come back rich beyond the dreams of salesmanship, and so dolled up that the girl and her parent, who wouldn't have her marrying a penniless sailor, never knew him until he revealed himself in this dramatic fashion. One song of Billy Wright's developed an intrigue, wherein the husband, surprising the lover, who went out of the

THE MINSTREL.

window, was recompensed and revenged on finding himself in possession of "more than a hundred pounds and a glorious pair of breeches. Tol, lolly dingdong, doddle O day, and a glorious pair of breeches." So the cash balance was on the side of virtue. Let it ever be thus.

Uncle Billy sang with pathos, while his fiddle made a harmonious noise:

"Oh, my name was Robert Kidd, as I sail'd as I sail'd,
Oh, my name was Robert Kidd, as I sail'd;
My sinful footsteps slid, God's laws they did forbid;
But still wickedly I did, as I sail'd.

I'd a Bible in my hand, as I sail'd, as I sail'd,
I'd a Bible in my hand, as I sail'd;
I'd a Bible in my hand by my father's great command,
And I sunk it in the sand, as I sail'd.

I murdered William Moore, as I sail'd, as I sail'd,
I murdered William Moore, as I sail'd;
I murdered William Moore, and I left him in his gore,
Not many leagues from shore, as I sail'd."

The refrain "As I sailed, as I sailed" haunted the reverie of men as that other ghost "Long, long ago, long ago" troubled the subconscious state of women. I have heard a woman do her whole morning's work to that dolorous monotony; and if "As I sailed" got into a man's head it would stay until there was a change of weather.

Other characters seen no more on those roads are the pack peddler, the codger, and the man who drove the tincart. The minstrel with his stringed instrument and the peddler with his fardel had survived from the middle ages. The codger gave way to the tramp who jumped freight trains. The tincart, like the wooden Indian in front of the cigar stores, disappeared for some subtle reason I cannot name. The junkman still goes his rounds in the suburbs and in the residence sections of cities. I believe that my old neighborhood changed more in the few

years after I left it than it had prior to then in all
the decades since the Revolution.

3—I GO OUT TO WORK.

In April, 1870, I went definitely out to work. A
young farmer who had got land and a house and
taken a wife, wanted a boy and came for me. Since
that spring I have never been jobless, never applied
for work, never had the experience nor the feeling
of being unemployed. Except for Sundays, holidays, and a half dozen vacations, a day's work has
always been ahead of me when I arose. This place,
in the edge of Walpole, was three miles away from
Clement's and some hundreds of feet higher up,
and even that was not the "height of land," for
wherever you go in New Hampshire there is more
altitude just beyond. This ablebodied, handsome and
intelligent young agriculturist, my employer, idled
away his evenings playing with a cat in his lap. At
my former home we had rushed for a book when
supper was over, but in this house there was no
book. The Youth's Companion that came to the
young wife I saw only when she enlisted my help to
work out the charades. She called me into the
house sometimes from a distance if her husband
was away, and asked me the names of authors,
rivers, cities, and so on, not occurring to her. I enjoyed these hours and worked faster to make up
for them when I got back to the field. Here was
a mismated couple that should have had a trial marriage first, or at least have followed the custom of
their forebears who sampled knowledge before they

became life subscribers. They had been differently nurtured, he on a rough hill farm, and she in a
home at the outskirts of a city where there was
plenty of "company" and a division of household
duties. Here, where her married life began, was a
lonely place, no neighbor within call, and all the
work to do that was known to a farmer's wife—
washing, baking, churning, sweeping, getting together a "mess of vittles" three times a day, and
answering a call into the field occasionally in haying
time. And he worked harder than she did. Whenever a horse was free from the team, she fretted
to go and visit her parents five miles away, preferably Saturday night and over Sunday, with her
husband left at home. She was unsocial with him:
one saw her evading him by day, and heard her
angry outcries at night. Things went to smash the
first year. Some would not say it was lucky, but so
it appears to me, that the teacher of the fall school
came to board with them—a fine big girl who had
lure and desire. She fell in love with the little wife.
(The wife was so diminutive that when she took a
husband they said he would have to shake the sheets
to find her.) And the husband fell in love with the
school teacher, and she reciprocated there also.
That would have been an ideal match, for they were
a couple of mated birds. There was need no longer
for the wife to evade him, nor occasion for her nocturnal murmurings. However, a woman can be
jealous if she can't be loving. Except in the love
game, persons who have rejected a proffered article are indifferent who gets it. My employer's wife,

on the contrary, begrudged this girl—who always managed to put herself in line to be held for a hug or chased for a kiss—the possession of the husband she herself did not appear to want. The girl became an eyesore and a bore, while the husband's evident content was more than the wife could bear. She went home to her mother and stayed until the ᴗacher, seeing it was improper for her to remain without another woman in the house, went somewhere else to board. Happily, the breach was mended before it got too bad for repair. Some wise woman must have given the wife valuable counsel, for in a few months she returned to her spouse; and whereas there had previously been no child or prospect of one, now there was one within the year, and others followed closely. The teacher married. It would not surprise me if she rejoiced in the thought that she had united man and wife, as was the fact, and had fun herself while performing that benevolent deed.

Three marriages are known to man—the trial marriage, the companionate marriage, and marriage; and yet there are not three marriages, but one, and that is a trial marriage no matter what you call it.

I have observed, living together, couples who were married and also couples who were not. All manifested the same devotion on an average, the excess of it, if any, being on the side of the unwedded. And they all had the same troubles.

4—A WOMAN OF SIMPLE SPEECH.

A strange lady lived nearby, there in Walpole—one known to a considerable distance abroad—if I may use the words of Howells, characterizing a certain piece by Mark Twain—for her "breadth of parlance." Mrs. Chandler Wilbur, she was, an exponent of the four-letter words. In our sophisticated speech, when speaking about the things of the flesh, we use words of three or four syllables, and of as many letters as may be needed to spell them. Mrs. Wilbur, in such emergencies, used no more than four letters and one syllable. Mrs. Angela T. Heywood, a Massachusetts woman of the past century, wrote much in advocacy of a return to these simple forms, and even ventured to print one of the least innocent of them. Mrs. Heywood may not have employed the terms in social intercourse, but this Walpole lady did, and they added piquancy to her conversation, unrestrained as it was by the presence of mixed company, young or old, friends or strangers. This foe of euphemism and verbal artificialities was a good woman withal, and the mother of men. The neighborhood contained no prettier or more modest girl than her little granddaughter.

Regarding Mrs. Heywood and her simplified vocabulary I find the following from the pen of Stephen Pearl Andrews in The Truth Seeker of August 11, 1883, more than a dozen years after Mrs. Wilbur had pointed the way to freedom from the babyish and silly restrictions against which the Princeton lady rebelled. Having visited the Heywood home and had conversation with Angela, Mr. Andrews wrote as follows:

"Mrs. Heywood is in a very high degree mediumistic, inspirational, and prophetic. Much of what she says and does merely flows through her as an instrument of some power which seems determined to break up the babyish and silly prudery of the people, and so lead the way to the free discussion of all physiological and sex questions, although, still, she is herself in full harmony with her inspirations. She is again utterly destitute of the sense of fear. She laughs and rollicks over what seems to the onlooker the edge of a fearful precipice. She would sooner see her beautiful home ruthlessly sacked, her children scattered, and be herself driven, as a drudge, into somebody's else kitchen than she would back down an inch from her full claim to the right to say her full thought in her own words."

Mrs. Wilbur made no claim to being inspired, and only the affiliation of her form of speech to that of revelation warrants us in attributing to its splendors an occult source.

The unlawfulness of the four-letter word where a sesquipedalian polysyllable might be used was the discovery of some one undoubtedly the enemy of direct speech. Had we not evidence of the fact in the existence of the various vice societies, could we ever believe that the choice of one word instead of another might adversely affect a man's life, liberty, and prosperity? The thing is beyond reason. The long substitute word will inevitably in process of time become coarse. How, then, will careful talkers express themselves when education shall have made their now refined terms the familiar idiom of the vulgar?

The Walpole lady's aforesaid breadth of parlance was no sample of the verbal tastes and habits of the New England women of her generation or the next. The contrast is beyond description. The

women affected a niceness that embarrassed them
and cramped their powers of expression. It was
ungenteel, for example, for one of them to say bull.
I heard my cousin Stephen's wife speak of the male
Holstein in her husband's herd as "the animal."
My aunt Louisa, who in a flash of temper used a
biblical word, felt so bad over the slip that she went
away and cried. Sensitiveness to all that is revolt-

MY GRANDMOTHER PREFERRED A PIPE.

ing ran in the family, my grandmother being so
afflicted, even though she indulged the now unfem-
inine habit of smoking a pipe, which I often lit with
pieces of split shingle kept on a shelf over the
fireplace for that purpose. But when grandmother's
mind decayed at the age of 95, what a change took
place! All the repressions of a lifetime were un-
loosed, and she chatted affably and familiarly on
forbidden themes. Told one day that the minister
was calling, she asked not to be left alone with him,

as she not only questioned the safety of any woman in his presence, but doubted he was sound. All this being true of my respectable old grandmother, it might be true of all the saints who happen not to have liberated their thoughts while with us. Do they ponder life, then, and the things of the flesh in terms they permit themselves not to utter? And if the mind is the soul, what a load the unexpurgated one must carry to the blest abode!

5—I LEARN OF UNCLE ELIPHAZ FIELD.

Before the season ended in Walpole I knew that my next place was to be with Uncle Eliphaz and Aunt Lucia Field in the South end of Surry. Uncle Eliphaz was grandfather to the children of two families in the neighborhood, and Lucia was the spinster aunt. One of the younger set, Sarah Ellis, dwelt with them and taught the school I attended in the little building just beyond the garden fence. The old gentleman was older than the Constitution of the United States, having been born but one decade after Independence. Any man above the age of seventy used to be spoken of as a "link" between the present century and the last. Uncle Eliphaz, having seen and admired the world so wide, found pleasure in relating his remniscences for my benefit, while I equally rejoiced to hear them. When company came Aunt Lucia warned me not to start her father agoing. Visitors from Boston surrounded the table on a day I call to mind when he was moved to give his experiences among the Indians. Now I had seen Indians in Maine in 1863. They were

basketmakers, to be met on the road, shouldering to
market a bunch of baskets half the size of a load of
hay and scaring horses into the ditch. But my conception of the noble red man had been drawn from
the books published by Mr. Beadle. The word Indians brought to my vision brave and dignified warriors of lofty mien, wearing eagle feathers from the
top of the head down the back, bearing a bow, and
sporting blankets and moccasins picturesquely
beaded. As I wished this impression confirmed I
asked him how his Indians were dressed. Immediately I knew it was a social error, for he replied:
"Some of the younger ones didn't wear nothin',"
and he mentioned the consequent exposures of both
kinds. Aunt Lucia looked at me in pain and be-
wilderment, as if it were beyond her to understand
why boys should be so indiscreet and untimely in
asking for information.

That winter was a round of doing chores, and
going to school.

The following summer, working for Henry T.
Ellis, brother-in-law of Aunt Lucia, and on the
same farm, I actually earned wages—no less than
$25 for the season. Mr. Ellis was a thinking man
with an intellectual curiosity about things, one of the
few my boyhood knew, and together we discussed
weighty subjects as we worked. He used to pooh-
pooh the pieties I brought from Sunday school and
from the reading of religious papers; but he noted
my advancement at school; told me to come around
when I reached college age, and he would help me
to see how far I could go. But instead of going to
college I went into a printing-office.

The winter following we buried Uncle Eliphaz, who died one day at 88, just after I had filled and lit his last pipe. It was the first time I had come personally into touch with the hour and article of death. The Unitarian "Priest" White of Keene preached the sermon, standing in the doorway between two big rooms of the old farmhouse that was built generations before for a tavern. He read that all the days of man were three score years and ten, or if by reason of strength he be four score, and so on. And then I went out and did the chores and life went on without Uncle Eliphaz. The family was Unitarian. There had once been a Unitarian society in Surry, and this old house held the remnants of its small library. The books were too dry for me.

6—REMINDERS OF MORTALITY.

On the road that ran back of this house, and close by the schoolhouse, the forefathers had walled in a small graveyard, where perhaps fifty of them lay buried. The dates on the slate-colored stones, along with comic sculptured angels, ran back into the seventeenth century and seemed to me as remote as creation. One emigrant was there—"Samuel Mc-Curdy, born in the north of Ireland, in the county of Antrim and the parish of Abobel." Verses were inscribed appropriate to young and old. For a young woman:

> "When blooming youth is snatched away
>   By death's resistless hand,
> We to the dust the tribute pay
>   That pity doth command."

And the visitor was reminded of his mortality:

"As you are now, so once was I"—

Words to humble the proud and to show them
they were common clay. The graveyard bank on
the side next to the road had been washed by a
century of rains, till at least one grave was un-
covered, and the small bones came to the surface.

THE SKULL IN THE WALL.

In time a skull followed, and rather than that it
should lie there exposed, all the privacy of the grave
invaded, I unearthed the skull completely and placed
it in a hole in the wall where a stone had fallen out.
While I remained in the neighborhood I went often to visit with that poor Yorick and to muse on
what and when he might have been in life. Somebody, doubtless the doctors, had sawed off the top
of his head, just as the stem-end of a pumpkin is
excised to put in the candle for a jack-lantern. The
sawn-off piece was there and could be lifted for a
view of the brain cavity.

On that farm lived a little girl named Mary Ellis, of my own age, who, with her features that were classical except for a nose which naturally turned up a bit, giving her a haughty air in the presence of boys, was a little beauty. But her soft eyes never lit up for me. In the year 1928, like myself, she is living on borrowed time, according to what Priest White read from the Bible at the funeral of her grandfather. Well, years later Mary took the skull of Poor Yorick from the hole in the wall, put it in a box, and sent it to me in New York. Until I left for San Franscisco in '87 it stood on the top of my desk, labeled, "He was a Good Man, but he *would* talk to the editor." It had disappeared when I returned from the West. What, I wonder, is the social or affective implication of a Skull sent by a young lady to a young man?

CHAPTER IV.

1—THE TRAVELER'S GHOST.

SWINBURNE'S three wreckers, "marriage and death and division," ended my stay with this excellent family. Uncle Eliphaz Field no longer sat in the sunny doorway, holding his cane upright in one hand while by its bent handle he turned it 'round and 'round with the other. He had read nothing, thought time wasted on "printing," and forbade me a candle when I had nothing to do but read. His death was the first break in the household. Then Sarah, his granddaughter, got married and took Aunt Lucia to live with her in Brattleboro, Vermont.

An abandoned house in that neighborhood had not been lived in for many years. When last occupied, by a family of strangers or foreigners, so the elder people said, a traveler passing that way had taken lodging in the house at nightfall, and had never been seen again. The family soon moved away. That the traveler may have been murdered in his bed, at first a suspicion, grew into a theory and a legend and then was accepted as a fact. Everybody that could deny it had died. Inevitably the ghost of the dead man took possession of the premises; it had indeed been seen at night wandering

65

through the vacant rooms by the light of a candle carried in its hand. At length, as nobody would live in the house, it was taken down and the lumber piled or carried off. But the barn on the premises they left standing, and rather than give up the ghost, the believers averred that the traveler done away with in the house now occupied the barn, as his candle, to be seen shining through the cracks between the boards, proved aplenty.

When I stayed in the employ of Uncle Eliphaz, or with his daughter Lucia, they sometimes sent me to the village on an errand, after supper and the chores were over. The village lay a mile and a half away, and the walk there and back took an hour. I enjoyed it greatly. Every boy likes to go to the village. But in the fall, when the days were shortening, it began to be dark before I got home, and I had to pass this "haunted" barn, walking on the other side of the road, of course, yet keeping an eye on the building to see the light the ghost carried. And one night I saw it before I got within ten rods of the place. I had not much courage, day or night, but I had curiosity. I felt willing to see a ghost or anything else if it did not see me first. So I crossed the road, ducked under the rail that was laid across the gap in the stone wall where the "pair of bars" used to be, and, making no sound with my bare feet, got close to the barn-doors and looked through the crack between them. Then I saw that the light was but a lantern standing on a box; and seated beside it, on a milking-stool, was an old fellow I knew, husking corn. Well, I had been that kind of a ghost myself, husking corn by lantern-light, and I felt cheap. If I had run away without looking I should have been a believer in ghosts at least until daylight the next morning.

2—MOVING ON.

But already my next home was in view—with Aunt Polly Abbott, widow of Daniel, and her invalid daughter Mary Ann, in a large house a few moments' walk north of Surry village. Aunt Polly, aged and obese, needed a boy to build the fire in the morning, supply the stove with wood, and run her errands. That was about all. There was no continuous work for me, and I went to school. The invalidism of Mary Ann originated in a broken heart. The young man whom she was engaged to marry fell in the Civil War, which seemed to me farther away then than it does now, and left her a maiden forlorn. But Mary Ann was in my opinion the victim of her own romantic ideas that had become a possessive mania and a chronic disease. She was extremely religious; had the minister there to pray with her every week. A modern doctor would have had her out of that bed in a month, and maybe an enterprising minister would have had her in another. The piety of the household found its outward and visible sign in my attendance at church, prayer-meetings, and Sunday school, where I made my best record as a student of the New Testament. The teacher of the boys' class, named Herman Streator, asked us to answer this one: "How was it possible for four different men, unacquainted with one another's work, to write the four gospels and make their statements agree perfectly?" He was obliged to give the answer himself, and he did it perhaps reverently, anyhow under his breath, as though it had been something improper but which a boy ought to know: "It was inspiration. The writers of the gospels were inspired." I trust he spoke in ignorance of the gospels' many inconcinnities. I now feel that I should have liked to put John Remsburg's "The Christ" into his hands, and then, naming four pupils after the evangelists, let him ask questions while the boys answered them according to their gospels.

3—I SUFFER OPPRESSION.

The life I led at Aunt Polly's was physically enervating. All it meant to me was sawing a little wood, shoveling a good deal of snow, and going for the milk, groceries, and mail. Her devotion to the cooking habit provided me with more food than any boy needs. She had two or three prosperous sons, one of them a big man in the county. Their advice to me when they visited their mother negatived too much exertion in the form of work—an obvious sarcasm unless they referred to my endeavors at the table.

Slowly as time passes with the young, those days of ease came at length to an end. A close neighbor named Britton got, that spring, the idea that he could save money by having a boy to do a hired man's work, and he elected me for the experiment. In his barn there was a forty-foot tie-up, with fifteen bovines to feed, eight of them cows to milk. Cleaning out the stable every morning caused me to

shovel nigh a cartload of green and very heavy
manure. Just ahead loomed the sugaring to be
done, and the summer's wood to be sawed. Britton's interests took him much from home, early
and late, which signified that Georgie did the chores.
Has a boy of 14 the right to milk eight cows? some
of them calling for a squeeze that would crack the
nib on a scythe snath; others so holding out on him
that it was like trying to strip milk from a rope's
end? I stayed for the sugaring, wading in deep
snow and guiding an ox sled to where the tapped
maples dripped their sap into twelve-quart buckets.
The days thawed and the nights froze. My

THE BOY WITH THE FROZEN PANTS.

trousers, hung on the bedpost when I took them off,
would stand alone in the morning. Shoving bare
legs into those icy garments—for that was before
I had learned to wear underclothes—imparted a
chill to the nether members. Stockings and boots
were never dry. The room I retired to at night by

the light of a candle showed bare walls except for one work of art, a picture, in pink and green, of a boy, with his surviving parent, visiting his mother's grave beneath a willow tree that wept over it. I hated that damned boy heartily with his trousers tied down and his little plug hat. At this place the food served to me was, for the first time in my life, inferior to that distributed to the rest of the family. Hitherto there had been none of that discrimination, or if so I had been insensible of it. Living, in those environs, was arranged on the principle that one man or woman was as good as another, as regards station. There were no servants, male or female. The male employee on the farm rated as hired man, the female as hired girl, by the old-fashioned called a maid. The man and maid sat at the table, or in the "other room," with the family and with the family's company, being formally and ceremoniously introduced to the latter. The girl would be a neighbor's daughter or the man a neighbor's son. They were never obsequious, no more than tractable, and at a word of fault-finding they quit.

The claim of the undistinguished American that he was as good as anyone else loses its apparent egotism by reason of the American's admission that any other man is as good as he. "To good Americans," said the Chinese diplomat, Wu Tingfang, "not only are the citizens of America born equal, but the citizens of the world are also born equal."

An exception as to station was the "bound" boy. A boy might be bound out to a farmer, working for his keep until he was of age, when custom allowed that the man he lived with should give him a hundred dollars and a suit of clothes. While he automatically got his "time" and became his own master at twenty-one, he might forfeit the bonus and have his time earlier. Nobody bothered to treat him differently from the unbound, yet the distinction could be observed. They had an ancestral repugnance for servitude. Some boys got their time from their fathers instead of waiting for their majority. The old man in that case put a paragraph in the papers saying he would no longer collect the boy's wages or be responsible for his debts. One fellow I knew said he wished his dad had done this for him, because, he grumbled, "I was married before I'd got to be twenty-one, and so I never really had my time."

An elderly woman, in the position of an aunt and a dependent, took sides with me against an overload of work, here at Britton's, and coming to me surreptitiously when I was sawing wood, advised me to "cut stick and run." I cut the stick I was working on, and then, feeling sorry for myself, began to blubber. With that spell of weeping I took leave of my childhood, even as I took leave of Mr. Britton.

4—JUST KEEPING STEADY AT IT.

As always, a place was provided for me and waiting, and as one liberated from servitude I went. I had been a misfit in that environment. From my stay there I cannot recover a single incident to be recreated as a pleasant recollection. Such is not true of the others, and I would delight to go back to any of them if I could. That Britton proposition was like the illustrious cold potato with no warm side. I dropped down the road a mile or two and worked that season out for Edmund Woodward, a solid and sedate old agriculturist with a gem of a farm. Nothing there dimmed the bright visions of one who took life for a picnic. The old man required only that, having started to work for him, I should "keep steady at it." He observed hours of labor, as was not the rule on farms. He began the day at 5 o'clock in the morning and ended it by knocking off at 6 P. M., two hours before sundown in summer time. At this house, when days were long, there was "baiting," that is, eating between meals. Mrs. Woodward shot food aboard the table in a way to make the eyes stick out first, and then the waistband—good food, well cooked, and plenty of it. Mr. Woodward called her Mother. About the house he conducted himself like an obedient boy. I conceived she needed correction for scraping iron cooking utensils with a silver spoon that had got worn out of its original ovoid form by such usage; but no man ever changed a woman's way of doing her work. Mrs. Woodward said "Humph!" and that was all. She kept on scraping the cooking utensils with her thin silver spoons. If her silverware passed to any of her descendants, they will know why one edge of her spoons is straight. They said of Mr. Woodward that he was saving of his money, yet for a New Hampshire farmer saving is a defensive instinct. He was just to me, if not generous. His birthday

fell on the Fourth of July. No one would believe
he gave me the day and bought me the powder to
celebrate the anniversary of independence, and
technically he did not. When I told him I wanted
to celebrate *his* birthday, he bought me the powder.
It followed that, with a double-barreled shotgun of
large caliber, I awoke the countryside at earliest
dawn. While he was not quite a link with the past
century, Mr. Woodward remembered the cold summer of 1817, when the hands in the hayfield sheltered themselves from the chilling winds by sitting
on the sunny side of a bank to eat their baiting.
Woodward, with his tuning-fork and his musical
"do," pitched the tune for the church choir. Another hand working for him awhile that summer
was Joe Jolly, who divertingly turned handsprings

JOE TURNED HANDSPRINGS.

on his way to the hayfield or did horizontal bar
work on the pole across the big barndoors. I simply

revered him. And yet Joe never was a mere gymnast. "No," he said, "when I followed the circus
I was the Chandelier." I assumed a Chandelier
might be an Entertainer, perhaps a Vocalist. He
indeed had a song which he sang with feeling:

> "The spring had come, the flowers had bloomed,
>   The birds sang out their lay;
> Down by the littul running brook,
>   I first saw Maggie May.
>   . . . Singing all the day
> How I loved her none can tell
>   Littul Maggie May."

In after years I inquired of another ex-circus
man what duties went with the title or decoration
of Chandelier. He replied that the Chandelier took
care of the lamps and hauled them up the center
pole of the tent to illuminate an evening's performance.

Here, to the house of Woodward, his grandfather,
came by coincidence the Sanger boy and his sister,
now of Boston, who had been schoolmates with me
ten years before. Their cousin, a large fat girl,
took her vacation with the old folks at the same
time. I stared at the girls without lighting a re-
ciprocating eye. The boy came to me one day with
the story that the girls were dressed in boys' clothes,
the Sanger girl in her brother's, and the other, I
supposed, in my Sunday suit, which young Sanger
intimated she overflowed. Unhappily, I missed sight
of that innocent masquerade, and the regret I nour-
ished has never been assuaged. Today a fat girl
poured into a pair of trousers, or knickers, is no
sight that a man or boy would go far out of his

way to view. All things come to him who waits, though they may not come up to expectations, for age never compensates the lost opportunities of youth. I learn that the Sanger boy is now a resident of Jamaica Plain, Boston.

5—OVER THE HILL TO EAST WESTMORELAND.

My wages that summer were $10 per month. Having seen Mr. Woodward pay the money to my uncle, and then forgotten it, I light-heartedly traveled five miles in a westerly direction to earn $25 more by working over winter for Deacon Jonathan Shelley of the London district in East Westmoreland. It was hilly country. The early farmers anywhere near the Connecticut settled on the hills to avoid contact with the Indians, who made expeditions up and down the river. Here I gained some schooling also while school kept, with Millie Aldrich for teacher. I think of the able Millie with respect; for it fell out that on that day when I got into a fight with Wallace Keyser, a boy of my own age and size, and a tough nut at that, and was on the point of going to the floor with him, Millie grabbed one of us in each hand and flung Wallace one way and me the other. Wallace grinned as we recovered ourselves; but Millie was pouting and her mouth wore a smile on only one side; for on putting forth whatever horse power per minute she registered, she had ripped a sleeve of her dress at the armpit.

That school is one of the considerable number of those country institutions where I spent a few weeks with my books that have long since been abandoned and let fall into decay, or have entirely disappeared, leaving none but a few gray heads, apart from fading maps and records, to retain the knowledge they imparted, or to testify to the fact that they ever existed.

Jonathan Shelley happened to be the first deacon I had ever worked for, and the last. He was a tremendously long-armed and long-legged individual, with a short backbone and a rather small head at the top of it. His church, Christian by denomination—the first syllable pronounced Christ, the same as when that name is used alone—stood in the Flat, down the hill less than half a mile away, and had as settled pastor the Rev. Jehiel Claflin. I enjoyed the religious privileges of that sanctuary.

The deacon conducted family worship in the front room of his house every Sunday morning, and often on rainy days. He always read substantially the same scriptures, selecting that chapter of the book of Matthew which says that these shall go away into everlasting life and those into eternal damnation. The chapter treats of the occasion when Jesus shall sit as a coroner over the spiritual remains of mortals who are divided upon his right hand and upon his left, as a shepherd divideth his sheep from the goats. Those on the left were the goats. Having thus segregated them, Jesus said to the sheep on the one hand: "Come, ye blessed of my father, inherit the kingdom prepared for you from the foundation of the world"; and to the other moiety: "Depart from me, ye cussed [so pronounced by Deacon Shelley], into everlastin' fire prepared for the devils and his anngels." (He said ann.)

The deacon seldom got out of this chapter. And having read the scriptures he knelt and prayed, with his elbows in the chair where his seat had been. He looked a good deal like a capital Z turned around and pushed up to the chair, save and except that his feet were larger in proportion than the serifs at the end of that letter. He thanked the Lord that we were still alive and on praying grounds and interceding terms for mercy. "We thank thee," he would say, "that thou hast so far spared our unprofitable lives that we live to see the comin' of another of thy Sabbath mornin's. We thank thee that while others have been stretched upon beds of sickness, we have been permitted to enjoy a tollable degree of health. . . . Hear us in these our feeble supplications. Grant us each favor as we ask it as far as is consistent with thy will; and finally save us in thy comin' kingdom, there to praise God and the lamb, world without end. Amen."

Those phrases were his reliance. In the course of the prayer he asked God to bless "our wife" and urged the merciful Christ to delay his judgment on the recreant youth there present who was carelessly putting off acceptance of the begotten son of God as his personal savior. Out of curiosity I once asked Deacon Shelley if he thought I should go to hell, and he gave me to understand that he was quite certain of it.

Deacon Shelley had a workshop where, in earlier times, he had made ox bows, casks, buckets, and piggins. A piggin is a small wooden bucket, of capacity from two quarts to a gallon, with one stave sticking up far enough to be used as a handle. His

chief output in my day was axe helves and hammer
handles, his steady market being the Cheshire Railroad.   The helves and handles used in that vicinity
bore his brand, "J.S.", or "C.W.", which latter
stood for Chandler Wilbur, husband of the Walpole
lady addicted to four-letter words.   Choppers
gravely discussed the reasons for preferring the
J.S. or the C.W. axe-helve.   Reeving, hewing, shaving, scraping, and sandpapering these articles was
rainy-day and evening work.   By such creative industry I earned what Deacon Shelley paid me for
allowing him to board me and send me to school.
The various handles I made were so like his that
no one could tell the difference.   I sledded the bolts
for them from a distance; went with him into an
adjacent swamp to cut the black-ash saplings to be
split into barrel hoops.   While gathering the little
black ashes I came near witnessing the fall from
grace of Deacon Shelley; for I knew and he knew
that we were poaching on Daniel Aldrich's premises; and more than that, in cutting the little trees
so low that the stumps would not appear, he chopped
into a rock with his best axe, and uttered the oath,
"By heavens!"

6—NEW AND TRUE LIGHT ON CHURCHES.

The church at the Flat had its large day when
a preacher named Emerson Andrews came from
somewhere "below."   Points south were below, and
going to Massachusetts was "going down below."
This man came and conducted the services, and none
of the congregation remained away.   A circus could

scarcely have drawn better than this eccentric preacher. From the time and place of its origin I have calculated that he belonged to the same family as Stephen Pearl Andrews of New York, who was raised in Hinsdale. An excellent farmer's wife named Andrews in that locality had sons who were approaching manhood sixty or seventy years ago, or so the story goes; and when she was asked about their prospects, she replied that the outlook for all but one of them was far from bright, for only the oldest was worth anything on the farm. The next oldest son threw his time away reading books, another had begun clerking in a lawyer's office with small promise of making anything of himself; the third sawed on a fiddle from morning till night, and the fourth, expecting to be a minister, was calling worthless sinners to repentance already. So she had but the one promising son out of the "passle," the son who stayed at home and worked the land. The rest of the story of this Andrews family tells that the bookish boy became the president of a university (E. Benjamin Andrews); the law clerk governor of Connecticut; the fiddler a great musician known in Europe and America; and the one with a hortatory complex, if the story is authentic, might be identified as this Emerson Andrews who preached at the Flat. I listened to him, but don't remember a word he said. What I distinctly recollect is that he sat in the pulpit before the afternoon meeting began and sang:

"Blow ye the trumpet, blow,
    The gladly solemn sound;
Let every nation know,
    To earth's remotest bound,
The year of jubilee has come,
    Return, ye ransomed sinners, home."

That was more than half a century ago, and the
hymn may have been sung for half a century before then. There was no sign of the Jubilee that
season, nor has any been seen since. It was a false
alarm. There was no observable correspondence
between the subjective order of thought and the
objective order of phenomena; but in religious
things there never is.

In that town of Hinsdale, pronounced Hensdil,
whence the preacher came, a mill or factory stood
beside the Ashuelot river. One of its hands, a
young woman, deriving her inspiration from the
turbulent stream, turned out a quite well known
poem while employed there. The poem began:

"Over the river they beckon to me,
    Loved ones who've crossed to the farther side:
The gleam of their snowy robes I see,
    But their voices are lost in the rushing tide."

The river which was the Ashuelot ran downhill
rapidly at that point, in a hurry to empty its waters
into the Connecticut, and was indeed noisy enough
to interrupt conversation.

No trace of Catholicism appeared in any of the
places where I lived, outside of Keene; but Keene
was a city, and all degraded forms of humanity
gather in those haunts of iniquity. However, at
the Flat was an Irish section hand (employed by

the Cheshire Railroad), who knew all about it and could tell me how "these here Prodestant churches" stood as compared with the true one. He had asked whether I ever had been baptized, and learning I had not, shook his head sadly and repeated, "Too bad, too bad, too bad!" Of course I asked why. "I will tell you," said this man, whose name I disremember except that it was Pat. "Ye see, it is this way. The Catholic church is the spouse of Jasus Christ, and Jasus is no Mormon to have more than one wife. Yer mother was yer father's wife, wasn't she, and what would other women be if he had 'em? They'd be just what all the churches be except the true one—they're all hoors." Residents of those rural areas knew of Catholicism as "the Irish religion," distinguishing it from Christianity. George Patten of Westmoreland more than once uttered the prediction that if there was ever another war in this country, it would be, by Godfrey, between these two, Christianity and Catholicism.

This man George Patten at times fell into profane and unlicensed anecdotes and speech. He was, I think, the author of a story about the deathbed of Ethan Allen. Anyhow, he told it. As it ran, the minister said comfortingly to the dying man: "The angels are waiting for you, Colonel Allen." And the hero of Ticonderoga shot at the ghostly counsellor the last beam of his closing eye as he responded: "Well, God damn 'em, let 'em wait." Colonel Allen lived to utter a few more mild cuss words, and then passed to his reward.

Knowledge of the institution of the papacy had escaped my inquiring mind until I was ten years old. The geography used in the school that summer asked the question, "For what is the city of Rome distinguished?" The pupils who answered said: "As the residence of the Pope." That word "pope" raised a laugh. None of us had intent to show disrespect toward the sovereign pontiff, whatever he might be, but that word pope was irresistibly funny. The fellow wearing the title vaguely existed in my thought for a moment as a superior kind of magician, an entertainer, because he gave audiences, which idea was again obscure to me; or a man rather more like God than the ringmaster at the circus with his high hat and swallowtail coat. Hence, when a year or two later the Vatican council affirmed the dogma of the pope's infallibility and my mother sent to the New Hampshire Sentinel some comments on that subject, I must suffer in silence while the ribald made merry over the locution "infallibility of the pope," which seemed to me just letters of the alphabet spilt on paper.

CHAPTER V.

D EACON SHELLEY stimulated a boy's energies and accelerated production at his hands by praising him. Mrs. Shelley believed that the more a boy ate the more work he would do. I trust I justified their methods. I knew not then what it meant to be tired after a day's work. One might be tired while working; but when a man complained, "I'm tired tonight," after work was over, I missed the sense of the remark. Tired, and doing nothing! It was too much for me. Work and weariness went together, but they ended at the same time. The deacon, when chores were done, could doze in his chair; I craved diversion, excitement, and found both at Thompson's general store down to the Flat, where men and boys gathered for exchange of thoughts and competition in feats of strength and agility. Deacon Shelley viewed this dissipation as the beginning of the downward path towards perdition; yet as all hired men were supposed to have their liberty evenings, he lacked authority to forbid my going there or even my attending a dancing school on Mutton Hill; tuition 25 cents a lesson; music by Ambrose & Higgins's Orchestra. That was a one-piece orchestra; the performer, Ambrose Higgins, fiddler. The Deacon refused me an

advance of two dollars for lessons, on the ground
that it would make him party to a form of frivolity
if not of sin. Still, I found the money where someone had put it, on the lightstand by my bed, and
asked no questions. The pupils at the dancing
school were young. The girls, slender and uncor-
seted, seemed too soft and fragile for rough hands
to grab in the hurried turning of partners and corners. There were, however, no injuries among them
traceable to that cause. Having been raised sister-
less, I had no familiar knowledge of the nature of
girls. Thoughts were engendered in my mind by
hearing one say to her partner: "I don't like to be
swung off my feet—not clear off, only almost, not
quite." As to girls without their encircling bar-
ricadoes, I doubt they donned them at that time as
young as they now put on the next-to-nothing corset. On a vacation ten years later, I went to town
with a farmer who had a daughter of 16 or 17.
While he did his trading at the store, I asked him to
suggest some useful gift of remembrance I might
send home to his folks. Falling in with the idea
as a good one, he remembered that the little girl
had been talking lately about a pair of corsets, so
long as other girls of her age were wearing them;
hence he concluded, "I dunno but what they'd suit
better'n anything else you could buy." I bought
'em, along with a bag of candy, binding him to say
only the candy was my contribution to the happiness
of his little girl.

The town spelling schools were held there on
Mutton Hill. A school teacher, two ministers, and

a doctor went down at the one I contested, and left me spelling words selected from the familiar Latin and French phrases in the back part of the book.

COMING SIXTEEN AND SPELLING GOOD.

"Who loosened and let down this brutal jaw?
Whose was the hand that slanted back that brow?
Whose breath blew out the light within this brain?"

(See Mr. Markham's Man with the Hoe, and various allusions to close relations with oxen.)

The term with Deacon Shelley went far enough into the spring of 1873 for me to help him shingle his wagon shed, a half-roofed building annexed to the barn. The job had a thrilling finish. The deacon nailed on the last course of shingles, tied them with a narrow board beveled and nailed down, and had unshipped all the staging but one bracket toed into the shingles, when his feet escaped from beneath him and he sprawled face downward on the

roof, catching hold of that last bracket to save himself from going over the eaves. At the moment this
befell, I was some distance away, carrying the old
shingles into the woodshed. I heard his yell; saw
what had happened, and slowly moved toward the
scene. The ladder, which he repetitiously ordered
me to fetch, was leaning against the eaves a dozen
feet from where those large extremities of his
were waving in an impossible attempt to reach it.
As there seemed to be no immediate danger that he
would let go of the bracket, and as he was perfectly safe while he held on, I continued to move
with moderation. I sensed that I was in the presence of a situation promising much that could be
communicated to the neighbors with advantage to
my reputation as a recounter. The faculty of observation and description which afterwards was to
help me as reporter, then and there began to develop. I lingered to fix in my mind such features
of this occasion as I thought would be most appreciated by Uncle Lewis Aldrich and old Zeke Woodward, who lived up the street and were prone to
draw me out on the traits and peculiarities of Uncle
Jock (for so they called my employer). Meanwhile
the Deacon on the roof demanded the ladder with
his voice and searched for it with his feet. Having placed the ladder where it touched him, I leisurely ascended it, noting by the way how the view
off toward Mount Gilboa and Albert Chickering's
place improved as I gained altitude. Then, arriving at the proper height, I assembled Uncle Jock's
feet and put them on the nearest round. Now the

doubt arose in his mind that he could let go his hold on the bracket and not slide against the ladder with enough impetus to tip it over backwards. He referred the question to my judgment. One could see, I reflected, that the factors of the problem were force, motion, and equilibrium. If in sliding to the eaves he gathered force enough to impart motion to the ladder, disturbing its equilibrium and carrying it past its center, then its top, with him on it, would describe an arc over the lane and above the wall on the other side and land him in the Greening tree, when he could come down out of its top in the way we did last fall when we picked the apples. "Consarn you, you young tyke," said the Deacon, "you go to work and shore up the ladder with one of them long boards." I did better by bringing a trace-chain and making the ladder fast to a tie-ring stapled to the corner of the building. With his feet on the ground again he sent me up to pry the bracket off the roof. He had the impulse, he owned, to carry off the ladder and leave me up there.

2—A DIGRESSION.

When I wrote the name of Albert Chickering a few moments ago, my mind strayed far from the incident then being related. Yes, over west across the valley, off the Gully road, on the brow of Mount Gilboa, lived Albert Chickering, a most substantial citizen, who had more cattle, they said, than he ever stopped to count, and owned, as they also said, "all the land that joined him." Does the unpredictable occur? Does it? About fifteen years later I was in line to be Albert's son-in-law, and silk for the wedding gown was in hand when the lure of publishing a paper in San Franscisco put the breadth of a continent between me and a very sweet girl who had courage stronger than her family's confidence in my future. She would almost have been a man's fortune in herself, for the Chickerings were thrifty and forehanded property-acquiring people. The girls taught school and invested their pay. This one married in due time, raised a family of bright children and died some years ago. One of her boys and one of mine were fellow gobs in the navy in 1917. They called each other cousin.

When Albert Chickering was an old man (he lived past ninety), he went to hear Ingersoll lecture. I judged that the lecture to which he had listened was "Which Way?" the one that closes with a vision of the future and a picture of the present, thus:

"I see a world at war, and in the storm and chaos of the deadly strife thrones crumble, altars fall, chains break, creeds change. The highest peaks are touched with holy light. The dawn has blossomed. I look again. I see discoverers sailing across mysterious seas. I see inventors cunningly enslave the forces of the world. I see the houses being built for schools. Teachers, interpreters of nature, slowly take the place of priests. Philosophers arise, thinkers give the world their wealth of brain, and lips grow rich with words of truth."

When asked how these sentiments fell in with his habit of thought, Mr. Chickering answered:

"Gosh! Bob Ingersoll said just what I've been saying all my life; and darned if he didn't say it in the same words."

3—IT SAVED FIREWOOD, ANYHOW.

Uncle Lewis Aldrich who is mentioned above as one who drew amusement from hearing of the notional ways of "Uncle Jock," was kin, probably uncle, to Nelson Aldrich, the Rhode Island politician who, having in time got into the United States Senate, provided some place such as doorkeeper for another nephew, one Wes Aldrich, then our neighbor.

In the days of the Fourth New York Liberal League I read before that society a paper on "New England and the People Up There." Into that youthful forensic effort I introduced the story how, when I drew the cider one evening there at Deacon Shelley's, and when melted tallow, dropping from the candle into the piggin, floated on the surface of the cider, an old fellow said to me: "I wish the next time you would bring the cider in one thing and the tarler in another, and let me mix 'em to suit myself." That was Uncle Lewis. All the old fellows were uncles or aunts to young and aged. He spent many a winter evening in Aunt Nancy Shelley's kitchen, droning over the topics of the times, past and present. I was reading a book by "Boz" (behind which name Dickens had concealed from me his authorship of the work) and I looked up at hearing Uncle Lewis's comment on Aunt Nancy's remark that a baby just born in the neighborhood was "a long time coming"—two or three years after the parents were married to each other. Uncle Lewis had said to Aunt Nancy: "It's different now to what it was. There ain't a man on this road but what didn't have his wife in a thrivin' way before he married her." Mrs. Shelley smiled at the stocking she was darning. The deacon didn't smile at anything. I promptly asked: "How about Uncle Daniel Abbott, over in Surry? He lived on this road when he was married." Uncle Lewis waved his hand: "Same as the rest."

The answer surprised and disappointed me. I didn't believe it. I had heard Aunt Polly go on about such doings; and I told Uncle Lewis I guessed if he knew what she said of girls that set the neighbors to talking about them, he would think different. For to tell the truth Aunt Polly said, "The sluts!" whereat her daughter Mary Ann would turn wide-open eyes on me as being present, and check her with an admonitory "Mother!" But Aunt Polly was only doing her duty. How could the old edify the young except by pointing out that their conduct is unprecedented? But the method isn't infallible, since the young, by reading or thinking, find out that their respected elders, now so ready to give advice, were once at the less blessed receiving end themselves. Parents who inform their children they didn't carry on like that when they were young, mean only that they were told they shouldn't.

To all young girls among my descendants who may be picked on I bequeath this:

Take heart, dear child; or should you chance to
　stumble,
While contrite toward yourself, don't be *too*
　humble
When parents are severe and elders grumble:
　"Such things weren't done by lassies with their
　　laddies
When *we* were young—such holding and such
　petting!"
They tell it thus, conveniently forgetting
　What cut-ups were the grandmas and grand-
　　daddies.

I ran over, mentally, the names of the elder offspring begotten of this custom of their sires to
which Uncle Lewis had recurred. They were then
from fifty to sixty years old, setting back their
births to 1820 and earlier. Aunt Polly's animadversions on the growing-up girls proclaimed her one
in habit and sentiment with all generations before
and since. No generation can grant anything to
the crop of youngsters it is raising. Listen to this!
In one of the plays of Vanbrugh (b. 1664) the virtuous Mrs. Cloggit exclaims: "Look you there
now; to see what the youth of this age are come to."
The lady was speaking of the youth of the seventeenth century—the century of our Puritan forefathers. And another of the same date protested:
"Girls were not wont to do such things when I was
young."

Uncle Lewis, whose age linked him with the previous century, had knowledge of an old custom
practiced in rural New England, and divulged to

him partly by his forebears and somewhat by observation, called "bundling."   Theodore Schroeder,
who has written much useful matter tracing the
erotogenesis of religion, thinks this practice religious in its origin. It may be, and yet one can see
how easily it might arise out of the conditions, the
necessities, and the opportunities of rural districts
two hundred or more years ago in those states.
Leaving out the side remarks and the individual instances, I will see if sense can be made of Uncle
Lewis Aldrich's rambling discourse on bundling,
delivered to me on an evening when I worked in the
shop scraping and sandpapering axe handles.   In
the first place (so he premised) they used to marry
younger than they do now.   Before the oldest boy
was of age his folks began to talk about his bringing
home a wife.   The girl he wanted might live a long
ways off.   Getting home again after spending half
the night courting her was a hardship and might be
"resky." Said Mr. Aldrich: "I've seen 'em goin'
home at sunup myself. If the girl's folks favored
the match they didn't object to his resignin' himself
to her society till the mornin' light appeared.   The
bundling may have been done partly to make them
safe and partly to keep them warm without burning
up all the firewood."   Here the use of large sacks
or sleeping bags is inferred, and you see the parents dropping the sacks on the floor in front of the
young folks, who step into them, and the tops are
brought up and made fast at the neck.   Uncle
Lewis believed they were oftener rolled up in quilts.
"Maybe their hands were out," he said, "I don't

know." It was expected of them that they would go
to sleep and be in shape for work the next day. No,
the fellow didn't stay to breakfast. That warn't
done. One of the old folks came around early and
turned him loose. The fellows then made a short
siege of it, Uncle Lewis said. Her folks were not
going to all that trouble for six months or a year
when there was nothing to prevent the young ones
from getting married. So they would learn them
by themselves and not go nigh them. "They might
have huddled each other," he surmised, "I dunno.
Folks can generally depend on a girl to make a fellow behave till they are about ready to be married.
And a young fellow without any experience thinks
he is favored a lot if she lets him hold her. Take a
sofa, not a settee that is nothin' but a wooden chair
stretched out, and mother's big shawl, and no matter then if the fire does go out. But if they hain't
these, and the courtin' wood is all burnt up, and
the fellow works his boots off and takes off her
shoes, why, the girl don't like him much or don't
want him if she makes any great kick when he picks
her up and carries her to her bed, and they get under the coverlids and keep warm. They got on all
their clothes except what they had on their feet.
Oh, I don't suppose they bundled except in winter.
The sofa done for summer time. I remember when
I was courtin' my wife that sometimes we'd fall
into a clinch and go to sleep. No. I never was
bundled, but I can guess how it turned out. That
there way the two on 'em would get to be jest like
one person, and resistin' him would be the same as

resistin' of herself, which is a delusion. What's the odds? They got married."

The records are said to show that the Puritans frowned upon bundling and its natural consequences. But the arm of Puritanism was not long enough to reach districts remote from Puritan centers. The objectors were bundled into their graves, and their bespoken daughters and sisters still throve. No stigma attached to the past of families on London Road, although their descendants followed other counsels. Good people may make their own customs, and their ʰ·ndicate them.

⸱rved Mr. Schroeder's treatise on bundling ⸱⸱ ⸱ibus origin for insertion at this point, but I c⸱ ᵓake his theory fit the facts as they were impart⸱ ⸱. Part of the treatise on the subject in Woodwaɪ⸱ "ʼashington" is more applicable. Woodward say⸱ "he nights were cold; there was usually only one ⸱ce, before which all the family sat. Squalling cʰ⸱ and prosy old men cluttered the stage and made ɪ⸱ ⸱⸱nder passages very difficult, if not impossible. ⸱ under the warm blankets in the darkness of the ʟ⸱ ᵓm, conversation was much more pleasant and dec⸱ easier."

Mr. Woodward's further quotations on the theme descend to ribaldry, and I cannot follow him. As one who in his youth performed much irksome labor in the preparation of fuel for stove and hearth, I am inclined to view bundling as a justifiable recourse to save firewood.

4—BROTHER TO THE OX.

In the spring of 1873, having turned 16, I commanded wages of $16 per month for the season, May-October inclusive. The situation had waxed serious. When every day meant half a dollar to the employer, or more than that counting out Sundays, one was expected to deliver the goods in the shape of service and performance. So from Deacon Shelley's I went down the hill and on beyond the Flat, and worked for Gene Fuller. Three generations composed the family: Christopher Fuller and his wife—he was a carpenter engaged in building a barn on the County Farm; Gene and his wife, and their children. Gene proved to be a boyish man who would rather stop and throw stones at a mark than assiduously cultivate crops. The farm was a large one; the soil fertile; the pasture ran further up on Mount Gilboa than I ever explored. Sheep, cattle, and turkeys flourished. That summer I learned to shear sheep. I have not since had enough use for the accomplishment to atone for the pain that Fuller's flock suffered at my hands. I harbored always a friendly feeling for oxen and they were patient with me. When quite a small boy I had been sent into the barnyard to yoke a pair of cattle that weighed about sixteen hundred each, and towered a foot or more above my head. To yoke oxen one withdraws the righthand bow from the yoke and carries it in his fist, while with the yoke and the undetached bow under his left arm, he approaches the off ox. The ox, which may be lying down, erects himself slowly, hind end first, and looks pla-

cidly and not with disfavor at this insect that has
interrupted his restful period. The insect hooks
this off ox with the bow, which is like the letter U,
and pulls the top toward him far enough almost to
twist off the animal's head, so that the open ends
of the bow may be inserted and pinned into the
yoke, which he is not strong enough to raise to a
level. The insect then goes to the other end of the
yoke, elevates it, and takes out the other bow. Having hooked the off ox, as aforesaid, he looks around
for the near one. That animal has been an interested

GOOD FRIENDS.

spectator of the proceedings so far, and when he
sees the insect making frantic demonstrations toward himself with the empty bow, he sighs and
moves forward, even lowering his head to lift the
yoke, in contempt of the insect's effort to raise it
to the level of his neck. The oxen may have mistaken the insect for a calf because of its knock-

kneed legs resembling their front ones. He gives the word in a small voice which he tries to make a large one, and the oxen humor him by moving ahead and letting him think he is driving them.

In Maine they handled oxen with a goad, a four-foot whipstock with a quarter-inch brad in the smaller end. The cruelty of its use caused me distress when I was yet very small, and I never forgot it. As in some ways the hired farm hand is brother to the ox, I became class conscious without knowing economics.

NOTE.—Out of a letter from a New Hampshire girl who long has been a grandmother I purloin a few words: "I think grandpa and aunt had quite a trial one winter when you and I were with them. 'George, have you watered the horse?'—'Sarah, have you got the potatoes?' 'No,' and it was every day. You loved to read and I loved to play. That was long ago."

Yes, it has been quite a spell since that winter. "George, have you watered the horse?" says grandpa. He asked again in an hour whether I said No or Yes. Sarah loved to play, certainly; she loved to laugh also, and she had the lips and the teeth to make a good deed shine in a naughty world. I married a girl who laughed like Sarah.

That old horse was a white one that gave a close imitation of a snowstorm when shedding his coat, unless I "carded" him with care and vigor. And we hitched him up to an ancient "pleasure wagon," or so grandpa called the vehicle used for driving rather than farming purposes. I was sometimes privileged to "carry" Sarah in it. There was room for four like us on its wide seat On one occasion, as we drove away, a girl without feeling or manners observed that we looked as if we were "going off to get married." And Sarah laughed. I hope she is laughing still.

4—THE WORTHY ELLIOTT WEYMAN.

On this road where my sixteenth season "fleeted" by (talk of the fleeting days of youth, they are the longest in life's calendar) a man lived named Elliott Weyman who was the first person I had ever heard to question the truth of the Bible and the justice of the God whose biography it contains. They called Mr. Weyman a spiritualist. Every doubter was a "spiritualist" to the church people there, who seemed not to have heard of any other unbelievers in the Christian religion than these and the heathen in distant lands. His skepticism had been excited by reading the book of Job. The devil harassed Job, he owned, but God "put him up to it." All of the afflictions of men, said Mr. Weyman to me, were due to the trickery and treachery of God, who also let his own son fall into the hands of his enemies, and then forsook him. Weyman regarded the future life of the individual as problematical; hence those Christians who were worrying about their title to the mansions they placed in the skies might be "barking up the wrong tree." On the other hand, the continued existence of people here on earth was assured by their propensity to reproduce themselves; therefore, any act, large or small, which improved the world was that much clear gain for the people. So Mr. Weyman, following out the thought, spent the last years of his life in planting small pine trees on some acres of his land that were too steep for cultivation. It was pure philanthrophy, for he could not hope to live until the trees grew large enough to add value to the land. Weyman, when his time came, was buried near the grove he had created. I saw his trees about 1914. They had grown up tall and straight, some of them near a foot through at the butt. His little saplings had become a stand of pine, a worthy memorial to a worthy man.

Of this season's experience, or want of it, there is nothing to report. There could be no story here except one of long days laboriously spent and oblivious nights. Late rising invited sarcasm. When my brother, employed in a printing-office, informed me that he went to work at 7 A. M., I inquired what he did with his spare time in the morning. An incident of this summer was my oversleeping once and hearing a querulous voice under my window inquire whether I cal'lated to stay in bed all day. Said the voice: "Come on, get up; it's 5 o'clock!" I was half an hour behind time. That season, for the first time, I went into the hayfield with a scythe, on equal terms with men; first cradled and bound oats and rye. The cradle was no new-fangled implement; on the contrary, quite ancient; yet some farmers there were who still reaped their grain with a sickle to save the stalk from breakage. Straw with its integrity so preserved commanded a sale for use in sucking lemonade.

Farmers raised corn for the sake of the grain; women would not make brown-bread or johnnycake with Western meal. The era preceded the introduction of the silo and the planting of corn to be cut when green, chopped and stored therein to feed milk cows. The furniture of barns included a "feed cutter" designed to prepare meals for horses. Came the thrashing machine and that later contraption, the hay press, with their crews of wild young men sophisticated by wide travel—they'd been in every town in the county, pretty near, they boasted. In Denman Thompson's "Old Homestead," Uncle Josh Whitcomb, who lived in Swanzey, next to Keene, says to a young man: "John, I was a wild coot when I was your age. Yes, sir. Ran with a thrashin'-machine three years!" The hay-pressing gang were equally untamed. They went as far north as Bellows Falls and south even to Fitzwilliam. One of them skinned me by selling me a watch, on which, the cases not proving to be of solid gold, I was out three dollars.

5—MY STATION RISES

I left the Fuller place, in the fall, with a flourish, in a very neat rig, a nimbly stepping roan horse and a single-leaf side-spring buggy, driven by Emerson Franklin, who had hooked me for the winter. This Franklin was a bachelor of near 50, who lived alone in a house he owned at Westmoreland village, doing his own housework and cutting men's clothes and hair. He offered no pay and required no service of me except taking care of his horse. What he wanted of a boy I didn't understand, as more than an hour a day spent on a horse would be idle time. I found out after I had been with him for a while. He had an epileptic seizure of a night, when all his muscles tied themselves into knots and had to be smoothed out. The first scare over, I came to view the infrequent seizures calmly as part of the job.

I remained with Franklin for two years; and this proved, as it were, the life. The days were free; after dark the boys came for company and to play eucher. He cut my clothes and taught me straight handsewing evenings and rainy days. By way of outside employment there were teams to be driven, wood to be sawed, and always farm work in season. The cordwood that I reduced to stove length filled large sheds. Old Doctor Simmons's work, most of which I did, included the sawing of ten cords of wood. The doctor prepared a nervine known as prickly ash bitters, a favored restorative in the hayfield. Traffic in it supplemented his practice and the sale of clocks. When clocks first began to be actuated by springs instead of weights, a good-sized mantel clock sold for twenty dollars. A younger physician had the practice in the village. The old Doc played it rather low down on me once, I thought and still think. A man who lived a mile out of town owed him a hundred dollars, borrowed money, and he sent me to see if I could collect it, with instructions to say that the doctor stood very much in need of the sum. The debtor was a deacon in the Congregational church, but sometimes called Colonel. Deacon was his Sunday title; Colonel his secular and military handle. They told of him the story that when he went to Concord as representative of the town, a Westmoreland woman at the capital saw him joining some other members in a drink of milk punch; and when she taxed him with the indulgence, he replied with dignity, and to her satisfaction: "Madam, I have never in my life taken liquor except as a beverage." Well, when I faced him with the request that he should liquidate Dr. Simmons's note, he was all the Colonel and the Statesman. "Young man," he said, "when I needed the sum of one hundred dollars, I went and borrowed it. You may return to Dr. Simmons and say I advise him to do the same."

In Westmoreland I came near losing my head, with the bell of the Unitarian church as the exe-

THIS IS THE CHURCH.

cutioner. Will Barber, the minister's son, was pulling the rope, "setting" the bell; that is, turning it mouth upward. When he eased off on the rope the bell came down and did its stuff with a loud double clang. Being ignorant of how this effect was produced, and wishing to learn, I climbed to the belfry and put my head through an aperture into the bell's apartment. The bell rope lay in a groove on the outer circumference of a big wheel, or spoked sheave, with the bell depending from its shaft. Pulling on the rope turned the sheave and oscillated

the noise producer. In introducing my head I must
have thrust it between the spokes. The bell being
"set" and at rest, I devoted a few seconds to inspection. Then a loud creak startled me and I
backed out. The bell was returning. The descend-
ing spoke of the sheave took my cap, but I got away
with my head.

On two occasions I naturally ought to have been
obliterated. The first one happened in old man
Brockway's sawmill in the South end of Surry. He

BROCKWAY'S MILL

ran an up-and-down saw seried with ferocious teeth
an inch long. I turned in to help him saw some
saplings that were so slender that, teetering with
the motion of the saw, they must be sat upon to
control the vibration. Brockway went to dinner and
left me sawing. The work had no difficulties, for
the saw stopped automatically at the end of the cut,
"niggering back" was a simple if thrilling adventure,
and the log could be moved over for the next cut

by raising and lowering a lever, while starting the
saw required nothing but putting the foot on a
wooden pin and bearing down. Continuous sitting
on the bucking saplings, however, tended to weary
the flesh. It also made the mind less alert, for when
Brockway came back he found me astride a log,
gazing intently at the teeth of the saw as each stroke
brought me an inch nearer to them, and utterly
oblivious of anything else. He grabbed my arm
and yanked me off the log, when I had come within
a few ups and downs of having my head split open.

Three times and out, considered as a rule, scores a
failure here. There are exceptions to all rules. I
escaped once more. Behold me carting phosphate,
with a yoke of cattle, from the North Depot to East
Westmoreland, and having a dozen barrels aboard,
weighing a ton and a half. Oxen hold back reluctantly when a heavy load is pushing downhill,
and small blame to them, with the tongue of the
cart thrashing about and the yoke knocking against
their horns. On starting down a sharp dip in the
road, I jumped off the cart to go to their heads,
for we were gathering speed. I landed on a rolling
stone, and sat down in front of a cartwheel. The
tire took the bark off by backbone; the hub belted me
in the head; yet I scrambled to my feet and got in
front of the cattle in time to slow them down and
avert a wreck. The performance could not be successfully repeated with a thousand chances. When I
dropped from the cart upon the rolling stone and sat
down I should have fallen backward in front of the
wheel and lost my daylights.

CHAPTER VI.

1—THE GIRL INTRUDES.

IN the next few years after I came to 14 I drew only feebly with the girls. They paid me no attention and but few times did I wish it otherwise. We he-fellows regarded as effeminate the boy whom the girls favored. As I advanced further into the adolescent period the gulf widened on account of the bluff I put up to mask my timidity when girls were by. The school girls of fifteen or sixteen without exception neither looked at me invitingly nor spoke to me. However, when I returned there with more assurance. after a stay in New York, they exercised their powers of speech and had learned to look. One of them, in a way, explained the cold spell between us at school. To my astonishment she said they considered me "too conceited" over a few times that, when the rest of the class hadn't the answer ready, it had been my luck to remember it. Those awful examples in arithmetic! Teacher called one scholar and then another to the blackboard; always it was an example they hadn't done. Teacher asked, finally, if anyone in the class had worked that problem, and my hand went up, followed by myself at the board, making homely figures, marking down the answer, known of course beforehand, and swaggering to my seat. It was simply, why—annoying! It would have been kinder on my part, this one thought, if I had kept my hand down and given them another try at the example. Thus I saw that in my nervousness, I had behaved like a chump—that Thackeray was right when he said a boy was an ass; and I have no hope at all that my error will help any other boy through that trying period of life and girls. One teacher at that epoch when I was in a state of ignorance as to the worth of a lass really made overtures toward comradeship. She raised my temperature by stopping beside my desk when going down the aisle, and brushing the shoulder of my coat with her hand or straightening the part in my hair by turning a hank over on the side where it belonged. With such contacts and with out-of-school meetings, or walks that just happened, we acted like one of those engaged couples where the man has lost his enthusiasm, for I was so much of an idiot as to take the passive and receptive part. Only boys of the age I had then reached will approve my attitude, or understand me. Later I wrote cynically of this episode:

> "The school is done and the winter sped;
>   The schoolmarm and I, we drift apart,
> And Romance I. lies cold and dead
>   On the fresh green grave of a broken heart.
> Go plant the willow and cypress tree,
>   Hang up the handsled out of reach.
> I will get the parson to measure me,
>   And take my size for a funeral speech."

My original offense is aggravated by this rhythmical performance and I now wish to register contrition and regret. What of merit has man ever done that he should be worthy to have a woman mindful

of him? And when a girl touches him and her hand
trembles and her color comes and goes, and she is
ready to forgive and weep for his faults, and then
he only grins at her, what does the overgrown lum-
mox deserve except that his neck should be quickly
and unfixably broken?

Yet others of womankind have a way of avenging
disregard of one—they are all for each and each for
all. It couldn't have been long before the goddess
of retribution took me in hand and reduced me to
a girlward condition so imbecilic that I could indite
the following defeatist verses:

> "If the love of another should gain you,
>   Let me dwell in your memory alone;
> Or if thought of my solitude pain you,
>   Forget me as one never known.
> As the flowers of last season have perished
>   That budded and bloomed and are fled
> So the blossom of love that I cherished,
>   When the summer departed was dead."

The time and the place and the girl have escaped
me. I do not know when or where or to whom I
inscribed these lines, nor can I explain now why I
ever came to write that mush. But I quote it so
that the worst may be over. This work is "The
True George Macdonald," and I have never done
anything else so bad that it wasn't a virtuous act
compared to that one.

Two young persons, girl and boy, see each other
at short intervals covering a considerable length of
time, and are as distant as though they had never
met, until all of a sudden something jumps across
between them, and at once they are appreciative

friends—chums. They find and confess that they
had always taken notice of each other, and "Don't
you remember?" coming from her to him reveals
that all the time he thought her indifferent she has
been taking notice and can recite his local history
more accurately than he could do it himself. And
then separation for all time—or death.

> "For some we loved, the loveliest and the best
> That from his Vintage rolling Time hath prest,
>   Have drunk their Cup a Round or two before,
> And one by one crept silently to rest."

The lovely girl who on my return so held the
mirror that I could take a look at myself as others
saw me was at the time she did so already on her
silent and pitiful way to the Great Rest, under sentence of death from tuberculosis, there known only
as "consumption," which was ever the scourge of
New England maidenhood. In a circle that would
embrace a population of scarcely one hundred, I
could name half a dozen young girls, pretty beyond
words, who died as virgin sacrifices to the white
plague.

2—THIS WAS RURAL NEW HAMPSHIRE.

That town of Westmoreland—and you must accent the *West* and almost ignore the second syllable
by calling it mer—has a small population, no common center, and many districts. I have mentioned
neither Parkhill, Poocham, nor the Glebe. Parkhill got its first name since my day. Formerly it
was The Hill. On its top is a Congregational church
where Samuel P. Putnam went once to preach. The

view up the Connecticut Valley from there makes the most beautiful postcard I ever saw. Poocham is a detached settlement; and what the Glebe is I never could find out. In England the income of glebe land is part of ecclesiastical graft. Once this glebe may have been so devoted, since New Hampshire formerly made public grants for the support of the Protestant ministry.

It irks me to shift from the subject of girls to the unrelated one of surviving Puritan manners and morals, now probably extinct, but my observations in the rural parts of New Hampshire, with reading extending further back, convince me that the customs and characteristics of the people down there who lived at a distance from the ignoble strife of the crowd had changed little since the Revolution, or even since the Colonial period; and they spoke the speech brought to their shores by the Pilgrim fathers; those living coastwise using the vocabulary of the sailors on the Mayflower. I sincerely believe that more changes have taken place there since 1870 than had occurred in the previous century. My boyhood saw the passenger and mail-carrying stage-coach go rocking by on thoroughbraces attached to C springs, the driver delivering parcels and collecting letters to be mailed. Would not Thomas Paine have seen the same vehicle in the New England of his period? The fathers of the families used flint-lock firearms, and neither the guns nor the flints had become antiques when I handled them. Manv a farmer's lantern was of tin, elaborately perforated —holes shaped like stars, crescents and triangles—

with a socket for a candle inside. The candle provided domestic illumination; snuffers, a pair of shears surmounted by a small apartment to receive the burnt wick, belonged to the outfit. The announcer of evening meetings ignored the sun and the clock, and called for a gathering "at early candle-lighting." I assisted, while in Surry, at candle dipping, which is the old way of manufacturing candles. Given a large and deep receptacle, a wash boiler, full of melted tallow, the dipper draped his wicks in a row over a stick, and lowered them into the hot fat. They were lifted out for the grease to harden, and then dipped again and again until they carried enough tallow for a candle. Lamps still burned whale oil. In Jonathan Shelley's house the kerosene lamp, lately acquired, was viewed with apprehension by the women. Only the deacon himself handled it, and he stood at arms' length to touch it off, as if its wick had been a fuse.

Professional men wore shawls as pictures show they did or still may do in Europe. Overcoats were called surtouts, and that is what George Washington called his. When Elijah Mason, a man of 60-odd, put on his best clothes to visit a lady and solicit her hand in marriage, he wore a low plug hat, a blue coat, much cut away as to the skirts, and a buff waistcoat, with close breeches that made him look like the picture of John Bull.

Manners were manners. A farmer's daughter, on my being introduced to her, cast down her eyes, put her right foot behind her left, and lowered herself until her skirts touched the ground. It was the polite gesture, of which old folks spoke, called "dropping a curtsy." Another reference: In a seventeenth century play a female character speaks: "Very well, and how did madam receive all this fine company?—with a hearty welcome, and *curtsy* with her bum down to the ground, ha?" That would be a deep curtsy. Uncle Eliphaz Field, who learned his manners just after the Constitution of the United States was adopted, having been born about 1785, responded, when presented to a lady from Boston, by bowing very low, putting out his hand to one side with a small flourish, and saying: "Your sarvant, Ma'am."

I saw no looms going, but spinning-wheels were in common use. My aunt spun and dyed the wool she knit into our stockings. In the attic were wheels like the distaff, and quill-wheels, and a hetchel for breaking up flax.

Nothing mentioned in New England history appears very old-fashioned to me, not even the new England morals lately described by Rupert Hughes. The scenes of my boyhood knew them all—including sabbath-violation by walking otherwise than reverently to and from church—but *without the penalties*. The Constitution, guaranteeing religious liberty, taken seriously by our New England ancestors of a few generations back, certainly did revolutionize their ideas in this respect; and to a large extent it killed off puritanism at the same time. "The right of every man to worship God according to the dictates of conscience" is a phrase I heard oftener sixty years ago then I do now. The descendants of the Puritans quoted it.

The new "religions" of the nineteenth century, Perfectionism, Mormonism, Eddyism, and virtually Spiritualism, sprouted from the free religious soil of New England; where also were cultivated Emerson and Theodore Parker and the Unitarians. I would not affirm that New England morals as I saw them had improved since the Puritans practiced them; but the witch-chasers were gone, if not all belief in witches. Our neighbor, Aunt Achsah Mason, who at sixty had never seen a railroad train, put a heated horseshoe in her churn before pouring in the cream. The efficacy of a hot horseshoe as a defense against witches is well attested.

A real Puritan reformer, a Cotton Mather, would have been kept as busy there in my country as the Watch and Ward Society was in Massachustes in 1927 suppressing modern fiction. The customs of the too ardent fathers, mentioned in connection with "bundling," had not passed away, yet nobody started a movement for their abolition. The people seemed to be wholly incurious regarding one another's sexual affairs. When they had anything to say about a birth closely following a wedding, they said it with a smile, and remarks when made did not go beyond broad joking. The selectmen investigated cases of illegitimacy on complaint, the man at fault paying the girl $300 if he did not choose to run or to marry. Being forced to make good in this amount was remembered longer against a man than the offense whereby he incurred the penalty; and a quarrel between neighbors must go far toward a personal encounter before he would be twitted of that.

3—THE PURITANS MADE A MESS OF IT.

Treatises of considerable volume on the morals of the Puritans, the colonies, and early New England have been written. Long ago were issued a few numbers of a magazine called "The Times," in which Professor Giddings of Columbia University began a promising string of articles on "The Natural History of New England Morals." The end of the magazine was the end of the articles so far as I am aware. Reading them was like reading about People I Have Known.

In 1925 Rupert Hughes devoted a series to "The Facts About Puritan Morality" in the Haldeman-Julius Monthly. Mr. Hughes quoted the list of offenses that had been committed not so much in

NOTE—When I was at Gene Fuller's in East Westmoreland, his oldest boy had reached the age of 10, and there were two younger. The second one has been gathered to his fathers in the little burying-ground where four generations of the Fullers are laid away. The youngest one is a school superintendent in Lancaster, N. H. The one who was 10, now 65, has learned of the publication of these memories and writes me at length from the Pacific Coast, where he occupies a responsible position in a medical institution. He has made good. . . . . The writer must watch his step. The husband of the granddaughter of one of the most interesting women I have mentioned as residing in Walpole is reading The Truth Seeker now. The Surry girl of classic beauty who forwarded the skull to me in New York about 1884 sends now an admonitory letter from St. Paul, in Minnesota, chiding this author a little severely for recalling forms of speech that were not nice, and censurable customs that have become obsolete in the old neighborhoods. She mentions at the same time a book with a religious motive which she prefers to my work.

spite of, as perhaps because of, the prevailing fun-damentalism. But the most hideous features of the record are not the offenses but the punishments in-flicted. Count all of the real crimes committed, and still the magistrates who imposed the harsh pen-alties for slight breaches of the moral code were really the infamous criminals. Here is a famous sentence imposed on the pioneer Secularist, Roger Williams, September 3, 1635:

> "Whereas Mr. Roger Williams, one of the elders of the church of Salem, hath broached & dyvulged dyvers newe & dangerous opinions, against the authoritie of magis-trates, has also writt letters of defamation, both of the magistrates & churches here, & that before any conviction, & yet mainetaineth the same without retraction, it is therefore ordered that the said Mr. Williams shall departe out of this jurisdiction within sixe weekes nowe nexte ensueing, which if hee neglect to performe, it shall be lawfull for the Governor & two of the magistrates to send him to some place out of this jurisdiction, not to returne any more without license from the Court."

If a person swore in 1635, as did Robert Short-house and Elisabeth Applegate, he or she was sen-tenced to have the tongue put into a cleft stick, "& to stand so by the space of haulfe an houre."

The penalties the Puritans inflicted cured none of the habits for which they were prescribed. Swearing was the rule two hundred and twenty-five years later, and punishment for it unknown.

So of the notoriety of public acknowledgment forced upon "Temperance, the daughter of Brother F———, now the wife of John B———, having been guilty of the sin of fornication with him that is now her husband." In those Puritan days Mis-

tress Temperance had to stand before the whole
congregation and profess to bewail her great wickedness; and this after her marriage to John! In
the seventeenth and early part of the eighteenth
century cognizance was taken of many such cases;
and there were plenty of them, for "the records of
the Groton church show that of *two hundred* persons owning the baptismal covenant there from 1761
to 1775, no less than *sixty-six* confessed to fornication before marriage." These were baptized persons who had received the Holy Ghost. At Braintree, Mass., of *sixteen* couples admitted to full communion, *nine* had confessed to premarital relations.
And they also had the baptism. The Braintree confessions belonged to the period of the Great Awak-
ening (religious revival), 1726 to 1744. The information is taken by Mr. Hughes from "A Social
History of the American Family" by Arthur W.
Calhoun, Ph. D. Dr. Calhoun opines that "discipline probably stiffened about 1725." Discipline
hadn't stiffened on London Road one hundred years
after that date unless Uncle Lewis Aldrich was an
untruthful man.

An exception to what a man could do in the
colonies and escape punishment was furnished by a
scalawag minister named Lyford, the first preacher
to be sent over from England, who, it is true, was
exposed and condemned by Governor Bradford and
Cotton Mather, but he never had to stand in the
pillory nor pay a fine. The faculty of preaching was
withdrawn from him, and he went to Virginia,
where, says Bradford, "he shortly after dyed, and
so I leave him to ye Lord." Cotton Mather, in his

account of the same Lyford, introduces a modern note by referring to the "eminent worthy stranger" as "this *bird*." The Rev. Lyford was a bird.

As to the particular misconduct of Lyford, Mather says: "But the sum of the testimonies deposed upon oath before the magistrate, December 7, 1699, by several women of unblemished reputation, is that he would often watch opportunities of getting them alone, and then would often affront them with lewd, vile and lasciverous carriages." Now, since the same sort of women-chaser is found every day among the clergy in our own times, Puritan morals cannot be especially taxed with Lyford. But Lyford after all had to go. To the contrary, in the town of Surry, N. H., in the '60s, such a preacher plied his trade and made his propositions to the women, and yet remained there till he died a natural death. He would "often watch opportunities of getting them alone." He got one of them alone at a house, where he stayed overnight, by pretending that he had a cold, for which the remedy was catnip tea, and asked to have some of that decoction brought to him after he had got into bed. A girl took the catnip tea to him, when he told her of his ruse and affronted her by saying that she was herself the medicine he desired. The girl made a disturbance, and the story got out. His lasciverous carriages ended his preaching, but not his residence in the vicinity, where he was afterward known as the Rev. "Catnip" Allen. He was a bird.

The Puritans, among whom illegitimacy was frequent enough, dealt sternly with the women. Calhoun says: "In 1707 a woman was sentenced to be

set on the gallows, received thirty stripes on her
naked back, and forever after to wear the capital
A" (for adulteress). Naturally the records are
loaded with cases of infanticide. The bearers of
illegitimate children took that chance to avoid de-
tection and to escape being set on the gallows.

As in the part of New England that I know the
girl who gave birth to an illegitimate child suffered
no physical punishment, tales of infant slaying never
reached my ears. In Westmoreland village I knew
four illegitimates, three of school age and one
younger. They held their heads up with the rest,
suffering no social disability. Being safe from the
gallows and stripes, the mothers had not tried to
conceal their error by committing infanticide. In
that same town of a thousand population, two
men lived in polygamy, having two women apiece,
spoken of as So-and-so's "wives," first and second.
Nobody cared. On the Surry end of the London
Road dwelt a farmer's son with the widow of a
neighbor, deceased. If they ever were married it
was not until she had borne him a boy, who lived
nearby the last time I was in New Hampshire. Right
there once lived also a good man with the daughter
of a neighbor as a maid. Tradition said she be-
guiled him into marrying her by going home to her
mother and disguising herself with a pillow. To the
contrary, another tradition, which might have been
a real slander, said that she worked for him under
promise of wages, and he reckoned it was more
economical to marry her than to pay the wages. At
any rate, they were married; and I heard a young
woman make merry over the guileless remark of the

wife that their marriage "did not change anything." They "went right on just as before." They were a worthy couple respected by their neighbors.

No longer ago than 1914, visiting one of these towns, I noted the comment of my hostess concerning a young couple domiciled within a few hundred yards—the man being employed by the lady's husband—that for the children's sake John and Marie ought to get married, as she was having a new baby every year or two. The lady's tone was judicial, not minatory, nor such as might be expected of the late Mrs. Elizabeth Grannis, who, with the cooperation of an upstate Episcopal bishop, procured the passage of a law by the New York legislature to abolish adultery.

I am not here "exposing" the morals of the New Englanders of my childhood. They had to live.

The blots on the reputation of the Puritans are not their human failings, but the inhuman punishments they inflicted. And of my own New England, or the part of it I know, I speak in praise for the forbearance that makes it gloriously different from the New England of the Puritans, and unspeakably more humane. They were the spiritual heirs not of Cotton Mather but of Roger Williams. The morality which the Puritan clergy and the magistrates under them tried to enforce, made no allowance for nature, which raised and asserted itself in spite of their ferocious discipline. Contemplating the variations from rule that I have mentioned as known personally to me, going on sixty years ago, I am moved to ask whether the happiness of mankind would have been appreciably enhanced if all or any of these people who had made mistakes in their pursuit of happiness had been dealt with according to the methods of the Puritans. The irregularities, after all, may not have been in sum more than one-half of one per cent. at any time, but what a mess the Puritans made of it with their scant material! When the punishment is twice as bad as the offense and the judge more vicious than the accused, I am not on the side of the court, nor enthusiastic for the prosecution.

4—"NEW MORALS FOR OLD"

If I wanted to argue that morality is dynamic rather than static, and may occasionally get a move on itself, I could point out that my predecessors in rural New England were progressive beyond their day.

In 1924 the New York Nation published articles on "New Morals for Old." Isabel Leavenworth contributed one on "Virtue and Women." Mrs. Leavenworth stated: "I recently heard an elderly Boston lady make a remark which expressed the horror commonly aroused by any conduct which endangered the distinction between the two classes [the respectables and the "other" or common women]. 'Do you know,' she said, 'I heard that a young man of our set said he and his friends no longer had to go to girls of another kind for their enjoyment. They can get all they want from girls of their own class'." Fifty-four years before the date of the paper printing the article by Mrs. Leavenworth, and in a New England city ninety miles from Boston, I was helping a farmer to deliver a load of hay. A house next door was occupied by the "other" kind of women. One of them made her appearance, and the farmer, agreeing with her that it was "a nice large day," and telling her where the hay grew and how much of it he was carting to market, inquired sociably, "How is business with you?" She replied that business was slow, and that to tell the truth there were "too many amateurs in that town for an honest woman to make a decent living at her profession." She spoke with scorn of women and girls "holding their heads up" and at the same time keeping the bread from the mouths of their betters, as you might say. Now if what this "other" woman said was true, and if what the elderly lady described was a phenomenon of 1924, then in "new morals for old" this New Hampshire town in 1870 was about a half century in advance of Boston, Mass. However, anyone who accepts either of these women for gospel does so at his own peril. But why take chances? Let a man make a guess. Mine is that the girl of a young man's own class cuts into the business of the other woman not by supplying the same kind of "enjoyment," but something better and finer. If a young man is in love with a girl of his own class, the other woman has lost him while he remains in that condition, even allowing the enjoyment is no more than the spectators see when lovers are on the stage. So that, let us say, if a young man can manage to keep himself in love with a good girl, he will not consider the "other" class at all, nor miss what they offer him.

5—THE APPEAL TO LANGUAGE

A famous passage in Lecky's "History of European Morals," where he speaks of the prostitute, reads as follows:

"Herself the supreme type of vice, she is ultimately the most efficient guardian of virtue. But for her the unchallenged purity of countless happy homes would be polluted and not a few who, in their pride of untempted chastity, think of her with an indignant shudder, would have known the agonies of remorse and despair. On that one degraded and ignoble form are concentrated the passions that might have filled the world with shame. She remains, while civilizations rise and fall, the eternal priestess of humanity, blasted for the sins of the people."

Mr. Lecky makes of the female members of the family alone the vessels that preserve the purity of happy homes, as if what the male members do outside had no bearing upon it; whereas the chance is there that the impurity personified and distributed by the woman representing vice will be brought home. No; as I have said in a preceding paragraph, the eternal priestess of humanity is the Good Girl. The others are only the revivalists.

On one of my last invasions of New Hampshire—maybe in Gilsum, maybe in Alstead—I saw a farmer who had gone to school with me in the winter of '69-70. Having shaken his rough but honest hand, I inquired whether anything worth mentioning had happened since we last met, which was at the date just given.

He thought for a moment and then replied: "Wal, I don't know as there has."

More than a third of a century had passed and nothing changed.

My hope to show that the rural New Hampshire people of seventy years ago were virtually what they had been before the Revolution, is strengthened by the appeal to language. They still spoke in the '60s the mother tongue the Pilgrims brought to America A book of plays (already cited), written shortly after the Pilgrims set sail, that is, in the Restoration period, is full of Yankeeisms at which English writers now poke fun. The Yankee "I guess" occurs two or three times in one play. The New England pronunciation of words like round is produced in the book by inserting the letter *a* before the *o*. I was shown when studying phonetics that the *ow* sound is made up of *ah* and *oo* (*ah-oo*), but for *ah* the Yankee pronunciation substitutes the sound of *a* as in cat, and makes it *a-oo*. Try it. There occurs too, in this book written when our Pilgrim ancestors were alive, the phrase "going snucks" or snacks, meaning equal division. I heard that in New Hampshire; and I also find the reproachful words "lazing 'round," which I myself sometimes provoked. And then the comparison "as mute as a fish." Who has heard that? If anyone in the 1920s had known of the phrase, it would have been applied to President Coolidge. A farmer's wife in Surry used it of persons who were not saying anything. So I found "bawl" as an alternative for cry or weep; and the phrase, "Let her bawl; the more she cries the less," etc.—a saying that cannot be completed without using biblical language, and I am not inspired. I have heard it in New Hampshire and nowhere else. James Russell Lowell's Introduction to "The Biglow Papers," gives many instances.

We boys and girls who had been to school were irreverent toward such pronunciations by our elders as sarvant, 'arth, clark, and ile (for oil.) After doing my share of the laughing, I came to New York and heard those words pronounced soivant, oith, cloik, and erl. The people of my country did not say "leave that alone": they said *let* it alone. They didn't "blame it on": they laid the blame to. They rejected *"like* he did" and *"like* it was," and said *as,* or "the same as." They correctly discriminated in the use of *shall* and *should,* which have now gone into the discard, "will" and "would" taking their places. The woman at the table did not ask, *"Will* I help you to some of this?" She said "shall," and that usage is characteristic of past generations.

Their stories and jokes were of an ancient flavor, belonging, like Dean Swift's, to an age when there were no modern conveniences, and were mal-odorous. The possession of a digestive tract they figured was a joke on one and all. Sex allusions were barred if women were present, and among men the digestive kind got the laugh.

They were competent swearers, but as they had no Holy Name Society to discourage the taking of ghostly names in vain, their oaths were non-sexual, though to the last degree blasphemous.

Located according to language, literature, and customs, these New Englanders represented the seventeenth century. They were true to their en-vironment. Nothing happened to change that, and they kept undeviatingly the even tenor of their way.

The vernacular was almost destitute of slang; so was the vocabulary of New Yorkers at the time I came here. Some Germanisms had followed the big immigration from the fatherland. The city accent and pronunciation misled me, and in one instance I set down a born and bred New Yorker for a foreigner, so different was his speech from my own. Some of its peculiarities survive, and I will mention them. Not long ago a youth employed by another tenant of the building I was in, came to me for the key to the hoistway door, explaining he wanted to "leave a case down in the hall." Now, what could be made of that? I let (he would say "left") him have the key, but asked him why the case (a box) should be disturbed if he wished to leave it down in the hall. It turned out he desired to lower the case, or to let it down into the hall. I surmise that "left" and "leave" came in with the Irish, because my friend Pat, the section hand—he who, leaving out the Catholic, impeached the virtue of all churches claiming to be spouses of Christ—was accustomed to use them; only he said "lift" and "lave." The difference between the two words is plain enough. To "let alone," for example, is not to disturb, harass, touch, or take. To leave *alone* any person or thing is to leave that person or thing in solitude. The terms are not interchangeable. A man says he can drink or leave it alone, but he cannot; he may leave the stuff himself, but it will always have other company. If his enemies cease to trouble him, he will say they have "left" him alone, meaning he is no longer harassed by them. But when, employing the term in the same sense, he remarks that since the death of his wife, rest her soul, he has been left alone, he implies that in

life she annoyed him.   So these locutions, which
I regard as highly unmailable, have not had access
to The Truth Seeker since I began reading and
revising manuscripts, if I saw them first.   I have
sworn eternal enmity to all of them, though it is
a losing fight when they are admitted to The Atlantic Monthly, published in the heart of New England.

6—SPEAKING OF THE PILGRIMS.

Between Pilgrims and Puritans there was a difference that no longer persists in the common mind
nor in all of the uncommon ones.   President Roosevelt, at the Pilgrim anniversary in Provincetown,
Mass., 1907, talked of none but the "Puritans."
Now the difference, supposing one may be pointed
out, is that the Pilgrims were an independent body
of believers something like the Congregationalists
(who are often as liberal as Unitarians), and that,
unlike the Puritans, they preached religious freedom for others as well as for themselves.   In England they suffered persecution, as much in proportion by the Puritans as by the Established church.
They left their native shores to escape both, and
went to Holland, where they found the people so
liberal that they (the Puritans) faced the prospect
of being absorbed and assimilated by the Dutch-
men.   Their young men and women took them
wives and husbands among the Dutch girls and
boys, so that had the Pilgrims stayed in Holland,
their organization would have gone to pieces, and

to save it they took ship for their native England,
making port at Plymouth, but not allowed to come
ashore. At that they up anchor and sailed away for
America, establishing another Plymouth here. That,
as the poetry of Mrs. Hemans puts it,

> "They left unstained what there they found —
> Freedom to worship God,"

may be true of them, though false as to the Puritans who came later. These Puritans never
harbored the impious notion of freedom of worship. They would not tolerate it when at home
in England, and so far as they were moved
by religious impulses, and not by the commercial
spirit and a desire to improve their circumstances,
they quit England because they were not allowed to
run that country. They were looking for a community where they could force the people to adopt
Puritan notions.

To the Puritans New England is indebted, if it
owes them a balance, for its Fast and Thanksgiving
days. Fast Day in New Hampshire was recognized
but not observed. They imported Christmas later.
The country *churches* possibly took note of it; the
families I happened to be with on that anniversary
paid it no attention, and the making of presents they
reserved for New Year's day, which indeed was as
happily celebrated as Christmas even by New
Yorkers when I came here. That the Pilgrim
fathers renounced Christmas observance is a matter
of record. At the end of December, 1621, Governor William Bradford, who wrote a history of

"Plimoth Plantation," which contained an account of the voyage of the Mayflower, made this entry:

And herewith I shall end this year. Only I shall remember one passage more, rather of mirth, then of waight. On ye day called Christmas-day, ye Govr caled them out to worke, (as was used) But ye most of this new-company excused them selves, and said it wente against their consciences to work on ye day. So ye Govr tould them that if they made it mater of conscience, he would spare them, till they were better informed; So he led-away ye rest and left them; but when they came home at noone, from their worke, he found them in ye streete at play openly; some pitching ye barr, & some at stoole-ball, and such like sports. So he wente to them, & tooke away their implements, & tould them, that was against his conscience, that they should play, & others worke; if they made ye keeping of it mater of devotion, let them kepe their houses, but ther should be no gameing, or revelling in ye streets. Since which time nothing hath been atempted that way, at least openly. (See next page.)

In the old country excess of conviviality marked the celebration of Christmas. Thomas Carlyle alluded to this feature. He himself forgot one season the significance of December 25 when it dawned, and went about his usual occasions until he noticed that the public houses, which is to say the saloons, were doing more than their average volume of business. He saw people in numbers going in and coming out, and then remembered that it was "the birthday of their redeemer."

Bradford was as oblivious as Carlyle. He could speak of December 25 without recognition of the redeemer's birth. So little mindful were the Pilgrims of the observance of this important anni-

GOVERNOR BRADFORD ON YE DAY CALLED CHRISTMAS.

From Bradford's
Of
Plimouth
Plantation
Facsimile
in the
New York
Public Library.

ons ȳ day called Christmas-day, ȳ Gou: caled them out to worke, (as was vsed) but ȳ most of this new-company excused them selues, and said it wente against their consciences to work on ȳ day. So ȳ Gou: tould them that if they made it mater of conscience, he would spare them till they were better informed. So he led-away ȳ rest and left them; but when they came home at noone from their worke, he found them in ȳ streets at play openly; some pitching ȳ barr, & some at stoole-ball, and shuch like sports. So he vvent to them, and tooke away their implemente, and tould them, that was against his consciencc, that they should play, & others worke. If they made ȳ keping of it mater of devotion, let them kepe their houses, but ther should be no gameing, or revelling in ȳ streets. Since which tims nothing hath been attempted that way, at least openly versary that the entry of this date the year before, i.e., 1620, does not name the day, and indeed they do on it heavier work than usual:

"On ye *.15. of Decembr* they wayed anchor to goe to ye place they had discovered, & came within .2. leagues of it, but were faine to bear up again, but ye *.16. day* ye winde came faire, and they arrived safe in this harbor. And after wards tooke better view of ye place, and resolved wher to pitch their dwelling; and ye *.25. day* begane to erect ye first house, for comone use to receive them and their goods."

Thirty years after Governor Bradford made his entry, that is, in 1659, a law was passed by the General Court of New Hampshire "for preventing disorders arising in several places within this jurisdiction, by reason of some still observing such Festivals, as were Superstitiously kept in other countries, to the great dishonor of God and offense of others." The court therefore imposed a fine of five shillings on whosoever should be found observing any such day as Christmas either by forbearing to labor or by feasting. The law may long ago have been repealed, but my people were abiding by it when I left the state.

Thanksgiving was the day the lid blew off, or was conscientiously removed. The laws of economy were for the time disregarded, and food set out with bewildering frequency, in large amounts and many varieties. I suppose that the fare provided by Aunt Nancy Shelley in 1872 duplicated that of the farmer's wife of one hundred years earlier— chicken potpie for breakfast, with hot biscuits and smoking johnny cake; apple-pie too, if one desired;

and for the midday dinner, chickens, roasted, a wide choice of vegetables, and the holy trinity of pies—mince, apple, and pumpkin—all three included in one helping. That the family repaired on Thanksgiving Day to its customary place of worship I cannot trust my memory to affirm or deny; but my recollection would be that the family, augmented by children and grandchildren not living at home, opened up the front parlor that had been closed since last year, unless there had been a funeral, and "visited" when not eating.

CHAPTER VII.

1—I TAKE LEAVE OF THE INVISIBLES.

SURVEYS in recent years tabulate the disappearance or the abandonment of hundreds of country churches. That movement had begun in New Hampshire before I departed thence, and some churches supposed still to be active drew a small attendance. The Walpole Hill church was empty and decaying when I passed it on my way to school at the Hollow in 1870, its closing preceding that of the district school by several years.

I went to Sunday school in Keene, Surry, and Westmoreland. Having thus heard a great deal about God's being everywhere present, I at the age of sixteen called on him for a showdown. The calling took place on top of Surry Hill, from which, as I have elsewhere said, all the rest of the universe was visible on a clear day. And this day was clear; the stillness so profound it could be heard. Having found a comfortable place to repose, on a mossy knoll, I bent my mind to the problems of the cosmos, to discover if peradventure I might think them out to a solution. Nothing having come of my mulling and pondering, I said aloud, addressing the welkin: "Here is the place and the moment for God to produce himself and to tell me about things. He

131

might speak or he might appear." And I was almost afraid he would. But my mind was made up and I persevered in the thought, keeping my eyes lifted and ears alert for about the space of half an hour. Still nothing happened. The sun continued to shine, and the wind to blow, and the heavens to remain empty. There was no such presence as favored Moses on Sinai. Not even the Devil came along, as I had heard he did to Jesus on an exceeding high mountain. I had said to God: "This is your chance to get me." Now I added: "You have missed your chance. Good-bye," and I arose from the mossy knoll and went my way, convinced that one of two things must be so: either I had been misinformed about the watchfulness of God over all my acts and his close attention to any prayers I might make, or else God had merely been imagined by the ministers; and I was a skeptic, a doubter, a disbeliever from that time on.

I had heard a good many sermons, all more or less Fundamentalist, the Unitarian ones being as bad as the others, except for kindly omitting threats of hell. The Unitarian minister cast no doubt on the inspiration and inerrancy of the Bible. Once the Rev. Mr. Barber of the Westmoreland Unitarian church, having asserted there was no passage of scripture not reconcilable with every other passage, had his attention called by Deacon White to Proverbs xxvi, 4, 5. Verse 4 reads: "Answer not a fool according to his folly, lest thou also be like unto him," and verse 5 reversed the injunction by enjoining: "Answer a fool according to his folly, lest he be wise in his own conceit." Dr. Barber labored the question for the best part of an hour, when he might have explained the contradiction in a minute by saying verse 5 was the comment of some other writer on the opinion of the author of verse 4. Or verse 5 might have been the second draft of the first writer, who forgot to strike out the words expressing the idea as it had come to him before. It made me tired.

The first preacher ever really to hold my attention was the Rev. W. H. H. Murray, who, being on a lecturing tour, addressed some remarks to an audience in Keene on an occasion when I chanced to be there. The Rev. Murray talked about the people of the Orient and their virtues, and having extolled them highly, told his hearers, no doubt to their amazement, that when Christians had learned to behave themselves as well as a Chinaman did, they might with less cheek say to the heathen, "Be like us." I was then more suspicious of Christianity than before.

The days I went to Keene, which was no mean city, were the largest in the Almanac. If any old citizen remembers seeing a half-grown boy sitting on the rail that enclosed the Common, eating P. B. Hayward crackers out of a bag, then I am his ancient acquaintance. He might have seen me again while the Cardiff Giant was in town. I distributed the handbills which notified one and all that this petrified proof of holy scripture—the one and only individual survival of the days before the flood— was now for a short time in their midst, and could be viewed for the pitiful sum of ten cents. I must ignore the conversation of an obscene old man who descanted on the incompleteness of the early Christians if this one was to be taken as a specimen of their manhood, and he proposed to take up a subscription to buy a better endowment for the giant than had been the puny gift of his mother. Should I visit Keene again, could I find anybody, I wonder, who remembers Rarey, the horse-handler, and his exhibition there? My uncle, who doubted that a boy could be properly trained without flogging and who worked out this scriptural theory on myself, had me go to witness the demonstration of this man Rarey who gentled horses without the use of the whip.

2—I MAKE A GEOGRAPHICAL CHANGE

As the summer of '75 waned toward fall, my New Hampshire days dwindled without my being aware of their approaching close. I had before me at one time the prospect that Emerson Franklin, with whom I continued to live, would buy for me the old Ezra Pierce place, then for sale, and that I would settle down there as a farmer, probably married. Already I had looked the place over and in my mind had cleared it of stones to admit of cultivation, when orders came to proceed to New York and be a printer. This news getting about, I assumed a considerable importance in the community, which now took more notice of me than it ever had before and made my going away the topic of conversation. My acquaintances wagged their heads; the idea was a large one, not easily grasped. Men who had never been farther away than Brattleboro said: "What business do you guess you've got going to New York? Them fellows there won't make two bites of you." Elias Chamberlain, a man of 80, had the curiosity to ask: "How soon are you expecting to go West?" York state was out West according to his memories of geography, which were as ancient as the century. So for the time I was an individual possessing interest, and more than one girl not previously eager for my acquaintance asked if I would write to her from the city.

I accumulated for my entry into the metropolis an outfit of clothes highly satisfactory in my own regard. The near-purple cutaway coat was of a ribbed material known as "trico," worn by the best dressers; under this a waistcoat of black velvet, cut very low to reveal the bosom of a grass-colored shirt with a real collar and a string tie; below, a pair of tight trousers showing a delicate green stripe; and then a pair of calfskin boots with high heels; on my head a black slouch hat, and to cover all but the hat and the boots, a brown overcoat of the broadcloth order. The color of some garment in that orgulous ensemble must appeal to any taste. There is preserved a tintype picture of myself as I then appeared. It could be used against me.

The sentimentalist is on the lookout for pathos when he scans descriptions of the parting of a youth from his old home and friends; but all the regrets remain behind, to be felt by those who may have cause for sorrow in the prospect that they shall not see him again. It is by them that tears are distilled. The one who is going away to new fields contrives to control his grief. His mind is on his venture. Melancholy, if ever, attacks him when in later years he turns to look back. For the moment he knows none of that regret which may come to him when he is mature and his own children drift away. The pang is always theirs who stay. Were it otherwise, nobody, I suppose, would ever leave the place where he was born.

I review my journey to New York with wonder that I should have ended it only twelve hours late, at my mother's house, instead of tying up in the port of missing gawks. My brother had written me full and sufficient directions, as they no doubt seemed to him, after he had made the trip twice; nor did he omit to urge upon me certain precautions which I was to observe. I had only, he wrote me, to take the train at Putney, Vermont, just across the Con-

BRITTON'S FERRY.

This is at Westmoreland, N. H. The State of Vermont begins at Putney on the other side of the Connecticut River.

necticut river by way of Britton's Ferry from Westmoreland (Putney is the town where the Oneida

Community began, the building that housed it being still there in 1875); to change cars at New Haven, and then, on arriving at the Grand Central Depot, New York, to board a Fourth avenue horse-car and get out at No. 338. I would then be there, he said, and he should be glad to see me. But on the way, or en route, as he chose to phrase it, I was to cultivate no acquaintances whatever, talk to no strangers, and to reserve all confidences with other people until I knew whom I was speaking with. All this is conventional and sensible advice, but had I followed it I should indubitably have been lost. However, the counsel was of no avail. I immediately forgot all those words of wisdom, and before the train had made its first stop I was chinning with a young fellow-passenger, a city chap at that, and smoking my first cigar, which he alluded to, airily, as a Havana. I can today place that cigar as one of the brand that used to be handed out when the loser settled for a game of fifteen-ball pool at five cents a cue, including drinks. In a little while the wight had my name and pedigree. His own name, he told me, was William Jones, and he was oftener called Willie. So commonplace a name awoke at once my suspicions. It must be an alias, I shrewdly divined, and yet, foolhardy as it might be, I would follow the adventure through. He was smaller than I, anyhow, and would need his gang to help him carry out any sinister intentions he might have toward me.

On the day's run from Putney to the metropolis, that boy told me more about New York than I have learned by being here most of the time for above fifty years; and I have not been unobservant. He must have got his impressions of the city and its attractive wickedness from reading The Police Gazette. He painted the female peril in lively colors, and before we got to the last stop I knew just how to elude the sisterhood, designing or sinful.

3—DROPPING THE PILOT

At the Grand Central, where I first heard the roar of the city, which I still catch at intervals, Willie tendered me his guidance, and asked, when we were in a street car, for the number of the house I got off at. I gave it as 335 Fourth avenue, and naturally we did not find the house, 335 being then the number of The Truth Seeker office on Broadway. We inspected 335 Fourth avenue. It was a business building deserted and locked up, and I had not the slightest notion where we went from there. "Never mind," said Willie Jones cheerfully, "I'll take you to my house tonight, and we'll have another look at this neighborhood in the morning." For such a little cuss, for so I looked upon him, he was very competent and commanding. He saluted a policeman with "Good evening, Officer," and urged the driver of the next conveyance we entered, which was a bus, to get downtown sometime tonight. It was 7 o'clock and dark, the month being November.

I had by now lost my sense of direction; knew not whither we were drifting; and Willie, having some surprises up his sleeve, smirked and was ret-

icent. We proceeded in fact to a ferry, over the
river to Brooklyn, and into the streets of that city.
He brought me soon to a building with a wide and
brightly-lighted entrance, and there came to a stop.
"This," I reflected, "is just one of those gilded
palaces of sin, and pitfalls for the unwary." Actually it was a variety theater, the first I had ever seen.
After a consultation as to financial resources, and
mine being found good, Willie did business at the
ticket window, and we went in. As an awed spectator from a gallery seat, I saw that evening the
play of Ali Baba and the Forty Thieves, with some
other sketchy work, and the performances of an
astonishing gymnast named Frank Gibbons. Willie
Jones said with pride that he knew Frank personally, and had even shaken hands with him.

When the curtain came down to rise no more for
me on those enchanting scenes, Willie and I walked
through the night to his house in Schermerhorn
street, which from my recollections of it must have
been a residence district of the first class. He let
himself in with a key at a door in a brownstone
front. We trod upon soft carpets and awakened
no one, till he led me up the stairs and into a room
which, as I saw when the gas had been lit, was
furnished in the best of style. He produced two
garments, since known to me as nightshirts. I let
him put on one of the effeminate things before I
committed myself to the other. He had seemed to
divine that I carried none in my valise.

Having slept as a tired boy was bound to do I
awoke in the morning in the strange quarters to
realize I had not been robbed; and after passing

through the first bathroom in my experience, and being well washed and combed, I tracked Willie to the dining-room, there to be introduced to an elderly female who might have been his relation but evidently not his mother. Her greeting to me lacked cordiality. Her manner said: "I wonder what ruffian has picked up Willie now," and held me responsible for his being out late. So the atmosphere of the dining-room wanted warmth. When she asked him if he had kept up his reading while away he replied that he had read matter both religious and secular, and found most enjoyment in the latter, which displeased her.

Overnight my mistake about the house number in New York had corrected itself. Willie took me again to the metropolis, rang the bell of No. 338 Fourth avenue, saw my mother greet me. And so, having violated all the rules of travel laid down for the guidance of greenhorns, I came safely through, though delayed in transmission. When I turned to say good-bye to Willie, he had disappeared and I never saw him again.

4—THE TRUTH SEEKER AND D. M. BENNETT

The Truth Seeker had been going for two years when I came to New York. D. M. Bennett began its publication in September, 1873, at Paris, Illinois, by way of replying to a clergyman who had access to local newspapers, while he had not. Bennett. having business instincts, capitalized his answers to the minister, and made his paper continuous. He was one of those who can make money, but not always keep it. In 1894 I prepared the biographical sketch of Bennett for S. P. Putnam's "Four Hundred Years of Freethought." The incidents of his life, which I now take from that sketch, are, first, that he was born in Springfield, New York, December 23, 1818, two months earlier than he should have been, for the reason that his mother overexerted herself in lifting a Dutch oven. Only for that maternal indiscretion he might have had a birthday in February with Washington and Lincoln. He took four years of schooling in Cooperstown, N. Y.; worked in a printing-office and also at wool-carding, although he preferably would have studied medicine. At 15 he joined the New London Shaker community; ten years later had risen to be head of its medical department, and at 27 was the community physician. But he fel lin love with the little Shakeress Mary Wicks, and she with him, and they left New Lebanon to marry, since Shakers had the eccentricity to be celibates. After a term as drug clerk in St. Louis, he went into business for himself and made money. In the '50s, having tried the nursery and seed line in Rochester, he took the road as salesman and collector. In Cincinnati he manufactured proprietary medicines, waxing wealthy, but as an investor, he lost $30,000. In 1868, in Kansas City, he dropped more money trying to sell drugs, and so went to making bricks on Long Island. Leaving this venture to go out as commercial traveler, he turned apothecary once more, in Paris, Ill., and again was partner in a seed firm. Thence, having started The Truth Seeker, in 1873 he brought

D. M. BENNETT IN 1873.

his paper to New York the first of the following year. About that time my brother, at 18, had set himself up as a printer. Bennett attended the New York Liberal Club that had been organized in 1869 and still continued. There he came into touch with the family. Eugene took the paper to print. In a short time Bennett bought Eugene out and engaged him as foreman. When I came on from New Hampshire to join the force, the paper was published at 335 Broadway, on the top (sixth) floor of a structure called the Moffat Building, corner of Worth street. The editor's visitors took no elevator; they walked up five flights of stairs. On another top floor, at No. 8 North William street, half a mile distant, east by south, I found the printing-office, with a vacancy for an able-bodied devil who could sprinkle the floor with a sponge and sweep it with the remains of a broom; and I answered the description. The approach to the Brooklyn Bridge, opened in 1883, now occupies the site of the building, and North William street is reduced to one short block. It was then as now the center of the printing business, and hard-by was the "Swamp," habitat of the leather trade.

Bennett, now 57 years old, was a man of average height, small-boned, and carrying more weight of flesh than he ought, for one of his feet was deformed and he walked with a limp. His gray hair, worn long and getting thin, was retreating from his high forehead. His eyes were small and twinkling, with the puffiness beneath them which physiognomists used to say denoted the possession of a large vocabulary of words. He dressed in a loose gray suit, and the fact that he habitually wore no tie or collar was concealed by gray whiskers. His picture shows what an observer first noted, that is, that he had a fine head. Not at all a full-blooded man was Bennett, nor of the sanguineous temperament, but pallid, with a translucent skin; his flesh not very solid nor his physique rugged. All of us called him Doctor. A man of humor he was, however; one who liked to poke the boys in the ribs and crack a joke. No man I ever saw could smile so genially or better appreciate the witticisms of the press. But he never wrote a piece of humor himself, except unconsciously. I one day put into type a piece of his copy in which he attributed the development of intelligence to improved means of observation; and he wrote gravely, in illustration: *The frog has opportunities for observation superior to those of an oyster.* Now I hold that the contemplation of an oyster, or even a frog, as an observer—the one viewing the world from the eminence of a log, the other suffering the serious handicap of being buried in the mud—has a humorous appeal, but I am morally certain that Bennett never saw anything funny in the comparison.

The Doctor did a great deal of writing by getting up early and working late. One number of his paper (March 23, 1878) contained this item:

"In a late Crucible [he said] we notice the following complimentary notice of ourselves: 'D. M. Bennett of The Truth Seeker is one of the greatest workers we ever knew. He generally commences at 4 o'clock in the morning and works till 11 P. M. He deserves all the success he gets.'

"We might amend this a trifle by saying that we have on a few occasions been known to lie abed until 5 A. M."

The paper quoted was Hull's Crucible, published in the state of Massachusetts, I believe, by Moses and Mattie Hull, advocates of Spiritualism. Mr. Hull acquired his knowledge of Bennett's working hours at first hand, for Bennett employed him for a while as a compositor. As a man of learning, he wrote and did public speaking. As a printer, he was far from being at his best. His proofs bore many marks, and I have somewhere else related, as touching on and appertaining to his skill, that one of the other printers took a proof that he had set, and pasting it on the wall, labeled it, "The Mistakes of Moses."

Mr. Hull wore a high hat. In this he was but one of three compositors known to The Truth Seeker printing-office who sported tiles. Another, a certain Mr. Clegg, not only came to work in a high and shiny beaver, but carried a cane for dress purposes. A third stovepipe compositor we called Professor, because he lectured at a Bowery Museum on the marvels there offered to view for a dime, but his hat lacked the glossiness of the one worn by Mr. Clegg, and was a habit of the professional man rather than of the natty dresser.

5—TYPESETTING MADE EDITORS THEN.

By the fact of Mr. Hull's being an editor, I am reminded of the numerous future editors who handled Truth Seeker type. An able and studious young man named Thomas was the first to be graduated into the editorial class. He did a little such work on The Truth Seeker, and then in turn on The Sewing Machine Journal, on Science, and on Power, a mechanical publication issued from the World building. An accomplished compositor named Moore, much interested in the fine points of the craft, got to be editor of a religious paper. Another, of the name of Hammond, did city editing for a Boston daily. John Bogert turned Labor editor on Hearst's Journal. Will Colby, once our office boy, was on the editorial staff of The Cosmopolitan when Hearst bought that magazine of John Brisben Walker. You can add the two Macdonalds to The Truth Seeker comps. who doubled in editing. For a small printing office it was a prolific school of journalism.

Truth Seeker printers became competent. John Reed, a boy from Pennsylvania, after serving as an apprentice, changed to Funk & Wagnalls', where, he told me, they gave him the worst copy on the Standard Dictionary. Tommy Blake, another Truth Seeker apprentice, was soon foreman on one of the floors of the Funk & Wagnalls establishment.

If Napoleon said of his soldiers, or of one division of them, that every man carried a marshal's baton in his knapsack, then it is not too much for me to observe that a printer's apprentice should carry in his head the possibilities of an editor or an author, or a critic, or at least an intelligent reviewer. A compositor like the one who set, and the proof-reader who passed, Fiske's "Comic Philosophy" and Spencer's "Social Statistics"* is a source of danger in a printing-office.

---

*The titles mentioned are old ones. The point is that the philosophy of which Fiske discoursed was Cosmic, and Spencer preferred the word Statics.

I changed the subject to say a few more words on my lamentable forgetfulness of good advice. Unless the reader skipped the part of my story that tells how I left New Hampshire, he knows that I went aboard the train across the Connecticut at Putney, Vt., en route for New York, well charged with precautions against getting picked up for a sucker, and that, disregarding the warning, I at once began to chum with a fellow I had never seen before in my life. As it turned out, I could not have done better. I have stated likewise that this youth, in his superior wisdom, took some pains to make me aware of the city's menace, including the female peril. I never thought of that again either. The fact is that such things are not recognized when met. That is why men read the newspapers all their lives and then buy a gold brick. With the money to spare I should have purchased the first shiny brass ring a man who confessed he was no better than a smuggler offered me at only a fractional percentage of its value; and less than ten years ago I gave a fellow 50 cents for a pair of gold-bowed glasses he had just picked up. I saw him pick them up. A bystander told me he saw him drop them. The trick was not new to my reading; it was new only to my experience, and I fell for it. The glasses were of my size and I used them with satisfaction until my wife took them away from me because they made a green stripe across my nose. The futility of the warning of Willie Jones will soon appear.

NOTE.— A Westmoreland lady finds my story not above criticism on the score of impurity; but another New England reader writes: "I've been reading the Memoirs aloud to my Missis—who is an invalid. 'Twould do you good to hear the poor lady laugh. One learns, too, for we are both New Englanders and all you write is in our family tradition. We are both keen on Yankee history—and you are certainly a 'document.' "

The reader will kindly accept the story as a narrative consisting of facts necessary to an understanding of the people it is about. There is no moral lesson in it.

My memory is jogged by one who points out that I have overlooked an interesting character in Westmoreland known as Thu Blanchard. His name was Bathual, but some, seeming to derive it from Methuselah, called him M'thu. He was a handy man about town, doing odd jobs like lighting the fire in the church. There was no fire when one meeting opened and he was asked why. "I'll tell you why there is no fire," said Thu. "There ain't any fire because I hadn't nuthin' to start it with but three matches and dam' green wood."

In Surry (1871) I spent a little time in the cider mill of Jonathan R. Field keeping a horse in motion to grind apples. The horse led itself as long as it kept the "sweep" in motion, but had learned that by stopping it relieved the pull on its halter. I was there to make the horse resume its travels in a circle, which must have been monotonous for the horse. I learn of a Jonathan R. Field III out in Idaho.

Memories are stirred in the breast of a Fall River lawyer, Milton Reed, Esq., who says:

"In your interesting Autobiography you refer to the Rev. Josiah Lafayette Seward of East Sullivan, N. H. He was my Harvard classmate and at one time intimate friend—a pragmatic, plodding, unimaginative chap. The last time I called on him in Keene he was plugging away at his History of East Sullivan, to which he had devoted years of his life.

"I never met the Rev. W. O. White, although by marriage he was connected with a branch of my family. I read his Life, written by his daughter Eliza Orne White.

"My father's maternal ancestors lived in Alstead, Westmoreland, and that region, named Granger. I never lived in New Hampshire, but have frequently visited the beautiful region in which those towns are set."

The Rev. Josiah Lafayette Seward was not, for God took him, before he had completed that opus, his History of East Sullivan, and it was finished by another hand. Priest White, Unitarian, was my pastor in 1862-'65, and preached the funeral of Grandpa Eliphaz Field. He was a slow and hesitating speaker.

CHAPTER VIII.

1—IN OVER MY HEAD

MY mother was fond of company. She liked the society of others so well that she took boarders and rented rooms. Often the paying guests and the visitors who remained to dine were advanced thinkers. A Mr. Brewster, partisan of the hollow globe theory, came among them. Mr. Brewster was persuaded that any one who should attain the regions of the North Pole would find there an opening through which he could sail his ship and navigate the hollow insides of the earth. He fancied this interior to have advantages over the outside as a place to live. He constructed a globe three feet in diameter, for use in illustrating his theory, with miniature ships, magnetized to keep them in their course, that navigated the outer surface and sailed bravely over the rim and disappeared through the north hole. For a time this globe was stored with us, to be moved with our household stuff the First of May. People abused mother's good nature in similar ways. One man induced her to entertain for a season his mother-in-law, a terrible old woman.

Of the 1875 group with whom I mingled socially at my mother's board was Osborne Ward, author of "The Ancient Lowly," a spare, sparsely-whiskered man with a prominent adam's apple and a resonant voice, who summed up the failings of mankind, obstructive of the ideal social state, as Intemperance, Concupiscence, and Irascibility.   Mr. Ward was the Socialist candidate for lieutenant-governor of the State of New York in 1879.

Another man, name now unknown to me, was interested in organizing the Sovereigns of Industry, a society of young working people, of the skilled class, I think, with aspirations to be literary and dramatic, or entertainers at least.   My brother was secretary of a branch that put up a very good show.

The Spiritualists had a society called a Lyceum, which met in Armory Hall on the west side.   They maintained a Sunday school that attracted me, especially when they had exhibitions.   I heard there lectures and debates.   Mattie Sawyer was one of their speakers, who professed to be inspirational. Poetry came to her out of the air, and I have heard her deliver verse of twenty minutes' duration that sounded like Poe's "Raven," if you did not notice the words.   Mattie was a social radical, but at that time most of the Spiritualists believed in social freedom.   Today their pastors have to walk straight, I understand, and they have ministerial scandals just like those of the Christian communions.   This is probably necessary in order to establish Spiritualism as a religion and get their churches exempted from taxation.

There were more women than men in the household group.   Among those who rallied round, the most surprising individual, to me, was Mrs. Cynthia Leonard, a very dominant person indeed, and I stood in awe of her.   In her vigorous tones she ad-

dressed me as "Young Man," and once passed me
fourteen cents and sent me out for a quart of
"lager," for so she termed beer, which till then I
had never tasted. The good old word lager went out
of our vocabulary even before the advent of near-
beer. A generation later Mrs. Leonard might have
put her motion in the form of a request that I should
fetch a scuttle of suds.

But beer, I supposed, was for common consumption; the immortals quaffed nectar. All of the great,
nevertheless, sometimes come down. The Rev. J. M.
Buckley, editor of The Christian Advocate, on a
visit to London, heard how a detail of Tennyson's
admirers followed him for a while as he was viewing
pictures in an art gallery, purposing, should he
chance to speak, to catch and preserve what memorable words he might let fall. Children and a maid
were with the poet. The persons trailing him heard
him say to the maid: "You take care of the children,
Mary, while I go and get some beer."

Mrs. Leonard, president of the Chicago Sorority,
was mother of Lillian Russell, a person destined to
become noted. Lillian never appeared as a girl at
our house, nor later at gatherings of Freethinkers,
whom she disdained, although her father was a
Freethinker and ardently approved of Ingersoll.
When Lillian herself had a child, a girl, she sought
out a Catholic institution and sent the adolescent
damsel to a convent school. Lillian's sister, Susie,
more companionable, would come with her mother
to the Liberal Club (in the '80s) and captivate the
audience with a song. So with her sister Leonia.

Mrs. Leonard, as listener or speaker was

to be seen at the Liberal Club and at most other gatherings I attended for years. That first season of mine in New York, in the circle about our table, an idealist who chanced to introduce the social freedom proposition might be abetted by others. My brother, young and conservative, withstood them. With the courage of his virtues he declared: "I have my principles and I practice them," and then he challenged his adversaries: "Do you people practice yours?" This caused embarrassment. Mother answered him: "My son, you are impertinent. Declare your principles, but omit the personalities." A good rule for all, considering the intimacy of the subject.

Amongst a half dozen contributors to the conversation, the dumb one was myself. Already I have certified to my profound ignorance. I knew nothing and had no material for opinions. Some persons, for want of intellectual stimulation, go through the world that way. I was shy and on the lookout for avenues of escape. If my interest in a topic led me to attempt the saying of something, the silence that fell upon the company caused the remark I contemplated making to go back down my throat. I was stumped, then, on an occasion when a deep-bosomed voice boomed: "Young man, tell us what they think of these modern ideas in New Hampshire." My New England conscience answered for me: "We have no use for them." The Voice (politely): "How interesting!" And then, addressed to another: "Mrs. Bristol, here is a man after your own heart." Mrs. Bristol confused me by blushing. She was an attached friend of mother's, though twenty years younger. I never knew what formed the bond between them. Coming of an old and patrician Massachusetts family, she had married a New York man, who brought her hither and then in a few short years let himself be separated from her by dying. At the age of twenty-five she was successfully fending for herself; achieving economic independence by overlooking the sales-ladies in one of New York's firms of purveyors to women who bought high-priced clothes. She was reticent, reserved, and distant. Ruskin said that architecture was frozen music. This woman's immobile face was congealed beauty. Mother called her Agatha. She garbed herself with elegance; and what a burden of dress-goods women then packed about with them. I get a vision of high-necked waist, sleeves inflated at the shoulders, skirt tightly drawn in behind the legs, so it snapped as they walked, and a superfluous quantity of the same material falling from the exaggerated projection of the sitting parts, and trailing half a yard on the ground.

Was this the bustle and pullback era? I fear so, for contemporary verse included the following:

> "You've pulled it back," he cried in grief,
>   "Much further than you'd oughter;
> Your front stands out in bold relief,
>   My daughter, O my daughter!"

No word or picture now seen in the advertisements of women's things hints at the volume and expanse of muslin, when it was muslin and not duck, that composed the white layers of feminine toggery

pinned weekly to the clothesline. And then that bas-
ket of reinforced tire weave called a corset that
women exhaled themselves into. "Willowy"? They
were as trees walking, with the bark on. They say
the filled-in terrain about the great cities of our land
is largely of corset formation, the discarded gear
being indestructible, and resistant to the processes
used to reduce old battleships to repair parts for
automobiles. The shoes they wore can by no means
be the stock from which their present insubstantial
footgear has descended. They were plain soles and
heels and uppers, just a good job by a shoemaker,
no strings or bows, but buttons, and the tops were
so high they would not stand alone but fell to one
side like the empty part of a bag half filled with potatoes. The tops were built to that elevation to insure that no stocking should be seen between them
and the hem of the skirt. To fasten them on, the
wearers used a hook maybe a foot long, so they
could reach the buttons while sitting on the floor.

2—THE WATERS DEEPEN

On stormy days a carriage called for Agatha or
brought her home. Until the Voice drew her attention to my existence, she had been unaware of me,
so far as I had any knowledge, and yet I surmise
she must have looked me over and gauged the
chances for my betterment in the same manner that
I had but recently inspected the Ezra Pierce place
in Westmoreland with thoughts of how it might be
reformed in appearance. I was a rather tall fellow
for my age, and by no means slim-built, and I had

of late resorted to shaving my upper lip to keep a mustache from pushing forth. I observed with admiration but with moderate interest this beautiful creature so nearby and so far away. She came to contemplate me with less preoccupation when a predatory individual—to wit a sneak thief—invaded our house and, while collecting portable property, strolled into an occupied room, and the woman he found there gave the alarm by screaming. Then, of course, I must blunder on the scene and for appearance's sake grab the thief. His physical condition being poor, I had no trouble in detaining him until the iceman, making a late delivery, took him off my hands and held him for the policeman on the beat. The household gathered for a review of the events and each one's part in them as the excitement died down. I believe that I was the only representative present of woman's natural protector except an anæmic or phthisicky young man who, contrasting them with his own, passed comments upon the capability of the tough-looking pair of hands that stuck out all too far from the sleeves of my coat. Agatha evidenced her curiosity by taking a seat beside me on the sofa and saying, "Let's look." As though my allegedly competent right flipper had been a sample of goods she was solicited to buy, she inspected it, turning the calloused palm upward, and, with no signs of approval, calmly advised that I wear gloves when handling coal. This she said with the quirk of the mouth and the wink of the eye I had seen other New England women execute with the mischievous intent to "plague" somebody. Said I, to reprove her and rather pridefully: "Printers do not wear gloves when sticking type. What you see on my hands is not coal; it is a mixture of ink, lead, and antimony; but," I boldly added, "I should not mind bringing up coal if you need some to keep your fire going."

My remark was not intended for gallantry. I merely had confidence in my capacity to fetch up coal with the best of them. I was sure that as coal-heaver I should shine more brilliantly than as a conversationalist. But, "Mercy," quoth Agatha, "I believe I am getting a compliment," and she smiled. "Two things," said Immanuel Kant, "fill me with awe: the starry heavens and the sense of moral responsibility in man." But what are the starry heavens to "the light that lies in woman's eyes," and what becomes of man's sense of moral responsibility when that light is turned on him? The presence of Willie Jones just then, or recollection of his warning words, would have been helpful to me. One and then another of the company went away, and the room emptied except for us two and mother, who was obliviously reading a book. Agatha held me in conversation, shrewdly controlled by herself so it would be all about myself and never personal to her, until I became restless with the pumping. Then she murmured that if I meant what I said about delivering coal to keep her warm, I could begin by filling the scuttle in her room, which was on the floor below. Doubting her sincerity I proved my own by taking the hod to the bin and loading it. She was in her room when I came back. Now, if this were alone the record it purports to be of my observations in the liberal movement, there would be no excuse for bringing Agatha into it, for she was no innovator, religious, social or other, and as little dreamed of espousing views that would not pass muster with the world as of wearing clothes odd and out of fashion. Her opinions were regular and conservative, and even though she herself neglected the means of grace, she thought people ought to go to church more. Advising me I should read Christian evidence, she presented me with a fine large work by Judge Greenleaf on the "Harmony of the Gospels"—a book I still possess. For reasons that will appear, I never read it through and was relieved, then, to learn that neither had Agatha. Concerning its subject matter, I may remark it can be made to appear that any two or more series harmonize, by excluding those which contradict each other. A colloquy like this occurring later on would further develop Agatha's views: Churches are a necessity to society. One meets there the best people. Evolution? One should know the titles of Spencer's and Darwin's books and something of what they contain. Freelove? I was glad to hear you say you had no use for it. Divorce? Some women have kept their social standing after being divorced once, not twice. The common women, the street girls! Why—my boy! (protective demonstration). What made you think of them? Have you spoken to one, or looked at one? Where were you last night? You went to see Frank Chanfrau in "Kit, the Arkansaw Traveler"? But you came *straight* home, didn't you? I have tickets for Gilmore's Garden tomorrow night, and we will go there if you like."

Gilmore's Garden was really the old Madison Square Garden, built by Barnum (his Great Roman Hippodrome) on the former site of the New Haven Depot. It was but a block from home and was called Gilmore's Garden because Gilmore gave popular concerts there that winter.

Agatha was one of the "If you like" and "Do you want to?" kind of women, if women are not all of that kind, who would appear to defer when they lead, and consent while they ask; to consult another's will or wishes while having their own way. That makes the other fellow responsible because he *would* have it so. However when I endeavor to coordinate my ideas and clarify the woman theme, my powers of construction leave me and my thoughts become coagulated.

Tennyson wrote:

> "Flower in the crannied wall,
> I pluck you out of the crannies;
> Hold you here, root and all, in my hand,
> Little flower—but if I could understand
> What you are root and all, and all in all,
> I should know what God and man is."

Easy enough; but what would you know about woman?

3—TO RESUME

As I said, Agatha had retired to her room when I reached it with the coal, and as I set the hod down by the fireplace (for all rooms had their separate heating plants), she said: "Let me see those hands again. You must have made them worse by handling the scuttle." Examining the soiled mem-

bers, she ordered my coat removed, when she rolled
back my sleeves, fixed some water in her bathroom
basin, led me to it, and applied soap and brush till
my hands were so clean and soft I was ashamed of
them. I ought to have resisted the rolling up of
my shirtsleeves, since it exposed the want of an
undergarment and provoked inquiry. "Why, your
arms are bare," said Agatha. "It's their week to
be so," I replied. My brother had given me two
spare suits to wear next to the skin. One was
woolen, fleece-lined for winter; the other summer
"gauze" and sleeveless. I wore them in alternate
shifts, and this happened to be the summer suit's
week. That was the beginning of the renovation
which Agatha forthwith worked on me. She discovered faults I never suspected anybody had.
They subsisted in the clothes I wore and the way
I wore them. My walk, mostly on the toes and
with eyes on the ground, she condemned, despite
my defense of it as the only way a fellow *could*
walk in the woods and on the farm; he had got to
see where he was putting his foot down. Still I
took thought and changed my gait. And as for
clothing, besides following her directions and obtaining gloves and cuffs at A. T. Stewart's, I found
a tailor, one Jerry McEvoy, on Stuyvesant street,
diagonally across Third avenue from the Bible
House, who made me a good suit, Prince Albert
coat and all, on easy terms. And I bought me a
derby hat. In that era, the accessories of a pro-
letarian shirt were conveniently made of paper.
With paper cuffs, and with a paper collar buttoned
to a separate and detachable bosom, a fellow was

dressed for a party if he kept his coat on. Agatha tolerated none of these fictions. When in the autumn of 1876 I returned to New Hampshire on my vacation, clad as she would have had me, my Aunt Louisa voiced her appreciation of the change for the better. "Have you earned the wages since you went away to pay for them clothes?" she asked. I said yes. "And you don't owe nothing on 'em, either?" No. "And besides that you've paid your own way here from New York and have money enough to go back there with?" Every cent I need. "Well, all I've got to say is you've done mighty good."

I applied myself—no, that is too feeble; I devoted myself to the maintenance of a fire in Agatha's grate. Having brought the evening's coal and put some on, I sacrificed the time to stay by the fire and see that it didn't go out. This may not have been necessary, strictly speaking, but it was immeasurably agreeable. She seemed to find it agreeable also to keep these watches with me, when she had unarmored herself as women were in the habit of doing, and put something on in the way of fatigue uniform, or négligé. She had books, her own or from the Mercantile Library in Astor Place, which we made shift to read by the shaded light of a gaslamp on a stand placed near the chimney, creating a fireside clime quite domestic. If she was to be late, I would find a card on the table asking if I would like to wait until she came. Agatha was seven years my

senior, yet I made the discovery that a certain sort
of consciousness, a consciousness of that nature
which may be induced by propinquity, the male and
female in close community of thought and person,
has the effect of reducing all the gentler creatures
to approximately the same age; the young female
becoming more staid and serious; the maturer ones
more girlish.   Agatha, when the ice was thawed by
this nearness and by the warmth of friendship,
with the intensity of her interest in citifying me
and improving my style, dropped off those seven
years.   The weeks passed pleasantly away, and by
the time six had gone I was spending at least three
evenings of each of them with her, acquiring a degree of proprietorship in the chair by the fire.   It
befell on one of these evenings that the room I
entered was empty; nevertheless I lit the gas and
sat down to read a book that I had begun.   She
came in later, very majestic in her impressive street
apparel, ornamented hat and costly furs, and with
her womanly bearing that restored her age.   Putting aside the book: "I have kept your fire for
you," I said.   "Yes," Agatha answered, "we must
not let the vestal spark expire.   I was kept late at
the store—too late for dinner, and I dined lonely
at a restaurant.   You need not go now."   (The
lady is recreated with strange vividness, as though
her "ghost" had appeared, from the fragrance of
the warmed atmosphere that was released when she
unfastened her furs, and the scent of the drop of
White Rose she had put in her hair, whenever I
come where those perfumes are present.)   She hid
herself for a brief period inside the half-open door

of her closet, audibly removing her rustling outer
garments, and came forth reduced to her easy home-
things that I have called her fatigue dress, or un-
dress—that "kimono," the integrity of which as a
covering of the person depended ultimately on a
clasp or pin she wore at the throat. "This is cosy,"
Agatha said, as she came to the fire; "but I wonder
if we ought." Then, apparently having resolved
her perplexity about the ought—for I only looked
at her without helping her with the problem, not
understanding what it was—she seated herself by
my knee on a footstool none too broad for a person
of her amplitude thereaways, and said: "You may
make me a back if you like. Do you want to?" I
responded by moving closer to furnish her the required support. "Turn out the gaslamp," she directed a few moments later; "I love the firelight."
There was enough of this light to shine on the
bosom pin she wore. The book I laid down when
Agatha came in was by a Victorian author whose
name I shall not attempt to give. It related that
one evening, the hero, seated by his lady, drew her
to him and unfastened the pin at her throat. The
Victorian author says to the reader: "And so
would you—at eighteen." Contemplating the glow
of the fire in Agatha's brooch, from which I could
withdraw neither my eyes nor my imagination, and
fumblingly extracting the pins from her hair (which
she protested would not do at all, but it did), I recited the Victorian scene. Then shakily I said to
Agatha: "I am eighteen." Agatha answered: "So
am I," and looked up at me. So we agreed we were
of the same age; and then we knocked off three

years and called it fifteen. The Intelligence Quotient at that moment would not have put us above twelve. But, Willie Jones preserve us! When she turned to the fire again there was no pin at her throat for the fire to shine upon. Rather its glow fell upon billowed whiteness, not all linen and lace, that the trinket had guarded.

4—ONE PROBLEM IS SOLVED ANYHOW

Another day followed. All was still well with the world. Reaching the office a moment late, I asked myself seriously whether I had come to New York to learn type-setting and to be an editor, or to let a woman occupy my mind. The inquiry ended in a compromise. I found that I could place a long take of copy on my case, after shuffling the sheets to get the gist of it, and then put it into type as usual, though allowing my thoughts to dwell pleasantly on the ulterior subject mentioned. As my work suffered no harm or delay, I saw that one does not reflect upon the subject of woman with that set of mental faculties the possession of which makes the Intelligent Compositor. Such is the wise provision of nature.

Home at the close of a successful day, I resumed the accustomed chair and book. Agatha, having come in and made herself comfortable, approached me, and tipping back my head, shook it by grasping the scalplock that would never lie smooth, and said: "Oh, chuck that book! What do we care about the Harmony of the Gospels?" Since she had been surprised or wheedled into admitting she was only eighteen, she had to act the part and be girlish—absolutely giddy. Her enthusiasm for the improvement of my mind by wide and constant reading, perceptibly diminished. She had been a New England girl and knew how to train. I recognized that signal.

Family concerns called Agatha to Boston; and I am compelled to say of her, as of others in those changeful days, that I never saw her again nor heard from her. While tender, she was practical. She did not demand that I should write. Letters that supply a bond between parted friends are futile, like all things else except time, to allay the hurt of separation in those who are wrenched apart by ineluctable circumstance.

But youth is buoyant and resourceful. In the days which ensued I resigned myself again to reading and philosophy, and might have learned to smoke a red clay pipe if the long bamboo stem had not turned out so bothersome. I was now eighteen, almost nineteen years old, and was through with women. I had solved them—penetrated their last disguise. The frozen-face was a girl at heart.

If Agatha survives, she is seventy-eight years old; but I have no such thought—cannot picture her as an aged woman. Nevertheless I have veiled her name and whatever circumstances might identify her. A writer may go too far, even in his eighth decade, in assuming that the older friends of his youth have all passed out. Since I began these memoirs I have heard from a woman, Sarah E. Holmes, now past 80, living in Pennsylvania, who recalls that she tried to teach me German long before I was married; and I have been married forty years.

Note.—To this chapter as first printed exception has been taken in certain quarters on the score of too close adherence to details. I am in receipt of criticism that is quite peppy from a New Hampshire spinster who quotes the best thoughts of E. V. Lucas as rebuking what she imputes to me as a penchant (excellent word!) for realism. "I realize," writes the lady, "that you are getting vast amusement out of this, but feel that I must state my attitude."

CHAPTER IX.

1—D. M. BENNETT'S WEALTH OF WORDS

D R. BENNETT possessed such facility as a penman that had he spent as much time at his writing as most editors are obliged to do, he easily would have filled the entire paper every week with his articles. He wrote, with rapidity, a round, even, and legible hand, his letters well formed; and he made few changes except in the way of additions. When not satisfied that a sentence expressed all it should, he wrote it over again, saying the same thing in a different way and letting both stand. One word led to another, and he put them all in, with their synonyms. And he wrote some more into the proof. His prodigality in dispensing his gift of words was evinced in the subheading of The Truth Seeker, which, omitting his picture, ran as follows:

"Devoted to: Science, Morals, Free Thought, Free Discussion, Liberalism, Sexual Equality, Labor Reform, Progression, Free Education, and Whatever Tends to Elevate and Emancipate the Human Race.

"Opposed to: Priestcraft, Ecclesiasticism, Dogmas, Creeds, False Theology, Superstition, Bigotry, Ignorance, Monopolies, Aristocracies, Privileged Classes, Tyranny, Oppression, and Everything that Degrades or Burdens Mankind Mentally or Physically."

This urge to give full measure he found opportunity to gratify when the office was on a ground floor with a street window for advertising purposes in Clinton Place. That window by his direction was soon gilded with lettering. Beneath the sign of THE TRUTH SEEKER, extending across the building, one read:

WORKS OF

VOLTAIRE	PAINE	DARWIN
VOLNEY	INGERSOLL	SPENCER
FEUERBACH	BRADLAUGH	R. D. OWEN
HUXLEY	DRAPER	HAECKEL
TYNDALL	BUCKLE	BUECHNER
LUBBOCK	FROUDE	J. STUART MILL
BOOKS	BOOKS	BOOKS
Liberal	*Science*	*History*
Spiritual	*Philosophy*	*Poetry*
Reformatory	*Art*	*Romance*

The period of succinctness in sign writing had not then fully arrived. Today we should hardly find so many substantives on any window except that of a railway and steamship ticket office. Profusion of words characterized early book titles also. The literary fashion put the contents to the front; and whereas the title now is likely to consist of two or three words in one corner of a fly-leaf, an author might then indulge himself in anywhere from sixteen to twenty-four lines on his title page.

Having learned the contents of the approximately one hundred and fifty boxes in the printer's case, almost my first "take" as a compositor was copy on Bennett's essay, "An Hour with the Devil," which he prepared as a lecture and delivered, or read, "before the New York Liberal

Association at Trenor's New Hall, 1266 Broadway, Sunday, December 5th, 1875." That Association, by the way, had been organized by my mother to provide a platform for Prentice Mulford, writer, lecturer and returned Californian.

Bennett promised his hearers "an hour." Actually it took him more than two hours to read the essay, which when printed filled almost fourteen columns of solid brevier (8 point) in the current number of The Truth Seeker.

I began setting type and editing manuscript at the same time. In the copy that came to me generally I saw room for improvement by correction and even by insertion. New York was still throbbing with the Beecher-Tilton scandal. The incontinency of Beecher had been established, it seemed, by a cloud of witnesses, and the press, especially The Sun, persisted in calling on him to confess or get out, or to get out anyway, and cease desecrating by his polluting presence a temple of religion. Mr. Beecher deigned no reply beyond authorizing his friends to state that he would observe *"the policy of silence."* An unsatisfied press was not so grateful to him as it should have been for providing it with this new phrase susceptible of daily repetition.

Now this discourse of Bennett's was a complete defense for the devil against all maligners and, as the author read it from the galley proofs, it contained the passage: "He [the devil] is too modest, or too peaceful, *or too much in favor of the policy of silence,* to strike back when he is smitten, even to uphold his own innocence." The italicized words were not in Bennett's copy; they were my contribution; and as it turned out they furnished the line that was rewarded with a laugh.

The lecture of Bennett's, "An Hour with the Devil," began: "As far back in the twilight of human existence as we are able to penetrate."

In the fifty years I have been handling manuscripts, how many of those submitted for acceptance, and for publication at an early date, opened with these same words; how many for that innocent cause have been recommended by me for immediate return to the author! When a writer asks the reader to go with him as far back into the twilight of human existence as we are able to penetrate with the eye of history, I know at once that he is going to be prosy.

Bennett was handicapped by prosiness and prolixity. The fact that he could be entertaining in spite of these desperate disadvantages, is an evidence of pure genius. What a man he was for trios of words! Reading some of his 1875 output, I find these sets of triplets in the space of a column:

> "Persecuted, tortured, and burned.
> Cruelties, wrongs, and outrages.
> Dogmas, superstitions, and errors.
> Dishonesty, fraud, and thieving.
> Honest, moral, and truthful.
> Fraud, dishonesty, or otherwise.
> Weeds, thistles, and nettles.
> Fruits, grains, and flowers.
> Elaborate, able, and exhaustive.
> Earnestness, honesty, and firm convictions.
> Sincere, honest-hearted, and well-disposed."

He named his first book "Sages, Infidels, and Thinkers." In the same number of the paper, introducing his report of an address by Hugh Byron Brown at the 320th meeting of the New York Liberal Club, he described the audience as "full, intelligent, and appreciative." Verbal triplets were the fashion. His contributors, too, produced them —if not following his example, then joining him in emulating the author of the Declaration, who wrote "life, liberty, and the pursuit of happiness."

2—THE TRUTH SEEKER AS IT WAS

The number of The Truth Seeker for December 1, 1875, gave eight columns to Mr. Brown's excellent paper above mentioned. At the end of the report are the two lines:

"CHARLES BRADLAUGH lectured before the club on Friday evening, November 26th, but too late for a report."

The next number, December 15, printed "an address on the anniversary of Thomas Paine," by C. A. Codman of Brentwood, L. I., ("Modern Times"), delivered on the previous January 29, and thus almost a year old; and also Bennett's fourteen-column "Hour with the Devil," with the editor's apology that because of its length "many articles are crowded out of this issue," and still *nothing about the lecture by Charles Bradlaugh* at the 321st meeting of the Club. I cannot see a man like Charles Bradlaugh coming to New York now, speaking before a Freethought society, and getting only two lines of mention. I hold myself excused by youth and ignorance for not attending and reporting the meeting. But then I had never heard of Bradlaugh. What a source of pride to me today had some good friend directed me to the meeting, so that this record might contain my impressions of that great English Freethinker and orator!

I missed Bradlaugh, but I heard the foresworn Victoria Woodhull speak that winter in Cooper Union (then "Institute"). The statements of that poor, misunderstood sister were a string of lies, as all her former acquaintances knew. She had now taken up the work of biblical interpretation, beginning at the Garden of Eden. The said Eden, with its rivers, so she told her interested audience, meant merely the regions of a lady's hypogastrium; a statement which I deemed both immodest and indelicate.

The first trace of anything that may have been written by E. M. Macdonald, who, in almost the next shuffle of destiny's cards, was to be editing the paper, is a paragraph, December 15, on "Sovereigns of Industry," a now extinct order then lately instituted for purposes of cooperative buying and selling. Eugene held the office of secretary to the Earl Council S. of I., and the members, young men and women, had a good time, whether they bought cooperatively or capitalistically.

The first sixteen months of The Truth Seeker's existence coincided with a very trying era for publishers. Bennett stated, in his solongatory for 1875, that during this period more than one thousand

papers had been compelled to discontinue; but The
Truth Seeker proposed to expand, to have larger
pages, and to come out every week instead of twice
a month.

On September 15, '75, he had announced himself
a convert to Spiritualism, saying: "For several
years we have felt that we had received proof of the
existence of an intelligence not connected with physical bodies, and the Spiritual theory accounts for it
to our mind better than any other." On account of
this confession of Spiritualism, Bennett was charged
with supernaturalism, which he denied, but had
considerable difficulty in explaining the difference.
He was a man with but one antipathy—the Christian system of superstition. Spiritualism convinced
him, a Mohammedan might perhaps have converted
him, and before he died he joined the Olcott-
Blavatsky Theosophical society.

For his sin in admitting proof of the existence
of intelligences not belonging to visible bodies, Bennett was denied membership in the First Congregational Society of the Religion of Humanity
formed by G. L. Henderson and Hugh Byron
Brown; while the Positivists of the New York
Liberal Club argued against holding meetings in
Science Hall because The Truth Seeker, with its
editor entertaining those views, was sheltered in the
same building.

All idealisms not included in the Christian scheme
might hope for Bennett's allegiance. He championed
Greenbackism when it came and supported Peter
Cooper for President. He listened to a speech by

Ingersoll in Cooper Union, and, in reporting the event expressed disagreement with the Colonel's opinions on finance.

3—I FIRST BEHOLD INGERSOLL

To me at that age monetary questions were nothing, but Ingersoll was much, and I feasted on that Cooper Union speech. Ingersoll, as an orator, was a great illusionist. He made you visualize what he chose. Remembering his illuminative "presence," I do not wonder that Mark Twain, supposing he thought of Abou Ben Adhem's visitor, could express it only by terming Ingersoll's appearance that of an "angel." A Republican in politics, he in this speech accused the Democrats of grabbing all their hands would hold, and then exclaimed: "And my God, what hands!" Now the hands of Ingersoll were large, like the rest of him, and when he spread them out some two yards apart to illustrate the size and capacity of those he had just spoken of, they seemed to grasp the whole audience and the earth and the firmament.

Disagreeing with Ingersoll in his advocacy of specie payment, Bennett said:

"His remarks upon finance scarcely convinced us of the superiority of gold as a medium of exchange, or that contraction is calculated to benefit the manufacturer or the laborer. It will benefit the capitalist and the banker, who of course will, after the contraction, have the same number of thousands as before; and the greater extent to which the contraction is carried the larger proportion will they hold of the whole, and the less will be obtainable by the working classes."

The Truth Seeker volume of 1876 contains as much "finance" as Freethought. Had Bennett lived to see Socialism sweep into popularity, I suppose he would have shared that vision the same as he saw eye to eye with those who beheld their salvation in greenbacks, and that his paper would have turned Socialist with him.

Besides the lecture of Bradlaugh, the series by Moncure D. Conway passed without my hearing them. Mr. Conway came from London, where he was a minister of the South Place chapel, and reported much fundamentalist opposition to the theory of evolution as presented by Darwin. Yet I absented myself from home one evening to hear the astronomer Richard A. Proctor, whose lectures were reported for The Truth Seeker by a young foreign lady, Miss M. S. Gontcharoff. The speech of Professor Proctor would never have betrayed him to me as a Britisher if he had not said "leftenant."

Huxley, whose Chickering Hall lectures on evolution were delivered in September, 1876, was less Yankeefied of accent. And he was humorous in spots. He resorted to Milton instead of Moses for a statement of the creation hypothesis opposed to evolution, and told us why he did so. Happily, he said, "Milton leaves us no ambiguity as to what he means," while about the meaning of the Mosaic doctrine, which some critics say Moses never wrote, two are seldom found who agree, notwithstanding they all consult the same Hebrew text. And then came Huxley's memorable remark: "A person who is not a Hebrew scholar can only stand aside and admire the marvelous flexibility of a language which admits of such diverse interpretations." He had been applauded when he came on the stage, but not again until he released this witticism, when the stenographer bracketed "Laughter and applause." Professor Youmans of the Popular Science Monthly, and Professor Marsh of Yale, enjoyed themselves.

4—THE PAINE HABIT FORMED

I first assisted by my presence at a Thomas Paine celebration in Ecclesia Hall, No. 8 Union Square, Saturday, January 29, 1876. I saw there Dr. Charles L. (Charlie) Andrews, son of Stephen Pearl. It was the 139th anniversary of the birth of Paine. I saw Dr. Andrews also on the 191st Paine anniversary, and doubt that I have missed seeing him at any of the intervening ones. The opening address by Mr. Bennett at Ecclesia Hall filled half the paper the next week, and what the other speakers happened to say was left over for a future number.

During that year (1876) Bennett survived periods of strong discouragement, being at times ready to suspend. In view, he said in one of his moments of depression, of "the large numbers on our list who decline to renew their subscription, though they must know they are several months in arrears; that many, if notified of their indebtedness, pay no attention to it"; that books and pamphlets "are allowed to quietly lay on our shelves" (despite their merits and modest price); "when our request for a little temporary aid is treated with utter indifference, we are able to appreciate the estimate placed upon one who has devoted every dollar he possessed and nearly every moment of his time to the cause of

Liberalism, and we would seem to be admonished that it is time for us to modestly retire from the position we have presumed to occupy, and to sell out our business to someone who can run a paper without money, and live upon air at the same time. If there are those who have a limited amount of ready money, and a large amount of courage, who feel like buying out a business which neither pays in the present nor promises in the future, let them send in their propositions."

A distant successor of Bennett has read those words with understanding.

As the postal regulations were then, a publisher might devote the whole of his paper to reading notices and advertisements of his own business—a privilege which since has been so restricted that this class of matter must be confined to a twentieth part of the paper's area, any excess of space devoted to business (except in religious publications) being penalized by postage rates increased in the proportion that this 5 percent limitation is exceeded. So all of The Truth Seeker's departments, editorial, news, correspondence, and miscellaneous, were utilized for the insertion of commendatory notices of Bennett's books and tracts, including price lists. Such freedom from editorial dictation by the government was a vast advantage to the publisher.

There was immediate response to Editor Bennett's plaint; the subscribers rallied and not only paid up their subscriptions but made him donations and loans. Ella E. Gibson, who wrote "The Godly Women of the Bible" ("by an Ungodly Woman of the nineteenth century"), lent him $300, and in a short time he had as much as a thousand dollars in gifts and loans. His most steadfast friend was a young Jewish merchant named Morris Altman, who supported him financially and ran a six-inch business card advertising his $50,000 stock of dry goods, millinery, etc., at 301-303 Sixth avenue. Altman was a humanitarian employer, an innovator in providing seats for his girl clerks, shortening their hours, and closing early on Saturday. Through all the years, his personal appearance is quite distinct to me, perhaps because he was a man of striking good looks and wore his clothes and his high hat so well, and flashed across his pleasant smile to us printers at our cases, with a bow as polite as he could have made anywhere. He died that summer at 39 years of age.

5—EVENTS AND OBSERVATIONS

The evangelist Moody, with his singing partner, Sankey, played New York the season of '75-'76, occupying the Hippodrome (heretofore mentioned as Gilmore's Garden) on Fourth Avenue for some six weeks at a computed cost to the angels of $250,000. His meetings were reported for The Truth Seeker by Prentice Mulford, who wrote under the name of "Ichabod Crane, a Christian Worker." I went one night, and thought the proceedings less entertaining, even, than Victoria Woodhull's lecture, which had proved, as it were, a "flop." To hear Moody at that time, Mr. William Plotts, now of California, came ashore from a schooner in the bay. Brother Plotts had his doubts about religion at the time, and they have not since been resolved. He

worked the oil fields of Pennsylvania as the Boy
Contractor, got a theory about oil drilling, and with
some well-digging machinery and bad notes went
West to try it out. Some years ago he sold his
properties to the Standard Oil Company.

It was in the early part of 1876 that a Scotch
Freethinker and Positivist, George L. Henderson, a
brother of the Iowa Representative, D. B. Henderson, speaker of the House, 56th Congress, leased the
building at 141 Eighth Street, which contained a
meeting room, 40 x 60, and good office accommoda-
tions. He named the premises SCIENCE HALL,
and The Truth Seeker moved thither, printing-office
and all.

Features of the Freethought work of the centennial year, besides the organization of the National
Liberal League, were the lectures of the former
Rev. W. S. Bell of Brooklyn, B. F. Underwood
of Massachusetts, and of J. L. York of San Jose,
Cal. Underwood told of being catechized by his
orthodox grandmother. "I hear, Benjamin," she
said, "that you have become one of those dreadful
Unitarians." He replied: "No, that is quite false.
I call myself a Philosophical Materialist." She took
comfort from his words, saying: "Well, I am glad
to hear that. I couldn't believe you had lost your religion to the extent of being a Unitarian."

Comstock was perniciously active. He put John
A. Lant of Toledo, Ohio, in jail for matter appearing in his paper called The Sun, and procured the
indictment of Dr. E. B. Foote for issuing "Words
of Pearl" in a small pamphlet containing hints for

the prevention of conception. Dr. Foote's trial before
Judge Benedict and the fine imposed cost him $5,000.
Comstock thereby made a formidable and implacable
enemy who in his subsequent prosecutions he was to
find facing him or working back of the defense. For
the full Comstock saga the reader is referred to the
book, "Anthony Comstock, Roundsman of the
Lord," by Heywood Broun and Margaret Leech,
1927, and The Truth Seeker files.

Liberal exchanges were the Boston Investigator,
Banner of Light (Boston), the Religio-Philosophical
Journal (these last two Spiritualist); Common
Sense, published by Col. R. Peterson, Paris, Texas;
Prometheus, a magazine, Charles P. Somerby, 139
Eighth Street; Dr. Foote's Health Monthly, New
York; Hull's Crucible, Boston, and Davis's Battle
Ax (location unknown).

What I call the best thing in the Third Volume
was Charles Stephenson's poem "Our Father in
Heaven" (p. 374). Stephenson died in 1877 at Rock
Island, Ill., aged 24.

Bennett began June 17 to reprint Haeckel's
"Doctrine of Affiliation or Descent Theory" out of
the "History of Creation," then just published in
America. It was my weekly "take" as copy to be
put in type. Quotations from Haeckel ran in the
paper so long that by the time they were finished
we had moved into Clinton Place, and I had become foreman and assistant editor. Then I wrote
a summary of them.

Bennett had published in 1876 his "World's Sages,
Infidels, and Thinkers," written by himself, by his

office assistant, S. H. Preston, by A. L. Rawson,
by numerous of the living characters mentioned
in it, and by other helpful friends.

6—ORIGIN OF A FAMOUS PASSAGE

In 1875, Grant sent to Congress his message
containing the famous church taxation paragraph.
In 1876, at Philadelphia, led by Francis Elling¬
wood Abbot, editor of The Index (Free Religious),
the National Liberal League was organized in Concert Hall, Chestnut Street, July 1-4, and there were
adopted the Nine Demands of Liberalism, which
The Truth Seeker has printed as its political platform for many years.

All this is familiar history. One interesting incident connected with Grant's message has never
been published. In seeking information from
Stephen Pearl Andrews with regard to govern-
mental or official affairs, I inquired whether he
thought it probable that the Presidents themselves
wrote all of the messages they transmitted to Congress. He replied it was certain they did not.
Heads of departments contributed to them, he said,
and recommendations by advisers were included.
For an example, Mr. Andrews then mentioned
Grant's church taxation paragraph of 1875, saying that he himself and a group of liberals had
prepared a statement on the subject, and procur-
ing an appointment with the President at the White
House, had brought it to his attention. So that was
the origin of Grant's recommendation that all

property, whether ecclesiastical or corporate, be equally taxed.

"I would call your attention," said the message, "to the importance of correcting an evil that, if permitted to continue, will probably lead to great trouble in our land before the close of the nineteenth century. It is the acquisition of vast amounts of untaxed church property. In 1850, I believe, the church property of the United States, which paid no tax, municipal or state, amounted to $83,000,000. In 1860, the amount had doubled. In 1875, it is about $1,000,000,000. By 1900, without a check, it is safe to say this property will reach a sum exceeding $3,000,000,000. So vast a sum, receiving all the protection of government without its proportion of the burdens and expenses of the same, will not be looked upon acquiescently by those who have to pay the taxes. In a growing country, where real estate enhances so rapidly with time as in the United States, there is scarcely a limit to the wealth that may be acquired by corporations, religious or otherwise, if allowed to retain real estate without taxation. The contemplation of so vast a property as here alluded to, without taxation, may lead to sequestration without constitutional authority, and through blood. I would suggest the taxation of all property equally, whether church or corporation."

This recommendation, as sent to Congress, was modified to admit of the exemption of a limited amount of church property. The body of it originated with the Freethinkers who organized the National Liberal League the next year.

The Truth Seeker of October 7, 1876, records the
death of James Lick, the Californian philanthropist
who had given $60,000 toward the erection of Paine
Memorial Hall in Boston.

James Lick was a native of Fredericksburg, Pa.,
born there August 25, 1796, and through his grandfather a son of the
American Revolution.
At 25 he was a New
Yorker, but not prosper-
ous. He went thence to
Buenos Aires, and made
pianos to sell to the
natives. He bought hides
and brought them to the
United States, and then
spent eleven years manu-
facturing and s e l l i n g
pianos in Peru. He went
to San Francisco (Yerba
Buena) in 1847, when
the place had only a
thousand inhabitants,
and bought real estate. He made millions selling
it. Amongst his later holdings was a flour mill
near San Jose, which cost him $200,000, but
brought only $60,000, when sold for the Paine
Hall fund. In his will he gave his money back to
California in the form of the Lick Observatory at
Mount Hamilton, which belongs to the California
University; donations to the Academy of Science,
a home for aged women, free baths, Pioneer Hall,
and other benefactions, none of them religious,

JAMES LICK.

but all, as he intended and hoped, contributing to human progress. He died October 1, 1876. There will be more about James Lick in subsequent observations.

NOTE—Lately I gave a list of editors who had first worked on The Truth Seeker as composers. I omitted one who resorted to the case only to set up matter for his own use as circulars. This was Edward Dobson, employed thirty years ago and previously thereto as book wrapper and shipper and a pick-up man. "Teddy" thought and discoursed on high themes, even then, and before he was twenty-one lectured at the Liberal Club on "Spontaneous Generation." An old-timer, in view of the lecturer's juvenility, said he believed the present generation was becoming altogether *too* spontaneous. I had not seen Teddy for about twenty years when he walked into this office (June, 1928), a man of fifty-two and whitehaired. He has had an editorial position on the Brooklyn Standard-Union for a quarter of a century, and is now dramatic critic.

CHAPTER X.

THROUGHOUT 1876 the heading of The Truth Seeker had presented each week a rather poor picture of Dr. Bennett with a book on the table before him, some chemistry apparatus on his right, a library behind him, and a globe and telescope on his left. We may infer that in commercial enterprises theretofore he had

AN IDEALIZED EDITOR.

followed the fashion and embellished his advertising matter with his portrait. Now, beginning with the first number in 1877, he substituted for his own a picture of Benjamin Franklin and made editorial mention of the change, saying "There is no more fitting man whose face should grace the heading of The Truth Seeker than the great American scientist and Liberal, Benjamin Franklin." When in the first week of '76 a duel took place between Fred May and James Gordon Bennett of the New York Herald, he took the precaution to write: "It is, perhaps, needless to state that there is no relationship between the Bennett of The Herald and he of The Truth Seeker." He would not be mistaken for a duelist.

I must quote a sample of the style of Editor Bennett's assistant, S. H. Preston. "But the great unwritten gospel of Nature," Preston wrote grandly, "revealed in the rock and the rose, in the intuitions of the human heart and in the fiery scriptures of circling suns and constellations, and uttered in all the myriad mighty voices of the wondrous Universe, shall never fail. To the bigot who would force upon us a self-contradictory, revolting old book (which men may mangle, rats may nibble, and time moulder) we offer the glorious gospels strewn everywhere by the generous hands of our universal Mother, whose sublime lessons speak to the consciences of men in the stars and sunbeams, in the winds and waves and woodlands, and which will be everlastingly taught by ten thousand tongues of Nature through all the corridors of eternity."

"Sam," as we called Preston, was a little man but he wielded a mighty pen. The boys used to say that he grasped it with both hands. He had the liquor and tobacco (chewing) habits, which made him not so agreeable to Bennett, who had neither.

Dr. Sarah B. Chase, who underwent some persecution at the hands of Anthony Comstock on account of a hygienic syringe which she advertised,
took Preston in hand and reformed him. He would
have been a miracle of grace had his reformation
been brought about by a conversion to religion.
Mrs. Chase had a little daughter Gracia, about ten
years old, who showed promise as an elocutionist
and recited verses at the Paine anniversary celebration. She adopted the stage as a career, and
was successful.

Bennett procured a copy of Viscount Amberley's
"Analysis of Religious Belief" and announced that
he should reprint it, a promise he fulfilled. There
was much controversy over the work, especially
among the Russell and Amberley families in England. The son of Amberley, Bertrand Russell, is
a distinguished mathematician and radical.

The Rev. G. H. Humphrey, author of an attempt
at constructive criticism entitled "Hell and Damnation," challenged the editor of The Truth Seeker
to debate Christianity and Infidelity with him. The
debate ran through many numbers of the paper and
was printed in a book of more than 500 pages.
Humphrey was a rare Fundamentalist, or would
be so reckoned today, but he and Bennett became
excellent friends. In the debate the minister
stressed the immorality of Infidels, and Bennett
replied with page after page of clerical offenders,
concerning whom Humphrey took high grounds,
declaring that their damnation was just; and then
he made fresh attacks on Infidels. The Truth
Seeker then ran a department of "Notes and Clip-

pings" on the front page, and here were gathered current instances of clerical delinquencies. Not many years later there was a report that the Rev. Mr. Humphrey had been found away from home, I believe with his wife's niece, and fragments of the seventh commandment in evidence. It looked like a point for Bennett, but he declined to publish the facts which I had handed in as a piece of copy. Bennett read the story and put it in the waste-basket. "George," he said, "I think the temptation was too great!" I asked: "Why, have you seen the young woman?" He said: "No, but I have seen Humphrey's wife." Bennett had great charity toward human weaknesses when he knew the cir cumstances.

The postal regulations in 1876 put no restriction on the amount of advertisements and paid reading notices a paper might carry at the rate of a cent per pound; and Bennett availed himself freely of these liberal provisions by placing commendatory notices of his publications, with prices attached, on every page of The Truth Seeker. All continued articles, and he had one or more of his own productions running most of the time, were made into tracts, pamphlets, or books. Production was cheap. The price of stereotype plates was under 20 cents a page; composition, 30 cents, as against a dollar in each case today. As a consequence he could price his tracts and pamphlets at the rate of four pages for one cent. The sale of cheap literature by mail was facilitated by shinplasters, paper currency in fractional parts of a dollar. The hours of labor were 7 to 6.

The interesting returns of the 1876 Hayes-Tilden presidential election were printed in The Truth Seeker's news column Nov. 11. As they were there given, Tilden had 197 electoral votes; Hayes but 158, and 6 were doubtful. A recount reversed the result; but such turmoil ensued that Victoria Woodhull, appearing upon the platform of Chickering hall, two weeks later, with a Bible in her hand, drew from the sacred volume the prediction that before New Year's the country would be involved in hopeless anarchy, revolution, and the most sanguinary war the world had ever seen. Not another President should ever be inaugurated under the dome of the Capitol at Washington, she said, but monarchy would be our next form of government, and Grant the dictator. The text which Mrs. Woodhull read from the Bible appeared to support that view.

Liberal papers making their first appearance in 1876 were: Evolution, Asa K. Butts, 34 Dey street; John Syphers' Agitator; The Radical Review, Boston, Benjamin R. Tucker; Freethought Journal, Toronto, Ont.; The Age of Reason, New York, Seth Wilbur Payne.

Among liberal writers and new contributors to The Truth Seeker were: A. L. Rawson, George Francis Train, E. C. Walker, S. H. Preston, Horace Traubel, Maria M. deFord, W. F. Jamieson, Susan H. Wixon, C. Fannie Allyn, James Parton, Benj. R. Tucker. Of these, Mr. Walker and Mr. Tucker are living at the date of this entry in 1928.

Of the surviving workers in the liberal field as far back as the Centennial year is Felix Adler, head of the Ethical Culture Society; while the man who reported his lectures for The Truth Seeker still has, I hope, "the cheerful habit of living." This is D. W. Craig, last of San Diego, Cal., who has wielded a fearless typewriter up to now. But he had no machine then. His handwriting, however, a discriminating compositor would prefer to either typewriting or reprint. He used the system of shorthand taught by Mrs. Eliza Boardman Burnz, teacher in Cooper Institute, the lady who later prevailed upon Bennett to introduce the limited spelling reform of dropping the final *e* from have, give, and live.

2—IT HAS COME AT LAST.

On November 1, 1875, Bennett had begun his "Open Letter to Jesus Christ." On January 15, 1876, he published an article which The Scientific American had declined, by the Hon. A. B. Bradford of Pennsylvania, a former clergyman, on "How Do Marsupials Propagate Their Kind?" He made these pieces into tracts and sold them. In the number of the paper for November, 17, 1877, he announced in the heading of an article, "IT HAS COME AT LAST," and wrote:

"One week ago was announced in these columns the arrest in Boston, by Anthony Comstock, of E. H. Heywood of Princeton, Mass. I was not then aware that the time of my own arrest was so near at hand, but at that very moment a warrant had been issued against me, and was only awaiting the pleasure of Mr. Comstock to serve it.

"On Monday last, a little after the hour of twelve, while busily engaged in my office preparing matter for this issue of the paper, that noted champion of Christianity, with a deputy United States marshal at his elbow, visited me with the information that he had a warrant for my arrest. I inquired upon what authority and upon what charge. He replied by the authority of the United States and upon the charge of sending obscene and blasphemous matter through the mails. In reply to my enquiry what the objectionable matter was he exhibited two tracts, one entitled 'An Open Letter to Jesus Christ,' and the other, 'How Do Marsupials Propagate Their Kind?' He then demanded the amount of those tracts that were on hand, which were delivered to him. He showed a package of tracts, etc., which had been put up at this office and sent by mail to S. Bender, Squan Village, N. J., and a registered letter receipt for the money accompanying an order for The Truth Seekers, tracts, etc., which was signed in this office. I asked him whether the party to whom the tracts were addressed was a *real* party, and he had opened his package, or a *bogus* party, and the letter ordering the tracts a mere decoy letter, such as he had used on other occasions. He acknowledged that it was the latter—that he had written the order in an assumed name."

Mr. Bennett passively accompanied his captors to the room of U. S. Commissioner Shields in the Postoffice building and furnished bail in the sum of $1,500. He did not name his surety, but of course it was Dr. E. B. Foote. He then, in The Truth Seeker, expressed his indignation that a man "hard upon sixty years of age, and who for nearly a half century have been a supporter of our government, am now arranged by it [he meant arraigned] as an offender against it for sending indecent and blasphemous matter through the mails."

Diligent in business, the Doctor closes the article by saying: "It is hoped that in the emergency that soon must come, those who know themselves to be indebted to The Truth Seeker will be prompt to pay, and that those who feel like subscribing for the paper to help it through its trouble will be ready to do so. . . . Those who send for books and pamphlets will also help push the cause along and render The Truth Seeker more able to weather the approaching storm. May it not be expected that every liberal in the country will do his duty?"

The firm of Henderson & Brown, proprietors of Science Hall and doing a coal and real estate business therein, started a defense fund with a pledge of $25 before the next number of The Truth Seeker went to press.

Bennett's temperature rose rapidly during the following week, and he had in the next number a white-hot article on the miserable Comstock's hideous offenses. The article was seven columns in length, and addressed to the proposition, "American Liberty: Is It a Sham?" He found much to be said in support of the proposition that it is. In prospect, following the successful prosecution of The Truth Seeker, he saw the writings of Darwin,

Spencer, Huxley, Tyndall, Proctor, Haeckel, Draper, Fiske, and others summarily squelched.

Meanwhile Comstock was prosecuting Ezra H. Heywood in Massachusetts for selling "Cupid's Yokes" and Trall's "Sexual Physiology."

The attack on freedom of speech in 1877 created quite a furor, and increased the circulation of The Truth Seeker, while letters of sympathy poured in and a defense fund grew apace. There have been so many such attacks on the freedom of the press in the half century which has since elapsed that the people have grown weary of protesting and little excitement is caused by them now. Occasionally we see statistics of the number of persons doing time for talking too much or saying the wrong thing, but we take only the mildest interest in the figures. In 1877 such outrages in the name of the people aroused indignation.

3—A FEW PARTICULARS.

To mention a few of the Events of 1877: Part of the Paine farm at New Rochelle was sold at auction; a split took place in the New York Liberal Club in May and the "radical" element decided to meet thereafter in Science Hall; it was reported from Revere, Mass., that Lemuel K. Washburn, a Unitarian heretic, was making things lively in his parish; in Bell county, Texas, a party of Ku Klux lured a Freethinking physician, Dr. J. A. Russell, from his house and binding him to a tree, gave him one hundred lashes. Dr. Russell had given "Infidel" lectures. The whipping party left a placard threatening to burn out or hang any Infidel lecturer who should appear in that neighborhood. A feature of The Truth Seeker was the Ingersoll-Observer controversy, later published under the title of "Paine Vindicated." The New York Freethinkers' Association was organized, with Dr. T. L. Brown of Binghamton as president and H. L. Green as corresponding secretary. The Rev. O. B. Frothingham, modernist or liberal clergyman, gave weekly discourses in Masonic Temple. The First Annual Congress of the National Liberal League was held at Rochester, N. Y., October 26. Henry Ward Beecher delivered his famous sermon, December 14, repudiating the doctrine of hell.

Walt Whitman made the principal address at the Paine celebration in Philadelphia. Horace Traubel recited the poem he had written for the occasion.

The Society of Humanity held meetings in Science Hall, addressed by Thaddeus B. Wakeman, Hugh Byron Brown and Albert L. Rawson.

A few weeks before the arrest of Bennett by Comstock he had begun a discussion with a man who signed his name Cyrus Romulus R. Teed, of Moravia, N. Y., on the proposition that "Jesus is not only Divine, but the Lord God, Creator of Heaven and Earth." That also was published in a book, "The Bennett-Teed Discussion" (1878). Teed was more interesting as a character than as a writer. He was another of those hollow-globe theorists, only instead of holding with Brewster that the hollow inside of the globe could be reached by sailing through a hole at the north pole, he taught that we were actually living there, that is, on the inner surface of a sphere. A few years after the debate with Bennett he moved to New York and appeared to be domiciled with some women he had converted to his views. He came occasionally to the flat where my mother and I were keeping house, and perhaps with a view to gaining my adhesion, set forth his pretensions. He had been understood to be a celibate like Paul, but he also claimed the Pauline liberty: "Have we not power to lead about a sister?" That he should allow women to feed him he argued from Luke viii, 2, 3, where certain women are named who accompanied Jesus and "ministered to him of their substance." What Jesus would accept Teed would not disdain. And the small matter of his relations with these females he settled by identifying himself as the man named in the first verse of the forty-fifth chapter of Isaiah: "Thus saith the Lord to his anointed, to Cyrus, whose right hand I have holden, to subdue nations before him; and I will loose the loins of kings, to open before him the two-leaved gates; and the gates shall not be shut." Giving the words a close anatomical interpretation, he found there his warrant for conjugal association with women. He founded a colony in Florida and for a long time published a magazine advocating his system of geology and of religion. When he died his followers looked for his resurrection on the third day. At the period when I was seeing him frequently the telephone had but recently come into use. He said that he knew how sight as well as sound could be transmitted, thus realizing television, but should leave that for others to work out, since he had a more important mission.

4—MENTIONED IN PASSING.

Our household, that followed the New York custom and got wheels under it regularly once a year, had moved in May, 1876, from Fourth avenue to apartments in East Eleventh street near Second avenue, a quiet and restful quarter of the city. While we lived there ghouls stole the body of A. T. Stewart from the churchyard of St. Mark's-in-the-Bouwerie, just around the corner. I am told that the name of A. T. Stewart means nothing to this generation. It must have been a household word in mine, for before I left Surry I had heard of Stewart's great white building occupying a block above Tenth street between Fourth avenue and Broadway. Stewart was the pioneer department-store organizer. His grave was robbed for ransom.

Of my own advancement there is nought to record beyond an attempt to read what books there were in the world, and a short-lived ambition to learn music and be a pianist—this and what came of it. Events I could not control led me to discontinue practice after a few unfruitful lessons. But then there was left my teacher, a girl of eighteen, answering to the name of Doris, who is not so summarily to be dismissed. She had been a music student under Gottschalk, who at his public concerts brought her out as a star pupil. Her hands, beautifully formed and remarkably developed as to the hitting power of their digits on a keyboard, had been modeled by the sculptor J. Q. A. Ward. She at this time gave pupils piano lessons in the morning, and in the afternoon posed for a class of art girls in Brooklyn. To ask such a being as that to spend her evenings drumming scales diatonic and chromatic into the head and hands of a boy who had no talent, and who would rather be reading or romping with her, seemed to me, to a growing degree, irrational, although there was half a dollar in it for her. The nearness, herself occupying a chair beside the stool I sat on, had danger in it, which I felt and suspected she did. One evening when the struggle between me and the instrument was more than usual disharmonious, I detected a quaver in her voice and tears in her eyes; and when I dropped my hands and swung about toward her, she manifested relief. Her face, I thought, expressed more than I had seen in it before, and her smile now was illuminative. We spoke to each other on new terms, with different words and accents. Performer and instrument also underwent a parallel change, for Love, as it were, took up the Harp of Life, and smote on all its chords with might. The result was the music of the player's old sweet song, the only one he knows. The roles of teacher and pupil then became one with my suspended study of the Harmony of the Gospels. So thoughtless, unstable and impulsive is youth. This young woman had been cherishing some depressive memories of a recent misadventure that would have caused a less spirited girl to hesitate between suicide and a fast life; she having, a short time before I knew her, felt obliged to rid herself of a lover who had brought her to New York. The man, twice her age, married and endowed with agreeable qualities that would content any woman who might be the exclusive beneficiary of them, turned out to be a rover in love as in business—for he was a traveling man; and when there came to her the clearest evidence of his perfidy, she dismissed him with finality. The tale that had won her sympathy, and so her consent to accompany him, was the old one, though doubtless new to her, and to the average woman once. Its theme is an uncongenial wife who won't divorce him. It transpired that this bird lived with his wife, who was a good sport. The one genuine thing about the man was his evident infatuation with Doris, but he had resorted to lying, which is a great aid in matters of the affections. In a certain behalf the novelists write with truth to life. They become authentic on the theme that the daughter who leaves home for the good times promised in the great city is reluctant to return thither when disillusionment comes. That was the case with Doris. Hence she took a room in the Eleventh street house; asked her father to ship there the piano she had left behind her, and with a strong resolve began "on her own." She had admirers, whom my watchfulness discouraged. I was so ludicrously exclusive I wouldn't even eat the candy they sent her. The parents were divorced and her mother, domiciled in nearby rooms, cooperated with her in music teaching, and chaperoned her at the art class. This mother, a Spiritualist and not bigoted, found no fault now with the domestic situation of her daughter; rather she thought it ideal, and was friendly toward myself. As when women start a fashion they go farther than men, who do not have to be told by the pope where to stop leaving off clothes; so when they are liberal they are more liberal than men also. I heard of a young woman in New York, living in bliss with the man of her heart; but being convinced that the exclusiveness of monogamy was contrary to the law of God, she sacrificed her happiness to go with one she merely respected, thus following her convictions. I never knew a man so conscientious as that. Women know more perhaps, or maybe less. I will not dogmatize on that point. I have met no other person who took Spiritualism so seriously as Doris's mother did. Where a devout Christian would see the hand of providence, she acknowledged the help of the immortals. I was no convinced believer, and neither was Doris. Nevertheless the mother gave the angels credit for bringing us "en rapport," as it were. A reader of The Truth Seeker and an admirer of Bennett, it was more than she had ever hoped that her daughter should find love and refuge and happiness in The Truth Seeker family. She was a lovely spirituelle being. Doris imparted to me, in such a manner as one would affect in saying that some things are unaccountable: "Mama liked you before I did and thinks you are smart. She says she wishes she had as bright a son—her way of telling me I am not so bright as you are." The light-hearted creature, I regret to say, saw in other young men certain qualities, such as style, speed, and spending-money, that to an extent compensated for inability to quote Spencer's definition of evolution, to argue abstractly, or to spell hard words off-hand, in which last accomplishment she acknowledged herself to be weak. By Doris Spiritualism was at times defended; at other times humorously viewed. She must have been in the latter mood when in the front room one evening our Spiritualist contingent had grouped themselves about the table, fingers and thumbs making contact, waiting for manifestations. Some of the sitters believed they were developing mediumistic powers. Doris wrote on a filmy piece of paper, just off a caramel, the words: "You are on the right track; meet every night." Standing on a chair I slipped the message into the seance-room by way of the transom, at the right moment for a draft of air to carry it to the center of the table. We heard next day that Brother David Hoyle, a firm believer in spirit intercourse, pronounced it a genuine communication. Doris had expected her playful act would be understood and merely smiled at by the indulgent sitters, and never dared to enlighten Mr. Hoyle.

After some months of such felicity for Doris and me as that which is predicated of companionate marriage, Doris's father, left alone, urgently invited her to come home. The mother preferred to take the daughter west with her, to the regions of Utah. For expenses she needed my help, and Mr. Bennett, asking no questions, lent me seventy-five dollars. He had no bank account; he carried his money in a long pocketbook, which, when I made the touch, he drew forth from an interior pocket, and then counted out the bills without comment. The divulging of this youthful experience is mitigated, I hope, because it brings out a characteristic of Dr. Bennett's that otherwise would not appear. He could do a favor without preaching a sermon on the imprudences that put people where they want favors. Mrs. Bennett, like him in being helpful, was as motherly as though she had learned the art by raising a family of sons instead of being childless all her life.

When Doris went West, I roped her trunk, which was uncertain as to hinges and lock. It was like winding heartstrings about it and pulling them tight.

Years ago I was admonished by a thoughtful friend that such mementoes of his youthful affairs as a man has retained ought to be destroyed for the sake of those they might possibly annoy if preserved to pass beyond his care. I thought the counsel good, and so, going often to a small box in which certain letters and pictures and verses had been kept for memory's sake, I at each visit drew something out for a last look or reading, and then ditched it for good. This braid of hair with its message I once carried to the fire and made the right motion for consigning it to the flame, but my hand refused to relax when it should

have done so, and came back with the words, "Remember me." Some day another hand than my own will grope in the pockets of clothes I am not wearing, nor am to wear again, and will bring forth a bunch of keys. One thin key will unlock the drawer in a safe that holds the original of this picture—this braid of brown hair, bright and glossy after all the years, stitched to a fragment of paper; the girlish writing almost unfaded. The hand that draws it out then may cast the relic where it will.

I was now nineteen, nearing twenty, and through with women.

5—FRIENDS.

When I say that in 1877 the family occupied a flat at 308 Third avenue, about Twenty-fourth street, I expect the old New Yorker to interject: "Near the Bull's Head Hotel, where the circus people used to bivouac." That is so, but for old New York, as I saw it, I refer the reader to James L. Ford's book, "Forty-Odd Years in the Literary Shop (1921), which covers the same decades as my own observations. Third avenue has decayed in the last half-century as a consequence of the elevated trains running close to second-story windows. Nearby No. 308, in the cigar store of Sam Schendel, I made the acquaintance of a boy of my own age from Tunkhannock, Pa., one Henry H. Sherman, who was a Munson stenographer of remarkable skill. We were chums from that time until his death more than forty years later. He lived in Gramercy square, near neighbor to Samuel J. Tilden, for whom he occasionally did short-hand work. He had luck in picking up positions. For a time he was secretary to a police commissioner of the name of McLean. In that place he was in receipt of tickets, which he shared with me, to all shows that required police attendance. I saw enough prize-fights then to sate my interest in the game, and have not cared to see one since. Perhaps the last public employment or office held by Sherman was undersheriff when Tamsen had charge of Ludlow Street Jail. Few will remember Sheriff Tamsen's notice to the police that "der chail is oud," when his prisoners got away from him, or the public reaction when a young lady stenographer resigned her situation because Sherman swore at her. The German influence prevailed so strongly in the jail during the Tamsen administration that The Sun spelled the under-sheriff's name Schurmann. After I had learned shorthand Sherman gave me remunerative work transcribing his notes. The typewriting of records was not then required. Typewriters did not at once displace script. They came into use in 1873 and their Golden Jubilee was celebrated the same year as The Truth Seeker's. Sherman, who professed the Episcopalian faith, worshiped at St. George's in Rutherford Place, under Rainsford. He never pressed too closely the language of scripture. His term for the unknown, for first causes and final results, was a "Jigger." Life began with a Jigger, he said. The soul? Oh, tha⁺ was a kind of a jigger. Gods, angels, spirits, all undefinable things, were jiggers, equivalent to the sailor's gilguy and gadget. I have found the word a handy one and use it every week when marking copy for the printer. He died about 1920.

It is impossible, as I may already have shown in these papers, for a writer to stick to his chronology. From the date of my first meeting with Sherman, I have just spanned forty-odd years to mention his death. And while in the second decade of the nine-teen hundreds for the moment, I will set down an in-cident of the century's 'teens. Four men whom I had met under divers circumstances had shown, in one way or another, that they regarded me as some-thing more than a speaking acquaintance. Their attitude was rather that of cordial friendship. I conceived the idea of making them friends of one another. They were Abel and Merriweather of Montclair, and Sherman and Coburn of New York. Abel was New York agent for the Titusville Iron Works; Merriweather handled the foreign trade of the Lucas Paint Company and was an Anglican by way of his wife; Coburn was an engineer who specialized in dams and is said to have planned more of them than anyone else. To the boys of the Massachusetts Institute of Technology, in my son's time, he was known as "Pa" Coburn. Sher-man was now a lawyer. I got these four good men together at a luncheon one day somewhere in the vicinity of Fraunce's Tavern. They seemed to be well met. It was worth something to me to hear them explain to one another how they happened to be friends with this harmless fellow "Mac." My presence embarrassed them not at all, nor restrained them in their drolleries of which I was the theme. Each found a different excuse for being found in my company, and then, momentarily serious, told why they had left their offices on a busy day to meet men who were friends of Mac. With roasting and toasting they did me up brown. On the whole it was so good to be there that Mr. Abel proposed future gatherings, and as the oldest man present he would invite the others to be his guests. So swiftly the years have gone that it seems only the other day, yet not one of my four guests survives. James Russell Lowell observed that the penalty for prolonging life's journey is that a man shall find every milestone marking the grave of a friend.

CHAPTER XI.

AMONG the persons who left an imprint on my memory by rallying round at this Third avenue flat was Joaquin Miller, Poet of the Sierras, not long home from his London "triumphs." While Miller bloomed modestly as a poet, he wore clothes not designed to escape attention. He was "loud" in this respect, I thought, and inclined to pose. His big slouch hat and long hair were never worn for comfort. He kept the hat on after entering a room in order that those present might admire the whole outfit, including his boots. I could have told him that men didn't wear their trousers stuck into the legs of calfskin boots where I came from. Calfskins as there worn were for dress occasions, and fashion required that the pants fall to the instep. His velveteen vest was crossed from pocket to pocket by a gold cable that might be a piece of chain-harness gilded over. "Mr. Miller is a gifted poet," said our nattiest dresser, Mr. Cooley, "but not the gentleman. A gentleman does not wear rings on the fingers of both hands." Miller professed to be a good deal of a puritan as regards women, who, he demanded, should before all things be modest. Mulford's wife told of his meeting a

206

woman author in London one evening, who shattered his illusions. This woman said to Joaquin: "Mr. Miller, do you know what line of poetry you bring to my mind?" He thought she meant one of his own creations, and blandly asked: "Which line is it?" And she gave him the bold eye as she quoted: "Make me a child again just for tonight!" Miller glared and left her. The lady was spoofing Mr. Miller.

There was John Swinton, the journalist, then on The Sun, probably—a casual caller; and there was a French lady, Mademoiselle Minnie Leconte, an acquaintance of the family or group, who appeared to be his protégée. Nobody commented on that, and I will not. But Minnie, flush with press theater-tickets that Mr. Swinton gave her, fixed upon me as her escort. Thus with her under my wing I went to see the elder Sothern who was great, and plays to which my means would not admit me; and it is probably by the same favor that I saw Janauschek and Modjeska, who, I have to admit, did not entertain me. About 1889 I attended a play where the younger Sothern took the part of an auctioneer, which was a thriller. Just the other day, as it seems, though it was five years ago, I saw this actor, not on the stage, and he was an older man than was his father when Minnie Leconte went with me on John Swinton's tickets to his performance in a play making fun of George the Count Johannes. This time the younger Sothern was attending the funeral of Mrs. Eva A. Ingersoll (Feb. 4, 1923).

Ned (Edward Fitch) Underhill, a boyish man of fifty, a stenographer of the old school, once a pupil of T. C. Leland, held an important position in the Surrogate's court. While I rarely saw him at public meetings, he foregathered with the Freethinkers socially. He had been through the fire a dozen years earlier when the police raided a club of social radicals in session in a hall on Broadway and he got taken along with Albert Brisbane, the father of Arthur, and other persons in attendance. He defended the club in the newspapers, admitting he had been present, not in his capacity as Tribune reporter (which was then his employment), but as a guest. The reformers didn't take it lying down so much then as they are inclined to do now. It is only a few years ago that at the behest of a Catholic archbishop in New York the police broke up a birth-control meeting in the Town Hall, and got by with less hard knocks than those got who sixty years earlier raided this social group on Broadway.

Underhill offered his parlors in a house on a downtown street for meetings of the Fourth New York Liberal League, and furthermore showed up very well as an entertainer himself, for he was a piano player, an expert whistler, and an excellent story teller. He had a red-haired and rather young wife named Evelyn, of whom I saw little, and heard more or less not to her discredit for benevolence. They held advanced ideas on social freedom.

ON PREJUDICE.

When I was talking with young Doctor Ned Foote one evening, he asked me if I really did not think that religion kept girls straight—such was

the word he employed—who without belief in it
would go wrong. Now take Catholic girls, he argued, and so on. I said: "I don't know anything
about the facts, do you?" He replied: "No, not the
facts, but it is the common idea, and I doubt if
I have ever heard it disputed, that Catholic girls
put a high value on chastity." We were sitting just
inside the door at the Liberal Club, waiting for the
audience to come and for the proceedings to open.
Doctor Ned, two years my senior, was a medical
student at Bellevue. There was more of the conversation, and I may come back to the subject of
it. Ned was brought up in the Unitarian church,
since that was his father's religious connection, and
came into Liberalism because he found there his
allies in the battle with Anthony Comstock. Now,
in New England, whence I lately had come, Catholic
girls bore another reputation than that he gave
them. They were in fact supposed to be on the
stroll; and a "History" compiled by Dr. W. W.
Sanger quotes statistics of a confirmatory nature.
Of course there is or was a reason. The kind of
people coming most numerously to this country at
any given time will, while adjusting themselves
economically and socially, furnish the largest additions to the outcast population; and that was the
period of Irish Catholic immigration. Later it was
German, then Jewish, producing a change in the
class of statistics gathered by Dr. Sanger. But this
phenomenon of adjustment, while it might explain
the Catholic girls in New England, had no bearing
on Dr. Foote's proposition, which concerned those
who had arrived.

However, old fellows have told me that street girls wore the usual Catholic beads, and that their rooms, like Catholic homes, contained religious objects and pictures.

At the time of this conversation with Doctor Ned I had known only one Catholic girl, and thereby hangs a tale appertaining to the year 1877, which the foregoing talk may excuse me for taking off the hook. Written some time ago, it has the appearance of interrupting the general narrative. Its opening is above the level of my style.

THE WIND AND THE CURTAIN.

Whoso searcheth the files of the Daily Graphic for the year 1877 shall at one place find, mayhap, words of praise bestowed upon a Swiss girl of eighteen years, member of a traveling musical ensemble which included her elder sister and that sister's husband, who by misdirection when her "people" moved on to fill their next engagement, got left in New York with nothing but a handbag for luggage and only carfare in her porte-monnaie. This girl, it will be learned, talented, refined and accomplished as she was, went direct to an intelligence office and, being aware that the situation of a servant promised immediate board and lodging, prudently registered as a domestic, and then sat down to wait for an employer. Prentice Mulford put the piece in The Graphic, both to commend the girl's quick wit and good sense, and to question whether there were many American girls who would have acted so promptly and wisely in a foreign city. Anticipating the younger reader's objection, at the mention of The Graphic, that Bernarr Macfadden had not at that date set up his tabloid newspaper, I will assure him there was a Graphic nevertheless—a pioneer illustrated daily; and to speak of it is to evoke the name of the Positivist David G. Croly, its distinguished editor, with that of his wife Jennie June, and of Dr. William Augustus Croffut, the member of his staff who composed the puns and paragraphs and verses that other papers copied. Freethinkers twenty years later read Dr. Croffut as a contributor to The Truth Seeker and heard him as a lecturer. Mulford did a daily column of news and comment and some reporting and dramatic criticism for The Graphic, and Arthur B. Frost (died 1928) was an illustrator on the same paper.

My mother, in quest of a maid, found the aforesaid girl at the intelligence office and brought her home. If all girls ought to know cooking and housekeeping, then this was exactly the engagement the otherwise well-trained Hilda needed. And yet, although the difference between her prepared dishes and mother's was certainly remarkable, the inferior nature of hers could be overlooked in view of the graceful way she put them on the table. Stage training teaches one to move inside a limited space without bumping into persons or objects. I had not yet taken the first glance at the new maid, or become aware of her presence, when her baby-sized hand, with its cocked little-finger, placed food before me, and I raised my eyes far enough to find out to whom the comely member belonged. I surveyed a slender figure, a head of unruly blond hair perversely waved, and a face that would sink a thousand kicks. No one sympathetic with beauty in distress could have the unkindness to suggest that her potatoes, adamant against the insertion of a fork, needed to be boiled longer than tea. I gave her a cheerful grin; she smiled back and blushed.

Hilda was still a new-comer when one evening as I sat reading in my room I heard unaccustomed notes issuing softly from the piano, which usually was mute. The sound soon drew me out of my seclusion, since the words of the book I was reading did not go to music, and opened the way for conversation with Hilda, who was doing the playing. Her first inquiry concerned the dinner that night, whether it had been well prepared. She let me know that criticism of the cooking was plainly heard by her in the kitchen and made her unhappy. That matter having been discussed, and when she had asked what tunes I liked and had played others which she held I ought to prefer, even singing a little, at my suggestion, in her small voice, the young lady related to me, as she had previously to Mulford, the events that had led to her trying housework. Hilda spoke precise English, with an accent that sweetened it. She understood the continental languages, learned in traveling over Europe since childhood. Her housework done, Hilda's evenings now were open; I was always at home (economizing that season to pay back a loan with which Dr. Bennett had accommodated me in a pinch), and the movements of the rest of the household left us to

keep each other company. She kind-heartedly offered to teach me if I wished to study any of the
varieties of speech that she happened to know. Or
if I didn't play the piano already, she would show
me how easy it was to acquire the art. On account
of previous attempts at the piano, and the failure
that had followed, I was dead as a pupil for that
instrument, and instinctively cut it out. The observant girl had decided I was reading too much in
my room. "A change," she said in her individual
English, "would do you so good." I ought to have
seen a warning in the teaching proposition, but her
lullabies had sung caution to sleep. She recommended French as a language one should know if
one would be erudite, and I agreed on that tongue
for study because I possessed a copy of Andrews
and Batchelor's French Instructor: D. Appleton
& Co., 1859. I have the same book by me now,
with my name as she wrote it on a card pinned to
a fly-leaf.

Here was a perfectly artless girl. All her life
she, like myself, had known nothing but work; and
on hearing of the amount of study and practice and
discipline she had been obliged to undergo, in familiarizing herself with the instruments she played,
from the slide trombone to musical tumblers, I
picked for myself, as preferable because easier, the
labor that comes to a boy raised on a New England
farm. We had only this one lesson book. My
erroneous pronunciation of the French words made
it needful that we should scan the book in unison,
and this propinquity, since it excused our sitting on

a couch together, or she on the arm of my chair, accelerated a familiarity with each other far surpassing mine with the French language. No success I achieved went without its reward from her, or the reward might be offered in advance as a stimulant, or as an encouragement midway.

We did not touch upon the subject of religion. I assumed she was an indifferent. That was an error. As an early riser, I left my room one Sunday morning at dawn to go for a newspaper and to enjoy the air while it was cool and fresh. Writers have described the streets of New York as pleasant and enjoyable at that time of day, and I know they tell the truth. When I came back on this particular morning I met Hilda coming out at her door, dressed for the street. I thought perhaps she had decided to walk with me, and would have greeted her joyously and appropriately, but she eluded me and ran down the stairs. Then I remembered she had a small book in her hand. She must be a Catholic and on her way to early mass!

At this discovery a cloud lowered out of the sky between Hilda and me. She did not see it, but for me it was always there. No doubt there is a rule against a Catholic's doing anything secular before mass. I have observed that the ingesting of food prior to receiving their savior is forbidden to those of that faith; but for a girl after many an evening's good-night to evade a morning's good-morning in order first to go and see her priest—well, I was no poacher. If he had the prior claim, let him hold it.

The French lessons went on, but the cloud did not lift. Without combating Hilda's Catholicism, which I so resented that I should surely have hurt her feelings if I had once begun, I made inquiry as to the restrictions preceding the taking of communion, and thus learned enough so I might infer why I had been dodged that Sunday morning.

Came the day when Hilda's sister got into touch with her, and it did not appear to be one of unrestrained delight for Hilda. Inevitably came also her last night with us, and with me the parting was no calamity. I thought of a woman as possessed already, who had given herself to the church, and didn't believe she ought to have two communions. She slept in the living room on the couch where we had sat to con the French Instructor, and where I had received so many encouragements to persevere and so many innocent rewards of merit. My room adjoined, being connected as to atmosphere and audition by a window which, when opened for the circulation of air, admitted of good-nights being said after both had retired. Anybody who has lived in those old-time flats, with dark bedrooms and a "well," knows the arrangement. To this room I retreated, promising good-byes in the morning. Lights were out. A voice said: "Good-night," and mine answered. In a few moments the voice repeated: "Well, good-night." I resolutely responded: "Oh, yes; good-night. Bong repose." Silence for a short space, and then the voice was heard again. "Are you asleep yet?" Trying to subdue the words drowsily: "Just dropping off; good-night," I replied, my resolution weakening. The voice: "What shall you dream of tonight—I mean who?" I made the polite reply. "I am so glad," said the girl, whose simplicity was her strong point, "for I shall dream of you too." Then sleep, but not undisturbed. Into the dream of her that I had promised there came the sound of sobbing. And then I dreamed that the deep and filmy lace curtain on my window—it must have been that—blown and twisted by the draft—the same draft which appeared to have blown open my door—had become detached from its supporting rod and had fallen upon my neck; and as if rain had accompanied the wind, the warm drops of a summer shower fell also upon one's face. Let the Catholic press shout "Prejudice!" but the fabric was in good time returned unrumpled to its place and the door closed. The cloud was too thick.

Dr. Ned Foote had said to me doubtingly, as we sat there inside the Liberal Club door, that he feared Liberalism would not have the hold upon "our girls," meaning Freethinker girls, to confine them, like the influence of the church, to the paths of prudence. "See, for instance," he argued, "how strong the Catholic girls are for being married by a priest." I saw, but what of it? A wedding is a ceremony premeditated and deliberately enacted; and it is not with premeditation or deliberation, but under the strongest of impulses, that the paths of prudence are temporarily abandoned; and there is no reason to believe that prospective marriage by a priest has any more strength, if as much, to overcome that impulse when it arises, than has sound secular common sense, or Rationalism. That which Dr. Ned Foote accepted as the virtues unerringly illustrated by girls of the Catholic communion was in fact merely the moral teaching of the Catholic church and the hope, frequently disappointed, of Catholic parents. The church points to its professionally continent women, the religious sisters, as a triumph of chastity. These women when abroad are too conspicuously clothed to permit of association with males, and their dormitories are "caverns measureless to man." They represent the so-called chastity of the ecclesiastical institution, and of their lay sisters—to the latter's full content, approval, and resignation. In my association as a workman for a decade with Catholic young men, I could not gather that to them the fact of a girl's being a Catholic rendered her the less liable morally to err. These men also believed in having the marriage ceremony celebrated by a priest. Did this prevent their anticipating it? Not observably so. Such is the moral—that religion holds its votaries to artificial forms, but leaves them on an exact equality with unbelievers, or maybe with less restraint, in the presence of intense emotions.

Following Hilda's departure letters came and went between us for more than a year. She would

Écris bientôt un petit mot de tendresse à ta pauvre amie qui languit, et t'envoie tous ses baisers

Hilda

have me keep up my French lessons, and, to insure this, every time she wrote, she gave me paragraphs to do and answer in that language. The sentiments expressed in them came not from her head, blond and wise, and level.

Now, I asked myself, why was this? Why this sustained intercourse by mail, in the present case, when in more serious instances there was no epistolary correspondence to follow? Some one will have to explain it. Usually when I can't point a moral I am ready to quit; but here there is none. The truth of Swinburne abounds: "Touch hands and part with laughter; touch lips and part with tears."

I handed the problem to a man of years and discretion, who reads my story because he happens to be from New England also, and since his young manhood a city resident. He professes to see through it, and so I will quote him:

"A man asks questions," he says, "that his own experience would answer if he reposed confidence in it. Maybe fifteen years ago, when my mind happened to wander back to the old home town, I thought of a woman who as a girl wrote me often when I had just gone to the city. She was still unmarried, a New England old maid going on sixty years, and while the mood was on I wrote to her. From her answer I could tell that my letter had created quite a tumult in her bosom. She said: 'I suppose you have not thought of me for an age before—you have had so many friends. But there has been none or few to put you out of my memory, and so there you have remained. Do you remember when you drove a team by our house day after day? I saw you every time—and heard you. You were singing—what seemed to be your favorite hymn—'There is a land of pure delight.' I thought that a land of pure delight would be any land, even our little town, if only those who were loved would understand, and if those who loved each other could live together always. I could write you often, but mustn't; for you live in that land, I hope.' There was nothing between me and that girl but a day's ride together, a hand-clasp at parting, and then the inane boy and girl correspondence by letter for a little while—no more than that for the material of a lifelong remembrance.

"And then there is another, where on her part it is more like 'you have forgotten my kisses and I have forgotten your name.' Says her letter: 'You should understand why I and *the others* [the catty emphasis is hers and does me great injustice] are resigned not to meet you again, or to write. We cannot revive the old thrill, we cannot meet on the old terms, we cannot sing the old song we sang so long ago; and never could after the parting.' So a man need only go back to his nonage to find the answer not plain to his matured wisdom. You will find that among the women you left in New Hampshire the one who knew you youngest will take the most interest in your story.

" 'Touch hands and part with laughter; touch lips and part with pain.' That is how it is if you just touch lips. You have told of a young woman in Surry who kissed her lover good-by when he enlisted for the Civil War, and because he didn't come back she went into a decline. There is pain anyhow, but it doesn't last so long when the worst that can be has been done. Very few war widows went into a decline."

Aversion for the other communion that claimed Hilda's first Sunday morning allegiance was in me a conscience with promptings stronger than those of instinct. "From the heretic girl of my soul should I fly?" asks Moore. Not necessarily, for that is different. As I have said, I went about among Catholic girls. A young fellow who was a foreman, a dues paying member of the typographical union, and carrying a card in the Socialistic Labor party, and besides this a contributor of signed pieces to the labor press, would have no difficulty in meeting them at their entertainments and dances or getting invitations to their homes. Those were days, I guess, when fewer girls than now were looking for a career, and fewer claimed a pay envelope with more money in it than the young men of their class were earning per week. The known fact that I did not "belong" created no religious prejudice against me in the minds of these girls, or at least none was shown in their attitude.

Regarding Freethinking girls, Dr. Ned Foote's apprehensions were totally unfounded. When a young man's life is laborious his circle of girl acquaintances, such as he will know the lives of for the next generation and after, is small. I can count all of mine on my fingers; but for what it may be worth to morality without religion, and to banish the misgivings of those who hold with Dr. Foote, I will say that I never knew one of them who afterwards was "lost." One and all, "our" girls, my contemporaries, have matured into superior women. Whom did I marry but one of them?

But the better morals of Catholics is a myth. If I were not trying to write these memoirs without recourse to slang, I should say it is bunk. Latin countries never made the claim and it has been abandoned in Ireland since statistics superseded Moore's poetry.

When Hilda went away I was twenty, going on twenty-one, and was through with women.

2—MY BROTHER TAKES UP THE PEN

E. M. Macdonald had in 1877 written articles in reply to the Rev. G. H. Humphrey's slanderous accusations against Infidels, and for his pains had been called by that controvertist a callow stripling who probably knew not the difference between Calvinism and Galvanism. In 1878 E. M. began to use his pen quite freely in a discussion of the Labor problem, which he identified with the population question, telling the workingman that his way out was to cease burdening himself with children. He also promulgated the dogma that "the causes of the present state of society are found in Tobacco, Rum, and Religion," he being at the time an abstainer from those vices. While living in Keene, N. H., my brother had acquired the smoking habit and also had experimented with "stone-fences" and other alcoholic mixtures and distillations that were dispensed by a local "publican." Now Bennett had bribed him to forswear both Tobacco and Rum, and he was hence in a position to give advice. Incidentally in his articles he seems either to have rapped or to have ignored the doctrine of certain propagandists called Land Reformers, a small group held together by the teachings of George H. Evans that met occasionally in Henry Beeny's fruit and candy store at Fourth avenue and Twenty-fifth street. Mr. Beeny, William Rowe, and J. K. Ingalls therefore labored with him in letters to The Truth Seeker. They had detected a slighting reference to themselves in his words, "while others will gravely assert that only by dividing this earth, including the sea, into ten-acre cabbage-patches, can man be rendered happy." Doubtless that is a travesty of Land Reform, the advocacy of which is now forgotten. E. M. next came forward with "A Plea for the Unborn," an undisguised word for birth control. "Will our workingmen," he demands, "go on raising slaves for the capitalists, criminals for our jails, competitors for the scanty subsistence forced from the grudging earth?" He found cause for commending the efforts of the Oneida Community, where "they allowed no children to be conceived till they were prepared to support and educate them."

In Putney, Vermont, on my way to New York in the fall of 1875 I was in the neighborhood of the house which the Oneida Community had occupied from 1837 to 1847. I knew of the association only by its name, which indicated a communistic society. But in New York, where some interest in the experiment survived, I learned that the community had been founded on the Bible and that its members were "Perfectionists," who had achieved "union with God" and were immune to sin. They were taught that the second coming of Christ took place in the year 70. The founder, John Humphries Noyes, may have entertained suspicions that to his followers he bore something like the relation of Christ to the apostles, or to the early church. The social scheme of these Perfectionists was called pantagamy—*pan* for all and *agamy* for marriage. That is, all male and female members were held to be married to each other. The leaders frowned upon that exclusiveness which embraces only one man and one woman. They had at Oneida, N. Y., since 1847, a farm of 650 acres, with 300 members; and in order not to overpopulate the land the men were expected to practice "male continence." And lest the young men and women might be imprudent, the elders of the community attended to the instruction of the young females, while women beyond child-bearing age educated the youth of the other sex. Thus was birth regulated, the father and mother acting only with the consent of the community. Dr. Lambert, a member of the Liberal Club, speaking from its platform one evening, accused the leading men of not allowing the women to choose the fathers of their children, and hinted that Noyes, patriarch of the community, was father of a disproportionate number of damsels' firstborn. Dr. Lambert said that if he were a praying man he should pray that every woman in the Oneida community might be "blessed out of it."

Could I locate at this moment a report I once

made of a few minutes' address by the excellent Mrs. Cynthia Leonard at the Liberal Club, I could present a view of these conditions the opposite of commendatory. Mrs. Leonard, then past fifty, inclined to sex asceticism. She failed to uphold, as I should do, the right of youth to be served by youth, but she denounced in the most scathing manner the commandeering of women past the child-bearing age to endow young men with experience. The implication of Mrs. Leonard's remarks that this would be uniformly unpleasant for the mature women, is accepted without comment. As for Noyes, I hardly see what claim he can have for the respect of mankind above that of Purnell, head of the Michigan House of David, except that the Oneida experiment was more of a highbrow affair. The Bible doctrine he prevailed upon his followers to profess had nothing to recommend it above that of Teed and Dowie and Mrs. Eddy and Ben Purnell. It would indicate as low a critical faculty in the Perfectionists as in these other groups, only that we may surmise many professed Perfectionism for the sake of the promiscuous Solomonic sexual privileges it conferred. We might expect such a scheme to fail for want of women going into it and from the number of young people going out; as in fact it did in 1881—its end being hastened by persecution. The Oneida Community still exists, but not as an experiment in Perfectionism, Pantagamy and male continence.

The right of birth-control—or of the same thing under its earlier and less acceptable name, "prevention of conception"—is so rational a proposition that its denial generally arises from some ulterior purpose or anterior cause, usually religious. However, if I have ever been found among its advocates as a social measure it was incidental to my resentment that legislators of the Comstock caliber should have the prerogative of dictating to the people at large what they may know. And this includes censorship of books—dictating what they may learn by reading. My contention has been that knowledge should be free and people left to make what use of it they choose. Birth-control might be taught in public schools and in Sunday schools along with the seventh commandment, and even then there would still be enough of those accidents that happen in the best regulated families, added to cases of parentage aforethought, to keep up the population of the country.

3—BIRTH CONTROL, COLGATE STYLE.

Mr. Samuel Colgate, was president of the Comstock Society at the time it was conducting prosecutions of men and women for imparting birth-control information. Colgate & Co., the well-known soap manufacturers, were in 1878 agents for "an article called vaseline," prepared by the Cheeseborough Manufacturing Company, which was extensively advertised in a pamphlet setting forth its merits and uses. A number of persons procured from Colgate & Co. copies of this pamphlet and, fortified therewith, The Truth Seeker quoted from page 7 the words of Henry A. DuBois, M.D., as follows:

"There is one use for this ointment that I have not fully worked out. Physicians are frequently applied to to produce abortion. Recently on the same day two women came to me; the reason assigned in the one case was that the husband was syphilitic; in the other, that pregnancy brought on violent attacks of spasmodic asthma. Of course I explained that the child had rights as well as the mother, but it was all I could do to prevent one of these cases from going to a professed abortionist. In some cases of this kind prevention is better than cure, and I am inclined to think, from some experiments, that vaseline, charged with four or five grains of [a certain] acid, will destroy," etc.

(The circular gave the name of the acid and employed language not adapted to a non-medical publication.)

Now, here was the prohibited information, or what appeared to be such, coming right from the head of the society at a moment when the society was prosecuting a case against one F. W. Baxter for communicating similar knowledge to the public. And that is not the worst, for if our pure drugs law had then been in existence Colgate could have been prosecuted for fraud, since the advertisement quoted, written to recommend the vaseline that Mr. Colgate sold, is a fake. Vaseline and the said acid, commingled, have not the virtues ascribed to them by the advertiser of the unguent. This truth, after a lapse of time necessary for the fact to be ascertained, was announced one evening at the Liberal Club by E. W. Chamberlain, who warned all and sundry to beware of relying upon the promises for which President Colgate of the Vice Society stood sponsor. That being the case, the publication was innocent, except so far as it was calculated to deceive. I will add a statement from Dr. Foote's Health Monthly, quoted in The Truth Seeker of June 8, 1878:

"It seems that a complaint was made against Mr. Samuel Colgate, president of the Society for the Suppression of Vice, for sending through the U. S. mails a pamphlet in regard to vaseline wherein it was spoken of favorably as a *preventive* when combined with a certain other drug. It is stated, however, that Mr. Colgate pleaded ignorance of the contents of the pamphlet, and the complaint was dismissed."

While D. M. Bennett, arrested by Comstock for selling his Open Letter and the Marsupial tract, awaited trial, he opened subscriptions for a defense fund and circulated a petition for the repeal of the federal law under which the Roundsman of the Lord operated. The petitions came back to the office with 50,000 signatures attached. All hands on The Truth Seeker worked at pasting them together, and they were wound about a reel constructed for that purpose. The length of the petitions thus made into one was estimated at "one thousand yards." Meanwhile petitions were sent direct to congressmen with twenty thousand additional signatures.

4—ONE CASE DISMISSED, ANOTHER STARTED

Bennett had hoped that Ingersoll would appear for his defense, when the case came up, but tradition has it that Ingersoll did even better—that he went to Washington and influenced the authorities to have the case dismissed, January 5, 1878, by U. S. Commissioner John A. Shields. The petition came before the House Committee on the Revision of the Laws in May, and on June 1 The Tribune and other newspapers announced that the committee had reported favorably a bill to repeal Mr. Comstock's law on the ground that it was unconstitutional and that "in many instances it has been executed in a tyrannical and unjust manner." Unfortunately, the announcement proved to be untrue, or the committee reversed its action, for the law was allowed to stand unrepealed and unmodified. So the agitation went on, T. B. Wakeman preparing voluminous briefs to show that the post-office had no such power as that which it conferred upon Comstock.

In August Bennett was again arrested, this time for handling a pamphlet called "Cupid's Yokes: or The Binding Forces of Conjugal Life," by E. H. Heywood. Miss Josephine Tilton, sister-in-law of Heywood, and W. S. Bell, lecturer, were taken at the same time. These arrests took place while Bennett and Bell and Miss Tilton were attending a Freethought convention at Watkins, N. Y. Says Bennett in The Truth Seeker of August 31:

"Miss Tilton had some of the books on the ground for sale, but no other person had any. We have a variety of the books of our publication for sale, but not a copy of 'Cupid's Yokes' was upon our table. Miss Tilton had a contiguous table, upon which she offered for sale several of Mr. Heywood's pamphlets, photographs, etc. Among the pamphlets was the tabooed 'Cupid's Yokes.' We are not sure that we sold a copy of it, but if we did it was to aid Miss Tilton when away or unable to attend to her customers. We put not a cent of the money for 'Cupid's Yokes' in our pocket, nor did we have a cent profit from the sale of them."

The prisoners were admitted to bail. They were all bailed by women; Bennett and Bell by Mrs. J. K. Ingalls, wife of the author of "Social Wealth," and Miss Tilton by Lucy Colman, the veteran abolitionist. At their arraignment, someone said the arrested trio looked like the Father, Son, and Holy

"THE TRINITY."
Left to right: D. M. Bennett, Josephine Tilton, W. S. Bell.

Ghost, and they were posed for photographs as "the Trinity."

The war against Comstock, which had not failed for a moment, "now trebly thundering swelled the gale." Bennett brought a libel suit upon himself by attacking a man named Chapman, who had resorted to a house kept by a Madam DeForrest and made arrangements for Comstock to hire three girls for $14.50 to parade naked before him so that he might arrest them for indecent exposure. Chapman gained the confidence of the "madam" by retiring with one of her girls—an act the morality of which Bennett severely condemned. This suit did not come to trial so far as I can discover.

When the Watkins case came up in December the three defendants appeared before the court of Oyer and Terminer at that place, Judge Martin of Elmira presiding. Says Bennett of these proceedings: "It seems Judge Martin did not think our indictments belonged to be tried in his court, and they ought to go back to the Court of Sessions, which is to sit in February next." One George Mosher, who had thought to turn an honest penny by selling "Cupid's Yokes," was arraigned with the others. All were required to furnish new bail. A worthy man of 83 years, Samuel G. Crawford by name, a resident of the town of Havana, offered himself, and being an honored and respected citizen, was accepted. I find no record of the case coming to trial.

5—BENNETT'S THIRD ARREST.

Meanwhile Bennett had defied the forces of Comstockery, and had been arrested again.

"Just as this paper is going to press, Tuesday, 4 P. M., December 10, 1878, the editor has been arrested on a bench warrant from the U. S. Circuit Court at the instance of Anthony Comstock, on the charge of sending a copy of 'Cupid's Yokes' through the mails. Bail was demanded in

$2,000. E. B. Foote, Sr., M. D., was accepted. The case may come to trial in one or two months. There may be more of these prosecutions than will prove interesting."

Bennett saw that this one was made interesting for Anthony Comstock. The year closed, so far as Comstock cases were concerned, with the pardon of Ezra H. Heywood of Massachusetts, who had been sentenced to a two years' stretch for selling "Cupid's Yokes" and Trall's "Sexual Physiology."

The year 1878 had been signalized by the most animated sort of discussion over the Comstock postal laws, with The Truth Seeker and its constituents battling for the repeal of the laws, and Francis Ellingwood Abbot, president of the National Liberal League and editor of the Boston Index, opposing the making of any fight. The ground which the conservative Mr. Abbot had taken for the Nine Demands and for separation of church and state was his limit. The state might be separated from the church but not from Comstockery. He was against God in the Constitution, but, as Leland said, "for the devil in the post-office." The 70,000 who had signed the petition for repeal were to him misguided persons, the victims of deception, or they were Freelovers and obscenists. There was really no occasion for Abbot to get into the fight, for no organized attempt had been made to involve the National Liberal League until he began the forming of auxiliary Leagues with a view to reelecting himself as president and casting out the anti-Comstock faction. Had he kept to the business of the League and allowed liberty of thought and action among members as regards the postal laws, he might have remained at its head. But his course so angered the anti-Comstock members, who happened to be in the majority, that at the Annual Congress in Wieting's Opera House, Syracuse, N. Y., October 26, the delegates, of whom there were 127 voting, elected in his place the Hon. Elizur Wright of Boston by a vote of 76 to 51. And then, instead of accepting the result and changing his tactics, Mr. Abbot took his minority with him to the Syracuse House across the street and organized a New National Liberal League. This he announced as a "victory" and asked the auxiliary Leagues to rejoice with him. Nearly all of the auxiliaries, however, remained with the Old National League. Mr. Abbot's "strategy" defeated its author and split the League.

In The Truth Seeker of December 9, 1878, Theron C. Leland said: "Never was a defeat so clearly due to the defeated hero himself," and these words were followed by the statement: "Had Mr. Abbot issued a straightforward Call, as he did last year, with no exhibition of nervousness about delegates, let the local Leagues represent themselves as they found it most convenient, let their delegates present themselves with the usual credentials at the Convention as they did last year at Rochester, and had hurled no flings at anybody, there would have been no special effort made by the repeal party to secure a majority of the delegates. The delegates would have met under no special urgency, no hot blood would have been coursing through their veins, not nearly so many delegates would have assembled, and

Mr. Abbot would have had an easy and a real instead of a fictitious 'victory'."

Mr. Abbot did not destroy the League he had done so much to create, but he materially weakened it by withdrawing from it himself and the able men who went out with him. As a consequence of alienating the majority of the members, his paper, The Index, declined toward suspension and of his New National Liberal League there are no reported conferences. I was a delegate to the Syracuse Congress; and while admiring Mr. Abbot for his ability was obliged to vote with the 76 because they were The Truth Seeker people.

6—MORE HISTORY OF 1878.

Ingersoll drew vast audiences in New York in 1878. The meetings he addressed at Chickering Hall were crowded. One of his lectures which I attended was on Thomas Paine. That was not long after his controversy with The New York Observer. Everybody was keen to hear what he would have to say about Paine's detractors, so that when he declared: "I am going to bring these maligners of the dead to the bar of public conscience and prove them to be common liars," there ensued the best demonstration I ever saw at a public meeting. The audience did not seem to be angry; it was delighted. The listeners did not hiss the men who had libeled Paine; they cheered his vindicator. They all wanted Ingersoll to see them and know they were there and that they approved his sentiments; so they got upon their feet; they stood in the seats to get more altitude, and then swung their hats or elevated them on canes or umbrellas.

The name of Samuel P. Putnam, who was afterward to become such a force in Liberal work, was seen in The Truth Seeker of April 20, for the first time, attached to a piece of free religious poetry quoted from the Boston Index.

The news came early in the year that since the will of Stephen Girard excluded ministers of the gospel from the college he founded, the trustees would build a chapel on the grounds.

The publication of Ella E. Gibson's "Godly Women of the Bible" began August 1878, producing a book that has been kept in print ever since. John Peck started his forty years as a contributor. An almost if not quite unknown, or at least forgotten, Freethought writer had a desk in the office—Thomas Cairn Edwards of Vineland, N. J. — a finished scholar (Edinburgh) who collaborated with Bennett in the production of his books. My own name as a recruit was first printed in a notice of the organization of the Fourth New York Liberal League, Daniel Edward Ryan president, that elected me treasurer. Thomas Edison was then unknown as a heretic, yet a paragraph in The Truth Seeker contained this intimation: "If Thomas A. Edison is not deceiving himself, we are on the eve of surprising experiences"—nothing less than having lights brought into our houses by means of a wire! Power, too, enough to run a sewing-machine! It has since transpired that Mr. Edison was not a victim of self-delusion.

NOTE.—"Your story this week is dull," writes a correspondent, referring to June 16. He wants more stories like the one of June 9. In that respect he differs from all other correspondents, for, besides his, my little venture in social pioneering hasn't got a hand since it was printed. In manuscript I showed it to a literary young woman, who pronounced it "an idol." I have learned to go behind girls' spelling, and I know she meant an idyl. A similar romance, submitted to a maturer woman, mother of a family of girls, was read with feeling and ordered to be printed on pain of losing a lifetime subscriber. On the third one I sought a professional opinion, and the verdict was "artistry." Now, to everything else I have written there has been response. Even my mention of an adventure with an up-and-down saw has brought two letters from Brother A. L. Bean of Maine, who knows sawmills from rag-wheel to cupola. If anyone missed my girl stories from The Truth Seeker, he has now read them all in the foregoing pages.

In the last or near last story of Surry, N. H., a picture was introduced: a grave and a weeping willow, and a boy. It hung in the room where I slept, and I remarked that "I hated that damned boy heartily." When I went to school in Surry one of the scholars was a mite of a girl who would have been described in the language of the day, which favored regular verbs, as "about as big as a pint of cider half drinked up." Having survived the sixty years that have since passed, the girl is now a woman; she writes me that she lives in that house where I was homesick; has found the picture (for there couldn't be two such things in the world), and that while the tombstone and the weeping willow remain, there is not a damned boy in sight. Therefore I either got this picture mixed with another, or else I killed the boy and put him under the stone. Or my mind may have projected "Rollo" into the scene. My description fits Rollo, if anybody remembers him.—The Truth Seeker, June 30, 1928.

WHO WAS WHO IN 1878.

A list of speakers and attendants, actual and announced, at the Watkins, N. Y., Freethinkers' convention held in August, 1878, shows Who was Who in the Liberal ranks fifty years ago:

Hon. Geo. W. Julian, Indiana.
James Parton, Massachusetts.
Hon. Frederick Douglas, Washington, D. C.
Dr. J. M. Peebles, New Jersey.
Elder F. W. Evans, Mt. Lebanon, N. Y.
Parker Pillsbury, Concord, N. H.
Hon. Elizur Wright, Boston.
Prof. J. E. Oliver, Ithaca, N. Y.
Hon. Judge E. P. Hurlbut, Albany, N. Y.
Horace Seaver, editor of The Investigator.
J. P. Mendum, publisher of The Investigator.
D. M. Bennett, editor of The Truth Seeker.
Col. John C. Bundy, editor of The Religio-Philosophical Journal.
G. L. Henderson, editor of The Positive Thinker.
Asa K. Butts, editor Evolution.
M. J. R. Hargrave, editor of The Freethought Journal.
G. A. Loomis, editor of The Shaker.
Benj. R. Tucker, editor of The Word.
Dr. J. R. Monroe, editor of The Seymour Times.
C. D. B. Mills, Syracuse.
Mrs. Matilda Joselyn Gage, corresponding secretary of the National Woman Suffrage Association.
Mrs. Clara Neyman, New York City.
Giles B. Stebbins, Detroit, Mich.
Charles Ellis, Boston.
William S. Bell, New Bedford, Mass.
Rev. A. B. Bradford, Pennsylvania.
Thaddeus B. Wakeman, New York City.
Dr. T. L. Brown, Binghamton, N. Y.

Rev. J. H. Horton, Auburn, N. Y.
Prof. J. H. W. Toohey, Chelsea, Mass.
Prof. A. L. Rawson, New York City.
Rev. William Ellery, Copeland, Neb.
T. C. Leland, New York City.
Ella E. Gibson, Barre, Mass.
Dr. J. L. York, California.
Mrs. Lucy A. Colman, Syracuse.
Mrs. P. R. Lawrence, Quincy, Mass.
Mrs. Grace L. Parkhurst, Elkland, Pa.
Hudson Tuttle, Berlin Heights, Ohio.
Rev. O. B. Frothingham, New York.
Mrs. Elizabeth Cady Stanton, New Jersey.
The Hutchinson Family, singers.

And the names of Liberal lecturers not included in the list were:

Charles Orchardson, New York.
Ingersoll Lockwood, New York.
B. F. Underwood, Thorndike, Mass.
Prof. William Denton, Wellesley, Mass.
W. F. Jamieson, Albion, Mich.
E. C. Walker, Florence, Iowa.
C. Fannie Allyn, Stoneham, Mass.
Moses Hull, Boston.
Laura Kendrick, Boston.
Mrs. Augusta Cooper Bristol, Vineland, N. J.
J. W. Stillman, New York.
Dr. A. J. Clark, Indianapolis.
D. W. Hull, Michigan.
C. L. James, Wisconsin.

EUGENE M. MACDONALD
Editor of The Truth Seeker, 1883-1909

PART II
MANHOOD'S MORNING

CHAPTER XII.

1—GOING TO JAIL FOR A PRINCIPLE.

THE events of 1879 tested the loyalty of many persons professing Liberalism. The year began with the trial in prospect that was to put D. M. Bennett in jail for thirteen months and subject him to a fine of $300 for mailing the pamphlet "Cupid's Yokes." All this trouble, as I have told, began at the 1878 Watkins convention of Freethinkers, when Josephine Tilton for a moment left her book stand, which was "contiguous" to Bennett's, and when in her absence he waited on an individual who called for a copy of that pamphlet. Of course the right to sell so innocuous a piece of writing deserved to be maintained, even at some cost; but as for myself I never viewed the production as worth quite the fifteen cents that was its list price. I read "Cupid's Yokes" as most persons would, because it had been pronounced indecent, licentious, and lewd; and thereby began an experience to which there has been no exception, i.e., that one who procures and reads any book or print having no other distinction than that of being obscene will be disappointed, as he deserves to be. The last book to catch me that way was "Women in Love," by D. H. Lawrence. Justice Ford of New York, in 1923, or earlier, discovered that his daughter, unmarried, had gained access to this book of Lawrence's at a library; and on the strength of that fact Justice Ford went to the New York legislature with his Clean Books bill. But "Women in Love" is the soporific kind of literature that appropriately has been called "chloroform in print," being so dull that no one of my temperament, craving action, could read it with sustained interest.

The first number of The Truth Seeker for 1879 announced President Hayes's pardon of E. H. Heywood, who had been jailed for writing and selling the pamphlet, and that Bennett's prosecution in the United States Court stood "in suspenso." The case was set for March 18. Bennett then said that he expected nothing but conviction from the presiding judge, the Hon. C. L. Benedict, in whose court Comstock had never lost. The suspense was brief. Bennett headed his next editorial "Our Trial and Conviction" (Truth Seeker, March 29), and the article began with the words: "It is over. We have been tried, and twelve men have pronounced us guilty. We are now a convict, and if the rulings and instructions of Judge Benedict cannot be set aside, a prison awaits us."

The rulings and instructions were not set aside. On the 15th of May they were upheld by Judges Blatchford, Benedict, and Choate, and on June 5 Judge Benedict pronounced the sentence: "You have been indicted by a grand jury, tried by a jury, and found guilty of violating a statute of your land. The Court has heard the arguments of your counsel and given the case serious thought. The sentence of the court is that you be confined, at hard labor, for a period of thirteen months, and to pay a fine of $300; the sentence to be executed in the Albany penitentiary."

There was malice in that *thirteen* months. A year's sentence might have been served in the comfortable county jail in Ludlow street.

Bennett came to court that day prepared with an article entitled: "What I Have to Say Why Sentence Should Not Be Passed Upon Me," in which he ventured to express the mild hope that the laws of the country might sometimes be administered by a better judge than the one that had tried him. He had with him these contemplated remarks in the form of galley proofs, having reduced them to print, and asked twice for the privilege of reading them; but "waving him imperiously aside," Benedict pronounced his doom, and a marshal took him to Ludlow Street Jail.

The Hon. Abram Wakeman, brother of Thaddeus B. Wakeman, who managed the outside campaign against the Comstock laws and their constitutionality, had conducted the defense. Abram was great as a man and a lawyer; his presence and his eloquence made Judge Benedict on his bench look like a child in a high-chair taking a scolding and occasionally saying "I won't." Mr. Wakeman endeavored to show that the indicted pamphlet contained no plain language that could not be paralleled in many other books. He tried to introduce expert testimony that "Cupid's Yokes" must be separated from the class of books recognized as obscene. He was stopped by Benedict's "I won't let you." The prosecuting attorney, Fiero, was one of those vain fellows whom for their incorrigible conceit and impudence you feel the desire to kick. Present and ready to testify to the literary character of "Cupid's Yokes," was O. B. Frothingham, lecturer for the large group of cultivated persons who met weekly in Masonic Temple to hear his scholarly discourses. He came pretty near to being the flower and the ripe fruit of his generation. Confronting such a man, Fiero seemed a small bad boy, insolent and precociously vicious. And this same Fiero, objecting to the introduction of competent testimony, told the twelve dolts sitting as a jury that they were to form their own opinion of the book, or take it from the court, regardless of the views of "Frothingham or any other ham." (Here the impulse to kick Fiero would have been too powerful for control had he not been out of reach.)

During the next lull in the proceedings the prosecutor approached Mr. Frothingham and said: "I hope you will accept an apology from me if, as I am warned, I have used your name in an insulting manner." Mr. Frothingham, without appearing to see him, replied that this was unnecessary; for, said he, "neither your insult nor your apology reaches me."

The prosecution had marked in the pamphlet the passages held to violate the law. Fiero declared they were too impure for the record; but Abram Wakeman read every one of them in a good clear voice, so that the jury and the audience could hear them; they all went into the transcript of his speech and were included in the report of the trial that Bennett made into a book, besides which all of the readers of The Truth Seeker saw them in the current number of the paper.

The secular press almost unanimously condemned the conduct of the trial, the conviction, and the sentence that followed. Indignation meetings were held in various parts of the country, while a petition for Bennett's pardon addressed to the President (Hayes) bore above two hundred thousand signatures. The protest that went up has no modern parallel except that which was aroused by the execution of Francisco Ferrer in 1909, or by the Sacco-Vanzetti matter of 1927.

2—FROM JAIL TO PENITENTIARY

At the Ludlow street jail Bennett at first was immured in a dungeon which from his description of it must have surpassed all his expectations as to noisomeness; but before the time for him to sleep in it arrived the turnkey summoned him to the jailer's office, where the sheriff's son let him know that by paying $15 a week for board and lodging, he might have better accommodations for himself and the privilege of entertaining his friends up to 10 o'clock at night. The prisoner closed at once with the offer. The cell to which he was now assigned had a comfortable bed, nicely whitewashed walls, and room for the reception of half a dozen visitors.

All the office hands, including the printers, surprised the doorkeeper by going in a group to visit

their employer in prison. Bennett paid a tribute
to the loyalty of these faithful employees, calling
them by name. "It is saddening," he wrote, "to
part with the excellent and faithful corps of assistants and compositors employed on The Truth
Seeker. Few papers have had a more faithful, intelligent, and honorable staff of assistants. We
have toiled together for years in perfect harmony
and cordiality. They entertain a high regard for
me, and I assuredly do for them. Let me mention their names, that you may at least know that
much about them: E. M. Macdonald, foreman;
H. J. Thomas, proof-reader and compositor; T. R.
Stevens, G. H. Weeks, G. E. Macdonald, T. Grat-
tan, J. Phair, and C. A. Wendeborn, compositors."
The loyalty of employee to employer is a phenomenon rarer now than then. The change has been
brought about through organization of the employees exclusively in their own interests. In the
smaller offices, of which this was an example, the
man and the "boss" were much of a family. The
oldest of the compositors in the list, T. R. Stevens,
lives to count his great-grandchildren. Tom Grat-
tan was first to die, being a consumptive. Thomas
has been dead for many years. Phair was killed
in a street railway accident in Canada, and Weeks
and Wendeborn have not been heard of for decades. As we are talking of a time fifty years
back, they more than likely have laid aside stick
and rule for good.

On Bennett's removal to the Albany penitentiary,
pursuant to an order of District Attorney Fiero
dated June 17, E. M. Macdonald took the editor's

desk. G. E. Macdonald then became foreman, yielding his compositor's frame to Ed. Hurd, who stayed with the family for a considerable time. Few years have since passed without a call from Mr. Hurd, who quit composition for proof-reading and found employment on the daily papers. He died May 30, 1928, in Colorado, at the Printers' Home, in his 80th year.

Bennett in the penitentiary was for the first thirty days incommunicado to his friends in New York, but a friend was nearby in the person of G. A. Lomas, editor of The Shaker Manifesto. Although Mr. and Mrs. Bennett had left the Shaker community more than thirty years before that time, all the members continued to express the sincerest friendship for him; and their editor, it seems, found a way of getting past the penitentiary guards. Elder Lomas reported to the outside world that "the old hero was in a most undaunted mood" and likely to remain so. "But it was terrible to my feelings," says the Shaker elder, "when he said, with deepest emotion: 'You know, Albert, I have not been used to being treated and spoken to like a dog.'"

While in the Ludlow street hostelry the Doctor's time was all his own, and having writing materials at hand his output was profuse enough to fill a half dozen pages of the paper every week. The writing appeared as letters from "Behind the Bars." At Albany, they allowed him at first a monthly letter covering an area described as a "half-sheet." On this he wrote so closely with a sharpened pencil that at a little distance the half-sheet appeared to be almost a solid black, and it assayed more than three thousand words. With practice he in the course of a few months raised this number of words to 3,250, which occupied more than a page of the paper in solid and by no means fat long primer.

Before the end of the year the keepers of the penitentiary relieved their distinguished prisoner of the duty of making shoes, to which they had first detailed him, and, perhaps because he knew drugs, placed him in the hospital, where the restrictions as to writing were removed. He now could receive papers and books and write unceasingly. Before he came out he had nearly finished, with exterior aid, a two-volume work entitled "The Gods and Religions of Ancient and Modern Times."

3—WHAT THE CAT BROUGHT IN.

In the fall a new complication arose. His enemies made public the intelligence that some two years previously Dr. Bennett had been "vamped" or seriously blandished, and that, while fearlessly acting out the maxim, "Do right and fear no man," he had neglected its no less important amendment: "Don't write, and fear no woman."

On page 265 of Volume V (1878) of The Truth Seeker, there is a brief article from the editor's pen, dealing in a strikingly sympathetic way with the unfortunate Bishop McCoskry of Michigan, who at the age of 70 had written a number of letters to a girl. Bennett comments:

"It is a dangerous business for a doting old man to write soft and silly letters to any lady, for he knows not, though they are designed for the eyes of but a single person, how many may be invited to peruse them. Witness the grief of the old bishop for this cause. He was obliged to resign the honorable position he held, with the promise to spend the remainder of his life in Europe, in exile and retired disgrace. Poor Beecher had lots of trouble about the letters he wrote. The Newell divorce case, now progressing in our courts, is bringing to light another batch of ridiculous love-letters, written by another old man. They may serve to amuse for an hour a giddy public, but it would have been far better to consign them to the flames. Were we to give advice to men of age, it would be: Write no love-letters.

That was the voice and warning of experience, for even then he was feeling disquietude over certain letters written by himself. A year later those missives were serving to amuse a giddy public, and for more than an hour too, for Bennett never undertook a series of writings that could be read in an hour. In his agitation for the repeal of the Comstock laws he had raised up two sets of opponents who agreed in nothing else but the sacredness of these laws. Those opponents of his were the Christian cohorts on the one hand, and the so-called Free Religious and conservative Spiritualist people on the other. The orthodox had backed Comstock all the time. Now the Boston contingent who read The Index and took the side of Francis E. Abbot in the debate, and the constituents of the Chicago Religio-Philosophical Journal (Spiritualist), Col. John C. Bundy, editor, espoused Comstock's cause against Bennett, and for downright meanness and conscienceless lying far surpassed

their ecclesiastical allies. The woman addressed
in the tell-tale letters first tried to blackmail Bennett, who wouldn't give her a cent, and then sold
the letters to Bundy, who made them public through
his paper. A fellow I have heretofore mentioned,
Seth Wilbur Payne, who started a paper called
The Age of Reason at 141 Eighth street, is supposed to have stolen The Truth Seeker's mailing
list and conveyed it to the enemy. So Bennett's
readers received copies of Bundy's paper containing the letters, to which Bundy had given the worst
interpretation possible, and added a score of lies.
In an article of thirteen columns' length Bennett
from his prison acknowledged the authorship of
the letters and supplied the circumstances under
which they were written. Why he wrote them,
he said, must forever remain a mystery, since it
was a conundrum to him. He believed himself to
have been afflicted with a kind of moral delirium.
Well, he was not going to try to lie out of it. Whatever may have impelled him to write them, the
letters certainly were from his hand. Then, pleading the right of every man to be a fool once in his
life, and saying he feared he had too fully availed
himself of that privilege, he gave all the details,
setting forth that in an evil hour, somebody, doing
the cat act, brought in this female. Describing
the occasion, he wrote: "One evening, while [I
was] writing in my office, an old friend and acquaintance of forty years' standing entered with
this person." The person was Miss Hannah Josephine McNellis—"unmarried," thirty-five years
of age, Irish by birth, raised in the Catholic church,

educated in a Catholic school, but now become, as
she stated, a Spiritualist, a Liberal, and a "medium." Personally Josie was to be inventoried as
"petite, lively, chatty, and agreeable." DeRobigne
Mortimer Bennett fell for Hannah Josephine Mc-
Nellis. The person desired employment, and he
invented for her the situation of canvasser for advertisements. At that she had no success. She
next accepted the proposition to work in the office,
"to assist at correspondence, proof-reading, copy-
holding, and making some selections of anecdotes,
etc., for the paper." She failed again, totally; and
as no more pretexts for employing her occurred
to him, he advised Miss McNellis "that she had
better discontinue," which she did. But in departing, this person left the miasma with him, he states,
and the infection worked. Then was it that he
wrote the letters as his part of the correspondence
which ensued. Bennett for some time had been
assigning causes for the acts of others, but he now
provided himself with a problem in behavior which
he could not solve. "How I could ever write so
much," says he, "and keep it up so long and for so
unworthy an object, is a mystery even to myself."
Why he discontinued the correspondence is more
easily explained than its inception. People who
knew the woman brought him proof of her deceit-
ful nature. They gave him the name and residence
of a man she had lived and traveled with, and the
testimony of attendants when "she was brought
to premature childbirth." The latter misfortune
was worsened to his mind from the circumstance
that before he discovered the cause of her illness

he had been solicited for a donation "to procure medicines, etc.," and "handed out seven dollars." It irked Mr. Bennett to say aught against a woman—"the male sex very naturally feel a commendable degree of magnanimity toward the opposite sex." But, he demands, "what am I to do? My reputation is grossly and dastardly attacked." He had been accused by the loathsome Bundy of pursuing, persecuting, oppressing, and trying to starve out a virgin; of importuning her to sacrifice her virtue on the altar of his lust, when there was no such person as a virgin concerned, and the letters and circumstances admitted of no such interpretation. Mrs. Bennett published a "card" in the paper, saying that she had known of the woman's influence over her husband and had been grieved by it; that he had long since told her of the letters. "But it is all past," she wrote; "the most amicable feeling exists between us; and I am sorry that other persons should make it their business to arouse and spread a scandalous matter that was all settled and overlooked." The ghouls were indifferent to the feelings of Mrs. Bennett, who suffered much more from this publicity than she had from the affair when it occurred.

4—STEADFAST FRIENDS.

If the publishers of the Bennett letters thought themselves repaid, then it was an instance of virtue, or meanness—often the same thing—being its own reward. Bennett lost no credit. Those who

had been his friends remained so still. When detractors asserted that the higher type of Liberalism had quit him and that only "the coarsest and
lowest species" remained, Bennett promptly named
as among the steadfast, whose absence he had not
noted: Colonel Ingersoll, who had worked for
weeks to procure him a pardon; James Parton, the
distinguished historian and biographer of Voltaire;
Thaddeus B. Wakeman, whose interest in The
Truth Seeker's welfare remained undiminished;
Theron C. Leland, who wielded the sharpest pen
then or since at the service of Liberalism; Mr.
Briggs of California, who, always generous, had
increased his donations; Courtlandt Palmer, of the
very heart of swelldom, who was writing a letter
nearly every week with a generous inclosure; and
Mr. A. Van Deusen, one of the "aristocrats," who
"drops in every now and then and leaves from $5
to $25." And as it was with the leaders, so with
the rank and file; there was no defection. My
own verdict in the case is that Bennett was a poor
judge of women. He ought to have sheered off
when he learned the McNellis woman's pedigree—
Irish, Catholic by education and training, and pretending to be a "medium." The Irish-Catholic female is not passionate but intriguing. An honest
man trusted the McNellis woman and she betrayed
him. Except for her treachery we might congratulate Bennett on the experiencing of so pleasur-
able a commotion of the senses at sixty.

In 1874 a large stuffed shirt known as Joseph
Cook was set up for a Monday lecturer in Boston.

Cook had a considerable vogue on account of his pretense that he was harmonizing religion and science. In 1879 he chose to "throw in" with Anthony Comstock against D. M. Bennett and all other Freethinkers. He delivered a special lecture on the subject, to which Bennett replied under the plain heading of "Joseph Cook, the Liar," and when Cook came to New York to address the annual meeting of the Comstock Society in the hall of the Young Men's Christian Association, the boys from The Truth Seeker office distributed the article, at the entrance, to persons going in and to passersby. Hundreds of copies had been handed out before the distribution could be stopped. Writing an account of this occasion was my first attempt at reporting. I learn from the effort that when Mr. Cook entered the hall he looked to me "like a cross between a pugilist and a cattle-drover," and that as seen on the platform making a speech he was "shock-headed, bull-necked, sledge-fisted, with a foot like an earthquake." He had certainly a big right foot, as I now recall, and he "stomped" on the platform to impress his points. Hence the simile of an earthquake.

S. P. Putnam had now come out of the church and announced himself as a lecturer not only on Liberal topics but also on "Free Marriage," "Marriage and the Social Evil," and "Times and Genius of Shakespeare."

Two Liberal papers were born but to die: The Pacific Coast Free Thinker, San Francisco, Byron Adonis, editor, and The Infidel Monthly, Albany,

N. Y., A. H. McClure & Co. John Brown Smith went to jail in Northampton, Mass., for refusing o pay a poll tax of $2. He stuck it out for eleven months, when a friend paid the tax and liberated him. This was the year of the memorable "Pocasset tragedy," when a man named Freeman, in Pocasset, Mass., killed his child in obedience to a "command of God," even as Abraham led his son to the sacrifice.

In this year of 1879 S. P. Putnam published his attempt at a serial narrative called "Gottlieb: His Life"; Mr. Wakeman wrote long and convincing articles on the iniquity of the Comstock postal laws; a numerously signed petition for the taxation of church property was presented to the New York legislature, sponsored by Senator G. E. Williams; an attempt made to break up the Oneida Community as "a form of organized harlotry" was denounced by Mr. Bennett editorially and by E. C. Walker in the correspondence columns. In these days appeared occasionally Mary E. Tillotson of Vineland, N. J., in skirts almost as short as 1928 fashions demand. But Mrs. Tillotson obviously wore pants. Crowds followed her on the street. Comstock bullied the American News Company into refusing to distribute The Truth Seeker.

5—I MAKE FORENSIC AND POETIC ENDEAVORS.

The Fourth New York Liberal League held regular bi-weekly meetings. This is the organization that met at Ned Underhill's house and at the home of its president, Daniel Edward Ryan, or wherever

hospitality was offered and space available. One
member after another prepared and delivered a
talk or read a paper, listening to all which gradually produced in my mind the conviction that I
could do that. I therefore gave notice to the secretary, who was my brother, that I should like to
step into the next vacancy and offer a few appropriate and well-chosen remarks. He and the other
officers consented, but he warned me I must not
expect him to stay. I withstood the pleasantries
of the boys in the printing-office while awaiting
my opportunity, and in the meantime conceived of
a paper under the title of "New England and the
People Up There." My chance came on March 9,
(1879). For the occasion the League, instead of
looking for a parlor to meet in, rented a small hall,
which was filled, the audience including, besides
Dr. Bennett, the noted lecturer B. F. Underwood
and the learned philosopher Stephen Pearl Andrews, as well as most of mother's roomers. I
marked with surprise the presence of Miss Ettie
DePuy, a magnificent young woman who might
have had a career as an actress in tragic parts if
she had not soon married and taken up domestic
life. Owing to my natural reserve I had not attempted to make her acquaintance.

Mr. Bennett reported the occasion in his next
editorial article, March 15. He wrote (this was
three months before his imprisonment):

"On Sunday night Mr. Underwood attended the bi-
weekly meeting of the Fourth New York Liberal League,
in Science Hall building. A paper was read by Mr.

George E. Macdonald—his first effort in that direction
—entitled 'New England and the People Up There.' It
was full of sparkling humor all the way through, and
brought out repeated laughter and applause from the
audience. We hope ere long to lay this lecture before
our readers. Hearty compliments were paid to the lecturer on this his first effort, and several predicted a bright
future for him in the humorous field. Among the complimentary speakers were S. P. Andrews and Mr. Underwood. They agreed that he would yet be appreciated by
audiences much larger than on this occasion."

I regret not to have fulfilled these predictions.
However, Ettie DePuy captured me and made me
walk with her to her door, alternately praising the
matter of my discourse and hinting how I might
improve my speaking voice. Miss DePuy offered
to give me a few lessons in Delsarte oratory, but I
had had two girl teachers. I was twenty-one and
was through with women. Bennett printed the lecture in the paper and then published it as a pamphlet. I feel no impulse to read it now. Sixteen
years passed before I "lectured" again, when my
audience had increased to eight hundred, all cheerful; and that was the last.

May was the fatal month when I wrote my first
"poetry," some stanzas inspired by the imprisonment of Bennett and the grief of his wife. George
Francis Train, who was contributing to The Truth
Seeker then, quoted three of them:

"Our statute books are stained by laws
    That make our honest thought a crime;
    That couple Freethought's aim sublime
With moral filth's corrupting cause.

The hand of persecution smites
  Our noblest leaders, men of brain,
  Who work for universal gain
And wage the war of human rights.

Then let the lamp of truth be trimmed;
  Let growing strength allay our fears—
  The light that beams from coming years
Illume the eyes by teardrops dimmed."

WHENCE THE IMPULSE TO WRITE?

I have often wondered how the writing game chanced to appeal to our family. Mother made the first venture; then my brother, and in the time I am now speaking of I felt the urge to take a few chances. We had no literary or more than literate antecedents; and not one of our kin, who were numerous, ever developed the writing faculty, or were equal to more than the composition of a decent letter hoping this finds you the same. However, a relative, nearby in space and time, but removed in kinship, won no inconsiderable reputation. That was Henry Harland, whose mother and my mother had the same grandparents, and were cousins, yet most sisterly in their intercourse. The Harlands lived at 35 Beekman Place, in a house that backed on the East River and commanded a view of Blackwell's (now Welfare) Island. The scene of Harry's novel "As It Was Written," put forth under the pseudonym of Sidney Luska, was laid in Beekman Place; and one summer when the family was abroad, mother and I lived in the house. Edmund Clarence Stedman tutored Harry. Next

to putting him in a printing-office his parents did
the best thing for their son. Having read his "Cardinal's Snuff-Box" I should have called it a perfect
piece of work if at one place he had not pictured a
cow licking a man's hand "with her soft white pad
of a tongue." A cow's tongue is no pad; it is exceedingly muscular; about as smooth as a rasp, and
two or three licks bestowed on a man's hand would
take the hide off. But the longer I live the more I
am forced to observe the ignorance of persons not
brought up on a farm. I have just found a high-
school graduate who has never seen a yoke of
cattle and doesn't know oxen from cows; who has
not seen a stone wall, a pile of cord-wood, nor a
woodsaw and sawhorse. A few years since a
painting deemed worthy of honorable mention by
incompetent judges placed the driver of a yoke of
cattle on the off side. Ben Ames Williams professed to depict farm and barnyard life in New
England (in The Saturday Evening Post) without being aware that the uprights which hold the
necks of kine at their manger are stanchions, and
so called them something else. The same writer
speaks also of barrel staves, released by their decaying hoops, falling into "shooks" again; which
would be like a piece of disintegrating statuary resuming the form and dimensions of the marble
block it was chiseled from. Then a Collier's artist painted a tapped sugar maple with a fire bucket
hung by its bail over the sap spile. And he had a
girl tasting the sap with a spoon, evidently supposing that the tree ran hot syrup which could not be
drunk from a dipper. I look in the current At-

lantic Monthly (March, 1928) and find Llewelyn
Powys writing: "And as I gazed upon this frail
human being, so purely winnowed by the harsh
flails of life," and so on. Winnowed by flails!
Fanned by baseball bats! Such exhibitions of ignorance broadcast in publications like The Saturday Evening Post, Collier's, and The Atlantic
Monthly are a cause of deep distress to the educated.

The home of his ancestors having been Nor-
wich, Connecticut, Harry Harland, though born
abroad, regarded that town as his birthplace. He
went further and traced his descent to the celebrated Pilgrims, John Alden and Priscilla Mullens.
I have not examined the genealogy to see if I am
implicated by it. The ancestors of the Hussey
family, to which his maternal grandfather and
mine belonged, were seventeenth-century pioneers,
not pilgrims.

NOTE.—The absorption just now of the Peter Eckler Publishing Company by The Truth Seeker makes it impossible for me to resist telling now an incident, and its relation to this deal, that happened the year that William
Green or William Green's Sons, printers, turned out the
first copies of the revised New Testament done in America.
One of the compositors in The Truth Seeker office mentioned by D. M. Bennett in his letter from Ludlow Street
jail quoted last week, had taken a job at Green's as proof-
reader. On the day the New Testament was up he could
not work and asked me to "sub." for him, which I did.
Now the foreman at Green's was Robert Drummond, a man
of such efficiency that employees and the craft spoke of
him as the "slave driver." When I entered his presence
that morning Mr. Drummond was spreading the gospel by

cutting up copies of it into takes for the men. His greeting to me was gruff; it assigned me to another place first, and then to a red-headed assistant foreman. Well, Mr. Drummond—ages later—bought the Peter Eckler Publishing business from the heirs of Peter and Peter's son Caryl, and managed it until November 1, 1927, when, just before his 79th birthday, he was killed in a street accident in Brooklyn. He liked the book trade, but printing was his profession, and a few years before his death he got to be almost a daily visitor at The Truth Seeker office, where he enjoyed sitting on a high stool and discoursing about old times and the newest refinements of the great art. He had forgotten the morning when in Green's big printing-office he officiated like a mate on a steamboat and referred the green hand to the place aforesaid. His son and son-in-law are the parties of the first part in the transfer of the publishing company to this address.—The Truth Seeker, July 14, 1928.

CHAPTER XIII.

1—A FREE PEOPLE IN A FREE LAND.

WHEN the Hon. Elizur Wright of Boston, president of the Liberal League, issued his call for the annual congress of 1879, he appointed also a national party convention "to give the Liberals of the United States an opportunity for consulting as to the propriety of taking political action." The invitation to this convention, evidently written by Colonel Ingersoll, was published September 6, 1879; it bore the heading, "A Free People in a Free Land," and to it were affixed the signatures of Robert G. Ingersoll, James Parton, T. B. Wakeman, E. H. Neyman, Parker Pillsbury, J. P. Mendum, Horace Seaver, and B. F. Underwood.

The regular League Congress met on Saturday, September 13, in Greenwood Hall, Mechanics' Institute, Cincinnati. The political Convention assembled on Sunday at the Grand Opera House, which was filled. Having completed the unfinished League business of the previous day by electing all of the old officers, the Convention proceeded to organize. The report of what was done occupied thirty-four columns of The Truth Seeker of September 20 and 27 and October 5. Gen. B. A. Morton of New Haven, Conn., presided, and Colonel Ingersoll spoke frequently, saying, for a last word:

"I think this convention has behaved splendidly. Let us give three cheers for the party."

No candidates were nominated, members being advised to interrogate candidates of the political parties and vote for such as accepted the principles of the Liberal League. The new party's "menace" appeared in the persons of Charles Sotheran and other members of the Socialist Labor Party, who demanded recognition of the "economic" question. The Cincinnati papers falsely reported that these Socialists had captured the convention. Colonel Ingersoll, however, handled the bumptious ones adroitly. They had been more welcome had they been less obstreperous, since "One Who Was There," writing in The Truth Seeker, said that "whatever prejudice there might have been in the convention against Socialists, as such, arose not from their principles but from their violent manner of announcing them, as also from their action in urging upon the Convention the adoption of measures and principles which, by their own confession on the floor of the Convention, the rules of their own organization forbade them to support."

As tried by the president of the League on Gen. Benj. F. Butler and the Hon. John D. Long, nominees for governor of Massachusetts, the experiment of interrogating candidates on their church-state attitude produced negligible results. Mr. Long declined to give a categorical answer, but asked Mr. Wright to call on him. Butler replied that he must refer the inquirer to his record.

A proposal from any hopeful member of the Liberal party to endorse candidates of either of the

old parties was sure to be met with heartfelt protest from some other member who could think of
such a proceeding only with pain. There were reports that Ingersoll had renounced his allegiance to
the Republican party. This was of course false.
Ingersoll for various reasons was dissatisfied with
Hayes, and held him in low esteem, as was shown
when a newspaper man asked him if he thought
there might be bloodshed over the late disputed election, and Ingersoll answered, "Who would fire a gun
for Hayes?"

2—STATE LIBERAL GATHERINGS.

One of the ablest and best-known Freethought
writers and speakers of the last quarter of the nineteenth century reported, in The Truth Seeker of
October 4, a Liberal Encampment, composed of
Materialists and Spiritualists, that had closed a
week's meeting at Bismarck Grove, Kansas, September 11. The reporter's name, evidently a new
one to compositors and proof-readers, was printed
J. E. "Kemsburg."

Mr. Remsburg, author of the report, named as
the moving spirit of the Encampment Gov. Charles
Robinson, Kansas' first governor, while among visitors from abroad were the Hon. George W. Julian,
who had been the Antislavery candidate for vice-
president of the United States in 1852; and George
W. Brown of Rockford, Ill., formerly editor of the
famous Herald of Freedom, the first Antislavery
paper published in Kansas, which was destroyed by
a proslavery mob in 1853.

Scores of the Antislavery agitators, when their cause had been won, joined the Liberal ranks. They were represented by such leaders as the two named by Mr. Remsburg (Julian and Brown) and by Elizur Wright, Parker Pillsbury, A. B. Bradford, Lucy Colman, Amy Post, and Lucretia Mott, and by hundreds of the rank and file who joined the Liberal League and subscribed for The Truth Seeker. The Abolitionists were in the main religious heretics, the single prominent exception being the outlaw John Brown of Osawatomie, who was a fanatical Presbyterian.

In the columns of The Truth Seeker thus far scanned I have not found the name of the veteran Agnostic, student of Spencer and exponent of Evolution, David Eccles, but on March 22, R. G. Eccles asks The Truth Seeker to publish his challenge to Charles Sotheran, a Socialist secretary, to debate economic principles. As R. G. Eccles writes as of New Castle, Pa., I do not completely indentify him with Dr. R. G. Eccles of Brooklyn; still his remark to Sotheran, "If your object was to obtain truth rather than to play the bully and obtain a bluff," etc., is after the forthright Ecclesonian manner, and I doubt not that this was truly the brother of David.

The organized Freethinkers of the State of New York held their convention in September at Chautauqua. George Jacob Holyoake of England was present and participated in the exercises. Page 66 of Mr. Holyoake's pamphlet "Among the Americans" (1881) is devoted to a not complimentary notice of the gathering. Mr. H. L. Green writing to The Truth Seeker said of Mr. Holyoake:

"So soon as I noticed in the investigator that George Jacob Holyoake was coming to this country I wrote a letter to New York for him, when he arrived, inviting him to attend the Freethinkers' Convention, and I rejoiced when I received his card accepting the invitation. His presence was a great addition to the Chautauqua entertainment. He has a great head and a greater heart. Everyone who came in contact with him fell in love with him; and after he had remained with us a number of days, and spoken so often and so well, it gave us all sad feelings to bid him farewell. The Liberal friends who met Mr. Holyoake at Chautauqua will always remember the time spent with him as the most pleasant period of their lives."

The "greater heart" that Mr. Green found in Mr. Holyoake did not save him from saying of the gathering: "I was surprised to find the Liberal convention I attended a great 'pow wow,' with no definite plan of procedure such as would be observed in England." That was unkind after the words of Mr. Green, who was the organizer of the Freethinkers' Association and of the convention and invited him there.

A debating Fundamentalist of the time, the Rev. Clark Braden, supposed to be a Campbellite, dogged Freethought lectures and defied them to meet him. He was a vituperative polecat, and Christians who engaged him to meet Underwood or Jamieson did not repeat the order. B. F. Underwood unveiled this honorless and characterless individual in The Truth Seeker of August 2, 1879.

John Hart of Doylestown, Pa., proposed to finance a pamphlet made up of the worst passages of the Bible to test the sincerity of the anti-decency crusaders. When Mr. Hart died in 1927 he had taken The Truth Seeker almost half a century.

There were no dull moments in 1879: the organization of a new auxiliary League was reported almost weekly. Conventions were held in many states, with indignation meetings here and there called to protest against the imprisonment of Bennett, or to censure President Hayes for not granting the pardon petitioned for by two hundred thousand citizens. All the "reformers," and there were many varieties of them, joined forces with the Freethinkers. The Spiritualists were an exceedingly strong division of the army, for as yet they had not experienced religion and turned ecclesiastics.

The last number of The Truth Seeker for the year 1879 makes a quotation from "Man," showing that a Liberal publication of that name then existed, the publisher of this small sheet being Asa K. Butts. Later, "Man" was edited by Theron C. Leland and Thaddeus B. Wakeman, and became the official organ of the League. The year closed with Bennett in the Albany penitentiary serving his thirteen months' sentence.

Reports said that Hayes declined to exercise clemency on the ground that his act would show disrespect for the court. Rumor said Hayes was willing, but Comstock plowed with his heifer and the Methodist Mrs. Hayes forbade her Rutherford to shorten the imprisonment of the Infidel.

Benjamin R. Tucker, John S. Verity, John Storer Cobb, and other Boston plumb-liners spent time and energy without stint in behalf of liberty.

They had their own local "case" in the arrests of Ezra H. Heywood, publisher of The Word. Verity

MY UNCLE BENJAMIN

and Cobb are to me only memories which mention of their names evokes, but "the subject of our sketch" is still a live one. Tucker was born there in the Bay state in 1854, and is like myself in being of Quaker stock on one side of the family. He was receptive to book learning and got a fine education at the Friends' Academy and the Massachusetts Institute of Technology. At 23, Heywood being in jail, Tucker edited The Word. He served on the staff of the Boston Globe eleven years, established The Radical Review and published that high-class magazine for one year, and also did editorial duty on The Engineering Magazine. He is best known as editor and publisher of Liberty from 1881 to 1908. I was writing for the darned thing at the time it suspended. Bernard Shaw and I were his only paid contributors. Long previous to that he had translated and published Claude Tillier's "Mon Oncle Benjamin," and Tucker has been my Uncle Benjamin ever since. Until a year or so ago he had refused to permit his biography to be written. I would not claim that my example has changed his mind, but I believe it is no secret that he has at length consented and placed the material for his Life in competent hands. The picture was taken in his insurgent youth, at least fifty years ago. He lives in France, and with him is Pearl Johnson, the mother of his now grown daughter Oriole. Pearl is another of our Free-thinking girls who just naturally expanded into the superior womanhood.

3—DOMESTIC AND LOCAL

When the family took its flight from the Third avenue place near the Bull's Head Hotel in the spring of 1878, it lit on Fourth avenue at the north-east corner of Twenty-fifth street, occupying rooms over and under Mrs. Stringer's drugstore, for we had two floors and the basement. Roomers were more numerous than ever before, and the dining-table longer. Mother's paying guests fol-lowed her. The additions were not all so interest-ing as the old ones. However, we had with us the newspaper man who did the column of Sunbeams in The Sun, whose name comes to my mind as New-bould; and a redheaded party known as Jim Ander-son, who had gained notoriety down South as an active member of the Louisiana Returning Board which so altered the election results in 1876 as to elect Hayes—the President who, said Charles Fran-cis Adams, wore upon his brow the brand of fraud first triumphant in American history. The news-paper man often contributed interestingly to the table talk; but Mr. Anderson appeared not to be exactly in his element. He was an adventuresome person, more executive than conversational. I was sorry to hear of his demise. It took place in the West, perhaps in Nevada, where he engaged in an altercation with a mounted desperado, and drew a pistol on his adversary. The latter, as I heard the encounter told by a man from Carson City, slipped off his horse on the further side, and pointing his gun across the saddle, "pumped" Mr. Anderson full of lead.

A character not to be overlooked was Dr. Charles DeMedici (pronounced demmy-deechy), a countryman of Hamlet and a peripatetic philosopher who taught languages without being able, in my opinion, to enunciate or articulate any of them distinctly. He confessed to being oblivious to the difference in sound between whale, wale, vale, and fail. Perchance his native Danske requires no such discrimination. One might acquire from him a short lesson in French by lending him a dollar overnight, for he acknowledged the favor with a "merci, mosur." Years after I had last glimpsed Dr. DeMedici, an advertisement canvasser named ˙Albert Leubuscher told me of an encounter with him. Leubuscher in a street car perused a pamphlet entitled "The Art of Conversation," when a voice beside him boomed: "Wrong! It should be the art of *conversing*." That was DeMedici, and he was right of course. Leubuscher then and there made his acquaintance and, much impressed with his merits, soon wrote a memoir on him. Albert Leubuscher died many years ago. His sister, Amalia, a lovely girl who attended our socials in Lafayette place, is the widow of the late Bradford DuBois. His brother Fred Leubuscher flourishes at the practice of law, and in 1927 was retained by the man whose wife shot Wallace Probasco. Dr. DeMedici turned chemist and invented certain cosmetics called Lelia Pith and Oxzyn Balm. He showed genius in gathering the last three letters of the alphabet into a short word.

The main room on the first floor of the Fourth avenue residence was capacious enough to be a meeting-place for the Fourth New York Liberal League and for other gatherings. There being a piano present and some of the guests being gifted and willing to oblige, these occasions had a tendency to become social. Why we always moved the first of May I never understood. As it was as regular a phenomenon as anything occurring in the astronomical world, I never thought to inquire. From this house we moved in due season to one in East Seventeenth street, owned by Mrs. Roberts, around the corner from Stuyvesant Park, and almost opposite a church. No more paying guests. Mother sold her boarding works to one of them at the Fourth avenue house. And listen to a tale of woe. To accommodate mother I had drawn thirty dollars of my savings account to deposit with the gas company on three gas meters, one on each floor. Too late I remembered this and went to recover. The new landlady had let her gas bills run till they ate up the deposit. I then drew the balance from the bank and closed the account. What was the use of saving? Forty years afterward the same bank asking me to have my signature verified, I told the cashier to look in his books for 1878 and he would find it, which he did. I presume that none of the men who were in the bank when I had my account and left my signature there was living when I referred the present cashier to it; a substance as perishable as paper lasts so much better than the stuff the average human is made of.

The Truth Seeker of June 7, 1879, recorded the death of the Hon. Ebon Clark Ingersoll, who had served six terms in Congress from Illinois. Then first appeared that immortal tribute of his brother, which was Ingersoll's most heartfelt utterance.

"And love taught grief to fall like music from his tongue."

4—LIBERATION OF DR. BENNETT.

As the topic most widely and warmly debated in 1880, as in the year previous, was the imprisonment of Bennett, which incidentally provided many a pulpit with its theme, I shall go to the end of the matter and then return to pick up the happenings passed by.

When Bennett in his cell learned that the President had deferred to his wife in the matter of the pardon, he wrote that he hoped after this no friend of his would ask Hayes for either justice or clemency, since a sense of justice was the quality the Executive lacked, and Bennett would rather stay in prison than accept clemency from that kind of a man. In his letter from Albany, Feb. 8, I remark this reflection: "Jesus once wrote in the sand. I wrote several times on paper. His was the easier rubbed out." He was thinking of his letters to the woman who sold him out, and wishing, no doubt, that they had been written in water.

In The Truth Seeker of May 8 Bennett broke the news, under "Home Again," that he had been liberated from his unjust imprisonment. A month earlier committees had been organized in New York to give him a proper reception. There were two of these committees, one representing the Liberal public, the other the Fourth New York Liberal League. The former was headed by Daniel Edward Ryan and included Ingersoll Lockwood, T. C. Leland, and the Drs. Foote, senior and junior. For the big demonstration the trustees of Cooper Union refused the use of that auditorium and the committee took Chickering Hall, a much finer place, though not so capacious. While members of the general committee went to Albany to escort Bennett home officially, the first reception he had in the city was private and unofficial. Let the guest of honor, Bennett himself, describe it:

"All the attachés of The Truth Seeker office were in waiting. The office was illuminated, speeches were made, songs sung, toasts given, etc. California wine in reasonable quantity was placed upon the large imposing-stone in the composing room, and I found a wineglassful did me no harm, it being the first drop of wine or beverage of any kind I had tasted for nearly a year."

Dr. E. B. Foote, Jr., who that evening was attending a meeting of the general reception committee in Science Hall, participated in this greeting by the attachés. He did part of the organizing, particularly the forming of the attachés in a line, with Bennett in the midst, and marching all hands in

lockstep formation around the imposing-stone, while
leading that popular chanty, "The Isle of Blackwell."
He took none of the wine but made most of the
noise. Bennett, for his indulgence in "a wineglassful," was appropriately rebuked by several of his
abstemious readers, who warned him solemnly
against acquiring the habit or encouraging it in
others. There has always been found a considerable
fringe of ascetics in the Freethought ranks—foes
of rum, tobacco, corsets, sex, meat, and white bread.
The good old Quaker lady, Elmina Drake Slenker,
having adopted what was called "Alphaism," wrote
unceasingly against "sexual intemperance," which
meant that men and women ought to let each other
alone unless they viewed with alarm the depopula-
tion of the earth and highly resolved to rescue humanity from extinction. Mrs. Celia Whitehead exposed the horrors of woman's dress. D. W. Groh
never allowed anyone to smoke a pipe with a clear
conscience. T. B. Wakeman advocated Prohibition,
and there were health-food people aplenty. For years
I have brought my luncheon to the office, the sandwiches being invariably constructed of mahogany-
colored bread. I long ago stopped eating white
bread lest J. E. Ismay, making a call, should surprise me in the act, or for fear George B. Wheeler
would hear of it. Their slogan is: "The whiter the
bread the sooner you're dead."

The Bennett reception in Chickering Hall, coming
off on the evening of Sunday, May 2, was an overwhelming success, only that the place was too small
for the crowd. "Long before the hour of eight arrived," says the report (Truth Seeker, May 8, 1879),

"the seats were filled, hundreds were standing up,
and large numbers were unable to obtain admittance." My friend Henry H. Sherman, whom I
have mentioned, reported the speeches stenographically. The Hon. Elizur Wright presided and made
the opening address. The speeches and letters filled
more than seven pages of the paper. Many of The
Truth Seeker poets, including Samuel P. Putnam,
exhaled themselves in verse. Outside the hall the
allies of Anthony Comstock circulated a pamphlet
prejudicial to the reputation of the guest of the evening. It was ineffectual.

In the midst of the report of the meeting is this
paragraph:

"The quintet next sang the following original song of
welcome by Mrs. Jennie Butler Brown of New Haven,
Conn.; music by Edwin A. Booth of New York."

This chap Booth, employed in the office as wrap-
ping and mailing clerk, had musical gifts and talent.
He invented a number of tunes, the words to one
of which I aided him in writing, and it was published by Pond or Hitchcock. It dealt with "a
little faded flower." By the time I had perverted
the words the way he insisted upon, nobody would
have known them for the song I composed. Booth
generously proposed my name on the published
work as co-author—a distinction which I resent-
fully declined. So the performance was printed
"Words and music by Edwin A. Booth." One evening when I went with him to see the light opera
"Iolanthe," at the Standard (?), Verona Jarbeau
sang this song for an encore. Booth listened in
the most exalted state, and was not himself again

for some days. The song under some such title as
"The Flower That She Gave Me" may be found in
the old catalogue of the music publishers of that
date. Booth went on the road as salesman for an
Ohio firm of stove manufacturers, and so disappeared from these records.

Bennett enjoyed other receptions. The National
Defense Association gave him one; but after all I
think he prized most his "Welcome and Installation"
by his own Fourth New York Liberal League. I
must quote the opening paragraph of his story
about it:

"Though one of the grandest and most enthusiastic receptions ever bestowed upon mortal man was given to
D. M. Bennett upon his emerging from prison—on which
occasion Chickering Hall could not contain more than half
the people who turned out to do him honor—it has been
supplemented by another which, if less magnificent in
point of numbers, was certainly as enjoyable to all who
attended it. The Fourth New York Liberal League decided, some four weeks ago, to give a private reception
to the returned convict, whom, during his imprisonment,
they had elected as their president, and to duly install
him in the office. At a meeting of the League held April
18th it was voted to give the private reception to Mr. Bennett on the evening of Saturday, May 8th, and Mr. Henry
J. Thomas, Dr. Charles Andrews, and George E. Macdonald were appointed a committee to perfect the arrangements for the meeting. On the evening of the 18th it came
off at the capacious and magnificent parlors of Mrs. E. L.
Fernandez, No. 201 Second avenue. The greater part
of the members of the Fourth New York Liberal League
were present, with many invited guests. About seventy-
five persons were present, and by common consent they
passed one of the most pleasant evenings of their lives."
(Truth Seeker, May 15, 1880.)

Vice- president Henry A. Stone read the address of welcome, at its close inviting Bennett to take the chair as president of the League. The latter complied, his voice trembling noticeably as he responded to the greeting. After that the affair became literary, musical, social, and convivial, there being served, as Bennett notes, "a fine article of light mountain wine of California." The reception was held, as above said, in the parlors of Mrs. E. L. Fernandez. Mrs. Fernandez, who was associated with the theatrical profession as a teacher, or adviser, needed only the call and the opportunity to place her parlors at the disposal of this auxiliary League for its meetings. The members carried good times with them; the occupants of her house, in the way of dancing and other entertainment, added to the joviality. She had at this time a small daughter, three or four years old, named Bijou, who was friendly withal.

5—WHAT LIBERALS DID AND TALKED ABOUT.

The English Comtean, Mr. F. J. Gould, will be interested to learn from these presents that there is a day named for Mrs. Fernandez in the Positivist Calendar. It is the 12th of April, on which day in 1880 her elegant and hospitable residence was open to a brilliant company representing "the press, the lyceum, the studio, and the stage," which was met there to present "a beautiful crayon likeness of Stephen Pearl Andrews to that gentleman in behalf of his many admirers." The artists were Miss L. E. Gardinier, Mr. Pickett, and Mrs. Varni.

I surmise that the reporter of the event was Mr. Courtlandt Palmer, and that the naming of the day was the inspiration of that other Positivist, T. B. Wakeman, who made the presentation speech. The report ends with the words: "It was eminently enjoyable to be there, and all who shared these delightful hours will long treasure the dedication of Fernandez Day in the radiance of Andrews' glory." I was not present, yet I have hanging in my house the picture of heroic size, presented to Mr. Andrews that day. The magnificent head and poise of Andrews was an unsurpassed model for something Jovian in the way of portraits.

A European committee called a Congress of the Universal Federation of Freethinkers to assemble in Brussels in August, 1880, and invited the National Liberal League to send delegates. President Wright replied that as the Liberal League was not an organization of Freethinkers as such, but a union of persons of all shades of thought and creed to effect an entire separation of church and state, sending a delegate to a purely Freethought congress would lead to misapprehensions as to its purposes. Mr. E. C. Walker, Liberal organizer for Iowa, differed emphatically with Mr. Wright, and not fearing the identification of the League with a Congress of Freethinkers, held that the League should be represented by delegates. At present, I believe, the views of Mr. Walker are much in harmony with the more conservative ideas expressed by Mr. Wright in 1880.

Mr. Walker in Iowa, Mr. H. L. Green in New York, and Mr. F. F. Follet in Illinois were the most industrious organizers of Leagues in the country.

D. M. Bennett and A. L. Rawson, secretary of the National Liberal League, set sail August 4 for Liverpool, thence to Brussels to attend the Universal Congress, dated for the last of the month. The letters Bennett wrote while absent were made into a book called "An Infidel Abroad." He reached home on November 9 to discover that he had "sent in letters more profusely than room has been found for them," and it was New Year's by the time the last of them appeared.

Bennett's fellow-delegate, Rawson, was an artist of some reputation, having illustrated a *de luxe* edition of the Bible, besides making the pictures for Beecher's "Life of Christ."

Little or nothing was heard during the year 1880 of the National Liberal Party organized in Cincinnati in 1879. Politics had proved a divisive issue. The fourth Congress of the National Liberal League assembled in Hershey Hall, Chicago, September 17-19, and reelected Elizur Wright president with T. C. Leland for secretary. Editor H. L. Barter of the LeClaire, Iowa, Pilot had just been arrested by a Comstock agent named McAffee and lodged in jail on a frivolous charge. The outrage acted as an irritant on the Liberal public, and the majority of Freethinkers said in their hearts that the Comstock laws should be repealed and censorship of the mails discontinued. That was their temper when they gathered in the Congress at Chicago. Ingersoll, who was opposed to the League's committing itself to that policy, found himself in a hostile atmosphere, for the first time among Freethinkers.

Secretary Rawson reported that of the two hundred and nine auxiliary Leagues eighty-two were represented by delegates. He had received twenty-five proxies, while fifty had asked him to appoint proxies for them. T. B. Wakeman of the Committee on Resolutions reported, with other recommendations: *"We therefore urge the repeal of the present United States postal laws known as the Comstock laws."*

Colonel Ingersoll opposed the resolution, asked the privilege of offering a substitute, and closed his participation in the discussion with the words: "If that resolution is passed, all I have to say is that, while I shall be for liberty everywhere, I cannot act with this organization, and I will not." Nevertheless the resolution for repeal went through "almost unanimously," and he withdrew his name as first vice-president from the list of officers.

In his speech Ingersoll said: "This obscene law business is a stumbling-block. Had it not been for this, instead of a few people voting here—less than one hundred—we should have had a congress numbered by thousands. Had it not been for this business, the Liberal League of the United States would tonight hold in its hand the political destiny of the United States. Instead of that we have thrown away our power upon a question in which we are not interested. Instead of that we have wasted our resources and our brains for the repeal of a law that we don't want repealed. If we want anything, we simply want a modification."

So the League was divided again, as it had been two years before. H. L. Green, who resigned along

with Ingersoll, tried ineffectually to organize another. The report of the proceedings was printed
in The Truth Seeker of September 25 and October
2, 1880.

Recalling today the odium suffered by the organization on account of its action on the Comstock
laws, and even by Ingersoll although he opposed the
motion to repeal, I conclude that it was an impolitic
course for the organization to pursue. Yet there
were thousands who believed that the work of
Anthony Comstock, with the approval and patronage of nearly all the churches, was indeed the most
dangerous form of union of church and state. Had
the religious public shown any inclination to treat
the League fairly, or to understand it, or to cease
lying perpetually about its objects, the stand of the
League would have been recognized as a very
courageous way of meeting a moral issue. But in
the circumstances the organization took a big risk,
and in view of the consequences I am inclined to
think it would have been better to take Ingersoll's
advice.

6—AU REVOIR TO ANTHONY COMSTOCK

During Bennett's imprisonment, members of a
"James Parton Club," headed by Parton himself,
sent a letter and a contribution every month. Courtlandt Palmer stood by Bennett through thick and
thin. Colonel Ingersoll wrote to Mrs. Bennett:
"When you write your husband tell him for me that
I have never joined in the cry against him and
never will." Ingersoll imputed no base motives to

those who differed with him. He said: "I do not, I have not, I never shall, accuse or suspect a solitary member of the Liberal League of the United States of being in favor of doing any act under heaven that he is not thoroughly convinced is right." There are few men with the nobility to take that position in a controversy, and Francis Ellingwood Abbot, Benjamin F. Underwood, and members of the Free Religious fraternity generally were not among them. These were frightened and hunted cover when their Liberal associate, Bennett, was accused. Had one of them, or any Liberal, been attacked on moral grounds, Bennett would have replied with an attack. He would have brought forward the names of five hundred ministers of the gospel who had done worse. They did not understand as well as he how to repel such assaults, which are inspired by the meanest reactions that take place in the visceral cavity of man.

Two newspaper editors in New York stood by the Liberal cause—Porter C. Bliss of The Herald and Louis F. Post of the Daily Truth.

As for Anthony Comstock, I would not speak with extreme harshness of any man, therefore I shall not say of him all the ill that I think. "De mortuis nil nisi bunkum." In his latter days he said in self-praise that he had sent enough men to jail to fill a long train of passenger cars. If among those hundreds of convicts there was one whose shortcomings could be so described that I should conceive of him as being a less desirable person than Anthony Comstock, I beg his pardon; I am doing that passenger an injustice. Within my ken, no

person has breathed the vital air who as a sneak
and hypocrite touched the low level of this repel-
lent blackguard—Anthony Comstock.   As a generalization, he summed up all the vile particulars
discoverable by close scrutiny of humanity perverted, degraded or perverse.   A man whose proud-
est boast might be that by tearing up a railway track
he had sent a large number of passengers to a hospital for terms averaging thirteen months, and simultaneously caused scores to be subjected to such
agony that they blew out their own brains—such
a man might be more of a hero and less the mis-
creant, in my judgment, than Anthony Comstock.
And when you come to analyze the motives of his
backers, aiders, and abettors, they are no higher
than the impulses of their tool, in all respects exe-
crable.   Conscious of baseness in themselves, they
hoped the world might mistake it for virtue if they
decried the manifestation of their own traits in
somebody else.   When legislators pass laws of the
Comstock variety they know themselves to be hypo-
crites and trucklers.   Judges who permitted Comstock to obtain convictions in their courts were brutal and stupid.   The offense penalized is wholly
imaginary, the injury purely hypothetical.   It is impossible to prove in any case I ever heard of that
anybody has been harmed—impossible to show that
the activities of Anthony Comstock throughout a
career marked by the deceit and treachery of the
sneak and the malice of the religious fanatic, and
causing more misery than an epidemic of hemor-
rhoids, have ever worked final benefit to any man,
woman, or child.   Such is the charitable view I am

able to take of a man the sight or thought of whom always aroused in me the impulse to give him a mighty swat on the jaw.

In 1928, while cogitating on the incidents of the past which I am now setting down, I received from Annecy, Haute Savoie, France, a letter written by one of The Truth Seeker compositors of 1878-9. This was that bird Henry Hoyt Moore, already mentioned as having later become a religious editor. In his letter, Moore indulges in the following reminiscence:

"Nearby where Sunset Cox's statue now stands unless it has been removed since I came to Europe, was a moving-van stand. I recall this particularly because it was from this stand that a husky young furniture smasher was brought into the composing-room on one occasion. The comps had become interested in the manly art and had bought a set of boxing gloves to use on one another 'after hours.' It was suggested that we should bring in one of these outside demons, accustomed to scrapping and perhaps to the more plebeian art of rough-and-tumble fighting, to show us the methods of a real fighter. He came, put on the gloves—and you walloped him all over the place."

I quote this to preface the statement that had Anthony Comstock occupied the place of that bewildered piano-mover, a fond ambition of my life would have been attained then and there. He would have received the afore-mentioned swat.

In the year 1913 I one evening heard a testy old man making a fuss in the middle of a group of passengers at the gate of the ferryboat I was on, and when I looked closer—it was Anthony Comstock. I wanted to merge with the crowd in which he was using his elbows and let what might happen; but when I got nearer I saw a gray and pallid and flabby and short-winded old party who tottered on his legs—no game for anybody but the undertaker at an early date. He died that year.

MR. DARROW OF HARVARD, ILL.

Notices of liberal lectures here and there brought out the names of Keresy Graves, author of "Sixteen Crucified Saviors"; George Chainey, a young clergyman of Evansville, Ind., who had renounced the Christian pulpit; John S. Verity, a sturdy defender of liberty; Dr. Sarah B. Chase, whose specialty was physiology; Mrs. H. S. Lake, who addressed either Freethinkers or Spiritualists; J. E. Remsburg, who appears to have made his first Infidel speech at Bismarck, Kan.; Van Buren Denslow, a journalist of Chicago, later of New York, author of "Modern Thinkers" (preface by Ingersoll); Juliet Severance, Augusta Cooper Bristol, Mrs Mattie P. Krekel, Mrs. O. K. Smith, Mrs. A. H. Colby, O. A. Phelps, John R. Kelso, A. H. Burnham, L. S. Burdick, R. S. McCormick—many of them Spiritualists who doubled in Freethought.

A few names appear once and are not seen again. Clarence Darrow, who signed himself C. S. Darrow, wrote from Harvard, Ill., Feb. 19, 1880, to commend the Freethought lectures which a young man of the name of Eli C. Ohmart had been delivering in northern Illinois and southern Wisconsin. Mr. Darrow saw in Ohmart not an equal but a rival of Ingersoll.

Except that Mr. Darrow, who is just a week my junior, had a father who was the village Infidel, while mine lay "in cold obstruction" by the rivulet of Bull Run, his boyhood was the same as what I have described as my own; and as Ohio, or the Western Reserve, was settled by Yankees, there would be nothing to differentiate its people from New Englanders. In February, 1928, he was quoted by the New York World as thus describing his youthful surroundings:

"I was born and lived for twenty years in a small country town. Generally, conditions of life have changed a good deal since that time. My family were poor and so were all the other families in the place. There was a blacksmith's shop, a wagon shop, a harness shop, a furniture shop, and practically everything that was used was made in the town. Nobody had a monopoly of either riches or poverty. Every one had enough to eat and all the clothes they could wear, which were not many, although the wardrobe was more extensive than at present, especially with the girls. I never heard of anyone dying of starvation or coming anywhere near it. The community was truly democratic.

"There were a few people who had what they now call a servant but what they then called a hired girl, and some had a hired man. These went to all the swell parties without evening clothes and they were in no way boycotted by the people who employed them and they had as good a time as the rest. Often a hired girl married her employer's son and the hired man married the employer's daughter and began creating the foundation of an American aristocracy.

"There was one railroad within ten miles of the place and I remember having a great thrill taking a long trip of twenty miles on the train, much more of a thrill than to travel half way round the globe today. There were churches in the town, of course, and there were people who didn't belong to the church, of which my family were a conspicuous example, my father being the village Infidel, which afforded him considerable occupation and enjoyment in a place in which there were few real pleasures. I don't remember that the neighbors ever refused to associate with him. They thought him queer but hardly dangerous, and at least didn't carry any dislike of him to his children."

The town of Darrow's birth and boyhood was Kinsman, Ohio. When writing him for information as to how far Eli Ohmart had got by now, I asked him for a picture of himself taken by the Kinsman photographer, and he replied that he had not preserved one; and as to Ohmart he had nothing further to report. Time's reversals are ironical. Mr. Ohmart did not write to The Truth Seeker to say that he had just met in Harvard, Illinois, a young Freethinker named Darrow who was destined to make his mark in the world. Darrow wrote that of him; and he didn't and Darrow did.

At the beginning of 1880 Bennett bought out Charles P. Somerby, who had conducted a Liberal publishing business and bookstore at 139 Eighth street. Spelling reform in The Truth Seeker was so extended as to drop *ue* from such words as dialogue; the final *e* from definite, etc.; *te* from quartette, and *me* from programme. These most excellent spellings, adopted at the same time by The Home Journal, would still be the rule in The Truth Seeker office but for our giving up the composing-room and sending the work out to be done on the machines by operators who cannot be expected to follow the style until it becomes universal.

On October 30, 1880, Ingersoll was one of the orators at the exciting political meeting in the Academy of Music, Brooklyn, where the great audience lost control of its emotions on his being introduced by Henry Ward Beecher, who presided. As the New York Herald said the next day: It was indeed a strange scene, and the principal actors in it seemed not less than the most wildly excited man there to appreciate its peculiar import and significance. Standing at the front of the stage, underneath a canopy of flags, at either side of great baskets of flowers, the great preacher and the great Agnostic clasped each other's hands, and stood thus for several minutes, while the excited thousands cheered themselves hoarse and applauded wildly. As Mr. Beecher began to speak, however, the applause that broke out was deafening. In substance Mr. Beecher spoke as follows: "I . . . now introduce to you a man who—and I say it not flatteringly—is the most brilliant speaker of the English tongue of all men on this globe. But as under the brilliancy of the blaze of light we find the living coals of fire, under the lambent flow of his wit and magnificent antithesis we find the glorious flame of genius and honest thought. Ladies and gentlemen, Mr. Ingersoll." Said the Herald reporter: "The enthusiasm knew no bounds, and the great building trembled and vibrated with the storm of applause."

Apart from some humorous verses appropriate to the occasion but of no permanent worth, with reports of meetings and unsigned notes here and there, I kept out of print and attended to getting the paper to the press. The foreman (myself) gave out the copy to the compositors after he had revised it; made up forms of the paper and books, and either held copy or read proofs. He was also expected to set the type for advertisements and title pages. Those were good times. He worked ten hours per day, got $15 a week, and saved money. The responsibilities and troubles of the world rested lightly upon young shoulders, and he rejoiced in his own works.

CHAPTER XIV.

ON his trip abroad, Bennett developed the *wanderlust,* and when, soon after his return, a friend suggested a journey around the world and an account of it, he accepted with no show of reluctance. His letters in ten weeks from Europe, printed as "An Infidel Abroad," had made a tome of 860 pages, but undeterred by the fact that they were asked to pay a dollar-fifty for this, and, in addition, to subscribe five dollars each for the globe-encircling journey, his readers fell in with the plan by hundreds. On the 7th of May, 1881, he reached the decision that he would go, the date of sailing to be determined by the tide of subscriptions. The next two months yielded seven hundred subscribers to the enterprise. His faithful Fourth New York Liberal League tendered him a farewell reception in the parlors of Daniel Edward Ryan, 231 West Thirty-seventh street, on the 24th of July, when there were speeches, songs, and recitations. He gave two pages of the paper to a description of the affair, concluding: "Many of those present expressed their determination to visit the steamer Ethiopia, of the Anchor line, which sails at 8 o'clock Saturday morning, the 30th, at the foot of Dey street, and see Mr. Bennett off." Forty were there to see him join Cook's Tourists. He wrote a Parting Word for the paper, giving his first foreign address as London, England, and the second as Jerusalem, Palestine. He resigned the editorial chair and the power of attorney to E. M. Macdonald.

The Ethiopia was an eleven-day boat. Bennett had time before making land to write a nine-column letter, and in addition to resume the series of articles begun three years before on "What I Don't Believe." Convinced of the infinitude of space, Bennett never quite understood why it should be limited by the chaces that inclosed the forms of the paper. I heard my brother try to make this clear to him by pointing to the foot of the last column and expounding the incompressibility of type.

It soon became evident that he had possessed himself of all the guidebooks accessible to tourists and was drawing upon them freely for ancient and modern history. He attended the International Freethought Congress held in the Hall of Science, London, with Charles Bradlaugh as chairman. He can have omitted few details of the proceedings, since his report, occupying parts of three numbers of The Truth Seeker (October 29, and November 5 and 12, 1881) filled sixteen columns, and meanwhile he was contributing two columns per week of "What I Don't Believe." When the paper had been printed the type was lifted, made into book pages and stereotyped.

Meanwhile Liberal speakers at home were busy East and West. George Chainey, the brilliant young minister who had left the church and turned state's evidence, lectured to large audiences in the West, and then came to Boston, establishing a lectureship in Paine Hall and publishing his paper called The Infidel Pulpit.

Samuel P. Putnam was burgeoning forth. He had experienced adversity since stepping down from the pulpit. The year 1881 is too early for a biographical sketch of Putnam, but since he was the coming man in Liberalism, I will say here that he was born in Chichester, New Hampshire, in 1838, the son of a Congregational minister; entered Dartmouth College in 1859; enlisted in the Union army, 1861; in 1863 competed for a captaincy and won it; experienced religion and resigned in 1864; later attributed his conversion to an attack of camp fever; took three years in a theological seminary, Chicago; married in 1867; served two churches as orthodox preacher; joined the Unitarians; wife divorced him in 1885 because of "religious and temperamental differences"; joined the Free Religionists and contributed verse to the Boston Index and Unitarian papers; from necessity took another Unitarian pulpit and built a church, but found himself unable to preach the religion required; entered the Liberal ranks just in time to share in Bennett's fight against comstockery; gained a precarious livelihood by lecturing, bookkeeping, and writing wrappers; in July, 1880, was appointed on probation to a clerkship in the New York Custom House; confirmed January 1, 1881; promoted on merit April 1, 1882. One of his college mates tells me that Putnam took the "big slate" at college in mathematics, and I certainly should suppose that he would, for no man I ever saw, except some lightning calculator, was so quick at figures as Sam. He habitually added two columns at once; or three when in a hurry. He was short, redfaced and chubby, and spry as a cat.

With his living provided for by his salary at the Custom House, Putnam now lectured, contributed

articles to The Truth Seeker, and further gave play to the exuberance of his poetic fancy. I prepared a long biographical sketch of Putnam for the memorial volume published with the report of the Secular Union Congress for 1896, and also for the Dartmouth Class Book of 1862. (Horace Stuart Cummins, Washington, D. C., 1909.)

In 1881, at 43, he still looked like a boy, and I might say he never really grew up. In spirit and manner and outlook he remained the boy all his life.

In certain quarters the year 1881 produced some trepidation as being the year when the famous Mother Shipton prophecy matured.

All of this prophecy, except the last two lines,

> The end of the world shall come
> In eighteen hundred and eighty-one."

having been written after the event, is fairly true.

The author was one Charles Hindley of Brighton, England, who published the lines in 1862, representing them to be a reprint of an old version of fifteenth century prophecies. So stated Ella E. Gibson in The Truth Seeker of January 22, 1881. Frauds are killed off with the greatest difficulty. They are championed with a zeal that rarely comes to the defense of truth. The credulous prefer to believe that the Mother Shipton prophecy was all written in the fifteenth century except the closing lines. The book of Deuteronomy is a parallel instance. The last chapter of Deuteronomy describes the funeral of Moses: and they say Moses wrote all the book but that.

In a spring number of The Truth Seeker I observe an apology for "imperfect bookkeeping." It says: "If we have had dishonest or careless help in our office, we have them no longer." Bennett in the Albany penitentiary made the acquaintance of several whose tales of injustice and injured innocence he accepted as they were told to him. One was a young fellow we will call Albert Smith. When Albert's term expired Dr. Bennett employed him in the office and gave him access to unopened mail and to postage stamps. Bennett's confidence in the honesty of the man was imbecile. E. M. Macdonald had him watched. He was glad to get off with only an exposure of his thefts. Anybody could impose on Bennett once.

At this period William Henry Burr, formerly a congressional reporter and pioneer shorthand writer, made the discovery, as he thought, that Paine was the author of the Junius Letters and of the Declaration of Independence. In an article of January 22, 1881, he flouts Ingersoll and Van Buren Denslow, who were unconvinced of Paine's identity with Junius. The controversy caused me to devote a number of evenings to a close examination of the Junius Letters laid beside the writings of Paine. I saw no correspondence of style whatever. The Declaration is reminiscent of Paine's writings prior to its date. One may agree that whoever wrote the Declaration of Independence, Paine was its author, yet I could not feel that he had contributed any of its paragraphs to that composite work.

A man destined to cause the Freethinkers much embarrassment ran, at Lamar, Missouri, a paper named The Liberal. He was G. H. Walser, who founded the town of Liberal, in that state, to be the home, exclusively, of Freethinkers. Incidents in the after fate of Liberal as a town must be mentioned in this record as they occur. In the beginning of 1881, Walser and his wife deeded Bennett "all lot No. three (3), in block No. seven (7) in Liberal." The Doctor printed the debenture and returned thanks.

2—PERSONS AND PROBLEMS.

All the economic reformers brought their doctrine to the Liberal Club, perhaps the only open forum in the city. Henry George, author of "Progress and Poverty," made a speech there on the 14th of January, the club having met to hear a lecture by Henry Appleton on Ireland. That was the first time I saw Henry George. His book, published two years earlier by the Appletons, New York, was then in its fourth edition, and coming out in London, Paris and St. Petersburg. Mr. George's head looked large for his body; he wore a presentable red beard, and spoke English with a pronunciation acquired abroad—perhaps of his mates on British sailing vessels. His book was reviewed in The Truth Seeker, April 16, by the lawyer and author, Edward W. Searing, who married the deaf and voiceless Laura Catherine Redden ("Howard Glyndon"), poet and newspaper correspondent.

This year a fund was raised—in The Truth Seeker of course—for the renovation of the Paine monument at New Rochelle, the Fourth New York Liberal League leading the enterprise. Exercises took place at the repaired monument on Memorial Day (reported in The Truth Seeker of June 4, 1881), the month before Bennett's departure. When most of the speeches had been made, the Doctor proposed a vote of thanks to the donors of the restoration fund, calling for "three sonorous ayes." He got them, and then, when the party had visited the old Paine house, he informs us, "we wended our way to the station, all feeling that we had enjoyed a very pleasant day, and that we would like to see returns of the same on every succeeding year."

A piece of ancient history worth picking up is Dr. Thomas P. Slicer's renunciation of evangelical orthodoxy. Dr. Slicer, pastor of a Brooklyn church, announced himself unable longer to preach the accepted faith. His name appeared many years afterwards on the list of speakers at Paine celebrations.

Ingersoll delivered his lecture, "What Must We Do to Be Saved?" in Wilmington, Delaware, about the beginning of the year. At the opening of the February term of the New Castle county court, Chief Justice Comegys, haranguing the grand jury on the subject of blasphemy, implied that Ingersoll ought to be indicted for blasphemy. Any officer, he said, might arrest Ingersoll without warrant if he again entered the state. The alarm of Comegys, with the accents in which he communicated it to the jury, brought upon the state of Delaware almost as keen ridicule, if not as much, as Tennessee endured forty-five years later because of the Scopes anti-evolution trial. Ingersoll closed an interview published in the Brooklyn Eagle by saying: "For two or three days I have been thinking what joy there must have been in heaven when Jehovah heard that Delaware was on his side, and remarked to the angels in the language of the late Adjt.-Gen. Thomas: 'The eyes of all Delaware are upon you.' "

In March T. B. Wakeman went before a legislative committee at Albany, N. Y., "in opposition to a bill to largely increase the criminal jurisdiction and powers of the Society for the Suppression of Vice." Under the heading: "Liberty and Purity; How to Secure Both Safely, Effectively, and Impartially," the address ran through five numbers of The Truth Seeker. Incidentally it exposed, by producing the affidavits of numerous honest citizens, the lies told by Anthony Comstock in his book entitled "Frauds Exposed."

3—THE INSPIRED ASSASSIN OF GARFIELD.

The two days of leisure and recreation promised workers by the Fourth of July falling on Monday in 1881, were turned to days of anxiety because the religious fanatic, Charles J. Guiteau, chose Saturday, the second, for the assassination of President James A. Garfield. The President was in the waiting room of the Potomac Depot at Washington when Guiteau approached him from behind with a heavy revolver and fired two shots, one entering Garfield's arm and the other his body. The President lingered for eighty days and died at Elberon, N. J., September 19. Meanwhile the churches prayed intensively. It was an orgy, a regular prayer drive. The splurge continued for two months, when the powers of the ministers were augmented by the state governors appointing September 8 for a day of prayer with a gesture of fasting added— all but one; Governor Roberts of Texas pleaded that his was a civil, not an ecclesiastical office, and he would attempt no control over the religious acts of the citizens of his state. The prayer promoters condemned him to perdition, but went on and perfected their organization. On the 8th of September they mobilized more praying people than had ever got together before on one day. The prayers placed end to end would have reached anywhere in or out of the universe except, as the event proved, the throne to which they were addressed.

Put on his trial in November, Guiteau offered the defense that God had chosen him as an instrument to carry out the inscrutable purpose of the divine

will. It was God's act, he said, and God would
see him through. Writing to George Jacob Holyoake of England, Ingersoll said: "It was fortunate
for me that the assassin was a good Christian, that
he had delivered lectures answering me, that he
was connected with the Young Men's Christian Association, and that he had spent most of his life
reading the sacred scriptures."

Religious demonstrations were confined to Guiteau and the churches. Garfield made none, invited
none. The Sun said, when the grave had closed
over the body of the President: "During the long
and trying illness which his chief physicians have
recently declared was incurable from the outset,
there is no record that he was ever visited by a
minister of the gospel, that religious services were
performed, or that his sufferings were soothed by
religious consolations in any form."

In August the Ingersoll-Black discussion occupied the pages of The North American Review, on
account of which the Appletons gave notice that
they would no longer publish that magazine. The
North American Review came out thereafter under
its own imprint, and with its editorial policy un-
changed.

The Rev. H. W. Thomas of Chicago, Methodist,
was featured as the heretic of the year. Charge.
with heterodoxy and threatened with expulsion, he
resigned and formed a People's Church, where his
audience and his salary were doubled.

The ranks of Liberal lecturers were recruited by
the appearance of John R. Kelso of Modesto, Cal.,

formerly a rousing revival preacher, and afterwards author of some excellent Freethought books. His arguments were as clear as mathematical demonstrations.

The Dominion of Canada woke up and barred the works of Voltaire and Paine's "Age of Reason" from its provinces. Canada for most of the time in recent history has had the meanest government on earth.

Moses Harman began the publication of the Kansas Liberal at Valley Falls, Kan.

A note in The Truth Seeker of December 24 states: "Sheriff Pat Garrett, the slayer of Billy the Kid, is a Freethinker and patron of The Truth Seeker. Billy the Kid was a Christian."

The monthly Iconoclast was started by W. H. Lamaster at Noblesville, Ind.; Remsburg entered the lecture field October 8, 1881; Judge Waite's History of the Christian Religion to A. D. 200" was reviewed October 8.

On the evening of Friday, September 23, I was early in a seat at the Liberal Club when notice had been given that Mrs. A. C. Macdonald would attempt a "Universological Explanation of the World and Man," and would answer the objections of Mr. T. B. Wakeman to the proposition that "the laws of thinking and the laws of creative energy in the universe are one." I listened closely and took notes, so that when mother reached home with the party of women who had accompanied her, I was prepared to tell her what I thought of her lecture. But she did not ask that. She asked, "How did I look?"

The annual congress of the National Liberal
League, held in Hershey's Hall, Chicago, September 30 to October 3, was pronounced "a most enthusiastic, harmonious, and successful meeting."
Secretary Leland reported 175 active auxiliary
Leagues, and 55 others that were no more inactive
than many branches of the Christian church. This
congress resolved that the resolution that had been
passed at a previous congress and had led to the
withdrawal of some members, embodied the opinion
of only the majority who voted for it and was not
a test of membership in the League. Owing to the
inability of the Hon. Elizur Wright to serve longer, the congress elected T. B. Wakeman president.
Other officers were T. C. Leland, secretary; Courtlandt Palmer, treasurer; George Lynn of Lock-
port, Ill., chairman of the Executive Committee, and
Mrs. S. H. Lake, Elgin, Ill., chairman of the Finance Committee.

4—I JOIN THE NONPAREILS.

A reading notice in a December number invites
the public to attend the annual ball of the Nonpareil Rowing Club at Tammany Hall on the evening of the 16th. As the name of this club would
warrant one in inferring, its members were in large
measure connected with the printing craft. The
invitation alluded to, having given the date and
place, went on to say that "those who like to dance
can find no better society to do it in than these
gentlemen, who erstwhile arrange the alphabetical
metal, and anon urge the propulsive oar through

the pellucid waters of the Harlem." I must have been at my best when I wrote that. The club was not exclusive; it admitted policemen. Nobody ever tried to explain why printers and policemen should flock together, but there they were.

Joining the Nonpareils for the sake of the exercise and to acquire the art of rowing with a sweep, I soon was a member of a scrub crew propelling a four-oared gig up and down the Harlem and looking for races with other crews of our class. Such rowing is enjoyed because it is a personal accomplishment. When one catches the water with the blade of a sweep, and feels the boat jump as he puts his back to it, he may get a thrill not to be had by stepping on the gas.

For several blocks above the Harlem Bridge at 139th street both sides of the river were lined with boathouses. The Nonpareils had theirs on the west side some two blocks away. If I may I will speak of my first appearance in the clubhouse after election to membership. My new rowing suit, a bright blue with pure white stripes about the terminals, drew undesired attention from old members whose suits, under water and sun, had turned all of one color, and that one only faintly suggestive of the original hue. As I advanced from my locker in the rear toward the front of the boathouse I found myself walking self-consciously between two lines of attentive spectators. Someone observed that the new member would now wet the new suit by going overboard, and that Mr. Halloran would assist. I went to the float with Mr. Halloran, but did not go overboard. Mr. Halloran went. Another name

was called and a two-hundred-pound policeman
came forward. I never resist an officer. He discharged his duty and I was duly ducked. But there
was some defect in his strategy, for he went also
into the rolling river, and when I let go of him and
swam out, regaining the float easily, the tide had
got him and he disappeared downstream. When he
came back by land twenty minutes later, he reported
that he had made a landing near the bridge. The
initiation being over, I received the greetings of
the president of the club, known as Charlie Gatta.

CHAPTER XV.

THE religious pathology of Guiteau was the subject of many communications to The Truth Seeker in the first half of the year 1882. The bloody assassin persevered, and ever grew more insistent, in his protestations that he was but the instrument of divinity in "removing" President Garfield. The identity of Guiteau's contention with that held for the patriarch Abraham was plain, and I am glad to find an article in The Truth Seeker of January 7 by that logical thinker Stephen Pearl Andrews, which puts the matter in a clear light and in the right words. Said Andrews:

"It strikes me forcibly that it is really not so much Guiteau who is on trial as the Christian church, and religion itself as it has been and is understood and taught in most countries. Especially is it Judaism, Mohammedanism, and Christianity, the three great religions of the occident, which are on trial; and to convict and hang Guiteau will go a long way toward rendering a verdict against the fundamental doctrine of these three great religions—the one doctrine in which they all agree, and by which they are affiliated as of the same descent. That doctrine is, faith in the direct inspiration of individual minds by the deity, which inspiration may and does in some supreme instances

306

lift the individual so inspired out of himself, cancel
his responsibility, and make him the mere agent
of the higher power; and further, that the grandest
and sublimest test of the overpowering presence of
such inspiration is its requisition upon the individual to some act so abhorrent to his natural affections and reason that nothing but such a divine
pressure upon him from without himself could have
induced him to, and have sustained him in, the act.
Such was the act of Abraham in his proposed sacrifice of his son Isaac at the supposed and assumed
command of God; and it was that supreme act of
faith in what came to him as an inspiration, and of
obedience to the command so communicated, sub-
jectively, or through the operation of his own mind,
that constituted and constitutes Abraham 'the father
of the Faithful,' and, as such, the historic head of
the three great religions above mentioned.   All of
them date back to Abraham for their origin, and to
this one act of Abraham as the sign and seal of the
divine sanction of their own faith—the very reason
of their own existence.

"What Abraham did, or proposed to do," continues Mr. Andrews, "Guiteau has done.   The cases
are as nearly identical as can well be imagined.
Abraham was the Guiteau of his day; Guiteau is
the Abraham of our day.   Guiteau and Abraham
are virtually one . . . Guiteau is logically and precisely right in affirming that there are two and only
two questions rightly before the court: (1) Was
he under a divine pressure, an overpowering influence, compelling him to do an act from which per-

sonally he would have recoiled, both in his sentiments and in his reason? and (2), Does the presence
of a divine inspiration, thus lifting a man out of himself, constitute such a variety of insanity as also
to lift him above all responsibility to human laws?"

That was the line of Guiteau's defense. It is
sound if the religions are sound. Naturally, however, The Truth Seeker denied the validity of any
such plea, while admitting to its columns argument
in Guiteau's behalf. A man named Wisner, of
Fordham, made out a strong case, theologically, for
the defense. "That it was God's will Garfield
should die," he wrote, "is already proven. Had the
bullet missed, would it not have been providential? As it hit, was it not equally providential?
All Christians agree that if God had willed it otherwise it would have been otherwise. Could he not
have palsied Guiteau's arm had he so pleased?
When Guiteau raised his weapon in his name,
would he not have stopped him as he did Abraham
of old, had it been his will?"

This letter, of a column's length, which The
Truth Seeker published in full, Guiteau incorporated into his statement to the press, accepting its
appearance as "providential." His own sister, convinced of her brother's divine mission, wrote him:
"You certainly deserve the commendation of all
people who profess to be Christians, for your un-
wavering trust in God's power when you shot the
President, as I sincerely believe you had. There
can be no condemnation on God's part toward you,
and no condemnation in your heart toward your-

self." In a special prayer, prepared by the assassin for use on the gallows, Guiteau implicated his deity, saying, "Thou knowest thou didst inspire Garfield's removal." He also composed a hymn with the closing line, "Glory hallelujah! I am with the Lord."

Socrates died like a philosopher, but Guiteau died like a saint.

Every generation, doubtless, produces its pulpit clowns. History sets them down as "eccentric preachers." Such was the Rev. T. DeWitt Talmage. Talmage at the height of his career as pulpit clown delivered his sermons in the Tabernacle church, Brooklyn, Presbyterian, and they were syndicated; that is to say, he prepared weekly a quantity of matter to appear in the newspapers as the sermon of "last Sunday." A series of his sermons in 1882 were on Ingersoll. That accounts for Ingersoll's "Talmagian Catechism" and "Interviews on Talmage" (see the fifth volume of the Dresden edition of his works). Talmage owes it to Ingersoll that his name is mentioned a quarter of a century after his death (in 1902). The next generation may ask the meaning of the words Talmage and Talmagian—whether they possibly are variants of Talmud and Talmudic.

2—INGERSOLL'S MEMORIAL DAY ADDRESS

The Grand Army of the Republic invited Ingersoll to deliver the Memorial Day address at the Academy of Music, May 30, which deeply stirred the souls of a number of nervous Christians. They demanded to know whether there was no Christian soldier who could have been asked to speak. The editor of The Sun, which printed numerous protests, saw in the event the doom of Christianity. Said he: "The fact that a professed Infidel, a man who denounces the scriptures and pours scorn and insult upon the Christian religion, could be brought forward as the chief orator on such an occasion as the services of Decoration Day in this city, appears to us something of far greater import than any of our correspondents have taken it for ... It means, in our judgment, that there has been a general decline in religion. ... If this process continues for fifty years the Christians will form a very small minority of the people of this country. But perhaps some new manifestation of religious life may arise to arrest the spread of Infidelity."

Besides this prediction that Christianity would be wiped out, there were warnings that Ingersoll's appearance would produce a riot; yet the day came and Ingersoll with it; and "there was not a dissenting voice amidst the thunders of applause that greeted him as he stepped to the reading-desk." One beholding the audience called it a "throng rather than a crowd." The speech delivered that day by Colonel Ingersoll was the one which, thirty years later, Christianity's most popular exponent, the Rev. W. A. Sunday, gave as his own at a Memorial Day observance in a Pennsylvania town.

The indignation felt by the religious people of the country that a man who denounced the scrip-

tures and poured scorn and insult upon the Christian religion should be publicly heard was shared
and voiced by Mr. Frank James, who, at the time
he so expressed himself, was an inmate of a jail
in Jackson county, Missouri, where he awaited trial
for several murders and numerous highway robberies. Said that bandit, as reported in the Kansas City Journal: "Ingersoll is a blasphemer, who
goes abroad denouncing the Bible, the most sacred
of all books. He ridicules its teachings and the
savior, and yet amid all this he has hearers to the
number of two thousand, while a man for using an
indecent word while drunk will be confined for
thirty days. My God! How can such a state of
affairs be? The Lord is my helper. I care not
what men shall say against me. Ingersoll is doing unspeakable injury to this nation. He is sow-
ing the seeds of iniquity in the minds of our
youth." This Frank James and his brother Jesse
being the most notorious criminals of their day,
his pious deliverance carries its own sarcastic commentary.

   Among the contemners of Ingersoll who threw
in with Talmage, Joseph Cook, Guiteau, and Frank
James, was the hereinbefore mentioned skunk and
scalawag, Clark Braden, who propagated falsehood
by pamphlet. Braden circulated the printed statement that Ingersoll was financially irresponsible and
his note unbankable in Peoria. In reply, Mr. Kirk-
patrick of Arrowsmith, Ill., published in The Truth
Seeker an open letter to the libeler, saying: "Mr.
Clark Braden—Sir: In your pamphlet you say

that Colonel Ingersoll's note is unbankable in Peoria, Ill. Now let me say that if you will go to the trouble of finding one of those unbankable notes, Mr. A. T. Ives of this place (formerly of Bloomington) will gladly trade a bill for house rent he holds against you for an interest in one of those unbankable notes of R. G. Ingersoll's."

The season's pulpit heretic was the Rev. George C. Miln, once a Congregational preacher in Brooklyn, and then of a Chicago Unitarian church, where he delivered a sermon renouncing belief in God and a future life. He stepped down and out with the full consent of his congregation. Miln at this time, the beginning of 1882, was a man of middle age and personally pleasing. As he appeared to me when he spoke before Felix Adler's Society for Ethical Culture, he more resembled an actor than a clergyman. I thought he intentionally strove after that effect. Soon we read: "The ex-Rev. George C. Miln has now definitely announced his intention of taking the stage this fall. He will appear as Shakespeare's Hamlet, of whose character he has an original conception." When the time came he appeared in several Shakespearean roles. His Hamlet was praised.

In The Truth Seeker a debate about prohibition got a start from the declaration of Mr. E. C. Walker that "prohibition involves a principle which, if carried to its logical conclusion, would stop every Liberal press in the country, and close the lips of every Freethinker." Mr. Walker quite convincingly defended this position. A Freethinker having doubts could hardly do better than to turn to

Mr. Walker's clear demonstrations of the character of prohibitory laws. The logic of prohibition, carried to a conclusion in New Jersey that year, brought about the arrest of W. H. Rosentranch of Newark for the crime of blasphemy, April 14, and in Massachusetts an attempted suppression of Walt Whitman's "Leaves of Grass."

There lived a man in France during a past century who thought the world would be happier when the last king had been strangled with the entrails of the last priest. Should an accident like that happen to the last amateur custodian of public morals and the last censor, we might go to hell with less friction.

William H. Herndon, for twenty-two years the law partner and intimate associate of Abraham Lincoln, and his biographer, appealed to The Truth Seeker (Nov. 25) to publish, with "a good little editorial," his refutation of the lies of pulpit and press that defamed him for speaking the truth about the religious belief of Lincoln. In a "card of correction" Mr. Herndon wrote:

"I wish to say a few words to the public and private ear. About the year 1870 I wrote a letter to F. E. Abbot, then of Ohio, touching Mr. Lincoln's religion. In that letter I stated that Mr. Lincoln was an Infidel, sometimes bordering on Atheism, and I now repeat the same. In the year 1873 the Right Rev. James A. Reed, pastor and liar of this city (Springfield, Ill.), gave a lecture on Mr. Lincoln's religion in which he tried to answer some things which I never asserted, except as to Lincoln's Infidelity, which I did assert, and now and here affirm. Mr. Lincoln was an Infidel of the radical type; he never mentioned the name of Jesus, except to scorn and detest the idea of a miraculous conception."

The Rev. Reed, whom Herndon names, endeavored to lay the foundation for a Herndon mythology—a reverse of the myth that Lincoln was a devout Christian and praying man—which should represent Herndon as a drunkard, a liar, a blasphemer, and a pauper, wholly unworthy of credence. If the Rev. Reed only knew it, he was libeling a man whose faith was much nearer his own than was Lincoln's.

3—THE LEAGUE STARTS A NEW ERA

The sixth Annual Congress of the National Liberal League—convening in the hall of the Young Men's Temperance Union (formerly a church), St. Louis, Mo.—opened on Friday, September 29, and continued until Sunday, October 1, with morning, afternoon, and evening meetings. Its proceedings were reported in The Truth Seeker of October 14 (1882). The officers elected for the ensuing year were: President, T. B. Wakeman, New York; secretary, T. C. Leland, New York; treasurer, Courtlandt Palmer, New York. E. A. Stevens of Chicago and Mrs. H. S. Lake of California were elected chairmen, respectively, of the Executive and Finance Committees. That, I believe, was the first recognition of Stevens, who in coming years loomed large in the affairs of the national organization.

The discussions of the congress were diverted from the subject of church and state separation by the introduction of proposals to take sides with the industrial cause in its various forms. But organized labor was not there to take the side of the Liberal League. The following paragraph in the report is significant:

"Another member arose and pointed to the vacant seats as a reminder to those present of the *interest* exhibited in their discussions and plans by the labor organizations and other societies the cooperation of which they expected to secure."

The situation warranted the inference that the various industrial organizations took then, as they continue to take, only the coldest sort of interest in the secular cause.

The congress of 1879 had tried without success to establish a National Liberty Party. The members had then listened to a very urgent member of the Socialist Labor party. That individual (Charles Sotheran), as Mr. T. B. Wakeman now asked the Congress to notice, had since accepted a position on a Tammany newspaper, was sending his children to a convent school, and "had spent much of his spare time in abusing his former comrades and Liberal movements and societies." Again, said Mr. Wakeman, in order to placate the respectable Liberals who deprecated the League's war on comstockery, and at the same time to please the Socialist element, the Congress of '79 had elected as chairman of its National Committee (Gen. B. A. Morton) a reformed capitalist who was at the same time an ardent admirer of the League's first president, Francis Ellingwood Abbot, the champion of purity. And shortly afterwards, when the National Committee looked for its chairman to lead the new party, he was discovered to be under indictment for forgery and bigamy, with some half dozen wives on hand to illustrate his aversion to the principles of that social freedom which was advocated by certain members of the League whom he despised. (I never heard before 1879 or since 1882 of Gen. B. A. Morton, chairman of the National Committee of the Liberal Party.)

Mr. Wakeman at this sixth congress expressed disappointment that Colonel Ingersoll had apparently withdrawn from the National Liberal Party of 1879, at the launching of which he had proposed three rousing cheers.

Viewing the character, hinted at above by Mr. Wakeman, of some of the persons who made themselves prominent in that 1879 party, I never supposed that Ingersoll's want of enthusiasm required any further explanation than his inability to work in harmony with them.

Mr. Wakeman still held that the labor organizations could be brought into the League, since "only those who have broken with imagined autocracy above the skies can lead effectively the break from the real autocracies and monopolies on the earth." They have never come in.

An old and experienced Freethinker, Thomas Curtis of St. Louis, a charter member of the

League, opposed a Liberal political party as being impractical; it would be obliged to move fifty millions of people, which was like the old story of the tail trying to wag the dog. "The trouble will be," Mr. Curtis said, "that these very labor and reform organizations you may try to combine in order to wag your dog are largely composed of your religious opponents. The thousands of Catholics in them will obey not you but their priests, and so with the Protestants and even semi-Liberals. Until these men are liberated from their old religious bonds they cannot cooperate with themselves nor with you."

At the request of Mr. Wakeman, the Congress committed itself to the use of the new "Era of Man" in place of Anno Domini. This era Mr. Wakeman reckoned from the martyrdom of Giordano Bruno in the year 1600 of the common chronology, and the League paper, Man, was so dated thereafter (282 instead of 1882). The reform calendar did not survive its founder.

4—THE WORSTING OF THE REV. JOSEPH COOK.

Bennett's letters of travel at the beginning of 1882 were from the Near East; and it was a short one that did not make four Truth Seeker pages. His articles on "What I Don't Believe" were meanwhile continued. His old enemy, the Rev. Joseph Cook of Boston, overtook him in Bombay. The Bombay Gazette had proposed a debate between Cook and Col. H. S. Olcott, the Theosophist. At the annual dinner of the Theosophical Society, Bennett being present, the colonel mentioned the Gazette's suggestion, and saying he had no time for a debate, invited Mr. Bennett to be his substitute. Bennett agreed, and then and there said a few preliminary words regarding the Boston Monday lecturer, following them with a challenge to Cook. The latter ignored the challenge, but took Bennett as his text when he spoke publicly again. The Christian minister made the mistake of acting uppish or arrogant toward the natives, with whom, on the contrary, Bennett immediately got upon the most friendly terms. Cook, irascible and quarrelsome by nature, could put up with no opposition. Some sort of an issue arising between him and his native audience at Poonah, as reported in The Theosophist, "Mr. Cook wrathfully advised them to pray to their 'false gods.' Then he quarreled with two of the Christian missionaries present, and insulted the chairman, a respectable European gentleman of Poonah; the remarkable lecture coming to a close, to the great delight of the heathen audience, amidst a 'general Christian row,' as the heathen editor of a local paper expressed it."

Cook having returned Bennett's written challenge unopened, Colonel Olcott and Dayanana Sarawati, a learned Parsee, each sent him a defi, which he refused to take up because he would not appear on the same platform with Bennett. So it was necessary to answer Cook in his absence, and Bennett had a walk-over. A crowded audience heard him flay "the falsifier, the defamer, the maligner, the slanderer, who with falsehood and malice in his heart wilfully attempts to injure and destroy the reputation of a fellow-being." I am quoting Mr. Bennett's language. After dealing with Cook, Bennett dealt with his religion, pointing out its errors and receiving "abundant applause."

Cook, coming well advertised to Bombay, charged upon the heathen like a warhorse. Bennett had no advance agent, but he got the decision. He went away with a testimonial, while to Cook the Native Public Voice addressed a farewell thanking him for coming, but hoping he was under no delusion that his "flimsy, unargumentative, and merely rhetorical lectures have produced any impression whatever on their minds with respect to the truth of Christianity."

On the boat he took from Japan to Sydney, the Reverend Joseph fell off the upper deck and landed so hard on a lower one that the ship's surgeon had to repair his ribs.

5—HOME AT LAST.

Bennett, the earth's circle completed, as far as might be by sea, touched land at San Francisco on May 30 (1882). He was two months crossing the continent to New York on account of the many receptions held for him on the way. His Fourth New York Liberal League awaited him with another reception, which was held at Martinelli's, in Fifth Avenue. The feature of this occasion, to me, was the presence of Horace Seaver and J. P. Mendum of the Boston Investigator, for I had been detailed to meet them at the Grand Central and lead them to the banquet. Mr. Seaver was a stout old gentleman, with a considerable mustach; Mendum slightly built with a not luxuriant brown beard turning gray. When I came upon them they were standing together like children lost in the crowd, timidly regarding their surroundings in the big station. They were of the age I have now reached myself, when a man is not so sure of himself as he is at twenty-five. I conducted them to Martinelli's and placed them in seats of honor at the speakers' table.

When Bennett was in Ceylon, and had addressed at a place he calls Panadure, an audience of two thousand, he relates: "Two persons came to the stand and chanted to me several stanzas in Pali, composed for the occasion by the two young priests in the pansala (Panchala?)." (Truth Seeker, July 8, 1882.) The eighth stanza ran thus:

"May Mr. Bennett, who is like unto the Sun which destroys the dew of superstition,
Is like a victorious general in engagements of controversy,
Who follows the teachings of Lord Buddha, which comfort the world,
And who well bears the pearl necklace of renown,
    Shine long."

At the reception we were giving him in New York, T. B. Wakeman read some of these stanzas very acceptably to the diners. The ceremonies lasted nearly six hours. Samuel P. Putnam was the poet of the evening.

The two thousand persons who attended the New York State Freethinkers' Convention at Watkins,

feted Bennett again, and he must have found it
hard, after all this, to get back to work at the desk.
In fact, he was already planning for a tour of the
United States with a stereopticon and slides pur-

THE TRUTH SEEKER OFFICE IN CLINTON PL.

chased abroad. But first he must oversee the removal of the office from the rooms in Science
Hall, which had long ago become too crowded
through his inveterate publishing of books. He
found new and larger quarters at 21 Clinton place
and moved in. The number of the paper for October 14 first bore that address.

A little while later the mind of Bennett seemed
to undergo a reversal as to the policy of bucking
the Comstock laws; for when on October 27 Ezra
H. Heywood of Princeton, Mass., was arrested
by Anthony and held in default of $1,000 bail,
for circulating selections from the poems of Walt
Whitman, Bennett wrote (Nov. 4): "We must

confess that we have wondered why Mr. Heywood should decide, under the circumstances, to mail such matter. He seemed to us not a man with a coarse, animal nature, but naturally as free from such tendency as one man in a thousand. We must say, however, that he chose to make himself most conspicuous by mailing Walt Whitman's most objectionable poem, and by publishing some things which we most certainly would not publish. We could not see what good was to be gained by it, what principle of Liberalism is involved, or how the best interest of any class of the community can thereby be served. There is no reason why anyone should unnecessarily thrust his hand into the lion's mouth."

Bennett did not in this article descend to the impeachment of Heywood's character; in fact, he gave him a clean bill of moral health, so far as he could judge; but otherwise he paltered very much as his timid friends had done not long before when his own hand was in the mouth of the lion, saying: "We are all in favor of free mails, the same as free thought, a free press, and free speech, but we are not in favor of sending indecent matter by mail, or any other way."

These remarks at once impressed me as invidious and while I pondered them, a printer who prided himself on the classical allusions at his command, said with a sigh: "Achilles had his vulnerable spot. and so has the Doctor. I'm afraid it is his vanity; he is in the limelight, and isn't encouraging any rivals in martyrdom." The uncompromising Benjamin R. Tucker, then publishing Liberty, replied to the article with heat and vigor. Writing of Heywood's arrest, he said: "In this connection we must express our indignation at the cowardly conduct of D. M. Bennett, editor of The Truth Seeker, who prates about Mr. Heywood's taste and methods. We do not approve of Mr. Heywood's taste and methods, but neither did we of Bennett's when we did our little best a few years ago to save him from Comstock's clutches."

6—THE LAST HOME.

Others expressed their astonishment at the change in Bennett's point of view. I lay that change to his last sickness, which attacked him while we were moving the office in October. We were still at 141 Eighth street when he began to hiccup, and the affection was never checked. It became a habit. I heard him say to Dr. Foote and his son (this was at 141): "If you boys don't do something to stop this hiccuping, I am gone." He was enough of a physician to know what to expect. The trouble was shaking him apart when he worked, or spoke, or ate. Criticism of his utterances then would be leveled at a dying man. About the last of November he left a piece of unfinished copy on his desk and went home. To get the conclusion of what he was writing I carried the last sheet to his rooms, where he dictated a paragraph to me. It is in The Truth Seeker for December 9, the shortest installment of anything he ever wrote to be continued. The same number of the paper announced his death, December 6, 1882.

We buried Dr. Bennett on the Sunday following his death, from the place where the Liberal Club met, German Masonic Temple in East Fifteenth street, Mr. Wakeman being the eulogist. Over his grave in Sylvan avenue, Greenwood Cemetery, stands a monument bearing his name and extracts from his writings, and the legend, "Erected by One Thousand Friends."

For a Bennett Memorial I composed an ode of many stanzas, closing with the apostrophe:

"Where o'er thy precious dust this shaft we raise
　To bear the record of a hero gone,
'Neath changeless stars, through ever-changing days,
　First in our heart of heart, sleep on, sleep on."

He sleeps on. And could he be awakened alone by the footfall above his grave of someone who remembers him, his slumbers have been undisturbed for many years. Until I went West—that is, for five years following his death—my brother and I were accustomed, once in a summer, to visit Greenwood Cemetery and delay our walk for a few moments at the place where he lies. I have not been there since the summer of 1887.

The inscription on the face of the monument underneath "Erected by One Thousand Friends" and the medalion reads: "D. M. Bennett, the Founder of The Truth Seeker; the Defender of Liberty, and its Martyr; the Editor Tireless and Fearless; the Enemy of Superstition, as of Ignorance, its Mother; the Teacher of Multitudes; the Friend faithful and kind; the Man honest and true, Rests Here. Though dead he still speaks to us and asks that we continue the work he left unfinished. When the Innocent is convicted, the Court is condemned."

THE GRAVE OF D. M. BENNETT

The monument stands at the corner of Sylvan avenue
and Osier path, Greenwood Cemetery, Brooklyn, N. Y.

Many young Freethinkers have expressed them-selves as desirous of knowing what kind of a man was Bennett who founded The Truth Seeker. In my attempt to answer the question I have described him as I knew him. I hope the picture presented and received is fairly accurate, which none can be when a man is overpraised. It would be useless for me to conceal any of his faults. He told them all or showed them all himself. Anything added thereto, to his discredit, may be dismissed as false. He owed the popularity he achieved partly to cir-cumstance, and more to his simple and honest na-ture, his industrious hand, his capable head, and his courageous heart. His success was all earned and genuine, for he had none of the tricks, either of speech or pen, that deceive the unwary, nor re-sorted to the "skilled digressions" which appeal to the passions or stir the emotions of the unthinking. He was a likeable man, and it did not embarrass him to be praised. His journalism was of the sort called personal. The Truth Seeker was Bennett, and in advertising himself he advertised the paper.

7—FOR THE RECORD.

I am writing of a year (1882) in which occurred many events that have their place in the annals of Freethought. John William Draper, author of "The History of the Conflict Between Religion and Science," died January 14; Bradlaugh was elected to Parliament for the third time; Charles Darwin died and was entombed in Westminster Abbey. Satirizing the burial and memorial of unbelievers in this sacred edifice, Thomas Hardy, speaking for the dean, said in 1924:

> " 'Twill next be expected
> That I get erected
> To Shelley a tablet
> In some niche or gablet.
> Then—what makes my skin burn,
> Yes, forehead to chin burn—
> That I ensconce Swinburne!"

The dean got his revenge on Hardy for this jibe by laying the author's ashes away in the Poets' Corner, in 1928.

Charles Watts of England and Charles Bright of Australia came to the United States to lecture. Herbert Spencer spent a few weeks here in the fall, and was dined at Delmonico's by the evolutionists. The attendants at the dinner included John Fiske, Editor Youmans of The Popular Science Monthly, Carl Schurz, the Hon. Wm. M. Evarts, Thaddeus B. Wakeman, Courtlandt Palmer, and Henry Ward Beecher. Carl Schurz said of Spencer: "We greet him as a hero of thought who has devoted his life to the sublime task of vindicating the right of science as against the intolerant authority of traditional belief." Beecher was a professed evolutionist from that date.

Otto Wettstein, designer of the Freethought badgepin, began writing for The Truth Seeker, as did also C. L. James, author of a History of the French Revolution. LaRoy Sunderland, formerly a hypnotic evangelist, wrote articles unveiling the philosophy of revival hysteria. Bennett made the experiment of reducing the subscription price of

The Truth Seeker to $2.50, but got no more sub-
scribers thereby, and the next year it was put back
at $3.   The surviving Liberal exchanges of The
Truth Seeker and Boston Investigator were: New
York Man, Boston This World, Milwaukee Liberal
Age, Indianapolis Iconoclast, Missouri Liberal, Val-
ley Falls (Kan.) Liberal, the Pepin Gazette, Texas
Agnostic, San Francisco Jewish Times, and Dr.
Foote's Health Monthly, New York.

In the pages of this ninth (1882) volume of
The Truth Seeker I come upon occasional contributions from my own pen in prose and verse. Visitors to the office began asking where G. E. M.
could be seen, and were brought into the printing
office, for purposes of congratulation.   The elder
Dr. Foote was the second person to encourage me
to write more and oftener; the first one being Bennett.   Bennett imprudently had said as early as 1879
that The Truth Seeker would print whatever I might
choose to write.

As a neophyte, I was an exceedingly enthusiastic Freethinker, justifying Ingersoll's similitude of
the bumblebee —"biggest when first hatched." However, nobody, I trust, will accuse me of shrinking
up any since.   The following sonnet, the form and
terms of which were lifted from Shakespeare, I
wrote in praise of Universal Mental Liberty.   It
is a fair transcript of my mental state at that period.

"Could half the joy a mind enfranchised brings
   Be told in numbers that to it belong,
The world would say, 'A poet 'tis that sings
   Whose wayward fancy hath betrayed his song.'

Too early still the day, too late the dawn,
  For all mankind yet to behold the light
That shines on those who know of coming morn,
  And greet its glow from Freedom's lofty height.
But time may come—when dust of ours shall lie
  Mute as our papers, yellowed with their age—
When those who now would plainest truths deny
  The present poet will esteem a sage.
His worth shall live upon the lips of fame,
And grateful praises consecrate his name."

As an exponent of Freethought I have had occasion to repel the insinuation that Freethinkers are without ardor, that emancipation from superstition as they deem it, is not with them an occasion for rejoicing. I put that sonnet in evidence to show what the wider outlook did to me, who am not emotionally effervescent, and never was.

Embalmed in the files of The Truth Seeker there are probably hundreds of testimonies to the "spiritual" uplift of Freethought. A convincing one came from a woman in Texas many years ago, who "thanked God," as she phrased her gratitude, for the day when her husband went to hear Ingersoll, some two years prior to the time of her writing, and became a Freethinker. She said that while a church member he had been the tyrant of his household, and had even beaten her. He came home from Ingersoll's lecture a different man, and had since been the kindest of husbands. She had not herself wholly given up the old faith, but she was ordering more of Ingersoll's pamphlets for him, and expected to enjoy them herself.

A perplexing phenomenon is the occasional rever-
sion of an apparently convinced Rationalist to some
form of mysticism. O. B. Frothingham, for years
a Rationalist lecturer, whose discourses made up
the bulk of a Truth Seeker book entitled "The
Radical Pulpit," turned in his last days to a form
of theism. B. F. Underwood, whose lectures in the
'70s made a lifelong Materialist of me, thought he
was taking a step forward when he embraced Spiritualism. Louis F. Post died a confirmed Sweden-
borgian, they say. G. H. Walser, founder of the
town of Liberal, Missouri, after being fooled by a
medium who later was exposed as a fraud, relapsed
into an orthodox fundamentalist. George Chainey,
who, as a Materialist, called Theosophy "mental rub-
bish" and said he hoped Bennett would write no
more about it, went to a Spiritualist camp-meeting,
found there the "mother of his soul," proceeded
from Spiritualism to Theosophy, and has been a
mystic of one sort or another ever since. I have
known men, once supposed Freethinkers, to lean
toward Christian Science, even Bahaism. And I
have ceased to wonder thereat, not because I can
explain their action, but because I have seen so
many of them they are no longer novelties—not
even an individualist turning authoritarian. Doubtless their state of reaction may be called a spiritual
second childhood, matching that of the body and
mind. Like children, the aged must play safe. I
once stood upon a bridge over a swollen river
watching two or three families of Indians hauling
ashore the drift and wreckage that came down with

the flood. While the vigorous bucks worked their canoes in the current of the midstream, the old men and young boys paddled about close inshore. The old men in their prime had breasted the current, and after a few years the boys would be doing a man's part also, but now the old and the young were in the same boat—the youth not yet competent for the battle, the aged owning defeat.

CHAPTER XVI.

1—I BECOME THE ASSISTANT EDITOR.

PROGRESS in these writings for 1883 is
hindered by my preoccupation with the
contents of the volume of The Truth Seeker
for that year. As an employee I had been taken
off stone-work in the printing-office, and to my
duties as foreman and proof-reader there had been
added the role of assistant to the editor, E. M.
Macdonald, much of whose time was taken up with
the business affairs of the paper. Mrs. Bennett,
as owner, took care of the receipts and expendi-
tures, but my brother understood the trade; and
while from some source she had brought in a
"business adviser," she found after a little experience that Eugene was her reliance. This "adviser"
and her relatives, I suspect, would have displaced
both of us if that had been practicable. As it was
not, they made her fairly suspicious of us; and
soon she endeavored to take the management from
Eugene by organizing the Truth Seeker Company.
The members of the Company, whom, with herself,
she called "executors," were Daniel E. Ryan, T.
B. Wakeman, her brother Loren J. Wicks, Eugene
M. Macdonald, and John V. Wingate. In announcing the formation of the company she said
that her brother and Mr. Wingate would relieve

herself and Mr. Macdonald of "much business and office work." The change gave Mr. Wingate a position with salary. Meanwhile the office had re-

A PICTURE OF MRS. MARY BENNETT

moved from No. 21 to No. 33 Clinton Place, and my brother and I had desks in the rear of the building. Visitors met Wingate and then came back to the editor's room to inquire who the hell Wingate was. The business adviser made a confidant of one of the compositors to keep him informed of all that was said in the rear, and receiving what could be measured as an earful, rewarded the printer with a job in the front office, at time work, and little to do. Mrs. Bennett lost confidence in Eugene—the influence of her relatives and adviser, I suppose. To place events in the right connection I will say here that she died in my brother's house, to which she had come in her last years, and gave him what they had left her of the estate.

To resume. I was assistant editor, and, to me, being assistant editor meant more than the leisurely preparation of a measured amount of matter per week, and handing it to the chief for revision and bestowal on the men who were to put it in type. My brother wrote his editorials, and with letters and articles for publication passed them to me. He could go fishing then, if he wanted to and had the time, which on account of examining contributions, answering letters and receiving visitors he usually did not. It was my pastime to take the writers' mistakes out of the MSS. by revising them, to supply the headings, and otherwise to prepare them for the printer. When they were insufficient for the available space, I must select the "fillers." I then took the printers' mistakes out of the proofs and overlooked the make-up. The editor might keep regular hours; the assistant was expected to stay for the last revise, and, when the forms were locked up, to test them and see if they would lift.

All the manuscripts for books as well as for the paper went through the assistant's hands for reading. To be a competent assistant editor the person in that position should have persuaded himself that he could do the work a little better than the old man, and should be watchful that none of the latter's errors get past him and go through.

The work was not burdensome. There was still time to indulge the itch for writing, which led to the production of editorial articles. The New York Times then had on its staff William Livingston Alden, who originated the famous "sixth column" feature, a humorous editorial. To bring The Truth Seeker to a level with the best journalism, I began making that kind of a contribution to the last column, when available, of the ninth page. The pieces are in the first few numbers of the tenth volume of The Truth Seeker, and are worth a chuckle today. But the space was not always available, for my brother's articles and selections often filled the pages, so that, dropping the column editorial, I devoted myself to writing editorial paragraphs of either light or serious import. I reflect with something of sadness on the fact that at the time in question I could turn off about twice the amount of work in a given length of time that I am now capable of doing. Then the thought went ahead of the pen. Now it does not keep up with the typewriter—and I am a slow typist. In these days of the sere and yellow, as the weeks go by, I am inclined to breathe a sigh of relief when the pagination of the editorial manuscript I am making lets me know that enough has been prepared for the next number of the paper. At that age (in 1883) I should have done this Fifty-Years narrative on spare time during the day, in the office. Now the preparation of it is home work—three hours in the evening, six Saturday afternoon, and twelve or fifteen on Sunday. About twenty-four hours are required to turn through a year's file of The Truth Seeker and to make notes, and the remainder of the week is not too much for elaborating them. With forty-five volumes yet to do, a year's travel lies between me and the colophon. And work on the volume in hand is prolonged by my dallying over the pieces that I wrote myself, to which I have not turned before for more than four decades. One feels a curiosity to see how he thought and wrote in his salad days.

Besides editorial paragraphs, there was verse, of which none I ever produced satisfied me. I found a market for some of it, but not a line contains the germ of immortality. My first commercial venture in "poetry" went to a trade paper, The Sewing Machine Journal, and produced ten dollars. It was embalmed in a "popular" publication called "Gems of Poetry and Prose." I have no inclination to disturb the remains.

That season I took up the study of phonography, or shorthand, with D. L. Scott-Browne (pioneer of the Haldeman-Julius form of matrimonial hyphenation), who charged me a dollar an hour for lessons and seemed surprised when I taxed him fifty cents an hour for making up the forms of his magazine at night. I contributed certain verses to his publication for which I received no thanks from the

young lady in whose behalf I invoked the muse.
One scrap of my rhyme—a parody—in The Truth
Seeker, Mr. Scott-Browne pounced upon to use
as a test for his advanced pupils. Entitled "How
to Be a Preacher," it ran:

> "If you want a receipt for a popular minister,
>   Skilled in expounding the doctrine of sects,
> Arrange a collection of expletives sinister,
>   Mingled with fragments of various texts;
> Take the last wailing of Christ in his agony,
>   Latin and Hebrew, original Greek—
> Eloi, Eloi, lama sabachthani—
>   Howl it and chatter it, mumble and shriek;
> Of Moses and Joshua study astronomy,
>   Copy the morals of David and Lot,
> Practice each day in Ezekiel's gastronomy,
>   Drink with old Noah, the bibulous sot;
> Gather some scraps of New England theology,
> Weak metaphysics, and Cook's eschatology;
> Fill your discourses with all that's fanatical,
> Rattle them off in a manner theatrical;
> Doubt every fact and believe every mystery,
> Meet modern learning with biblical history,
> Praise all the actions of pious rascality,
> Damn every heretic as a finality.
> These qualities constitute, blended in unity,
> The joy of the modern religious community."

A Boston lawyer named James W. Stillman surprised me one day by coming unannounced to the
door of the room where I was at work and then
reciting the lines in a thunderous voice. It embarrassed me, of course; but still and all, that was better than being in ignorance as to whether anyone
ever noticed the verses or not.

2—THE MAN WITH THE BADGEPIN

With my shorthand notebook and several carefully pointed lead pencils in my pocket, and nothing
to do with them but a little occasional transcribing
for my friend Sherman, the stenographer by profession, I bethought me to go and get some practice
for speed at the Liberal Club, which met in East
Fifteenth street every Friday night. It was my
fortune first to hit the club with this purpose in
view on a night when a controversy was going on
between Mr. T. B. Wakeman and another legal
gentleman named Shook, a professed Christian;
Mr. Wakeman being the speaker according to the
program, and Mr. Shook there to controvert him.
I am not going to quote the report I turned in at the
office to be published with the foreword: "Reported
for The Truth Seeker by a Young Man Whose
Veracity we have hitherto had no Occasion to
Doubt."

In my notebook were the speeches of the evening nearly verbatim. Transcribed, they would
have filled many columns, and, for the purpose of
a descriptive report of the meeting, were wholly
useless. However, I had written some asides in
"English," and from these made up the printed
account. When Mr. Wakeman saw it a week later
he pronounced it unsatisfactory. Young Dr. Foote,
who was present at the meeting, said it was better
than the speeches. With some further encouragement I repeated the performance, and the report of
the Liberal Club became a feature of the paper, im-

proving, I hope, from week to week. Shorthand
being an obstruction to descriptive reports, I discontinued its use in doing the story of the Club.
This was the beginning of my career as the Man
with the Badgepin.

3—MEMORABLE LIBERAL CLUB MEETINGS.

Three meetings of the Club in 1883 were in a
way historical. The speakers severally were Albert
Brisbane, Dr. Dio Lewis, and Samuel P. Putnam.
Mr. Brisbane spoke on "Modern Scientific Specu-
lations—Their Superficialities." His lecture was a
review of philosophies ancient and modern, none
of which satisfied him. He examined and rejected
Comte, Hegel, Spencer, Darwin. They had settled
nothing, he said. As near as I can say, Mr. Brisbane, being a Fourierite, rejected observation and
experiment as methods of ascertaining the ultimate
truth, and relied upon thought or excogitation. The
problems of the universe were to be solved by
thinking—by discovering "the designs and laws of
cosmic wisdom." Mr. Brisbane was one of the
notable men of his generation. In discussing his
speech Stephen Pearl Andrews referred to the
French philosopher, Charles Fourier (1772-1837),
as the greatest genius the world had ever produced.
Occasionally the reader finds in the writings of
Arthur Brisbane, son of Albert, the same unquali-
fied praise of Fourier. But Mr. Andrews dissented
from the dictum of Mr. Brisbane, speaker of the
evening, that the law of cosmic wisdom remained

yet to be discovered. "As a matter of fact," said Mr. Andrews, "I have discovered it and am now teaching it to a small class."

Did all these philosophers labor in vain? It would appear so, for who now quotes Fourier to prove a point? What did Hegel demonstrate? Who works out a problem now by applying the thoughts of Kant? What is of most human interest today in the career of Albert Brisbane—the advocacy of Fourierism which he conducted, or the fact, to be verified by reading the files of New York newspapers for 1855, that on an evening when he was meeting with a society of social radicals at 555 Broadway the police raided the place and arrested him with the rest of those present?

Seeing how soon philosophers are forgotten, Omar Khayyam was not irrelevant when he said that the revelations of the learned are no more than "stories" which they wake up and tell before going to sleep for all time.

Beholding Dr. Dio Lewis in the flesh was like witnessing an incarnation. He had been one of the myths of my childhood. His name I had known for twenty years, for he was head of the school for nurses attended by mother just after the war; but here he was in proper person, speaking from the platform of the Liberal Club on the announced subject of "The Function of Civil Law in Human Government." He declared that all rights belonged to the individual, none whatever being vested in that vague abstraction called society. We must learn, he said, to distinguish between crime, which may properly be dealt with by force, and vice, which we should seek to eradicate by persuasion. A crime must have the element of malice prepense and of injury toward another person. VICE IS AN INJURY WE DO OURSELVES IN A MISTAKEN PURSUIT OF HAPPINESS. The law cannot properly deal with vice, because vice is not a crime, and law has only to do with crime. Rum-selling and rum-drinking are vices, but the sale of liquor should no more be interfered with by law than the sale of potatoes. Gluttony is a vice fully equal, in the extent of harm it does, to intemperance in the use of alcoholic liquors, yet no one believes gluttony should be punished by law. We have all more or less vices, and if vices were to be punished with imprisonment the whole world would be in jail, and the last man would have to put his hand out through a hole in the door and lock himself in. Thus spoke Dr. Dio Lewis at considerable length. He was a health reformer, a dietician, heartily opposed to the use of rum and tobacco; and as for selling either, he said he would prefer to be a horsethief. His differentiation between vice and crime suited me then and does now.

When Samuel P. Putnam spoke in the fall, Benjamin R. Tucker had just translated and published Bakounine's "God and the State." Putnam took the book for his theme and was full of his subject. At the outset he announced himself to be an Anarchist—of course of the school later known as Philosophical—a godless, churchless, stateless Anarchist. Society, he said, very much in the vein of Dio Lewis, did not exist. It was a myth. The church and state were relics of a barbaric

342 FIFTY YEARS OF FREETHOUGHT [1883

past, born of ignorance and fear and brute force.
Give us freedom of thought. Yet freedom of
thought is born to blush unseen unless we have
freedom of speech, and freedom of speech is
nipped in the bud if it be not supplemented with
freedom of action. The church would control our
thoughts and the state our acts. Away with both.
The Anarchist will brook no authority except that
which is accepted in freedom. Enforced equality
of men is a humbug. Liberty first: equality if you
can achieve it as an outcome of that liberty. Liberty is the means, not the end. The state is un-
trustworthy and cruel. It has been guilty of every
enormity. It is a giant monopolist. It uses brute
force in order to compete with private enterprise.
Even the postoffice has to protect itself by law
from individual competition. The state has made
fishing or attending a theater on Sunday a crime.
It is a tyrant and usurper.

Those were some of the points maintained by
Mr. Putnam; and I have never been a more violent dissenter from such views than from those of
Dio Lewis. The ideal condition of man would be
stateless and churchless, realizable when each shall
have become orderly enough to respect the liberty
of all. For some years I even advocated these principles myself and would now rejoice could it be
seen that any progress had been made toward their
general adoption. But "progress" has gone in the
opposite direction. Before the people can get
fairly set in opposition to one bad law, the legislative bodies divert our attention from it by enacting
a worse one.

Fifty years ago a voice might hopefully be raised in behalf of libertarian ideas, but no more. The time when those ideas might have had a China-man's chance has gone by. We have reached a point, with respect to the conflict between liberty and authority, where a man found himself on the morning after he had bet on the Dempsey-Tunney prize fight at Chicago. The man I speak of was a passenger on the train which takes me to New York. He acknowledged he had placed his money on Dempsey and lost; but, he said: "I still think Jack Dempsey can lick Gene Tooney." And a train hand who had been listening turned away saying: "Aw, it is too late to think." So it is too late to think that liberty can beat force. Liberty, in whose eyes shines always "that high light where-by the world is saved"—Liberty is licked.

4—A PAPAL EMISSARY AND ADVENTURER

A package of bad medicine shipped from Rome entered our ports under the label of "Mgr." Capel. The monsignor, a French Jesuit, was on a mission from the pope to work amongst Protestants and make as many converts as he could. The Protes-tants gave him a hearing, and the better-fixed en-tertained him in their homes and invited their friends to meet him. Episcopalians afflicted with the Catholic itch were especially cordial. He gave in Chickering Hall a lecture on divorce, making the point that when a divorced man marries a sec-ond time the woman he takes is a concubine. The good and polite Episcopalians applauded the monsig-

nor. In addition to indulging in this sort of blackguardism, Capel ventured to sound out the country
on the question of state support for Catholic parochial schools. Catholic statisticians in 1883 laid claim
to only 8,000,000 adherents of the church in place
of the 20,000,000 they are talking about now, and
the parochial school was in its infancy. Speaking in Chicago, Mgr. Capel condemned the public
school and the school laws that compelled the attendance of Catholic children. He then gave his
American hearers due notice that there was going
to be a fight. The American public school, he said,
was no place for Catholics and they were going
to leave it. He proceeded: "Suppose that the
church sends out an authoritative command to the
Catholics to start schools in every parish and support them, and send all Catholic children to them.
It can be done in the utterance of a word, SHARP
AS THE CLICK OF A TRIGGER." Had Herr Johann
Most, a contemporary bumptious anarchist, talked
about "the click of a trigger" a policeman would
have pulled him down and put him in jail. But
this emissary of the pope was permitted to proceed. Said he: "That command will be obeyed.
New schools will spring up everywhere. What
will be the result of that? A FIGHT! Do you
suppose some millions of people are going to pay
taxes twice over—once for their own schools, and
again for Protestant schools from which they get
no benefit? If it isn't a downright fight, it will be
at least a WARLIKE CONDITION—a million or two
of voting, tax-paying citizens HOSTILE TO THE GOV-
ERNMENT." He promised that Americans should

see Catholic parents pressing the muzzles of their guns against the breasts of the state tax-collectors.

The threat contained in this incendiary language of the pope's emissary went unheeded. The proposal to relieve Catholics of the burden of supporting their religious schools met with no public response. Thirty years later (in 1915) Mr. Alfred E. Smith, then a delegate to the New York state constitutional convention, moved to strike out the clause prohibiting state support of sectarian schools; but Smith's motion never got a second. Thus Capel exposed the hostility of Catholics to the government without gaining anything thereby. Notice, however, that the Catholics are not making their demands and threats so loudly and defiantly as in 1883.

In his mission as proselyter, Capel's best catch was the widow Hamersly, an Episcopalian lady of New York whose husband had left her four millions. Her bishop, Dr. Horatio Potter, had been expecting that his church would come in for a large share of the Hamersly money. The widow disappointed him. The French Jesuit had been there, and the Catholic church got it; which showed the error of the Episcopalian fashionables in lionizing Capel.

Again, in the furtherance of his mission Capel appealed to the government at Washington in the name of 8,000,000 American Catholics to arrest the Italian government in the act of taxing propaganda property in Rome. That failed despite its approval by a big Catholic mass meeting which he arranged.

The late John R. Slattery, a former Catholic clergyman and a contributor to The Truth Seeker at the time of his death in 1926, related to me that Capel, while in New York, declared himself to a Catholic married woman and proposed an intrigue. Being repulsed, he professed to be mystified, saying he did not understand New York Catholic ladies. Mr. Slattery remarked that the woman told him of the incident in order that she might disclose the name of another New York Catholic woman with whom Capel came to an understanding. That Capel was a woman-hunter appears not only from testimony but from what happened to him in California, where the pursuer seems to have been pursued. Anyhow a woman there took him into camp and he never got back to Rome with a report to his holiness the pope. So far as I know or care he lived with this woman on a ranch in California until 1911, when he died. So all is well that ends well.

Capel is dismissed for the present with the following excerpt from the News of the Week in The Truth Seeker November 4, 1911:

"Monsignor T. J. Capel, the Catholic preacher, died in Sacramento, Cal., Oct. 23, at the age of 75. Capel was the Catesby of Disraeli's satirization in 'Lothair' because of his success as a social lion in the English society of his day. He appeared in New York nearly thirty years ago, and in his lectures talked about putting muskets to the breasts of representatives of the government who came to collect the school tax from Catholics who were supporting parochial schools. He argued at the same time in favor of putting irreligious persons to death as homicides because they 'murdered the soul.' He was a high liver and hard drinker, and had the reputation of being 'the devil after women.' He went west from here, and it was reported that he had annexed a wife and a farm in California. He drank heavily in New York, appeared in an intoxicated condition at a dinner of police captains at Delmonico's, picked up a woman afterwards, and disgraced himself generally. He beat everybody who would lend him money. His priestly function was at length taken from him by Cardinal McCloskey."

5—FOR THE RECORD OF 1883

W. H. Herndon of Illinois contributed to The Truth Seeker, February 24 and March 10, articles on the religious belief of his friend and law partner, Abraham Lincoln.

The Catholics pushed their "freedom of worship" bill in the New York legislature. It provided that the wardens of state prisons should be compelled to give clergymen access to prisoners. The drive ended years later with the appointment of Catholic prison chaplains salaried by the state.

Peter Cooper, the philanthropist, died in April. When testimony was taken as to Mr. Cooper's views, they were found to be substantially those of Thomas Paine.

A strange figure called the Dude made its appearance in the early part of the year. The New York Tribune, after describing the genus, said that "he gets his religion from Colonel Ingersoll." The Tribune had taken Courtlandt Palmer for a pattern. Mr. Palmer to some extent dressed the part.

George Chainey discontinued publication of his paper, This World, which was consolidated with the Radical Review, edited by E. A. Stevens and George Schumm.

The death of Dr. George M. Beard, Materialist and one of New York's most eminent men of science, gave opportunity to Joseph Cook to put in circulation a story that the doctor had come to Jesus on his deathbed. The religious newspapers caught by the Rev. Cook's falsehood later repudiated it and expressed regret. Yet it is still going.

Religion was injected into the political campaign in Ohio by the nomination of Judge George H. Hoadley for governor. Mr. Hoadley being a Freethinker, the Cleveland Leader declared the nomination to be "the deepest and most outrageous insult ever offered to the God-fearing people of the State." Judge Hoadley was elected.

H. L. Green began the publication of a Freethought Directory, the forerunner of his Freethinkers' Magazine that continued through many volumes.

The International Federation of Freethought Societies held its fourth Annual Congress at Amsterdam, August 31 to September 2. Charles Bradlaugh and Dr. Ludwig Buchner, author of "Force and Matter," were among those present.

Kersey Graves, author of "The World's Sixteen Crucified Saviors" and the "Bible of Bibles," died September 4 at his home in Richmond, Ind., at the age of 70 years.

The Liberal League Congress for 1883 was held

at Milwaukee, Wisconsin, September 21-23, in Freiegemeinde Hall. Largely attended by Germans, it could adopt a resolution declaring: "No so-called temperance (prohibition) law shall be passed." The resolution caused animated discussion. T. B. Wakeman, T. C. Leland, and Courtlandt Palmer were reelected president, secretary, and treasurer respectively, and E. A. Stevens chairman of the Executive Committee.

On October 13 Mrs. Bennett announced that she had disposed of her pecuniary interest in The Truth Seeker and its business to The Truth Seeker

THE MANAGER AND THE EDITOR.

Company. Charles P. Somerby became business manager, E. M. Macdonald continuing as editor. The company paid Mrs. Bennett $10,000 for the property, Ephraim E. Hitchcock furnishing the money and being the actual owner. Mr. Hitchcock was wealthy and supposed to be conservative. The public was surprised at his death in the '90s to learn that he was proprietor of an Infidel paper. Mr. Hitchcock made the company a present of the $10,-000.

The famous Nineteenth Century Club, Courtlandt Palmer president, came into notice the early part of the year 1883. The meetings were held in Mr. Palmer's parlors. Carrying Freethought into swelldom, as it were, it was the means of causing some plain people to put on swallowtails who had never worn them before. It admitted the commonality to the presence of the exclusive. Here Ingersoll in 1888 debated with the Hon. Frederic R. Coudert and former Governor Stewart L. Woodford "The Limitations of Toleration."

In London, George William Foote, editor of the Freethinker, underwent prosecution and conviction on a charge of blasphemy and served a year in jail. A religious commission was appointed to examine the works of Mill, Darwin, Huxley and others, with a view to bringing blasphemy prosecutions against their publishers.

The Seymour Times, Indiana, took the name of The Ironclad Age and was published as a Freethought paper until merged with The Truth Seeker a decade afterwards.

William Denton, author, geologist, man of science, and Freethinker, died while conducting explorations in New Guinea, August 26. "His death," said The Truth Seeker, December 22, "was a sacrifice to science."

The Children's Corner of The Truth Seeker, edited by Susan Helen Wixon, began Nov. 10. The department was continued long after her death, which occurred in 1912.

On December 8 The Truth Seeker announced that the Bennett monument "now stands in Greenwood cemetery." On the 23d, it being the 65th anniversary of Mr. Bennett's birth, the Fourth New York Liberal League, rechristened the Bennett Auxiliary, celebrated the day with a meeting in the hall of the Liberal Club.

CHAPTER XVII.

1—KEEPING HOUSE IN THIRD AVENUE.

VIEWING Third avenue, a few blocks above the Bible House, in 1928, the spectator might guess that the thoroughfare had seen better days, but he would have no idea what a "homey" aspect those precincts wore forty-five years ago. While the same houses are there now as then, most of them, they are not in good repair. The class of tenantry has changed, and not for the better. It was a good neighborhood when mother and I kept house at No. 78 in the '80s, and those may have been among the most restful and contented years of that active woman's life, since she had no responsibilities but myself, who paid the rent and the household expenses, while she was free to answer calls from her old patients, who never forgot her when ill, or to visit her relatives near and far. She seldom stayed long with her relatives; they were so surprised at her views, which it was against her nature to conceal, that they lived under some strain while she remained with them, especially those in the South. She had a pension of $12 a month. It is surprising today to know how far that amount would go toward the upkeep of a woman who was independent of the dressmakers. And, always remindful of me, or else of the other party concerned, she never left me without a house-keeper. On one of her most extended vacations she installed a Miss Dalrymple, a girl employed on part time at demonstrating an invention of young Dr. Foote's called the polyopticon, of which one might see the advertisement, with occasional mention, in The Truth Seeker. The device reflected pictures on a screen. The doctor introduced it at entertainments given by the Liberal Club. Miss Dalrymple showed it at fairs. I never saw her before or since the month or more she cared for my rooms, prepared my meals, and read to me evenings for shorthand practice. I faintly recall May Sinclair, who came for a short time and then passed out of my ken. And after her Mrs. Mina Egli, a Swiss woman who had enjoyed a varied experience among reformers; had been with the Kaweah colony, an enterprise of Burnett G. Haskell of California; had in that state joined an Adamic or Edenic society wishful to restore the innocence of primitive man and woman with respect to clothes; had ranched in Dakota. Her remarks were generally cast in German, and she set me the task of translating Heine's verse. I also, at her suggestion, began to turn a German version of David Copperfield back into English. By looking at the book I observe that I turned the hard words into shorthand in the margin, and now I can't read that. Mrs. Egli cooked my steak by frying it in a tin pieplate on top of the stove. Otherwise this very bright lady is but a vague recollection. Came later Mrs. Britton, an actress, who was a Grahamite, with prejudices against bakers' bread. To convert me she once made a batch of Graham biscuits. Not being a good judge of quantity, she mixed dough enough to make half a peck of them, and baked it all. When fresh from the oven the Graham biscuits were assimilable; when cold they had the resistance of the packing that is put on a horse's foot under the shoe to protect the frog. To utilize them I set a plateful by the window to shy at cats frequenting the roof of the Charities and Corrections building just below. From this I was compelled to desist when the janitor came up through the hatch, and having examined the tin where I had made a hit, looked accusingly in my direction. Mrs. Britton removed my ammunition. Not seeing the biscuits again on the table, I asked for them; but Mrs. Britton said she had given them to the man who brought the kindling-wood. He had thanked her, too, saying he could feed them to his horse. He never came back, and I suspected, without imparting my suspicions to the lady, that the horse had not got the better of the biscuits.

2—A DISTURBING CHURCH

On Twelfth street there was and now is St. Ann's church, one of the miracle-joints where they hold novenas and expose, for the healing of the faithful, an alleged bone of St. Ann. That church had the worst bell I ever heard. The body of the the church extended deep into the backyard space, and the noise of the bell came in at my windows with such an irritating effect that I was obliged to emit a rhymed objurgation and send it to St. Ann's pastor. Called "The Protest of a Disturbed Citizen," it was thus conceived:

"By heat oppressed, and disinclined to roam,
I spend the Sabbath in my humble home.
Borne to my windows, looking toward the west,
Come anthems rising to the winged and blest,
And organ's peal that quivers on the air,
The drone of human voices blending there;
The shriek of tenor, orotund of bass,
Soprano screaming in Jehovah's face,
And wail of preacher supplicating grace.
A church looms skyward, mocking Babel's height;
Through windows stained pours in the varied light;
An uncouth tower, offensive to the eye,
Gives shelter to a bell whose agony
Finds voice in rasping and sepulchral sound
That grates the nerves of all the dwellers round.

O pile of brick and monumental stone,
Thou'rt reared of martyrs, from their blood and bone;
For every brick a sacred life they gave,
And for each stone some hero found a grave.
The window-panes that tint the sunlight's flood
Have caught their hue from sacrificial blood;
The chime, the chant, and mammoth organ's tone,
Seem echoes from a dying martyr's groan.
Nuisance thou art to deity or man,
Thou church of God Almighty and Saint Ann."

3—HEALTH EXERCISES AND A VACATION

While I was taking one of my infrequent vacations in New Hampshire, a demure young schoolmarm whom I had for company in my rides about the country said to me that she supposed I took advantage of the opportunites which city life affords for being naughty. And when I answered with dignity touched with indignation that I did nothing of the kind, she replied: "Well, if I lived there you bet I would." But in the days now being recalled I was potipharically speaking a Joseph, though taking little credit therefor, since I never had to slip out of my coat to get away. My membership in the Nonpareil Rowing Club had lapsed before 1884. The literary game was more to me than sport on the Harlem, if not so stimulating to health. I came to New York weighing 160 pounds. In the spring of '84 I weighed 145; had a pain in my chest, and a cough tinted pink. My maternal guardian, taking the situation under advisement, recommended that I should go out more evenings, that I should get a wife, or stop sitting up so late at night to read; meantime swinging Indian clubs would straighten the shoulders. She practiced laying poultices on my chest at night, arguing that adjacent irritation would be good for the lungs. The Indian club notion seemed best to me. On the block below us the well-known Coroner Brady had set up his son-in-law in the hardware business. As a pair of clubs were part of his window display I went there to buy them. The coroner, who happened to be present, tried to sell me a zinc washboard, bringing out a specimen, casting it to the floor, and then jumping on it with both feet to show how substantial it was and how unlikely that a woman would rub a hole in it by bearing on it too hard. His enthusiasm came near making a purchaser of me. I escaped when he said he would lay it aside till I came again; and then he followed me to the door and said in confidence that he was just trying to show his son-in-law how to sell goods.

Our living room afforded space for the swinging of clubs if mother would retire for the nonce into the kitchen. From that vantage point she watched me through the window between the two rooms. I can still see the flash of her spectacles out of the gloom beyond. To these recuperative measures I added a long vacation in the farthest reaches of the state of Maine—away off in the Aroostook (native pronunciation Aroostick, with the accent on *roos*). There lived the uncle who more than twenty years before had wanted to take me with him, and also the aunt who as the big girl Amanda Dunn had dragged me to school in Sullivan for the first time, at the age of 3. North from their house lay fifty miles of woods, and then the Canadian border. Twenty miles west arose Mt. Katahdin. We were on the east branch of the Mattawamkeag.

The first stage of the trip to Maine was made aboard the old steamboat Franconia, then plying between New York and Portland. We had aboard a dogmatic old Scotsman from Brooklyn named Matthews. He carried a Bible for light summer reading and confined himself closely to the Psalms. For a joke, I inquired whether he were consulting the Book of Jonah. He shook his head, but a few minutes later asked sternly: "Am I to understand that your question was meant to be personal and suggestive?" Before we were out of the East River our boat went into collision with the Sound

steamer Rhode Island, so that the Franconia made
the rest of the voyage with a battered nose. Arrived at Portland, this old Scot, feeling sure
that his family had read of the accident and might
want to know whether he had escaped with his life,
made haste to mail home a postal card. A few
minutes later he mailed another. I asked him why
the second one, and he explained that on the first
card he had forgotten to tell his wife he was alive.
While his conversation was very dry, his actions
provided me with amusement. The car we rode
in out of Portland had double windows. Mr. Matthews, wishful to throw away a half glass of water,
raised the inside sash and let fly; and he was bewildered when the water came back and took the
starch out of his shirt. Nearing his station, and
aiming to brush up a little, he produced a whisk
broom, removed his coat, and tried to hang the garment on the top of the open door of the car. He
stood on his toes; he even hopped into the air, in
his endeavor to make the coat stay there for him
to brush it. The top of the door was oval. He
gave the door many reproving glances as he returned to his seat. Somewhere along the journey
the hat went 'round in behalf of a boy who had
lost a leg. Mr. Matthews saw it coming and opened
his Bible. Just before the hat got to his part of
the car he closed the book and his eyes and indulged
in silent prayer which lasted until after the collection. I had supposed that kind of a Scotch Presbyterian to be a mythical figure.

At Oakfield Plantation, where I stayed a month,
there had lately been a Baptist revival and no con-

verts, as a swearing man told me on oath. This blasphemer had attended one evening and put in a request for prayers, which somehow the parson missed, so it went unheeded. The next day a neighbor inquired whether he should renew the request. He replied: "No, b'God, I shan't. Last night I was in a state of grace if any one ever was, and if the elder'd buckled down to it and prayed for me like a man, by Jesus Christ, he'd 'a' got me; but b'damned if he can get me today."

The farm of one hundred and seventy-five acres, mostly woods, where I took this vacation, had at the time a market value of perhaps five hundred dollars. In a few years the railroad came into the neighborhood; potatoes were "discovered," and the farm about 1920 sold for ten thousand. Living on farm, garden, and dairy products, with mutton when someone killed a sheep, or "beef" when an overcurious deer came too close and got shot by chance, I gained weight and forgot about my health. I have seldom thought of it since.

The following piece of poetry, which excites tender recollections, should have been inserted before unless the morality of it ought to exclude it altogether. Since such works belong not to a man's years of discretion, this will be assigned to youthful days regardless of the date it was committed:

To a Lady Who Would Not Permit Herself to
Respond to the Poet's Passion, Lest It
Might Prove Fleeting.

"Gather ye Rosebuds while ye may;
    Old Time is still a-flying,
And this same Flower that smiles today
    Tomorrow will be dying."

Since Love is Joy, how short so'er its stay,
    Why seek a fleeting passion to subdue?
The longest life we reckon but our *day,*
    We spurn not roses though their hours be few.
All things are transient—happiness or grief
    Hath morn, hath eve declining from its noon;
And things most sweet are fleetest; mark how brief
    The moment's ecstasy of love's deep swoon.
The passing passion sleeps; it never dies.
    The stars that are Her eyes, her gentle breath,
Dwell ever in the dream-world of the skies.
    "Dear as remembered kisses after death."
When Cupid knocks, throw open wide the door,
Lest Love, affronted, should return no more.

4—AFFAIRS OF THE LIBERAL LEAGUE

Messrs. Wakeman and Leland gave notice that
they should not be candidates for reelection as
president and secretary of the National Liberal
League. The Truth Seeker nominated Samuel P.
Putnam. It was also proposed that the League
drop divisive issues, like prohibition, and confine
itself to the Nine Demands of Liberalism. The
proposition was hotly debated. More than the usual
friction could be noticed between Spiritualists
and Materialists. Some of the "hard-headed" ones
seemed to exert themselves to make impossible the
cooperation heretofore practiced by the two divisions of Liberalism. The Truth Seeker took no
editorial part in that debate. The Spiritualists
were loyal and practical Secularists. After a manner, it seemed to me, they contributed to the cause
a feminine element of rare value. The women who
at a Spiritualist gathering were liable to go into a

trance and deliver an inspirational address knew how to leave out the spirits when speaking before the Liberal Leagues. The Truth Seeker carried a full column of meeting notices, about half of which were Spiritualist. Announcements of deaths were equally impartial. It was deemed no unusual thing to see a death notice begin "passed to spirit life." Twenty-five per cent. of the readers of The Truth Seeker were Spiritualists, and ninety per cent. of the Spiritualists of the country were with Bennett in his fight for free press and mails.

Other nominations for next president of the National Liberal League included George Chainey, by Putnam, with the endorsement of the Boston Investigator. No one hastened to demand that the nomination be withdrawn when the news appeared that Chainey had been converted to Spiritualism. The eighth congress of the League met, September 8 and 9, 1884, "on the grounds of the Cassadaga Lake (N. Y.) Free Association, to which it had been invited by the officers of the Association." That is to say, the hosts of the Congress were Spiritualists, and Cassadaga Lake was the Spiritualist camp-meeting ground. George Chainey had gone early, attended the camp-meeting, and to the surprise of the Liberal world experienced conversion to Spiritualism. Proceeding to a confession, he declared that "the horizon of his mind had previously been bounded by the limits of this mundane life; now his mental vision pierced beyond the grave, and in the abyss of eternity he saw gleaming the star of immortal life." His speech at the Congress demanded a reply, and a reply he got from T. B. Wakeman and Charles Watts. These speakers expressed as they would not otherwise have done their unflattering view of Spiritualism in general.

And all this on the grounds the Spiritualists had invited the Freethinkers to occupy.

I suspect that the other-world people thereupon walked out on the Congress, which then went into executive session. The Committee on Platform reported a short program inoffensive to Prohibitionists or "modificationists" of the Comstock law. The Congress proposed to change the name of the organization to the AMERICAN SECULAR UNION, elected Ingersoll president, Putnam secretary, Charles Watts first vice-president, and Courtlandt Palmer treasurer. It raised $1,200 on the spot and voted to put Putnam and Watts into the field at salaries of $1,500 each. (T.S., Sept. 20, 1884.)

Liberals who would read the story of an interesting year in the history of Freethought will consult the files of The Truth Seeker for 1884. Agitation for statehood in Utah stimulated a drive against the Mormons, who were the Bolsheviki of the period, and there was as much opposition to admitting Utah into the Union of States as ever there was to the recognition of the Soviet republic in the League of Nations. But while the Bolsheviki are said to be atheistic, the Mormons were orthodox to the point of Fundamentalism. A clergyman named Gallagher, who spoke at the Liberal Club, proposed very drastic measures for their control if not extirpation. Sanity talked back at the excited preacher in the eloquence of Stephen

Pearl Andrews. Mr. Andrews protested we could hardly spare Mormonism, which was an object-lesson on the rise and growth of religions. In reporting the meeting I must have resorted to my shorthand notebook, for the Pantarch's speech is given in full in my report of the discussion. Of the Mormon church Mr. Andrews said:

"It shows us precisely here and now the whole method and process by which a religion founded in faith in the supernatural takes its rise in the subjective illumination of a single individual. Now Mormonism has given us during the last half-century, right here, in modern time, the opportunity to witness the precise way of this immense phenomenon. One hundred years ago nobody knew or could know what we now know of the engendering, gestation, and ultimate evolution of a great religious movement. Mormonism has contributed to us that knowledge."

It followed that Buddhism, Christianism, and Mohammedanism could be accounted for in the way which the rise of Mormonism illustrated to all. It was better to observe Mormonism and learn from it, said the wise Mr. Andrews, than to destroy it.

The editor of The Truth Seeker came out strongly against the Mormon church as being, like other branches of the Christian church, a menace to the republic. He charged that the crimes of the Saints were due to their religion, and cited facts to prove it. Had Mr. Andrews lived another quarter century he would have seen the phenomena attending the rise of a religious integration repeated in Christian Science.

5—FOR THE RECORD OF 1884

Conventions were held in several states and lecturers were busy. Ingersoll spoke sixty times in three months. New organizations sprang up, among them a pioneer Freethought Club in Toronto, Canada. Helen Gardener made her first appearance as a public lecturer at Chickering Hall in January, Colonel Ingersoll presiding. The press hailed her as "Ingersoll in soprano."

We issued a fine large Truth Seeker Annual at the beginning of 1884, containing a review of the previous year and some contributed articles. It was a Freethinker's Almanac, with a calendar. Five thousand copies were sold. In this annual T. C. Leland reported that some two hundred and twenty-five Liberal Leagues had been organized.

New York State Superintendent of Public Instruction Ruggles had rendered a decision ordering the discontinuance of Bible reading in public schools. The editor of The Truth Seeker mentions the fact that the predecessors of Mr. Ruggles —John A. Dix in 1838 and John C. Spencer the year following—had issued similar orders. "We presume," the editor observes, "that as little attention will be paid to Mr. Ruggles's decision as was paid to his two predecessors' orders." This proved to be the fact.

Charles B. Reynolds, ex-Rev., who had made a good impression at the Salamanca Convention of Freethinkers in 1883, now took the field as a lecturer. George Chainey gave a Sunday evening course in New York. Remsburg visited the East and spoke at the Liberal Club. Henry Ward Beecher, having abandoned in succession the doctrines of hell, the fall of man, the atonement, and the trinity, now added to his heresies the rejection of the resurrection story. The Rev. Dr. R. Heber Newton, Episcopalian, was rebuked by Bishop Horatio Potter for destructive criticism of the Bible, and forbidden to allow Henry George to speak in his church. Oscar Straus of New York read a paper eulogistic of Thomas Paine before the Brooklyn Historical Society. Mr. Straus was heard again on the same subject before The Thomas Paine National Historical Association in 1921.

Wendell Phillips, the great antislavery agitator (b. 1811), died in February, 1884, and was eulogized as a distinguished Liberal. In February, G. W. Foote of the London Freethinker was liberated after a year's imprisonment for blasphemy. In March the Bennett Monument had been completed and an extended description published*.

---

* The monument stands at the junction of Sylvan Avenue and Osier path, Greenwood Cemetery, some ten minutes' walk from the main entrance. "It is distinguishable from the other monuments in the vicinity by its massive proportions and severe plainness." Its total height is thirteen feet, six inches; the cost, some $1,500, made up of contributions by "one thousand friends." Dedicatory services were held at 220 East Fifteenth street, June 13, 1884. The Truth Seeker of June 28 reported brief addresses given and the fine oration by T. B. Wakeman. The same number of the paper printed a beautiful full-page picture of the monument, the work of the Moss Engraving Company, which by a coincidence is now making the pictures which appear in these reminiscences.

It diverts me now to observe that the companionate form of marriage is quite old in principle. In April, 1884, at Dover, N. H., a man and a woman appeared before a clergyman and asked him to marry them for six months. The groom explained that a previous marriage that he contracted for life had ended in divorce and he didn't purpose to take any more risks. The lady, confident it would be renewed, was willing to enter into the limited contract. The minister withheld his approval, as did a justice of the peace. As another instance, there had been a companionate marriage in 1877 between Mrs. H. S. Lake, a Liberal lecturer, and Prof. W. F. Peck, the parties agreeing to continue it "so long as mutual affection shall exist." The Massachusetts Supreme Court five years later, when Mrs. Lake asked for a separation, decided that such a contract required no divorce proceedings to terminate it.

Before Paul Carus ever was known as Dr., or had married a fortune and begun the publication of the monthly Open Court to expound "the religion of Science," that intelligent and learned German spoke before the Manhattan Liberal Club on "Education and Liberty," or, as he gave us the more comprehensive title, "Wohlstand, Freiheit und Bildung." He observed that the English language contained no equivalents of these terms. Dr. Carus lived and died loyal to the Kaiser, and during the World War his Freiheit was gravely menaced by the Espionage Act.

An editorial article in The Truth Seeker of July 26 began: "At her home in St. Cloud, N. J., on

Sunday, July 13, after suffering for several years with consumption, Jennie Macdonald, wife of E. M. Macdonald, passed to her rest." Jennie had been a singer. "She sang," the article reads, "at Chickering Hall when thousands gathered to welcome home the founder of The Truth Seeker; at Watkins, when the Freethinkers went there to their annual meeting; at all our League meetings here; and at home she filled her house with music like the warbling of a bird." That was so. No babies ever had sung to them sweeter lullabies than hers. She lost one baby by death when it was a year or two old. That led her to ponder the question, whether it would live again. And Mr. Bennett, who had been but a short time dead, would he not, she inquired, find her little babe and care for it there as she knew he would in this life if it had no other friend? How could a man answer that question from a dying woman? I said to Jennie that one of two things was undoubtedly true— either that her baby was with the Doctor over yonder, or it had passed beyond the reach of harm or need of care.

Jennie was a Southern girl who came to New York as a concert singer. Her singing voice, which might have made her a reputation had it been trained, took the grades without effort. She could sustain B flat with a smile. The features of many singers wear a look of agony while holding that note.

Among the 1884 obituaries was that of John P. Jewett (b. 1816), the original publisher of "Uncle Tom's Cabin"—a Freethinker, a cordial friend of

D. M. Bennett, and a caller at the office when in town. He was a native of Maine, and a resident of Orange, N. J., at the time of his death.

Philip G. Peabody advocated in The Truth Seeker the adoption of cremation in place of earth burial.

The Freethought Association of Canada, which in December held a largely-attended convention in Toronto, affiliated with the National Liberal League. Mr. William Algie of Alton erected a Freethought hall, contemporaneously dedicated to the cause. The speakers at the dedication were Mr. Algie, William McDonnell, author of "Exeter Hall," Charles Watts, and Samuel P. Putnam.

The Nineteenth Century published the historic debate on religion between Herbert Spencer, Agnostic, and Frederic Harrison, Positivist. When The Truth Seeker had reprinted the discussion, Stephen Pearl Andrews intervened to reconcile the antagonists. The Pantarch was given to the use of unusual words. This essay on Spencer and Harrison, being so marked, drew the following letter from "A Spencerian Positivist" (William Henry Burr) of Washington, D. C.

"A SLANDER NAILED."

"To the Editor of The Truth Seeker: In his communication last week Mr. Stephen Pearl Andrews characterizes Auguste Comte as a 'comprehensive agglomerative conceptualist,' and intimates that Mr. Herbert Spencer is no better. The charge furnishes ground for an actionable cause against the publishers. So far as is known, the character of Mr. Spencer's mother is above reproach. Let the politicians have a monopoly of slander."

The Andrewsian phrase "comprehensive ag-glomerative conceptualist" is seldom paralleled. However, one may cite a near approach to it by the Hon. John M. Robertson, who, quoting Pope on Bacon, "the wisest, brightest, meanest of man-kind," remarked on "the monstrous parallogism of the collocation."

The League organ, Man, suspended in the fall of 1884, and The Truth Seeker took over its assets with the exception of its boom for Ben Butler, who was running for President with the sanction and encouragement of Mr. Wakeman. Just before the election, James G. Blaine, the Republican candi-date, was Burcharded. I quote my report of the incident:

"Blaine received the benefit of the clergy at the Fifth Avenue Hotel last week, being waited upon by a committee of about two hundred Protestant ministers. The chairman, the Rev. Dr. Burchard, assured Mr. Blaine that they were loyal to him, and had no sympathy with the opposite party, which had always been the party of RUM, ROMANISM, and REBELLION. Mr. Blaine thanked the reverend gentlemen for this sympathy, and challenged the world to point out an act of his own or of the party he represent-ed that could not receive the sanction of the clergy, the church, and the Almighty." (T.S., Nov. 8.)

The political referees decided that Burchard had beaten Blaine. Owing to disillusionment regarding the merits of his party's candidate, Colonel Inger-soll took no share in the campaign. In the course of a lecture in Chicago he put the question: "What minister has ever done as much for the world as Darwin?" and when a voice sang out "Burchard!" he joined in the laugh that followed.

The ministers were for Blaine, and he lost. They were against Grover Cleveland, who won. They opposed Cleveland on moral grounds, assuming as true the campaign story which they aided in circulating, fixing upon him the guilt of bastardy. The Truth Seeker said: "These clerical gentlemen flooded the country with obscene literature, slandered candidates without stint, and while ostensibly working for morality, did more to corrupt the public mind than all the literature Comstock has been able to suppress." The New York World put it felicitously thus: "Slander was backed by sanctity; defamation and regeneration walked hand in hand; lying and praying mingled. The 'family purity' dodge was practiced by those [the clergy] who have, unfortunately, contributed their full share to family impurity." In the end Cleveland's one effective clerical helper was Henry Ward Beecher. Mr. Beecher had at first refused to endorse him, on the grounds alleged, but came around to his support with the powerful argument that if every man in New York who had broken the seventh commandment once, twice, or even thrice, should vote for Mr. Cleveland, he would carry the state by two hundred thousand majority.

CHAPTER XVIII.

1—GIORDANO BRUNO'S PHILOSOPHY.

THE year 1885 starts with the item that Dr. Woodrow has been removed from the faculty of the Presbyterian Theological seminary at Columbia, South Carolina, for teaching that the Bible can be reconciled with the theory of evolution. Dr. Woodrow was a mistaken prophet, for the reconciliation has become more hopeless with the years; but he had the spirit to retort on the trustees of the seminary that they might take their places with the Wesleyans who only a century before had declared that anybody disbelieving in witchcraft denied the truth of the Bible.

This year began the raising of a fund to erect at Rome a statue to Giordano Bruno, the Italian philosopher, father of pantheism, who had been burnt at the stake as a heretic in 1600. The first subscriber to the fund was George N. Hill of Boston, who shared with T. B. Wakeman the glory of proposing a new calendar, to wit, the Era of Man, beginning with the death of Bruno.

This martyr to Freethought, Giordano Bruno, was born at Nola, Italy, in 1548. His name was Filippo. The name of Giordano was adopted when he became a Dominican monk. He had a theory of his own

371

about the infinite, and once made the dangerous remark that a priest could be in more profitable business than contemplating the seven joys of the Virgin Mary. He also hinted that the theory of transubstantiation was to a certain degree absurd. Only his youth preserved him from the inquisitors. Finally, on account of his outspoken heresy, Italy waxed too tropical for him, and he turned wanderer, supporting himself at one time by teaching, at another time as a proof-reader. He taught grammar to the young and astronomy to the men. At Milan he became the intimate friend of Philip Sydney, whom he afterward saw in England. At Geneva he met with no better reception from the Protestants than he had found with Catholics at Rome. He therefore journeyed to France, to Lyons and thence to Toulouse. At this latter place he had the audacity to remark that the earth revolved continuously and persistently upon its axis. The Aristotelians tackled him upon this subject and he was obliged to flee. From one place to another he went, either led by his desires or forced by the enmity of the church, until in 1593 he was placed in the dungeons of the Inquisition. Seven years later, being condemned to die for heresy, it was ordered that he should be put to death without the shedding of blood, which meant the stake. He informed his judges that they inflicted the sentence with more fear than he received it. A crucifix was held up before him as he stood bound to the stake, Feb. 17, 1600; he told them to take it away. He was burned to ashes and his dust scattered to the winds.

I take this little sketch of Bruno from my report of a lecture before the Manhattan Liberal Club, October 30, 1885, by the Scotch-American philosopher, Thomas Davidson (1840-1900), who was himself a good deal of a Bruno and expounded a philosophy as baffling as Bruno's own. And judge by this what a heretic he was: "Giordano Bruno, said the lecturer, was a greater savior and nobler martyr than Christ. The crucified Galilean did not suffer a tithe of the torture endured by Bruno, and with his latest breath he inquired why God had forsaken him. Bruno died composed; having a God within, he knew that God would not forsake him unless he forsook himself. Incidentally the lecturer remarked that the church claimed to be the representative of the theological God, and the worst thing to be said about the church was that it represented him very faithfully."

Professor Davidson's interpretation of the philosophy of Bruno may be regarded as authoritative (or should I say "authentic"?). Knowing that the more I said about it the greater number of errors I should fall into, I merely observed in my report that it "consisted of being, process, and result"; that different philosophers had taken up separately the three postulates of Bruno, and had founded a system on each of them. For instance, Hegel's philosophy was that of pure being; Leibnitz's of process, and Spinoza's of result. Twenty years later I composed an extended biography of Bruno for "A Short History of the Inquisition."

It was as reporter of the proceedings of the Liberal Club that, as heretofore stated, I came to be

called the Man with the Badgepin. Mr. Otto Wettstein, the Liberal jeweler of Rochelle, Illinois, had
just designed and introduced that emblem, which
I have worn ever since.

2—WERE NOT THESE FEMINISTS?

Rereading the reports of this famous Club's affairs, one realizes how little there is which is new
to reformers of advanced age. Woman speakers in
rational dress appeared on its platform, and the garments of 1928 were advocated. Mrs. King, who
spoke at the first meeting of the new year on
"Rational Dress Realized," would have been in style
today had she omitted her "pants," which descended
a few inches below her short skirt. But Mrs. King
foresaw the day when the skirt would disappear and
only the trousers be retained. Mrs. Leonard made
a better guess by saying the short skirt would come
but the trousers would be dispensed with. "There
was no reason," Mrs. Leonard implied, "why the
great works of nature should be concealed." The
ladies refused to consider the objections of men.
Mrs. King would reassure the men by suggesting
that if they feared to be shocked they might put on
"blinkers." That was forty years before the girls
of Somerset, Pennsylvania, issued their declaration:

"We can show our shoulders;
We can show our knees,
We are freeborn Americans,
And can show what we please."

All the eccentric personages of any note came to see us at The Truth Seeker office. Have I mentioned Mary Tillotson, who risked arrest by wearing bloomers on the street? She never missed us when in the city, and was an occasional contributor. A less conspicuous person was Mrs. Vosburgh, a woman who, like Joanna Southcott, manifested the virgin-mother complex. Presumably disappointed in her hope, Mrs. Vosburgh soon retired from view. Dr. Mary Walker was much better known and had a longer career. She frankly wore clothes in the similitude of male garments, topped with a high silk hat. If I am not mistaken she suffered arrest, but vindicated herself by arguing that the clothes she wore were not a disguise. Moreover, she declared she would "wear trousers or nothing," so that on the whole it was deemed advisable to let the doctor have her way.

3—THE TRUTH SEEKER'S HEATHEN.

We had a compositor unique among New York printers—an educated Hindoo named Amrita Lal Roy, a non-graduate of Edinburgh University. Amrita was a good compositor and moreover spoke and wrote English with precision. In religion he was pagan. In one of my sixth-column editorials I brought him to the attention of the Baptist Foreign Missionary Society, which was boasting, in a report on results, that it had made more converts among the heathen than all other denominations by their united efforts. To convert a heathen to Episcopalianism, so the Baptist Society urged, cost on an average, as statistics showed, not less than $592.03; to Congregationalism, $248.14; Presbyterianism, $224.91; Methodism, $117.91; Campbellism, $72.88; but Baptists were bringing them into the fold at $37.05 per convert.

Casting doubt on its being worth even that sum to a heathen to be turned into a Baptist, this is the proposition I caused The Truth Seeker to put before the missionaries:

"To tell it just as it is, we do not believe that a heathen can be converted to Christianity for $37.05, and to afford them an opportunity of testing the matter, we will make the Baptists an offer. We have in this office, bowing down to the wood of his case and the stone of the imposing slab, a full-blooded royal Bengal Heathen. He is of high caste, ranks next to the Brahmans for style, and bears credentials to that effect. He is without religion, neither drinking intoxicants nor smoking or chewing tobacco. He does not swear by heaven above nor by the earth below. Jehovah and Jesus Christ rank in his mind along with the mythical Giascutis and the apocalyptic Boojum Snark. There is but one obstacle to his becoming a Christian, and that is the fact that he is well educated, and has probably in his comparatively brief existence forgotten more than the ordinary minister ever learns. We say this without meaning to impeach the retentiveness of his memory. He is conversant with Greek and Latin, and with Sanskrit, Begalee, and Telegoo, besides writing English of the purest kind. In disposition he has the mildness peculiar to his race, and buckles down to reprint or the Spencerian copy of Mr. Charles Watts with equal humility. Taken all in all, he is a rare heathen. We could scarcely conceive of a more desirable subject for the proselyting zeal of a missionary.

"What we propose is to throw open the door of our composing-room and give the Baptist missionaries a chance at this heathen. If he has a soul that is likely to be d—d, we would by all means prefer that it should be saved. It is a sad sight to see a pagan of his mental caliber going down the dark valley unprepared and neglecting the means of grace.

"The financial arrangements for the test are immaterial, perhaps, but it is well to have everything done decently and in order. Let the Baptists deposit $37.05 with some responsible person; we will do the same. The heathen may be allowed $3 per day for his time; the missionary 50 cents. Heathen and money to be found any day at 33 Clinton Place. If by the time the sum of $37.05 has been exhausted the heathen shall have knocked under and consented to be baptized, the Baptists take the money. If. on the other hand, he still remains the heathen that he is, we take the cash.

"We urge our brethren of the Baptist denomination to come forward and prove their claim to converting heathen at $37.05 per head. Our heathen, so to speak, is white unto the harvest, to say nothing of the other compositors who might casually experience. a change of heart. Here is a soul for ministers to save, and we presume, in the words of the immortal Webster Flannagan, that is what they are here for."

Amrita Lal Roy remained a heathen. He wrote a number of excellent articles for The Truth Seeker, and for John Swinton's paper, and sold one to The North American Review.

I have before mentioned John Swinton and the paper bearing his name. The Truth Seeker had numerous occasions to chasten Mr. Swinton for suppression of the fact that many of the men whom he honored with his notice were Freethinkers. That designation did not appear at all in Mr. Swinton's paper. One would sooner expect to see it today in the New York Nation. And still, when subscrib-

ers were coming in slowly, Mr. Swinton's friend,
Madame Henri Delescluze, took the platform at the
Liberal Club and canvassed the audience for recruits. She got twenty of them, and in acknowledging the favor said she "would make the labor unions
blush for their lukewarmness when she recounted
to them the generosity of the Freethinkers." It has
always been the weakness of Freethought societies,
or perchance it is to their praise, that they invariably have been hospitable to outsiders who had no
further interest in them than to secure their help.
Freethinkers in those days as in these were often
accused, falsely, of being as narrow-minded as the
orthodox. Mr. Swinton was asked in The Truth
Seeker to make the test as to who were his friends
by requesting the use of a New York pulpit in which
to plead for support of his paper. As for open-
mindedness, as between the Liberal Club and the
labor unions, that might have been ascertained by
applying for a chance at one of their meetings to
canvass for a Freethought paper.

The evening just referred to was the one at which
John E. Remsburg gave his lecture on "Sabbath
Breaking," and Madame Delescluze had the grace
to object to all he said and to defend Sabbath observance! Mr. Swinton was the lecturer at the next
meeting of the Club.

4—PRIEST LAMBERT'S BOOK.

A Catholic priest named L. A. Lambert of Waterloo, N. Y., wrote a book called "Notes on Ingersoll"
which was so cordially received by the Christian

world as the finishing blow for the blasphemer that
its author became boastful. Freethinkers had paid
small attention to the performance; but when Lambert's organ, The Catholic Union and Times, edited
by a priest named Cronin, made the statement that
their silence was due to their inability to answer the
Waterloo priest, The Truth Seeker challenged him
to debate the matter with Charles Watts. Lambert
declined on the ground that an oral discussion gave
too much room for blasphemous declamation on the
part of the Infidel. However, if Mr. Watts would
publish his side of the debate in The Truth Seeker,
then Dr. Lambert would reply through the same
medium. The editor at once accepted, with the
proviso that the articles by both Mr. Watts and the
priest should be published simultaneously in The
Truth Seeker and in The Catholic Union and Times.
To this perfectly fair offer no response came from
the boasting editor and priest. It met with the
same joyless reception that a similar one would get
today from a Fundamentalist journal asked to print
one of the Truth Seeker's Fundamentalist-Atheist
debates.

The mendacity of the Lambert book would surprise and abash any common liar who could understand it. A religious person recommended it to
my notice and I secured a copy which I carefully
read, and having done so wrote my opinion of Lambert. It ran: "On questions of fact he is mali-
ciously and I think knowingly dishonest. As to
scriptural quotations, he forces into them meanings
which the authors could not have designed to convey, and denies to them the interpretations which

anyone can see the writers intended should be made. Having by these methods formulated replies to Colonel Ingersoll's statements, he crowns mendacity with audacity and challenges his opponent to answer him. In nearly every case where opportunity is afforded for a direct issue, Lambert has saved his cause only by direct or indirect falsification of the authorities which he quotes. I say nearly every case. I mean every case which access to the records has permitted me to examine. I believe that his statements are not to be relied upon in any instance. He who runs may read his arguments and detect their fallacy without pausing to give them a second reading. In proportion to its size, Lambert's 'Notes on Ingersoll' probably contains more sophistry, more captious criticism, more misstatement of fact, and, in a word, more slush, than any other volume printed during the present century. It will no more bear replying to than a sieve will hold water."

That was my opinion when I read the book in 1885, and I presume it is right. I place much confidence in first impressions.

5—THE DYNAMITERS.

The disturbers later more frequently called anarchists, or propagandists by deed, were in the early '80s known as dynamiters. There was O'Donovan Rossa, an Irishman, who reaped profitable publicity as a dynamiter until a woman with the attractive name of Lucille Yseulte Dudley came by and missed several shots at him with a pistol. A Washington newspaper headed its account: "Woman Empties

Four Chambers at Irish Agitator." Mr. Rossa seems soon to have subsided: the woman, after an amusing trial, was acquitted as irresponsible.

A dynamiter who made himself known to Liberals by joining their societies and appearing at congresses was William J. Gorsuch. Gorsuch attended the Milwaukee Congress of the League as a Freethinker with Socialist and anti-prohibitionist leanings. In '85 he came out as a dynamiter and was the English speaker at a New York meeting of Herr Johann Most and his followers in commemoration of one Reinsdorf, whom the German government had put to death for attempting to remove a crowned head. My brother and I were present at this meeting and were entertained with beer by Herr Most. There was much blood-curdling oratory in advocacy of destroying by "blind, brutal, barbaric force," within the week next ensuing, all the existing governments of the world. The dynamiters were known as Internationals. Reporting a call by Gorsuch at The Truth Seeker office, the editor wrote:

"In religion, Mr. Gorsuch told us, the Internationals are about half Atheists and half Christians. But the Atheists among them never attend Freethought meetings, read no Freethought papers or books, of course take no interest in constructive Liberal work, and remain Atheists for the same reason the French peasant did— 'If there were a God, he would give us bread, wouldn't he?' Not getting bread, the peasant was an Atheist."

A later note reads: "There was a meeting of dynamiters at Paris the other day called the Council of Eleven. Three American delegates were present. During their deliberations one of the American delegates wanted to 'embrace the occasion' to say that they (the dynamiters) were not Atheists."

Gorsuch achieved arrest at Newburg, near Cleveland, Ohio, in July, for advising strikers to put dynamite on the street car tracks and blow the cars to pieces. He appears not to have been prosecuted, for in August he spoke at a workingmen's meeting, when he exhorted his hearers to "arm themselves with rifles, visit the warehouses, and take whatever they wished, shooting down all who opposed them." He had spoken before the Manhattan Liberal Club advocating these sentiments without creating a ripple. The old Club was not a place where a speaker could talk utter nonsense and not have the defects of the presentation made clear to him. Dr. R. G. Eccles, a Brooklyn member, qualified as a specialist in the treatment of certain forms of delusion. The Liberal League of Chicago appeared to be less fortunate in the handling of its menaces, and a not good-natured discussion was had over the policy of excluding them. "Dynamiters" were the heralds and prophets of the Haymarket tragedy that was on its way. Had Gorsuch been in Chicago at the time of the bombing of the police he undoubtedly would have suffered with the four who were hanged. But the nerve of Gorsuch failed him. He abandoned his radicalism, struck his colors, and got a kind of religion, and the last time I saw him, say in 1920, he told me he was writing a book to "expose" Ingersoll.

An apostasy took place among the Freelovers that went unnoticed in The Truth Seeker because the

male party to it was pious. About 1875, one Leo
Miller, then of New York, free, white, and married,
entered into illegal conjugal relations with Martha
or Mattie Strickland, spinster. They suffered a certain martyrdom for their principles, being jailed,
and were canonized by the social radicals. Then in
1885, Miller, under conviction of sin, dissolved the
union and published a letter in The Sun confessing
marriage to be a divine institution established by
our heavenly father.

5—THE DEPARTING VETERANS.

The leaders of Liberalism were lessened in num-
ber during 1885 by the death of Porter C. Bliss,
J. S. Verity, Theron C. Leland, LaRoy Sunderland,
T. W. Doane, and Elizur Wright. This was the
year also of the death of General Grant and Victor
Hugo.

The death of Mr. Bliss took place in February.
He was a journalist, explorer, archeologist, historian, and Freethinker. His Liberal editorial work
on the New York Herald has been mentioned. In
philosophy, he was a Positivist. Mr. Verity died
in Lynn, Mass., February 10, at the age of 62.
Horace Seaver conducted his funeral in Paine Hall,
which was draped in mourning. Verity was an
able, useful, and much respected member of the
Boston Liberal Club, and a good writer. T. W.
Doane, who died in Boston, August 8, at the age of
34, was the scholarly author of "Bible Myths and
Their Parallels in Other Religions."

Elizur Wright   *T. C. Leland*

Theron C. Leland died June 3 of this year at the age of 64. The rudiments of knowledge came to this farm boy without effort on his part and his first consciousness of himself included being able to read. At eighteen, he entered the Wesleyan Seminary at Lima, N. Y., being graduated with highest honors. But the virus didn't "take," and we find him soon afterward an ardent convert to Fourierism in which he became expert as he did in everything he undertook. So much so that he developed into an expounder of this social philosophy and it was while lecturing upon it that he came to know A. F. Boyle, the partner of Stephen Pearl Andrews in the teaching of phonography, or shorthand. Leland speedily gained first rank in the winged art. He in turn taught phonography to men who themselves became experts. Among those whose speeches he reported were Daniel Webster, Rufus Choate, and William Lloyd Garrison.

The year 1851 was marked by the arrival of Kossuth, the great Hungarian statesman-refugee, whose statue was in 1928 unveiled in New York. Leland attended his receptions, taking notes for the New York Tribune and Courier and Enquirer. A list of his engagements as stenographer shows that he stood almost above and beyond the heads of his profession. The frequent mention of Leland in these pages indicates how active he was in the Liberal movement. With Wakeman he conducted the League organ, "Man," devoting all his daytime to that and the secretaryship, and supporting himself by teaching evening schools of shorthand. His wife was Mary A. Leland, a woman of no small literary capacity, and a natural poet, whose gift has descended to her daughter, Grace D., best known to Truth Seeker readers for her "Ingersoll Birthday Book," and as the life-partner of the editor for more than a few years of a national Freethought weekly published hereabouts. Leland was a wonderfully bright and witty man, of buoyant spirits and a sense of humor that constantly bubbled over. A birdman, gay, active, and swift. But deep and serious withal, a valiant fighter and a rock in time of trouble.

Elizur Wright, who several years held the office of president of the National Liberal League, and had come to be called the Nestor of Liberalism, died in Boston, Dec. 21, 1885.

Mr. Wright was born in South Canaan, Conn., on Feb. 12, 1804. He was graduated at Yale College in 1826, and for two years was a teacher in Groton, Mass. From 1829 to 1833 he was professor of mathematics and natural philosophy in Western Reserve College, Hudson, Ohio. In

1833 he came to New York, and was for five years secretary of the American Antislavery Society, editing, in 1834-5, a paper called Human Rights, and in 1834-8 the Quarterly Antislavery Magazine. He went to Boston in 1838, becoming editor of the Massachusetts Abolitionist. In 1846 he established the Chronotype, which he conducted until it was merged in the Commonwealth in 1850, of which he was also for a time the editor. From 1858 to 1866 he was insurance commissioner of Massachusetts, and was thereafter connected with insurance interests. Mr. Wright published, in 1841, a translation in verse of La Fontaine Fables, a work entitled "A Curiosity of Law" in 1866, and many pamphlets and reports. The part taken by Mr. Wright in the antislavery contest was conspicuously heroic and the black race of America owes to but few men more than to him. After the abrogation of slavery, Mr. Wright devoted himself largely to the discussion of Freethought.

In the latter part of 1884, following the defection of Chainey and the controversy it engendered, the Spiritualist papers and some of their contributors announced that the hour had struck for the separation of Spiritualism from Liberalism. In June, 1885, the Banner of Light declared:

"It is time Spiritualism obtained a full and absolute divorce from what is miscalled Liberalism, says the Spiritual Offering—and we have about come to the same conclusion. Spiritualists offered them the right hand of fellowship in opposing bigotry and superstition, but they have of late ignored it by traducing our mediums in public, in private, and in the columns of their newspapers, and calling us all delusionists! This is a quality of Liberalism we do not understand. No wonder The Offering wants the two divorced."

The editor of The Truth Seeker, commenting upon this, saw no reason for the separation. "Liberalism," he argued, "is not particularly Materialistic any more than it is Spiritualistic." Moreover,

he thought that the space in the Liberal papers given
to the discussion of Spiritualism had been about
equally divided between those in favor of it and
those opposed. However, there was a difference.
The Spiritualists were less dogmatic than certain
of the hardboiled Materialists like Otto Wettstein,
T. Winter, and Dr. Titus L. Brown, who could not
view the other-worlders as anything but a deluded
lot of victims of their own credulity and the trickery of their mediums. The first of these writers
always signed "T. Winter, Materialist," as though
a man might be under suspicion of being something
else unless he labeled himself, and the matter of
his communications was uniformly offensive to
such Spiritualists as might be readers of The Truth
Seeker, and these were not few in number.

6—FOR THE RECORD OF 1885

Someone proposed to the ex-Rev. C. B. Reynolds,
who had become an effective Freethought lecturer,
that he should travel with a tent as a Liberal evangelist. He seized upon the idea, and through The Truth
Seeker raised the needed funds. William Smith of
Geneva, N. Y., paid for the tent with a contribution of $300.

In Mr. R. B. Butland of Toronto the Freethinkers
found an excellent reporter of their activities. They
held a well-attended convention in Albert Hall,
Toronto, in December, 1884, at which eleven local societies were represented (T. S., Jan. 19) ; Mr. J. Ick
Evans was elected president, Mr. Butland secretary,
and the name changed from the Freethought Association to the Canadian Secular Union.

The Museums of Art and Natural History in New York—the former in Central Park, the latter just outside of it on the west—had been closed on Sunday. The park commissioners passed a resolution to open them. Then ensued a fight, the obstructionists being the soap man Colgate, who was a trustee; Morris K. Jesup, and the Rev. Dr. John Hall. In cooperation with Samuel P. Putnam, secretary of the National Liberal League, The Truth Seeker printed and circulated a petition supporting the commissioners and asking for the Sunday opening. The long contest that following brought public attention to the question and in the end the closers were defeated. That was one case where Liberalism won. How many Sunday visitors to the museum know to whom they are indebted for the opening of the doors?

The suggestion of a reader that the Society of the Religion of Humanity hold regular meetings and install T. B. Wakeman as "pastor" met with approval by the editor, who added: "Let us have a temple without a priest; religion without theology; morality without dogma; a social organization that meets the emotional and artistic wants of the people without degrading their mental faculties by a blind faith." The idea was to some extent realized the following year.

A paragraph in the same number announces the removal of "Mr. Replogle and his wife" from the editorship of the Missouri Liberal, the paper established at Liberal, Mo., by G. H. Walser, founder of the town. "The Liberal," says the paragraph, "opens war on the Freelovers, announcing that it

has in preparation a series of articles against them."
This course divided the town of Liberal against itself with injurious results.

Besides Ingersoll, the active Liberal lecturers
regularly reporting to The Truth Seeker in '85 were
S. P. Putnam, C. B. Reynolds, Charles Watts, Helen
H. Gardener, E. C. Walker, W. S. Bell, W. F.
Jamieson, J. L. York, Mattie P. Krekel, and J. E.
Remsburg. In the three years since he left the
school room as teacher for the field as lecturer,
Remsburg had traveled nearly fifty thousand miles
and had delivered from one to twenty lectures in
one hundred and fifty cities and towns.

A well attended convention of New York State
Freethinkers at Albany was reported in The Truth
Seeker of September 19; the Canadian convention
at Toronto in the October 3 number. A new weekly
called The Rationalist appeared in Auckland, N. Z.

The report of the proceedings of the New York
Liberal Club on the occasion of the inauguration
of T. B. Wakeman as president gave the following
brief history of the club: This organization was
started by seven persons, including Mr. Wakeman,
who met in a little hall in Third avenue, Sept. 14,
1869. Henry Edger was one of the prime movers.
T. D. Gardener was the first secretary, and J. D.
Bell the first president. The second president was
Horace Greeley, who presided at several meetings
and presided at a dinner while candidate for President of the United States. The next president,
W. L. Ormsby, gave place to James Parton. Mr.
Wakeman's election as Parton's successor took place
in the spring of 1885.

Judge Hoadley, running for Governor of Ohio, engaged in a debate with his opponent, Foraker, who attacked the judge's well-known views on the separation of church and state and the exclusion of God from the Constitution. Foraker won the election.

At the annual congress held in Cleveland, Ohio, October 9-11, the National Liberal League adopted the name of the American Secular Union, as proposed the year before and elected as officers Robert G. Ingersoll, president, and Samuel P. Putnam, secretary. A woman suffrage plank met with opposition from but one member. Ingersoll closed the meetings with a lecture. The Truth Seeker, October 17-24, reported it as the largest congress in the history of the League.

7—ENTERTAINED BY INGERSOLL—AN INTERVIEW.

In August I took part in an event which I recognized as the greatest thing that had ever happened. I interviewed Ingersoll for The Truth Seeker. With his family he was at Long Beach, New York, and included me in an invitation to S. P. Putnam to visit him at his hotel. They were supposed to talk about the affairs of the national organization, Ingersoll being president and Putnam secretary. The members of the family were assembled on the hotel veranda when we arrived. One of the young ladies, sitting by her father, arose and offered me the post, which I hesitated to accept until the Colonel drew the chair a little nearer to him and beckoned me to take it. Mrs. Ingersoll made the same provision for Putnam, and the girls, Maude and Eva, beautified the group. The Colonel asked me questions that seemed to be only such as I was prepared to answer readily. Mrs. Ingersoll gave a homy turn to the conversation by asking her husband if he had put on his heavy underclothes, according to her advice. When Ingersoll got an answer to a question he expanded upon it, as though he were just continuing the other's line of thought. His conversation was as well organized as his lectures, and he spoke as entertainingly to one as to a thousand —which is to say his thought was as clear, his words as well chosen, and his sentences as perfectly formed. I showed him a newspaper clipping of which he was the subject and inquired whether he would confirm or add to its statements, so that I might reprint it. When he had read the piece he slipped it into his vest-pocket, and said: "Let's have something original. Write out a few questions and I will answer them." And so in this manner I got an interview with Ingersoll that filled six columns—his first contribution to The Truth Seeker.

On the way home in the train Putnam expressed his admiration for the Colonel and Mrs. Ingersoll, and then fell to praising the daughters. I responded by mentioning one of them, with whom I had spoken, as certainly a lovely girl, and he declared the other one glorious.

Here is ancient history. November 7 The Truth Seeker announced: "The Rev. Mangasar M. Mangasarian, who has been pastor of the Spring Garden Presbyterian church in Philadelphia for three years, has publicly renounced the doctrines of Presbyterianism and tendered his resignation to his congregation. In his sermon he said: 'I have ceased to be a Calvinist. If Calvin, Wesley, and Edwards had the right to make articles of faith and differ with good and holy men who went before them, have I not the same right to make articles of faith and differ with Calvin, Wesley, and Edwards? I have outgrown the creed of Calvin. I shall have no creed save the words of Christ'." Mr. Mangasarian, progressively skeptical, soon surrendered the words of Christ as his creed. He does not now, in fact, believe that the Christ of Christianity is anything but a myth.

CHAPTER XIX.

1—THE MIXED ECONOMIC SITUATION.

THE Truth Seeker Company issued another Annual at the opening of the year 1886 and the paper began to be illustrated every week with Heston's cartoons, to which were added pictures by an artist named John, and with others taken from the comically pictorial French Bible. One of Heston's pictures entitled "A Contribution to the Irish Question," showing Uncle Sam putting money in the hat of Pat while Bridget handed the gifts out of the window to a priest, caused a fellow named Blissert (a sort of agitator) to promise he would see that the labor unions put the boycott on The Truth Seeker. (See T. S., Mar. 20, 1886.) Events justified the picture, for while a league of Irishmen in America were soliciting funds for their friends on the other side, the Vatican was sending a deputation to Ireland to beg funds for the erection of a church in Rome.

Agitation for the opening of the Museums in Central Park was continued by Putnam, as secretary of the Secular Union. In opposition the churches organized the New York Sabbath Committee, at a meeting of which, reported by myself, there appeared as a speaker the famous Congressman Breckinridge of Kentucky. Mr. Breckinridge will "get his" at the proper place in this record. A bill passed the Assembly appropriating $20,000 annually for the cost of Sunday opening of the museums.

Oppression of the Mormons under the Edmunds act began to take the form of persecution. Edmunds proposed that the President be empowered to appoint trustees to take charge of Mormon church property. John Swinton's paper asked, "How about trustees for other churches?" The Edmunds act provided that if any male person in a territory (this was years before the admission of Utah as a state), over which the United States had exclusive jurisdiction "hereafter cohabits with more than one woman, he shall be deemed guilty of a misdemeanor." The penalty was a fine of $300 and six months' imprisonment. The Truth Seeker said: "Supposing this law was enforced in the District of Columbia?"

A new contributor to the paper appeared with the signature of Si Slokum. He was one of those prolific writers who could turn out a good story every week for boys' papers of the Ned Buntline make and had a great number of readers. This year saw, probably, the first of the contributions of L. K. Washburn, who had begun a lectureship in Boston under the auspices of The Investigator.

Our Hindu printer, Amrita Lal Roy, left us to return to his native land. We gave him an evening of festivities called a "Chapel Send-off." A number of well-known labor leaders were present, including a Russian named Leo Hartman but known as Somoff, for whose return a large reward had been offered by the czar. Everybody made a speech and signed a testimonial. The account of the occasion closes thus: "Beyond anything that was expressed in words, the loss of Mr. Roy is felt in The Truth Seeker office; for, somehow or other, the little chap, in spite of his dusky face, had worked himself into the regard of all who associated with him." The Russian known as Somoff told the assemblage that his stay in America had banished Nihilism from his mind and he was now prepared to be a good and conservative citizen of the community. But Roy, on the other hand, had been changed from a mild Hindu to a revolutionist and he was returning to India to stir up the natives.

In December, 1887, the New York Sun reported that "the talented, learned, and gentle young Hindoo, Amrita Lal Roy . . . recently started a paper in the English language in Calcutta called Hope." His book, "Three Years Among the Americans," appeared in 1889. Said Amrita in this book: "I spent my most peaceful days in New York as a printer at The Truth Seeker office. At this date I cannot help comparing the conduct of these so-called 'Infidels' with that of the pious Christians of New York to whom I had applied for a situation on my arrival in America, very much to the prejudice of the latter. Nor can I refrain from acknowledging with gratitude that by few persons in New York were the peculiar circumstances in which I was placed so considerately recognized, or so much facility for making my way given to me, as by the Infidels of The Truth Seeker office." (T. S., March 30, 1889.)

The obstreperous dynamiters, now called anarchists, were making a good deal of trouble in the ranks of industry, especially in Chicago and Milwaukee. Discussion of the propaganda was quite continuous in The Truth Seeker, the editor holding that while their ideas were wild, their right to express them could not be denied, and he therefore denounced as an outrage the arrest of Herr Johann Most, who was advocating the policy of violent resistance to authority. The Chicago Liberal League had been obliged in self-defense to exclude them from its platform (T. S., '86, p. 359) and from membership, but in spite of these measures, the League was fired from Dearborn Hall, where its meetings had been held. In May occurred the riot at a labor meeting that has since been known as the Haymarket tragedy. A bomb was projected into a crowd and five policemen killed. It is the tradition that the police were the aggressors, the disturbers of an orderly meeting, and that they had no call to be there. The Truth Seeker said: "A mass meeting from which no riot promised to spring was in progress when the police charged upon the assemblage. In what followed the rioters were in the wrong. Even in war no nation would use such horribly murderous weapons as dynamite bombs." The editor did not live to observe what missiles were used in the World War, 1914-1918. In the News of the Week a paragraph said that "August Spies and Sam Fielden, the men who made so much trouble in the Chicago Liberal League, are in jail and liable to be tried for murder. Nothing is heard of Gorsuch in these troublous times." E. A. Stevens, president of the Liberal League, wrote that but for the fortunate ejection of the trouble-makers, the League meetings would doubtless have been prohibited and its officers arrested. Who threw the bomb was never known, but on August 19 a jury returned a verdict of murder against August Spies, Michael Schwab, Samuel Fielden, Albert R. Parsons, Adolph Fischer, George Engel, and Louis Lingg. In passing sentence Judge Gary said: "The conviction has not gone upon the ground that they did have actual participation in the act which caused the death of Deegan" [one of the policemen killed].

Somebody not known did throw the bomb. Spies, Parsons, Fischer, and Engel were ultimately hanged. Lingg committed suicide or was killed, while in jail. The police professed to know that he was the actual bomb-thrower. Fielden and a man named Neebe were sentenced to prison terms, and later pardoned by Governor Altgeld.

Early in the season Henry George began his canvass for nomination and election as mayor of New York on a Labor ticket. In April the following occurred, as I find on page 263 of The Truth Seeker:

SUPERSTITION IN THE LABOR MOVEMENT.

I followed the crowd into Irving Hall one night last week when the workingmen had their mass meeting in favor of the eight-hour system. The hall is one of the largest in the city, and it was full. It looked to me as if this ought to be a great day for the movement, and maybe it was, but I don't think so. A certain Mr. Quinn had been chosen chairman of the meeting, and when I entered he was contending for the abolition of poverty on the ground that

"God Almighty never intended for men to be poor," which was rather a novel proposition to lay before a multitude of intelligent people. The position of God on the labor question is not of the slightest importance, but it may be suggested that he would scarcely have given the assurance that the poor we would always have with us if he had intended wealth to be universal. There is nothing quite so tiresome as listening to those dogmatic persons who attribute their own conceits to God and deliver them as revelations of the divine will.

Mr. George was received with overwhelming applause, and was listened to with the closest and most respectful attention. It soon transpired from the direction of his remarks that he favored an act of the legislature which should make it a misdemeanor for an employee to work more than eight hours out of the twenty-four. Leaving in the background the fact that we already have in this state a similar law, to which no one pays the slightest attention, Mr. George went on to develop his argument in support of such a statute. And what grounds do you think he based it upon? He placed it plumb beside the Sunday laws, whose beneficence he defended with all the strength of his lungs. To the Christian sabbath, he held, which had its sanction and authority "among the thunders of Sinai," from the Creator himself, the world owed all the progress which it had achieved. Except for the Sunday laws, he argued, mankind would still be in the degraded state industrially, whatever that may have been, in which it was situated before the Sunday was established. Such was Mr. George's main argument in favor of an eight-hour law, and it is due to the intelligence of the audience to say that it was not received with marked enthusiasm. The remainder of the address was good in a general sense, but it had slight reference to the eight-hour movement.

Mr. George is one of those who hold the superstition that the religious and labor questions are one; that the ministers are the workingman's best friends, and that the Salvation Army fanaticism is of vast industrial signifi-cance.—G. E. M.

Mr. George delivered a lecture on Moses as a great statesman, political economist and law-giver, and defended Sunday laws. There should be no campaigning on Sunday, he said, except to discover the will of God. And yet he was generally supported by Liberals. Shortly after his nomination the editor of The Truth Seeker addressed to him a letter inclosing the Nine Demands of Liberalism, and inquired whether he thought his prospects of election would bear the strain that would be thrown upon them by his endorsement of these principles. Mr. George was shrewd enough as a politician to ignore the letter. The editor waited three weeks for an answer and then said: "The treatment which our letter has received at the hands of Mr. George is unworthy of a man asking the votes of the people because he is a Reformer." Mr. George's rivals for the office of mayor were Abram S. Hewitt, Democrat, described by the editor as "the fussy gentleman who refused to rent Cooper Union for the reception of D. M. Bennett when he came out of the Albany bastile"; and Theodore Roosevelt, Republican. Mr. Hewitt was elected with 90,000 votes. George had 68,000, and Roosevelt 60,000. Colonel Ingersoll, analyzing the result, said: "Several objections have been urged, not to what Mr. George has done, but to what Mr. George has thought; and he is the only candidate up to this time against whom a charge of this character could be made."

The Rev. Edward McGlynn of St. Stephen's church had been a popular orator at George's meetings, and publicly announced his conversion to the

Single Tax. The pope, assuming to be more of a political economist than Moses or George, suppressed McGlynn. This seemed inconsistent, for George contended that God owned the land, and the pope as God's representative on earth would be in a position to make terms for its occupancy.

2—LIBERAL AND SOCIAL QUESTIONS.

A quite notable occasion was the meeting for discussion, at Courtlandt Palmer's Nineteenth Century Club, between Prof. John Fiske and Chauncey M. Depew. Fiske defended a kind of deism, or near-pantheism, based on the proposition that God is "an infinite and eternal power which is manifested in every pulsation of the universe." Mr. Depew presented Fundamentalism in the manner of the best after-dinner speaker of the period. Mr. Palmer had brought there T. B. Wakeman to show the gentlemen where they got off, as it were, at. The eminence of the debaters, with the distinction of the audience present, left Mr. Wakeman powerless. He did not like to tell Professor Fiske and Mr. Depew that from his point of view they were Sunday-school scholars in the infant class. He must have longed to meet them at the Liberal Club where critics were not too reverential. He contented himself with presenting the superior claims of Positivism and the Religion of Humanity.

During this year the difficulty of maintaining freedom of opinion in a small community became apparent in the experience which the town of Liberal, Missouri, was going through. The father of the town, G. H. Walser, had been converted to Spiritualism by a tricky "medium" named Bouton, and had displaced Henry Replogle, a Materialist, as editor of his paper, The Liberal. Mr. Replogle began to print a paper of his own called Equity, devoted to the principles of libertarianism. Mr. Walser objected to Equity, first, because he did not think the town needed two papers; second, because Equity was labor reform, while he was a capitalist. Add to this the fact that Replogle advocated social freedom, and Walser had a case with which he could go before the community. He had employed a lecturer named C. W. Stewart, who, addressing a Sunday night meeting in the Opera House, proposed that the persons holding objectionable views about sex and marriage should be led to the outskirts of the town and invited to keep going. Mr. Walser indorsed the speech and called for a rising vote of approval. This brought to their feet as many as did not wish to be understood as approving of free love. Of the contrary minded, four persons arose, including Mr. Replogle. Two days later a mob attacked Replogle's house, heaving rocks, firing guns, and sticking a dagger in his front door. The demonstration divided the town. Mr. Chaapel, Spiritualist but Liberal, resigned from the editorship of Mr. Walser's paper. The disputants brought their deplorable quarrel to The Truth Seeker, July 17 and July 31. Then came the exposure of the medium Bouton, who had converted Walser and been indorsed under oath by Stewart and others, with a diagram of the premises and test conditions. (T. S., June 27, 1886.) But the exposure, occasioned by a fire in the medium's house which brought to light the devices of Bouton, was so complete that Walser himself wrote to The Truth Seeker about it, and Bouton acknowledged his deceit. That was another blow to the town of Liberal. A still harder one was delivered by the local railroad company which, itself being in the coal mining business, refused to transport Walser's coal except at discriminatory rates, and Liberal, being a coal town, suffered accordingly. Its industry was crippled. Freethinkers were compelled to sell their property and look elsewhere for employment; and as no one else would buy, they sold to Christians.

Mr. Walser's belief in spirits survived the exposure as fraudulent of the phenomena upon which it was established. Instead of returning to Rationalism he appears to have become more credulous and more fanatical. I am unable here to tell what became of Mr. Walser, except that within the past few years I have seen a pamphlet containing religious poetry of his composition that showed he was out of touch with Freethought and was as religious as a hymnbook.

Mr. Edwin C. Walker, divorced from his wife, and receiving the hand of Lillian Harman, bestowed upon him by her father, Moses Harman, suffered arrest along with Miss Harman, because they "did then and there unlawfully and feloniously live together as man and wife, without being or having been married together, contrary to the statute in such case made and provided, and against the peace and dignity of the State of Kansas." This

took place at Valley Falls, September 20. Lillian
was soon liberated. On trial in October, both
were found guilty and sentenced—he to two and
one-half months' and she to one and one-half
months' imprisonment. Mr. Walker determined to
appeal his case on the ground that the marriage
was valid. We read in The Truth Seeker, November 5:

"One of the incidents of this affair is the desertion of Mr. Walker by his old friend Tucker.
Hitherto Mr. Walker and Mr. Tucker have been
mutual admirers of each other. Mr. Tucker now
parts from Mr. Walker, sadly but firmly. Why?
Because, in claiming that his marriage is valid, Mr.
Walker submits to the state, and in so doing makes
dependants of himself and Mrs. Walker, and Mr.
Tucker will never contribute money for the vindication of the right of men and women to enslave
themselves." This union of Mr. Walker and Miss
Harman, entered into without ostentation, advertising or publicity, became the subject of a long
and interesting discussion. Because the parties to
it were associated in the publication of the paper
Lucifer, Dr. Juliet Severance named it the Lucifer
match.

"Dr. Edward Aveling, Socialist and Freethinker," says The Truth Seeker of September 18,
1886, "arrived last week from London." But that
was the sort of arrival that, like a rise in temperature, announces itself. Dr. Aveling and his lady,
who was Eleanor, daughter of Karl Marx, blew into
The Truth Seeker office one day, or should I say
blossomed? They made quite an appearance; he,

the perfect stage Englishman as done by our best comedians, with his "bowler" hat and a bit of a cane which he carried by the middle, and clothes of a pattern like a yard-square cross-word puzzle; and she in a gown conceived in the height of the Dolly Varden mode, bearing figures of bright roses nearer the size of a cabbage than anything that a rosebush could produce or support. Passers-by who saw this attractive couple enter the office waited for them to emerge, as when Dr. Mary Walker in her male attire or Mary Tillotson in pantalets would call. As they were engaged to speak for the Socialists, I wondered how the proletariat would receive persons in such gorgeous raiment. With Dr. and Mrs. Aveling came Herr Wilhelm Lieb-knecht, member of the German parliament. The Karl Liebknecht who was assassinated in the Spartacide uprising in 1919 was his eldest son. Mr. Aveling, on his return to England, wrote a book on how America struck him. It was deprecatory of our customs, habits, manners, and institutions. He spoke of the difficulty he experienced, in local option towns, in obtaining champagne, and stated that when strolling in Fifth avenue he met with more "stares" than he had encountered since he climbed the monument (for he had visited Washington).

3—STEPHEN PEARL ANDREWS.

After having been for some weeks reported absent from Liberal meetings, on account of illness, Stephen Pearl Andrews died on May 21 (1886).

The Truth Seeker said: "New York does not appreciate it, only a few know it, but the city has lost one of her greatest men. If Mr. Andrews had been a politician representing greatn e s s achieved through ways dark and devious, or if he had posed as a philanthropist w h o h a d squeezed the life-blood out of what people he could reach, and had

then given them a statue on some street corner, or a few pictures for the museum in the park, New York would be dressed in mourning. But the city has few tears for reformers and it was left for the heretics to do honor to his memory. The funeral was held at the Liberal Club rooms on Sunday afternoon, the 23d. T. B. Wakeman pronounced the oration, and the brotherhood and sisterhood of born radicals filled the hall to more than overflowing. After Mr. Wakeman had concluded, the Rev. G. W. Sampson, president of Rutgers College, spoke of his friendship for the dead man." Friends had long been aware of the close sympathy between Dr. Sampson and Mr. Andrews, and were not surprised when the clergyman appeared; but the scandalized Dr. Buckley of the Christian Advocate sternly inquired: "Can this be true?"

When Stephen Pearl Andrews passed away, he had just rounded out seventy-four years of an active and intense life. No field of thought was alien to him. Dictionaries of biography still carry, in connection with his name, the legend "eccentric philosopher." Eccentric he was, if by that appellation is meant refusal to let others do his thinking for him, or to order his actions. Perhaps the adjective "eccentric" will do as well as any for a man who liked to go where trouble was and help straighten it out. Thus we find him an active Abolitionist, and this in the southland where he stood an excellent chance of being suddenly and completely abolished himself, and he not yet thirty. He went to England in 1843 to enlist the aid of the British Antislavery Society that he might raise sufficient funds to pay for the slaves of Texas and thus make that "republic" a free state. While in England he learned phonography, becoming the founder in America of shorthand reporting substantially as we have it today. Mr. Andrews was a man of vast learning, a forceful speaker, and had a remarkable command of the philosophy of language, through which he achieved intimate knowledge of thirty-two tongues, speaking several fluently, Sanskrit, Hebrew, Greek, Latin, and Chinese among them. He came later to study the thinkers of all schools and was convinced that he had found the principles underlying them.

Stephen Pearl Andrews did more than other teacher to broaden my education. The writings of D. M. Bennett made me an unbeliever in the Bible. Ingersoll gave me Freethought touched with

emotion and adorned with beauty. From reading
and hearing B. F. Underwood I became a Materialist. Dr. W. A. Croffut saved me from embracing certain economic fallacies; Herbert Spencer led me into individualism; and Mr. Andrews
liberalized my mind so that I could look on all sorts
of conflicting views without any great amount of
astonishment or exasperation. He had charity for
all manifestations of belief, whether material or
spiritual, yet for anyone who designed by force of
law to impose religious belief or social conduct on
another he had a club, intellectually speaking. I
am thinking of him on the platform of the Liberal
Club. He was a tall man with a large frame and
a head to match. His command of language was
extraordinary, and when he employed it in denunciation he made the best choice of words. One
thought that thunder was rattling and crackling
overhead. He was very strong on social freedom,
so emphatic in fact that it was years before I could
listen to him without wishing he wouldn't say it.
The spying of neighbors on men and women's relations moved him to profanity. "That," he once
said publicly, "is none of their damned business."
I shuddered to hear him. That was long ago. In
1928 Arthur Davison Ficke, in an article "featured"
by The Outlook, which once was the Rev. Dr. Lyman Abbott's paper and had President Theodore
Roosevelt for a contributing editor, writes of that
"absolutely individual problem, marriage," and
says: "To discuss marriage in public is an essen-
tially foolish undertaking. But the necessity of doing so has been forced upon the individual, every-

where in the world, by *the prying and bullying power of the neighbors.* The thing which we call 'society' is only the neighbors. *The sooner we slap the neighbors' noses, the better for them and for us."* (Italics extra.)

That is substantially what Mr. Andrews held. As for his philosophy of Universology, I thought his language unnecessarily obscure, and said so. When he replied that only babies needed to have their food mummed for them by some old granny, I dropped that objection; still when one meets with such a phrase as "convoluto, evolutive, spiroserial progression direct and inverse," he finds the thought requires clarifying. But Universology had more contacts with the common mind than Einstein's theory of relativity, which the inventor said would not be understood by more than twelve living persons. Some previous study is necessary to the explanation of many problems. For illustration, a professor of mathematics remarks that he would not attempt to describe the cosine to a person who has no geometry. However, I once wrote for The Truth Seeker a digest of a lecture on Universology. Mr. Andrews made a trip to the office to tell me it was correct and to enlist me if he might as his interpreter, but I made excuses. I felt incompetent for the undertaking. Today I might be unable to interpret the piece that I wrote myself. After a lapse of time a student asked the philosopher Hegel to unfold the meaning of something he had said. He replied that when he wrote it there were but two who knew what it meant—himself and God; "and I have forgotten," said Hegel.

4—RANDOM OBSERVATIONS.

No fission so nearly complete had occurred forty years ago between the Freethought and economic advocacies as has since taken place. Radicalism has gone in the opposite direction, into regions where Freethought cuts no figure, and where some sort of religion prevails. We have only to compare the defense of the Chicago anarchists with that made in the Sacco-Vanzetti affair of 1927. The accused in Chicago never were suspected of being hold-up men. Fielden, a former Methodist exhorter, owned a team and carted stone. Parsons was a printer; Spies, an editor; Schwab an assistant editor, and so on. They could not be connected physically with the bomb-throwing. No one "identified" them as witnesses professed to identify Sacco and Vanzetti. The Intellectuals in those days gathered no great defense fund. The Socialists and the labor interests raised money enough to retain General Butler. I suppose The Truth Seeker, for the reason that there was no evidence whatever to connect the accused with the crime, devoted as much space, editorial and other, to the defense, as any paper then published. The prosecution was regarded as solely an assault on free speech. The "highbrow" magazines were silent or hostile, according to my recollection; but this class of magazines in 1927 and later opened their columns to the Sacco-Vanzetti partisans. I think the Chicago anarchists had the better case. I never doubted their innocence of the actual crime, which the court itself admitted.

To be friendly I carried a Socialist card and bought stamps to stick on it to show my dues were paid; and attended the Socialist and labor meetings and festivities. Seeing his name in The Truth Seeker in 1886 reminds me that at a big meeting in Cooper Union I heard a distinguished foreigner named Shevitch, who had with him on the stage the woman over whom Ferdinand Lassalle fought his fatal duel. She was a beautiful woman, a stately German blonde. I acquired a prejudice against Shevitch. The Leader, a Socialist daily started during the political canvass of that year, held a protracted fair in the Lange & Little Building, 20 Astor Place, to buy itself a press. Shevitch, a big, handsome, imposing, and even pompous person, attended, and the Socialist girls went weak in the knees when he came near them or deigned to notice them. He picked as a favorite one very pretty German girl, and buying wine induced her to drink glass for glass with him till she got fuddled, and then he took her away. I heard no criticism of him for this, but formed my own opinion. He did not bring with him to the fair the Lassalle relict, who, I heard, was a titled or aristocratic woman. The Pressmen's Union voted not to attend the Leader Fair for the reason that the press the paper intended to buy was a self-feeder and would throw a hand out of work.

The year 1886 was an uneasy one for persons who are troubled by the Friday superstition. It came in on a Friday, went out on a Friday, and the day occurred fifty-three times. Four months had five Fridays each; the moon changed five times on a Friday, and Friday was the longest and the shortest day.

The New York State Freethinkers held their annual convention, September 2-12, at White Sulphur Springs. E. M. Macdonald as treasurer reported that the association had profited from a lecture by Colonel Ingersoll to the extent of $736.50. The president of the association was Thaddeus B. Wakeman; the secretary, Mrs. F. C. Reynolds.

There were items in the paper now and then concerning the defalcation and death of Archbishop Purcell of Cincinnati. This ecclesiastic had swindled the people of his diocese out of about $4,000,-000, and his assignee, named Mannix, turned out to be no better. It happened that George Hoadley, the Freethinking ex-Governor of Ohio, had gone upon the bond of Mannix, and was mulcted for $62,000. The church itself, though also on the bond of Purcell, never settled with its dupes.

The Secularists of Canada, holding their annual convention in Science Hall, Toronto, September 10-12, reelected William Algie president and J. A. Risser secretary. Mr. R. B. Butland, a former secretary and long-time correspondent of The Truth Seeker, died during the year, bequeathing the sum of $7,000 to the Toronto General Hospital.

John Peck, the Learned Blacksmith of Naples, N. Y., became a prolific and very popular contributor to The Truth Seeker, and continued so for twenty-five years.

John H. Noyes, founder of the Oneida Community, died April 13, at 74. William Rowe, the

old Land Reformer, died June 24, aged 68. Burnham Wardwell, Prison Reformer, died October 3,
after having been supported by the charity of Freethinkers for some years. The Boston Index expired December 30.

A leaf in a scrapbook, the making of which contributed for a time to the diversion of my better
element (Mrs. M.), preserves a piece of my rhyming dated 1886.

THE OLD MAN'S CHOICE.

"There are three things of
beauty I have seen—
Three things beside
which other beauties pale.
One is a ship at sea
beneath full sail,
When all her canvas draws,
whose tall masts lean,
While in her cordage sings
the rising gale.

"The second is a field of
waving wheat,
Grown tall and bright,
and golden in the sun.
A fair young woman is
the other one,
Which ends the trio of my
graces sweet
That with the full-rigged
vessel was begun."

With four-score winters battered, bent and gray,
So spoke this man passed far beyond life's prime,
Yet answered, with a wealth of nerve sublime,
Unto my query: "Which is fairest, pray?"
"My son, give me the woman every time."
                                        G. E. M.

The theme of the verse was furnished by an old
fellow named Maxwell, met on a vacation in the

Aroostook, who asked if I knew what were the three handsomest things in the world. As I had not at that time segregated all the lovely objects to be seen, I replied that I could not name them offhand. "Well," he said, "I can. They are a ripe field of wheat, a full-rigged ship in a breeze, and a woman who is a wife; and the last one is the prettiest." I sold the poem to Puck for about half my vacation carfare.

The Freethinkers of Petaluma, Cal., established a Free Secular Library in the store of Philip Cowen, who acted as librarian. The largest contributor was William Pepper, the friend and patron of Luther Burbank, and probably the man who made an "Infidel" of the plant wizard. Mr. Pepper was a nurseryman and left large bequests to charity.

The 1886 Congress of the American Secular Union was held November 11-14, in Chickering Hall, New York. Among those attending were Robert G. Ingersoll, John E. Remsburg, Horace Seaver, William Algie (Canada), Samuel P. Putnam, Charles Watts, T. B. Wakeman, James Parton, Parker Pillsbury, Robert C. Adams, Helen Gardener, L. K. Washburn, J. P. Mendum, and Courtlandt Palmer. There are no survivors of this group, and among the delegates I find the name of but one now known to be living, Miss Kate Booth of the Boonton, N. J., Secular Union. Kate is now Mrs. George Gillen of Nutley, N. J. It was at this congress that Ingersoll gave his lecture entitled "A Lay Sermon" to an applauding house.

Ingersoll had been president of the Union for two terms, and declined a third in favor of Courtlandt Palmer. Mr. Putnam continued as secretary. I conclude from an entry by the directors that Colonel Ingersoll paid the local expenses of the Congress.

In July the earnest Christians of Boonton, New Jersey, contributed to the history of religious persecution by wrecking the tent in which C. B. Reynolds held his meetings, and then causing his arrest on a charge of Blasphemy. Reynolds was held under a bond of $400 to await the action of the Morris county Grand Jury. Mr. Edwin Warman offered bail. Ingersoll agreed to undertake the defense. On the 19th of the following October an indictment for blasphemy was placed by the Grand Jury in the hands of the district attorney. Mr. Reynolds renewed his bail and awaited the action of the court.

In March the Committee of ·Ways and Means of the New York Assembly gave a hearing on a bill to abolish the exemption of church property. Samuel B. Duryea appeared, representing the Constitution Club. T. B. Wakeman represented the American Secular Union, and Gilbert R. Hawes the Liberal Christians. The editor of The Truth Seeker, who was present, received the impression that "the real sentiment of the Assembly is in favor of this bill, but legislators have such a fear of the religious element that we cannot expect it to pass." It did not pass.

CHAPTER XX.

1—GOOD WORKERS AND WORKS OF 1887.

A DOZEN or more Freethought lecturers were in the field and were heard during the season of '87 in nearly every northern and western state. In April The Truth Seeker gives these laborers in the vineyard the following mention:

Judging from the number of papers containing favorable reports of their lectures, the Freethought missionaries in the field are not only winning fame for themselves, but are having a good effect upon the population they visit. Mr. Charles B. Reynolds is called "able and eloquent," and his manner of presenting his themes "dramatic and picturesque." Mr. Samuel P. Putnam is described as "of pleasing address and a finished orator." His style, we are told, "is cultured and refined," and his action "graceful and expressive." Mr. John E. Remsburg sustains his reputation for presenting "masses of facts in a scholarly and eloquent way," and Mr. W. F. Jamieson is set down as "eloquent and solid." Mr. W. S. Bell pleases the timid ones of the fold, because his "scholarly periods do not offend." Dr. J. L. York is very generally called the "Ingersoll of the West," and Mr. Charles Watts is reported from Canada as "holding his audience in rapt attention." He has challenged all the ministers of Toronto or of any other city throughout the Dominion, to debate with him, but so far without finding a victim. Capt. Robert C. Adams of Montreal is doing yeoman service in lecturing to the intelligent of his city and in writing letters to the Montreal journals. One of his recent letters upon the Sabbath question—which is up for discussion there—is the best, for a short review, that we have seen. Mr. J. D. Shaw, of the Independent pulpit, has taken the field in Texas, and the papers say he gives excellent satisfaction, being a "logical, forcible, and pleasant speaker." His oratory is "chaste and refined, and he wins many warm admirers. It is pleasant also to learn that he obtains many subscribers to his Independent Pulpit wherever he lectures. Of the other speakers we hear less; but Dr. Juliet Severance was a power in the recent Labor Convention at Cincinnati; E. C. Walker is fighting the best he can from behind the iniquitous bars of a Kansas county jail; J. H. Burnham occasionally emerges from his retirement at Saginaw City, Mich., and electrifies an audience; Col. John R. Kelso keeps the church stirred up around Longmont, Col.; Mrs. M. A. Freeman of Chicago speaks for all who wish, and her auditors, we are told, are more than pleased. Helen Gardener is at present living here in New York, but when she does go out the reporters hasten to throw themselves at her feet. Mrs Lucy N. Colman is warned by age not to tax her strength upon the rostrum, but her reminiscences are enjoyed by a larger audience than any grand opera house would hold. She has had her share of aged eggs and crowns of glory for her magnificent work for liberty, and now lives quietly in Syracuse. L. K. Washburn is going West, and when he gets where Liberal lectures are appreciated, we shall expect to see in the papers of all the towns he visits, appreciative reports of his ornate, epigrammatic, and beautifully-rounded sentences, delivered in a musically ringing voice. For Mr. Washburn is second to but one as an orator, and piles up his facts in rivalry of Remsburg. We wish we had space to reproduce all the good things the press say of our missionaries, but they must accept the will for the performance, for there is a limit to the columns of even so large a journal as The Truth Seeker.

The Society of Humanity had acquired the three-story and basement building at 28 Lafayette street, through a donation or bequest of $10,000 by a Mr. Habel, and on the parlor floor meetings and so-

ciables that might almost be called receptions were
held. Birthdays of Paine and Jefferson were celebrated, their services and principles expounded, and
then there were musical and literary offerings, followed by dancing. They were quite brilliant functions. I discover that I reported these affairs for
The Truth Seeker, with lists of those present. Casually it is observed that "Henry George, Jr., and
his pretty sister made many friends." Among the
elders but one survivor can be named, Mr. Ed.
Wood, who still makes his yearly visit to the office
of The Truth Seeker, which he has bound and
mailed for nearly half a century. It is the only
paper among those he was handling when he took
it, that is still alive. It is his mascot. When the
Society suspended its formal meetings for the season, the younger set rallied and kept the dances
going. Mothers seemed pleased to bring their bud-
ding daughters, whom for form's sake they watched
from the side lines, besides having, I hope, a good
time themselves. The rooms were free. There
was no necessity for advertising to fill them completely, and no undesirable intrusions resulted.
They were joyful occasions.

Henry Ward Beecher grew more rationalistic in
his utterances. One of his sermons must have been
annoying to Catholics, who address the mother of
Jesus a hundred or a thousand times to once for
his Father in heaven. Beecher said:

"The mother and brothers of Christ did not believe him to be what he declared himself to be,
and surely his mother should have known. Between this Mary," Beecher went on, "celebrated in

the Magnificat for two thousand years, and the real Mary, there is a wide difference. That she had the slightest spiritual perception or insight there is no proof, and she and her other sons thought Jesus was 'cracked.' When he was good and great they said that he was crazy, and begged him not to tramp around and exhibit himself to the common multitude. They wanted him to stay at home and be a good citizen." One could see that Mr. Beecher had set aside as negligible the story of the angel's appearance to Mary with the news that she was the mother of God. A daily newspaper observed that he handled the holiest mystery of Christianity "with the carelessness of contempt." If Beecher's treatment of the incarnation was not blasphemy on the virgin, it was vergin' on the blasphemous, said a humorist. "Beecher should not be condemned for speaking the truth," said The Truth Seeker. But while the public was puzzling itself to reconcile Beecher's preaching with orthodox theology, he took sick and died March 7, 1887, in the 74th year of his age. The Congregational ministers of Chicago charitably refused to send a message of condolence to his widow. In the Beecher memorial volume shortly compiled thereafter, the only tribute that has lived is Ingersoll's.

2—THE ANARCHISTS, HENRY GEORGE, THE CHURCH.

The discussion over the question whether or not the Chicago Anarchists ought to be hanged continued through 1887. Henry George, who was con-

ducting The Standard, denounced all the proceedings that had been taken against the accused men,
and declared their defenders to be the party of law
and order. The police had acted without provocation, the jury was chosen in a manner shamelessly
illegal, and it would be charitable to suspect the
judge of incompetency. The Truth Seeker maintained vigorously that the men had been convicted
for their opinions and not for the commission of
crime. On the result of the appeal the editor said:
"The police by perjury connected the defendants
with some wretch who threw a bomb, the lower
court by partiality secured their conviction, and the
higher court by sophistry sustains the verdict."
And later. "The Chicago tragedy is over. Oscar
Neebe is serving his fifteen years' sentence in Joliet
penitentiary; Samuel Fielden and Michael Schwab
have been sentenced by the governor (Oglesby) to
life imprisonment instead of death; Louis Lingg is
dead by his own hand; August Spies, Albert R.
Parsons, Adolph Fischer, and George Engel were
hanged on Friday (Nov. 11, 1887), as commanded
by law." The Haymarket bombing had occurred
May 4, 1886. I wrote some verses on the hanging,
one couplet of which fixes in the memory the names
of the men who were hanged, and corrects the
common mispronunciation of one by rhyming it:

> "Four corpses swing in the morning breeze:
> Engel and Parsons, Fischer and Spies."

Throughout the year the heretic priest, Rev. Edward McGlynn, pastor of St. Stephen's Catholic
church and land reformer of the Henry George

school, was the center of a religious, economic, and political disturbance. McGlynn was a better secularist than George. The editor of The Truth Seeker laid the Nine Demands before George and he dodged them, but Father McGlynn had come out for similar principles in 1870, and in 1887 added: "I am glad to know that what was said so long ago is in substance and spirit and largely in phraseology the same as the Nine Demands of the American Secular Union. I can cordially and unreservedly subscribe to those demands, and I should be glad to see them granted by appropriate changes in our constitutions, state and federal." His defiance of his ecclesiastical superior, Archbishop Corrigan, was expressed in a current conundrum: "Why is the Rev. Dr. McGlynn like a stray goose?" The answer was that he didn't follow the propaganda. In association with Henry George he organized the Anti-Poverty Society, which elected him president, Mr. George being the leading member. John Swinton alluded to the combination humorously as "the bald-headed prophet and the pot-bellied priest." At the first meeting, which filled Chickering Hall, Henry George said: "This society does not propose to ask what beliefs its members hold. If Archbishop Corrigan wishes to join, good and welcome; if Colonel Ingersoll wishes to join, good and welcome." The archbishop's name was received with hisses and Colonel Ingersoll's with "prolonged and tremendous cheers." Hugh O. Pentecost, then a reverend, addressed the society a few weeks later. Pentecost, besides preaching anti-poverty doctrine, made a plea for the Chicago

Anarchists. When he added that he was "no longer in sympathy with the church as an organization or with evangelical Christianity," his congregation in Newark permitted him to resign. Dr. McGlynn was ordered to Rome, but publicly refused to go. The Christian Advocate said: "A few years ago Dr. McGlynn would have been undergoing torture at the hands of the Inquisition, and if he refused to recant, the fagots for an auto-da-fé would soon be collected. As Rome is infallible, and never changes, the only reason it does not do this now is because it cannot." Dr. McGlynn remarked: "In the good old days of Galileo they could take a layman to Rome in chains for what they think I am guilty of." Continuing obdurate, he was formally excommunicated.

The followers of Henry George charged that the Catholic church, through its tool, Terence V. Powderly, had enlisted the Knights of Labor to destroy the George land movement. This proved to be the fact. There was a conflict between the George party and the Socialists as to which should send delegates to the convention of the United Labor party at Syracuse, for the nomination of a state ticket. George also contended with the Socialists for control of The Leader newspaper. The Socialists prevailed in both instances. Mr. George started The Argus as a campaign paper. Both The Argus and The Leader suspended before the end of the year, and so did John Swinton's paper, which in the squabble between the church and George took the side of the church and the Knights of Labor. George atoned for his disrespect for

the Catholic machine by emphasizing his own part-
nership with God. His proposed reforms, he said,
were "God's will," he was carrying out "God's intentions" according to what "God designed." He
phrased his theory thus: "I have never stated that
the land belongs to all men. Rather I believe it
belongs to God and that all men are his children to
tenant this world for a little while. This is a new
crusade," said George. "As in the old crusades the
cry was 'God wills it!' so in this crusade the cry is,
'God wills it!'" The will of God counted little, as
George's party got few votes. The Truth Seeker
noted there were two Infidels on his municipal
ticket, that of the Union Labor Party—Louis F.
Post, candidate for district attorney, and Fred Leubuscher, nominated for the General Sessions judge-
ship. Thaddeus B. Wakeman, who the year before had been a George man, was now with the
Socialists. The Truth Seeker gave space to the
issues of the campaign because of the amount of
religious controversy the participation of Dr. Mc-
Glynn brought into it.

3—BLASPHEMY AND OTHER PROSECUTIONS.

The case of C. B. Reynolds, arrested the previous
year for blasphemy, came before the court of Morristown, N. J., on May 19, with Ingersoll for the defense. It lasted two days. Judge Francis Childs,
presiding, cautioned the jury not to violate the law
by acquitting the defendant. The obedient jury,
after an hour's deliberation, brought in a verdict of
guilty. The judge imposed a fine of $25, with costs,
which, duly juggled, made the whole penalty $75.

Ingersoll drew his check for the amount, and the prisoner was free. His address to the jury is contained in the Dresden edition of his works.

The Rev. Hugh O. Pentecost, who was becoming extremely radical, wrote to the New York World: "I think some one ought to express the disgust and shame which many Christians must feel at the proceedings. How silly and stupid it is to fine a man for expressing his honest opinions, in whatever bad taste, so long as he infringes on no one else's equal rights in doing so. Will men never learn anything from history? It seems incredible that a statute against blasphemy can be operative in this or any state. This silly and wicked statute has succeeded in giving a thousand times the circulation to Mr. Reynolds's pamphlet that it otherwise would have had. I am a Christian minister, but in my opinion if God and the Christian religion cannot take care of themselves without a resort to courts of human law, both are in a bad way. Truth can take care of itself. If we have the truth we need not fear blasphemers. If Reynolds has the truth, judges and jurors will not suppress it. That cause is a very weak one which will not bear discussion. I venture the opinion that there are many Christians in New Jersey who are ashamed of the Reynolds trial and conviction, as I certainly am."

Pentecost was right. When Ingersoll had finished his address to the jury, professing Christians to a considerable number, and some of the clergy of Morristown, presented themselves before him to register the protest that they had had no hand in the prosecution and did not believe in it.

Mr. Edwin C. Walker of Kansas, who in 1886 had lectured industriously to Liberal audiences

MR. WALKER AT 35.

wherever he could collect them, spent New Year's in jail at Oskaloosa. He had effected a marriage union with Lillian Harman in a way that apparently violated no law, and yet involved no recognition of the right of the state to intervene in such relations. Miss Harman, sharing his imprisonment, declined to purchase her liberty by paying her half of the costs. The prisoners were placed under regulations more severe than those usually enforced in civilized lands, being denied the privilege of either writing or receiving letters.

This "Lucifer match," as it was called because of the connection of the parties with the radical paper, Lucifer, published by Lillian's father, Moses Harman, at Valley Falls, lit the fires of revolt among social radicals, and was the subject, of course, of discussion in The Truth Seeker, where the grievances of all were heard. The editor advised the prisoners to submit to the money extortion, as the least of two evils, and pay their fines. In February their hands were forced by the arrest of Moses and his son George Harman, on a charge of using the mails for the circulation of obscene literature.

The matter complained of was an article headed, "An Awful Letter." The editor of The Truth Seeker described it as "a coarsely written and exclamatory denunciation of the abuse of marital rights." Following this arrest Edwin and Lillian paid their fines under protest and came out of prison to help fight the battle of the two arrested Harmans. Mr. Walker wrote to The Truth Seeker: "The accursed church-state monster has separated us, has murdered our happiness, but it has not made us love and respect it, and it cannot. We are pledged by our sufferings and our devotion to liberty and justice to do all that we can through all the years of our isolated lives to destroy it." Mr. Walker was immediately rearrested on the same charge as that for which the Harmans had been held, and in November he was indicted with them to appear for trial in April, 1888.

In May Mrs. Elmina D. Slenker, of Snowville, Va., who had been contributing to The Truth Seeker for ten years or more, was arrested by an agent of the Comstock society, accused of contaminating the United States mails. Mrs. Slenker was an Alphite, or one who admitted the legitimacy of marriage for no other purpose than to perpetuate the species. She circulated literature bearing on this question and probably treated of the propagative act with considerable freedom. The agent of the Vice Society got her into the trap by pretending to be interested in her work. The Truth Seeker came out with the searching inquiry: "What shall be said of the dirty agents employed for years in ensnaring an aged woman—inducing her, by

pretending to be students of her special hobby, to
write such words as should place her in their power?
What shall be said of the society that employs
these foul creatures? What of the Christians who
support this society and urge the prosecution of the
miserable work? Their actions sink them beneath
the notice of clean and honorable people, and they
are best left to fester in their own corruption. No
words can express the contempt in which every decent man must hold them."

The National Defense Association, E. B. Foote,
Jr., secretary, E. W. Chamberlain, treasurer, conducted the defense of Mrs. Slenker and Truth
Seeker readers paid the expenses. Her most ardent
advocates were women. She was indicted on July
12 and held for trial in the United States District Court for the Western District of Virginia
at Abingdon. She was arraigned October 21 before Judge Paul and a jury, which found her guilty.
When the judge postponed sentence, Chamberlain
argued a motion in arrest of judgment on the
ground of defective indictment and the court
granted it and discharged Mrs. Slenker from custody. Henry M. Parkhurst, one of the old-time
stenographers, a Freethinker like nearly all pioneers of that art, reported the trial for The Truth
Seeker.

4—PERSONAL AND REMINISCENT.

The matter written by myself and published by
The Truth Seeker in 1887 would make a small book
if collected for that purpose; but it was mainly topi-

cal and of no permanent value. There were verses and stories, reports and special articles. Because in those years my brother and I could do each the other's work, vacations of some length for both were feasible. When I returned from mine I offered him congratulations on having conducted the paper as ably during my absence as I had when he was away.

I quote here a paragraph in one of my letters to Eugene written from our old home on Surry Hill, for the effect it had on two old men—Peter Eckler of the Eckler Publishing Company, and Dr. J. R. Monroe, editor of The Ironclad Age. The paragraph reads:

"I sat under the old apple-tree in the dooryard, where we used to roll about when we were boys. The tree is dead and furnishes hardly any shade; so I sat in the sun and watched the summer clouds go over, like ships sailing in the sky. The old times came back, and old familiar faces clustered around, and I saw them but with closed eyes. The hum of bees and the drone of vagrant flies sounded now and then, and with their music came memories, floating, drifting, appearing and disappearing like things seen through a glass reversed—distant but distinct. Thus I saw my friends not only as they are now, but as I knew them then; not only those who still walk the earth, but those who have sunk back to that dreamless sleep from which they first awakened on this life. So under the apple-tree I dozed and dreamed."

Monroe said in his paper: "We confess to the weakness of having critically read his communications over the second time, merely for the pleasure his style of writing imparts." That called out Peter Eckler, who wrote Dr. Monroe a letter indorsing his commendation. It appeared that Mr. Eckler both read the vacation letters and preserved them, so that he could quote not only the paragraph I have reproduced, but another from my vacation letter of the previous year.

Having reached the age these men had attained forty years ago, I probably understand better now than I did then why the description of a visit home appealed to them.

In one of the old numbers of The Truth Seeker I find this quoted by a contributor in order to expose its false reasoning:

A certain Infidel, calling upon his friend, an astronomer, noticed several globes lying upon a table, and admiring their appearance, he inquired as to where they had been obtained and who was the maker of them.

"What would you say were I to tell you that no one made them, and that they came here of their own accord?" questioned the astronomer in reply.

"Such a thing would be impossible," answered the Infidel.

It reads like a story prepared for Sunday-school consumption a century ago. Ingersoll had been dead but a short time when the Rev. Dr. Charles Parkhurst adopted the narrative to hortatory uses by repeating it with Henry Ward Beecher in the place of the astronomer and with the name of Ingersoll given to the "certain Infidel," the conversa-

tion taking place in Beecher's study where Ingersoll was represented as calling upon the Brooklyn
preacher.

5—FOR THE RECORD.

Another death which took away a man in whom
the liberal world felt an interest was that of Prof.
Edward Livingston Youmans, editor of The Popular Science Monthly (Jan. 18), which he had
started in 1872. Professor Youmans is remembered by those who observed his work for the fact
that he created for Spencer, Darwin, Huxley and
Tyndall an audience in America almost before they
had achieved one in England. He was 67 years old.

Activity on the part of J. D. Shaw, lecturer, editor, and organizer, was frequently reported from
Waco, Texas, where his Religious and Benevolent
Association met in Liberal Hall. In his monthly
Independent Pulpit for January he spoke of the
goodly number of youth in attendance at his meetings. "Now," he says, "we have many young people, and a more orderly, well-behaved, and attentive
company it would be hard to find."

"Our Canadian friends," announces our editor under date of January 15, "have another Freethought journal, and we trust it may be longer
lived than its predecessors. Mr. Charles Watts
and Mr. H. C. Luse have begun at Toronto the
publication of Secular Thought, and the first number
is out." Secular Thought under Mr. Watts (who
returned to England in 1892) and his successor
J. Spencer Ellis, continued to be published well
into the twentieth century.

Lucy N. Colman, who was born in 1817, and was in the anti-slavery reform with Garrison, Phillips, Frederick Douglass and others, published her Reminiscences in many numbers of The Truth Seeker during 1887.

In March The Truth Seeker moved its office from 33 Clinton Place to 28 Lafayette Place, which was to be its home for nearly twenty years. The editor wrote:

"Our new quarters are commodious, consisting of a large store and basement, and a new building in the rear for a printing-office and editorial rooms. The neighborhood is very religious and literary, but we hope to survive the former fault and add to the latter good quality."

St. Joseph's Union and the Mission of the Immaculate Conception were a block below. The Episcopal clergy house was across the street. There was an old church nearby. The Christian Union, The Church Press, and The Churchman were neighbors, as was also the Astor Library. Lafayette Place, now no more, ran between Broadway and the Bowery, from Great Jones street to Astor place. The great event connected with the removal was the Printers' Ball in the new building, attended by the elite of Typographical Union No. 6 and enough ladies and gentlemen from the Society of Humanity to make up twenty couples. Ed. King, the philosopher of the workingman, made the dedicatory address. The curious reader will find the report of this soiree in The Truth Seeker for March 19, 1887.

Felix Oswald's "Bible of Nature" ran in The

Truth Seeker as a serial, beginning July 16. Dr. Oswald (1845-1906) termed it "a contribution to the religion of the future." It was purely rationalistic and therefore hopeless as a religion.

The paper now published in Liberal, Mo., was called The Ensign. It reported "the first annual commencement of the first Freethought University in the world" as occurring every evening from June 28 to July 2. Evidently The Ensign was short-lived, for the next reference to the town (Sept. 24) states that C. M. Overton and M. D. Leahy have resuscitated the Liberal, Mo., paper under the title of "American Idea." "Mr. Overton's greatest effort," we read, "thus far has been to endeavor to prove that Liberal is a Christian town, and its people Christians."

There was great mortality among the Spiritualist papers, marked by the demise of Light in the West, Spiritual Offering, Light for Thinkers, Current Fact, and Mind and Matter. A new one was started at Cincinnati called The Better Way. In Melbourne, Australia, the Anarchists published a 12-page monthly which they named Honesty, and the Freethought lecturer, Thomas Walker, started a monthly illustrated magazine, The Republican. For some years L. V. Pinney conducted The Press at Winsted, Conn., as what Mrs. Slenker called "the most radical of radical papers."

One of the curious events of the year was the confiscation of all Mormon church property by the U. S. government. This was in some way the outcome of the attempt to prevent Mormon men from cohabiting with more than one woman.

On the death of John Swinton's Paper, August 7, which The Truth Seeker attributed to the George furor and false issues raised by Labor leaders, our editor said: "It was better edited, contained more labor news, and had more editorial vigor than any labor paper now in the field." Mr. Swinton said: "I have been wrecked by this paper and by the labors associated therewith—in which during the past four years I have sunk tens of thousands of dollars—all out of my own pocket." Mr. Swinton was one of the great editors, of the Horace Greeley and Charles A. Dana class, but had the misfortune to be an idealist.

Dr. Titus L. Brown, the Binghamton, N. Y., Materialist who had served six terms as president of the New York State Freethinkers' Association, wrote his funeral sermon and died August 17. His family, with a treachery common to religious survivors of deceased Freethinkers, gave him "Christian" burial.

The International Freethought Congress was called by Charles Bradlaugh to be held in the Hall of Science, 142 Old street, E. C., on September 10-12. One hundred delegates attended according to a report copied from the London Freethinker into The Truth Seeker of October 1.

The annual Congress of the American Secular Union, held in the rooms of the Chicago society, October 15 and 16, elected Samuel P. Putnam president (Courtlandt Palmer resigning) and E. A. Stevens secretary in the place of Putnam.

The Canadian Freethinkers held a convention in Toronto, October 29 and 30.

"Mr. and Mrs. B. F. Underwood have resigned the editorial control of The Open Court (Chicago). The reason is that Mr. Hegeler, the proprietor, desired to associate with them Dr. Paul Carus, his secretary and future husband of his daughter, to which they objected. This will, probably, end The Open Court."—Truth Seeker (Dec. 17).

Mr. Hegeler fixed The Open Court so it could not fail by endowing it with a million dollars. His son-in-law, Dr. Carus, remained the editor until his death in 1919, and it is still published.

After thirteen years Mrs. Besant resigned her place as coeditor of Bradlaugh's paper, The National Reformer, to take up the advocacy of Socialism.

The last important news item for 1887 is the resignation of Andrew Carnegie and Judge George C. Barrett of the New York Supreme Court from the membership of the Nineteenth Century Club, "the upper-tendom of heresy," of which Courtlandt Palmer was president. Mr. Palmer in a letter to the New York Tribune had stated his opinion that the Chicago Anarchists did not deserve death. Mr. Carnegie brought this question up at the club and was personally unpleasant. Mr. Palmer declined to admit that his private views were any concern of Mr. Carnegie, who thereupon resigned. The discussion reached the newspapers and the publicity caused the resignation also of Judge Barrett, who on account of his judicial office was in no position to face the music. Mr. Palmer said that two qualifications for membership in the club, according to its motto, were "courtesy and courage." He would say

he thought Mr. Carnegie was wanting in the one
and Judge Barrett in the other. The ruction proved
an excellent recommendation for the club, which
moved to larger quarters and flourished up to the
time of its founder's death the following year.

Mr. Carnegie, as a large employer of labor and
as a target for the Anarchists, was excusably prejudiced against men believed to have advocated the
removal of capitalists by means of bombs. Judge
Barrett was merely placed in an embarrassing position and took the easiest way out. I recall the
amusement evoked among his acquaintances by the
notion that he could not sanction radical thought or
expression. If those from whom he thus separated
himself had retaliated by telling what they knew
about his social views as exemplified in his private
life, he might have been severely damaged. But
telling tales was opposed to their principles. I can
almost, not quite, vizualize the excellent lady and
speak her name; but I wouldn't if I could.

*   *   *

And now, after a few preliminary remarks at the
beginning of Chapter XXI (next number) I close
twelve years with The Truth Seeker and am off to
the Pacific Coast for six years of experience on the
other side of the continent.

CHAPTER XXI.

WHEN two men, both known to readers by name, are at work upon a paper, one being the editor and the other an assistant who writes articles for the editorial column but puts his brightest ideas somewhere else and signs them, then all the good stuff that appears stands a chance of being credited to the assistant. Such is my experience. Ever since I came to be the Hyas Tyee of The Truth Seeker, with an assistant off and on, pieces of my writing that attracted attention by their merits have been passed to the credit of my confederate for the time being. But if somebody did wrong, that was the editor. For instance, an article by one in 1913 got me summoned by a priest; another in 1918 caused the postoffice to refuse the paper distribution in the mails, and a paragraph done by a third in 1925 is the basis of a libel suit by a preacher now pending. Two of the assistants were lawyers who ought to have known how far they could safely go, and the other was a minister who had hitherto preached the gospel for thirty-five years. Thus was it, in a measure (though I never wrote anything actionable), when I served as assistant to my brother. He stood sponsor for whatever appeared editorially, for, like his model, Mr. Dana of The Sun, he held that a paper had only one editor. We were so much alike in style that at this day I cannot tell our articles apart. His were likely better to maintain sobriety throughout, but ofttimes he wrote with enjoyable humor.

So in The Truth Seeker of December 24, 1887, Dr. E. B. Foote, Sr., having seen certain lightly conceived notices on the editorial page, wrote Eugene to inquire whether I had taken a seat at the editor's desk or he had borrowed my pen. The editor replied:

"We regret to be obliged to state that when the notices were written our brother was on his way to the limitless West, where he proposes, in company with Samuel P. Putnam, to start a Freethought paper and grow up with the country, or walk back to New York."

He to whom Charles Watts so often alluded when to the editor he wrote: "Give my regards to your funny brother," was now off The Truth Seeker, and had not been missed. Such is our little life.

On the 16th of December I parted from the boys in the office by the usual sign of shaking hands. That evening a few intimates attended a dinner at Mouquin's in Fulton street and at its end, with expressions of good-by and good luck, Putnam and I crossed the Hudson to the West Shore and were off for the coast, which we believed offered a field for another paper.

Our train, crossing Niagara River, gave me my first sight of the Falls. Unfortunately I viewed this marvel of nature just after I had been charged the extraordinary sum of sixty cents for a plate of corned beef and beans, and my capacity for admiration and wonder at anything else had been diminished by the size of the restaurant check. One should see the Falls first.

At Chicago, reached on a Sunday morning, we met E. A. Stevens; that is, he met us. Stevens was secretary of the American Secular Union and president of the Secular League of Chicago—a most efficient man in all respects. The Liberals of the city on that morning attended the meeting of the Ethical Culture Society to hear Mr. William M. Salter's comments on the current discussion in The North American Review between Robert G. Ingersoll and the Rev. Henry M. Field. Mr. Salter was as far from indorsing Ingersoll as his successor, Mr. Bridges, is from approving Darwin as a philosopher. All of his discourse that remained in my mind was his denial of the Colonel's dictum that happiness is the greatest good. Mr. Salter maintained, with superb disdain for this plebeian sentiment, that the greatest good is "character." And yet character contributes to human happiness, or it is a nugacity or an evil. Convinced that Mr. Salter was getting us nowhere, I inquired of Putnam what he thought of the argument. He said he hadn't heard it, being asleep during its delivery. Putnam traveled much, by day and night, and improved all his opportunities to make up for lost sleep.

That evening's meeting of the Chicago Secular League, at which Stevens presided, was different, more like the New York Liberal Club—a lecture and then discussion. A young fellow of about my own age arose on the floor and offered a few pertinent remarks. I reported his name as Darrell. It was Clarence Darrow.

2—VARIETIES OF PASSENGERS.

After a twilight breakfast, Putnam and I took a train out of Chicago and shortly ran into a blizzard that stalled our engine. We ate next at 10:30 that night. I quote from an account I wrote for the first number of our new paper FREETHOUGHT:

"When the train got under way its progress was slow, and Kansas City (Mo.) must have started out to meet us or we never should have seen it. The city is away up on a bluff, out of sight of the depot. It is evidently a large commercial center, doing an extensive business in a product labeled 'Relief for Kansas Sufferers,' put up in bottles for residents of the adjoining state. The Kansas unfortunates referred to were supposed to suffer from thirst, their state being dry and Missouri wet. And yet a brighter side of the situation in Kansas had been turned to me. In that state I overheard an argument on prohibition between a resident and a stranger. The resident bore a bottle, which he shared with the other. And as they swigged it off, he said: 'I am a prohibitionist from principle. I have drank prohibition whiskey for fifty-seven years, and it never hurt me; but a quart I got once in Missouri made me sick for a week'."

Kansas must have been a tough state at that time (1887). Two passengers who evidently were natives lured a brace of Easterners into taking a hand at old sledge. After a game or two that the tenderfeet won, a Kansas man picked up three of his cards and said he wished the game had been poker. One of the Easterners held three aces, and agreeing to call it poker, bet a dollar in confidence that no other three cards could beat his hand. His opponent raised him ten, and being called, laid down three hearts, saying "A flush," and took the money.

That was the now-past cowboy age. Through Arizona and New Mexico the train picked up men wearing white, wide-brimmed felt hats. These were cowboys off the range. But of the "cowboy," it soon appeared, there were two classes—genuine and bogus. The real one, as I observed, was a healthy specimen, and though his legs sometimes got beyond his control and stretched themselves across the aisle of the car, he would make an effort, without taking offense, to coil them down when politely requested to do so. He wore an expensive band on his hat; carried no visible weapons, and seemed to be an educated and agreeable person, speaking grammatically in good English. "The bogus cowboy," to quote from notes I made, "is different. He is not a cowboy at all. He only calls himself one and wears a cheap sombrero. He is an imitation bad man, an all-around tough, who never mounted a horse in his life and when at large is seldom sober enough to keep the saddle if lifted into it. Description of a meeting-up with one of them who surged into the smoking-car near Flagstaff may be excused because it developed my partner's unexpected resourcefulness and nerve."

Apart from his jag the fellow brought with him only annoyance and discomfort. He bulldozed the passengers, lounging up and down the aisle with his hand on his hip. The discomfort arose from the probability of his being armed, and no one could tell what a mean souse might do with a gun. As I sat next to the aisle, he paused to inquire whether I would prefer to fight or to lend him four bits for a couple of drinks. I replied that he misjudged me

if he supposed that I would do either to oblige
a man in his condition. His subsequent remarks
interested Putnam more than they did me, for when
he had moved along to propose that the next passenger either fight or "pungle up," Putnam exchanged seats with me. "If that fellow comes this
way again," he said, "I'll down him and you can
sit on him and take away his gun." A carpenter
from Chicago volunteered: "And then I'll kick him
off the train at the next station." We had no need
to carry out this fell conspiracy, for when the train
stopped again at a place called Williams, the disagreeable passenger dropped off for a drink and
made such a belated return that he missed the
train, which was just moving out. He chased us
a little way, but only the words that came out of
his mouth got aboard. A new passenger said:
"Hell! him a cowboy. The son-of-a-gun is a section boss on the Santa Fé."

I asked Putnam, skeptically, whether he really
had designed to climb the front of that low-life had
he come back. He replied: "You would just have
found out I would if he gave me the chance. I
can't fight, but I can down a man quick as lightning. But don't write anything about it." I
thought of his collision with the author of "Helen's
Babies" and believed him.*

*If readers have forgotten this incident, which I believe
I have somewhere already mentioned, I will repeat that
the "collision" took place while both men were in the army.
Putnam on one side of the campfire played cards with
comrades. John Habberton on the other side annoyed the
players by tossing small, smoking brands upon the blanket

3—THE NATIVE LAND OF THE HUALAPAI.

Of the country we passed through I wrote, while the impression it made on me was fresh:

"This southwestern land, New Mexico and Arizona, is a land of poetry and mystery and terror. It is full of fearsome mountains and chasms and precipices. Along the line of the railroad nothing appears to grow, and the soil is of a rich brick color, as though it had been baked in a kiln. Bluffs rise near you hundreds of feet high, in such layers as are sometimes seen in the high banks of a river. Rocks turned on edge stand off by themselves with no relative, perhaps, within a hundred miles. Then there are rocks weighing thousands of tons arranged in all manner of queer forms, helter-skelter, in pyramids, in circles, as we see cobble-stones beside the road where children have been at play. The sandbanks do not slope from top to base; they are straight up-and-down, or overhanging. The mountains often have no foothills but rise from these plateaus like the pyramids from the plains of Egypt. Solitary peaks stand treeless from the foot to the white summits that wear their caps of snow in very presence of the regal sun. Again, there are canyons deep enough to put a good-sized mountain into. How these gorges ever got scooped out in their present fashion is a matter of great mystery. The train crossed one called Canyon Diablo, 285 feet deep.

"The natives of this land are much the color of the soil, somewhere between copper and chocolate. From their adobe huts these natives came out to meet the train and sell their wares to the passengers. The Pueblo Indians were,

where the cards were dealt. When words failed to abate the torment, Putnam arose and capturing Habberton by a leg dragged him through the fire on his seat. Habberton bore malice and perhaps scars all his life, and showed the former many years later by voting against the admission of Putnam to an author's club.

if I recollect accurately, the first we saw. All the business enterprise of this tribe seems to have been given to the women, who had bits of pottery, volcanic glass, and some colored stones, the which they desired to convert into the currency of the East. The tawny damsels were the least attractive of all human females that have appealed to me. Old or young, they showed no trace of past or promise of future good looks. The male Indian was content to let the women support the family. I saw one absurd old Indian astride a small donkey, and addressed him as Powhattan. He replied, 'No savey.' He wore a white man's necktie, the string about his forehead and the ornamental part falling behind In these Indian villages were adobe churches for baptizing converts, but no facilities for washing them. The Mojave Indian girls painted and penciled their faces to imitate the front of a brick house. Both these and the Mojave women dressed carelessly. They drew about their bosoms, beneath the arms, what passed for a shawl that was somehow fastened behind at the top. This was an adequate covering while it hung straight down, front and back. It failed to be such when the wearer stooped. In my notes is the entry: 'Before the average Indian maiden can make her debut in paleface society, she must spend more money for buttons and adopt some form of trousering.' To the old Indian who didn't 'savey' I made the proffer of a dime for the purchasing of pins with which to fasten the back of her dress for his daughter, Pocahontas. The train lingered at its stopping-places as though reluctant to leave, giving passengers plenty of time for fooling. There was a long wait at Mojave, where an enterprising farmer had struck a furrow around one hundred and sixty acres. He could go around twice a day, they said, with a horse-drawn machine that sowed the seed, which was barley, and covered it two and a half inches deep. He carried four furrows. In a beauty contest among the Indian women and girls there assembled, some Hualapai maiden would have been crowned as Miss Mojave, for the women of that tribe were a laughing lot, and had the reputation of being companionable.

"Some of the places marked on the Arizona map as towns were deceptive, for when reached they were found to consist of a single building and to contain a single inhabitant. Such were Chino and Aubrey, each with a population of one. Cactus as big as apple-trees made spots in the absolutely Saharic desert look like orchards. There is a great deal of that sort of illusion in that country where trees subsist almost without water."

4—IN A HISTORIC PRINTING-OFFICE.

I liked San Francisco at first sight, and like it still, although fire and progress must have changed it greatly in forty years. We had the best of luck in finding an office room at 504 Kearny street that was precisely what we wanted. In a jiffy we had a corner curtained off for trunks and sleeping quarters, a long table brought in that would serve for the uses of a desk and to display books, and chairs enough to seat ourselves and visitors. In the search for a printer our good luck still went with us, steering us away from the wrong place and into the right one. The one positively not It, but first entered, was run by a man named Bacon, a deacon. We were to hear of him later as Deacon Pork. We got out of there without coming to terms with him. I could see he had a good outfit. Nevertheless we withdrew. And then we came to William M. Hinton's, 536 Clay street, below Montgomery. Both those printers were, as you might say, historic. Bacon put his shop on the map by rejecting the manuscript of Bret Harte's "Luck of Roaring Camp" as irritating to the modesty of his young lady copy-holder. The deacon had his meed of

praise for taking this protective attitude toward
the girl employee, who seemed as safe with him as
anywhere except in the arms of Jesus.   On the
other hand one not impressed by the piety of Deacon Pork, but professing that the fact was of common knowledge, told me that this employer had
himself betrayed the confidence of the girl, and sent
her East in that condition.

A few moments' speech with Mr. Hinton was
enough to satisfy me that this was the printing-
office we sought.   He told me more papers had
been born in his office and buried from the same
than anywhere else on the coast.   "But, *semper
paratus,* we are always ready for one more.   We
will set all the matter for you or you may set part
of it, and what you earn we will knock off your
bill.   There's a spare frame over there.   Henry
George set up the first edition of 'Progress and
Poverty' at that frame."

Here seemed to be established a sort of affiliation, George and his book being no strangers.   Mr.
Hinton had been in fact the partner of George in
publishing a daily paper.   He printed four numbers of Freethought, enough to convince me that
owing to the dolce far niente way of running his
office, I must spend my time there as foreman, compositor, and stone hand.   While the fifth number
was in hand and the work far in arrears, I asked
Mr. Hinton if he would disclose to me, as one friend
to another, why the paper was late.   He replied
that he was unable to explain the circumstance.
Looking about him he said: "Here we stand in the

presence of enough material to print the largest
paper in the country. Here are from fifteen to
twenty men, all at work, many of them sober. I
cannot understand why your work is behind. You
think it over and come back and tell me." In five
minutes, having looked at the copy on the cases
of the compositors, I returned to say that his men
were working on a job of city printing, putting in
type an extended list of delinquent tax-payers. He
waved his hands, but said: "If you know what to
do in this exigency, do it. The office is yours."

Who could say an unkind word to a man like
that? In a few minutes, then, the men were busy
on my copy in place of the list of delinquent tax-
payers, and having read and corrected the matter
and made up the forms, I put the paper on the
press. But this arrangement, so ideal from Mr.
Hinton's point of view, could not last. It gave me
no time for reflective thought. We rented another
room on the floor at 504 Kearny; bought an outfit
of type, and hired Frank L. Browne and his wife
to set up the paper. This relieved Mr. Hinton
of all but the presswork, which he continued to
do excellently well and quite promptly throughout
the life of the paper. Some years later, on the occasion of a political overturning, he was elected
as supervisor of San Francisco.

Putnam early in the year departed upon a lecture
tour of the coast, drawing good audiences, selling
books, taking hundreds of subscriptions, and earning generous lecture fees. He thus virtually supported the paper. Neither of us drew a salary
above expenses, and for my part I knew how to

live economically. There came in all the literary
contributions and letters admissible to a paper of
our size, which began with twelve pages, 10x12
inches over all. The city had one Labor paper,
The People, which soon suspended, for no Labor
paper lives long, and The Weekly Star, independent-
political. published by James H. Barry and edited
by F. B. Perkins, the father of Charlotte Perkins
who has been successively Charlotte Stetson and
Charlotte Gilman, a remarkably brilliant writer and
poet. Mr. Perkins was a Freethinker and available for lectures when meetings were held. A
fierce remark about Mr. M. De Young, one of The
Chronicle brothers, was accredited to him. According to the tradition De Young started The
Chronicle in a small way as a gossipy sheet, being
aided or financed by a lady vocalist known as
Madamoiselle Celeste, who sang at the Bella Union,
a concert hall near the Barbary Coast. The paper
scored a success. In the course of a year or two a
news paragraph stated that a well-known sculptor
had executed a bust of the founder of The Chronicle
which was to be seen in the office of the paper, and
copies thereof were for sale. Mr. Perkins commented: "Not so: the bust of the founder of The
Chronicle is to be seen at the Bella Union, and
we believe it is for sale."

Barry was aggressive, attacking injustices in vigorous terms. Usually he had a fight going, and
once got into jail. The Star employed Alfred Denton Cridge, a veteran writer and printer, and a former friend of D. M. Bennett.

5—CALIFORNIANS CORDIAL AND TRUSTING.

Our business for the first year was to make acquaintance with the town and the limited number
of Freethinkers there and in the vicinity, as well
as in the state. We found them hospitable and
helpful. Some were "forty-niners." Numbers
were miners, ranchers, wool-growers, orchardists,
pioneer merchants, old settlers, and all were interesting. Out-of-town visitors selected the Freethought office as a place to leave their trappings.
One day a man of about 60 entered, wearing an
overall suit, which, having introduced himself as
Thomas Jones of Independence, Inyo county, he
asked my permission to remove. Then he stood
revealed as very well dressed, a wealthy man and
liberal with his money, but he did not propose to
spoil a set of glad rags by exposing them to the
wear and tear of railroad travel. On another day
there came in a rough-looking individual so dis-
guised by drink that his faculties wandered. He
seated himself for a short period of repose and
then coming to life inquired if this were the Freethought office and myself Putnam or Macdonald.
Set right about that he proceeded in a drunken
man's fashion to say: "I don't know you and you
don't know me, but we both know my partner Bill
Reed. Bill says that you are a man that can be
trusted with money." And he drew from his
pocket a heavy buckskin sack and emptied therefrom two hundred dollars in double eagles. These
coins he poured upon the table, and drawing out

some of the pieces, pushed the rest toward me with the command: "Take care of that until I call for it." With the sum which he returned to his pocket, he proposed to fight away dull care. I suggested that a man might dissipate considerable gloom with less money, provided the effort were not protracted beyond reason, but he replied that he wasn't looking for an argument; that his plans were laid and couldn't be changed. And thereupon he departed, while I gathered up his gold and put it away. Once during the following week I caught sight of him firing a rifle in a shooting gallery near the office, and went in with the idea of accosting him. He saw me but there was no recognition in his eye. His shooting, I noticed, was good. The muzzle of the gun cut circles in the air larger than the target, yet he would apostrophize himself: "Fire when she bears," and so turn loose at the right moment and make a fair shot. At the end of the week he paid me a second visit, being sober but cheerful, and saying, with no reference to his previous call, that he had come to greet me in behalf of his partner, Bill Reed, who took the paper. "A pretty good town, this is," said he, "for a man to spend his money in. I come here a week ago as near as I can figure, with a couple hundred dollars in the old sack; and I am going back to camp with less than fifty of 'em—broke—damn a fool, drunk or sober." I suggested he might have deposited a part of it with some friend for safe keeping, but he replied regretfully that there was no chance. To determine whether his expedition was

at a sure-enough end, I asked: "Are you dead
certain you are on your way back to the camp, or
wouldn't you extend yourself another week if you
had the dinero?" Said he: "No; I am not quite
broke yet, but I know when 1 have had enough.
Well, I'll tell Bill I met you, Mr. Putnam. Good-
by." I stopped him and he never suspected why
until I brought his money out and asked him to
take care of it for me until we met again. It took
an argument to convince the man that the wealth
was his and that he had seen me before. San Francisco was a comparatively safe city at that time.
He had been bemused for a week without being
robbed.*

The contents of The Truth Seeker show that
during the first part of 1888 I wrote several letters
to the brother I had left "back in the states," as
was the phrase of the Californians. They were
written, probably, to occupy time spent alone, Putnam being absent filling lecture engagements, and
I was never keen on hunting the society of my fel-
low-beings or inflicting my own on them. Was I
homesick? The closing paragraph of one letter to
The Truth Seeker runs:

"I am several thousand miles away from The Truth
Seeker office, but am often with the boys in the light and
bright composing room, and see the familiar 'forms,' as it
were. I see Stevens tapping around the stone, Colby making eccentric and apparently unnecessary marks on the

*The amount, of this man's deposit was much larger
than I have indicated, but I would not put a strain upon
the reader's credulity by naming it.

proofs, Mellis groaning over a take of long primer, B ake
snatching the type from his case, and looking forward to
four figures in Saturday's bill; and the rest with contracted brows studying the quirks and turnings of their
manuscript. I attend again the little parties at the Society's
parlors and see all the faces there—Dr. Foote head and
shoulders above the rest, Brother Eckhard walking through
the Virginia Reel with stately motion, Philosopher King
lost in the wilderness of the Saratoga Lancers—the room
full of girls and melody and laughter and light. And
sometimes I find myself once more up in your editorial
room, resting my elbow upon your desk and stretching
out an inky and black-leaded hand for copy. And as the
answer sometimes came then, 'No more tonight,' I take
your words to close this long letter with. No more tonight.
But yours always."

A degree of lonesomeness may be implicit in
those lines, but if so the presence was at hand to
relieve it.

6—SHOULDERING THE WRONGS OF SOCIETY.

Mrs. Mary A. Leland, widow of Theron C. Leland of New York, had come to San Francisco to
live, with her two daughters, Rachel and Grace, and
they had a house on Taylor street, at the north end.
Mrs. Leland had been a quite remarkable woman;
like another Frances Wright, an agitator for the
rights of the female sex. In 1859 or earlier Josiah
Warren, an apostle of equitable commerce and
complete individualism, furnished the ideas on which
to found a community at the place now called
Brentwood, Long Island, under the name of "Modern Times." It was one of the numerous social
experiments of that epoch. Moncure Daniel Conway accepted an invitation in the summer of 1860

to go to Modern Times and address the inhabitants. The story he told afterwards was printed in the Cincinnati Gazette of February 27, 1860. On the evening of his arrival, he says, he was taken to visit the Queen of Modern Times. Following is the picture he draws of that royal personage:

"The Queen of Modern Times was in truth every inch a queen. She was a most beautiful woman, in the prime of life, who was born and reared in the Cotton States. She had at an early age married a rich man in the South, who in the end proved himself an utterly worthless man and a tyrant. From him she separated, and the law which gave him her children gradually schooled her to sum up all the wrongs of society in the one word 'marriage.' If she was the champion of any popular cause Mary Chilton would be regarded as the leading female intellect of her country; and it would be impossible for anyone to see her in her in-spired mood, and to hear her voice as it sweeps through the gamut of feeling, rehearsing the sorrows of her sisterhood, without knowing that she brings many momentous truths from the deep wells of nature."

Mary Chilton was Mrs. Leland. Twenty-eight years later, that is when I found her there in San Francisco, the queen had grandchildren for her sub-jects and seemed to be somewhat mollified. I sent her an invitation to drop in at the Freethought office when downtown. She replied that she went forth only occasionally, and would prefer to have me call, which I did, and soon persuaded her younger daughter (Grace) to come to the office and write wrappers. She was then typing the manu-script of her sister Rachel's (Lilian Leland's) story of a trip around the world entitled "Traveling Alone." I discovered the work needed revision by a practiced hand, as most all writing does (and this which the reader has now before him has so profited). The arrangement resulted in the young lady's bringing her Remington No. 2 to 504 Kearny street and working at my elbow, almost, when I was there, and greeting callers when I was out. The meeting in San Francisco was not our first. It was probably our fourth. Years before, when spending the end of a week at a farmhouse on the Schraalenberg road, in Closter, New Jersey, I observed a small girl playing croquet. She belonged there,

GIRL.   SCHOOL GIRL.

and acted the hostess by chasing the arrows I shot at a target. We got along well. Soon after that I encountered her as she walked with her father on the street. In another period of years, I undesignedly wandered into a place in New York where a society was giving a dance, and finding her there

renewed the acquaintance. A married couple who
were chaperoning a collection of girls obligingly
surrendered to me the privilege of going home with
her, as the hour was late, the night cold, and her
house far beyond theirs. It wasn't so far as I
wished it had been by the time we got there. That
was an evening in the year 1884. The next day

THE GIRL.   WIFE.

I informed my brother, and was ready to tell the
world, I had found the Girl, but he coldly restored
me to sanity by saying: "You poor chump; don't
you know she was bespoken long ago?" That was
the reason why a marriage that was evidently or-
dained at the time she chased arrows for me was
not fulfilled until four years after this 1884 date,
when it might have taken place. But now, here
in San Francisco, I had her isolated. At her house
I detected favorable signs. In a little red album

that held tintypes an inch square, mine was inserted beside hers. She had been observed to write our names together, one imposed on the other, Grace

THE BENEFICIARY, 1888.

D. Leland and George E. Macdonald, and then to perform the operation of canceling identical letters, with the happiest results. The name of Leland disappeared unless preserved as a middle one.

Plainly it was all over but the formalities. If the former Queen of Modern Times still held that the wrongs of society were summed up in the word marriage, she made no objection to our taking them all on at once. The inevitable took place on the July 20 following, establishing an anniversary I have not since been permitted to forget. I say inevitable because as I have stated to Marshall Gauvin of Winnipeg, Canada, and to Ernest Sauve of Iron River, Wisconsin, all men marry their stenographers. Inevitable again for the following reason: Said Mr. Bird of The Truth Seeker office to me a few years ago: "Did your boy get married?" Said I: "Yes, when he let his eye fall on that normal school girl, there was no escape." Said Mr. Bird: "There never is."

While composing this truthful record I have asked her whether she would have accepted me at any or all of our previous meetings, and with confidence and no hesitation she replied that she would.

7 —MY PARTNER'S COLLISIONS WITH THE ENEMY.

Satisfaction is always felt in mentioning instances where persons who have made themselves conspicuous by their unfair courses against the advocacy of Freethought have got their comeuppance. In May, 1887, while Putnam was delivering a lecture in Ukiah, Cal., on the Nine Demands of Liberalism, a local scamp named Hamilton arose and denounced him as a scoundrel, and to emphasize his displeasure he seized a lighted kerosene lamp and threw it at Putnam's head. Putnam dodged and the lamp went through a window and exploded outside. The interference of bystanders prevented Hamilton from trying to improve his aim with another lamp. Putnam finished his discourse, while his assailant ran away. Afterwards the man was placed on trial for his murderous assault, but escaped punishment. His conduct may have had the approval of the Christian part of the community, for when the citizens of Ukiah organized to purchase the right of way for a railway to a nearby town they elected Hamilton secretary with power to raise funds. He collected a few thousand dollars and departed for San Franscisco, soon followed by a sheriff. But he had taken ship for Australia, carrying with him the funds of the Ukiah and North Cloverdale Railway Extension Company.

A meeting addressed by Putnam in Oakland in May, 1888, was interrupted by the intrusion of the Christian champion and rapscallion, Clark Braden, reinforced by a local preacher named Sweeney and one Bennett, local agent of the Comstock society, with a demand to be heard and a challenge to debate. Mr. A. H. Schou of Oakland, who was presiding, said he would leave it to the audience whether these persons should be allowed to take up the time of the meeting, since the character of Clark Braden was well known throughout the coast. The audience voted a loud and unanimous No. The minister Sweeney begged he might inquire what was Mr. Putnam's objection to Clark Braden. Mr. Putnam replied: "I will tell you why I will not debate with him. I refuse to meet Clark Braden in public debate because he is a blackguard and a liar.'

There was curiosity to know how the Christian champion would take that. He shouted something at the speaker and then walked stiffly forth, followed by the Rev. Mr. Sweeney and Comstock's young man. As they went, Mr. Schou sent after them the reminder that if a Freethinker had entered Mr. Sweeney's church and created this sort of disturbance of the meeting, he would have been placed under arrest instead of being allowed peacefully to depart.

This man Braden, whose argument consisted in an attack on the good name of Freethinkers, usually did not return to serve the same Christian community twice. The religious people who employed Braden had a custom of meeting afterwards to pass resolutions repudiating him as too rank to be borne with. He professed to be a Campbellite, or "Disciple," and when the churches of that denomination could be worked no longer, he went to the Methodists. A religious paper in Winfield, Kansas, The Nonconformist, gave him this piquant mention: "It is yet to be reported that Clark Braden was ever received in a community the second time, except in company of the officers, with jewelry on his wrists." At one place, where he debated B. F. Underwood, the Christians who employed him told him he was injuring their cause, and he had to borrow $20 of Underwood to get out of town. In return he sent to Underwood a letter in which he told how the Rev. John Sweeney, Underwood's next opponent, was to be defeated. There was absolutely no good in Braden. His backers in Oakland came to grief. The Rev. Sweeney involved himself in an affair that

laid him under charges of financial crookedness and
vice, and Comstock's agent Bennett gained publicity
by means of rascally proceedings, the nature of
which will later appear.

8 —IRELAND AND THE POPE.

It became my duty to review on its first appearance Judge James G. Maguire's pamphlet "Ireland
and the Pope," being "a brief narrative of papal intrigues against Irish liberty, from Adrian V to Leo
XIII." That was a work of considerable importance, although written, as its publisher, J. H. Barry
of The Star, explained, on Daniel O'Connell's
principles—"as much religion as you please from
Rome, but no politics." That dictum of O'Connell's was a slogan among the supporters of Father
McGlynn in New York in the earlier '80s, without
the very hearty indorsement of thoughtful Freethinkers. That the taking of religion from Rome
involves the same surrender of independence as receiving politics from that quarter needs no argument, especially when no Catholic is allowed to decide for himself what belongs to religion and what
to politics. Judge Maguire's book had a large run
and is of permanent worth for the history it gives
of the plundering of Ireland with the pope's connivance.

John Alexander Dowie, who afterwards as
Elijah II, was to make a considerable splurge in the
country and to found Zion City, Illinois, appeared
that season in San Francisco, where he "unmasked
Spiritualism" and boasted himself to be a faith

healer. Reports that followed him from Australia were unflattering. San Franscisco clergymen published him as a "tramp and impostor." I attended one of his meetings in Irving Hall. In appearance he reminded me of Clark Braden, and he was a dull preacher.

I observed that there was a Greek Catholic church in San Francisco, and wrote to the resident bishop, one Vladimir, to inquire if he would not lay before the readers of Freethought the difference between the Greek church and the Roman. The bishop complied at some length, supplying the interesting information, verified by profane history and sacred scripture, that the Greek was the original Christian church, founded by an apostolical council at Jerusalem, as related in the fifteenth chapter of the Acts of the Apostles. Christians from Palestine, having fled there to escape the persecuting Jews, founded a church in Rome, Bishop Vladimir wrote me, but fell into many errors, apostatized from the faith of the true church, and invented doctrines too monstrous for the human conscience, as witness the dogma of the infallibility of the pope. The bishop of Alaska and the Aleutian Islands, for such was Vladimir's title, proved clearly that the bishop of Rome, which is to say the pope, was an arrant impostor.

On the eastern lecture tour Putnam in September attended a meeting of the Chicago Forum, a former church turned into what he termed a "temple of humanity," for social purposes, and spoke there twice on Sunday. His report to Freethought contained this note of prophecy: "Young Darrow, formerly of Farmdale, Ohio, of heretic blood, is going to the head of his profession. Law, and politics, and reform are his forte, and he is bound to be one of the brightest leaders of the people." As Putnam always predicted fair weather, he was bound to make some good hits, as in this instance.

9 —THE RIGHT OF AFFIRMATION.

The editor of The Truth Seeker made a little record for Secularism that year of 1888, which was noticed throughout the length and breadth of the country, by contending for the right of a citizen to register as a voter without swearing, or to affirm without raising his right hand. The Board of registration demanded that he should make oath on the Bible and then catechized him on his "belief in God." He declined to answer and the board refused to register him. The following paragraph tells what ensued.

"From the decision of the board the editor appealed to the Supreme Court, as represented by Judge George C. Barrett, for a mandamus compelling the inspectors to register him, and in opposition those gentlemen sent in their affidavits stating that he had refused to swear or to affirm in the usual manner. The judge was a righteous one. He said that the chairman of the board had no business to ask a man to uplift his hand; a citizen had been denied his legal rights, *and the board must reconvene and register the applicant.* In his written opinion Judge Barrett said: 'Inspectors have no right to require a man to affirm with uplifted hand, nor was it their province to demand the religious test. Indeed, their interrogations about the relator's belief in the existence of the deity was an impertinence to which no citizen, in the absence of any suspicion of untruthfulness, should be subjected.' "

The Board of Registration was therefore compelled to reconvene, without pay, for no other purpose than to register the editor of The Truth Seeker as a voter. Judge Barrett, who rendered this decision was the jurist previously mentioned who resigned from the Nineteenth Century Club with Andrew Carnegie because of the economic radicalism of the club's president, Courtlandt Palmer. The judge's membership in the Nineteenth Century Club had done its perfect work of liberalizing his mind on the relations between church and state which were there discussed.

10 —COURTLANDT PALMER DIES.

Unfortunately Courtlandt Palmer, former president and long the treasurer of the American Secular Union, did not live to applaud the decision of the judge. He died, July 23, 1888, at the early age of 45 years, in New York, the city of his birth. For a man born on the conservative side of the fence, and reared, as one biographer said, "amid the giddy whirl of fashionable society," besides being a member of the Dutch Reformed church until after he was married, Mr. Palmer underwent a considerable mental and social transformation. John W. Draper's "History of the Intellectual Development of Europe" made him a religious skeptic, and the So-

ciety of Humanity and his association with Freethinkers did the rest. A biography evidently prepared by himself was printed in the Social Science
Review for February, 1888. In it the writer dwells
with obvious pride on his
relations with the Free-
thought movement. That
was all the experience he
had. Up to the time he read
Draper, except from his college courses, his life had
been a blank. There was
nothing to record. After
that he had the full intellectual life. Ingersoll spoke at
his funeral. Palmer had
put in writing his wish not
to be buried from any Chris-
tion church nor to have any

Christian hymn sung. His survivors hardly kept
faith with him, for they called in the Rev. R. Heber
Newton to read the Episcopal service. He had discussed with Stephen Pearl Andrews, whose Collo-
quium suggested the Nineteenth Century Club, the
subject of Spiritualism and survival, in which he
did not believe. They agreed that the one who
first died should communicate with the other. Andrews preceded Palmer by two years, and no word
came.

Other Freethinkers to die in 1888 were Judge
Arnold Krekel of Kansas, July 14, aged 73, at the
end of a long and honorable career in the Missouri
legislature and on the bench; and Richard A. Proc-

tor, the popularizer of astronomy, New York, September 12, at 51. Proctor was an Englishman, and
reared a Catholic, but he wrote some observations
on the Ingersoll-Gladstone discussion which showed
that with respect to the Bible and the god that
book depicts he was on the side of the unbeliever.
B. F. Underwood wrote of Professor Proctor in
The Investigator: "I was acquainted with him personally. I had conversations with him, one fully
two hours in length, and corresponded with him
from the spring of 1887 until a short time before
his death. Professor Proctor was a radical Freethinker, an Agnostic. He had no belief in a personal God and none in a personal immortality. He
regarded the whole system of Christianity in its
theological aspects as a system of superstition. He
regarded Herbert Spencer as the greatest philosophic thinker of any age."

In Freethought for November 10 I began to
write under the head of "Observations," where I
stated my views and opinions with unrestricted
freedom and restricted responsibilty. These observations were kept up in Freethought for above
three years, and later in The Truth Seeker. I may
be a mesozoic precursor of today's colyumist.

11 —A PEEP FROM THE POPE.

Apparently Pope Leo XIII put out an encyclical
about this time in which he laid down the law on
liberty. Said his holiness as I find him quoted
(Dec. 1): "The state must profess some one religion, and the Catholic being that which alone is
true, should be professed, preserved, and protected

by the state, and false doctrines should be diligently repressed by public authority . . . I anathema-
tize those who assert the liberty of conscience and of
religious worship, and *all such as maintain that the
church may not employ force."* No man with that
stuff amongst his mental furniture, if discovered,
could get past our immigration officials today.
Archbishop Riordan of San Franscisco issued a
circular letter, read in all the churches of the city,
saying that marriage between a Catholic and a
Protestant, the ceremony being performed by a
Protestant minister, was "horrible concubinage."
Would a pope or an archbishop say the same things
today for American consumption? It seems to me
the boys are losing some of their courage.

In The Truth Seeker for 1888 are numerous en-
tries concerning that experiment in churchless
towns, Liberal, Mo. C. B. Reynolds having visited
Liberal, reported that its progress was checked by
the restraining hand of its founder, G. H. Walser.
"If he [Walser] would absent himself from Liberal for a few years," wrote Mr. Reynolds, "he
would be better appreciated, the citizens would become more self-reliant, and on his return he would
be surprised and delighted at the progress the town
had made." Prof. M. D. Leahy of the Liberal University felt compelled to resign as the alternative
to advocating Prohibition, which had become an
issue. There was no academic freedom for Professor Leahy.

Charles Watts, who was publishing Secular
Thought in Canada, filled lecture engagements in
the States. The Canadian government refused a

charter to the Secular Thought Publishing Company. The Freethinkers of Canada held a successful convention at Toronto, September 15. The Manhattan Liberal Club elected Dr. E. B. Foote, Jr., president, to succeed Van Buren Denslow. The New York legislature unanimously requested Ingersoll to deliver the memorial address in honor of the late Roscoe Conkling, and the Colonel accepted the invitation. The Rev. Hugh O. Pentecost proclaimed himself an Agnostic. John R. Charlesworth, an Englishman, who said that he had done talking for branches of the National Secular Society, announced in December that during the winter months he would lecture for American Freethought societies for the expenses of his journey. All of Mr. Charlesworth's connection with the Freethought cause, as I remember the circumstances, did not redound to its glory.

E. A. Stevens, secretary of the A. S. U., began proceedings to make the churches of Chicago pay taxes on property unlawfully exempted.

The Liberal papers existing in 1888 were The Truth Seeker, Boston Investigator, Ironclad Age, Indianapolis; Freethought, San Francisco; Secular Thought, Toronto, Ont.; Independent Pulpit, Waco, Texas; Lucifer and Fair Play, Valley Falls, Kansas; Liberty, Boston; The New Ideal, Boston; The Open Court (then a weekly, now a monthly), Chicago; I name also the Spiritualist papers, Banner of Light, Foundation Principles, Olive Branch and Better Way, and Dyer D. Lum's Alarm, which was Liberal with something to spare, being violently anarchistic.

The Congress of the American Secular Union, toward which Putnam lectured his way East, was held in Lafayette Hall, Pittsburgh, Pa., October 5-7. Putnam had declined reelection as president of the Union, and after a series of meetings which a local Freethinker named Harry Hoover canvassed as a candidate for secretary, creating something of a diversion and causing controversy, the delegates re-elected E. A. Stevens, and put in R. B. Westbrook, LL.D., of Philadelphia as president. The anti-religious addresses and general proceedings at this Congress were reported to the police, and it appeared afterwards that the assemblage barely escaped being raided and its speakers arrested. The new president, Dr. Westbrook, was a native of Pike county, Pa., born in 1820. Princeton college conferred on him the degree of A.M., New York University that of LL.D., and he got a D.D. from the Presbyterians, who fired him in 1864 for "abandoning the ministry and engaging in a secular profession." He wrote "The Bible: Whence and What," a book that enjoyed a vogue among liberals; attacked the trustees of Girard College in public lectures for their violation of Girard's will in introducing religious teachings, and then published the book "Girard College and Girard College Theology," a clear exposure of the whole situation. Secretary Stevens wrote eulogistically of Dr. Westbrook and predicted a good record for Secularism under his presidency.

12 —LOCAL SEISMIC DISTURBANCE.

The climate of California requires that in order

to preserve its reputation there shall be rain early
in November. The vegetation well watered by the
rains that continue from September till June can
stand a long dry spell, but in October, unless raining is resumed, there comes the sere and yellow
leaf. In the autumn of 1888 it was dry. John
Robinet, sheep man of San Luis Obispo county,
gave me a call about the 10th of November, just
after the election, and discussing results said that,
still and all, the prosperity of California depended
less upon the triumph at the polls than upon our
having a little rain in the near future. Said I:
"You probably have heard that the ministers prayed
for rain last month?" He said: "Yes, but what I
think is that instead of praying, some one ought to
do a good job of swearing, as for instance"—and
in eloquent swear words he condemned the protracted dry spell; in the language of the statute he
did unlawfully, wickedly, profanely, premeditated-
ly, and spitefully utter with loud voice, in the
presence of divers of the citizens of the commonwealth, publish and proclaim, concerning the
weather, certain wicked, profane, and blasphemous
words, to the discredit and contempt of the same.
Forty-eight hours had not passed before rain began falling and falling hard, and there was a great
storm, with vast commotion. One may read in
Freethought that I had just written the heading
of an article on supernatural interference with the
weather "when my ear was struck by a sound that
might have been made by a trainload of steam
boilers coming up Kearny street over cobblestones.
The telegraph pole across the way waved like a

cattail in a breeze, and the building I was in appeared suddenly to move about six inches to the
south, stopping with a bump that nearly slid me
out of my chair." The next day's papers reported
the severest earthquake since 1871, and the Berkeley University professors laid it to "the late heavy
rains diminishing the barometric pressure," and
so on. I remembered the fervent swearing of Mr.
Robinet, and recalled the prayers of the ministers
for rain. Why not swear for rain? The ministers had indeed offered up their petitions, but nothing happened to the barometric pressure prior to
the time of Robinet's profanity.

Our landlord while we were at 504 Kearny street
was a man of the name of Von Rhein, and he was
an argumentative Christian. The first time I went
to pay the rent he asked me how Freethinkers accounted for design in nature unless they believed in
God, or would account for the existence of a watch
if it had no designer. I replied that Freethinkers
recognized design in manufactured articles, but
not necessarily in raw material, which was about
all one could make out of nature. He dismissed
the subject then by saying that of course I had
given it more thought than he had, but he believed
I could be answered. Again, on a similar occasion, when the rent money passed from my hands
to his, he inquired whether I fully realized what
the fate of a scoffer was likely to be. I said no,
that I was not quite clear on that point, and he
tendered the information that all who denied the
divinity of the Christian religion were destined to
be damned. He said he did not mean perhaps.

When I inquired if persons who had never heard of the Christian religion would share the same fate, he said they most undoubtedly would. "To illustrate," quoth Mr. Von Rhein, "it is as if a person were approaching a deep hole; the fact that he does not know the hole is there will not save him from falling into it, however honest he may be." Said I: "One can't reply to an argument like that except by saying that parties who prepare deadfalls are more culpable than those who ignorantly walk into them, and that an infinite being who would play that sort of trick on a blind man could not be depended upon to do the fair thing in any case." Mr. Von Rhein answered that the arrangement was sufficiently equitable to satisfy his sense of justice.

Not so very long after this discussion occurred, Mr. Von Rhein, while inspecting a building on Montgomery street, illustrated the argument, as might be held, by walking through a skylight and taking a drop of some twenty feet to the floor below. When making an observation on the incident I said: "His fall did not result fatally, but considerable blame is attached to the owners of the building for neglecting to provide proper safeguards against such accidents, while Mr. Von Rhein is entirely exonerated. When he is recovered from the shock I may take occasion to ask him whether he holds himself or the owners of the building responsible for his drop through the skylight. If he takes the blame to himself I shall then understand how it is that he believes in the culpability of people who, as he imagines, walk blindfold into the everlasting pit."

CHAPTER XXII

1—WE ORGANIZE AND CELEBRATE.

THE year 1889 opened cheerfully in the Freethought office, San Francisco, under the influence of a pleasantry neatly turned by Mr. Channing Severance, the Carpenter of Los Angeles, who wrote that he had within the week beaten the best six days' record walking for work, and added: "The thought has struck me several times that if Jesus Christ found it as hard to obtain carpenter work as I have, his going to preaching may have been a necessity on his part instead of a desire to save the world."

I still see occasionally the name of Mr. Severance attached to an article in a Spiritualist exchange.

Fifty of the Liberals of San Francisco subscribed a fund of $100 to finance a series of Sunday Freethought lectures by Putnam in Irving Hall. The first lecture, January 6, drew an audience of three hundred. Those which followed were still better attended. Within the month more than nine hundred citizens of California had signed a call for a State Convention, which was held on Sunday, the 27th, to organize the California State Liberal Union. There were two hundred and fifty attendants at the morning meeting, four hundred in the afternoon, and in the evening a thousand. I assume it was the largest gathering of the kind yet held in San Francisco, for an old-timer observed to me that he had never before tried to attend a Freethought meeting in a hall that would hold a thousand when he couldn't find a seat. Judge J. W. North of Oleander, in Fresno county, was the unanimous choice for president of the new union. Judge North in many respects reminded me of the Hon. Elizur Wright, president of the National Liberal League. The judge in his younger days had been an anti-slavery lecturer in Connecticut. He went out to Minnesota and founded the towns of Faribault and Northfield, the latter taking its name from him. He went to California and founded the town of River-side. I believe I heard him say that a rascally court, that had been bought up by land stealers, robbed him of most of his property. Feeble health and old age, he being now about 75, prevented Judge North from accepting the presidency of the California State Liberal Union, which he handed to Putnam with a graceful speech and amidst cheers. As a Freethinker, Judge North, again like the Hon. Elizur Wright, went all the way.

This convention drew part of its numerical strength from the local Turners, and a member of that Bund, a young architect named Emil S. Lemme, was elected secretary.

The Paine celebration immediately following the convention was a tumult. A German speaker named F. Schuenemann-Pott made an address, following opening songs by German singing societies. Mr. Schuenemann-Pott, a well-known Liberal leader of those days, and a man of experience, said he had never seen such a demonstration on a similar oc-casion.

In New York half of the audiences assembled at
Liberal meetings were women. In San Francisco
female attendants were rare. Here at this Paine
celebration where we had an audience of a thousand,
less than one hundred women could be rallied for
the grand march that preceded the dancing after the
literary and musical exercises were over.

A series of local Liberal meetings followed, inaugurated by Prof. Herbert Miller, a scholarly
young man who for his unbelief had found himself set outside a religious institution where he had
been teaching. In another month the professor
had raised funds and organized the San Francisco
Freethought Society, meeting regularly in Irving
Hall, with P. O. Chilstrom for president and himself for regular speaker. Of itself, with its membership made of the pleasantest sort of people, with
a full quota of girls and women; with a scholar for
a lecturer and musical talent enough for a concert;
with a generous patronage that made the expense
only a trifle, this started out to be a model Freethought society. It wanted only the right hall, and
such a one we supposed it would be easy to find in
the place that had been provided by the money of
James Lick, Freethinker and philanthropist—
namely, Pioneer Hall. There, however, we were
in for a disappointment. Some of the members of
the Pioneer Society were willing to allow the Freethought Society to occupy the hall rent free, except for the mere cost of janitor and light. But the
committee in charge of the building would not consent on any terms. They had a reason, which,
while not a good one, served their purpose. The

Freethought Society had an open platform, not for the exclusive use of members or invited guests, which in my opinion was a mistake. The lectures of Professor Miller, condensed, made admirable editorial articles not below the standard of any paper anywhere. But the discussions that were allowed to follow them when they were delivered spoiled their good effect and lowered the quality of the meetings as a whole. These discussions, participated in by such "protagonists" and "menaces" as we have always with us, diminished our audiences in size and led to the inquiry whether we called that sort of wild speculation "Freethought." Possibly the not always dignified proceedings suggested to the committee a reason for not renting us the hall. The situation discouraged Professor Miller, who relinquished his lectureship. His after fate is unknown to me, but I should be surprised to be told that he had not made his mark somewhere.

2—SAN FRANCISCO FREETHINKERS.

A variety of speakers followed on the platform of the society, which still met in Irving Hall, one of the best being Mr. F. B. Perkins, whom I have already mentioned. It was written of him in one of my Observations: "Mr. Perkins is a big man, with broad shoulders and a broad mind, and he is one of the ripest scholars I have ever met." He was a nephew of the Rev. Henry Ward Beecher. In former times he had been librarian of the San Francisco Free Library and of the Boston City Library.

We had another good man in Mr. Junius L. Hatch, who had studied for the ministry when young, but missed ordination. He told me he lost out on one question. They asked him if he believed unfeignedly that God created the world in six calendar days, and he answered that he did. "But I don't believe he could do it again," said the candidate. So he became a journalist. In 1889 he was fixed apparently for life by getting a place in the Custom House.

The cornerstone of the Lick Academy of Sciences was laid on July 12 of that year, 1889. Irving M. Scott, president of the Union Iron Works, gave the principal address, on "The Development of Science." It was the story of the church's warfare on science, but Mr. Scott did not mention the church. He called the hostile forces "Patristic," which few understood as of and appertaining to the holy fathers of the church. He thus escaped criticism at the expense of not being comprehended.

There were eminent Freethinkers to be found in San Francisco, though some of them suffered from shyness. I came into possession of a small book entitled "The Evidences Against Christianity," written by John S. Hittell and published by him in 1856. It was as strong an attack on the Bible as Paine's "Age of Reason," but more condensed and therefore less readable or "popular." I had heard Mr. Hittell, who was a historian, in an interesting lecture at Pioneer Hall on the discovery of Humboldt Bay, and finding him to be a Freethinker invited him to speak for the Freethought Society. He declined on the score of having more important work to do. Later I discovered that he deprecated aggressive Freethought work. As the author of "A Code of Morals," in which he dismisses the Golden Rule as "not sufficient for the guidance of humanity," he laid down enough maxims, drawn from the pagans and his own consciousness, to make everybody good, if followed. But as to propagating Freethought, he said:

"You are under no obligations to proclaim doctrines that, by the people around you, are regarded as criminal or injurious to the general welfare. If your neighbors accept false and debasing opinions, you can presumably do more good by teachings that will please and gradually elevate them than by offending them so that they would at once burn, banish, or avoid you."

On the other side to this proposition I named for the benefit of the author of those discouraging sentiments the examples of Socrates, Jesus Christ, Servetus, Giordano Bruno, and Mr. Hittell in 1856, who had proclaimed doctrines calculated to provoke burning, banishment, and avoidance.

On June 9, 1889, the Freethinkers of the world unveiled a statue to Bruno in Rome, with the financial encouragement of a thousand dollars sent from the Liberals of the United States. It is not the reformers that follow Mr. Hittell's advice who get the monuments and so perpetuate their influence.

3—TRIBULATION OF SINGLE TAXERS.

One of the careless Freethinkers who turned up in San Franscisco was Frank McGlynn, a real estate dealer and brother of the Rev. Edward McGlynn who had recently distinguished himself in the Henry George campaign back East. The wife of George McGlynn was suing him for a divorce, or an annulment of their marriage, because he would not go to church, because he "made their home a house of blasphemy," and because he was in short an Atheist. He professed the Single Tax, which put him on the church's bad books without further argument.

An adventure, rather comical on the whole, involved another Single Taxer. There appeared at the California State Convention in January "an evoluted preacher," as he described himself—the ex-Rev. J. E. Higgins, who in the course of his speech, which made an excellent impression, declared that he had found his right environment among Freethinkers, and believed he would do a little lecturing if he could find audiences. Soon after the convention he brought to the Freethought office a notice that he had an engagement to lecture in Eureka, Humboldt county, and along the Eel river, under the patronage of Robert Gunther. Having delivered this message to me, the ex-Rev. Mr. Higgins remained to impart a lecture on Single Tax, which he had recently espoused. Said I: "If you are going to meet Robert Gunther, take a fool's advice and leave the Single Tax behind you. Gunther has a hundred thousand dollars' worth of unimproved land." He promised faithfully to hold that thought. Anyhow, he said, his mind was so stored with other useful precepts struggling for utterance that he would hardly get around to economics. Only the worst of luck, including rain, pursued Mr. Higgins on this expedition. He was compelled to spend two or three days and nights under the roof of Mr. Gunther, and to defend the Single Tax or let Mr. Gunther get away with the proposition that Henry George was crazy. After the discussion he moved his quarters to the hotel and waited until the weather had cleared, when he came back to San Francisco and reported. Later Mr. Gunther reported also. The Single Tax had proved so divisive an issue between them that the two men had been unable to get together on any other. Mr. Gunther, in his description of their falling out, seemed to be the more outraged of the two. Mr. Higgins perceived in the adventure enough that was funny to compensate for his loss of time, but Mr. Gunther was too hot ever to cool off.

4—THE ADVENT OF BELLAMY.

The book "Looking Backward," by Edward Bellamy, that got to San Francisco early in 1889, raised a commotion more or less homogeneous with the revival conducted there that year by Sam Jones. According the volume a fair review, I still pronounced it a work inferior to "Rational Communism," by Alonzo Van Deusen, which The Truth Seeker Company had brought out in 1885. The emotional collectivists immediately staged "Looking Backward" as a Socialist revival under the name of "Nationalism." As such it had drawing power enough to fill the largest hall in the city. But Nationalism was nothing new, being merely a more theatrical presentation of an old idea.

478   FIFTY YEARS OF FREETHOUGHT   [1889

The Hon. John A. Collins was one of the best
and clearest headed friends of Freethought. As a
social student, he had written, a half century ago,
a work entitled "A Bird's-Eye View of Society."
Toward Nationalism I found him cool, if not indifferent. I asked if he had read "Looking Backward, the Uncle Tom's Cabin of Industrial
Slavery." He said he had glanced at it, and added
rather wearily: "I went through all this turmoil and
excitement fifty years ago." He had doubtless been
a Fourierite, and any Fourierite will admit that
Fourier said the last word on the problems of human society. I attended a Nationalist meeting
where speakers defined the term, and came away to
write the impression that Nationalism was "razzle-
dazzle Socialism." An enthusiast named Haskell
stated at this meeting that Nationalism promised
"two hours' work per day, luxuries for the poorest
equal to those now enjoyed by the richest, rare exo-
tics in every man's front yard, carpets in the house
ten inches thick, fare to New York, $12," and so
on. I predicted: "The Nationalist movement in
San Francisco will soon be where Croasdale said
he found the Single Tax Movement in New York,
namely, in a howling dervish state of emotional insanity. A rabbi asserted the new Socialism—that is,
Nationalism—to be synonymous with Judaism; the
Eddyites said it was Christian Science; Theos-
ophists recognized it as Theosophy; it was generally
accepted as harmonizing with the Spiritualist philosophy, and orthodox ministers were heard to affirm they were Nationalists because they were
Christians. I risked the surmise that the leader of

the cause, Mr. Haskell, was a "four-flusher." The
confirmatory testimony on that point from persons
having knowledge of Haskell's past performances
was so voluminous that it could not be printed.
Nationalism as manifested in San Francisco goes
into the museum labeled as an interesting phenomenon while it lasted.

5—THERE WERE DIFFERENT KINDS OF SPIRITUALISTS.

A society of Liberal Spiritualists in San Francisco sent notices of their meetings to Freethought;
some of the members came to Freethought meetings, and the same singers assisted at both. Outside these Liberals, the Spiritualist leaders in San
Francisco were about as hopeless a collection of
bamboozlers as could anywhere be found. Dr.
Louis Schlesinger, who published The Carrier
Dove, could hardly be called anything that would
write him plain but a humbug and grafter. For his
printing-office in the old St. Ignatius church on
Market street he solicited orders, yet one who gave
him an order, as I did just to be friendly, would
be hooked for twice what the job was worth. His
stunts as a medium, for he professed to be such,
were transparent frauds.

Mr. J. J. Owen published The Golden Gate,
Spiritualist, and sold lots in Summerland, Santa
Barbara county. The Celestial City, a Spiritualist
paper published in New York, viewed Summerland
and reported:

"Far out on the Pacific slope, hemmed in between a homely range of rugged, knotty, infertile mountains on the one hand, and on the other a dreary expanse of endless sea that has not even the activity of a surf, there lies a miserable, barren waste. Four consecutive months of each year no rain falls upon this parched, far-off land, while the sun's bright rays beat down and dry to pulverous dust the burning soil. Here is wanted to be established the new colony of Summerland, the future home of the Spiritualists of the world. No native fresh water is found within the border lines of this would-be city of the future. All the fresh water it gets for the irrigation of this unfruitful land is forced there through pipes, from a distance of four miles; and year after year has this sluggish soil sung its melancholy soliloquy in unison with the listless waters of the calm Pacific. To this forlorn and ragged edge of the western world are the owners and propagators of Summerland trying, by the wholesale suppression of all information relative to its disadvantages, to induce the people to come, trying to inveigle the innocent and the uninformed into giving up comfortable homes in the fertile fields of the East, and taking up their abode in this wretched colony."

Editor Owen of The Golden Gate, who was putting this thing over upon the hopeful, had no part or parcel with the Freethinkers and named them but to mispraise. He informed his readers that his editorial articles were messages from the angels, inspirational, and obtained by "secluding himself from the world and becoming passive and receptive to those higher and better influences and thoughts which he endeavors to express through the columns of The Golden Gate." Thus he wrote while promoting the Summerland scheme described in the language just quoted by the editor of The Celestial City.

The Summerland development may have been a
bona fide endeavor to found a Spiritualist colony,
or it may have been merely a real estate speculation with Spiritualists appointed to be the victims.
Probably it was the latter, since there is at the present time a place in Santa Barbara county of that
name, and colonies never last the length of time
that has elapsed since the date of which I am writing. The rival Spiritualist papers in San Francisco
stated that Summerland was a swindle. Some of
the Liberals who were also good Freethought
workers "fell for" the various schemes that were
floated by idealists or by cheats. One was the
Topolobampo venture, a plan with considerable
backing from the East, to establish the Sinaloa
colony in Mexico. John Lovell, publisher of
Lovell's Library, was interested in it, and I had
heard him talk on the Credit Foncier of Sinaloa before the Manhattan Liberal Club. I met numerous
returned Sinaloists who were known as Topolobampo Sufferers. One recounted that a woman,
Marie Howland, more or less an authoress, had
gone there to preside. He told me she was too advanced to meet his approval, since she attempted
to introduce mixed bathing among the colonists
"doffed of their clothes."

The Golden Gate advertised the medium Fred
Evans, a more versatile workman than Schlesinger,
but without the old doctor's blandness. I think
Schlesinger would perform his solemn tricks as
often as he could get a dollar a throw, even if he
knew all the time that the sitter was "onto" him;
but Evans was suspicious of anyone who asked him

to do that again and do it slow. Having one day, at
the solicitation of an earnest believer, sat at Evans's
curtained desk and got some slates with writing
on them, all in his own hand, as an observing
printer could tell, I wrote him a request to give me
another sitting, merely exchanging seats. I desired
to be on the side of the table where the works
were. He declined, making the excuse that he was
soon going to Australia and his dates were full.
At the same time he solicited more patronage
through newspaper advertisements—which showed,
anyhow, that he was lying when he pretended to
be too busy. I had solved his slate trick and
wished to have him see me do it and correct me
where I was wrong.

Meanwhile a friend with a totally unexplainable
confidence in Evans had sent me some slates firmly screwed together to be taken to the medium. My
friend assured me that in the presence of Evans I
should undoubtedly receive messages. I believed,
and still do, that nothing could be written on the
inner surfaces of the slates without taking out the
screws. As Evans was now out of the question,
my friend directed me to a medium named Colby,
with almost as good a reputation for slate-writing
and other psychic powers. I found Colby and
liked him personally. He did not, like Evans, remind me of a weasel. Had I seen him dealing faro
I might have asked for a look at the box before
putting anything down; still, one could recognize
in him certain qualities of a good sport. His rooms
were not far from the Freethought office, and
more than once after luncheon he came in to have

a chair and a chat and smoke his cigar. Then a
visitor from the South recognized him as a Baptist clergyman, named Rains, of Texas, who had
been in prison for holding up and robbing a passenger train. That put an end to my friendly relations with Mr. Colby. He had deceived me about
his past. He never told me he had preached. Mr.
Colby left San Francisco. Evans met in Australia
some one a little keener than himself who solved
his method.

6—MR. BAILEY SOUGHT SAFETY AFLOAT.

The shipping disaster in Port Apia, Samoan
Islands, when a terrific hurricane drove three German and three United States men-of-war upon the
reefs, with the loss of one hundred and forty men,
took place in March, 1889. Among the survivors
who somehow won through when their vessels
went down was an old man-o'-warsman named Bailey. He had "been to sea" all his life, but now
counted it time to quit, especially as he had reached
the age for retiring. Mr. Bailey, being a reader
of Freethought, deemed it neighborly to call on us
when he reached San Francisco on his way to join
his people in Oregon, with whom he expected to
spend his remaining days. He told me that for
some years he had held the thought of leaving the
navy, and when his ship foundered and he had to
swim for his life, and then barely saved it, because
he tired easy these days, the time seemed to have
come for him to lay up ashore. He gave me his
future address, where the paper was to be sent,

and departed for the State of Oregon, bidding all a final good-by and last farewell. I am uncertain about the length of time, but it seemed only a few months later, when the aged Mr. Bailey reappeared at the Freethought office with cheerful greetings. I asked him the question which he must have expected in view of the above farewell, and he replied that he was now on his way to the naval station at Mare Island to reenlist in the navy. How come? Well, it was like this: When he had got to the place in Oregon where his daughter lived, they had given him a little cabin all by himself on the side of a hill that showed a good prospect on pleasant days, and where, furnished with all the supplies he needed, he had settled down to a life of ease. But it rained and it rained, causing occasional landslips that changed the scenery about him. They assured him, however, that these things were always happening and were no cause for anxiety. But weren't they? Mr. Bailey testified that one night when he thought he was snug in his berth the ground under his cabin went adrift, and the next thing he knew he was at the foot of the hill, house and all. He pulled himself out of the wreck, spent a week making repairs, and took up life anew in the valley. It kept on raining, the streams rose till his house took in water, and had to be abandoned. The day after he got out of her she floated and went downstream. Then Mr. Bailey communicated with his shipmate Purdy, aboard the Independence, to see whether there was any berth for him there, and finding a chance to ship again, he came back. "Of course," said Mr. Bailey, re-

membering Samoa, "a fellow that goes to sea takes
some chances, but folks that live ashore aren't safe
at all. Whether it's a gale or fair weather, war
or peace," he concluded, "the deck of a man-o'-war
is good enough for me. I've seen battle and wreck
and sudden death at sea, and been cast away, by
thunder, but I got the scare of my life right on
terry firmy."

The Liberal activity stirred up by Putnam and
reported in Freethought drew the country's force
of lecturers in our direction. C. B. Reynolds came
first, followed by his wife, who was also a good
speaker, and they located at Walla Walla, Washington. B. F. Underwood made two tours. W. S.
Bell came and stayed; W. F. Jamieson arrived in
November, and the eloquent Mrs. Mattie P. Krekel, widow of Judge Arnold Krekel of Kansas City,
was on the way. The one lecturer left to the East
was L. K. Washburn. On July 1, Putnam had
seventy-five lecture engagements booked. Dr. J.
L. York of San Jose, with almost the whole field
to himself prior to Putnam's advent, and known to
those who read his announcements as "the Ingersoll of the West," appeared aloof and on the whole
unfriendly. George Chainey, was still going from
one perishing superstition to another. Just then
he was reported to be a Christian Scientist.

One day in the middle of the year G. L. Henderson, copartner in the old days with Hugh Byron Brown in the proprietorship of Science Hall
in Eighth street, New York, spoke for our Freethought Society and paid me a call at the office. A

decade had not yet passed since we met, but all things had changed. "If the friends of the beginning of the decade were to meet again in Science Hall," we said, "how many distinguished ghosts would be among them—Stephen Pearl Andrews, D. M. Bennett, Theron C. Leland, Courtlandt Palmer, Henry Evans, Porter C. Bliss, Tom Mc-Watters, and many another." Henderson had moved to Yellowstone Park, Wyoming, and the Religion of Humanity interested him no more.

A "character" known in San Francisco then was an old gentleman of the name of Choynski, who published his weekly "Public Opinion." He may have taken in subscriptions, but mostly, it was said, he took in his subscribers. He sent his paper for a year and then went and collected three dollars. The postal law allowed that as long as a paper was received, and the publisher not notified through the postoffice to discontinue it, the receiver was liable for the price. Mr. Choynski made the price high enough to pay him for the trouble of collecting. He was the father of Joe Choynski, pugilist, and said in his paper that every time Joe was going to fight, papa and mamma prayed he would get licked.

Occasional reference was made to the dilatoriness of the Lick trustees in carrying out the will of that Freethinker and philanthropist who had died thirteen years before. They held in their hands $1,650,000, yet half the bequests had not been carried out. The old ladies still waited for their Home, there were no Free Baths, nor any Manual Training School for the boys and girls of San Francisco. The monument to Francis Scott Key had been erected, and the Lick Observatory, containing the most powerful telescope in the world, completed and presented to the University of California.

One of our Oakland subscribers, Mrs. Dolly Broneer, was a descendant of Good Abner Kneeland, founder of the Boston Investigator, who back in the '30s had been a prisoner for blasphemy in Massachusetts. Mrs. Broneer showed me an acrostic written by Uncle Abner when he was 68 (two years before his death) to Dorcas Jane Rice, who was Dolly Broneer's mother. It ran thus, in quite classical form:

> "Delightful theme as e'er engaged the tongue,
> Or more sublime than ever poet sung,
> Remote from bigotry or slavish fear,
> Conjoined with love and all that men hold dear,
> Are modest virtue, pure in every sense;
> Sincerity of heart, benevo'ence,
> Justice and kindness join to make the sum,
> As all the graces harmonize as one.
> Now the result of all is happiness—
> E'en bigots here must surely this confess.
> Rejoice, then, now that we have found the road,
> Immortal bliss is ever doing good;
> Contented in its lot, does not repine;
> Enrobed in truth the graces ever shine."

Signed "Abner Kneeland" with a neat and proper flourish and dated at Salubria, I. T., the initials standing for Iowa Territory.

NOTE—These chapters of "Fifty Years of Freethought," which I have thrown into the form of an Autobiography to make a human document, have drawn more comment from readers, in their letters, than anything else that I can remember in The Truth Seeker. That is, more than have been received regarding anything the writer approved. People are inclined to animadvert more frequently than to commend. Regarding these chapters, one friend has indeed said they contain too much sex stuff, but that is characteristic of our species, being due, as the poet Milton divined, to the original error of Omnipotence in creating that "fair defect of nature," woman, without whom the history of the race, as well as these memoirs, might have been materially modified.

The temptation to print the commendatory words of readers that has been overcome hitherto, conquers at sight of these lines in The Literary Guide, to wit:

"Mr. George E. Macdonald, the editor of the New York Truth Seeker, is contributing to this journal some autobiographical chapters which are intensely interesting. For nearly fifty years he has been identified with the Rationalist Movement in America, and his pen becomes more gifted as time passes."

The year of my beginning to be identified, or affiliated, with the Movement was 1875—fifty-three years ago. The second half of the last sentence in the paragraph quoted from The Literary Guide brings the comfort which one past the meridian of life extracts from the assurances of polite and he hopes not insincere persons that he does not look his age.

The man writing in his eighth decade knows production is slower than in his fourth. He trusts it isn't inferior, but doesn't know. Hence the yielding to the temptation to print what is said by The Guide. I am not prepared to debate whether reprinting it makes it any nearer true or not. Still there is a feeling that an idea comes closer to being fixed as a fact, when put into type once or twice, than when it exists only as a hope.

8—CLOSING EVENTS OF '89.

Free as was San Francisco in the realm of personal liberty, there were streaks of religious bigotry such as that which excluded the Freethought Society from the hall built with the money of James Lick; and the town had Irish Catholic policemen, who could not see our right to sell the paper on the street. An old man named Ketchum attempted this, and one of "the Pope's Irish," as The Argonaut named them, ordered him to be on his way. Being stubborn, the old man suffered a clubbing. Not only that, but some influence prompted his neighbors to trump up charges of assault against him, and without defense he would have been indefinitely jailed. I testified as "character" witness for him, visited the prosecuting attorney at his office, and hired a lawyer. When I told the prosecutor that Ketchum was an industrious person who made his living selling our paper, the official replied that he must be industrious and a crank besides. An idealist of any sort in San Francisco was a crank and an object of suspicion. There was no more protection for Ketchum. When he came to the office on a later day with his bundle of papers ruined by the blood he had allowed himself to shed on them when a Catholic rough in a policeman's uniform beat him up, I advised him to desist.

The reading of The Truth Seeker and Freethought for 1889 is calculated to exasperate the Secularist who pays attention to what the churches were then doing. The effect of beholding all at once, instead of week by week, the year's sum of the church's stealings, invasions, abuses, persecutions, is impressive to the last degree. The church as an aggregate, backed by its millions of adherents and more millions of money, was achieving a record of infamy—grafting, grabbing, and for a pretense making long prayers. Deacon Benjamin Harrison occupied the White House, and the Sunday-school teacher Wanamaker a place in his cabinet as postmaster-general. Opposed to this predaceous combination were a few hundred Freethinkers, belonging to an organization, the American Secular Union, that could not raise ten thousand dollars; the secretary, E. A. Stevens, fighting a lone battle in Chicago to head off a little of the stealing if he might; the president of the Union, in Philadelphia, preoccupied with a book of Moral Instruction for the schools to displace the Bible and religious teaching; as if the promoters of those things—Bible and religion in the schools—cared a snap for moral instruction, or enjoyed anything better than to contemplate the feeble efforts of the Freethinkers with their half-dozen newspapers of limited circulation to prevent the incessant hold-ups and robberies in the name of religion. But what was going on then and has been ever since, and by what we behold today, doubts are raised whether Secularists can form an organization large enough to win by force of numbers. They will not for centuries be as numerous as the religious people who insist that whatever they believe as Christians ought as far as possible to be crystallized into law, and that what can't be enacted should be propagated at public expense. However, if Freethinkers cannot put the Bible out they can expose it. If they cannot exclude religion, they can at least show it up. I am not hopeful of settling the question of union of church and state while believers are in the vast majority, and not reached by the voice or literature of unbelief.

The workers of the American Secular Union that year appear to have been divided, though not at cross purposes. In Chicago E. A. Stevens, secretary, agitated for the taxation of church property and exposed the graft of the Catholic institutions that enjoyed appropriations of public money. In Philadelphia, R. B. Westbrook attacked the trustees of Stephen Girard, who were violating the provisions of his will by giving religious teaching in the college built with money Girard had left the city of Philadelphia for a wholly secular institution. Judge Westbrook also collected a fund to be offered as a prize for the above book of Moral Instruction in the schools. Mr. Stevens resigned before the next Congress, which, held in Philadelphia October 25-27, reelected Judge Westbrook and picked Miss Ida Craddock for secretary. The Rev. Father Edward McGlynn of New York, now a good Secularist, addressed the Congress.

A well-attended convention of the Oregon State Secular Union met at Masonic Hall, Portland, October 12. Putnam said of it:

"The Portland Convention was a happy success. Hundreds were present from all parts of the state, and the Liberals of Washington were generous in their attendance. It was an event for Liberalism, a representative assembly that in itself would mean much, but in its relation to future work it has a much grander significance. It is the beginning of many such mass meetings by which there will be more active union among Liberals and greater work

accomplished. The impulse and attraction of this convention will be for practical advancement . . . I have not
attended any national convention where there were greater
numbers or more interesting addresses."

He speaks of the "impulse and attraction" of
the convention. But the impulse and attraction of
the work on the coast was Putnam—the tireless
worker, the eloquent speaker, the ready, learned,
and effective writer. The men liked him; so did
the women. He might have kept the work buzzing
in Washington, Oregon, and California if he could
have remained there and borne the burden. There
was plenty to do. The Sabbatarians of California
were agitating for a Sunday law, without which
the state had got along very well theretofore, everybody being free to go to church who wanted to,
or to the theater, or to work. The Rev. Wilbur F.
Crafts, field secretary of the American Sunday Association, sent a questionnaire all over the world
to find out where Sunday was best observed, and a
San Francisco pastor answered: "Among the Christian people of California." With this proposed
Sunday law to fight in California, the Blair Christian Education bill in Congress, and the Western
States of Washington, Wyoming, Idaho, and New
Mexico holding constitutional conventions and voting for theological preambles, there was much to
comment upon.

The Museums in Central Park, New York, were
finally opened on Sunday in 1889.

Abroad in 1889, the International Freethought
Federation held its Congress in Paris in September;
Charles Bradlaugh resigned as president of the Na-

tional Secular Society of Great Britain, to be succeeded the next year by George William Foote; and the Swedish courts sentenced Victor E. Lennstrand to six months' imprisonment for publicly speaking against Christianity in Stockholm and Malmo. Lennstrand's health failed and the King pardoned him at the end of three months.

The Truth Seeker printed Ingersoll's only oral debate, the one he held with Frederic R. Coudert, a Roman Catholic, and Gen. Stewart L. Woodford, a Protestant, before the Nineteenth Century Club, on "The Limitations of Toleration," and Remsburg's "Abraham Lincoln: Was He a Christian?" A letter by Lincoln's law partner Herndon appeared, testifying: "Let me say that Mr. Lincoln was an Infidel. He did write a little work on Infidelity in 1835-6, and never recanted. He was an out-and-out Infidel, and about that there is no mistake."

The death of Mrs. Amy Post of Rochester, N. Y., early in the year, called one of the good old mothers in Israel to her rest at the age of 86 years. Mrs. Post had always been a reformer, beginning as an Abolitionist and closing her life as a radical Freethinker. It was said of her that as an "underground railroad" station keeper she harbored in her house for more than a dozen years, an average of one hundred and fifty runaway slaves each year. I believe that her last dear enemy was Anthony Comstock. Being a suffragist and a friend of woman, her remarks on that individual were replete with sentiments of pity for his mother.

The cause lost by death in 1889 that son of thunder, Horace Seaver, who had been editor of the

Boston Investigator more than fifty years. He died August 21, four days before his 79th birthday, for he was born August 25, 1810, in Boston. His inclination in youth was to be an actor, his parents' wish was that he should be a minister. Fortunately he became a printer and at 27 took work on The Investigator. He remained there while Abner Knee-

HORACE SEAVER.

land served his term as prisoner for blasphemy, and when the liberated Kneeland retired from the editorship in 1838 Seaver took his place. Ingersoll once wrote to Mr. Seaver that the distribution of the Boston Investigator had made it possible for him to travel through the country and lecture to thousands. Mr. Seaver was buried from Paine Memorial Hall, Ingersoll being the eulogist.

Late in 1889, the support of our paper Freethought having become rather burdensome to my partner, Mr. Putnam, who was sinking $1,500 a year of his earnings in it, we concluded to form a Freethought Publishing Company. Putnam had kept the lecture field almost continuously, selling books and taking subscriptions, and remitting the proceeds along with his lecture fees. The Free-thinkers were loyal and liberal, but there were not enough of them. Although church members are in the minority, there are not many Freethinkers, and never were, who could be signed up as sub-scribers to a Freethought paper. In my letters to Putnam acknowledging his remittances I ma.ry times protested against his working so hard and giving his wages to pay the bills of the paper. I had the feeling of being supported by his labors rather than my own. He was getting along in years, I reminded him, and ought to lay aside some-thing for the time when he could not do so much remunerative work. So we formed the company, issued stock, and moved to larger quarters, namely 838 Howard street, where there was a vacant store in a new building.

CHAPTER XXIII.

1—MEETINGS AND THE GIRL PROBLEM.

ON December 2, 1889, the Freethought Publishing Company had been organized and had filed incorporation papers; president, Samuel P. Putnam; vice-president, Frank L. Browne; secretary, George E. Macdonald. The names of W. H. Eastman and Emil S. Lemme, two excellent young men, were added to complete the corporation. One hundred and fifty persons bought shares. January 1, 1890, found us doing business at 838 Howard street. The company voted me a salary of $20 a week. Mrs. Macdonald kept the books and met the visitors. Outside my inclosed editorial corner I hung a basket marked: "Please leave poems here and go away." At that period Edwin Markham, distressed by one of Millet's pictures, wrote "The Man with the Hoe." I had a Millet picture, "The Angelus," showing a man and a woman, evidently farm hands, standing with their eyes attentively upon the ground, as though searching for something. The poem appears to have caused to be reproduced thousands of copies of this picture. I marked mine "The Lost Angleworm" and hung it in a good place.

The California State Freethinkers' Convention, held in San Francisco January 25 and 26, was a

Redrawn from a faded photograph, the picture shows the front of the office of Freethought, 838 Howard street, San Francisco, in 1890. The figures represent (from right to left) Putnam the Lecturer, the girl Compositor, Browne the Printer, and the Editor.

gathering of local Liberals. It must have been a memorable year in the history of the climate of California, for all places more than a day's journey from the city were cut off by landslides, washouts, and snowdrifts. The elder Dr. E. B. Foote of New York convened with us and served with me on the Resolutions Committee. We had enough present to elect ninety vice-presidents, an executive committee of nine, and Putnam for president, Lemme for secretary, and A. H. Schou for treasurer. The Liberal Spiritualists were there with their speakers and singers.

The extraordinary weather conditions and the advent of influenza or epizootic, under the new name

of *la grippe,* operated also adversely on the Paine
celebration that followed the convention. In my reports of meetings I sometimes felt it my duty to rebuke the girls who were due to be there for their
non-attendance at lectures on serious topics, whereas when singing and dancing were promised they
outnumbered the young men two to one. At the
state convention they might have heard the able addresses of W. S. Bell, the Hon. F. B. Perkins, and
various other speakers who never failed to instruct
an audience, but they were not present, while at the
Paine celebration, with a short program of educative talk and many musical numbers and a social
dance for good measure, they were plentiful and
happy until midnight's hour had come and been
chased away. Young married men and the fathers
of daughters were equally at a loss to explain why
this should be so.

On girls absenting themselves from Freethought
lectures I wrote in another place: "It seems to be a
settled fact that young women don't want public
lectures, and that they won't even attend a sociable
for pleasure when an instructive lecture must be
taken as a penance. If I were a safe man to send
into our families, I should be glad to inaugurate a
crusade among the girls for the purpose of quick-
ening their minds on the matter of mental improvement. They will go to church without urging, and
to the theater when urged to stay away, but they
seem to look upon an educative lecture as an un-
necessity and therefore to be avoided at any inconvenience."

A young woman who read this asked me how

many girls we had among our officers or on permanent committees. By a sad blunder we had omitted
to elect or name any.

Annually in San Francisco occurred the Bohemian ball in the same Union Square hall where the
Freethinkers met, and so many of our Bohemian
readers invited us that we must attend or explain.
They were joyous routs where one was allowed to
dance Bohemian figures he had never seen before.
Why my report of the 1890 affair should have run
into rhyme as it did is a wonder to me. I read:
"The band was playing all the night, and if feet
were heavy, hearts were light. The music told the
tale of him, yclept McGinty, who never rose, since
he went down into the swim, dressed in his Sunday suit of clothes. Then it related with toot and
blare, how the rollicking razzle-dazzle boys went
wandering off on a terrible tear and awoke the
night with their joyful noise. Ah! life is a dance
and the figure a reel; Time is the fiddler, gray and
grim, whose music we follow with toe and heel, till
foot is weary and eye is dim. We waltz and polka,
fast or slow, chassez and balance, cross over and
turn. New faces arrive and old ones go, but the
set moves onward in unconcern."

Versification and rhyme dribbled uncontrolled
from my pen in those days, while only under the
greatest provocation have I made two measured
lines rhyme in the past twenty-five years. E. C.
Walker told me a while ago that verse-making was
connected with the activity of glands.

2—OBSERVATIONS ON THE STATE.

From reading Herbert Spencer, who was and

is my favorite philosopher, and in companionship
with a considerable number of bright writers, I fell
into ways of anti-government dissertation from
which I have never fully returned.   Take this example from one of my Observations in Freethought:

"If there is any conspicuous evil that should be done
away with as fast as possible, it is government.   Thomas
Paine called it a necessary evil, and declared that in its
best form it could be nothing else; but since his time
people have got into the habit of treating government as
though it were something to be proud of.   They dress the
government in fine clothes and parade it through the
streets as Chinamen do their devil.   They give it the best
buildings in the country, and do not appear to realize that
the state house is half-brother to the penitentiary.

"No good reform can come through the legislatures—
the tendency is the other way.   Are the people enjoying any
liberty, a bill is introduced to restrict it.   If they demand
more chains, the legislature will hasten to accommodate
them; if they desire more liberty, they must fight for it.
The people of this country fought for their independence
of Great Britain, for the rights of American citizens in
foreign countries, for their protection on the high seas,
and for the abolition of human slavery at home.   These
epochs, marked by wars, are the only periods when liberty
has been achieved and personal rights guaranteed.   It
seems to be the lot of the people to acquire liberty, and
that of legislative bodies gradually to filch it away.   The
legislatures give us Sunday laws, oath laws, blasphemy
laws, Comstock laws, protective statutes, medical laws, and
unequal taxation.   The legislature kindly takes from us a
part of our earnings for its support, and another part for
the support of superstition.   It lets us pay for religious
services for its own so-called benefit and for the benefit
of all inmates of public institutions.   It gives us the privilege of voting if we are males of twenty-one years and

upwards, and denies suffrage to females of all ages. Where it got the right to grant the one or to deny the other nobody knows. Our legislatures know that the ballot amounts to nothing in the hands of a man in any large community where it is worth using, and that they should withhold it from women is explainable only on the theory that they never make even a seeming concession to the people until the worthlessness of the concession has been demonstrated."

There was much to a similar effect in my output for the dozen years following. I learned with gratification that my writings carried comfort to those who were in prison. Benjamin R. Tucker's paper, Liberty, brought me the news that Freethought was received weekly in Joliet, Illinois, and was read with pleasure by Messrs. Fielden, Schwaab, and Neebe, life prisoners and alleged participants in the Haymarket affair.

3—DEDICATED TO GIORDANO BRUNO.

The Freethought Society made the two hundred and ninetieth anniversary of the Martyrdom of Giordano Bruno, burned at the stake in Rome February 17, 1600, the occasion for a large memorial meeting. Thomas Curtis, with his fifty years' record as speaker and worker for Freethought, delivered the speech. I copy the last paragraph of the report of the proceedings: "This was one of the best meetings the writer has ever attended. The addresses, songs, and recitations were of such high merit, the audience was so large, so attentive where close attention was called for, and so generous in awarding praise to its entertainers—everything indeed passed off so brilliantly and harmoniously that many a day may pass before we see the like again."

Emotions stirred by the enthusiastic response of the big audience to a Bruno poem I had written and Putnam read, had not subsided when I wrote that paragraph. The verses are too many to be copied here.

It was ordinary, unimaginative verse, yet on the whole, dramatic; appropriate to the recent erection of the Bruno monument in Rome, to which many present had contributed, and Putnam put the needed energy into his rendering of the lines.

This year the California State Secular Society lost one of its best members by the death of the Hon. J. W. North of Fresno, who died February 21, in his 76th year. Another death soon followed —that of the Hon. John A. Collins of San Francisco, April 3. The judge, nearly 80 years old, had made a record in liberal and progressive work. As a boy he was an associate of Horace Greeley. A student for the ministry at Andover Theological Seminary, he failed of his purpose to be a preacher and took up anti-slavery work; also temperance, woman suffrage, Spiritualism, and industrial co-operative reform as a co-student of Fourier along with Albert Brisbane. Details of his professional and political life made a half-column in the daily papers.

Judge Collins was legal adviser without pay to the Freethought Publishing Company. I consulted him when the Freethought Society was troubled by John Alexander Dowie, who held his faith-healing services in a hall that was next to the one we occupied for our meetings, separated from it by doors that could be removed. His services were so noisy sometimes that our lecturer had to raise his voice. We bore the nuisance without complaint. And then this imported impostor (he came from Australia) proposed to enjoin us from advertising meetings at the same time and place as his. He complained of our holding Sunday night dances, threatening to be mean about it. Judge Collins thought of the facts a few moments and said we might advise Dowie it was his first move. Meanwhile we pushed our piano as far away from the partition between the two rooms as it would go. There was in town a rival faith-healer, Mrs. Anna Johnson. To discredit her work Dowie called her an impostor, a Jezebel, and, moreover, unchaste. Thus defamed, Mrs. Johnson, remarking that Dowie was a beast, a devil, and a liar, sued him for fifty thousand dollars. That diverted Dowie's attention from the Freethought Society.

4—AN EXPONENT OF EGOISM.

Henry Replogle shared our printing-office at 838 Howard street and there resumed the publication of his paper called "Equity," which was suspended when he left Liberal, Mo. The house Henry occupied at Liberal had been mobbed on account of his social views; hence he departed that town. He advocated in "Equity" a philosophy called Egoism, which runs more or less like this: Every man should be able to give a reason for the course in life that he chooses, and should be prepared to explain his conduct when he does good as well as when he does what is thought to be evil. To do good for the sake of good, or to do right "because it is right," is unphilosophical. Self-denial is unnatural, and therefore unwise unless some benefit results to the self-denier sufficient to pay for the inconvenience. Life has no object, but may have uses. Uses for what? To give the means of happiness to its possessor. One thing is not "higher" than another, but may be more complex. That is the difference between mud and brains. Intelligence is the result of complexity, and is the recognizable manifestation of the working of the brain. There is no design, but a natural process. Therefore we are not required to indulge in a sentimental adoration of genius. We need only to recognize it as a natural outcome of prior conditions, the same as virtue. Life has no purpose, but shall we therefore spend it riotously? No; that will not pay, as witness the wrecks on the shores of dissipation. Shall we practice self-denial as regards the pleasures of the world? Certainly, if it gives us happiness to do so; in which case we have used life to the point of its highest productivity, and in denying ourselves one pleasure we have achieved a greater. If the monk in his cell, the anchorite in his cave, the priest among lepers, were not happier than he thinks he would be somewhere else, he would not be there. To be what we call virtuous, not for virtue's sake, but because experience has taught us it brings most happiness, pays us in the end, and is without credit. It is no more praiseworthy than the act of paying our board in advance when we have no credit. To practice what goes under the name of morality is simply to prepare conditions for selfish benefits. The duty idea has nothing in it. If a person would be happier otherwise than in the performance of what he calls his duty, he would never perform it. What is life for? It is *for* nothing. We have legs adapted to locomotion, and we use them for that purpose. We find life adapted to the pursuit of happiness; therefore let us so employ it.

Horace Seaver, for more than fifty years editor of the Boston Investigator, is said to have produced his editorial articles by setting the type of them from notes. I sometimes preferred that method to writing an article in full and then revising it. I was at the case one day with Replogle alongside, running off a page of his "Egoism" on our half-medium Universal, when news came that a brother editor of liberal tendencies, T. L. Mc-Cready of The Twentieth Century, was dead. Said I to Henry as I spaced out a line, "McCready is in luck." Said Henry: "Yes; only being dead he can't appreciate it."

And holding these sentiments, that it were better not to be, we kept on working for dear life!

Henry had as his companion a sweet and lovely woman named Georgia. As she was the faster compositor of the two, and hence had the greater earning capacity, she held a frame on an Oakland daily and he did the housework. Not being married, they were so absorbed in each other that when Georgia died, Henry nearly lost his reason through grief.

In one number of Freethought I published a note of thanks to my wife for a gift of roses which she had placed on the editorial desk. Georgia Replogle remarked that probably editors' wives had brought them roses before, but my acknowledgment of them was an original thing for an editor to do. So far as I have known, it is the only instance recorded.

LILIAN LELAND
Author of "Around the World Alone."

I quote myself as reporter when I say that Lilian Leland bloomed on the platform of the Freethought Society one Sunday evening like a blossom in a hedge, and told in simple language the story of "Freethought Around the World." Miss Leland prefaced her address by saying that she had the good fortune to be born of Freethinking parents, who left their children's minds unfettered by any creed or belief, so that the Sunday-school stories of cross and crucifixion took no more hold upon her unterrified mind than the fairy tale of Jack the Giant Killer. In her journey around the world the first heathen country she visited was Japan, whose people she found more ideally Christian than those she left behind. The Japanese were the kindest people on earth, and suffered more than they gained from the in-

troduction of Christianity. She saw in Japan more
missionaries than converts. In China the people were
different. Their cities and their habits were inde-
scribably unclean, and it was scarcely possible for
the missionaries to make the inhabitants worse—or
better. She visited Benares, in India, the oldest and
holiest city on the globe. It stands upon the Ganges,
the impurest river in the world. In both India and
Japan she was warned against the native who professed Christianity. The uncivilized Hindu could
be relied on for a certain amount of fidelity, but the
converted Hindu had lost faith in his own gods'
power to punish and had learned hypocrisy. Palestine Miss Leland found the barest, poorest, stoniest
country on earth, and Jerusalem the least tidy city
with the possible exception of a walled one in China.
At the alleged tomb of Christ in Jerusalem warring
Christian sects were prevented from killing one another by the presence of a Mohammedan soldier
who guards the holy sepulcher. In concluding, the
speaker said her experience all over the world had
taught her that it is a good thing to be an American, because independence in an American woman
is not only forgiven but admired, while it would
subject a European woman to suspicion.

There was no discussion of the lecture, but when
Putnam had paid a brief tribute to the late T. C.
Leland, father of the speaker, and had said that the
daughter was a worthy descendant, Thomas Curtis
offered a resolution, which was adopted without
dissent, that the Christian parents of the country
be challenged to prove by comparison that they
could show a brighter example of womanhood, men-

tally, morally, and physically, as a result of a religious training, than Miss Leland afforded as a result of escaping it.

5—AN UNGRATEFUL INSTITUTION.

I violate the chronologies once more to say that early in 1928, a professor in Mills College, Oakland, resenting the act of an acquaintance who had sent him The Truth Seeker, which he pronounced "ignorant trash," thus showing that his reading of the paper had been confined to the affirmative of one of our Fundamentalist debates, wrote me to take his name off the list.

The discourteous language of the professor, whose name is Linsley, almost caused me to regret the defense of a Mills College president that I put up in 1890.   The president concerned was the Rev. Dr. Stratton, charged by a girl with going into her room when she was abed and the lights out, and kissing her while allowing his hand to wander.   I held that the Rev. Dr. Stratton was a misunderstood man; for it appeared that the apartment occupied by the complainant contained a telephone, one of the old-fashioned kind, of course, that had a little crank on it, to which the accused clergyman had frequent occasion to repair.   Admittedly the light was insufficient; and this fact, so ran my defense, added to absent-mindedness—an infirmity which is known to accompany great learning, or to result from habits of pious abstraction—doubtless caused the clergyman to mistake the young lady's face for the receiver, while the movement she resented as an ulterior design, may have been but a well-meant endeavor on the clergyman's part to ring up central. I submitted this explanation in lieu of Dr. Stratton's alibi and general denial, for it looked to me like a complete and triumphant vindication of a man cruelly misjudged, leaving no stain on the record of an institution with which Dr. Linsley has now the questionable honor of being connected.

The faculty never in gratitude asked for my photograph to put in the college album, or for the purpose of having an oil painting executed to hang on the walls. It should at least have my name enshrined among the defenders of its fair fame.

In September Mayor Pond of San Francisco summoned me before him for examination as to my capacity to act as judge of elections. A qualification for that position was being a taxpayer. I passed, and was O.K.'d on the English language, along with Mr. James Corbett, a prominent and gentlemanly exponent of pugilism, who a while later was roughly K.O.'d by Mr. Fitzsimmons.

D. C. Seymour, a traveling lecturer, who reported the incidents of his itinerary through Freethought, challenged Putnam to a debate on Spiritualism before our society, but appeared not when came the hour. Putnam made it a lecture. Not attacking Spiritualism as a theory, a religion, or an inspiration, he took the ground that its alleged facts were so far from being demonstrated that Spiritualism was not entitled to be called a science. Among those present was an ingenious chap named Kellogg, who asked permission to demonstrate certain

of the facts which Mr. Putnam had set aside as un-
proved. Mr. Kellogg hoped that for the production of harmonious conditions some Spiritualist
would assist. Our believing member, Mr. James
Battersby, consenting to the sacrifice, Mr. Kellogg
asked him to write a few questions on slips of paper, or "ballots," and while he did so the ingenious
one went to the piano and played the music of a
hymn. When the ballots had been prepared, the
"medium" and sitter placed themselves at opposite
sides of a table on the platform, their fingers touching. Kellogg apparently picked up one of the close-
ly-folded slips of paper and held it against his head,
looking serious. Loud and seemingly causeless raps
were heard, then the voice of Kellogg reading the
message, which he passed to Putnam to be read to
the audience. Mr. Battersby attested its correctness. Repeating the demonstration by request,
Kellogg sat at the table in such a position that persons nearby could see his work. Instead of putting the ballot to his head, as he appeared to do, he
dropped it into his left hand, unfolded it and held
it where he could read it. What Mr. Battersby
held down carefully under his fingers on the table,
supposing it to be another ballot, was a blank piece
of paper. Kellogg spoke of a local medium with
whom he had enjoyed a sitting that cost him a dollar and a half. The medium was making $15 a
day by means of this self-same "demonstration."

6—A JAMES LICK INCIDENT, AND OTHERS.

The Nationalist movement, founded on Bellamy's
Looking Backward," ceased not to spread, nor

clubs to multiply. One of the principal clubs had
for president Mrs. Addie Ballou, a Spiritualist and
Freethinker who was active as member and speaker
at our society. Her daughter, Evangeline, who
sang in opera, came frequently to sing for us.

A word more about Mrs. Ballou. She was an
artist and had painted a fairly good portrait of
Thomas Paine from her personal impression of
how the Author-Hero probably looked in life. Being acquainted with James Lick, she acted on his
suggestion and offered the portrait to the committee
in charge of the Centennial celebration, to be carried in the parade with banners representing other
Revolutionary fathers. The committee, which maybe never heard of Paine, or were against him if
they had, rejected her offering and she went back
to the Lick House to report. Lick was then suffering from his last illness at this fine hostlery he
had built on Montgomery street. Said he: *"Well,
if they will not march with Paine, they shall march
under him"*; and he had a line led across the street
from his window to a window opposite, and ran the
painting out on it. The procession marched underneath.

There were five Nationalist clubs in San Francisco in the spring of 1890. Henry George, then on
the coast, pronounced Nationalism a castle in the
air. Hardly a year later but one club remained,
and in place of the thousands who had thronged
Metropolitan Temple, there was sometimes no quo-
rum present. Dr. J. L. York had gone over to this
movement and to Spiritualism.

The Blair Christian Education bill met its fate

in the Senate at Washington on March 20, 1890; ayes 31, noes 37. The history of that bill, outside the then current issues of The Truth Seeker, is told in a book on "Religious Treason in the American Republic," by Franklin Steiner.

The Protestants and Catholics at Edgerton, Wisconsin, quarreling over the Bible in the schools, carried their case to the supreme court of the state, which decided that any reading of the Bible necessarily involved the reading of a sectarian doctrine. Therefore Bible reading in the schools was unconstitutional and prohibited. That was a famous decision.

There was in Boston an aged Freethinker named Photius Fiske, some of whose many philanthropies were occasionally discovered. He possessed wealth, and pensioned a number of indigent persons, besides making generous donations to Liberalism. When he died on February 7, 1890, the Boston papers reported that he had left a great fortune and had willed it to "Boston's deserving poor." He may be named among Freethinking philanthropists when Christians ask what Infidels have done for charity.

The first number of Freethought for the year 1890 announced the death of Mrs. Elizabeth H. Church, aged 81 years, whose father had been a consul in France, and her grandfather consul-general at Lisbon during the administration of George Washington. She made small bequests to Freethought activities and requested a secular funeral conducted by Mr. Putnam. She had one relative, the Rev. Edward B. Church of San Francisco, who faithfully carried out her will, attending the funeral to hear Putnam's Freethought discourse, and handing me the amount of her bequest as soon as the will had been probated. Mr. Church was a preacher who did not preach, but held the position of principal of the Irving Institute.

Some books with a vogue came out that year: "John Ward, Preacher," by Margaret Deland; "Robert Elsmere," by Mrs. Humphry Ward; "Story of an African Farm," by Olive Schreiner, and "Cæsar's Column," by Ignatius Donnelly. John Wanamaker, postmaster-general, took the Sabbath school view of books. He barred from the mails Tolstoy's "Kreutzer Sonata," "An Actor's Wife," "The Devil's Daughter," "Thou Shalt Not," one of the Albatross (Albert Ross) novels, and "Speaking of Ellen" and "In Stella's Shadow," by authors whose names have not endured. Joseph Britton, fugleman of the Comstock Society, arrested Patrick Farrelly, president of the American News Company, for handling them. Farrelly was a Roman Catholic, and made no defense, as a man of principle should have done. He "pulled" Lilian Leland's "Around the World Alone," after publishing it, on complaint that, like Mark Twain's "Innocents Abroad," it ridiculed sacred objects and pictures in Palestine and Rome.

7—THE CHINESE PRESS.

At the corner of Washington and Dupont streets, in San Francisco, a visiting Colorado editor and I one day in 1890 discovered a printing-office like no other in the country at that time. It was the office of a Chinese newspaper. The tall hand-press, made in Edinburgh long before the Chinese trade, was surmounted by a dragon. A compositor at his labors wore a yellow silk cloak with flowing sleeves, and his blue trousers were tied about his ankles with white tape. He wore a silk skullcap having a red knot at the crown, thus contrasting strongly with such members of the typographical union as I have been privileged to know. The Chinese comp, it could be seen, was one of the higher class, perhaps entitled to wear the mandarin-button, as in Franklin's day the printer, being a gentleman, wore a sword on dressy occasions. This compositor was surrounded by sixty type cases, each divided into 196 compartments, or "boxes." Job cases held display type awaiting sensational news, like the Second Coming. The Chinese compositor, when we observed him, happened to be distributing, or throwing in his case. He carried his type in a stick, from which he extracted it with nippers. Not beginning with the end of a line and throwing back the letters as they had been set, he rather planted himself in front of a case and stayed there until all the characters he had with him that belonged to this particular case were returned to it, when he proceeded to another. He may have distributed as many individual pieces of type in an hour as it would take an American printer five minutes to throw in. The Chinaman's type-face was on a square body of soft metal, bigger than pica. In his takes he got no "fat," no poetry, no italics, and no punctuation. The heading of the paper he produced, The Oriental News, appeared on the last column of the last page, and looked like the tail of a kite. I saw not the editor, but some of his copy hung on the hook. He had written it with a small brush and a box of blacking. A stone-hand carried a form on a tin galley held above his head like a tray borne by a waiter. He put no trust in his lock-up; he slid the form from the tin galley to the bed of the press, which was of the "Washington" pattern, but older. I have not watched the progress of the art preservative among the Chinese. It may have advanced and left this office in San Francisco in 1890 the last of its kind.

Our Freethought paper never looked like itself unless it carried a glowing report of Putnam in the lecture field. But one week when he was somewhere in Oregon, it contained only this card:

"DEAR GEORGE: I have struck it rich. Lectured three times and am only fifty cents behind expenses. No postage stamps. Yours forever,   SAMUEL."

Assuming it was my duty to write something for him to keep up the enthusiasm, I added to his card:

"The future gleams with promise, and the earth trembles beneath the tread of the advancing hosts that fling to the glistening sun the radiant banners of progress. Morn spills its goblet of effulgence over the mountain tops; the chariot of day mounts the heavens to high noon; the declining orb in majestic splendor sinks below the western clouds that lie in banks of red and gold above the far horizon's rim; the pale moon, like a silver scimeter, cuts through the sky's serene and vast abyss; the stars peep brightly from the void of space; night stretches forth her laden scepter o'er a slumbering world; and the Pilgrim dreams of a postage stamp large as a quarter-section of government land."

We called Putnam the Secular Pilgrim. He went wherever there was a call, and often had to take a loss.

From publications fifty years old readers discover how few of the lies told of Infidels in the twentieth century are new. President Calvin Coolidge in 1927 made the unfounded statement that doubters do not achieve. The San Francisco Monitor in 1890 said: "The achievers of great things have never been Infidels." At the New York Press Club that year Ingersoll said: "And after all, gentlemen, I call upon you to witness that there is nothing so weak and helpless as the truth. She goes into the arena without shield or spear. A good healthy lie, clad in complete armor, with sword and shield, does the business." Two of the principal achievers in San Francisco, James Lick and Adolph Sutro, were Infidels.

Thus far I haven't mentioned Henry Frank, known to all readers of The Truth Seeker. I supply the omission now from an article in Freethought of July 19, 1890: "The Rev. Henry Frank of Jamestown, N. Y., has been denounced as a heretic and expelled from relationship with the Western New York Association of Congregational churches." The title of one of Mr. Frank's books, "Doom of Dogma," stimulated many years ago the mind of the Rev. Dr. A. Wakefield Slaten, who in 1922 was also fired.

8—PROPHETS OF DISASTER.

Eighteen ninety was the year of many dire predictions, forerunning a historic "messiah craze," especially among the Amerinds. Mrs. Woodworth, a revivalist, foresaw a tidal wave that was to drown Oakland for its sins. In the August Arena, Dr. Joseph Rodes Buchanan, Spiritualist and psychometrist, in a twenty-page article on "The Coming Cataclysm of America and Europe," laid down the disastrous future for a period of nineteen years and after. Dr. Buchanan saw the Republican party hurled from power by the Democratic party, which would make things worse, and then yield to the Labor party with no better results. Meanwhile the seasons would so mingle with one another as to destroy all crops and make large regions of the United States barren. He had the Atlantic seaboard swept away from Maine to New Jersey, but forgot to mention Galveston on the gulf. "The Mississippi will be a scourge like the Yang-tse-Kiang in China." Here he came near the truth, since in 1927 the Mississippi-Kiang did overflow its banks. For the Pacific coast Dr. Buchanan duplicated substantially the prediction of Mrs. Woodworth. Occasionally someone recalls Dr. Buchanan and his prophecies. He has been dead many years and his psychometry (soul-measuring) died at about the same time. I saw him often in the early '80s when he had an Eclectic School of Medicine in Livingston Place, on Stuyvesant Square, New York City, and walked about the Park with Hope Whipple, who I believe was his psychic.

The former Reverend Hugh O. Pentecost was now conducting his paper, The Twentieth Century, as an Atheist and Materialist. He soon added Anarchist and defied the world. He held a meeting in Newark, N. J., on the 7th of November to commemorate the Chicago victims. It was stopped by the police, who clubbed the members of the assemblage and locked up Lucy Parsons, widow of Albert, hanged in '88.

An absurd manifestation of Comstockery showed itself among the principals of schools in Brooklyn, who wished to have Longfellow's poem, "The Building of the Ship," withdrawn from the text books as a menace to the morals of their pupils. Longfellow had been so indelicate as to call his Ship a young bride and to represent the Ocean as the ardent Swain. Quite lost to considerations of modesty, he wrote:

"And for a moment one might mark
What had been hidden in the dark.
That the head of the maiden lay at rest,
Tenderly on the young man's breast."

"She starts—she moves—she seems to feel
The thrill of life along her keel,
And, spurning with her foot the ground,
With one exulting, joyous bound,
She leaps into the ocean's arms!"

"Take her, O bridegroom, old and gray,
Take her to thy protecting arms
With all her youth and all her charms!"
"How beautiful she is! How fair

She lies within the arms that press
Her form with many a soft caress
Of tenderness and watchful care."

Often in my youth had I read that poem unconscious of its voluptuous theme. And at the Union

Iron Works, out at the Potrero, I later had seen
ships launched without indulging an impure thought.
I did not even think of Longfellow's verse.   One
day they put overboard the cruiser Charleston,
which instead of leaping into Old Ocean's eager
arms, moved out a little distance into the slough
and came to rest with her bottom in the mud, and
the groom, Old Ocean, miles away.   On another
day it was the cruiser San Francisco they launched.
Substantially the same story; but as she slid down
the ways a 100 per cent American leaped upon the
timbers she had left and frantically waved the flag
of his country.   His feet slipped their hold and he
went into the water after the bride.   But the exhibition was moral, even if the hands who pulled
him out were profane.

9—FOR THE RECORD.

The American Secular Union held its fourteenth
annual congress in the Grand Opera House, Ports-
mouth, Ohio, October 21-23, 1890, the attendance
being large.   "The opera house was packed," and
the old officers reelected—Dr. R. B. Westbrook,
president; Miss Ida C. Craddock, secretary.   The
congress discussed the policy of appointing a Field
Secretary and sending him forth on a salary to
work in the name of the Secular Union.   The
choice fell on Charles Watts, editor of Secular
Thought of Toronto, Ont., to be confirmed when
the funds for his salary should be collected.   Mr.
Watts already occupied the field, with half a dozen
other lecturers.   Dr. E. B. Foote, Jr., questioned

the justice of paying a salary to one and lending no assistance to the rest. Better, he thought, to subsidize them all. Dr. Westbrook had stressed the necessity of appointing a man of the best moral character. As all of them were of good moral character so far as known, this seemed a reflection on the unchosen. The fund to provide a salary for Mr. Watts failed to be subscribed.

The birth of a son to George E. and Grace L. Macdonald became known when the editor of The Truth Seeker, November 29, published a letter from me saying that I had made him an uncle and given his nephew the name Eugene. My letter said:

"The subject of these remarks [that is, the infant Eugene] became a resident of California on the eighth of the present month of November, and, I am informed, favors his father in the matter of sex. He was too late for the election this year, but will vote in 1912, provided he is not himself a candidate for any high office. This native son of the Golden West was recognized at once as Eugene Leland Macdonald, although he has so far declined to acknowledge his identity. The mother is happier than she ever was before. She is also in her right mind, and I would that I could say as much for the father, who has been in a state of wild excitement since the eighth. In acquiring a son I fear that I have lost many cherished friends among my male acquaintances on account of my inclination to thrust information upon them about the said son. When they see me coming nowadays they make haste to get upon the opposite side of the street or to conceal themselves where I cannot find them. Even my friend Burgman, the tailor, with whom for many months I have been accustomed to exchange theosophic thoughts, now turns upon me a cold ear and a deaf shoulder, says goodbye and skips around the corner at my approach. Putnam hurrayed as I did at first, but he has now departed for

Texas, and the time is near at hand when I shall have
to howl alone or hire somebody to shout with me. I shall
be pleased if you or any of the boys in The Truth Seeker
office will kindly make a little noise on my account. When
you see Counsellor Sherman and Harry Thomas, convey
the tidings to them. We were young together ere wives
and families had set their seal upon our brows. When we
all have scant soap-locks above our ears we will meet
again, and refer casually to the halcyon days of youth."

The interested mother of the boy has preserved
a Swinburnian travesty with the suggested title
of An Infant Son-(net). It might be entitled "A
Burden of Paternity":

> "Lying asleep between the sheets of night,
>   I heard a sound arise beside my bed,
>   Faint first, but swelling as I lift my head;
> And growing fiercer till I strike a light.
> It issues from a mouth not made to bite
>   Nor yet articulate, but small and red,
>   With voice imperative, which spoke and said
> I wist not what, save something to incite
> Me to a livelier motion, and I haste,
>   Without formality of donning shoes
> Or coat, or vest, or any other clothes,
> To warm a jolt of milk, in toilet chaste,
>   Which quickly in a bottle I infuse,
>   And thrust the same beneath that infant's nose."

The Oregon State Secular Union, C. Beal, president, and Kate Kehm, secretary, called a convention to meet in New Orion Hall, Portland, October
11, 1890. Putnam attended and reported that it
"added a bright page to the history of Freethought."

For all that California had no Sunday law and
made a pretense of taxing churches, San Francisco
was afflicted with the same meanly pious gang of

officials that get into places of authority in other
cities. I have said that the trustees of James
Lick's various bequests, taking a salary from the
estate of the Infidel, refused to let the Freethought
Society occupy Pioneer Hall, which his money
built, but they rented the front store in the building to a liquor dealer, who named his place the
Pioneer Saloon. I have told how the pope's Irish
on the police force clubbed off the street an old man
who sold our papers. The press was not much to
rely upon in 1890; we could get no notice taken of
meetings that drew sometimes as many as eight
hundred or one thousand attendants. To help news-
dealers sell Freethought, I printed posters they
might hang in conspicuous places. On their own
authority the police, being Irish and Catholic, ordered these taken in, although they bore nothing
more offensive than "Read Freethought: 'To Plow
is to Pray; To Plant is to Prophesy, and the Harvest Answers and Fulfills.'—Ingersoll." Catholic
roughs defaced the poster fastened to a board in
front of the office, and threw the board into the
street. There were more papists in San Francisco
than in any other city of its size, and they got the
political jobs. Ward politicians, controlling the
schools, made the teachers pay for appointments,
in money or otherwise. One teacher who had paid
in money and then lost the appointment, exposed
the system; and those that had paid in another
way and been cheated, naturally had nothing to
say. Men were placed on the school board who
were not fit for the police force. One of these
whom I met personally was a regular rounder, and

I heard him boast of the perquisites of his job. I exclaimed somewhat loudly in the paper against the suppression of Freethought by "office-holding politicians ready and seeking to be debauched by coin or concupiscence." The old part of the city contained a nunnery called Visitation Convent. One could learn from persons of long residence in San Francisco that the priests and some laymen had carried keys to its doors and lodged their mistresses there—a practice that might not have been wholly discontinued.

The local Comstock agent, C. R. Bennett, patron of Clark Braden, tried so many times to win his cases by lying that the courts ceased to act on his testimony. "He has been proved to be a man who cannot be believed under oath," said Prosecutor Mott, and Mott refused to prosecute a case with Bennett in court as witness.

CHAPTER XXIV

1—MY PARTNER REPULSES THE SABBATARIANS.

THE religious element in California, as elsewhere, was as unappreciative as it was unworthy of the free institutions, the gift of a more honest generation, which the bigots with a zest for persecution were preparing to slaughter. They had picked the free Sunday for their first victim. As no law exempted church property or parsons from taxation, it might be supposed that release from the civic duty of helping to support the state that protected them would be the first concern of the ecclesiastical parasites. But the nominal taxes, which in so many instances were never paid, worried them less than their lost grip on Sunday liberty. They could enjoin the collector of taxes by pleading oppression, or practice on the city officials to have their ratables overlooked, but they could hardly put barbers, bootblacks, or merchants in jail for Sunday work without some sort of statute to plead in their complaint. Therefore, in order to procure such a law the ministers formed a Sabbath Union, prepared a bill, and sent their secretary and several assistants to argue its passage before the joint committee of the legislature at Sacramento. Advices from the capital foretold a hearing, in February, 1891, when the advocates of the Sunday bill "expected to have it their own way." But to the displeasure if not dismay of the holy men, the Freethinkers sent Putnam, and the Spiritualists

524

Addie Ballou, to speak for the opposition. And, unexpectedly, the bill was for the time defeated. Mrs. Ballou told me that Putnam did it, and gave so lively a description of the scene in the Senate chamber that I forthwith celebrated the victory in a poem of sixteen stanzas. I quote the opening one and some of the others:

The Christian hosts had massed their force in Sacramento
    town,
And they had brought great orators of merit and renown;
And they had vowed a Sunday law they straightway would
    enact,
And all the Senate chamber with their followers was
    packed.

A half dozen stanzas give the argument of the Reverend Thompson, secretary of the Sabbath Union, and introduce Putnam and what he had to remark about the proposed law.

He said it had its origin along the pagan line,
And was imposed upon the world by Emperor Constantine;
And that when we observe the day, as under law we must,
We strike our colors to a knave and trail them in the dust.

The Fathers of the nation never dreamt of Sabbath laws,
And in all the Constitution there was not a Sabbath clause.
The gonfalons of ancient Rome might make a Christian
    flag,
But he would not consent to march behind a pagan rag.

He's stood beneath the Stars and Stripes upon the battle
    field,
And while *that* was triumphant he did not propose to yield.
Freethought, religious liberty! was his motto in this
    fight,
And Sunday laws he held to be subversive of his right.

When Putnam first began his speech, he scarcely had a
    friend
In all that vast assemblage, but when he reached the end,
So persuasive was his eloquence, so righteous was his cause,
From gallery and chamber rose the salvos of applause.

Oh, there are victories of peace, and victories of war,
And there are victories that hold the whole great world
    in awe—
Great triumphs for the men who win, aye for the men who
    fall,
But a victory for Freethought is the greatest of them all.

Putnam rightly estimated the value of the temporary success. "The snake is scotched, not killed,"
he wrote. "The combat will be renewed. But I
hope that at every session of the legislature there
will be a debate like this. It will educate the people.
It will set even the Christians to thinking. Agitation is the best thing for progress." When the
combat was renewed, Put was not there to engage
the enemy, and the ministers got their Sunday law.
Henceforth there could be no more sociables and
dances at the Freethought Society Sunday night to
disturb the faker Dowie. Malignity, spite, and
stupidity, on which Sunday laws are begotten and
thrive, had given the joy-killers their way. And
long they have had exemption too. The passage of
a law making legal deadheads of them was hardly
more than a ratification of an existing condition. It
legitimatized the skinning of the taxpayers and of
the treasury by the churches, which they had been
doing unlawfully hitherto.

2—RHYMES THAT RETURNED.

Of my rhymes, some that I considered the neatest were not so esteemed by anybody else, and they never got farther than the columns of Freethought. Others went about everywhere that papers like Freethought were circulated. In quoting my verse, then, I choose only such pieces as had the approval of reproduction elsewhere. There was one about 1890 that came back to me in the exchanges. It bore the title "Christian Faith" and evidently was a reply to a religious rhymer.

There is no Christian faith:
A man may say all increase is of God,
But he who plants not seed beneath the clod
    Reaps barren sod.

That man who hastes, when clouds are in the sky,
To house his grain, knows that no God on high
    Will keep it dry.

The mariner seeks Heaven's aid no more,
But life-preservers, when the breakers roar
    On leeward shore.

"The wind is tempered," says the Christian seer,
Yet prudent herdsmen scarce are known to shear
    At fall of year.

We go to rest with prayer when day is o'er
But seldom lock our sense in sleep before
    We've locked the door.

Believers rear their temples high and broad,
And then attach, not having trust in God,
    A lightning-rod.

And who has read of flaming holocaust,
Nor noted, touching churches that were lost,
   "Insured for cost"?

Whoever for another day prepares,
And guards 'gainst dangers coming unawares,
   God's word **forswears**.

He rises from his knees when prayers are said,
And, shunning Heaven, to whom he prayed,
   Seeks human aid.

There is no Christian faith;
Men with their lips may trust a God on high,
And by their every act their word deny,
   I know not why.

There were diversions occasionally, or they might be created. A subscriber in British Columbia discovered some lines of verse 'which he sent me saying that he thought them worthy of a place in Freethought, but if I did not agree with him, I might return them. They were as follows:

We stand by the graves of the old-time gods
   Who sleep with their prophets and seers,
Whose crowns and kingdoms and scepters and rods
   Have passed with the vanishing years.
And we know they are gone, and that even so
Shall ours and the gods of our children go.

Yet man shall abide, though his gods be dead
   And he bury them one by one;
He shall witness the last of the triple head,
   The Father and Spirit and Son;
And shall cry as his deities disappear,
"The gods have departed, but I am here."

We stand in the valley, or on the hill,
    Or move by the rolling stream;
And we query: "All these, are they older still
    Than the gods of the prophet's dream?"
Vale, river, and mountain as one reply:
"Before Jehovah was am I."

I sent the poem back to my correspondent telling
him I thought it rather poor, the theme not being
original and the versification and rhythm faulty. He
replied that of course he respected my judgment,
but still had confidence in his own; and, another
thing, he believed that our Freethought papers
would please their readers by publishing plenty of
good poetry. Editors arrogated to themselves more
than was warranted, he believed, by their qualifications as critics. He was sending the poem again,
and hoped I would find room for it, not alone to
humor him but at the same time to compliment the
unknown author. An adroit letter and the publication of the poem pacified him. To excuse the liberty I had taken in so freely criticising the verses, I
said I had written them myself in 1879, twelve
years before, which was the fact.

James Barry of the San Franscisco Star, who
had suffered imprisonment for publishing his opinion of a judge, went to Sacramento (1890) to argue
before the Senate Judiciary Committee in favor of
a bill designed to take from judges the power to in-
flict fines and imprisonment, with no trial of the accused by jury. When addressing the committee he
was interrupted by the chairman, a man named
Sprague, who asked with sarcasm if Mr. Barry

"gave the committee no credit for possessing intelligence." Mr. Barry requested that he might
be excused from answering immediately, as it was a
question yet to be determined. He said that the committee appeared to be lacking in something, but he
had not yet made up his mind whether it was intelligence or honesty. He then resumed, and soon
came to the reading of an extract from Ingersoll
on the matter of contempt of court. The chairman
again interrupted him, this time to inquire: "Who is
this man Ingersoll you are quoting?" Then Barry
stopped and announced that he was ready to answer
the preceding question concerning the intelligence
of the committee. His mind was now made up. If
that committee was fairly represented by its chairman, and if the chairman did not know who Ingersoll was, then the committee did not possess intelligence enough to carry thistles to a jackass.

3—FOR THE RECORD.

Moses Harman, editor of Lucifer, Valley Falls,
Kan., who had been arrested in 1887 for publishing
a coarsely-written letter on marital abuses, was sentenced in April, 1890, to serve five years in the
penitentiary and to pay a fine of three hundred dollars, and was taken to Lansing on May 4. Ezra H.
Heywood, editor of The Word, Princeton, Mass.,
appears to have courted arrest by publishing indicted matter from Harman's paper. He got it. E.
C. Walker, who had separated himself from Lucifer
and started Fair Play, later removed to Sioux City,
Ia., in order to pursue another policy than that of

using words morally certain to provoke arrest. I
maintained the not original position that these venturesome men who drew the attention of the sadists
to themselves were buffers for the rest of us. Anyhow their persecution marked the limits of safety
for us. B. R. Tucker of Liberty took a little different view. He said (I quote from memory) that
by putting themselves recklessly where they needed
defense, they halted the advance and sapped the
strength and resources of the main army of progress, which was under no obligation to halt or turn
aside for their relief.

Throughout the year 1891 The Truth Seeker
agitated for the Sunday opening of the World's
Fair in Chicago. Sixteen Liberal societies published notices of regular meetings. In Tennessee
a farmer named R. M. King, Seventh-day Adventist, of Obion county, was prosecuted for plowing
on Sunday. Convicted of Sabbath-breaking by the
county court, he took his case to the supreme court
of his state, where the sentence was confirmed;
he then employed Don M. Dickinson, former U. S.
postmaster-general, to carry it to the United States
Supreme Court, alleging that the conviction was
contrary to the Bill of Rights. In August The
Truth Seeker said: "Only the merest outline of the
opinion [by Justice Hammond] has reached the
public, but it appears to be in keeping with our
United States Court decisions, that the United
States constitutional amendments are binding on
Congress only, and not upon state legislatures. The
justice ruled that King was convicted under due
process of Tennessee law, and that it was not the

province of the federal court to review the case."

Hugh O. Pentecost, who for the past few years had been lecturing against the state, now took up the practice of the law. Asked his reason for doing so, he replied that the class people for whom he had been suffering martyrdom were not worth it. "They are wedded to the clergymen and the politicians," he said. "They will follow a black gown and a brass band into slavery, and they enjoy their servitude. They like to be humbugged, robbed, and ruled, and they love the men who humbug, rob, and rule them. When I did not know this I was willing to suffer, if need be, for the working people. Now that I know it, I am not."

Liberal lecturers in the field and reporting to The Truth Seeker at the end of 1891 were, first and foremost, Putnam; then, Dr. Henry M. Parkhurst, John R. Charlesworth, C. B. Reynolds, Mrs. Mattie P. Krekel, W. S. Bell, and John E. Remsburg. Henry Frank, lately fired by the Congregationalists of Jamestown, N. Y., announced himself ready to found the New Society of Human Progress and preach the New Liberalism. He has continued to do such preaching off and on up to the time of this writing.

In the line of duty during these closing years of my stay in San Francisco I had to record that Mrs. Annie Besant, once rational, had gone theosophist; that instead of emphasizing the neomalthusian doctrine taught in her "Law of Population" she now insisted that to be perfect one must be sexually inert;

That Edward Bellamy, publishing his "New Nation," preached the second coming of the spirit of Christ, incarnated, one inferred, in the person of Mr. Bellamy, while Nationalism was the name of the new dispensation;

That the always hostile Rev. J. J. Owen, once editor of the Spiritualist paper, The Golden Gate, when he received his editorial articles by withdrawing himself from disturbing influences and allowing thoughts to flow into his mind, now conducted the aggressive Better Way in San Jose and made war on a brother editor who accused him of leaving his hat and shoes behind when interrupted in a pastoral call;

That Col. M. E. Billings, compiler of the original edition of "Crimes of Preachers," had been prosecuted for shooting somebody and had made a profession of Christian belief;

That Tolstoy's "Kreutzer Sonata" had been vindicated as mailable and that Wanamaker repudiated all responsibility for giving the book a boom by ordering it thrown out;

That the trustees of Kaweah colony, established in Tulare county to exemplify Nationalism, had been arrested for poaching on government land (probably a bit of persecution).

The Liberals of Oregon rallied at a good convention at Portland, October 3-5, and elected J. Henry Schroeder of Arago, president. The American Secular Union Congress was held in Industrial Hall, Philadelphia, October 31 (1891). The editor of The Truth Seeker headed his report of it "I said in My Haste, All Men are Liars," and in his opening sentence pronounced this "the shortest and meanest congress" ever held by the organization. Thirty-four persons entitled to vote attended, about one-half of them, including the whole Truth Seeker office force, being from New York. President Westbrook tried to control the proceedings in such a way as to give no offense to the clergy. The Freethinkers were paying all the expenses and wanted some Freethought remarks, which Dr. Westbrook held to be improper. The delegates took counsel with one another and decided to move the headquarters to Chicago. To that end they elected Judge C. B. Waite president and Mrs. M. A. Freeman secretary. Dr. Westbrook had spent something like $5,000 of the Union's funds on a Manual of Morality. The New York Independent, then a religious paper, reviewed the work as follows:

" 'Conduct as a Fine Art,' by N. P. Gilman and E. P. Jackson, is a book composed of the two essays which shared equally the prize of $1,000 offered by a Philadelphia organization for the best manual to aid teachers in public schools to instruct children in morals without dabbling in religious details. We heartily recommend the volume as one to which the average school teacher can turn with certainty of gain. Both essays are clear and forcible; the one by Mr. Gilman is strikingly so."

The essayists are said to have been liberal clergymen. Mr. Gilman referred his readers to the Apostle Paul, who refers *his* to God, said The Truth Seeker, and assumed the immortal soul of man as a certainty. The book had no useful future.

4—THE PASSING OF VETERANS.

Death took its toll of veteran Freethinkers. On January 10, 1891, J. P. Mendum, proprietor of the Boston Investigator, died at his home at Melrose Highlands, Mass., in his 80th year. Mr. Mendum was born in Kennebunk, Me., July 7, 1811. As Abner Kneeland's successor in managing The Investigator, he enlarged the field of the paper, and published the works of the great Freethinkers— Voltaire, D'Holbach, Paine, Robert Taylor, Volney. He proposed the Paine Memorial Hall in Appleton street, raised the money with which it was erected, and owned it at the time of his death. He left a son Ernest (born 1853) who inherited the hall and The Investigator, which he conducted until it was consolidated with The Truth Seeker in 1904. Ernest disposed of his interest in the hall to Ralph Chainey, son of George.

Distinctly remembered events attended the receipt of news in San Francisco that Charles Bradlaugh was dead, January 30, 1891. The following paragraph recounts my participation in the publishing of the startling intelligence:

"It is a sign of enterprise in a daily paper to publish, on the day following his decease, the likeness and biography of a distinguished man. It was the enterprise of the San Francisco Examiner, which never spares its employees on great occasions, that caused a reporter of that paper to extract me from my bed on the night of Friday, January 30, in order that I might provide him with a portrait and sketch of Charles Bradlaugh. I made the nocturnal

CHARLES BRADLAUGH

This is believed to be Bradlaugh's best portrait. It was submitted to The Truth Seeker by his daughter Hypatia Bradlaugh Bonner for an anniversary edition, September 25, 1909.

visit to the office, hunted up the etching and the
facts, and sent the reporter upon his way rejoicing.
Otherwise he would not have gone back to The Examiner office, such being his orders. The paper
contained the next day the only accurate likeness
and biography of Bradlaugh published in the city.
The Post, having no picture of Bradlaugh, published Ingersoll's likeness with Bradlaugh's name."

The Examiner appreciated my assistance enough
to give me its cut of Bradlaugh to publish in Freethought.

There are biographies of Bradlaugh in all the
encyclopedias. He was born in East London, Sept.
22, 1833; became a great orator and established The
National Reformer, 1860, on the staff of which
were employed Bernard Shaw, John M. Robertson,
James Thomson, Annie Besant, and Bradlaugh's
daughter, Hypatia. He was many times elected to
Parliament, being a member at the time of his
death. He was a great man—the English compeer
of Ingersoll.

In June Mary A. Leland, having enjoyed and
suffered a life of near sixty-eight years that covered all the experiences of wife, mother, and grandmother, with the trials of a reformer besides, said
good-bye to all and closed her eyes not to open
them again. We held the funeral in the house
where she had lived, at Filbert and Taylor streets,
with the family and the near neighbors by the coffin while Evangeline Ballou sang an evening song
and the venerable Thomas Curtis, himself not having far to go, spoke the few words the occasion re-

quired. A memoir of Mrs. Leland, her personal history as Mary Ann (Brush) Torbett, so long ago that no one now living can remember the woman reformer of that name, would make a better biography than you could find by looking at a hundred that have been written.

I went to the office the day of the funeral and came to the house in the afternoon to attend the services. The family help, according to a San Franisco custom, was a Japanese boy; and this particular one, for certain advantages which thereby accrued to him, had joined the Salvation Army. The Jap had a surprise for me, for when I went up the steps he opened the door in a very formal way, and displayed himself in the full uniform of a Salvation Army warrior. Why he donned that rig for the occasion of a funeral I was never able to make up my mind. He may have thought the services religious, and hence calling for a religious garb, or he may have noticed the absence of religious preparations, and decided to add the missing touch himself.

To the list of deaths in 1891, Col. John R. Kelso, of Longmont, Colorado, contributed his. Colonel Kelso was a man of great mental and physical energy, a tall, soldierly man, with a limp from a bullet in his leg, who had been in the Civil War and in Congress. As I remember seeing him, he always wore a high hat and a ribbon in his buttonhole. Seventeen years after he was born, near Columbus, Ohio, Kelso was a teacher in the public schools and a licensed exhorter of the Methodist church. His mind was analytical. Analysis may be said to have been his middle name. As a preacher he applied it to the Bible, and came near committing suicide when he found the holy book wouldn't stand it. He quit exhorting, but kept on teaching until 1885—thirty-seven years. Then he published his books—Analysis of Deity, of the Bible, of the Devil, and finally, of Government—this last unfinished at the time of his death, January 26, 1891. He had a wife who helped him in his literary labors, and who adored him; so that his life was a great success.

The world lost James Parton, beloved of all Freethinkers, October 17, 1891, in Newburyport, Mass., where he had lived since 1875, and wrote his life of Voltaire. He  was born in Canterbury, England, February 8, 1822. After coming to New York at five years and receiving his education here, he began teaching and pursued that calling until he took the editorship of The Ladies' Home Journal, a very important periodical of its day. He adopted the profession of letters, lectured on literary and political topics, and became one of America's biographers of the first class. In 1854 he married the lady, then a widow of the name of Eldredge, who was born Sarah Willis, a sister of the poet N.

P. Willis and known throughout the country as "Fanny Fern." She died in 1872, and three years later he married her daughter, Miss Ellen Eldredge, by her previous husband. Parton was a fearless man. He wrote energetically in defense of D. M. Bennett, and sent The Truth Seeker a money contribution every month of 1880-'81 that its editor was in prison.

Dr. J. R. Monroe died November 9, 1891. The doctor had been in Journalism for many years. He started the Rockford Herald in 1855, moved it to Seymour, Ind., in 1857 and changed its name to the Seymour Times, and on removing it to Indianapolis in 1881 called it The Ironclad Age, which it remained until his death and its later absorption by The Truth Seeker. He had an honorable, not to say distinguished, record as an army doctor during the Civil War. A eulogist states that he stood at the head of his profession as a physician. Dr. Monroe, born about 1825, was a native of Monmouth county, New Jersey, of Revolutionary stock. His paper, The Ironclad Age, was a great favorite with Infidels.

5—ACCEPTING THE INEVITABLE.

If there had been enough interested Freethinkers on the coast to support a paper by renewing their subscriptions year after year, I should be there now editing the weekly Freethought; but it appeared there were only about two-thirds of the required number. The receipts and Putnam's earnings paid the paper's bills, but left out the editor. Putnam had earned and turned in some $3,500 in cash. I had put in only my time. He more than once murmured that if he had known the difficulties and the unrewarded work of getting out a paper, he wouldn't have proposed starting one, nor have lured me to the coast. He was past fifty years: it was time to collect for his old age. The expert accountant put on the books discovered that subscribers owed two thousand dollars, and the company owed, say, $200.

The meeting decided that were the friends of the paper to be told that I needed a salary they would subscribe it. I protested that I had a good trade, was in the best of health, and capable of earning an independent living. Besides, there was an attractive job, down at the water-front, loading angle-iron on a scow. However, against my vote the proposition carried that a salary fund be solicited in my behalf. A considerable amount of money came in. I agreed, nevertheless, with one man who wrote that if I could not make a go of it editing a paper I had better try something else. That looked like a sound economic principle. I therefore resigned. The company appointed Putnam as editor. I took a job setting type, but continued my contributions to the paper. Frank L. Browne assumed the management. Browne thought the paper could be made to pay. Putnam took the editorship, but was obliged to keep the lecture appointments he had made. In one of my contributed editorials I reviewed with approval an article by Herbert Spencer on Nationalism. Mr. Browne in the next number apologized for the editorial, being convinced that the hope of the race lay in Socialism. I am giving only an impression of the situation. There was no quarrel, no warm words. But I never could write Socialist articles. If a Socialist policy would be helpful to the paper, I was in no position to object.

I have an idea that 1889-'91 were years of failing prosperity in California. Men who had been flush of money found themselves getting short of that commodity and were apologetic about it. Papers without capital discontinued. Unemployment prevailed and the population drifted; old friends disappeared, went away in search of work, and new ones were few. Subscribers wrote that while our struggling paper enlisted their full sympathy, we must not forget that they had their own troubles. They could no longer raise the money for lectures, which had been so easy a year or two before. That card of Putnam's that I have quoted, saying that he had struck it rich, having delivered three lectures and found himself only fifty cents behind, was a shadow of coming events. In 1888 he might have come out fifty dollars ahead on each. He had a theory about this being a period of liquidation following one of credit. I never went into it deeply with him. I knew that we were printing a good paper that was praised and quoted by our exchanges East and West, and concluded that if the Western Liberals didn't support it, the cause lay in their financial inability to do so—in the visible change that had come about in their circumstances. They were embarrassed. There had been unprecedented weather conditions, and more subtle causes for a reversal of prosperity. The political economists may now have the floor.

The number of Freethought containing my last contribution bore date June 20, 1891. The last number of the paper published was dated August 15 of the same year. It said there would be a consolidation with The Truth Seeker, and the statement to that effect, written by Putnam, was congratulatory. He saw how the merger was destined mightily to advance the cause.

The Truth Seeker, announcing the Concentration of Effort, said: "The past two years have been hard ones for the few journals upholding Freethought. There has been much to distract the mind to other issues. Business has been poor, merchants finding but few customers, while the farmers have been compelled to sell their crops for little or nothing. Under these conditions the efforts of Liberals have relaxed, with unfortunate results Charles Watts, one of the ablest men who ever stepped upon a platform, has found it necessary to go back to England, where he could better provide for his family; and though his work in Canada is to be continued, we very much fear that it will not be possible to hold the Liberals of that country as he has done."

On looking at the Freethought subscription list my brother found a "few hundred of them who had paid nothing for a year or two," which, he obtested, was not the way to promote Liberalism. Putnam from time to time invited the "few hundred" to send in their arrearages to The Truth Seeker, and I don't doubt that those did who had it.

As I remarked of my boyhood situations, that I always knew where I was going next, so when San Francisco discharged me I had another place in sight. It was Snohomish, Washington, where as city editor of a weekly and tri-weekly small-town paper called The Eye, I began life in circumstances about as new to me as when I came into atmospheric existence in 1857 or to New York in 1875. An account of that will begin in Chapter One, Volume II. My newspaper partner in Snohomish, 1891-1893, was Clayton H. Packard, who still survives. Mr. Packard has read the fifty-odd pages of manuscript covering our association in Independent Journalism, and returned it with few corrections. This is a story of wide-open spaces, surrounded by tall timber, where men wore mackinaws. The moccasin tracks were there visible, as well as the Indians who made them.—G. E. M.

Fifty Years of Freethought

BEING THE STORY OF *THE TRUTH SEEKER*, WITH THE NATURAL HISTORY OF ITS THIRD EDITOR

BY GEORGE E. MACDONALD

VOLUME II

Foreword by CLARENCE DARROW

NEW YORK:
THE TRUTH SEEKER COMPANY
1931

To the Readers
of
The Truth Seeker

"Of what we give up, let us not try to fill the place with figments."—GOLDWIN SMITH.

FOREWORD

THIS book, in which Mr. Macdonald tells of the struggle in America against superstition for the past fifty years, will be interesting to many men and women. It contains the story of constant progress in the realm of human thought. The Author has been connected with The Truth Seeker, a consistent Freethought paper, for more than fifty years, most of the time as an editorial writer. The book is a work, of two volumes, which tells in a straightforward, simple manner the story of Freethought, mainly in the United States. Many of the struggles for religious freedom in America, especially of the early days, are exceedingly interesting, and the friends of Freethought are fortunate that a man like Mr. Macdonald has been willing to spend the time and care in writing the story.

From very humble beginnings the movement in this country, as well as the world at large, has had an enormous growth. Within the memory of many living men the story of creation as told by the Bible was not even doubted. The Old Testament and the New was the literal work of the Almighty. God wrote it with his own hand. The punctuation marks were about the only portions subject to doubt. Every part of the holy book was of equal worth. Not only was the whole story inspired but the translation as well. There was no difficulty about believing every miracle. All the evil in the world came from Adam and Eve's eating of the Tree of Knowl-

edge in the Garden of Eden. Few doubted that
all the women of the earth who suffered the pains
of childbirth were tortured because Eve handed
the apple to Adam. The serpent and Balaam's ass
talked with human beings. The only question raised
was as to whether they spoke in Hebrew. The
story of the flood was true. Joshua made the sun
stand still while he finished the carnival of slaughter. Jesus had no human father; he cured the ill
by driving the devils out of the afflicted and into
hogs. Jesus fed the multitude with the five loaves
and two fishes. When he was born a star led the
camels and their riders across the desert and stopped
over a stable. The author, of course, thought that
the stars were sticking in the firmament just above
the earth. Now we know that they are billions of
miles away and that if one should come near the
earth our planet would be instantly converted into
vapor.

These stories were taught in nearly all homes
and practically all the churches. Heaven and Hell
were both fixed places for the abode of the dead,
who were not separated according to their deserts
but according to their beliefs. Today few of the
churches talk about Hell, and not many have much
to say about Heaven. If either abode is mentioned,
no information is given about these mythical realms.
Many of the churches are now liberal and aggressive. In every city and even in the smaller towns,
there are churches that have maintained their names
but are the headquarters for doubt and the interpreters of scientific thought. Many of them openly
deny miracles, but some "liberal preachers" have

tears in their voice when they speak of Jesus.

It is only seventy years since Charles Darwin published his first book. It was everywhere met with ridicule and abuse. No one then questioned but that it took away the foundations of Religion. In that short length of time the whole scientific world has accepted his conclusion, and his theory of evolution is taught in every school worthy of the name. Amongst the intelligent people of the world it is almost as well established as the once heretical doctrine that the earth is round. It is well to take a look at the story of privation and suffering of the early apostles of freedom and science who at great risk and through dire privations went up and down the world seeking to emancipate the human mind.

Some of the men and women of whom Mr. Macdonald writes are:

Susan B. Anthony,
Harry Elmer Barnes,
Edward Bellamy,
Heywood Broun,
Luther Burbank,
Samuel L. Clemens
  (Mark Twain),
Moncure D. Conway,
Ernest Crosby,
Eugene V. Debs,
David and R. G. Eccles,
Thomas A. Edison,
Geo. Burman Foster,
O. B. Frothingham,
Helen Gardener,

Horace Greeley,
Thomas W. Higginson,
Gov. Geo. Hoadley,
Elbert Hubbard,
Rupert Hughes,
J. P. Mendum,
Courtlandt Palmer,
Samuel P. Putnam,
John Emerson Roberts,
Margaret Sanger,
Carl Schurtz,
Horace Seaver,
Elizabeth Cady Stanton,
Charles P. Steinmetz,
Henry W. Thomas,

Hon. W. J. Gaynor,   B. F. Underwood,
Thos. B. Gregory,   Andrew D. White.

It is well for us to remember these men and women who have made it safe to think. The world owes an enormous debt to the fighters for human freedom, and we cannot suffer their names to be forgotten now that we are reaping the fruits of their intelligence and devotion.

The Author, Mr. George E. Macdonald, is not a college man, but he is an educated man. He has read good books all his life. He has read them without fear and with a full understanding. And as a writer he has always been loyal to the truth as he understood it. He has clung to this ideal in spite of all handicaps, disapproval and danger. He has been a valiant soldier for human liberty. He tells the story well. I want especially to commend his literary style. It is simple and direct. It is never obscure nor clouded. He writes to be understood. No words was wasted or used only to adorn. His history is absorbing throughout, and everyone who reads it will realize that he is reading the words of an honest man who believes that disloyalty to truth is the highest aim. The possibility of quibbling or lying never enters his head. It is a plain and interesting story told by a man who has lived a plain life and has written for the sake of telling the truth and nothing else. I commend this rare production to all who want to know something about the struggle for truth and freedom in America, and the devoted men who made it.   CLARENCE DARROW.

Chicago, April 15, 1931.

PREFACE

THIS history ends with 1925. It began with 1875 and professes to cover but fifty years of my participation in the Freethought movement, though those years now number fifty-six. Occasionally, for the purpose of terminating a subject, I have alluded to events occurring later than the end of the century's first quarter. These could hardly be ignored by one writing in 1928-1930. I will cite for an example the necessity for changing my answer to the inquiry whether there are any towns in this country that have no churches. The disappearance of the rural church began to be remarked upon after a survey made in 1916. That whole communities were left altogether churchless did not so plainly appear. One of the few towns I have been able to mention as destitute of religious privileges is in Bergen county, New Jersey. Churches were barred "by original deed and contract." Reports say that the ban is lifted and this borough, once godless, now has a church in the form of a community center with a pastor. Some writers, not sensing the need of facts upon which to base their statements, have denied the possibility that any community can live without a church, and have asked one and all to picture, if they can, the sunken condition of the churchless town. But this town, founded in 1848, was so for more than a half century, and no evil was reported as coming out of it. We may now set aside the New Jersey hamlet as negligible, for the 1931 report of the Home

Mission Council of North America made public the fact that "there are 10,000 villages in America without churches of any kind," and three times as many "without resident pastors of any faith." Theoretically, as per the writers who prescribe religion as a preventive, those towns of unknown name should be engulfed in a wave of crime. No one foresees that this will happen, but rather that religious centers will continue to be the most criminal.

The Truth Seeker changed its class while printing "Fifty Years of Freethought" serially. A weekly for more than half a century, it for good reasons has been issued as a monthly since January, 1930. My first volume is inscribed to its readers. I feel like dedicating this one to their memory and to that of writers whose work The Truth Seeker has published; for many of these whom, when writing, I could describe as still surviving, have gone the way of all souls. Lemuel K. Washburn, mentioned early in Volume I as a heretical Unitarian minister, and in 1925 a contributing editor to the The Truth Seeker, died in 1927 at the age of 81 years. His death was the most important single loss to the cause since the death of E. M. Macdonald. A year earlier died Luther Burbank, whose answers to the Questionnaire fill some pages of this volume. I am not writing their obituaries; but because they are characters in this work, and outlived the period it covers, I will name, as no longer with us, David Eccles, an old contributor; Thomas B. Gregory, Garrett P. Serviss, James A. Hennesy, William Connolly ("The Spectator"), George B. Wheeler, Channing Severance, William M. van der Weyde.

And with the record of Edwin C. Walker left out
these annals would be considerably shortened, but
Walker died in his 82d year, in February, 1931.
Inscribed to the living, let "Fifty Years of Freethought" be a memorial to the dead who were of
its family. I bequeath the rest to the historian of
the ensuing fifty years of Freethought (1925-'75).

Volume I, largely descriptive and autobiographical, and bringing the reader to the year 1891, has
been criticised as conceived in too light a vein, too
"intimate." The author's years of youth and adoles-
cence, with the part which the opposite sex had in
them, are described. Why he should have rehearsed those passages so indiscreetly he is now
wholly unable to explain. There is none to expose,
or "debunk," his youthful courses were they to be
pictured as more staid than he recalls them to have
been. For the man in middle life, conscious that
he might have done better and wondering if he ever
will, there is stimulating medicine in one of Huxley's letters where he says: "Kicked into the world
a boy without guide or training, or with worse than
none, I confess to my shame that few men have
drunk deeper of all kinds of sin that I." What
Huxley was moved to "confess to my shame," as he
says, fell under my eye in the '90s; but despite my
inability to say no when a distinguished lady asked
me at 18 to go for a pitcher of beer; despite my
early addiction to a pipe; despite those domestic
experiences told all too frankly in Volume I; despite the admission in verses forty-five years old
that—

"I'm out some nights with the other boys,
    And come in, like Solomon, filled with dew,"

a confession like Huxley's I could not truthfully make. I at least had never smoked cigarettes. Looking at the eminence to which Huxley had risen, seeing how he had climbed back, and only a few slips withal, hope triumphed, and I now project my vision backward over a vista where there is nothing to tell that might paint a blush on the reviewer's cheek.

Another taking up the recording of events in line with those this book recounts, will not overlook, I trust, that singular one of 1928 in the history of the American Association for the Advancement of Science. I allude to the occasion when the president of the Association appealed to the clergy to "relieve the public mind concerning the possibility of any antagonism between science and religion." The author of that appeal is to be reminded that if there had been no conflict between religion and science, the Association of which he was president might never have been called into existence.

In preparing the Index for these volumes I discover omissions not now to be supplied in the text. Philadelphian readers may miss the name of the late George Longford, secretary of the Friendship Liberal League for a generation, and that also of its president Hugh Munro. Space or opportunity was not found to mention the organizer of the Detroit, Michigan, Freethought society, Mr. Edmund Marshall; nor Mr. William Brenner of New York, always in years past the reliable secretary of one society after another, including the Thomas

Paine Historical Association (1918-1924). As
early as 1921 Mr. Irving Levy began collecting material for the Freethought section of the New York
Public Library, and his work being well seconded
by Mr. K. D. Metcalf, chief of the Reference Department, that library may now be regarded as
complete in this respect. As I stated in a Note
(Truth Seeker Nov. 24, 1928), the persistent Mr.
Levy (a frequent caller) urged upon me the writing of "Fifty Years" until resistance was overcome,
and I began and completed it with the result which
the reader sees.

Born at Exeter, N. H., in 1842, Mr. Edward
Tuck, in years the oldest American resident of
Paris, the one member of the Dartmouth Class
of '62 who subscribed himself a Freethinker, is the
"without whomer" as related to the publication
of this volume. Biography of the undistinguished
or unpopular is not the kind of book on which the
publisher makes money, but may lose more than
he can afford. From the liberal impulses of Mr.
Tuck, science, art and philanthropy have benefited,
while a timely gift determines the fate of "Fifty
Years." Vol. II. A further evidence of his generosity is permission to make a frontispiece of
his picture, forwarding which he says: "The rav-
ages of time have not disfigured me greatly. I am
neither deaf nor blind, nor rheumatic nor gone
bughouse. In fact I am a lucky dog all 'round."
Freely construing the word "bughouse," I take it
to mean that Mr. Tuck has prepared no recantation of his cosmic theories for immediate release
upon his demise.

New Castle, in Pennsylvania, has a hospital to the founding of which one of her citizens, Mr. David Jameson, gave the better part of a million. His townsmen call it the Jameson Memorial. The name of Mr. Jameson, who has died since these memoirs closed, is to be read among those associated with liberal donations for the maintenance of The Truth Seeker through dull times. The drawings in both volumes are by Myer Kanin.

Although I lived through, witnessed, or "assisted at" the happenings herein revived and reviewed, many had passed from my memory and reappeared as a surprise when the veil was lifted. They will be an astonishment to younger spirits. The record of the Freethinkers is honorable. While they have never sought by force of law to deprive any person of his right to the pursuit of happiness, their opponents, the forgers of gyves in the shape of dogmas and ordinances against the freedom of thought, speech and press, have perpetually wrought handcuffs for the wrists of Liberty. A discriminating future may know whom to honor. I make no predictions as to that, but in hope and trust submit the names of a few of the deserving.

April 11, 1931.   G. E. M.

CONTENTS

CHAPTERS I-II—City Editor of The Eye, Snohomish, Wash. (1891-3)..............................p. 1

CHAPTER III (1892)—Sunday Closing of the World's Fair—Madrid Congress—Freethought Federation Organized 59

CHAPTER IV (1893)—Short History of Sunday—I Return to New York............................ 71

CHAPTER V (1894)—Value of Church Property in U. S.—Kentucky Blasphemy Case—Wise-Bible Case... 79

CHAPTER VI (1895)—Mount Ingersoll—Blasphemy Law Invoked in New Jersey—Truth Seeker Prohibited in Canada 93

CHAPTER VII (1896)—Influence of W. A. Croffut —I am "Office" Editor of The Truth Seeker—Liberal University Project—Watts and Foote in America— Death of S. P. Putnam............................113

CHAPTER VIII (1897)—Dr. Abbott and Jonah— The Brann Iconoclast—Girard's Will Attacked—Anarchist-Communist Arrests 137

CHAPTER IX (1898)—The Methodist Steal South— Government Lands Alienated to Churches—Spanish American War 153

CHAPTER X (1899)—Roosevelt and Paine—Death of Ingersoll—West Point Chapel Steal—Edison Characterizes Christianity 175

CHAPTER XI (1900)—Congress excludes a Polygamist—Skeetside—The Regicide Philosophy—Bootlegging Religion into Schools...........................189

CHAPTER XII (1901)—Mark Twain and the Missionaries—The McKinley Assassination Not by an Anarchist 203

CHAPTER XIII (1902)—Herbert Spencer's Religion —Martyrdom of Ida Craddock—Drama of the Crucifixion—Martinique Holocaust 215

CHAPTER XIV (1903)—The Anarchist Scare—"Religious Associations" Laws of France—Stuart Robson and the Ministers...................................229

CHAPTER XV (1904)—Soul Snatchers Struggle for Herbert Spencer—Carnegie, Atheist—The Offspring of Freethinkers—International Congress—Haeckel's Propositions 241

CHAPTER XVI (1905)—A Catholic Steal West—The Professional Parasites and Their Press Censorship—The Truth Seeker's Removal to Vesey Street—The Sex of Angels—New Rochelle Accepts Paine Monument 258

CHAPTER XVII (1906)—The Crapsey Heresy Charges—The Fake Franklin-Paine Letter—Short History of the Inquisition—The Christian Country Dictum —Exclusion of Mark Twain from a Library—San Francisco Disaster and the Almighty.....................271

CHAPTER XVIII (1907)—"In God We Trust" Removed from Coins by Roosevelt and Restored by Congress—The Infidel Town Myth—The Valley Forgery...292

CHAPTER XIX (1908)—An Atheist Mayor of Rome —Acts of Comstockery—W. J. Bryan Wars on Evolution—Ripe Ages of Freethinkers...................307

CHAPTER XX (1909—Death of E. M. Macdonald —Paine Centenary—Military Assassination of Ferrer— Colleges Accused of Teaching Infidelity—Paine Recantation Story Told of Herbert Spencer................323

CHAPTER XXI (1910)—The Ingersoll Recantation Affidavit—A Freethinker for Mayor of Topeka—Drews' Christ Myth—Roosevelt and the Pope—Bible Excluded from Illinois Schools...............................346

CHAPTER XXII (1911) — Edison Disturbs the Clergy—The Monistic Congress in Hamburg—Ingersoll Statue Unveiled in Peoria—Death of My Mother.....366

CHAPTER XXIII (1912)—The Incompetence of the Clergy—Haeckel's Church Departure—An Ingersoll Oration Stolen by an Evangelist........................386

CONTENTS   xvii

CHAPTER XXIV (1913)—Mr. Morton Characterizes a Priest and I am Summoned for Libel—Crimes of
Preachers—Where the Day Begins....................402

CHAPTER XXV (1914)—The World War and Its
Religious Side Shows—Catholics Trusted in the Kai-
ser—The Mexican Zapatistas and the Nuns—The Church
Protests Mayor Nathan as a Commissioner to this
Country 420

CHAPTER XXVI (1915)—The Lusitania Affair—
God Seen to Be on the Side of the Central Powers—
The Bill to Curb Criticism of Religion—Many Free-
thinkers Arrested—Revolution in Portugal and a Free-
thinker Made Provisional President—Death of G. W.
Foote 437

CHAPTER XXVII (1916)—Continued Activity of
the Arresters—Mockus Blasphemy Trial—The Kaiser
Invokes Jesus Darwin and Huxley Myths—Haeckel's
"Eternity" 451

CHAPTER XXVIII (1917)—Free Speech Suppression—Freethought Books for Soldiers—A Pest of Army
Chaplains and Testaments—Compulsory Church Attendance—Herndon Memorial 466

CHAPTER XXIX (1918)—Exclusion of The Truth
Seeker from the Mails—Its Triumphant Vindication—
The Y. M. C. A. in Disgrace—The Patriotic Activity
of Freethinkers—Mark Twain Fellowship............484

CHAPTER XXX (1919)—An Epidemic Among
Small Newspapers from Legislative and Economic
Causes—The Boys Come Home—Ernst Haeckel Dies..504

CHAPTER XXXI (1920)—A Preamble on Suckers
—Post-War Grafts—The Cross Officially Above the
Flag—The Questionnaire 518

CHAPTER XXXII (1921)—The Truth Seeker
Moves—Ingersoll Birthplace Dedicated as a Memorial
—Bishop Brown's Book.............................530

CHAPTER XXXIII (1922)—The Advent of Fundamentalism—Indifferent Reaction of Men of Science—Response of Luther Burbank to the Questionnaire—Towns
Without Churches 548

CHAPTER XXXIV (1923)—Our Golden Jubilee—
Progress of Fundamentalism—The Millikan-water
Irenicon—Tablet to Paine—Death of Mrs. Ingersoll..570

CHAPTER XXXV (1924)—Bishop Brown Heresy
Trial — Crime, Evolution, and Religion — American
Rationalist Association 587

CHAPTER XXXVI (1925)—Tennessee Anti-Evolu-
tion Law Passed—Scopes Conviction—Tablet on Site of
Ingersoll Home—Ground Broken by Edison for Paine
Memorial Building—Week Day Church School Decision
—Conclusion 605

PICTURES IN VOLUME I.

Andrews, Stephen Pearl.405

Bennett, D. M......142, 184

Bennett Monument 325

Bennett, Mrs. Mary....333

Bradlaugh, Charles 536

Britton's Ferry 136

Freethought Office 497

Leland, Grace L....452, 453

Leland, Lillian 506

Leland, Theron C......384

Lick, James 183

Macdonald, E. M...239, 349

Macdonald, G. E.....85, 454

Palmer, Courtlandt 462

Parton, James 539

Seaver, Horace 494

Somerby, Charles 349

Truth Seeker Office in
    Clinton Place 321

Tucker, Benj. R.........270

Walker, Edwin C........424

Wright, Elizur 384

PICTURES IN VOLUME II

Bradley, J. D...........442
Bryan, William J........611
Burroughs, John 545
Conway, Moncure D....304
Darrow, Clarence 608
Darwin, Charles 248
Edison, Thomas A..367, 614
Ferrer, Francisco 331
Foote, Edward Bond...399
Foote, G. W...........449
Galois, Marguerite 413
Gauvin, Marshall L.....597
Greeley, Horace 379
Griffith, J. I............. 33
Haeckel, Ernst, w i t h
    group, Jena, 370; in
    church departure car-
    toon 395
Holyoake, G. J..........281
Huxley, T. H...........112
Ingersoll, Eva A.......584
Ingersoll, R. G., at New
    Rochelle, 86; 181; fam-
    ily at statue, 377;
    Birthplace at Dresden.536
Macdonald, E. M., 324;
    monument .... .328
Macdonald, G. E. Males
    of Family, 473; with
    former Editors, 624;
    Family in 1825, 629;
    Residence 631

Macdonald, Mrs. Grace
    L. 633
Mark Twain.......362, 498
Muzzey, David Saville..614
Packard, C. H.......... 3
Paine Monument 269
Pentecost, H. O........301
Purdy, G. H............166
Putnam, S. P..........133
Remsburg, J. E........516
Ricker, Marilla M......528
Robertson, Morgan 88
Schroeder, Theodore ...461
Seibel, George 434
Skeetside 195
Steiner, Franklin 69
Stevens, Col. E. A.....482
Thomas, Norman 614
Tree in Snohomish..... 49
Wakeman, T. B........418
Waite, C. B............340
Walker, Ryan 223
War Cartoon, R y a n
    Walker 440
Ward, Lester F. at
    Haeckel Home, Jena,
    Germany 371; 417
Watts, Charles, w i t h
    group 226; 284
Wheless, Joseph 616
Wooden Ships and Iron
    Men 166-167

FIFTY YEARS OF FREETHOUGHT

CHAPTER I.

JOURNALISM IN THE FAR NORTHWEST.

IN JUNE, 1891, Clayton H. Packard of the thriving city of Snohomish, State of Washington, sent me an invitation to come and be his partner in the publication of The Eye, weekly and tri-weekly. I knew of The Eye from the exchange

OFFICIAL PAPER

OF THE CITY, AND OLDEST PAPER
IN THE COUNTY.

ISSUED EVERY MONDAY, WEDNESDAY
FRIDAY AND SATURDAY

—BY—

C H. PACKARD AND GEO. E. MACDONALD

lists of The Truth Seeker, and of Freethought, our San Francisco paper, and saw evidence of the use of the mind in its production. I had never been a small-town editor, and knew nothing of the routine duties of one following that profession. I therefore accepted the invitation of Mr. Packard. This might be the life. My wife Grace's attachment to San Francisco had been weakened by her mother's death, and she was easily lured aboard a steamer bound for Seattle, with such of our goods as we cared to take along, which included the baby. San Francisco and Seattle, viewed from the East, without laying a yard-stick on the map, appear to be neighboring cities, or no farther apart than New York and Portland, Maine. But a thousand miles of water stretches between them, going by boat—a four day's trip. After leaving America you go ashore first at Victoria, B. C., hard by Esquimault Bay, if you are tired of walking a ship's deck, which was my feeling. And there, I took notice, we had arrived where the days were long. It was evening when we docked, and I sat on the pier and read a book while the crew discharged freight. When the passengers were piped on board again, I closed my book and looked at my watch. It was near ten o'clock, and dusk coming on. In the middle of the summer, in those latitudes, there was no all-seeing hand of night till the hour after twelve. Unless a citizen got home before one o'clock, his all-hours return could be seen and reported by the neighbors.

Beyond Victoria there is another ocean to sail, one that is called a strait—San Juan de Fuca. You sail till morning and then all day, and stop in Seattle overnight. We stopped over a night and a day and went to a ball game with C. B. Reynolds, then a resident and a fan. Passengers went from Seattle to Snohomish, thirty-five miles off, by rail, and sent their goods up the Snohomish river by boat, the charges therefor being more than they had been on the same freight from San Francisco to Seattle.

Snohomish in 1891 was not to be classed as a quiet hamlet. It was full of people, all moving. A desperado with a hotel hack seized us at the station, outside the business belt, and set us down in the center of population. While we gave admiring attention to a rider who managed his "loping" horse with a single line around the animal's lower jaw, Packard rushed up and named us. In him I saw a man of forty per cent smaller build than myself, about two years younger, and more prone to rush. If he was not always in a hurry, then his gait betrayed him and his speed was deceptive. He had selected a room for us at the Maple House, a hotel overhanging the river, and to the Maple House we went. Main street, Snohomish, is closely companioned for a little distance by the Snohomish river. I felt at first that if I should step off the sidewalk with the wrong foot I would step into the river. An old subscriber to The Truth Seeker, J. S. Martin, lived on that river in a stationary houseboat fastened by hoops to cedar piles that rose eighteen feet out of the water at low

C. H. PACKARD,
"The Eye Man."

tide. I have seen the hoops go to the top of the piles when the river was up and the tide high.

Having been introduced to the printers in the office on the following morning, and not knowing what next, I inquired which type was dead and "threw in a case." It lay before me to learn what was news in that town and where to look for it, and then to divide my time between gathering it and putting it to press. Mr. Packard wrote a paragraph for The Eye introducing me as the new City Editor. He did not forget to name certain well-known publications, Puck, Judge, and so forth, to which I had contributed. The City Editor, when city editing, went to the justice's court, or to the superior court, or to a meeting of the city council, or to the opening of a new store or café, or he might absorb an item from observation or interview, and returned with the proceeds to the office. He there turned his notes into copy, and helped to put them into type; he proved the galley with a towel wrapped about a planer, read and corrected proof, transferred the matter to the forms and locked them up, put the forms on the press, and perhaps took a turn at feeding. Before I became accustomed to press-work, I spoiled a set of rollers by starting the press when they were lifted at one end. The sentiments that Packard managed to contain regarding a man, drunk or sober, who would start a press without looking at the rollers, did him honor.

The first event of importance that took place (a country editor would change that to "transpired") in Snohomish after I went into local journalism was

the presenting a coat of tar and feathers to the priest
of the parish, the Rev. Father Francis Xavier Guay.
I received no invitation to the party, nor notice that
it was about to take place. Anyhow I should not
have attended. If Catholics will have priests, let
them take what comes to them, or lay their troubles
before the bishop, and not call upon the secular
public to avenge their grievances. Packard as a
notary public gathered a sheaf of affidavits based on
the attitude the priest had taken toward penitents,
male and female, children and youth. Catholic
mothers were ready to furnish the feathers for the
occasion, but a heathen saved their beds by getting
the feathers at a furniture store; and then Catholic
men rolled the priest in them after tarring him.
Father Guay observed silence for two or three days;
then he wrote in a letter to The Eye, that he had
suffered distress of mind from accusations circulated to his prejudice, and from the harsh treatment
undergone at the hands of men not known to him.
He then migrated, but appears to have been retained
in the priesthood, as somebody from Southern California brought to Snohomish the news that the
priest with whom we had parted was serving a
congregation there.

There was in our city another paper, the Daily
Sun, upon which Packard looked with disfavor. The
picture of its editor formed in the mind from the
way Packard spoke his name fitted the man himself
pretty well when one came to see him. He must
have met with disappointments in life that had disillusioned him, for he had a saturnine countenance, a
harsh laugh, and the morose outlook of a cynic. He

was thought, in The Eye office, to be fit for treason, stratagems and spoils, and suspected of being on the outlook for opportunities to practice them. Before I had ever laid eyes on the individual, Packard one day said to me: "Here, Mac, is something on Frank Mussetter that I want you to write up. I have to go out and do some collecting." I asked: "What infamy has Mussetter been up to now?" and Packard replied: "Why, God damn it"—and then outlined in expletives the character of Mussetter, and went forth on his collecting mission. Our contemporary, it appears, had suppressed or misstated facts of public interest in order, as it was our place to allege, to curry favor with a certain low element and put The Eye in wrong. Hence I wrote the article, unconsciously using fighting language, and our afternoon edition gave it circulation. The consequences were set forth in the next number of our publication, in an editorial which read:

"A fierce-looking individual, loaded with several inches of adulterated hydrant water and a big revolver, which he said he had borrowed especially for the present crisis, awaited the senior Eye man's return from breakfast last Saturday morning. The distinguishing features of the combination were those of Frank Mussetter, editor and reputed owner of our at times luminous contemporary. Mussetter was evidently riled. He reads The Eye and thus keeps thoroughly posted on local and domestic affairs, although the scarcity of news and original editorials in his own paper might lead subscribers to doubt it. As we said before, Mussetter was riled. It might have been The Eye's scoop in exposing the priest and The Sun's supposed connection with the affair, but he didn't say so directly. Placing his good right hand on his pistol pocket, he inquired in a fierce, double-leaded voice fortified with beer if The Eye had a gun. Being informed that the chief engineer of this great moulder of public opinion (for our subscription rates see card at head of editorial column) was not in the habit of having such dangerous things in his possession when inside the city limits (*vide* ordinance No. 4), Mussetter cautioned us to procure a weapon. He said he had come to shoot us; that he had borrowed a gun from Charlie Cyphers with that object in view, and he proposed to use it. He was informed that he would probably never find a better time and opportunity than now presented themselves; also that he was making a damfool of himself. The Eye man explained that he was not a shootist, but would try to accommodate him with all the satisfaction he wanted in any other way. Mussetter averred that both he and his paper had been greatly hurt (we don't doubt it) by The Eye's articles, the truthfulness of which he did not deny; and that he would be satisfied with nothing short of shooting us. However, he graciously concluded to postpone the killing, and gracefully withdrew, remarking in a four-to-pica tone of voice, that he would surely open fire the next time he met us, and that we had better be prepared to meet our God, or words to that effect."

As the conscious author of the strictures on the worth, abilities, and good faith of Mr. Mussetter, I expected to be included in his graveyard list, and felt keenly the slight implied by his partiality for my senior, and his want of recognition of my merits and claims. A joker told me that Mussetter had left me to the mercy of his City Editor, whose name was Immanuel Joseph, and that I should keep an eye lifted for a fellow wearing an ulster and a Hebraic cast of countenance. Then a sincere friend who once lived in Virginia City, Nevada, where shooting had been popular, offered to lend me his gun, a short one that could be detonated from the pocket. He thoroughly explained the method of taking aim with the "gun" so masked. It consisted of laying the forefinger alongside the barrel and "pointing same," as one could do automatically and without sighting the weapon. But already I knew but feared not Joseph. He was more likely to borrow money of me than to pick a quarrel. I gave Joseph credit for having some sense.

But Mussetter's state of mind meanwhile must have been wholly unenviable. By warning Packard that he should shoot him on sight, he had conferred upon his adversary the right to do the same to him And if he were to make good his threat to shoot a man who had not menaced him, he could be hanged for it; whereas, according to the code, Packard might kill him with impunity and without warning wherever encountered. Mr. Mussetter may or may not have been handy enough with firearms to hold a gun on a man and fire it; but Packard was something of a mountaineer, a prospector accustomed to handling weapons, and while packing no gun for social purposes, yet when outside the city limits, on one of his trips into the wilds of the Cascades, where catamounts abode and wild goats offered themselves for targets, he wore strapped to his side a "shooting-iron" which, in its scabbard that projected a foot below the tail of his coat, looked to be twenty inches long. If so minded the senior editor of The Eye could have drilled his contemporary a block away. But instead of making Mussetter bite the dust Packard chose to hector the editor of The Sun, "our luminous contemporary," in the columns of The Eye. He did it well, too. Claiming as the challenged party the right to a choice of weapons, he advanced various absurd propositions calculated to make Mussetter look ridiculous, such as repairing to the Bon Ton restaurant and heaving 45-caliber fishballs at each other, or seeking the headwaters of the Stillaguamish river, with no doctors or priests—medical and spiritual advisers sternly excluded; and there exchanging double-leaded tariff editorials until one or both combatants received and acknowledged a mortal wound. "If either shoots his mouth off," said Packard, in naming the conditions, "before the proper signal is given, it shall be the privilege of the other, before the fight proceeds, to draw on the offending party for drinks enough to irrigate all readers of both papers for a period of three months next ensuing."

"Our luminous contemporary" came out daily, pushed by the faithful Joseph, with its usual scant measure of local news and a good political article on the editorial page clipped from some mid-western exchange; but although I pursued my diurnal canvass of Front street looking for subjects to write about, I never once saw Mussetter. At the end of a week the office telephone rang, and the bartender of the Penobscot, speaking, said: "Well, the enemies have met." Myself at the receiver: "And what happened?" Penobscot House: "Why, Mussetter rushed at Packard with one hand up and the other stretched out a yard in front of him to shake. And now he's trying to buy Packard a drink, but Clayt is a teetotaler and is taking a pocketful of cigars. And he don't smoke, neither. You'll fall heir to them cigars. Mussetter is happier than Clayt is."

Early in October (this was in 1891) my former San Francisco partner, S. P. Putnam, sent me word he was in the far Northwest and would like to speak in Snohomish. I telegraphed him to come a-running. Then I interviewed the known Freethinkers, took up a subscription, got out posters, advertised the meeting in The Eye, and hired Odd Fellows Hall. The house was full beyond capacity. Putnam had been there before, and had then been introduced to the audience by the mayor. But that was before the churches came in so strong. Now that there were four or five of them, representing considerable piety, the mayor hung back, with the consequence that Putnam had to introduce himself, which wasn't so bad an introduction. He spoke on the philosophy of camp meetings and revivals, drawing a strong contrast between Christianity and Freethought, to the disadvantage of religion. The audience took it with applause, except a real estate dealer named Sweeney, who interjected "No, that's not so," a few times, causing Putnam to pause in his discourse, and inquire whether, in commenting upon the fundamental truths of religion, he had misrepresented Christianity. Sweeney voted Aye, and was invited to take the platform at the close of the lecture. Thus Sweeney did, and it was the unwisest course he could have chosen. He announced himself as "a sort of a Christian," who believed that the story of Jonah's living three days inside the whale, and thereby becoming an authentic sign of the resurrection of Christ, was literally true. He charged Putnam with garbling the words of Jesus and misrepresenting Christianity. Pointing the finger of accusation, he declared that Putnam had quoted Christ as saying "blessed are the poor," when what the son of man really said was "blessed are the poor *in spirit.*" Putnam grinned, as Sweeney went on to affirm his belief that God halted the progress of the sun while Joshua in safety crossed the Red Sea! Having thus innocently confounded the army of Joshua with the children of Israel, Mr. Sweeney was bewildered by the immoderate laughter of the audience.

When Putnam replied, a good time was had by all except Sweeney, who as "a sort of a Christian," Putnam said, was not the kind of a Christian he had been describing. It was the "sort of a Christian," and not he, who misrepresented Christianity and always would because he didn't know his own faith. Putnam then picked up his Testament, turned to Luke vi, 20, and asked him to read it. Sweeney did so, and was humiliated to discover the words were "Blessed be ye poor," with no "in spirit" anywhere near them.

My report of Sweeney's speech, with his Joshua crossing the Snohomish river while the moon stood still on Pillchuck and the paralyzed sun forgot to set over the Olympics, was unsatisfactory to him, and he wrote a reply.

I have no file of The Eye for 1891; and when a writer quotes with no check but memory, it is his own fault if the events are not described as they ought to have happened.

Siwashes (the name for Indians on that part of the Pacific coast) lived in wickyups along the banks xx

of the Snohomish river, and paddled up and down the stream in dugout canoes. "Canoe" brings to mind a kind of small and light craft, generally employed for idle uses, like taking a girl out on the Charles river. I have seen a Siwash canoe probably eighteen feet long and of four foot beam, that carried the load of a moving-van, including the family. These aborigines were known as Snohomish Indians after the river. The Indian bands in those regions carried with them the names of the streams whose borders they inhabited. The student will see in *siwash* a form of the French word *sauvage*. The Siwashes were savage as to their mode of life, but peaceable and friendly toward their fellow man. I made no study of them, as to how they subsisted. So far as I could make out, they had solved the problem of living without labor. With so many salmon in the stream they did not have to work; they went fishing. Nevertheless, civilization was in the process of absorbing them. Younger men went out as farmhands; the old men and the womankind were most numerous in the wickyups. A government reservation at Tulalip where Indians who disliked tribal life could go drew many away from the streams. Early settlers, who, according to ancient history, were deserters from British men-of-war had found their way up the rivers from the Sound and lived with the Siwashes, squatting on the land or buying it of the natives. The white men bought their Indian wives of fathers, brothers, or perhaps of husbands. The sale of a girl by her father to a man who said he wanted her for a wife was upheld by the courts as legal in that country, which in 1891 had been a state for only two years. A young man settling there on a farm seventy years ago could make no better investment of his money or spare stock than to buy a wife with it, for the Indian women were good helpers about a place, and the children also could be worked as they grew up. How many wives some of them bought I am not interested to know. The federal law that was passed for the abolition of polygamy in Utah in the '80s did away with the plural wife system among these old settlers in Washington, who were expected to acknowledge the wife they had taken first and discontinue the others. They obeyed the law in the matter of establishing the senior spouse as wife. As regards the rest, it was said that to avoid inflicting hardships on them they were retained in the family as maids. None of the so-called squaw-men lived inside the city limits; they were ranchers. One of them, when his elder wife died, moved into town and married white. But he kept his ranch, and how large a population of secondary wives and their children the ranch maintained you could only judge from appearances. The man kept a general store in town. I saw one day a troop of mounted Indians galloping through the streets, and inquired of an older resident whether this was probably a massacre. He said no, it was only So-and-so's family going to his store for an outfit. In the East we hear of no prejudice against Indian blood; in Snohomish any reference to the fact that a person had a trace of it in him or in his family was forbidden as "ancient history." Some of the best-looking girls in town were half or quarter Indian. The red cheeks got from the white parent showing through the dusky coloring from the other side of the family produced a beauty that belonged to neither of the races unmixed. And yet one was not allowed to mention it. While I was yet new to my surroundings, an old and respected settler named Charles Short died and was buried from the Methodist church, where his family as chief mourners occupied the front pews. They were of much interest to me, both from their numbers and from their parentage, which was half Indian. The funeral sermon was preached by a young minister from Arkansas named Feese, who looked like a cowboy and had as dark a complexion as any white American I had ever met.

Surviving contemporaries of Mr. Short had related his history to me, speaking very highly of him. In reporting the funeral for The Eye, after sketching Mr. Short, I made reference to the picturesque group in the front pews, and remarked with reference to the general color scheme, that the swarthy preacher in the pulpit might well have passed for a member of the family.

When the report of the funeral had been read, one person after another stopped me on the street to inquire why I had given that dig at Short. All I could think of to apologize for was the implying that the fellow in the pulpit bore some resemblance to Mr. Short's family, and I admitted I ought perhaps to have left that out. But that was not the point. One man squared himself in front of me and implored that I reveal to him what I had against Charlie Short—what old Charlie Short had ever done to me that I should slur him after he was dead.

That was the way they felt. I had violated the tabu on a squaw man's family and had opened the tomb of ancient history. The fuss was silly to me then and still has that appearance. Likely enough the present generation of the Shorts, if they have fared East a thousand miles, are putting on dog about their Indian ancestry.

The first year was the hardest, for The Eye was a Republican paper, and took sides in politics. I had been voting the Republican ticket every four years since 1880, but saying why I did so was something else, and when it came to writing a party editorial I simply didn't know how. The title of a book in The Eye library showed that the work professed to be a History of the Republican Party. That book was the source of all I wrote in defense of the Grand Old Party. By good luck the need for these difficult editorial labors was shortly relieved, for Packard espoused the cause of Populism and wrote with such zeal that The Eye thereafter was never short of timely political matter.

The Eye was a good paper too. We brought it out as a tri-weekly, filled with local and county news, and every issue had a real editorial; and all that had been in the tri-weekly went into the weekly edition, where the accumulated editorials made a full page, as in the best city papers. It was the paper the old residents took and swore by; and it deserved their confidence. No man in the county had a better reputation for honesty and squareness than Packard. His probity was unimpeachable.

The press is said to be for sale. I never heard of

any schemer trying to buy the opinion of our paper, and I was myself corrupted but once. That was when a man just starting a game down the street and mistakenly supposing that I was going to make an outcry over it, took me aside and said that as The Eye had always used him well, he would like to show his appreciation. He was opening a little place to give the boys a chance to get action on their money; and while it was not the kind of proposition that competed for advertising space, still the press ought to be supported by all good citizens. Then to my surprise he passed me a twenty-dollar piece. As the first proffer of a bribe in my newspaper experience it produced in me a reaction hitherto unknown. On the spur of the moment one was not sure what he ought to do with the money or to the base wretch offering it. While I mulled over the situation he invited me inside and showed me his roulette layout. And now my course became clear. I changed the twenty into iron men and, picking number 27, told the man who turned the wheel to let it spin. He complied and announced "little 2-O." The other plays which I then tried were like that one, and in half an hour I walked virtuously forth, carrying with me none of the wages of corruption. Temptation no further assailed me until a few years ago, when a minister offered me fifteen dollars to print an article I had decided was unavailable for The Truth Seeker.

For another new experience I was once asked by the county medical superintendent to be his assistant while he reduced the dislocated shoulder of a man in

jail. The patient, a two-hundred pound Swede, out of the logging-camp, whose misfortune had come from a fall while intoxicated, lay on a mattress, on the floor. He appeared dead to the world, but for safety the doctor chloroformed him. The doctor then directed me to remove a shoe, to sit on the mattress beside the patient, facing him; to put my stockinged foot under the arm of the Scandinavian, and then, grasping his wrist with both hands, to give a strong and steady pull. Meanwhile the doctor squatted by the fellow's big blond head and slipped the bones back into place. Being City Editor contributes to a liberal education.

As impinging on "ancient history," that is, alluding to the circulation of aboriginal blood in the veins of persons who preferred not to have it mentioned, I committed another serious error when reporting a ball game. The game was played at Tualco, on the Skykomish river, ten miles away, and I had to go horseback to the grounds. The horse that carried me had a forward-and-back motion like the bed of a Campbell press, and an up-and-down one like a milk-shaker. I returned very sore, but I heard the next day that the Tualco players were sore in a different place, because I had christened their team "the Chinooks."

Now, there visited those parts at times a balmy wind called the chinook—an agreeable condition or movement of the atmosphere sometimes said to presage snowslides in the mountains. Our team bore the name of "the Cyclones"; the Tualcos' want of a name I supplied by calling them the "Chinooks," having reference to the aforesaid breeze, so that I could subhead my report: "Cyclones and Chinooks Play a Whirlwind Game." Thus, while Chinook is the common name for the Indian jargon of the Northwest, or for those to whom it is the native vernacular, I thought that in apposition with the Cyclones, and with whirlwind added, making a very neat collocation, its technical and ethnological

JIMICUM FIELDS THE BALL.

use might be overlooked. But not by the Tualcans, never! They made war talk and sent word that if they ever found the reporter again on the Sky-

komish they were likely to get his scalp. They had
no eye for the literary quality of the heading I
had written on the story of their game. But I came
near doing worse than that, for I received the impression, and was tempted to say so, that the chase
after a fly ball had a tendency to bring out the primitive qualities of the redman. Because: At one
point in the play, a pop fly was settling near where
I sat keeping score, and a Tualco buck named Jimicum came running to field it. His cap was off, his
hair was long, and his face flushed, and with every
bound he emitted a deep "How!" If I had not
known that his objective was the ball I should
either have fled or placed myself in an attitude of
defense. When the two teams next played I reported that the Cyclones had run into a Blizzard.

The Salvation Army came to Snohomish in '92
and made such a blare with its trumpets that it got
a hallful of spectators at ten cents. Moreover, it
took permanent quarters and having enlisted a few
recruits, left one of its warriors in command. My
reports of the meetings were so irreverent that the
officer in charge of the invasion wrote to The War
Cry that the work was difficult here on account of
there being a Satan in the place. The one that remained, who bore the name of Happy Bill, alleged
in the same publication that Snohomish was a
"tough" town. He meant, as he later was at pains
to say, in assuagement of public criticism, that the
town was "tough" in the sense of being hard to pull
apart, like deer-hide, and the editor of The War Cry
had imported another meaning into his words. He
never was forgiven, for Snohomish held itself to

be an orderly city, as indeed it was, and pointed with pride to its freedom from lawlessness.

Besides the Salvation Army organizers there came Joseph Murphy, said to be the son of Francis, the great temperance apostle. He made a strong religious plea, based ostensibly on the Bible, which gave me an opportunity to unfold some Scriptures on the subject. Mr. Murphy dropped in at the office to propose an armistice and to leave an order for job printing. Our "luminous contemporary," The Sun, now no longer conducted by the truculent Mussetter, but in the hands of W. M. Sanger, an altogether decent sort of chap, boldly championed Murphy, gospel temperance, prohibition, and the Good Templars. The town cared little for either, but liked the debate. Before this date my rival City Editor, Immanuel Joseph, had left the employ of The Sun and had started on a career of swindling, was after a while put in prison for taking human life, and finally locked himself in for good by killing a guard in an attempt to escape. The frontier is no place for an isolated Jew of Joseph's class. I imagine it was the new and gun-toting country that made him turn to deeds of violence.

Joseph with sardonic humor once handed in my name along with his own, as an applicant for admission to the Good Templar Lodge. Since membership with the Good Templars merely implied but did not guarantee abstinence, I was pained afterwards to learn that I had been blackballed by Walter Thornton. The more so because I held I had recently done Walter a favor. To relate the circumstances, Mr. Thornton, being out late one evening, was passing on the other side of the street from John Gillis's place, when he heard, issuing through the hospitably opened front door of that house of cheer, the sound of bagpipes played by a man in kilts who stood before the bar. Walter, staying his steps, plucked a large apple from a tree overhead, and threw it at the performer. The apple missed the musician by a foot and then went through a window in the rear of the saloon. The hurler was unseen, but John Gillis did some figuring. The facts showed that the apple, starting thirty feet from his door, had entered his premises at an elevation not above seven feet, and that on nearly the same level it had traveled the length of his saloon, at least forty feet, and had passed through the rear window some four feet from the floor. Gillis knew that no one in town but Thornton could make a throw like that. He therefore took counsel of the city marshal, who straightway found Walter and summoned him for malicious mischief. And now, while the incident was legitimate "news," and the pinching of our star pitcher a sure sensation if known (and it appears that Marshal Brown spoke to no one but myself about it), The Eye never mentioned the affair. Surely, I thought, my reticence deserved other recognition than a blackball.

I last saw Thornton in 1900, when he was pitching for the Chicago Nationals and his team played in New York. He called on me at 28 Lafayette place. He told me then, or previously had told somebody else, that he never would have blackballed me as an applicant for admission to the Snohomish Lodge

of Good Templars if that night he had not
happened to be a little full. In 1927 a reader of
The Truth Seeker in Southern California sent in a
newspaper clipping containing part of a sermon by
the Rev. Walter Thornton, who had used selections
from Ingersoll. Walter, I remembered, had Ingersoll's pamphlet, "How to Reform Mankind."

In May, 1892, I read in the Congressional Record
a speech that had just been delivered in the House
of Representatives by a young fellow named Bryan,
from Nebraska, on a day when members of Congress were filling the pork barrel—that is to say,
were discussing the Rivers and Harbors bill and
making appropriations of money to carry out its provisions. Bryan—it was William J.—introduced an
amendment to include the rivers of his state, more
particularly the Platte, the bed of which stream, he
declared, plainly showed that it must once have had
water in it, as it might again were the necessary
moisture to be supplied by artesian wells. Bryan
went on to tell his colleagues how the Platte, so
improved, and situated midway between the two
great oceans and equidistant between our northern
and southern frontiers, would be unsurpassed as a
harbor of refuge, "where, Mr. Chairman, our navy
might float in absolute security in time of war."

That speech remained to Bryan's credit in my
mind when he delivered the one that brought him
the nomination for the Presidency; and I was for
him. And why not? He was on The Truth
Seeker's list of book buyers and had ordered the
works of Paine. I could hardly be expected to fore-
see that he would read them without profit.

The Eye of July 7, 1892, published a card from the Presbyterian minister addressed to the editor.

"DEAR SIR: I wish, through the columns of your paper, to publicly express my righteous indignation and solemn protest against the act of certain of my fellow townsmen, in erecting a flagpole, on the first day of the week, commonly called Sunday, in front of a house of public worship in the city of Snohomish, at the hour of regular service, thereby disturbing the officiating minister and the congregation in the exercise of their civil and religious liberty, and as I interpret it was a menace upon the ife of both the civil and religious institutions of the United States of America. Yours respectfully, J. W. DORRANCE."

The first day of the week, commonly called Sunday, was in 1892 the day before the Fourth of July, when the E. W. Young camp, Sons of Veterans, had promised the town a flag-raising that would knock its eye out. The corner of Second street and Avenue A had been assigned by the city council as the place to plant the mast, and it was no fault of the Sons that the place selected was in front of a house of worship. The Presbyterian church stood on the opposite corner of Avenue A. Really that flag-raising was the job of the Grand Army of the Republic, which had planned it for Memorial Day, but for want of funds or enthusiasm had let the project fall through. However, a Grand Army man who owned timber had hauled to the spot a mainmast seventy-five feet long, and a topmast at least fifty. Councilman Knapp, the Tubal Cain of the combination, had hammered out a huge iron stirrup for the topmast, and if the two sticks had stood erect, one on top of the other, why, there would have been a flagpole one hundred and twenty-five feet over all. But two pieces of timber lying in the gutter of Second street were just two spars, and not a flagpole, although representing the substance. A week before the Fourth there was not even a hole for a pole to crawl into. As captain of the camp we had a Blethen from Maine, a tall fellow who could march the boys up the street in good order and shift them to the sidewalk with the command, "Left oblike," but he was no specialist on flagpoles. He held the office of jailer at the county lockup, which furnished him with an alibi, and left me, as first lieutenant, in full command of the Sons, who gathered around me looking wistful, and inquiring what was to be done about raising that pole. The answer was the formation of a pick and shovel brigade, headed by myself, to dig the hole, which had to be ten or twelve feet deep. We began thirty feet from the site selected, sank a shaft, and into it rolled the mainmast, which at my expense had been dressed and painted. The foot lay twelve feet below the surface and the top slanted into the air seventy feet away. Without derrick or "gin pole" we were thus far and no farther when the commanding officer and a detail of his subalterns in uniform marched in good order to the office of the electric light company and asked for the use of its derricks and tackle. The company readily made the donation; the mayor granted the use of the city team. I assumed responsibility for the wages of linemen, who had to do the work on overtime. Saturday afternoon proved too short; only the mainmast was in place at quitting time.

I quote from The Eye: "The writer of this

account, taking the initiative in the absence of a
more competent person, requested the men to resume
work Sunday morning in order that the program
for the Fourth might be carried out." I took the
time to call on the Rev. Mr. Dorrance and let him
know that we should work Sunday morning. He
replied that the act could not be excused on the
ground of either mercy or necessity, and I rejoined
that the same could be said of Presbyterian preaching, which was never necessary and seldom merciful; and yet inasmuch as the liberty pole was to be
presented to the city, which was destitute of such an
ornament, I held that the erection of one and its
presentation to the municipality would be a work of
charity. To quote again: "The next morning some
twenty young men were on the ground, and at about
9 o'clock the writer was shoveling gravel in a way
that excited the commiseration of all beholders,
when the Rev. Mr. Dorrance appeared. The gentleman planted himself upon the sidewalk, removed his
hat, and, in the name of God and the Christian
religion, commanded the boys to desist."

The boys looked at me expectantly. I replied to
the clergyman with some heat that the flag which
the pole would support aloft was designed for the
protection of Mr. Dorrance in his religious worship,
and that the Grand Army, the Sons of Veterans, and
American citizens at large would claim under that
flag the same right which they guaranteed to him.
Therefore, if he demanded religious sanction, then
in the name of the Great Jehovah and the Continental Congress, the work would proceed.

Dropping his argument from the gospel, the

minister withdrew and appealed to the authorities.
He visited the home of the county's prosecuting
attorney and called for an injunction against
Sabbath-breakers. The attorney, Heffner by name,
declined to act. He was just getting ready, he said,
to go fishing, and was late at that. Mr. Dorrance
saw the sheriff, Jimmy Burton, who shrugged his
shoulders and grinned. Burton was a Freethinker,
and, anyhow, it was outside of the sheriff's line of
duty. The man of God went to the city attorney,
who told him the town marshal might do as he liked
about it. Marshal Brown appeared, and while avoiding my eye and gazing at a new moon making itself
visible in the sky, said the work would have to be
stopped. It stopped. I asked him to take cognizance of the fact, and having done so not to look our
way again. He walked back to his post and was
seen no more, but he must have heard my order to
resume firing.

The pole went up, and it was a stick to be proud
of, towering one hundred and twenty feet or so in
the air; and before nightfall we had rehearsed the
next day's raising by sending up a banner with a
twenty by sixty foot spread, the largest in the state.

Our Fourth of July literary program was much
to my liking, for I had arranged it myself, and it
included neither prayer, invocation, benediction,
nor doxology. No minister had been invited to
participate.

When next I met Mr. Dorrance he halted, removed his hat, and astonished me by saying: "I
have an apology to offer. On my way home from
the city attorney's office last Sunday I saw a deacon

of my church extirpating weeds in his garden; and
it came to me that my work lay in my own congregation, not with those who make no professions of
respect for the sanctity of the Sabbath." I then and
there also expressed regret if in my comments on
the incident lately closed, I had said anything that
might be construed as personally disparaging to
himself.

♣

TO GEO. E. MACDONALD.

From The Eye.

Good-bye. And though we should not meet again,
And though your future leads you among men
Of more productive brain, and should your pen
Bring forth truth and legends which will stem
The tide of contradiction, and nobly stand
Forth on the pages of freedom's history. Grand,
Fearless, though alone, forget not our little band
Of fellow thinkers, Here, take my hand;
You've earned respect which will not die.
Once more farewell—farewell—good bye.

—GEO. JONES.

CHAPTER II.

ATLASES of late date locate the City of Ocosta on the Washington coast where the Pacific is joined by that estuary of the Chehalis river known as Gray's Harbor. During my City Editorship of The Eye I made an excursion to that point, or to the beach named in prospectuses as Ocosta-by-the-Sea. Mr. Henry Ford holds that people do not make mistakes; they have experiences. The trip to Ocosta-by-the-Sea was an experience. The attractive name the projected resort then bore was the gift of Tacoma realtors interested in adjacent lands. The promoters organized a committee to entertain the gentlemen of the press on the beach and at a hotel in Hoquiam. By error, invitations were sent to the newspapers of Snohomish and Seattle, promising transportation, hotel accommodation, and entertainment to editors and their wives "free as air." The City Editor of The Eye and Mr. Sanger of The Sun answered the invitation by letter, saying they would be glad to meet with their fellow press men of the great State of Washington. The committee in rejoinder gave them to understand that railroad trains were waiting for them to hop aboard. But conductors must have come from some other part of the state than Tacoma or Ocosta-by-the-Sea, since they declined to pass the editors and their wives on the strength of the committee's promises. So each of the editors paid $30.20 for carfare. The further "hospitality" of the committee was enjoyed at an average cost of $15 per editor and wife. Ocosta, when reached, we observed to be a marsh, with raised wooden walks, to which the appearance of being lined with trees had been given by spiking evergreens, or small saplings, to the stringpieces of the walks every ten or fifteen feet. The editors stopped, looked, and gave judgment. Said Mr. Sanger: "We have walked into the jaws of a big fake."

The committee had made provisions for fifty guests, and six hundred strangers were present. The committee compromised by selecting for its hospitality the newspaper men who came from Tacoma and points south. This did not include the Seattle and Snohomish editors. An enterprising gentleman from Westport, which resort was perhaps a rival of Ocosta-by-the-Sea, engaged all the teams and rigs at Gray's Harbor to give the women, at least, a drive on the beach. Being one of the left after the party had gone, I was strolling along a sort of wilderness road when I observed an unusually handsome lady sitting upon a wayside log in utter loneliness, looking like Misery waiting for the company which she is said to crave. I looked twice and lifted my hat. The lady began conversation. She asked me: "Do you know anything about this dreadful place?" I denied knowledge of it, saying, "Who would be here if he did?" "That," she replied, "is what I think; but I do wish I had acquaintance enough with the locality to find a drink of water." Said I: "I can guide you to a spot where there is beer. It can be seen through the trees." She arose, and we went and got the beer. Said the lady: "This is the first place I have been with my husband where we were regarded as outsiders." I guessed that they had come from the Queen City, as Seattle was surnamed. She said: "Yes, my husband is the Senator," and told me the rest of it. We walked to the beach. Years before that day a sailing vessel had been cast ashore there, and was imbedded in the sand, keel upward. The senator's wife sat down on the sand nearby. I pointed to the wreck and recited:

> "It was the schooner Hesperus,
> That sailed the wintry sea."

Said the lady: "Was that the name of this poor vessel?"

Ah, well! Women who know Longfellow are more plentiful than those with the personal gifts of that amiable one who, though the wife of a senator, was not superior to enjoying a glass of beer and a walk on the beach with a City Editor from the sticks.

I never went back to see how Ocosta-by-the-Sea came on. After what I said of the place in The Eye I couldn't look for an invitation to return, except to explain myself.

Nearer home, I witnessed the transformation of a wilderness into a city. Downstream a few miles from Snohomish there used to be a landing-place called The Portage. Between the Snohomish river

and the waters of Puget Sound lies a peninsula like
the one formed by the Hudson on one side and Long
Island Sound and the East river on the other, which
is called Manhattan island.   Mud and sand flats at
the mouth of the Snohomish River interfere with
navigation.   For that reason, at this place a few
miles downstream from Snohomish city, freight
and passengers formerly were taken overland to
deep water on the sound side, which was Port
Gardener.   The Portage and Port Gardener are no
more.   When I reached those regions a land company had bought the peninsula to start a city on.
The ground had to be cleared of stumps by uproot-
ing or burning, and the first time I saw the place it
was smoking.   A few weeks later a wide planked
thoroughfare a mile and a half long bearing the
name of an avenue ran lengthwise the neck of land,
and there being no buildings as yet, merchants carried on business in tents.   They christened the place
Everett, after a future New Jersey politician
named Colby, whose father was chief promoter.
Word went out that the Great Northern railroad,
then under construction by Jim Hill, would have its
western terminal at Everett.   They built a wharf
and advertised that whaleback ships from Duluth or
Superior, in Wisconsin, would make port there.   It
was going to be the first city of the sound, with
Seattle second.   Everett never fulfilled ten per cent
of the predictions and ballyhoo.   Nevertheless in a
remarkably short time it had a resident, maybe, for
every stump that had been pulled, or a population
of 7,000, twice that of Snohomish, while the Everett

Land Company controlled county politics and patronage.

Living two years in Snohomish, I knew all the residents by sight, and spoke to most of them, without seeking close acquaintance with more than a limited number. The pastor of the Congregational church, the Rev. Mr. Merritt, showed a friendly disposition. He had been a missionary in the Sandwich Islands; he could give first-hand information about the natives, and he rejoiced in the revolution that occurred there early in 1893, when the islands came under the protection of the United States. While holding the Snohomish pastorate this minister was called to another county to conduct the funeral of an old Indian chief who had professed Christianity and led his tribe into the church. Mr. Merritt said he thought he was making out a good case for the deceased chieftain, and wafting his spirit to the happy hunting-grounds with the approval of the surviving Siwashes, when one of their own medicine men set up a lament according to the Indian custom, and the minister and his choir had no further part in the proceedings. The grief-stricken congregation turned pagan in a jiffy and gave their dead *hyas tyee* a pagan funeral then and there. Thus it was in Hawaii, said the returned missionary; the conversion of heathen must be regarded as highly superficial.

And there was a local justice of the peace named J. I. Griffith, with whom I came near to being intellectually chummy. I went daily to Griffith's court to report police cases, some of them funny ones. He suspected me of making a joke of his court. Once as I was leaving it he asked me to drop in for a talk when he was at leisure. Judge Griffith had a bald head, but wore the best growth of sidewhiskers I had ever seen. There had been a heavy wind, and I wrote an account of what it did. After telling of the disturbance the breeze kicked up in the Siwash wicky-ups, how it unroofed a shack, tore down a sign, blew away somebody's back porch, and raised an embarrassing situation for several ladies

J. I. GRIFFITH, J. P.

on the street, I added: "It violently oscillated the whiskers of the handsomest justice of the peace in Snohomish county."

When I met the Justice alone he said he had been watching my work on The Eye, and liked it.

We had in that county one of the most solemn and serious of school superintendents. In company with Griffith I heard him open an address to the teachers at an annual institute with the words: "Another year has rolled into the dim vista of the past," and I glanced at the Justice to see how he was receiving that schoolgirly sentiment. He smoothed out his visage with his hand, turned to whisper "dim vista," and shook in his seat. I returned, "dear dead days beyond recall." The superintendent's rolling year and dim vista were an addition to our vocabularies. I believe the Justice found it difficult to keep them out of his remarks from the bench (the said bench being a flat-top desk with a chair behind it).

In Snohomish they "regulated" vice by bringing the housekeeper to court annually and imposing a fine. The city marshal arraigned her before Griffith one day, myself being present, and when she had taken a chair beside the desk she affably greeted the court: "Well, judge, another year"—and paused. I supplied the remainder—"has rolled into the dim vista of the past." The Justice averted his face. "The marshal," he said, "will see that bystanders do not harnass the court." The housekeeper paid and was escorted outside by the officer, while the court made dire threats of getting even with the reporter who had no respect for its dignity. Nevertheless the Justice and the reporter continued to be the best of tillicums, often tightening the bonds of friendship by wetting them.

Justice Griffith contributed special articles to The Eye, and expressed surprise to see them printed exactly as he wrote them. From experience with the country press he supposed perfection in proof reading impossible. He had been a school teacher in the middle West, and had a headful of knowledge. Although a just man, learned in law, and quite a pioneer in the county, the new influence in politics defeated him for reelection as a justice of the peace—a thing he found it hard to accept, and in desperation he went to Kokomo, Indiana, and

got married. Not long before his departure, when
I called in the morning to ask if anything was doing
that day, Justice Griffith said he hoped I would tame
my muse, and instead of composing rhymed advertisements and putting ridiculous things and trivial
incidents into verse, would produce something
serious and "elemental."   He challenged me to
write sober verse on any but a funereal theme.
"Why not," he said, "celebrate our noble river
down at the foot of the street?"   When I left him
I stood a few minutes on the bridge, looking upstream, and then went to the office, and, sitting at
my table in the corner of the composing room, while
work and conversation went on about me, committed the following to paper:

THE RIVER AND THE RHYMER.

Majestic river, that drains the hills
    And moistens the valley of fertile lands,
That leaps from the mountains down and spills
    Its crystal flood o'er the western sands,
Forever your waters go sweeping by,
Forever they picture the bending sky;
They turn the wheels of the mighty mills
    Of the gods, unguided by human hands.

The ages knew you ere foot of man
    Had touched the banks that you wind between;
Your waters sparkled and slept or ran
    Ere lips had tasted or eyes had seen.
Like serpent gliding through field or wood,
In voiceless and soundless solitude,
The same wide river our bridges span
    Rolled on 'twixt borders of living green

You are mine today; I see the gleam
　　Of currents and eddies, tides and whirls,
Where sunlight glitters upon the stream
　　As on a necklace of endless pearls.
My mind falls back from the ungrasped thought
Of untold ages when men were not
　　But placid river and angry swirls
Flung to the heavens the self-same beam.

O friendly River, so clear and cold,
　　By snows and springs of the mountains fed,
Flow through my life with your stream of gold
　　And leave it white as your fountainhead.
You bear away from the homes of men
The dross, and you make them clean again;
I would that your waves, as they pass, enfold
　　Each unjust act or a word ill said.

A 3 o'clock I carried the Justice a copy of the paper containing the poem he had ordered.

Packard had mining partners whom he grub-staked while they prospected or did assessment work on claims. One of them, a quiet and likable man named James Lillis, was killed in August, 1893, by falling rocks. He stood high in the estimation of other prospectors and miners, who thought him worthy of more than a formal obituary notice. Therefore one of them, whose name, except that the first part of it was Charlie, I do not remember, brought in a piece that he had written about Jim. Having mentioned Lillis's characteristics, which were those of the ideal man and miner, the piece closed with this paragraph:

"It is sad that as he was about to realize on the hopes justly built on years of toil, he should so suddenly be ca'led to the unknown country. He prospected Life's mountains and gulches; he located his claim on honor's vein; his location notice was plainly written; his corner stakes were plainly marked; he has driven the tunnel of life and driven it well; he has timbered it substantially, with timbers that will stand as an everlasting monument to his memory; he has fired his last shot; his assessment work on earth is well done, and he has gone over the range into the unprospected country from which none return; but so long as the rugged hills of Snohomish county shall know the sound of the miner's blast, the ring of the pros- pector's pick, or the tread of the fortune-hunter's feet, his memory will live in the hearts of his fellowmen as a beautiful picture framed by his deeds of kindness as last- ing as the gold that poor Jim sought."

The author doubted its quality, and submitted his offering with diffidence, not being a writing fellow. I had no doubt of its being as fine a tribute as any man ever had, no matter what his life or station.

I said at the beginning of this section of my journalistic experience that The Eye was a good paper. Rereading the crumbling fragments of its various numbers that are preserved confirms that opinion.

More than merely passable, too, was the report- ing. In writing today about life in Snohomish county my progress is delayed by taking the time to go over the stories of daily happenings there, either incidents on the street, or cases with unusual features that came into court. These stories, then, have a permanent interest which must inhere in their quality, since the now forgotten characters are becoming as unreal as those in fiction. I have in mind a report of a political meeting, or convention, on which Packard and I collaborated, that raised the price of the paper containing it to a dollar per copy.

That could happen but once in a paper's lifetime.

The following police court case is a specimen of the daily pabulum:

CHARGED WITH MAYHEM.

A peculiar case came down from the Tualco hop fields yesterday and landed in Justice Burton's court. The indictment charged one John Ward with malicious mayhem, in that, on the 26th of September, in the county of Snohomish, he did then and there bite off the ear of the affiant, Frank Lewis, against the peace of the people of the state of Washington and their dignity.

The scene of conflict was the bunk-house on Johnson's hop ranch in Tualco. The complaining witness, Frank Lewis, came into court with five other witnesses, and with John W. Frame as his chosen vindicator of the law. Ward had also a cloud of witnesses, and was represented by Oliver Thornton as attorney. The case had been set for examination at 10 o'clock in the morning, but as Colonel Thornton desired to associate Colonel T. V. Eddy with him as counsel in the case, he asked for a continuance until afternoon, and his request was granted.

When Lewis came to tell his story, it appeared that on the day of the alleged crime he was in Snohomish with his girl. Ward was also in town, and being offered fourteen watermelons for a dollar he surrendered to the temptation, bought the melons and got Lewis to carry them to Tualco, promising him half of them for his trouble. On the way home Lewis and his girl ate one melon and gave one away. Others were broken in transportation and thrown out, so that he reached the bunkhouse with only nine, which he stored under his bed. That night Lewis went to a dance, and when he returned, remembering that there were two more melons coming to him as his share, he asked John Ward's brother George to give him one. It appears that on a hop ranch the pickers lodge in a bunkhouse, which is how it happened that the parties concerned in this case were domiciled together. George Ward refused to give Lewis the fruit, and Lewis said that when he carted any more melons for Ward the latter would know it. Thereupon John Ward, who was playing cards, jumped up, jerked off his coat and said, "If you want to fight, come on." Then he slugged Lewis, clinched with him and bit off his right ear. Lewis threw Ward and thumped him until he acknowledged he had had enough, and then let him up. The account was corroborated by other witnesses, including Miss Louisa Sherman, who testified that when hostilities began she climbed to an elevated place in order not to be hit in the fracas.

The theory of the defense, as disclosed by the cross-examination, was that Lewis had knocked his ear off against a trunk in the room, but testimony did not support it; and when the state rested, Colonel Eddy said the defense would waive examination and give bonds to appear for simple mayhem. This being perfectly satisfactory to all concerned, Justice Burton placed the bonds at $250.

The bitten-off ear was not introduced in evidence; but a young man named Sherman testified that on the morning following the "scrap" he picked up the sundered member and upon examining it saw that it bore the imprint of teeth. He showed it to James Betts, who threw it over the fence. Later Mr. Betts picked it up and laid it on a rail, where it has since remained for aught Mr. Betts knows to the contrary.

Lewis's ear, as it appeared in court, looked exactly as if a mouthful had been bitten out of it. Mr. Lewis did not say how it felt to be here in Snohomish while his ear was lying on a rail out on Johnson's hop ranch in Tualco.

It was only courtesy to invest any man practicing law with the title of Colonel. Hence Colonel Thornton, a brother of the National League pitcher, Southpaw Thornton, gets the title, although until he took this case he was a clerk. One of our contemporaries, editor of a local paper, was William B. Shay, of whom I must say more later. I breveted him colonel also, and he appeared in The Eye as Colonel W. Bill Shay.

The Indians had learned to look for justice to the Boston man's courts. I reported a hearing in a justice's court where plaintiff and defendants were aborigines. A serious crime had been committed—that of robbing a grave. The report contains some account of Indian burial customs which I had forgotten until I read it over. The reader may be interested. Summarized, the story ran:

The examination of the four Indians charged with exhuming and robbing the dead body of Lincoln Pliney, held before Justice Smith last Saturday, was pronounced by the bystanders to be one of the most interesting trials that they had ever attended. John Pliney, father of Lincoln Pliney, whose grave was violated, is an old and well-fixed Indian rancher living near Haller City, in this county. He kept his boy out of the company of other Indians and sent him to school, and the lad became so fond of his books that when he died the old man put them with him in his coffin so that he might continue his studies in the happy hunting-ground in case he should find no library there. It appears to be the theory of the Indians that death is the beginning of a journey for which the deceased needs to be accoutred as though about to migrate from one country to another. As dangers might be encountered, John Pliney provided his son with a pistol and winchester rifle. In former days, before the Indians had become acquainted with cars and steamboats, they covered the grave with a canoe or killed a horse over it; but of late years, it would appear, the more civilized of them find traveling by rail and steamer much less laborious than by horseback or canoe, and so, as John Pliney desired that in the great hereafter his son should travel in the style he had been accustomed to on earth, he put fifteen dollars in his pocket for expenses.

The Indians do not have almanacs and calendars, and

their chronology is quite primitive. Those who knew Lincoln Pliney say that he died just before the big snowstorm.

Even the religious announcements in The Eye were not without pomp, as for example:

"The Eye is able to announce a new feature shortly to be added to its other attractions. Hereafter, with the cooperation of Lieutenant Brown, we shall publish regular notice of Sunday services at the Salvation Army barracks. We don't like to brag, but The Eye keeps up with the procession, and everybody reads it, ads. and all.

Meetings of all churches were advertised under the heading: "The Means of Grace."

A man afterwards to be a United States senator from Illinois and celebrated for his "pink whiskers," canvassed Snohomish county for votes in 1892 and practiced law in the county court the year following. The hostile camp knew him as J. Ham Lewis. Of course he was a colonel. This item mentions him, with the implication that Mr. Lewis did not hate himself:

"While Colonel Lewis was examining J. B. Carothers in the Robinson trial the other day, it became necessary to send for some of the surveyor's instruments, and H. Perry Niles was asked to bring them. As Mr. Niles arose to do the bidding of the court, Colonel Lewis caught sight of his beautiful red whiskers, and mistaking the countenance of the ex-surveyor for his own, reflected in a glass, he made it a profound bow."

Making a good figure on horseback, Colonel Lewis was not averse to posing that way for the admiration of beholders. His political promises were not good. He sent to The Eye a clipping about himself from another paper, indorsed: "Run this in The Eye and there is a cigar in it for you." The clipping appeared: the cigar did not. He was ungrateful. A few years later, when he was in Congress and I in New York, I wrote him to ask if he would send me a copy of The Congressional Record. He never replied.

An item about the town's single Chinaman has ethnological interest:

"Sing Sing Henry is regarded with much curiosity by the Siwash, who, it is said, have set him down as a no-good Indian."

A legal document published as issuing from the Skagit county superior court is important as law and inveigling as literature. I clip it from The Eye (April 13, 1892):

Judge Henry McBride of the superior court of the state of Washington for Skagit county, has written what is probably the most readable and entertaining legal document in the world. The document alluded to, now on file in the clerk's office, sets forth the findings of fact from the evidence in a case wherein "Kitty," the Indian widow of a Skagit rancher named Wilbur, applies to Judge McBride for the appointment of some administrator other than the surviving white wife of the deceased. A good deal of testimony was heard with a view to establishing the Indian woman's claim as the original widow of Wilbur, and when he had heard it all, Judge McBride found as follows:

"One day in the early summer of the year aforesaid [1867], the said Wilbur, while presumably in search of clams—although the evidence is strangely silent upon this point—espied sporting upon a sandspit near Utsalady, a dusky maiden of the forest, whose supple limbs had been molded by the heat of thirteen summers, and whose cheeks were uncaressed by aught save the gentle [chinook] zephyrs. Deeply impressed by her [very] visible charms of person, and being besides of a bold and venturesome spirit, he then and there resolved to claim her for his own. He made a liberal offer, but she—modest maiden—not considering it a good plan to yield too readily, rejected with seeming disdain his amorous attentions. He returned to his lonely ranch on the Skagit, there to devise stratagems new to encompass his end. He heard her sweetly guttural accents in the sighing of the wind, and in the floating mist he even beheld her voluptuous form. Later on, with a retinue consisting of two noble red men from the Snehosh— oh, the music of these Indian names! he set out to visit his sable [why not ruddy?] enchantress at her home upon the fir-clad hillside of the Swinomish reservation, near the banks of the murmuring slough of the same name. Arriving there, without incident worthy of relating, he raised his former offer, now tendering to her parents the princely sum of fifty dollars. But they looked coldly upon this suit, and the dutiful Kitty would not surrender herself to his ardent embrace, unaccompanied by the paternal blessing. The date cannot be determined from the evidence, but Kitty, who ought to know, says it was just when the salmon were beginning to run. Desiring to be exact in all things, it occurred to the court that it might be well to continue the hearing of this case for a few years while studying the habits of the salmon, but the litigants, anxious for the spoils, objected. An attorney, when a fee is in sight, seems to care but little for scientific observation.

"Once again he returned to his lonely ranch. There, in the solitude of his cabin, with no one to spread his blanket, no one to weave him mats, he brooded over his state of single unblessedness, until at length he determined to make one last despairing effort. This time he would go in state. So he consulted 'Chip' Brown, who had taken unto himself as a wife a child of the stream and the forest, and it was arranged.

"One day as Kitty sat upon the bank, viewing her own charms as reflected in the waters of the Swinomish, she was startled by the approach of a canoe containing her amorous

KITTY.

swain, 'Chip' Brown, Mrs. Brown, and a large number of Indians from a neighboring tribe hired for the occasion. On one side were ranged Kitty, her father, mother, relations and friends, and Joseph, their tribal chief. On the other, Wilbur, 'Chip' Brown, Mrs. 'Chip,' and his mercenary train; and the prize contended for was none other than Kitty herself. Mrs. 'Chip' being retained to act as interpreter, advanced to the center, and the battle of words which was to decide the fate of the dusky maiden began. The interpreter, the court is grieved to say—peace to her ashes!—abused her position of trust to descant upon the charms and graces of Wilbur and inasmuch as she herself had tasted the delights of wedded life with a paleface, her words had great weight. 'Twas long doubtful to which side victory would incline, but at an opportune moment, Wilbur himself advancing with sixty dollars in his outstretched palm, the battle was won. Chief Joseph thought the sale a good one, and her father was satisfied with the price, so the money was divided between her male relations; and Kitty, according to the laws of her tribe, was a wife."

In 1874, after Kitty had borne him three children, Wilbur took a white wife. In 1883 Wilbur died. The heirs of the Indian woman claim a $10,000 ranch, the property of Wilbur, and the white wife claims it also. Judge McBride says: "In conclusion, the court finds that Kitty is still alive and well, although somewhat tanned by exposure to the elements, and that all parties to this action want the ranch."

We have omitted a good many of the judge's philosophical remarks about the case, and have given only the statement of historical facts, to which it should be added that when Wilbur discarded Kitty she married an Indian. The findings should be extensively published for the instruction of other judges and lawyers. The style in which they are written gives them a literary finish that most legal documents lack. Every case at law has a story, which, by being well told, might make lawyers' briefs salable and thus repay the cost of printing them.

One number of The Eye during 1893 speaks of a debate before the local camp of Sons of Veterans, "for the good of the order," between the Hon. Christopher T. Roscoe and Capt. Geo. E. Macdonald on the question "Resolved, That Grant was a greater general than Napoleon." I had the affirmative, and proved that Grant must have been the greater general because he got the final results, that is, victory, which Napoleon missed. Neither Roscoe nor I knew enough about military generalship to say which planned his campaigns and handled his troops best; we could judge only by the outcome— the presidency for Grant, and death in exile for Napoleon.

Our baseball team, known as the Jays, having Thornton for pitcher, won most of its games, and when it didn't win the game it won a report in The Eye that plausibly accounted for its defeat. Of all the days in baseball annals, that was the greatest when the Jays beat the crack Y. M. C. A. team of Seattle, which would not play on Sunday and pulled our boys away from their work for a Saturday's game. That victory deserved a hymn, and got it.

The town was fundamentally democratic. When the mayor, the Hon. E. C. Ferguson, walked down the street, the ditch digger looked up from his labor and said: "Hullo, Ferg," and went on with his digging. At the ball the mayor's lady danced with Andy the bartender.

When I recorded the death of one of the frail sisterhood I placed after her name the words "a public woman." I would not do that now and would not then if I had stopped to think a moment. Her favors were for sale, it is true, but there were public men in the place, office holders, who apparently were also for sale in whatever way anyone would pay for them, and maybe the purchaser got less for his money at that.

A rival editor, already mentioned, Mr. Sanger, was a confirmed churchman and out of harmony with local customs. When he stated in his paper that he had had "a thousand invitations to drink, to one invitation to attend church," and a Seattle paper quoted him to that effect, I made the comment that this was the first thing Sanger had ever said or the Seattle paper reprinted that would make people want to come to Snohomish.

George Morrill, another young fellow, functioned at Haller City as commissioner of deeds and published the Haller City Times. Morrill was indifferently called Judge and Attorney-General. We distinguished his weekly paper as The Whoop in Haller.

We often entertained at our house William B. Shay, a youth of twenty-three, from Roxbury, Mass., who like so many others had come to the far northwest to go into journalism. He was rather exceptional in being equipped with a college education and knowing how to write. Called upon to compose his obituary, for he died during the smallpox epidemic, I said: "He was a quiet young man, who talked but little, yet was possessed of a certain energy that kept him always at the front in the enterprises which he undertook. His gentlemanly manners, his genial presence, his broad information, his cultivated thought, his ready wit, rendered him wonderfully companionable and equal to all occasions." As "Colonel W. Bill Shay" he figured in the reports of the meetings of the Omega Whist Club that attracted the earnest players to my residence. There was a sort of society whist club called the Alpha that got dull reports of its meetings into one of the other papers; the Omega achieved publicity through The Eye. My wife has preserved the score book and a framed copy of "The Irish Jubilee, as sung by Colonel W. Bill Shay." Our members were quite distinguished—a county commissioner, a justice of the peace, a county school superintendent, all the male teachers, and the newspaper men.

The enthusiasm called Populism seized the people of the Sound country in 1892, and every farmer and artisan became an orator and a politician. Puget Sound Populism meant currency revision and the free coinage of silver, which made it endemic in that region where there were silver prospects. To be a Populist was immediately to become wise to the tricks of government. The story of the puppies that got their eyes open was told again and again. The Populist speaker would state the pretensions of the old parties, what they deceitfully promised the people; and then he would relate that one about how a certain alumnus came back to the scenes of his college days and asked to see again the room where he had spent his evenings and nights. The boy tenant, as the story went, admitted the visitor, and when he had exclaimed, "The same old bed," "The same old chair," and "The same old bookshelves," he spied a door in the corner and repeated, "The same old closet"—opened it and found a girl therein. "Ah," said he, "the same old trick"; but the boy said, "This, sir, is my sister," and the visitor added, "The same old lie."

That one never missed fire. The orator, recalled to the seriousness of the situation, went for the oligarchy, the autocracy, the bureaucracy. He assailed the plutocracy that threatened the liberties and the prosperity of the people. He gave it to the shylocks and denounced the rule of Wall street. He would recover the republic of the fathers from the keeping of caste and class. He attacked patronage and privilege. He pointed to the shameless and brazen carnival of corruption at Washington, yea, in the very capitol that had housed Washington, Adams and Jefferson He would restore the government to the people who built it by their sacrifices and cemented it with their blood. In times like these, God give us men. Give us an elastic currency. A crisis in the affairs of the nation now exists. Put Americans on guard. He who dallies is a dastard, he who doubts is damned. The keynoters who said the same thing at the last national convention were echoing the Populists of forty

years ago, with the difference that the Pops did not
then know it was hokum.

Snohomish real estate was solid stuff in 1892,

LARGE TREES WERE THE RULE.

This big cedar had been sawed down before I reached the
spot. To preserve its memory the stump was turned into
a dancing pavilion and the four couples in the picture used
it for that purpose. The tree once stood on the main
street a few minutes' walk from the office of The Eye. Not
far outside the city limits were others approaching it in
size, and the locality where they grew was referred to as
"the bush."

when I bought a lot and built a house in a sightly
place three minutes' walk from the main street,
whence I could view Mount Ranier, the Olympics,
the Coast range, the Cascades, and Mount Pillchuck,
all white-peaked and tinted by the most glorious
sunsets. At that slight elevation there were neither
flies nor mosquitoes, nor fleas or other personal insects, nor were there parasites upon the fruit trees.
Vegetation flourished in tropical luxuriance. The

ground yielded a good quality of native grass that would outgrow anything else. Before I occupied the lot and fenced it, cows that browsed along the roadside intruded and fed the grass down short, giving thistles, which cows avoided, a chance to grow six feet high. When I built a front fence to keep out the cows, the grass sprang up and killed the thistles. Watermelons reached the size of pumpkins, and pumpkins were as big as flourbarrels. A man brought to the office a vegetable larger than any pineapple and inquired if I recognized it. He cut it in halves, showing an interior as white and solid as that of a potato, and then told me it was a radish! I saw a man on horseback ride through a field of oats so tall that only his hat showed above the grain. When grass was cut and rolled into tumbles, the carter drove around them, there not being space to drive between. Salmon populated the river in season, and salmon trout the small streams. An Indian might capture a big salmon and hooking a finger in its gills walk along the street offering it for sale. He was satisfied to get twenty-five cents for the fish. Beef sold at two pounds for a quarter, flat, and you could have Delmonico steaks if you preferred them to chuck.

Until the city of Everett was built up, a few miles away, Snohomish had been the county seat and the center of traffic for that region. Now business departed. The hotels emptied, houses became vacant, the merchants lost their trade, labor was idle. The election went against The Eye, which without the city printing must take in its sign as official city paper. Advertisements disappeared from its pages or were run free to economize on composition and boiler plate. Lawyers and lodges, moving away, withdrew their cards. The character of the population changed and fewer knew or cared for The Eye as the historic county paper. Two other journals survived: The Democrat, which fed on public pap, and The Tribune, which had been "purchased" by a couple of enterprising young men who knew what sort of a paper such a town as Snohomish was destined to become, a village of families, would read. In past times, if I said to Justice Griffith: "Have any items of news come under your judicial cognizance today?" he was likely to reply, "You may say that out-of-town relations named Farnum bummed a Sunday dinner off our local society leader, Mrs. Barnum, yesterday." That was the kind of news Packard and I overlooked, and it was the sort, less cynically worded, that the young fellows of The Tribune featured. A woman could not go for a horseback ride on the Pillchuck road without getting her name in The Tribune. Conducting The Eye was a two-man business no longer and likely to become less so. I communicated with my brother in New York, who said The Truth Seeker stood in need of my services at the time. I then let Packard know that I was leaving. He fain would have condoled with me over the outcome of my venture in country journalism, but I wouldn't dole. I felt like repeating to Snohomish and its remaining people the formula of the departing guest: "I have enjoyed my visit very much, and it was so kind of you to have me."

Packard sat down and wrote and signed the

kindest editorial "Farewell" that cold type could express.

I was captain of the camp of Sons of Veterans, and since I was leaving them the Sons called for a farewell reception. The hundred persons who assembled at Burton's Hall to help make the parting a success included two ministers, both of whom did as well as the circumstances and their consciences would permit in the little speeches they made. Professor Sinclair, then county superintendent of schools (not he of the "dim vista"), in a few remarks he had craved liberty to make, begged leave to count the guest of the evening as an important adjunct to the educational privileges of the community, and therefore to say that his departure was to the community a loss. But I will say right here that my contributions to the education of the community were but slight, fortuitous, and varied. It is true that the professor and I had held disputes and high discourse over the proper pronunciation of certain words, and I regretted he had lost a substantial wager on his contention that "combating" contained two t's and should be accented on the second syllable. To add another instance or two, The Eye had invited the early retraction of a brother journalist who scornfully repudiated "cag," seen on the price tag of a small cask of nails, as an allowable spelling of keg. The City Editor had won the gratitude of sign-painters by not allowing them mistakenly to put wrong letters into their work, and he was flattered by their coming to him for verification of their spelling and punctuation, lest some damned error be immortalized by their art. Better, he placed the Dictionary at their disposal. He, the said City Editor, had likewise unfolded scriptures, in The Eye, that were withheld by the pulpit, and he had guided lodge members in the preparation of resolutions of sorrow or regret. And once The Eye sent the lawyers of the place to their books with an item that ran about like this: "The Presbyterian minister, now giving his church a fresh coat of paint, is using the fire department's ladder, borrowed from Chief Knapp. Such devotion of the public ladder temporarily to sacerdotal uses involves a moral hazard; for if the minister should accidentally fall off and break a leg, he could claim the piece of city property, forfeit to the church as deodand."

"Now, who the devil," said the county attorney, "ever heard of deodand as a term in law?" The superior judge reminded him it was his business to know, but left him to find out for himself. Meanwhile his honor consulted his own dictionary.

The captaincy of the Sons of Veterans had made me the custodian of the camp sword and belt, which I wore when on parade. In resigning I surrendered the accoutrements to First Lieutenant Dick Paddon, who thereby automatically became the captain, enjoining him to employ the utensil mercifully and with discretion. Dick, instead of strapping the sword to his side, bore it to an engraver, to have inscribed on the guard this legend: "Camp 13, to Capt. Geo. E. Macdonald, '93"; and when, at this farewell reception, our past captain, the Hon. Christopher C. Roscoe, had made a speech containing quotations of poetry both from my own works and from those of Lord Byron, he summoned me to the platform and gave me the sword for keeps. It was my turn then to make an acceptance speech, like a candidate.

What followed was reported by Packard, who wrote:

"The response was typical of 'Mac' and was frequently interrupted by laughter. He is not a polished orator, and will probably never be as successful in wielding his tongue as he has been in wielding his pen. He has that classic, awe-inspiring style of delivery and gesture which is so noticeable in a bashful schoolboy. With a preliminary blush and stammer he said"—

It was an extempore speech, yet not wholly unpremeditated. Before coming to the hall I had taken out of stock in the printing office a dozen or more blank cards and written it upon them. These cards I placed in my trousers pocket and tightly gripped them in my left hand, thrust there for that purpose. This may have cramped my style but it fortified my spirit. If the words I had written had not come out of my pocket faster than I could repeat them I should have drawn forth the pack, made the pass to the place I wanted, and refreshed my memory. This is the substance of the speech that Packard so lightly characterized:

CAPTAIN ROSCOE, BROTHERS, COMRADES, FRIENDS, LADIES AND GENTLEMEN: I never was the subject of a reception and presentation before, but I have been to funerals, and the solemnities of this occasion remind me of a funeral. A few days ago I read in The Eye quite a flattering obituary notice of myself. It was written by my friend Mr. Packard, and spoke so highly of the deceased that I expected to find at the end of it those lines which were addressed by Fitzgreene Halleck to Joseph Rodman Drake:

> "Green be the turf above thee,
>   Friend of my better days!
> None knew thee but to love thee,
>   None named thee but to praise."

And then tonight when I heard the first note of the organ, I should not have been surprised if the choir had arisen and sung:

> "How blest the righteous when he dies,
>   How sinks the weary soul to rest;
> How calmly beam the closing eyes,
>   How gently heaves the expiring breast."

I see, though, this difference: At a well-conducted funeral the corpse is not expected to respond. On this occasion, I might as well be stricken with the dumbness incident to complete demise if I could not express my appreciation of the kindness shown me and the honor bestowed by this gathering. I might tell you that this presentation was wholly unexpected, but such language could be held only with the intent to deceive. Though I am something of a liar, there is a limit to my strength as such. There are moments when one might as well tell the truth. The boys told me they would give me this sword, and in accepting the token I would express the hope that I may never be called upon to give it warmth and color by sheathing it in the system of an adversary. Also that no enemy of mine nor foe of my country's will ever deem it necessary to take the chill and glitter off a similar weapon by inserting it between the ribs of your retiring captain. I shall keep the sword as a memento and souvenir. I can never look at it without remembering the boys with whom I have been associated for the past two years in this camp. When I see it I shall recall the members of the Grand Army of the Republic who have honored us with their presence. It will bring to my mind some of the most prized associations. I shall see friends who still walk these streets; others who have gone east of the mountains, and yet others who have passed beyond the "purple twilight" of those hills that separate us from the place "where the in numerable dwell." On week days I shall think of the people here as I have known them at their ordinary avocations, in stores and offices. On Sundays I shall remember the ball players, putting up games of League ball and humiliating the pride of Seattle. On the Fourth of July, I shall see the great flag floating from the top of the liberty pole on Second street; I shall see it floating and catch the rippling of its folds in the loyal winds from off these hills. The recollections will be pleasant to me. They will remind me of a community in which I have been welcomed, entertained and amused. And this evening's long-to-be-remembered reception, given without stint—this night's farewell, unaccompanied, I trust, with inordinate regrets on the part of my entertainers—is one of the happiest occasions I expect ever to enjoy. With best wishes I say good-by, and gratefully I thank you.

A number of my prized contemporaries were at the farewell reception. One of them, Mr. Gorham of The Tribune, made a speech. A choir and an organ led the congregational singing of Civil War songs, in which "When Johnny Comes Marching Home" recurred. The Sons had a bright colored member named Vey Stewart, whose family were all singers. Walter Thornton sang everything, including the dance tunes. As one will learn from Mr. Packard's report:

"A military lunch of hardtack, coffee and beans followed, after which some of the younger folks became tangled for a short time in the giddy mazes of the waltz and a few new round dances."

Mr. Gorham had thus moralized in his Tribune:
"Geo. E. Macdonald, editor of The Eye, will leave next

week for New York. Mr. Macdonald has been a resident of Snohomish for over two years, during which time he has had the editorial management of The Eye. He is well known among the fraternity of the state and is recognized as one of the best journalists on the coast. Although he has advocated, both orally and through the columns of his paper, ideas on religion and politics of the most radical kind, antagonistic to the established social condition of mankind, and opposed by the great majority of the people, Mr. Macdonald has made many personal friends in this section among those who have the most bitterly and publicly condemned his teachings. A man who will sacrifice unusual ability, the means with which to make wealth—which seems to be the one object among all classes these degenerate days—for the sake of principle, is ever to be commended, although not always applauded."

The intimation regarding my departure for the East was verified. On the 8th of November, the third birthday of my son Eugene, the train bearing in that direction the City Editor of The Eye and family moved out of town in the early morning, while "a number of their personal friends," to quote Mr. Packard once more, "were at the station to bid them farewell." And a guard of the Sons of Veterans, in full uniform and with the camp colors displayed, stood at salute.

Packard from force of habit kept on getting out The Eye. He owned the building in which it was published, a two-story structure on the main street, with a store to let on the street level and rooms upstairs, a small office building to one side, and a rear extension for the presses and printers. He owned city lots as valuable as any and had an interest in mining properties said to be promising.

I have a suspicion that hopes for prosperity through the development of mining industries in that region were largely illusive. The silver-bearing ore was of low grade and inaccessible. Packard's mines never produced. Indications were just strong enough to keep up interest. One town in the county took the name of Silverton, one of Goldbar, and there was a postoffice called Galena. The cause of free silver, an issue in the next national political campaign, may have reanimated The Eye and strengthened Parkard's determination to keep it going. And then there befell the most desperate county seat fight known to history, Snohomish battling for the retention of the courthouse as for its life. Snohomish citizens stood under arms, guarding the county records against removal. The matter came to a vote and the election into the superior court. There the judge threw out enough Snohomish votes to give Everett the county seat. The Eye, begun in 1882, suspended publication in 1897. Packard took ship for Alaska, and nearly lost his life on a "windjammer" that was blown ashore, leaving him a castaway among the Indians. Finding no gold in paying quantities, he returned to journalism and to his trade as a printer in the Sound country. Afterward he visited the East and read proof for the concern that prints The Truth Seeker. Having in his later adventures in the Far Northwest met with an accident that permanently paralyzed one of his legs and his right arm, he in his seventies is an inmate of the Home for Union Printers in Colorado Springs.

CHAPTER III.

THE Freethought part of this history for 1891 was completed with Volume I, before I went back to July of that year and started the intercallated story of life in Snohomish, state of Washington. Now, having closed that experience, I resume the history of Freethought where it was discontinued, and write as of 1892.

The Chicago World's Fair having been decreed, the kind of church people who adopt meddling as a means of grace saw that now was their day of salvation. Hitherto, with their fussy restrictions on Sunday work and amusements, they had been obliged to function merely as local nuisances. Now they would close the World's Fair on Sunday and make themselves felt as pests by all nations. They succeeded to that extent, if they did not make quite so complete a desert of the fairgrounds as they hoped. The stay-at-homes who could not get to the show were with them. So were the Chicago ministers and saloon keepers. Both the spiritual and spirituous could see more trade moving their way with the World Fair's entrances blocked. The meddlers resolved to memorialize Congress to pay no money, make no appropriations in behalf of the

Fair, save on the promise that the key should be turned on the exhibits every Saturday night, with no relief until Monday morning. They circulated petitions to this effect, and did such a business in collecting names that in some places they claimed more signatures than there were people. A Michigan paper, The Industrial News of Jackson, indulged in adverse reflections on the petition-circulating industry, saying:

"It begins to look as though people who are clamoring to have the gates closed on Sunday are stuffing the ballot boxes. It is considered somewhat peculiar that a number of petitions from several states exceed the total population as shown by the census of 1890. The states in which the petitions seem to have been padded out of all reason are Ohio and Michigan. The tally sheets in Secretary Dickinson's office [Col. John T. Dickinson was secretary of the National Commission] show that 4,053,425 citizens of Ohio have signed petitions. The census of 1890 gives Ohio a population of 3,673,316. On the face of the returns it therefore appears that if every man, woman and child in that state had signed the Sunday-closing petitions, the population of Ohio must have been swelled by the advent of nearly four hundred thousand souls. The returns from Michigan are even worse than those from Ohio. Mr. [Census Director] Porter's census takers found 2,093,899 people in the state, yet the petitions contain 4,050,518 names. This is a sad commentary upon closing the Fair on account of morality when Christian people will resort to such measures."

On the strength of these fraudulent petitions and for other considerations no more creditable to an honest and intelligent body of men, the United States Senate, having apportioned five millions for the Fair, made the payment contingent upon Sunday closing. The counter movement of the Free-thinkers had in its favor the opinion of nearly all the more important newspapers. The Freethink-ers also circulated petitions emanating from The Truth Seeker office; but what could honest workers do against competitors who presented the fraudu-lent signatures from Ohio and Michigan? The anti-openers so far had their way, as regards the closing of certain exhibits and concessions, that even with the gates open there was nothing to be seen worth the price of admission.

The annals that mention the early Christians of Rome and tell of the troubles they brought upon themselves, explain that they were punished not so much for their crimes as for their hatred of mankind. Having in mind the snouty Christians of our time, it is easy to imagine their first pred-ecessors as fanatical persons who went about de-nouncing people who liked to enjoy life on the Lord's Day. So if the Roman public lost patience, and made it sultry for the most vociferous yam-merers among them, what else could one expect?

Two Liberal enterprises that sounded good in the prospectus were heralded in 1892, both in New York. The first was "a movement looking to free thought, free religion, and social reform, under the management of Henry Frank," to be started at a meeting held January 10 at Hardman Hall, Fifth

avenue and Nineteenth street. The invitation
printed in The Truth Seeker bore the signatures
of Ingersoll, Mrs. Stanton, Samuel Gompers, Edgar Fawcett, Eugene M. Macdonald, Helen Gardener, Dr. E. B. Foote, Charles Broadway Rouss,
Hudor Genone, and other representative persons
and celebrities, including, for an oddity, the name
of C. H. Ingersoll, not elsewhere, to my knowledge, associated with Liberal movements.

Although the initial meetings had been "greatly
successful in attendance and practical support,"
there was doubt in the editor's mind as to the permanence of the Society of Human Progress. Mr.
Frank conducted it in connection with The Twentieth Century, the weekly established by Hugh O.
Pentecost, who had withdrawn from the paper, as
well as from the lecture platform, to enter the
practice of the law as better calculated to furnish
support for himself and family. In May The
Truth Seeker records that Mr. Frank's attempt has
failed after costing its generous backer, "supposed
to be Miss Helen Weston," a good many thousands
of dollars.

The second Liberal enterprise of this year looked
even better. Says The Truth Seeker of September 17, 1892: "It was one of the dreams of the
Freethinkers of this city a few years ago, when
Science Hall was leased and used as a Liberal headquarters, to have a theater where science and morality should be taught through stage representa-
tions. The dream is to be partially realized
through the labors of Garrett P. Serviss, for many
years night editor of The Sun, and known as one

of the most accomplished astronomers of the country. The daily papers announce his retirement from journalism to devote his time to the development of the Urania Scientific Theater."

When the editor adds that "Mr. Serviss has made arrangements to take hold of the work, and soon the theater will be allied to the Liberal press in disseminating scientific facts," the dreamers of a close alliance of Freethought and scientific representation by way of the theater must have been considerably cheered.

Professor Serviss no more than Mr. Frank was an out-and-out Freethinker of The Truth Seeker school. Mr. Frank retained a sort of theism, was metaphysical and probably socialistic—inclined to dismiss Freethought as destructive; or if he was fully in sympathy with The Truth Seeker himself, the character of his discourses then and for many years afterward showed that he appealed to audiences who were not. His late writings, however, would convict him before any ecclesiastical court as a hopeless Infidel.

Dr. Serviss, still making contributions to popular knowledge of astronomy, died in 1929.

Correspondents of The Truth Seeker alluded to the American Secular Union in 1892 as a defunct organization. Judge Charles B. Waite was president, Mrs. M. A. Freeman secretary, the office in Chicago. This organization, formerly as the National Liberal League reporting nearly three hundred auxiliaries and pledged to the Nine Demands, was showing little present animation and but a lax adhesion to its original aims.

The Union held its sixteenth annual congress in the Old Forum, Washington boulevard and Sangamon street, Chicago, October 23-25. The city had been crowded by hundreds of thousands of visitors to attend the dedicatory exercises of the World's Fair. Mrs. Freeman reported that some twenty-five Freethinkers remained to attend the Congress of the Union. Ten of them, members and delegates entitled to vote, reelected Judge Waite president, Mrs. M. A. Freeman secretary, and Otto Wettstein treasurer.

While the Secular Union functioned to this limited extent, Samuel P. Putnam called for a meeting of all liberals to organize as a political and voting force under the name of "The Freethought Federation of America." The meeting and organization took place in Chicago, September 4, when the delegates elected for president Samuel P. Putnam; for secretary John R. Charlesworth; treasurer, George L. Robertson of Chicago. Said Mr. Charlesworth in his report: "Together with those who signed the constitution at this meeting, and those who had sent their names by mail, over one thousand have already been enrolled."

Mr. Putnam said in his keynote speech that the Federation was for political action, to supplement the legal and legislative work of the Secular Union. "We must take our position," he said, "and fling our banner upon the political field." Mr. Putnam was as hopeful of organizing Freethinkers into a political party as though the attempt had not been made in 1879 with Ingersoll as leader. Yet what he said had reason in it. "The Farmers' Alliance," he argued, "would never have voted unanimously in favor of closing the World's Fair on Sunday if Liberalism had been organized as a voting power."

The California State Liberal Union, of which Putnam continued to be president, called and held a convention in San Francisco on January 30 and 31, 1892, preceded by a Paine celebration with an attendance of one thousand under the auspices of the San Francisco Freethought Society. The State Union reelected Putnam as its president. He was now registering as S. P. Putnam of California. The New York Paine celebration for '92 took place under the management of the Manhattan Liberal Club, Dr. E. B. Foote, Jr., being president, and engaging Chickering Hall for the occasion. The speakers were Robert G. Ingersoll and Moncure D. Conway.

Ezra H. Heywood, editor of The Word, was The Truth Seeker's imprisoned correspondent in '92, and wrote from the State Prison at Charleston, Mass., where he was serving a two years' term under a Comstock conviction. The National Defense Association labored diligently to obtain a pardon for Heywood, but there was no chance. President Harrison, hopelessly pious and puritancial, from whom the pardon must come, never overlooked the religious aspect of anything. He took the narrow Presbyterian view, and even favored for the District of Columbia a law that would prevent a mechanic from collecting pay for work done on Sunday. He was a hypocrite, of course, for he worked the government printing-office one Sunday to put in type his message to Congress on the Chilean difficulty. He issued a proclamation on the observance of October 21, 1892, as the four-hundredth anniversary of the discovery of America, and in it instructed the people to go to church and "express their gratitude to divine providence for the devout faith of the discoverer and for the divine care and guidance which has directed our history and so abundantly blessed our people." Quite consistently he refused to shorten the radical Heywood's stretch, which lasted "six hundred and fifty-eight days."

This was one of Ingersoll's busiest years. The controversy started by his 1891 Christmas Sermon in The Evening Telegram continued far into 1892. Besides lecturing constantly, he prosecuted a suit for libel against the Rev. A. C. Dixon, who had publicly accused him of "representing publishers of impure literature, paid to pollute the minds of children of this generation."

The Massachusetts supreme court rendered a notable decision on the status of "companionate" marriage. In 1877 Mrs. H. S. Lake, a noted Spiritualist and Liberal lecturer, entered with Prof. W. S. Peck into a "copartnership on the basis of the true marriage relation," agreeing "to continue the copartnership so long as mutual affection shall exist." Now it appeared that Mrs. Lake desired a legal separation, and the Massachusetts court declared that a mutual agreement marriage, when limited by the clause "so long as mutual love shall exist," is not a legal marriage, and therefore requires no divorce proceedings to terminate the relation.

During the year the Catholic church procured the passage of its "Freedom of Worship" bill by the

New York legislature. It provided, as outlined in
The Truth Seeker, "that the Catholics can set up
their religious plants in state charitable and penal
institutions by furnishing the capital themselves.
It is but a partial victory for them, but better than
nothing, they think; though if Tammany Hall continues its ascendancy they will unquestionably make
a strike for all that they desire, which is that the
state shall compel convicts to attend Catholic worship and also pay the priests who conduct it." That
prediction was fulfilled long ago.

Part of the history of 1892 has since repeated itself. The Canadian customs held up and refused
to deliver to R. M. Morrison of Quamichan, B. C.,
a copy of "Stories of the Old Testament" (illustrated), from The Truth Seeker office. The same
reasonless action was taken by the Canadian customs in 1928.

The Truth Seeker of June 4 (1892) said: "This
Sunday deviltry has been greatly helped along by
the decision of Judge Brewer of the United States
Supreme Court in the case of the Church of the
Holy Trinity. The church had been found guilty
by a lower court of violating the law against imported contract labor by hiring the Rev. E. Walpole
Warren from London. Judge Brewer reversed the
decision, writing also an opinion which has cheered
the Sabbatarians greatly." Brewer's opinion affirmed that this is a religious people and the United
States a Christian nation.

The Truth Seeker in April commented editorially
on the fall of the Rev. Dr. Charles Parkhurst, Reformer, who organized the Society for the Preven-

tion of Crime. In a suit brought to dispossess a woman who was keeping a disorderly house, Dr. Parkhurst, appearing as a witness, testified that he and a young male member of his congregation visited the premises in dispute, had three rounds of beer, and paid five nude girls fifteen dollars to perform an indecent dance, or do a "circus" turn as he described the act, which lasted half an hour. The Truth Seeker deplored the fact that Dr. Parkhurst, of whom better things were expected, had fallen to the level of Anthony Comstock.

The trial of Moses Harman in Kansas, when means and methods of defense were exhausted, terminated in his going to the penitentiary at Lansing on two convictions, one carrying a sentence of five years and the other one year. Mrs. Lois Waisbrooker of Antioch, California, took charge of his paper, Lucifer.

In November Charles P. Somerby retired from The Truth Seeker Company and ceased thereafter to have any connection with the paper or business. Mr. Somerby filled, in his way, the position of Business Manager after the Company purchased the paper from Mrs. Bennett in 1883. He understood the technical part of book and newspaper production, being a practical printer. His management, I understand, was not so good. His health lacked something of being robust. As a Positivist and Socialist he had other intellectual interests than those The Truth Seeker sought to advance. After leaving the company he occupied himself with the publication of The Commonwealth, a magazinelet. He died in 1915.

In 1890 Franklin Steiner delivered his first Free-thought lecture, became an occasional correspondent of The Truth Seeker, and took the field. Steiner, raised in the church, had risen in it, being at one time secretary of the Sunday-school. Now he was

just approaching his majority, and having heard Ingersoll lecture and done some reading and thinking for himself, he cast his fortunes with Freethought. A likely-looking lad with a good voice, his appearance on the platform satisfied the eye and ear. No one could deny his energy, earnestness, or sincerity. But as it hap-pened the demand for

FRANKLIN STEINER, '93

Freethought lecturers at that period was not on the increase. The speakers in the field were Remsburg, Putnam, Bell, Mrs. Krekel, and Charlesworth. That Steiner lasted but a few years is not evidence he was not a success at lecturing; rather that lectur-ing was not the road to success.

The International Federation of Freethinkers that assembled at Madrid in October was dispersed by order of the Spanish government before it had finished its program. Adhesions of societies and individuals were received from about twenty coun-tries, according to the official report in *La Raison* The Truth Seeker was first on the list; the Freethought Federation next. Gen. Porfirio Diaz, president of the United States of Mexico, headed the adhesions from our sister republic. Portugal was honorably represented by Dr. Theophilo Braga, professor at the University of Lisbon, who was to be the provisional president of the Portuguese republic, 1910.

Mrs. Ernestine L. Rose, who worked with Elizabeth Cady Stanton to inaugurate the Women's Rights movement in the United States about the middle of the nineteenth century, died at Brighton, England, Aug. 4, 1892, aged 82. She was the author of a "Defense of Atheism" that was one of the Freethought pamphlets in circulation in the early times of The Truth Seeker. J. M. Wheeler of the London Freethinker wrote that only six weeks before her death she presented him with a copy of that work and said she had nothing to alter. Her birthplace was Peterkov, Poland.

The Liberal societies publishing notices of their meetings at the end of 1892 were the Manhattan Liberal Club, New York; the Ingersoll Secular Society, Paine Hall, Boston; the Ohio Liberal Society, Cincinnati; the Chicago Secular Union; the Liberal League, Philadelphia; the Philosophical Association, Brooklyn; the Liberal League, Newark, N. J., and the Secular Union, Tacoma, Wash. The Canadian Secular Union, Capt. Robert C. Adams, president, held its annual convention at Toronto, September 10. The Toronto Secular Society held regular meetings. C. B. Reynolds, secretary of the Washington State Secular Union, accepted an engagement as lecturer for the Tacoma Secular Union.

CHAPTER IV.

THE division of this work which undertakes to tell the story of Freethought in 1893 ought to give first place to the historic Sunday fraud, with animadversions thereon. Fraud being a characteristic of things religious, the singling out of this one might be invidious except that this year it happened to be the great cause of war between Protestant church forces and Secularism. It is not out of place, then, for a Secularist to say that Christians keep Sunday under false pretenses. As a sabbath, Sunday has not a biblical leg, line, precept, or event to stand upon. They tell an idle tale about Jesus, crucified, dead and buried, having arisen from the tomb on the first day of the week, making the first day of the week holy. The Bible does not say that. The Bible says the body of Jesus was placed in the sepulcher Friday night, and that when late on the Sabbath day (Saturday) a couple of Marys came to see the sepulcher they found it vacant and an angel on guard who told them: "He is not here; for he is risen." The day or the hour of his rising is held back. It might have been any time Friday night, or during the following day. The text (Matt. xxviii, 1-6) makes it certain, if the Revision is accurate, that "late" on

Saturday the body had disappeared; and with it disappears the ground for pretending that Jesus hallowed the first day of the week by arising from the dead. And a truthful historian of Sunday as the Protestant Christian Sabbath would point out that the first emperor of note to die a Christian had proclaimed the first Sunday law, describing Sunday, not as the day of the resurrection, nor making any reference to the risen Lord, but as "the venerable day of the Sun"—and that is where it got its name, being dedicated to the sun god Apollo. And if it may be inferred that the pagans were already keeping Sunday, then why is it not reasonable to suppose that Constantine's purpose in issuing the edict was to bring into line the Christians who were not observing the day? The Christian church that later assumed the style and title of Catholic took its Sunday law from the pagan emperor, and to give it a Christian character called it the day of the resurrection of Jesus. The Catholic church, claiming authority in all matters of religion, thus coolly changed the "Sabbath" from the seventh to the first day of the week. Protestants, then, against all scripture, keep and enforce a pagan day preserved for them by a church they repudiate.

Liberals devoted the year 1893 to agitating against extending the Sunday law of Constantine to close the World's Fair at Chicago on Sunday, and Samuel P. Putnam, president of the newly organized Freethought Federation of America, took up his station at Washington in January to help push a joint resolution that if adopted by Congress would leave the matter of Sunday observance "entirely within the power of the regularly constituted authorities of the World's Columbian Exposition."

They did worse in Tennessee, for in Chicago there were no prosecutions for Sabbath-breaking. But in a circular issued by the National Liberty Association, under "The Chain Gang for Conscience' Sake," this story was told:

"July 18, in the year of our Lord 1892, witnessed a sight that revives the memories of religious persecution in the Dark Ages. At Paris, Tenn., four Christian men had been lying in jail since June 3, 1892, for the crime of following their common vocations on Sunday by working on the farm, plowing, hoeing, etc. The term of one having expired, the other three, after lying in jail forty-four days, were Monday, July 18, marched through the streets in company with some colored criminals and put to work shoveling on the common highway. All three were men of family, one 55, another 62 years of age."

And all this because in the year of grace 325 or thereabouts a pagan emperor issued an edict for the observance of the venerable day of the sun.

The International Congress and Congress of the Freethought Federation of America at Chicago are reported in The Truth Seeker of October 7, 14, and 21, 1893. The gatherings were held in the hall at 517 West Madison street because President Bonney of the World's Fair Congress Auxiliary was hostile and refused the use of the Art Institute.

Judge C. B. Waite presided at the sessions of the International Congress. The American Freethought Federation Congress followed the International one. The officers elected were Samuel P. Putnam, president; John R. Charlesworth, secretary, and E. C. Reichwald, treasurer. Reichwald was a newcomer, but he stayed with the organization until his death.

Ezra H. Heywood of Princeton, Mass., editor of The Word, died at his home on May 22, 1893, from a cold contracted while attending a Land Reform meeting in New York, at the age of 63. His life had been devoted to labor and social radicalism, and he paid the penalty by undergoing prosecutions and imprisonments, at the instance of Anthony Comstock, for several years following his first arrest in 1878, each of which has been mentioned in these memoirs. Heywood was related to United States Senator George Frisbie Hoar, and was born Hoar, not Heywood. Other members of the family thought the name was altogether too suggestive, and changed it against his protest. His wife was Angela Tilton, whose characteristics and advocacy have been dwelt upon heretofore in the account of my earlier New England days. They had children whose names are unknown to the annals of reform. Mr. Heywood was the author of the book, "Cupid's Yokes," the selling of which cost D. M. Bennett a sentence of thirteen months in the penitentiary.

The American Labor Reform League held its twenty-second annual convention at Science Hall, 141 Eighth street, with Col. Henry Beeny of New Jersey in the chair, May 7-8. We have met Colonel Beeny before. Evidently he is one of the last survivors of the group, composed of Ingalls, Rowe, Evans, and himself, who in the '70s met at his store in Fourth avenue to discuss Land Reform. The names of the speakers and officers are new, but today the only one of them represented by the living is that of Clarence L. Swartz of California, who in recent years has written an interpretation of the philosophy of B. R. Tucker. Beeny was elected president and E. H. Heywood, secretary.

The Rev. Charles A. Briggs, a higher critic, whom the New York Presbytery had acquitted of heresy in 1892, was put on trial before the General Assembly of the Presbyterian church in 1893 and suspended from the ministry. A few years later he joined the ministers of the Episcopal church.

The Rev. Dr. McGlynn, the excommunicated Single Taxer who had declared himself a Secularist and attended the congress of the American Secular Union of Philadelphia, was restored to the priesthood after going to Rome.

The important book, "The Dynamic Theory of Life and Mind," by J. B. Alexander of Minneapolis, came out early in the year and was reviewed in The Truth Seeker by Albert Leubuscher, January 21.

In 1893 Moses Harman, who for some years had either been going to prison for his plain speaking, or just coming out, was "liberated" (March) from his second term of imprisonment.

Dr. Titus Voelkel, on a conviction of "blasphemy," went to a German prison for thirteen months.

Samos Parsons of San Jose, Cal., "one of the most generously persistent supporters of Freethought in the country, giving largely of his means each year, and bestowing good advice with fatherly freedom," died about June 1, 1893, in his 90th year. I met Mr. Parsons in San Francisco. He gave more than a tithe of his income to the cause, apparently having no favorites among the workers and the publications, for, as he said, he "sprinkled" his gifts over them all.

Matilda Joslyn Gage's book, "Woman, Church and State," was warmly welcomed this year by the Freethinkers. Later The Truth Seeker acquired proprietorship of the work and published a new and corrected edition. Its typography as brought out by a Chicago firm was terrible, and "would have been terrible if printed twice as well." I read it for correction and found a thousand errors. The publishers had promised the author so large a royalty that The Truth Seeker could not afford to keep it in print. It was threatened but never prosecuted by Anthony Comstock.

The Freethinkers of Oregon organized the First Secular church of Portland and appointed Katie Kehm Smith lecturer. Mrs. Smith had long been secretary of the Oregon State Secular Union, and was thoroughly devoted to the work.

In June Governor Altgeld of Illinois pardoned the anarchists Schwab, Fielden, and Neebe, who had spent several years in jail on conviction of complicity in the Haymarket tragedy in 1886.

The National Reformer, London, England, the editorship of which on the death of Bradlaugh had been undertaken by John M. Robertson, suspended on October 1.

The Freethought events of 1892 and 1893 took place without my participation or observation, since I was at the time engaged in local journalism in the Far Northwest.

With a hearty "Welcome Home" by the editor, and a reprint of the Snohomish send-off, with letters from correspondents, including Peter Eckler, who agreed that I should not have gone away in the first place, I landed back in The Truth Seeker office with a satisfactory splash. Putnam would have called the return providential if that word had been in his vocabulary, for he was projecting a big book entitled "Four Hundred Years of Free-thought" to celebrate the four hundredth anniversary of the discovery of America, and there were occasions where I could be of assistance to him.

So once more I was foreman of The Truth Seeker's composing-room, sharing the proof-reading with Walker, and giving Putnam the benefit of what I knew about preparing manuscript for a book. "Four Hundred Years of Freethought" is a work of 874 large pages, mainly biographical, containing sketches of Freethinkers from Columbus to the author's contemporaries of 1894.

During my absence in the West, the editor's assistant had been William L. Colby, a competent printer and proof-reader, something of a student, and an accurate writer. He had a side interest, perhaps a central one, in Socialism. Succeeded as assistant editor by E. C. Walker (October 1), Colby found his work in demand at other publishing houses. As a proof-reader he was the next thing to infallible. But Walker was of course his superior by far in an understanding of Freethought principles and in the art of expressing them.

At the compositor's case was a printer I had not left there when I went West, namely, Herbert Bird of Washington Courthouse, Ohio. He is still to be met in The Truth Seeker office.

Prof. John Tyndall, at the age of 73 years, died at his home in Haselmere, county of Surrey, England, December 3, 1893.

One of the old Californian Freethinkers, Owen Thomas Davies, of Brighton, died on November 28, after 73 years of life. Davies was a Welshman who came to America at 30 on a ship that brought Mormon immigrants and he went with them to Salt Lake City. His leaving the Latter Day Saints a few years later was an escape, which he shared with another Freethinker named Thomas Jones, who settled in Inyo county. A generation later they met by chance in the office of Freethought and told thrilling tales of their adventures in getting away from Utah with the Saints on the lookout to stop them. The ex-Mormons were usually very good Freethinkers. One of them in San Francisco named George Thurston, a man of 60, had been an elder and once was sent on a mission. He had a faculty for relieving pain by "touch," and while a Mormon attributed it to his faith. He found that it worked with equal efficiency when his faith departed and he had become a Thomas Paine Infidel.

The Truth Seeker in December, 1893, announced a lecture in New York by Dr. J. H. Duren Ward. The Truth Seeker current as I write these notes, August 18, 1928, reports a lecture by Dr. J. H. Duren Ward.

CHAPTER V.

MY elder brother, E. M. Macdonald, directed the policy of The Truth Seeker one year after another, and wrote leaders, but the work of E. C. Walker, 1894-5, with the special articles which he prepared, strengthened the editorial department and lent variety to the rest of the paper. He started two new departments, viz., "Freethought Progress" and "Churchly Purpose," one to be pointed to with pride and the other to be viewed with alarm. He also collected matter every week for a column of "Not for Parsons," the same being items running from humorous to blasphemous. He compiled from census reports the important series of articles entitled "Church Property: Should It Be Exempt from Just and Impartial Taxation?"

The value of church property in the United States in 1890 was $679,694,439, according to the census returns. The analysis and compilation and tabulation of the figures through the industry of Walker, with his argument from history and justice, brought forth material for the best pamphlet on the subject of exemption ever prepared and published. No one has since attempted to duplicate the performance. In fact, the government appears to have discontinued the gathering of the statistics of ecclesiastical wealth. In 1931 the American Research Foundation issued a statement from which it could be deduced that in 1930 the value of all such wealth would not fall far below six billions.

There were two prosecutions in 1894 to be defended by Freethinkers. In Lexington, Kentucky, Charles C. Moore, who had been a preacher, but now described himself as "a durned old Infidel," began The Blue Grass Blade, a weekly paper in which "I" took the place of the editorial "We." It espoused Prohibition.

In April a local preacher, the Rev. E. L. Southgate, served notice upon Moore that suit would be filed against him in the civil court for blasphemy. Two indictments followed, one for "blasphemy" and the other for "nuisance and annoyance." The one was based on language in his paper of March 18, 1894: "When I say Jesus Christ was a man exactly like I am and had a human father and mother exactly like I had, some of the pious call it blasphemy. When they say that Jesus Christ was born as the result of a Breckinridge-Pollard hyphenation between God and a Jew woman, I call it blasphemy; so you see there is a stand-off."

Moore's case came up on July 2, on demurrer, in the circuit court at Lexington, Judge Parker presiding. In a decision that was a model of secular argument, the court sustained the demurrer, quashed the indictment and the bail bond, and dismissed the defendant without day. The Truth Seeker printed the decision in full, July 21, 1894, and it is in The Truth Seeker Annual for 1895. "Blasphemy," said the judge, "is a crime grown from the same parent stem as apostasy and heresy. It is one of the class of offenses designed for the same general purpose, the fostering and protecting of a religion accepted by the state as the true religion, whose precepts and tenets it was thought all good subjects should observe. *In the code of laws of a country enjoying absolute religious freedom there is no place for the common law crime of blasphemy.* Unsuited to the spirit of the age, its enforcement would be in contravention to the constitution of this state, and this crime must be considered as a stranger to the laws of Kentucky."

One "blasphemy" of Moore consisted, according to his accusers, in his likening the generation of Christ to the "Breckinridge-Pollard hyphenation." To explain the allusion: A notable breach-of-promise case was on trial in Washington, a woman named Pollard having sued Congressman W. C. P. Breckinridge of Kentucky on that complaint. The unfortunate statesman had already exposed himself as a legitimate target for the scoffers at the notion of any relation between religion and morality by fathering a Sunday law for the District of Columbia, well known as the Breckinridge bill, and by demanding the closing of the World's Fair on the first day of the week. Furthermore, he was a pillar of the Young Men's Christian Association and its "silver-tonguedest orator," and had been counsel for the prosecution of the Rev. C. A. Briggs for heresy.

On his trial Breckinridge acknowledged his fall, but laid it to the woman, whose character he impeached. He was convicted of adultery and perjury and then went back to his constituents, likening himself to the biblical David, and nearly persuading them to return him to Congress.

At about the time the Kentucky blasphemy case had been disposed of, another involving the arrest of an "Infidel" occurred in Kansas. Mr. J. B. Wise, an aged citizen of Clay Center, engaged in correspondence with a minister, the Rev. H. B. Vennum, over the inspiration of the Bible. They were shooting texts at each other by post, when Mr. Wise indiscreetly copied Isaiah xxxvi, 12, on a postal card and mailed it to the clergyman. The latter then abandoned argument and appealed to law, causing the arrest of Wise on a charge of misusing the postoffice. For weeks the old man lay in jail at Leavenworth as a United States prisoner in default of $300 bail. He was even held there for some weeks after bail had been furnished.

The National Defense Association, E. B. Foote, Jr., secretary, took charge of the defense and provided counsel for Wise, Truth Seeker readers paying the expense by subscription as usual. The prosecution was characterized as "the Christian onslaught on the Bible." The case went over into 1895.

The cause of the People's Party lured numbers of Freethinkers into politics. At Yonkers on the Fourth of July the party nominated Dr. E. B. Foote, Sr., for Congress, and Thaddeus B. Wakeman allowed his name to go on the state ticket for judge of the Court of Appeals.

Hugh O. Pentecost, once publisher of The Twentieth Century, and the disillusioned advocate of labor, joined Tammany Hall, and did such good work for the organization that Richard Croker instructed District-Attorney-elect Fellows to appoint him as assistant. Colonel Fellows did so, and then reconsidered his act. The opposition was too sharp.

The affiliation of Freethinkers with people's and populist parties was never enduring. Every representative of Populism in Congress voted to close the World's Fair on Sunday; its senators, like Kyle of South Dakota, were champions of Sunday laws, and it incorporated "divine sovereignty" as a plank in its party platform.

Senator Frye of Maine introduced in the Senate (Jan. 25, '94), and Representative Morse of Massachusetts on the same day in the House, the National Reform Association's God-in-the-Constitution amendment. The amendment proposed to put into the preamble of the Constitution the words: "Acknowledging the supreme authority and just government of Almighty God in all the affairs of men and nations; grateful to him for our civil and religious liberty, and encouraged by the assurance of his Word to invoke his guidance, as a Christian nation, according to his appointed way, through Jesus Christ."

That is the notorious "Christian amendment," and it was the battleground of the secular and theocratic forces during the first part of the year, when President Putnam made his headquarters in Washington ready to appear before the House Judiciary Committee, to which the amendment was referred.

The National Reform Association is still bringing to Washington every year or so this amendment which was not reported out of committee in 1894. There is a tradition that once, when sponsored by Blair of New Hampshire, it came within one vote of passing the Senate. Senator Gallinger introduced a District of Columbia Sunday bill that went to the Senate Committee on Education and Labor. That does not appear ever to have come to a vote. Recording the bills and pious amendments introduced in Congress year after year will at length become a monotony.

As long ago as 1894 the Sabbatarians, led by whatever professional parasite it may have been who preceded the Rev. Harry Bowlby as secretary of a Lord's Day Alliance, began presenting petitions to Congress to abolish Sunday carrying and distribution of mails. Mails are still carried, but no one can get his mail on Sunday unless he has a postoffice box, and not then unless the local postmaster chooses to open up. The District Sunday bill that Populist Kyle championed in the Senate had been framed, as the District Women's Christian Temperance Union interpreted it, "to stop the Sunday evening lectures of Ingersoll."

The Fifth Avenue Theater, New York, announced a four-weeks' engagement of a company to present "Hannele," a play translated from the German. Commodore Gerry, at the head of an organization called in derision the "Society for the Prevention of the Intellectual Development of Children," declared the piece to be blasphemous. A little girl (Alice M. Pierce, aged 15) in the title role supposedly died and was brought to life by Christ, who appeared in person. Thomas J. Gilroy, at that time mayor of New York, agreed with Gerry that a stage miracle might have a tendency to destroy the girl's belief in the biblical ones, and so weaken her morals. The play, then, was forbidden on that and the additional ground that the representation of Jesus on the stage would be blasphemy under common law. Not long afterwards the New York legislature passed a law prohibiting the representation of the "divine person" on the stage. (Penal Law, Section 2074, 1911.)

When officers of the American Secular Union called the eighteenth annual congress, to be held in Chicago, October 26-28, 1894, they invited the Freethought Federation of America to unite with them. Attendance was good, the addresses able, and a set of resolutions rightly called "ringing" was adopted. A number of Spiritualists arrived early, bringing a cordial greeting from their National Association. The A. S. U. by acclamation elected Putnam president and Mrs. M. A. Freeman secretary. The subsequent proceedings were those of the Freethought Federation, which also elected Putnam for president and Mrs. Freeman secretary. The two organizations differentiated as to treasurers, Otto Wettstein serving for the old society and E. C. Reichwald for the new.

In the spring of 1894 the Brooklyn Philosophical Association undertook to renovate and beautify the monument of Thomas Paine at New Rochelle, which had been neglected, it appeared, since 1881. A meeting was held there on Decoration Day. To

THOMAS PAINE
AUTHOR HERO OF THE
AMERICAN REVOLUTION

─ BUT KILL ─
MONARCHY.

INGERSOLL AT NEW ROCHELLE.

The platform was near the monument of Thomas Paine; the address delivered Memorial Day, 1894. As a photograph of Ingersoll speaking to an outdoor audience, the picture is probably unique.

render the occasion perfect Colonel Ingersoll came and brought his family. A report of the event is in The Truth Seeker for June 9, 1894. That was the first of the Memorial Day gatherings at Paine's monument, and the only one at which Ingersoll spoke.

Charles Watts was sending The Truth Seeker a weekly contribution of "Freethought and Secular Notes from England."

As a writer and speaker Mr. Watts was the most serious of men; in congenial company, the jolliest. During one of the seasons he spent in America, there also reached New York, playing with Henry Irving's company, an actor whom he called Old Tom Mead. Mr. Mead was full of stories. Mr. Watts's contribution to the entertainment of a group was less of anecdote and more of witty comment. Between them they banished dull moments. All of Mr. Watts's letters to the editor bore postscripts making reference to the "funny brother."

In Mr. Watts's July "Notes" he reported: "On Monday, June 25, the Bradlaugh statue was unveiled at Northampton in the presence of a vast crowd of over twenty thousand admirers of the late great English Freethought leader."

In 1894 Morgan Robertson, writer of famous stories of the sea, began his literary career by contributing poetry to The Truth Seeker, his first offering being "Church Bells" (August 11). He soon brought out his "Tale of a Halo," with The Truth Seeker imprint. This was the diverting story, told in rhyme, of a visit by Beelzebub to heaven. His "Extracts from Noah's Log" came as a contribu-

tion for May 18 in the following year. Besides knowing all about ships, from his years afloat, Robertson was a fine mechanic. Rec e i v i n g more or less help from E. M. Macdonald, including the gift of a typewriter, Morgan in return made for the editor a fine nautical watchchain in the form of block and tackle, all shipshape, even to the seizing. It is a curios-

MORGAN ROBERTSON.

ity and a keepsake, but not a practical watchchain, on account of its tendency to become tangled or "fouled." The editor's namesake, Eugene L. Macdonald, has it. Robertson lived and wrote just before the era of highly paid "topnotchers," or he might have died wealthy. His writings passed the test of permanency and were gathered into a "set."

Pennsylvania's eminent war governor, Andrew G. Curtin, died in 1894 and at once became a character in the Ingersoll mythology. In an article in the New York World was the following:

"Mr. Curtin had no patience with anyone who did not believe in the Bible. Once when personally requested by Colonel Ingersoll to sit on the stage during one of the

Colonel's lectures he flatly refused to even attend the lecture."

Declaring that the World's statement contained not the slightest truth, Colonel Ingersoll wrote: "I never requested Governor Curtin to sit on the stage during one of my lectures. I never invited him to attend one of my lectures. I never spoke to him about one of my lectures. I never invited a human being to attend one of my lectures."

Governor Curtin sometimes figures in a well-known fabrication as the man who accused Ingersoll of taking away the crutches of a cripple.

James Russell Lowell had died in 1891. In 1894 the following passage gained circulation:

"Some gentlemen tell us very complacently that they have no need of religion; they can get along well enough without it. Let me tell you, my friends, that the worst kind of religion is no religion at all. All these men who live in ease and luxury, indulging themselves in the amusement of going without religion, may be thankful they live in lands where the gospel they have neglected has tamed the beastliness and ferocity of the men who, but for Christianity, might long ago have eaten their bodies like the South Sea Islanders, or cut off their heads like the monsters of the French revolution."—*James Russell Lowell.*

And there was another like unto it:

"When the microscopic search of skepticism, which has hunted the heavens and sounded the seas to disprove the existence of a creator, has turned its attention to human society, and has found a place on the planet ten miles square where a decent man can live in decency, comfort, and security, supporting and educating his children unspoiled and unpolluted; a place where age is reverenced, infancy respected, womanhood honored, and human life held in due regard—when the skeptic can find such a place on this globe where the gospel of Christ has not gone and cleared the way, and laid the foundations and made decency and security possible, it will then be in order for the skeptical *literati* to move thither, and there ventilate their views." (Etc.)—*James Russell Lowell.*

Since Lowell never claimed the title of Free-thinker, he will not be invested with it by me, but he uttered unorthodox sentiment enough to clear him from the guilt of having written these passages. It is doubtful that Lowell called himself a Christian, or was one. The Freethinkers of fifty years ago found much in his writings that they could quote.

As to the fraudulency of the foregoing quotations, I condensed the evidence from The Christian Advocate completely disposing of them. James Russell Lowell never wrote or spoke as quoted. With a fine exhibition of nerve, the coiners shoved their counterfeit on the public before his death and he repudiated it in his grand manner by saying he was not accustomed to discuss religious questions in that tone.

On December 28, the Manhattan Liberal Club, then probably the oldest Liberal organization in the United States, celebrated its twenty-fifth anniversary. No original member was there; but Mr. T. B. Wakeman had with him and displayed his certificate of membership signed by Horace Greeley, the second president. The club had met regularly in German Masonic Temple for seventeen years.

In 1894 the place now held by the Ku Klux Klan so far as it is anticlerical was occupied by the "A. P. A." (American Protective Association). The

Truth Seeker took the position that such an organization would justify its existence to the extent
that it curbed the church and its stealings from the
state.

John Burns, Labor member of the British Parliament, came to New York in 1894, and out of
curiosity to see what a British legislator is like I
went to Cooper Union and heard as well as saw
him. His appearance was not striking, but when
he called his audiences "fellow citizens" and then
said that was right—they were his fellow citizens
because the world was his country and to do good
his religion—it became apparent he was an exceptional character. He further justified that view by
proclaiming: "The day of the Labor agitator is past.
It is time, also, to quit dreaming. When a man
with a sudden rush of brains to the head wants to
give you a plan whereby all social difficulties may
be adjusted at once, don't waste your time listening to him." Mr. Burns, a trades-unionist, left a
good impression. And, I think, that cannot be said
of Keir Hardie, the Socialist member who came
the next year. Personally Hardie was commonplace, intellectually he was about the same. Just
then, under the police commissionership of Roosevelt, New York suffered from the Sunday-enforce-
ment terror; and Hardie's first "crack" was to applaud the official terrorists and to express the hope
that the assault on Sabbath-breakers by the New
York police was "the beginning of a fight that is
to extend all over the country." He committed the
absurdity of saying that "Socialism is Christianity," and that he had the same faith in Christianity

as a system of economics that he reposed in it as a way of salvation.

After my appraisal of Mr. Burns appeared, Benjamin R. Tucker, editor of Liberty, reminded me that while I had condemned Lady Somerset for her crusade against the concert gardens of London, I had spoken highly of Burns, who was her assistant in the matter. Burns was not a plumbliner, but some of the labor radicals were corkscrews.

Charles Robinson, the first governor of Kansas and a helper in the first Freethought organization in that state, died August 17, at the age of 76 years. He had a long record in pioneering and in politics; had been a doctor practicing medicine in his native state of Massachusetts; had served in the California legislature, and was one of the founders of the Kansas State University.

CHAPTER VI.

FEW lecturers were in the field at the opening of 1895. Ingersoll was, of course, and the man who fixed his route said that were it possible to answer all calls, the Colonel would have his work laid out for him twenty-five years ahead. The speakers who sent their engagements to The Truth Seeker for publication were John E. Remsburg and Franklin Steiner. L. K. Washburn, who had been editing the Boston Investigator since the death of Horace Seaver in 1889, now also announced himself as in the field.

A meeting of Catholic priests, bishops, archbishops, and cardinals in New York excommunicated all members of Masonic lodges, together with Odd-fellows, Knights of Pythias, and Sons of Temperance. The organizations thus banned are said to have had a membership of two millions. All of that number who have died in the past thirty years —and we can scarce hope that half of them still live—have gone to hell, according to the logic of Roman Catholic theology. If you are not an obedient Catholic the church will see that you are kept out of heaven; but she will libel you as "prejudiced"

and worse if because you don't like a Catholic's religion, you vote to retain him in private life.

Pope Leo XIII issued an encyclical to his bishops
in America setting out principles regarding the relations of church and state that American Catholics
would be glad to obliterate. His holiness in the
following manner felicitated the reverend brethren
whom he ostensibly was addressing:

> "The church among you unopposed by the Constitution
> and government of your nation, fettered by no hostile leg-
> islation, protected against violence by the common laws
> and impartiality of the tribunals, is free to live and act
> without hindrance."

That would look like an ideal situation for any
church that could be satisfied with an even break.
"Fettered by no hostile legislation, protected by
the impartiality of tribunals," and "free to live
and act without hindrance"—if religion would show
the liberality that the pope then professed to admire, Freethinkers might relax their vigilance. The
pope, who was an exceedingly dull writer and
therefore such hard reading that he expected no
one but his bishops to smoke him out, went on:

> "It would be very dangerous to draw the conclusion that
> in America is to be sought the type of the most desirable
> status of the church, or that it would be universally law-
> ful or expedient for state and church to be, as in Amer-
> ica, dissevered and divorced."

No; freedom, protection and impartiality do not
glut the appetite of the pope for what America has
to offer. He asks that his church, "IN ADDITION
TO LIBERTY," shall enjoy "THE FAVOR OF
THE LAWS AND THE PATRONAGE OF

THE PUBLIC AUTHORITY." That is to say, Pope Leo XIII wanted Roman Catholicism established as the official religion of the United States. No representative of the church ever called for a square deal.

In February, J. N. Locke of Quiniault, Washington, reported the naming of a mountain for Ingersoll. According to Mr. Locke, Mount Ingersoll is the highest peak in that spur of the Olympics between the Quiniault and Humptulips rivers, and is situated in Chehalis county. Mr. Locke stated that the elevation is best known as "Colonel Bob." A few weeks later I added this note: "Mt. Ingersoll in Chehalis county, Washington state, is not the only mountain on the Pacific coast that bears the name of the loftiest of men. In the year 1890 a party of prospectors in the untrodden portions of Fresno county, California, outlying the mining camps of Grub Gulch and Fresno Flats, ascended one of the high peaks of a spur of the Sierra Nevadas, and, formally erecting a monument thereon, gave to it the name of Mount Bob. And not less graceful was the further act of these hardy climbers in selecting the highest eminence contiguous thereto and bestowing upon it the name and distinction of Putnam's Butte."

And again "your mountains build their monuments though you destroy their dust." Looking forward to 1910, here is another: "From our surveying friend, William F. DeVoe, some of the time of Victoria, B. C., a man of many adventures by flood and field, as well as by woods and hills, comes word that a mountain has been named after the editor of The Truth Seeker—Mount Macdonald. Mr. DeVoe has lately returned from above the Skeena river, where, finding a peak some six thousand feet high, at the head of the Schulbuckhand creek, Lakeke lake—an eminence having no better cognomen than Old Baldy—he rechristened it as above."

A correspondent of The Conservator, Horace Traubel's paper, communicated the fact, as appears in The Truth Seeker of January 8, 1898, that the handsomest group of big trees in the Santa Cruz mountains, California, is known as "Ingersoll's Cathedral."

By quoting the blasphemy law and appealing to the chief of police, the ministers of Hoboken, N. J., attempted to prevent Ingersoll from delivering his lecture on "The Holy Bible." As a result the lecture, which the chief of police confessed himself unable to forbid, contained new matter devoted to the Hoboken clergy. Ingersoll said:

"In this state of New Jersey, more than one hundred years ago, when the people were pious savages, there was enacted a law that allowed no discussion of some questions —on one side.

"That statute sleeps in its grave until it is invoked by some narrow-minded gentlemen who should have lived and died three hundred years ago. Some of these good men have so little confidence in their God that they feel he ought to be protected from ridicule. They feel their infinite God cannot write a book that does not need protection. It has never occurred to anyone that the works of Shakespeare, Shelley, Burns, and other great writers should have any assistance that it was in the power of legislators to give. One can hardly imagine that the Infinite should be under such deep obligation to the legislators of the state.

"Some clergymen are intelligent and educated. I don't refer to the clergymen of Hoboken, but there are some such. Most of them are not. They have a very narrow horizon and are not at all broad. Most of them feel that they are called to the ministry because they have not the constitution to be wicked. They go to the sectarian college, which is the storm center of ignorance, and, after they are graduated, they are like the lands along a part of the Potomac, as described by a writer: 'Almost worthless by nature, and rendered entirely so by cultivation.'"

Strong religious demonstrations took place. The Christian Endeavorers of the United States and Canada, the Salvation Army, and other bodies of religious enthusiasts appointed days and seasons of prayer for the conversion of Ingersoll. When they failed at that, a woman writing to a daily paper suggested that they should ask the Supreme Power to make them, if it was his will, "as noble in character and as useful to the world as the Colonel had shown them how to be." That also failed.

The Rev. Dr. Ward, editor of The Independent, explained the non-conversion of Ingersoll by saying that "when God omits to grant our petitions, he shows not that he has failed to answer them but that he has responded in the negative."

One purpose for which "Fifty Years of Freethought" has been attempted is that of supplying writers in this field with a certain amount of data. I have seen new recruits proceed as though the cause had no past. To illustrate I will quote the man, C. C. Moore, who ran a paper in Lexington, Ky., in the

'90s. Moore was once unjustly incarcerated for a term by his religious enemies, and while in prison wrote a book. Referring to this book, he stated in his paper that, apart from "Fleta," a work on law, and Bunyan's "Pilgrim's Progress," his was the only volume composed when the author was in prison. Moore here evinced ignorance of the fact that Paine wrote Part II of his "Age of Reason" in the Luxembourg prison; that in Oakham jail Robert Taylor produced his "Diegesis" and "Syntagma"; and that D. M. Bennett in the Albany penitentiary gave his leisure to a series of letters entitled "Behind the Bars," and to writing the two-volume octavo, "The Gods and Religions of Ancient and Modern Times." This is but one instance showing the Freethought writer's need for a background of Freethought history. A more recent writer, proceeding independently of history, has said that only one Freethinker of his time, namely, George Jacob Holyoake, enjoyed the friendship and esteem of Ingersoll. The truth is that Ingersoll fraternized with all of the leaders and workers, spoke and wrote in their praise, had them at his house, encouraged and entertained them. To emphasize: If you go back to the '80s of the past century, you will look in vain for me in the front ranks and conspicuous places. Ingersoll discovered me nevertheless, wrote a cordial letter, sent me one of his books, autographed—all without my ever having communicated with him or sought to obtain his notice—and invited me to visit him and his family at their seaside hotel. In addition to that, answering questions prepared by me, he wrote an interview of half a dozen columns, his first contribution to The Truth Seeker. Would he have done that and ignored the Freethinkers who were known? He did not. He showed his friendship in commendatory letters and in the hospitality he extended to them. The statements which these few lines are written to refute are without the shadow of a foundation in historical truth. Ingersoll's tributes to American Freethinkers—Courtlandt Palmer, Elizur Wright, and Horace Seaver—in the standard edition of his works, disprove them.

The Christian Statesman, organ of the God-in-the-Constitution party, opened a campaign of whoops for the suppression of The Truth Seeker by the civil power. From the 1928 appearance of The Christian Statesman, formerly a fat monthly but now reduced to less than half the size of The Truth Seeker, some power greater than the civil is pursuing to suppress it.

The week following our reply to The Statesman's frantic outburst, The Truth Seeker came out with the three-column streamer: "Prohibited in Canada."

A Truth Seeker subscriber, Robert Mitchell of Guelph, Ontario, having failed to receive his paper, made inquiry of the Canadian postoffice inspector. That official replied to him under date of August 24 that "this paper is prohibited transportation by mail in Canada." Along with a copy of the inspector's letter Mr. Mitchell sent one of his own containing the information that "our Postmaster-General Adolph Caron is a French Canadian papist of the densest ignorance and full of superstition, who gets his instructions through Cardinal Taschereau." The great minds of Canada were once more revealing the thickness of the bony process in which they are encased. The authorities there were deaf to the criticism of their own press and that of the United States. The brightest man in Canada, Goldwin Smith, wrote to the euitor of The Truth Seeker:

"There is much to which believers in Christianity would object, as they would to the utterances of my late friends, Professors Huxley and Tyndall. But there is nothing, so far as I can see, to justify or excuse the exclusion of your journal from circulation."

Charles A. Dana of The Sun gave an editorial to the case. "We hold to liberty," said Mr. Dana, "and we revolt at the arbitrary act of the Canadian postmaster-general." Mr. Dana declared that The Truth Seeker was "undoubtedly an honest and candid paper," "not adapted to suit a pious Catholic like M. Caron, or a pious Protestant either," but not given to "scurrility and blackguardism."

The order to keep out The Truth Seeker has never been changed, but we mailed the paper to Canadian subscribers every week, and they appeared to get it. Some years later, the postmaster at New York informed The Truth Seeker Company that publications prohibited in Canada would not be received for transmission here. On that the editor appealed to the postmaster-general at Washington and got a favorable ruling. The postmaster-general was Winne, a Roman Catholic. A few years ago The Truth Seeker learned that by a ruling from the Department at Washington it would no longer be received at the New York postoffice for distribution through the Canadian mails. Here no appeal remained, for the postoffice refused to take the weekly bundle marked for Canada; orders had come from higher up. A fresh clerk at the New York office once said to the messenger proffering copies for dispatch: "You have a noive to publish a paper like that. It ought to be suppressed in this country."

The order of Sir Adolph Caron prevented many Canadian subscribers from renewing, but I am of the opinion that those who stood by continued to get their paper. Postal clerks and carriers could hardly examine each piece of mail matter as it came to their hands. Perchance if the knowledge that The Truth Seeker is "Prohibited in Canada" ever percolated down to the men in Canadian postoffices they have by this time forgotten it. The residue of meanness abides in the Canadian customs, which will not pass a bundle of papers; which throws back "Bible Stories Comically Illustrated," and has been known to seize and destroy copies of Paine's "Age of Reason." In due time and place I shall quote from an editorial article which I had the malicious joy to write entitled "A Knight's Night Out." It celebrated the event of Sir Adolph Caron's visiting New York and being picked up by the police while drunk and unable to take care of himself.

The government excluded Mrs. Elizabeth Grannis's paper, The Church Union, from the mails for running a lottery. Mrs. Grannis, a purity reformer, had recently rushed a crusade against "living pictures" and low-necked dresses.

The Rev. Dr. Isaac K. Funk conducted in the last decade of the nineteenth century a paper called The Voice, with two major fads—one the prohibition of the manufacture of alcoholic beverages, the other the sterilizing of men who violate the marriage vow. The Voice was the organ of the Prohibition Party, which put planks in its platform indorsing the Christian religion. Unable to approve of the principles of Mr. Funk, I showed from the Bible that had the manufacture of liquor been prohibited and the sterilizing of adulterers enforced in Bible times, there never would have been any Christian religion, for Jesus would have been without ancestors. That is to say, Jesus descended from Solomon, whose father was David; and had David suffered the penalty prescribed for adulterers, he being one, Solomon would not have been born. To go back from David, he was the descendant of Moab, and Moab's birth was the consequence of Lot's becoming intoxicated and in that condition generating a son with his own daughter, which he would not have done when sober. This unavoidable conclusion hangs upon the statement of the first verse of the New Testament that such is "the book of the generation of Jesus Christ, the son of David."

The trial of J. B. Wise of Clay Center, Kansas, for letting the light of scripture shine from a postal card on which he had copied Isaiah xxxvi, 12, was announced in March as "approaching." The Truth Seeker raised a fund for Wise's defense. On the 11th of April, in the United States District Court for the Eastern Division of Kansas, the attorney for The Truth Seeker, Adolph Bierck, appeared on behalf of the defendant. Mr. Bierck thought it an appropriate time to relate this anecdote: "The poet Goethe was once invited to attend a conference oi ministers at Kiel, called for the purpose of suppressing obscene literature. Goethe suggested that they begin with the Bible, and the conference adjourned." But, Mr. Bierck added, the work prematurely abandoned by that conference has been taken up by an evangelical clergyman of Industry, Kansas, and he now, through the medium of this prosecution, invokes the jurisdiction of the District Court of the United States for the Eastern Division of Kansas to sustain him in his contention that this particular verse of the scriptures is obscene and indecent." Thus the Rev. Mr. Vennum had adopted the suggestion of Goethe to "begin with the Bible." The case went to the Court of Appeals.

Editor Brann of The Iconoclast, Waco, Texas, began this year the assault on Baylor Baptist University that led on to what his partisans spoke of admiringly as his hot finish. A young girl, Antonia Teixeira, had been brought from Brazil to be educated in the university, and then returned to her people as a missionary for their conversion and baptism. The girl became a mother. President Burleson of the university laid the paternity to "a

negro servant," but the scoffer Brann asked how
then it had been possible that the child should be a
Caucasian with the "blue eye and wooden face" of
the president of the faculty. I chided Mr. Brann
for his hasty conclusion, arguing that a man (Dr.
Burleson) good enough to be the president of a
Baptist theological seminary would of necessity impress his personality upon all who came within the
sphere of his influence and who shared the light
of his countenance; and Editor Brann, even though
immured in Texas, could not be so unfamiliar with
the laws of heredity and prenatal influence as never
to have heard how much environment had to do
with determining the features and complexion, the
blue eye and wooden face, in such instances as this.
I shall relate the sequel when I come to it.

"An exceptional Universalist minister" is named
in The Truth Seeker, June 1, to wit, the Rev.
Thomas B. Gregory of Halifax, N. S., who was
preaching "trial sermons" in the Church of the Redeemer, Chicago, and bade fair to cinch the job.
Mr. Gregory's name soon was seen as one of the editors of The Freethinkers' Magazine. He is that
facile writer whose syndicated articles have been
favorites with Freethinkers from that day to this.
He is no reconciler and, what is exceptional among
popular rejectors of orthodoxy who do syndicate
work, he never compromises his Freethought principles by talking about evolution as "God's Way."
At least I have not detected him in that offense and
hope he hasn't committed it when I was looking the
other way. (Mr. Gregory died in 1929.)

Samuel P. Putnam made a voyage to England,

lecturing in London and the provinces to very cordial audiences, writing his "News and Notes" weekly to The Truth Seeker, and returning in September. On his leaving Albion, seen to the Waterloo
station by Charles Watts, Editor G. W. Foote of
the London Freethinker wrote: "Thus ends a most
interesting episode in the recent history of the Freethought movement in England. Mr. Putnam has
returned to the land of his birth, but he has made
an indelible impression upon the Freethinkers of
England. They like his eloquence and they love his
personality. He carries with him their unanimous
good wishes. They hope he will live long to lead
the army of Freethought in America, and they also
hope he will come over again to old England. Whenever he comes he will find a host of eager hands
stretched out in glad welcome."

The Arena published an "Age of Protection for
Girls" symposium—relevant here because the Freethinker, Helen Gardener, took a leading part in it.
Miss Gardener was the only one of the disputants
who assumed an attitude toward the question other
than theological. I took a position which was this:
"It will be conceded so far as I am concerned,
that when the age indicated by nature is expunged
and the attempt is made to introduce another age
arbitrarily, one's opinion as to what that age should
be is as valuable as anybody's else; but each should
be supported, when practical, by something besides hysterical whoops."
By a strange oversight, I thought, nobody consulted the opinion of the girls, and they must have

thought it odd to be the excluded subjects of a discussion by people who could not know so much
about the facts as they did. A professional friend
looking over my shoulder says: "Girls of 12 or
under should *not* be consulted." But how about
girls from 18 to 21? If not they, then whom? I
asked my wife at what age a woman was able to
make a judicious decision, and she said: "Never."
The agitation led to the correction of abuses in
some of the states where there were no laws to protect female children of twelve years. It would be
difficult now to reproduce the state of the public
mind on the question. Not all of the discussion was
without humor, inappropriate as humor may be to
such a theme. I quote a paragraph in my Observations:

"I suppose that few Kansas people know how
much they are indebted to the Boston Arena for its
successful agitation in favor of raising the age of
protection for the girls of their state. The following anecdote bearing on the matter is told in Washington city by Representative Mercer of Nebraska:
An old Kansas couple who had a son living in California wrote to him requesting that he should return and take up his abode with them during the
remainder of their declining years. The son was
dutiful, but he preferred California for ranching,
even if he had to bring the old folks thither; and so
he wrote: 'I am surprised at your asking me to return. I own a ranch here and am happy. If anything is lacking, it is having you with me. I would
dearly love to be with you again, but, as said before, I am surprised that you should ask me to re-

turn to a state where they raised nothing at all last year except the age of consent.' "

A committee of women in '95 brought out Part I of "The Woman's Bible," the revising committee being headed by Mrs. Stanton, who had twenty assistants, including Mrs. Robert G. Ingersoll. The Morning Journal's symposium on the book in November would have been a totally hostile work except for an appreciative contribution by Mrs. Anna H. Shaw. "The Woman's Bible" showed that the Bible is not a woman's book. Of the suffrage movement at that time there were two divisions. One demanded suffrage in the name of right and justice, regardless of consequences. This division was led by Freethinkers like Mrs. Stanton. The other division demanded suffrage in the name of Christ in order that God might be voted into the Constitution, the Bible into the schools, and Christian doctrine generally into civil law. The second division was led by the churches, Anthony Comstock, and Dr. Isaac K. Funk, and women like Mrs. Grannis, Mrs. Livermore, and Miss Willard, W. C. T. U.

The annual congress of the Freethought Federation and American Secular Union was held the 25th, 26th and 27th of October in Hardman Hall, Nineteenth street and Fifth avenue, New York. On paper, as described, it appeared to be the biggest congress the national organization had held in years, probably because it happened in New York where I could attend and report the proceedings at length. My account was as long as those of former congresses that T. C. Leland used to turn in.

The hall seated about eight hundred, and the audience that filled all the chairs looked like a million on the evening Putnam put me up to read a lecture on The Judicial Oath. Since my essay on New England and the People Up There, in 1879, I had done no public speaking. I guarded against a breakdown by writing my lecture out in full, but had it fairly well committed to memory, and besides I brought some notes of extraneous matter calculated to relieve the monotony of too much argument. As to the necessity of raising my voice, I had the admonition of young Dr. Foote to gauge it by the auditor nearest the door in the rear, and in another matter the counsel of Ingersoll to discover some appreciative listener and talk to him. Capt. Silas B. Latham, proprietor of a fishing-smack, with whom I had made voyages of a week at a time, down to the banks off Atlantic City, sat halfway up the aisle, with his head listed to port, regarding me quizzically. So the lecture went over. The extraneous matter suited the Captain. Some verses I had written on "Putnam at Sacramento," part of it quoted in my reminiscences of the San Francisco experience, fixed the attention of L. K. Washburn, who applauded before I had really made a good start, and I let him have that part with what force I could put behind it. I never had any voice, either for strength or durability; so I am not an orator like other men. On that evening John McDonald sang a song I had written; M. Florence Johnson recited my poem on Bruno; Libby Culbertson Macdonald made a speech and included another of my rhymed performances; and that was the situation when I came on the boards and observed that if this was an election the Macdonalds would be accused of repeating.

A Committee on Amendments—E. B. Foote, Jr., Franklin Steiner, and Henry Bird—reported a new name for the organization, "The American Secular Union and Freethought Federation," and an amended and abbreviated constitution. Officers elected were President, Samuel P. Putnam; secretary, E. C. Reichwald; treasurer, Otto Wettstein. The report is in The Truth Seeker of Nov. 2 and 9, 1895.

Dayton, Tennessee, had put itself on the scroll of fame before it ever tried John Scopes for violating the anti-evolution law. The town won distinction in '95 by prosecuting five Seventh-Day Adventists for working on Sunday. The acquittal of the accused failed to vindicate the right of any person to do Sunday labor. They got off because the judge, whose name was Parks, intimated in his charge that "the cases were trumped up on questionable testimony procured at the instigation of witness-fee speculators and fee-grabbing officers." Did any one ever hear of a Sunday prosecution actuated by any more respectable motives than these?

St. Patrick's Day in '95 fell on Sunday, putting the celebration over to Monday, but for the faithful it was a two days' fiesta. The Irish from Ireland, of whom there were plenty, put on high hats and green sashes and marched in parade along the line where most hospitality was dispensed. A New York Irishman in court on Tuesday morning, with a "d. and d." against his name, received from the judge a reprimand for not confining his celebration to the appointed day. The defendant replied: "Maybe I was wrong, but someone told me St. Patrick had two birthdays because he was twins."

Mrs. Elizabeth Cady Stanton celebrated her 80th birthday Nov. 12, '95. That was perhaps the last meeting of the three pioneer suffragists, Mrs. Stanton, Susan B. Anthony, and Matilda Joslyn Gage. Miss Anthony read a list of "pioneers either present or sending greetings, and also of those whom death had taken from the ranks." Of the living she mentioned, paying tribute to each: Parker Pillsbury, Amy Post, Lucy N. Colman, Matilda Joslyn Gage, Mrs. Olive H. Fraser Ingalls (wife of J. K. Ingalls), who was at the first woman suffrage meeting held in the state of New York, and C. B. Waite, who had fifty years previously published the Liberty Banner at Rock Island, Ill. These were Freethinkers already named in my story. William Lloyd Garrison, Jr., was there and read a poem. A daughter of William Lloyd Garrison, Mrs. Villard, died in 1928, and was spoken of as liberal and progressive. I never heard of her until she died.

An item dated June 8 bore the news: "United States Judge John F. Phillips of the Western District of Missouri has just resentenced Moses Harman, editor of Lucifer, Topeka, Kan., to one year's imprisonment at hard labor." That was another stage of the prosecution of Harman for publishing the ' Markland letter," a protest against a husband's assault on his wife. I read the letter. The writer said the right thing in what the court thought was

the wrong way—an instance of questionable diction. As old Peter Bayle maintained, it is no more
than a question of grammar.

The convention of the New York Populists at
Syracuse nominated, August 30, the philosopher
Thaddeus B. Wakeman for secretary of state. New
York city gave him 625 votes.

If anybody remembers it, an absurd French scientist, M. Ferdinand Brunetière, professor at the Sor-
bonne, announced in 1895 the "bankruptcy" of
science, and the phrase won popularity with the
piety-enders. Science has accomplished so much
since then, that if Brunetière were to come again
on earth it would take him quite a while to learn
the latest terms necessary to describe the new business of the "bankrupt" concern—its progress and
discovery.

The editor and his constituency waged the fight
of the year to expel the Bible and religious exercises from public schools in states where they were
unlawful and unconstitutional. The history of that
fight alone would make a book. There were favorable decisions by courts, but the bootlegging went
on, and the victory in certain states was later
thwarted by the legislatures enacting laws, as in
Pennsylvania, making Bible reading compulsory.

The Kansas Freethought Association held its
annual convention in Forest Park, Ottawa, August
6-11. Mrs. Etta Semple gave the address of welcome, and was elected president. Mrs. Semple took
an active part in Freethought affairs and began the
publishing of a paper.

The first death of '95 to stir Freethinkers was Prof. Thomas Henry Huxley's, June 29. The ceremonies at the funeral according to the ritual of the

THOMAS HENRY HUXLEY.

Church of England were resented as a mockery and an insult to the memory of the dead Agnostic and to the Agnostics among the mourners. A pious inscription is written upon his tombstone. Huxley was born May 4, 1825, at Ealing, England. He once "stood" for a professorship in Natural History at the University of Toronto, Canada, and was rejected for want of a reputation for sanctity. He and John Tyndall, who had also applied for a professorship, were "charged with no religious convictions," and the chairs denied them. The great minds of Canada are permanently encased in impenetrable bone. The applications of these men, which were rejected, conferred more distinction on the Canadian college than all the applications that have been accepted.

A man who seemed to belong to another century died in Vineland, N. J., August 31, at the age of 94. In the '40s he started a Liberal paper in Portland, Maine (the state of his birth), and ran it for sixteen years. Through his labors he secured the passage of a law "to give every landless man in Maine, who would settle on it, one hundred and sixty acres of land at fifty cents an acre, to be paid in work on the roads." Among the contemporaries of my parents his name was a household word. The destitution of his last days was relieved by funds raised through The Truth Seeker. This was Jeremiah Hacker. His paper was The Pleasure Boat.

And we lost, in the bloom of her young womanhood, Katie Kehm Smith, who gave Freethought lectures throughout Oregon, and organized in '93 the First Secular Church in Portland, where she gathered a congregation of hundreds, as large as that of any orthodox church in the city, with a flourishing Sunday school attached. She was born in 1868 in Warsaw, Illinois, and at 17 took up teaching, then lecturing, then organizing. Katie served for years as secretary of the Oregon State Secular Union and industriously reported to The Truth Seeker the progress of the movement. She was the wife of the Hon. D. W. Smith of Portland, who fully approved of her work, and was proud of her.

After the death of Mrs. Smith the First Secular Church of Portland and its Sunday school were conducted by Mrs. Nettie A. Olds. The convention of the Oregon State Secular Union was held at Portland in September; president, W. W. Jesse; secretary, Pearl Geer, who thereafter reported progress; treasurer, C. B. Reynolds.

Lulie Monroe Power, daughter of J. R. Monroe, founder of the Ironclad Age, Indianapolis, who had continued the paper after her father's death, died in April, '95, age 45 years. In December, The Age ceased publication.

Victor Emanuel Lennstrand, whom G. W. Foote of the London Freethinker termed "one of the founders and martyrs of Freethought in Sweden," died in the fall of '95, in his thirty-fifth year. He published in 1889 Fritankaren, a journal of Freethought, and was subjected to eight prosecutions for blasphemy. Not of strong constitution, he was broken down by the prosecutions and his life ruined and shortened by his nine months' imprisonment.

N. D. Goodell, the California pioneer-architect of Sacramento, died at 81, in December. The report of his funeral said: "Mr. Goodell was honored by all the people of whatsoever belief." He gave liberally to the paper Freethought on the coast.

CHAPTER VII.

WHEN the year 1896 began President Cleveland and Congress had come near involving the United States in war with England. Beyond saying that whatever could be done to avert such a war should be done at once, The Truth Seeker avoided comment on the situation. Its fight was with traitors at home, not a "traditional enemy" abroad. The Christian or God-in-the-Constitution amendment had been introduced into Congress by Representative Morse of Massachusetts and Senator Frye of Maine. Our paper asked for funds to put Putnam on guard in Washington, where he could oppose the measure when it should come before the committee it had been referred to. Putnam took up his residence at the capital and on March 11 made a great speech before the Joint Judiciary Committee of the House. The bill perished, and The Christian Statesman and The Christian Reformer, its newspaper sponsors, discovered that the measure had been killed by "Infidels or even Atheists, Spiritualists, Freethinkers, and Agnostics."

To head off a few score of the lies that were in circulation about the chief exponent of Freethought in America, E. M. Macdonald prepared and published the book "Ingersoll as He Is." In April Ingersoll wrote him this acknowledgment:

"MY DEAR MR. MACDONALD: I write simply to thank you from my heart for your generous defense.

"I have never felt like answering these slanders, and yet I know that my silence would, by many, be misunderstood.

"There are some things that one can scarcely deny without the denial itself leaving almost a stain. Now and then I have answered some slander, but for the most part I have made no reply.

"Your splendid defense will make it unnecessary for me to say anything. Nothing need be added to what you have so generously said.

Again and again I thank you, and I remain, as ever,
"Yours always,   R. G. INGERSOLL."

It came out in one of the religious papers that "on Sunday, December 15, 1895, Grover Cleveland, President of the United States, returning from a duck-shooting cruise, and arriving at Washington at 2 P. M., made his way through the streets of the capital, accompanied by his fellow-sportsmen, laden with the ducks he had shot." And The Christian Statesman exclaimed: "What an object lesson to the young men of America does this Sabbath-breaking President present!"

Mr. Cleveland was an indifferent Sabbatarian and an inconsistent Christian. Nevertheless I considered it no more than his due to cite the following precedent from The Columbian Centinel of December, 1789, to wit:

"The President on his return to New York from his late tour through Connecticut, having missed his way on Saturday, was obliged to ride a few miles on Sunday morning in order to gain the town at which he had proposed to have attended divine service. Before he arrived, however, he was met by a Tything man, who commanding him to stop, demanded the occasion of his riding; and it was not until the President had informed him of every circumstance and promised to go no further than the town intended that the Tything man would permit him to proceed on his journey."

This particular Sabbath-breaking President of 1789, the occasion of whose riding was demanded by the Connecticut Tything man, was George Washington.

George, it must be remembered, could not tell a lie; but his declaring before the Tything man that he "proposed to attend divine service" at the next town, instead of confessing his intent to get a good swig of hard "cyder," was a noble attempt to accomplish the impossible.

From time to time ministers were quitting the pulpit, turning liberals, and saying they would never preach again One of these in '96 was the Rev. J. Ira Maltsbarger, Baptist, of Turner, Kansas, and significant were his remarks thereon. We hear much of the joy felt by those who are converted to Christianity, but Mr. Maltsbarger, on becoming, as he said, "an out-and-out Infidel," declared: "I feel as though a yoke had been cast from my neck. I am now a free man; can think as I like and can work conscientiously. I never was happier in my life."

It was during the years '95-'96 that Dr. W. A. Croffut emerged as a leading Freethinker in Washington, D. C., which event to me had the same likeness to a resurrection as my meeting with Dr. Dio Lewis at the Liberal Club when I had reached my majority after having been made familiar with his name at about the age of six. For many years I had lamented Dr. Croffut as one who had passed away.

Croffut exerted considerable influence in molding my youthful mind. When as a writer on the editorial staff of The Graphic in the '70s, he produced squibs and puns in poetry and prose, I recognized him as great, and bought the paper. I was a promising Labor radical until I listened to him before the Liberal Club in Science Hall, 141 Eighth street, on the problem of wages and strikes. It agitated me greatly, for nothing so disturbs one as an adverse argument which cannot be refuted. As an admirer of his poetry, I tagged him about to Memorial Day celebrations and other public affairs where he read it, though I did not regard him as at his best when he was exhausting along metrical lines. In 1874 or 1875 I perused this verse of his while visiting in a section of Westmoreland, N. H., known as Poocham:

> "Said a great Congregational preacher
>   To a hen, 'You're a beautiful creature.'
>   The fowl, just for that
>   Laid an egg in his hat,
> And thus did the Hen-re-ward Beecher."

Poocham critics condemned the lines as "ridiculous."

Croffut was versatile. He wrote essays on farming, a military history of Connecticut, a novel about the Mormons, and works on political economy. He experimented in hypnotism and recorded his observations, and he guided parties of Americans, of the Innocents Abroad variety, who went prospecting over Europe and Asia. After his 1895 voyage he wrote for The Truth Seeker on "The Holy Sepulcher a Historical Humbug."

The School Board of Kansas City, Mo., in March '96 refused the petition of the A. P. A. and the Protestant ministers to reintroduce Bible reading into the public schools. Having chronicled this as "Right on the Throne for Once," The Truth Seeker said:

"There is hope for Kansas City, for besides having a school board that rejects the Bible as a text book, it has a prominent clergyman who rejects the doctrine of the fall of man and the atonement which the Bible is alleged to teach. The clergyman is the Rev. J. E. Roberts of All Souls Church." Mr. Roberts had just put forth a volume of extremely heretical sermons, saying therein: "With the fall of man, which never occurred, must go the doctrine of the atonement, which was never needed; and with that doctrine goes the greatest moral enormity that ever gained currency among enlightened men." Not many years later, as we shall see, Dr. Roberts established his Church of This World, Rationalist, of which he still is minister.

Said an item in the News of the Week, March

28, '96: "The Rev. William T. Brown of the Congregational church, Madison, Conn., is to be tried
for heresy." One charge against Mr. Brown was
that he had said some parts of the Bible were not
"fully inspired," and another that he used the Revised version of the Bible instead of retaining the
old version "just as God wrote it." The next
week's item appertaining to Mr. Brown stated that
he had been acquitted "as an indorsement of the
advanced theology of the most radical thinkers in
the Congregational church." A third mention of
the Rev. Mr. Brown declared his acquittal a white-
wash, for it was admitted that he had said that "if
God called upon Christ to sacrifice himself for mankind, he was a devil," and that "the birth of Christ
was the same and no different from that of any
other child." This was the William Thurston
Brown who in 1913 lectured weekly for the New
York Freethought Society.

The number of The Truth Seeker for March 21,
1896, was the last to be printed from movable types,
and all the compositors but one went elsewhere.
We retained T. R. Stevens, who as an employee
dated from 1875, when the composing-room was at
No. 8 North William street, to make up the forms
with the metal delivered from a machine shop.
With my small family I had lived on the upper floor
of the building in the rear of 28 Lafayette place,
the printing-office being on the floor below, ever
since my return from the West. The typesetting
machine shops were in many instances only com-
posing-rooms. They set, corrected, and delivered
for 35 or 40 cents per thousand ems. The paper

then ran some sixteen columns of advertising per week, with much of the reading part, as in the days of Bennett, devoted to good words for books published by the Company. Weekly bills were about thirty per cent what they are now, and naturally all this advertising allowed by the postoffice in papers mailed at the minimum rate brought trade.

In '96 Mr. Walker left us and the editorial work became mine. I was sorry to displace Mr. Walker and held the thought that if the opportunity ever came I would proffer him the job again. That opportunity came in 1909, when he declined it. Being a practical printer, a keen and prolific writer, with many years of experience in the liberal field, Walker brought to the work more than could be expected of any other man.

The Evangelist, a religious paper, published the statement that the late O. B. Frothingham had discontinued the preaching of Freethought because he had come to the conclusion that truth was to be found in the church. In New Unity, Chicago, Mr. Charles de B. Mills of Syracuse, New York, an old friend of Frothingham, wrote upon his death: "It is grateful to know that the light that had illumined his path continued still to shine. He had not wandered from home, now in age seeking to retrace his steps and get back into the comfortable beliefs of an indolent and artificial religion; he had advanced much beyond the Ultima-Thule of the ancestors that had gone before, and never again could be taken with what the old and outgrown faiths had to offer." Mr. Mills confirmed the statement of the Rev. Minot J. Savage that Frothingham "never retracted any of his opinions. He has grown more radical from day to day the longer he has lived." He may, indeed, have grown too radical for the congregation he addressed. One explanation of his ceasing to maintain a radical pulpit was that he had inherited money and no longer needed to struggle. No radical preacher ever made it pay.

In February, 1896, Ingersoll lectured in ten of the larger cities of Texas, drawing so well that his manager declared that should he go there again he would have a "four-acre tent." In due time a letter came to The Truth Seeker from Mrs. Anna M. Brooks of Howe, in that state, who told of attending the lecture in Sherman.

"I must not forget to tell you," wrote Mrs. Brooks, "that I made the acquaintance of R. G. Ingersoll and his wife, and heard him deliver his lecture on 'Liberty of Man, Woman, and Child' to a densely packed house. I was invited to their room at the hotel and visited with them three hours. Oh, was not that a glorious opportunity—so unexpected by me! . . . I went directly to the hotel where I knew they would take dinner. I waited in the sitting room until they came back from dinner, and then, when Mrs. Ingersoll came in, I introduced myself, telling her I was one of her husband's numerous admirers. She laughingly said: 'Come right to our room.' We went in, and she said: 'Robert, here is one of your sweethearts.' We shook hands, and when I told him how far I rode through the mud to see and hear him he said he would give me a pass to the lecture. I thanked him, but told him I thought myself fortunate that I had already bought my seat in a good place. He said he was sorry I had been in such a hurry to pay out my money. Oh, we had a delightful time—so many of the city celebrities came to interview them, and I was introduced to them all."

As printed in The Truth Seeker there was an editorial elision in the letter. The editor had scratched out a line; and taking advantage of my knowledge of the fact, I wrote an Observation as follows:

In looking over some copy for the printers I observe a letter from a Texas woman who paid Colonel Ingersoll and his family a call when they were in her state, and I see that the Editor's pencil has been drawn through this line:

"*I gave Mrs. Ingersoll my recipe for biscuit.*"

At first the words may appear to be incongruous or mere gossip, but the more you look at them the more significant they become. Colonel Ingersoll and his family have had a good deal of mouth praise, much of which they are obliged to be grateful for when they know it is formal, perfunctory, and not straight from the liver. We can vision the honest Texas woman, living on a ranch, perhaps traveling miles on horseback and by rail to meet them; knowing that they were surrounded by people who would give them more flattery than they would enjoy, in language and with flourishes which she could not command; feeling that words were cheap, and that everything costing money was at their disposal; and yet, wishing in some signal way to attest her friendship and admiration, she bestows—not for what it is worth to them but for what it is valued at by herself—a formula the surrendering of which destroys at once and forever her pre-eminence among housekeepers and makes another woman her equal. It was not flattery or patronage. It was a tribute, beside which the widow's

mite is without moral value. In the creation legend to be
read in Genesis the gods drove man out of the garden lest
through eating the fruit of the tree of knowledge he
should become as one of them. Christ imparted to none
the secret of his remarkable power. Christian women
carry cakes or biscuits to their pastor's donation party,
but did they give his wife directions for making them?
These are the models of devotion held up for us to admire; but, after all, it has been left for the unbelieving
woman of the Lone Star State to perform an act of self-
sacrifice which should illustrate the real meaning of renunciation. She gave Mrs. Ingersoll her receipt for biscuit!

Mrs. Nettie A. Olds of McMinnville, Oregon,
reported in a letter published January 11: "We feel
especially thankful to those who have made it possible and are so energetically erecting the First Secular Church and Science Hall of McMinnville (70 x
40 feet, with gallery, large stage, full set of elegant
scenery, and kitchen with all modern improvements,
and sitting rooms), soon to be dedicated to the
service of humanity."

On April 13, at Topeka, Kansas, J. B. Wise of
Industry, under bond for having written a verse of
the Book of Isaiah and mailed it to a minister, was
found guilty by a jury and fined $50 by Judge Fos-
ter. Wise's counsel gave notice of appeal to the
United States Supreme Court; but the case never
was carried up.

The Supreme Court of California, in a decision
full of sound sense, quoted in The Truth Seeker of
May 9, declared unconstitutional a law forbidding
the opening of barber shops on Sunday. Said the
editor: "There is one sentence in the opinion delivered by the California judges which should be

conspicuously engraved where all the labor agitators, the legislators who pass labor laws, and the courts that affirm their constitutionality can see it daily. It is this: *'It is a curious law for the protection of labor which punishes the laborer for working.'*"

Mr. J. E. Hosmer of Portland, Oregon, state superintendent of Secular Sunday schools, reported the receipt of contributions for the creation of a Liberal University at Silverton, in that state.

Cyrus W. Coolridge, a capable young Russian Jew, had come to The Truth Seeker to learn typesetting. He soon began to write. His name was not Coolridge, nor Cyrus, and the W. stood for nothing in particular.

Joseph Dana Miller contributed articles in 1896. He was distinguished as an advocate of the Single Tax.

This was a presidential year, a year of Bryan's candidacy, and the issue between "sound money" and free silver. Freethinkers were divided. Both sides wrote letters, which became rather acrimonious after Ingersoll had written one to the editor condemning free silver coinage at 16 to 1.

The Secular Union and Freethought Federation congress in Chicago, November 13 to 15, had a larger attendance than any previous one. An audience of two thousand gathered to hear Foote and Watts in Central Music Hall. Mr. Pearl Geer, the young secretary of the Oregon State Secular Union, reported upon the work that was being done in his state. The Liberals there were publishing their paper, The Torch of Reason, conducting Secular

Sunday schools, and were going to establish a Liberal University. On the morning of Sunday, the 15th, the attendants at the Congress, out of courtesy to the Spiritualist contingent, adjourned to Schiller's Theater and heard a discourse by Mrs. Cora L. V. Richmond. Putnam was reelected president, and E. C. Reichwald, secretary.

Two distinguished visitors from England, George William Foote, editor of the London Freethinker, and Charles Watts, reached our shores on October 22, and the Freethinkers of New York gave them a cordial reception at Chickering Hall on the Sunday night following their arrival. The addresses by Henry Rowley, who presided, and of Putnam, Watts, Foote, Ingersoll, and T. B. Wakeman were stenographically reported in The Truth Seeker of October 31. Watts and Foote were entertained by the Drs. Foote in this city and at Larchmont Manor and by the Ingersolls at Dobbs Ferry. They went to Toronto for the convention of the Canadian Secular Union, to Chicago to attend the congress of the A. S. U. and Freethought Federation, and spoke at the Liberal Club and the Brooklyn Philosophical Association, besides Washington, Philadelphia and other places. Mr. Watts had previously spent years in America; it was Mr. Foote's first visit. I quote my impressions of the editor of The Freethinker as written down at the time:

Mr. G. W. Foote, president of the National Secular Society of Great Britain, has been looking over New York for several days previous to this writing, and New Yorkers have looked over Mr. Foote during that time. He has not told how our "institutions" impress him, but if they stand the scrutiny as well as he does their permanence is in no danger. The word "imperturbable" describes him fairly. Other Englishmen, I have observed, are at times impatient. They are choleric or jolly as the occasion may dispose. Foote is bland and humorous. We were on the way to New Rochelle, N. Y., by rail to visit the Paine monument. The weather should have been pleasant but was not. As the train passed gloomily through the land of melancholy days, somebody apologized for the rain. Foote paid interested attention and replied: "Well, you can't help it, you know," and then composed himself for forty winks. You see, he might have said "beastly," but he scored a point by not offering that criticism.

But although oblivious or indifferent to what can't be helped, and while he would not ostentatiously defy meteorology, Mr. Foote is obviously alert and curious. He observes and inquires, and before he had said so at the Chickering Hall reception, I had received the impression that he would be more grateful for a fact imparted than for a detailed expression of thought. He is quite candid. His criticism of American ideas is that they are superficial, and he has a right to that opinion, for America has no thinker like Spencer, nor any observer like Darwin. We don't encourage the domestic culture of that kind of people on this continent, although we sometimes take them "second-hand," as Wakeman says, from elsewhere. If one of these "first-hand souls" should venture to be born here, he would starve, or be stunted, or winter-killed on his native soil. Our religious population has seen to it faithfully that no Bradlaugh ever represented a constituency in the national Congress.

Personally, Mr. Foote is handsomer than he looks— that is, than he looks in any of his pictures. He would be taken for a doctor, or at least a professor, for he has the manner of the learned. He is cosmopolitan, and might be a German or an American except for his speech, which is United States with only occasional lapses into English. He brought the necessary number of *h's* with him and uses them in their appropriate connections. His dress is not peculiar. He is a man above nationality, so far as I can judge. On all topics of interest he is radical to the verge of reasonableness, and his thought is trammeled only by obstructive facts. Wherever he may go he will not attract attention as a "stranger in these parts."

I heard Mr. Foote before the Manhattan Liberal Club on "The Irreligion of Shakespeare." Mr. Foote met Ingersoll and pronounced his personality commensurate with his genius.

The Rev. T. DeWitt Talmage had been called from Brooklyn to Washington, D. C. He took his pulpit falsehoods with him and retold them. They included the myth of Ethan Allen's advising his daughter: "You had better take your mother's religion."

Dr. W. A. Croffut temporarily disposed of that yarn by writing Talmage a reply, printed by the newspapers, in which the following paragraphs occur:

"Around me as I write are trunks full of the literary remains of Major-General Hitchcock, a distinguished grandson of Ethan Allen, and in his written diary I find this alleged incident repeated, with the following words added:

"'I had often heard my mother speak of the death of that sister, and remember having heard her say that she attended her in her last moments, I desired to know whether there was any foundation for the story. My mother told me on two occasions that there was none whatever. I regard the story, therefore, as pure invention in behalf of certain opinions to which my grandfather was supposed to be unfriendly.'"

Talmage was a pulpit liar of more than common versatility.

In the summer, for a week's vacation, I went on a fishing cruise with Capt. Silas Latham of Noank, Conn., and wrote the story of the voyage for The Truth Seeker. The Coast Seamen's Journal of San Francisco, whose editor, Mr. McArthur, afterwards went to Congress, reprinted the account and invited me to become a contributor to his paper. Having all the engagements I could handle, I turned the invitation over to Morgan Robertson, who as we all know had been a seaman. At that time, Robertson had published no sea stories, but now he wrote one and offered it to Editor McArthur in exchange for a modest advertisement of his rhymed skit, "A Tale of a Halo." The proposition not being accepted, and Mr. Robertson having a story on his hands, he submitted it to the editor of McClure's Magazine, who gave him $200 for it and a commission to write others.

The Johns Hopkins University at Baltimore announced the publication in the fall of a "reconstructed" Bible under the direction of Prof. Paul Haupt, who had been working on the scheme for six years with groups of scholars in Europe and America. The reconstructed Bible was to be at the same time a new English translation embodying the latest scholarship. The projectors outlined their plan: "The attempt will be made to show at a glance the net results of modern criticism upon every line of every book of the Old Testament. This will be done by printing the text in different colored backgrounds; and the interpolations, additions, notes, and comments and various changes that are believed to have been made subsequently, will each be printed upon a background of a different color. It is from this that the new translation gains its name of the Polychrome Bible." Dodd, Mead & Company were selected as the publishers, and much was expected of the new version. I became interested and asked for Genesis, but that book had not appeared in polychrome form. I doubt whether it ever did appear. The first to come out was Ecclesiastes, translated by Professor Haupt in 1896; the next, Professor Cheyne's Isaiah. I waited until 1898 for Judges, by the Rev. G. F. Moore of Andover Theological Seminary, and another year for Joshua, by the Rev. W. H. Bennett, London. The production of the books must have been expensive, for on some pages the variety of sources required nearly all of the seven colors used, and in addition to these italics, fullface, ecclesiastical, superior figures, and Greek letters were employed. Introductory and explanatory remarks and notes filled twice as many pages as the text of Judges, and there were maps and numerous illustrations. Limited sales and want of popular interest in the scriptures prevented the completion of the Old Testament canon. Dr. Haupt found the public so ignorant and dumb that in his haste he declared that the state should make the study of the Bible compulsory—in which The Truth Seeker did not agree with him, and said so.

One of the prominent Liberals who died during the year 1896 was C. B. Reynolds, the veteran lecturer, at his home in Seattle, Wash., July 3. His death was caused by a fall from a swing in which he was sitting while in McMinnville, Oregon, whither he had been called to deliver the funeral address of an old-time L i b e r a l. Concussion of the brain resulted fatally about a week after he reached his home. Mr. Reynolds was born in New York in 1832. In 1868 he became an Adventist preacher. In the early '80s he began delivering Freethought lectures, having been

C. B. REYNOLDS.

"converted" by reading the Boston Investigator and The Truth Seeker. His career for the next few years, including his prosecution in New Jersey for blasphemy, has appeared in these pages. He lectured eight months of 1889 in Walla Walla, Wash. In 1892 he lectured for the Tacoma Secular Union. Afterward, till the time of his death, he was speaker for the Secular Church of Portland, Oregon. Reynolds was a man of character and courage and culture, with an uncanny knowledge of scriptural texts and ability to locate them; an always ready speaker, a good friend and companion, an honest, worthy, and sincere Freethinker.

Allen Pringle of Selby, Ont., president of the Canadian Secular Union, died on the 22d of July at the age or 55 years. Mr. Pringle was a native of the town of Richmond, born April 1, 1841. He studied medicine but abandoned it for farming and bee-keeping, and became the leading apiarian of Ontario. Freethinkers attending the World's Fair at Chicago in 1893 found him there in charge of the honey exhibit for the Canadian government. He was a student and a contributor to numerous newspapers and magazines.

On December 11 came the tragedy of the year, the death of Putnam by accident while in Boston. He died poisoned by illuminating gas at 47 St. Bartolph street. He had just returned from the Chicago congress to fill lecture engagements in the vicinity of Boston. His presence there coincided with that of Miss May Collins, the Kentucky young woman who had recently come into prominence as a writer and speaker, and now had decided to try lecturing in the North. Putnam that day visited his sister Caroline in Boston; and took dinner, or supper, with friends in Stoneham, one of the friends being Moses Hull. Just after his 7 P. M. arrival at No. 47 St. Bartolph street, the janitor of the building traced an odor of gas to the rooms where Putnam awaited Miss Collins's readiness to accompany him to the theater. The bodies of both, dressed for the street, were found on the floor.

The funeral of Putnam was held in Boston on the 15th, L. K. Washburn pronouncing the eulogy. They bore the body then to Forest Hill crematory.

Miss Collins was buried in her native state, Kentucky. Mr. Charles Moore of the Blue Glass

SAMUEL PORTER PUTNAM (1838-1896).

Blade, who attended the funeral, said that the address of Moses Kaufman, a Freethinker and friend of the family, was beautiful; that "the beautiful chapel of the most beautiful cemetery was comfortably filled with representatives of our best society." Miss Collins was but twenty years old, having been born in Midway, Kentucky, in 1876. She was intellectually precocious and her writings were mature.

As the place where Putnam lodged while in Boston was never discovered, the personal effects he carried there were lost. His satchel contained a collection of his poems that he was revising for publication in a volume with my own. The Truth Seeker had announced "The Poetry of Freethought," or Selected Poems of Putnam and Macdonald, and had booked columns of orders for the work. But no one knows what became of Putnam's selections. His death caused the plan to be abandoned. We were collaborating at the same time on what we had determined should be the great Freethought novel.

The life of Putnam was a perpetual protest against puritanism. I never heard criticism of him on any other score. He was a man of scholarship, ability, eloquence, sensibility, honor; a tremendous and tireless worker. As a lecturer he traveled more than one hundred thousand miles and spoke in all but four states of the Union. The names of the leading Freethinkers living during the twenty years of his labors will be found in the reports of his work that he communicated to Freethought and The Truth Seeker. He was 58 years old when he died. . . .

The farewell dinner to G. W. Foote and Charles Watts, at the end of their stay in America, took place at the Hotel Marlborough, New York, on the evening of December 15. Dr. E. B. Foote presided. The guests numbered sixty. The Liberals, owing to Putnam's death, were not inclined to anything festive. It was a funeral. Young Dr. Foote, responding to a toast to "The American Secular Union," whose president (Putnam) had just died, nearly broke down. L. G. Reed spoke on "Decaying Dogmas," Watts on "Waning Orthodoxy," Wakeman on "The New Religion," Henry Rowley on "Our Departing Guests." I made my theme "The Departed Guest" and talked of Putnam, the partner and "pard," the poet, the orator, the man of intellectual gifts, the comrade, my friend "Sam." And I read a poem I had composed entitled "The Spot Where He Made One." I had written it with a feeling of resentment that some of Putnam's friends, suffering from the timidity complex, were saying, "Let us wait for all the facts, before rendering judgment." The presumption of them, I thought, to judge Putnam! In one of my stanzas I acquitted him of any such righteousness as that:

Too well I know you for my heart to hold
  One doubt that had your sudden fate been mine,
  Though hatred, malice, circumstance combine
With voice of forsworn friendship to malign;
If I, as you, lay in obstruction cold,
Then would one thought, one pen and voice ring true
In memory of this friend who mourns for you.

Disclaiming the ability to add a leaf to his laurels, I said in other stanzas:

Since each of all the immemorial dead
  Hath found his eulogist, an advocate
  To plead the virtues common to the great,
  How shall I now some tribute fresh create—
What pæan is unsung, what word unsaid?
I can but echo oft-renewed acclaim,
Ancient as death, and evermore the same.

Yet let me wish that those hid hands which guide
  The way we tread on—which do leave or take,
  Which do this life reject, or that one make
  Rich in great actions for the whole world's sake—
Might deem mine worthy to be so applied
That it abound with service to mankind,
And like your own leave fruitful deeds behind.

And so close the Memoirs for the year 1896.

CHAPTER VIII.

FOR many weeks in 1897 The Truth Seeker was an In Memoriam for S. P. Putnam. Countless letters came, with many poems, some of them good. I remember how one by Anna Pritchard, which George Long illustrated with an impressive mourning group, and another by Sharlot Hall, surprised me by their excellence. I had not before heard of either writer. Sharlot Hall kept Putnam's death in mind for many a year and sent other poems for the anniversaries of it. Evidently Miss Hall was not without honor in her own country, since she was afterwards chosen to be poet laureate for one of the Western states. The Freethought societies held memorial meetings and the demand for a Memorial Volume to Putnam, as well as to Miss Collins, who had "added the name of a Kentuckian to the roll of the thinkers of the world," was general. I prepared the volume with the help of the Collins family and Putnam's sister Caroline.

Putnam's life after the year 1879 has made a part of this story. He was born July 23, 1838, in Chichester, N. H., his father being a minister. After attending common schools and the Academy in Pembroke, he entered Dartmouth in 1858. In 1861 he enlisted as a private in the Fourth New York Heavy Artillery. In 1863 he took rank as captain of Company K, Twentieth United States Colored Infantry. The next year he had a call to preach the gospel and resigned. He then took three years in the theological seminary in Chicago; was married in 1867 to Miss Louise Howell. After preaching in two orthodox pulpits, at DeKalb and Malta, Illinois, he joined the Unitarians, occupying pulpits at Toledo, Ohio; North Platte and Omaha, Neb., and at Northfield, Mass. In 1885, upon her application, and in default of his appearance to oppose, a divorce was granted Mrs. Putnam. Two children, Henry Howell and Grace, remained in the care of the mother. For a half dozen years he had been writing and speaking for Freethought, and in 1884 was made secretary of the National Liberal League when Ingersoll was elected president. His subsequent history has been told.

A discussion, part serious but mainly funny, followed a sermon by the Rev. Dr. Lyman Abbott, the successor of Henry Ward Beecher in the Plymouth pulpit, Brooklyn, in which the preacher moved his congregation to laughter by preaching on Jonah and the whale. He gave what looked like a critical commentary on the myth by saying that the book of Jonah "was written as a piece of satirical fiction, to satirize the narrowness of certain Jewish prophets." As The Sun had pronounced Dr. Abbott an Infidel for rejecting the Jonah story, so unmistakably vouched for by Jesus Christ (Matthew xii, 39), it printed a letter from myself stating that Dr. Abbott was an Infidel to the same degree as Paine, whose words he appeared to have borrowed, since Paine had said of the Jonah book: "It is more probable . . . that it has been written as a fable, to expose the nonsense and satirize the vicious and malignant character of a Bible prophet or a predicting priest."

The Sun deigned or feigned to take the matter seriously. In an editorial Mr. Dana gravely said: "Our correspondents who discuss the case of Dr. Abbott have no conception of the tremendous revolution in sentiment of which it is a symptom. All the Infidelity of past periods has been of no consequence as compared with the present Infidelity, of which, for the moment, he has made himself the example. It is an Infidelity which strikes at the supernatural basis on which Christianity rests, and therefore relegates the religion of Christendom to the position of mere mythology and fallible human philosophy."

The Times-Herald (publication place not identified) made the following metrical remark:

"The Reverend Lyman Abbott says of Jonah and the whale
That he's looked the fish all over, and he can't indorse
        the tale."

The discussion, which became widespread, was dismissed from The Truth Seeker with a quotation from Dr. Abbott a few years earlier when he had declared: "Christ gave his personal sanction to the account of this miracle, which, more than any other in the Old Testament, has been subjected to criticism and even ridicule. We must either accept the Old Testament history of this miracle, or believe that Jesus was a deceiver or was himself deceived."

President McKinley called a certain Judge Mc-

Kenna from California to a place in his cabinet as attorney-general, thereby causing severe criticism to be leveled at him by the Protestants of his party. I note the remark in The Truth Seeker that the objectors appear to be oblivious to the weighty principle that "when an archbishop of the Catholic church consents to throw his influence to the side of a candidate, he does not do it without some assurance that the claims of his church will be recognized in the event of the candidate's election." The archbishop alluded to was Ireland, who delivered the goods.

Daniel Lamont, secretary of war in Cleveland's cabinet, had given the Catholic church permission to erect a cathedral on the West Point military reservation. His successor, General Alger, confirmed the gift, and then to the surprise and consternation of Tom Watson, who was running an A. P. A. paper, the Roman Catholic Attorney-General, Judge McKenna, nipped the scheme at this stage by pronouncing the grant unconstitutional, although it had been extended to provide building sites for churches of all denominations. Later President McKinley nominated Attorney-General McKenna to be an associate justice of the Supreme Court of the United States. Though some of the judge's colleagues of the California bench protested that his legal attainments did not fit him for the place, he was confirmed by the Senate and took his seat in 1898.

While the public debated the proposed church grab at West Point, Senator Gallinger of New Hampshire introduced a measure described as an "amendment," as follows:

"Article XVI.—Neither Congress nor any state shall pass any law respecting an establishing of religion, or prohibiting the free exercise thereof, or use the property or credit of the United States, or of any state, or any money raised by taxation, or authorize either to be used, for the purpose of founding, maintaining, or aiding, by appropriation, payment of services, expense, or otherwise, any church, religious denomination or religious society, or any institution, society, or undertaking, which is wholly or in part under sectarian or ecclesiastical control."

The amendment got as far as the Senate Committee on Judiciary. Later, we shall see, the substance of it was enacted as a United States statute, March 3, 1897, to the provisions of which not the slightest attention has since been paid either by Congress or state legislatures.

Concerning Brann's Iconoclast, Waco, Texas, The Truth Seeker said editorially: "We have never regarded anything that Brann might say, on any subject whatever, as worthy a moment's notice."

Brann (if I may anticipate history) came to a bad end on the first day of April, 1898, being shot and mortally wounded by Tom E. Davis of Waco, a business man who had said he should be driven from town for his attack on the Baptist University. It was a street fight and Davis was also slain.

Alleged rightful heirs of Stephen Girard gave notice that a move would be made for the restoration to them of property which Girard, dying in 1831, had bequeathed to Philadelphia for the establishment of a college from which religion and preachers should be excluded. At the time of his death, Girard's heirs tried to break his will because it was unchristian. Now they were attacking the college trustees for not carrying out the will in the unchristian way prescribed by the testator. They had a strong case, if hopeless, for the systematic perversion of Girard's gift to the uses of religion by those who have had the management of the college is a scandal. In May, 1897, the city of Philadelphia unveiled a statue to Girard's memory. United States District-Attorney James M. Beck, the orator of the day, said of Girard: "What his religious convictions were no one will ever know." The fact of Girard's having been a Freethinker is never mentioned in the college. The pupils are taught religion, but the religion of the founder is concealed from them.

The case of J. B. Wise of Kansas, who had been in the meshes of the law for two years, reached its quietus in The Truth Seeker of January 30, 1897. Wise had used a postal card to convey to the Rev. Mr. Vennum of Clay city the twelfth verse of the thirty-sixth chapter of Isaiah. The scripture was adjudged to be obscene and Wise on conviction fined fifty dollars, which, with the costs of his defense, was paid by Truth Seeker readers.

From Florida the Mental Scientist, Helen Wilmans, spread her philosophy through a publication she called "Freedom." Mrs. Wilmans ultimately was charged with false pretenses and her business broken up. For a time she was a promising rival of Mrs. Eddy, who chose the word Christian instead of Mental to qualify her science.

The present editor of the London Freethinker, Mr. C. Cohen, first was introduced to the readers of The Truth Seeker as one of the National Secular

Society's speakers who had been warned off Chatham Lines because of a disturbance raised by "a handful of ill-bred Christians."

Governor Bradley of Kentucky vetoed the appointment of a chaplain by the legislature—an isolated example, too ideally honorable to be emulated by other governors.

The presidential chair of Leland Stanford University came near being taken from under its occupant, David Starr Jordan, following his remarks before the Unitarian Society of Berkeley, where he said:

"Stimulants produce temporary insanity. Whiskey, cocaine, and alcohol bring temporary insanity, and so does a revival of religion, one of those religious revivals in which men lose all their reason and self-control. This is simply a form of drunkenness not more worthy of respect than the drunkenness which lies in the gutters."

The ministers of California united in a demand upon the Methodist Mrs. Stanford, widow of the founder of the University, for the removal of Dr. Jordan. Rumors were about that he would be fired, but they died down and he stayed.

The ministers of Washington, D. C., procured the adoption of police rules prohibiting newsboys from selling papers on the street on Sunday. The Washington Secular League, of which D. Webster Groh, Dr. W. A. Croffut and Gen. William Birney were active members, took the part of the boys and provided them with counsel and bail when arrested. The boys became attendants at the meetings of the League, fifty of them being present to hear Dr. Croffut's lecture for their benefit.

Ingersoll's lectures in 1897 drew record crowds.

In both Boston and New York he packed houses as they had never been packed before. Representative Keliher of Massachusetts placed before the legislature a bill "to stop Bob Ingersoll from lecturing Sunday evenings if possible." Elijah A. Morse of that state, and of Rising Sun Stove-Polish fame, who when in Congress championed the God-in-the-Constitution amendment, wrote an article for the Chicago Christian Citizen proposing that the sale of Ingersoll's books be prohibited by law.

"There can be no such thing as personal liberty in civilized society," said True Reform, a Prohibition paper. The editor was a prophet. Destruction of the personal liberty delusion preceded the adoption of the eighteenth amendment to the Constitution, the establishment of collectivism in Russia, and the election of Mussolini to be dictator in Italy.

Henry Addis, a son of discontent, published in Portland, Oregon, his paper called The Firebrand With him were associated Abner J. Pope and Abe Isaak. All three were arrested in October, '97, for alleged violation of the postal statutes, the charge being indecency and literary incendiarism. Pope, a man 74 years old, a Quaker and Spiritualist, welcomed the martyrdom. Offered his liberty if he would agree to appear for trial, he refused to treat with his captors. Addis and Isaak gave bail. The Firebrand was anarchist-communist in sentiment.

The list of Liberal papers of 1897 included The Freethought Ideal of Kansas. The officers of the Kansas State Freethought Association for 1897 were Mrs. Etta Semple, president, and Miss Laura Knox, secretary-treasurer.

The Freethinkers of Salt Lake City, Utah, organized as The Free Lance Society, with Alexander
Rogers as president and a constitution embracing
the Nine Demands. Plans were laid to establish a
Church of This World with Dr. N. F. Ravlin of
California as minister. Ravlin was a Spiritualist
and Rationalist who had renounced the Baptist
pulpit.

The cartoons by Watson Heston, with which The
Truth Seeker had been illustrated for some years,
were discontinued in February. With Mr. Heston's salary added, the illustrations were burdensome at a time when The Truth Seeker was raising
a Sustaining Fund for itself under the head of
"The Helping Hand." Probably half of the readers, with whom the pictures had never been popular, were satisfied to see them dropped out, while
others lamented.

Percy Fitzhugh, a writer of stories for boys, who
jumped into popularity with "Mohawk Trail," got
some practice by writing articles for The Truth
Seeker. Six of them appeared in 1897.

The Freethought societies announcing regular
meetings at the close of 1897 were the Manhattan
Liberal Club, the Brooklyn Philosophical Association, the Friendship Liberal Club (Philadelphia),
the Chicago Liberal League (Mrs. Zela Stevens,
lecturer), the Washington (D. C.) Secular League,
the Ohio Liberal Society (Cincinnati), the Freethinkers' Association of Manchester, N. H., and
Liberal Associations at Springfield and Lowell,
Mass. Ingersoll and Remsburg were publishing
lecture engagements, and Steiner was in the field

looking for dates. Mrs. Mattie P. Krekel also offered her services to Liberal societies.

Atrocity stories that began coming from Cuba early in the year were unsuspiciously printed. They prepared the public mind for the war with Spain and the occupation of Cuba.

The season for the annual congress of the American Secular Union and Freethought Federation having arrived, and there being only the memory of Putnam instead of his living voice for an inspiration, and none to take the lead in making the arrangements, the editor of The Truth Seeker assumed the responsibility and hired Hardman Hall, New York, for the meetings (Nov. 19-21). Judge C. B. White of Chicago, acting president, issued the call. Liberals came from far away, and those of New York got together. The women trimmed the stage with bunting, flowers and banners, the American colors predominating, while the Freethinkers of a dozen European countries were represented by their flags. On an easel in the midst stood a large portrait of Putnam.

Prof. Daniel T. Ames, editor of The Penman's Journal, took the chair. I note among those present "Putnam Foote Macdonald and parents." That was our second son, and as he was born on the 17th of February of the then current year, it was his first attendance at a congress. We named him for Samuel P. Putnam and our good friend, Dr. E. B. Foote, Senior.

Moncure Daniel Conway, the biographer of Paine, spoke at this congress. So did W. A. Croffut of Washington, and numbers of the regulars, for the Manhattan Liberal Club met with us. Mr. James F. Morton, who talked about Massachusetts Sunday laws, may be singled out as the survivor of those who addressed the assemblage. It was at this congress that John Hutchinson, last of the famous Hutchinson family of singers, appeared. He gave a brief address, and then, accompanying himself on the piano, sang "One Hundred Years Hence." There I met for the first and only time Charles Chilton Moore, editor of The Blue Grass Blade, Lexington, Kentucky. The officers elected for the ensuing year were: President, John E. Remsburg; vice-presidents, W. A. Croffutt, T. B. Wakeman, Franklin Steiner, and Susan H. Wixon; secretary, E. C. Reichwald; treasurer, Otto Wettstein. The report is given in The Truth Seeker for November 27, 1897.

Charles Anderson Dana, editor of The Sun, died October 18. Mr. Dana, born in Hinsdale, New Hampshire, August 8, 1819, was 78 years old. Besides reaching the top of the editorial profession, he made himself acquainted with most phases of social, industrial, and religious reforms, and had been as many kinds of a "crank" as any other man. While something of a cynic, after his various disillusionments, he still appeared to have retained a certain sympathy for reformers of the unpopular kind. The Truth Seeker, on the occasion of his death, acknowledged that, in its more or less rocky career, it assuredly had been indebted to Mr. Dana for "brave words spoken at the right time." He kept his columns open to the expression of radical thought and to defense of the liberty of the press. I do not remember who passed to me the following observation on Mr. Dana; it might have been Stephen Pearl Andrews, who also was from Hinsdale, and knew Mr. Dana long and well (as an antagonist). I quote: "They say that many years ago (it must have been before the Civil War), when the Hon. Elizur Wright, several times president of the National Liberal League, was running an orthodox paper called The Chronotype, in Boston, he employed Dana as his assistant editor, and that during Mr. Wright's temporary absence Dana wrote an editorial treating of hell as a myth, thus provoking Mr. Wright to wrath and securing Mr. Dana his walking-papers."

Henry George was but 58 when he sustained an attack of apoplexy, as the papers reported, and passed away at the Union Square Hotel, New York, on the morning of October 29. He had delivered an address on the previous evening. The Truth Seeker quoted several eulogies of George, including that of Dr. McGlynn, who said the world would love and revere his name when the names of Presidents were only historic allusions. As I like best my own eulogy of Mr. George, I will quote from it:

"When hereafter I shall recall Henry George to mind, I prefer to remember him by his last speech, made the night before his death, when he said:

"'I am opposed to all things which conflict with the liberty of this people. I believe in freedom of thought and speech and trade. I believe in the freedom of men and the affairs of men as far as one man does not overstep the rights of another.'

"On that rock [I wrote] mankind, emancipated from

religious and political superstition, will some day stand with Henry George; and it will furnish the material for his enduring monument."

Three lines announcing the death of James G. Clark, poet and singer, were utilized as a "filler" at the foot of a column in the paper for October 16. Mr. Clark died in Pasadena, California, the 18th of September. I presume that nowhere will be found so much of an obituary as I made up for him later, and published October 30. I had known of him all my life, and then about 1892 I saw him in Washington state where rolls the Snohomish. He must have been past 80.

W. J. Freeman, of Stockton, California, pioneer and one of the old Guard of the Pacific Coast, died June 21.

The light that was Henry Morehouse Taber, Freethinker and author, went out on December 24. Mr. Taber died at his home in New York at the age of 72. His book, "Faith or Fact," had appeared earlier in the year. It comprised articles he had contributed to the Liberal periodicals.

My oldest boy, Eugene, born in San Francisco in 1890, was now of school age. I recorded his progress from time to time. This is the December report:

"As I have mentioned before, a small scion of my family is attending the public school. He has received some instruction at home, and I am not going to say he has forgotten any of it; nevertheless, when I endeavor to ascertain what he has added to the original stock, my research is unrewarded, as I view results. His 'vaccinate' (compulsory) he took with him as a condition of admittance to the mysteries of learning. In a few days he had a morning hymn at the end of his tongue, which he sings at home because his parents have disapproved of his singing it in school. I may here say that his experience as a pupil of the city has had a surprising effect upon his conduct. Obliged as he is to be in order five hours per diem, he refuses to restrain himself at other times. Having brought home each day a Good Boy ticket, with a big blue blanket-ticket every Friday night to cover the whole week, he deposits these certificates of behavior and abandons himself to making things hum. Reproof is met with the argument that a boy must be bad some of the time. To his repertory of hymns he has subjoined "America" and a fugitive piece setting forth that all things that are wonderful, likewise things which are great, or even small, the Lord has made them. Add to these the Lord's prayer, in his version of which 'deliver us from evil' comes out as 'vivvers ferneevers,' while another familiar part is rendered 'furvivers our lets as we forget our letters.' I have not corrected him—his rendering is authentic as any.

"So much he has acquired of a literary nature. His latest catch is the measles, contracted at school, to which he may not return until January, 1898. Here, then, is the record for nine weeks: One bad case of vaccination; three hymns; a corrupted version of the Lord's Prayer, and a case of the measles. He blandly informs his mother that he is learning to swear."

If the parents could have looked forward to what was to happen to the boys twenty years later they might have been worried. Eugene passed his examinations with A marks through grammar and high schools, got his ribbon and his letter in athletics, edited a department of the Bulletin, was a "math shark" and president of the "math" section, was class historian, was recommended by his teachers to the high school Alumni, who staked him for entrance to the Massachusetts Institute of Technology, where he won a scholarship and a degree, and remained a year after graduation as assistant instructor; enlisted three years later as private in the Eleventh Engineers, A. E. F., saw fighting in France, participated in several major operations, was promoted to be captain, was sent into occupied territory to superintend public service in a German town, acquired a speaking acquaintance with two languages, and on his return home unscathed, fell upon the field of matrimony, August, 1919. Since then several conspicuous bridges 'have been constructed in part according to marks that he has made on paper. His vision of the future, I believe, is a competency won by hard work, and then teaching in the later years. The boy Putnam, who took his parents to the Liberal Congress held the year of his birth, enlisted in the navy before he was of age, served on ships in the Suicide Lane between Cardiff and Brest, where few vessels won through because of the Kaiser's submarines, was prostrated with the "flu" at the latter port, and came home a skeleton, after long hospitalization, deaf in one ear from gunfire, with a case of established tuberculosis, now happily arrested. Electricity is his line. Married? An idle question.

If the boys sprouted no wings, they sowed no wild oats. For all the sins wherewith the face of their sire is illuminated when he remembers and laments them, they never took to liquor or tobacco, wine or beer, or even tea and coffee till they went overseas where water is worse. Their estate is that of the natural man, negative to piety, and their moral code is as religionless as the pagan puritanism of Mark Twain. I never asked why ministers, whose business is the selling of religion, should insist on the necessity of it in the education of the young. The public men and educators who write uncompensated testimonials to its efficacy are more of a puzzle. If it pays them, how do they collect?

CHAPTER IX.

TWO major church-government scandals came into the record for 1898—the Methodist Steal South and the alienation of government land to the churches.

The Methodist Book Concern of Nashville, Tennessee, presented a claim of $288,000 for damage to its property through occupation by Union troops during the Civil War. The concern was Southern in sympathy. No one denied its disloyalty to the Union. Despite this, Congress allowed its fictitious claim for damages and voted to pay the Methodist Church South the whole of the sum demanded. The steal met with opposition in the Senate, which had once referred it to the Court of Claims, and the Court of Claims turned it down. The Truth Seeker called on Liberals to make their protest to the Senate, saying:

"The grounds on which the robbery is to be opposed are that the Methodist Church South was a disloyal body; that its claim to indemnity is no stronger than that of any private citizen of the South in sympathy with the Confederacy; and that payment will open the way for similar demands now on file, which, according to a statement made in the House, aggregate more than nineteen millions of dollars."

The Senate passed the bill, McKinley signed it, and then came a rehearing. The public learned now that the revival of the measure was the work of an attorney, a Tennessee claim agent named E. B. Stahlman, who had undertaken to see it through for a commission of $100,800. Stahlman had received his commission as soon as the claim was paid by the government.

Methodism became a synonym for falsification. The lies told worked injury to the survivors of the wrecked battleship Maine. Congress was debating an indemnity for these men, when Mr. Boutelle proposed that each of them should present his claim. This followed:

"The debate on Mr. Boutelle's bill gave an opening for Mr. Steele of Indiana to deliver an awful jab at the Methodist church, though it was a shameful reflection on Uncle Sam's tars. Mr. Cannon of Illinois had prudently suggested that to allow the survivors of the Maine to state the amount of their loss *might tempt the men to overvalue their outfits,* whereupon Mr. Sims of Tennessee desired to know if the crew were to be charged with dishonesty in advance; and it was then that Mr. Steele ventured to remark: *'They are no purer than the Methodist Book Concern.'* "

The College of Bishops of the Methodist Episcopal Church South issued a statement saying that "as the bill was passed, in the latest judgment of Congress, on misleading statements and recommendations, the Methodist Book Concern would refund the whole amount appropriated by Congress." That only added another lie. Half of the amount had passed into the hands of Stahlman and the crooks associated with him, including, it was believed, one or two of the senators. Instead of returning the money, or recommending that it be returned, a committee of ministers "vindicated" the good name of the Book Concern's agents.

The Truth Seeker was virtually alone in pointing out the progress of this piece of rascality step by step. I got the facts from The Congressional Record, received daily through the courtesy of Represenatative William Sulzer, of New York, who, I observed, voted for the steal.

The church-government steal I have referred to as the second one in the record of 1898 was the giving of property of the United States to the Catholic and other denominations for chapels. Attorney-General McKenna having declared unconstitutional the attempted alienation, by Secretaries of War Lamont and Alger, of a building site for a Catholic chapel at West Point, a Catholic member of Congress introduced a special bill for that purpose, and it was carried. Of course the law was equally as unconstitutional as the gift without warrant of law, but it went through and became effective. When other sects complained of favoritism shown the Church of Rome, Secretary Alger, on the strength of the new legislation, threw open the reservation at West Point to all denominations and invited them to erect their chapels there in the name of "freedom of worship." The government also began the expenditure of large sums for the erection of chapels and churches at the homes for old soldiers, placing them under ecclesiastical control.

These proceedings involved the same violation of the Constitution and the United States statute that the drys might complain of were the government to grant some corporation the privilege of erecting and maintaining a liquor saloon on one or many of the reservations.

The first amendment to the Constitution denies to Congress or government the power to establish any religion. A United States statute designed to give force to this amendment even as the Volstead act puts teeth into the eighteenth, was enacted, I believe, in 1897. It runs:

"And it is hereby declared to be the policy of the Government of the United States to make no appropriation of money or property for the purpose of founding, maintaining, or aiding by payment for services, expenses, or otherwise, any church or religious denomination, or any institution or society which is under sectarian or ecclesiastical control; and it is hereby enacted that after the 30th day of June, 1898, no money appropriated for charitable purposes in the District of Columbia shall be paid to any church or religious denomination, or to any institution or society which is under sectarian or ecclesiastical control."

The statute has been as ineffective in stopping ecclesiastical raiders as the amendment it enforces had been without it. The law and the amendment have been flouted by Congress and the courts, and the ecclesiastical bootlegging continues.

At 2 o'clock in the morning, May 25, 1898, a drunken man in New York fell against an iron fence and cut his face so that from the station house, where the police brought him, he was taken to Roosevelt Hospital. The doctor wrote him down: "Lacerated wound in cheek; acute alcohol-

ism." He had been booked as Adolph Karol, and
allowed to go to sleep when the laceration had been
attended to. On waking he asked that reporters
be excluded while he told his right name; but he
was too late. The reporters had been there and
recognized him as Sir Joseph Philippe Adolphe
Rene Caron, M.P., P.C., Q.C., Knight Commander
of Michael and St. George, Lord of the Ionian
Isles, ex-Minister of Militia and Defense, ex-
Minister of Railways, and *ex-Postmaster-General,*
Ottawa, P. Q. That is to say, this "casual," picked
up from the street in New York and booked as a
common drunk, was the Sir Adolphe Caron,
Canadian Postmaster-General, who had excluded
The Truth Seeker from the mails of his country.
The account appeared in The Truth Seeker under
the head of "A Knight's Night Out." He had
come to New York to celebrate the queen's birthday. I wondered whether, if we could have caught
him at the right moment, we might not have got the
excluding order rescinded by appealing from
Philippe sober to Philippe drunk.

During the year I edited, with Introduction and
Notes, a Presentation Edition of Paine's "Age of
Reason," Part I being based on a unique Paris edition of 1794, a copy of which had come into my
hands in a pleasant way. This copy, outwardly
stained and defaced, had been the property of a
certain James J. Jordan, who kept a saloon at Seventh street and Hall place, adjacent to the meat
store where I purchased my family supplies. Mr.
Jordan bought it at a book stand, and having pe-

rused it, recommended it to me as something worth my notice. When I saw the imprint, "Paris, printed for Barrois, senior," . . . "second year of the French Republic, one and indivisible," I agreed with him that it was worth noticing, and at a later time, in lieu of accepting a Bottle with the compliments of the season, I inquired whether he would not consider giving me his "Age of Reason" for Christmas. He appeared relieved, and hastily withdrawing the proffered gift handed me the book.

I was persuaded that this was the correct edition of the "Age of Reason"; the proof, perhaps, had been read by Paine himself; and thereupon various other editions were diligently compared and revised by me, including Moncure D. Conway's, published by the Putnams. At his request I showed him the errors and departures that had taken place between 1794 and the year his was published. Few were serious, but the least of them troubled him. He magnanimously complimented the Presentation Edition as the best that had ever been printed.

From Paris, Dec. 27, 1898, he wrote: "DEAR SIR: I have received the new edition of the 'Age of Reason' which I ordered, and consider it not only the most artistic book by Paine ever manufactured, externally, but intrinsically an invaluable contribution to Paine literature." The letter gave me a sense of considerable importance and great pleasure; and if I have made too much of it, I can only inquire again what there is better than that a man should rejoice in his own works.

The authorities on purity pronounced unmailable "The Old and the New Ideal," a book by Emil F. Ruedebusch, of Maysville, Wisconsin, and held the author under a two-thousand-dollar bond. Later Mr. Ruedebusch paid a fine of $1,200 and served a day in jail. It was a harmless book, decently and correctly written. I wrote of it then: "I would rather see my boy reading it than smoking cigarets or drinking beer. I should say the same if the hopeful were a girl, adding that it were better for both to be convinced by it than to join the Christian Endeavorers. If this son of mine would agree to forgo Fourth of July firecrackers on condition that he might peruse the pages of 'The Old and the New Ideal,' I should close the bargain with him at once."

I am not a believer in "private" reading for man, woman, or child. The Bible has always been accessible to my boys; so has every other book in my library. They have had my consent to read anything they chose provided that, avoiding secrecy, they would bring it to the common reading table and under the family lamp.

In London, England, there flourished at this date a Legitimation League which had bestowed the honor of its presidency on Lillian Harman of America. In the spring of 1898 Capt. Robert C. Adams, American by residence, in an address before the League told how many victims the delusion known as comstockery found in this country, and his British listeners were horrified, as they well might be. Sarcastic comments were offered about our boasted liberty, and allusion made to the sinister significance of the stripes upon our flag as duplicated by the stripes on citizens in the penitentiary for exercising the freedom of the press. The Legitimists asked Captain Adams to tell his countrymen, on his return, how much more liberty was enjoyed by a British subject than by an American sovereign; and in other language they rubbed it into Captain Adams pretty hard. But they did not fool Lillian Harman, who soon thereafter wrote from London: "There is more liberty in the United States than here, though that is saying very little." And Lillian was right, for just after the Legitimists had reviled us American sovereigns through Captain Adams, their own secretary, George Bedborough, was arrested for selling a book by Havelock Ellis that American comstockery has never molested! There are people in England still, including George Bernard Shaw, who imagine that the thing called comstockery originated in this country and has not operated over there. The contrary is the fact. It began there with the suppression of Paine's "Age of Reason," never prosecuted here. We got our Puritans from England, but some stayed home and are still active. I think their record worse in England than in America.

In Utah, Warren Foster, Freethinker and Populist, ran unsuccessfully for congressman at large against Brigham H. Roberts, Mormon and polygamist. The election of Roberts brought the religious question into Congress, along with the bogey of polygamy. My reflections made at the time require little revision:

"As always, it will be inquired whether, on the whole, polygamy is a more serious offense against moral sanity than the celibacy, miscalled chastity, practiced by the Catholic clergy; and attention will be called to the domestic wrecks strewing the trail of the Protestant clergy from one end of the country to the other. Some will say, as they have said before, that they would as soon see their daughter in the home of a polygamist as in a nunnery or a house of assignation. There are more mistresses in New York than plural wives in Utah, more mistresses here than there would be plural wives if polygamy were one of our state institutions; and they are supported by Christians."

(In The Truth Seeker, probably of 1897, I came upon a statement by a pious lady reformer who was starting a new society to improve morals, to the effect that fifty per cent of the churchmen in New York, who were wealthy enough to afford to do so, were keeping secondary wives and paying their rent.)

Congressman-elect Roberts from Utah had not prepared himself in advance to meet the opposition to his taking his seat among the good and virtuous members of Congress, and was therefore chucked out. The Mormons came back later with Reed Smoot, who was fortified by preliminary researches among senators to ask why a Mormon should be excluded for having more than one woman. He was never called upon to expand his argument.

An author so disposed might write an entertaining and informative book on the phenomena taking place this year of 1898 in the Spanish-American War. Secretary of War Alger continued to manifest the concern characteristic of him that the churches and ministers should get theirs. As an administrator he was simply rotten, and his mis-management of detention camps cost twice as many lives as the fighting.

The Catholic priests of all foreign nations were inimical to the United States. This included the pope, who was obliged to stand idly by while one of the last of the officially Catholic countries of the first class got licked. Our Archbishop Corrigan at the time was expecting soon to wear the red hat of a cardinal, but never got it. The priests of Mexico inflamed their followers against the United States. When Spain sent troops to Cuba, the pope "like a new Moses," as the Archbishop of Damascus phrased it, "had raised his hand toward heaven and was praying that the angel of victory might accompany the Spanish army."

Our warship the Maine, lying at anchor in Havana Harbor, had been blown up on the night of February 15, and on March 8 Congress appropriated fifty millions for national defense.*

---

*Feeling against Spain for her treatment of Cuba had run high for many years, particularly during the Ten Years War, 1868-78. Midway in this, viz., in '73 the Virginius massacre which cost the lives of American citizens, intensified the anger. The Cuban War for Independence, 1895-98, added fresh fuel. The treatment of the Cubans in the concentration camps, with pictures of the starved "reconcentrados" made Spain's name anathema. The Maine was lying in Havana Harbor on a "friendly call." That was the official explanation. Really, trouble was brewing and she was there to keep order. Cuba and Spain were at war, but Spain and the United States were officially at peace, though the United States had made suggestion.—B. R.

President McKinley suggested to Spain that she get out of Cuba, but received no answer, and the United States declared war. Dewey took Manila, capital of the Philippines, Sunday, May 1, and fighting lasted all summer. Many Truth Seeker readers bore a part, most conspicuously G. H. Purdy of Dewey's flagship Olympia—an old man-o'-war-man, a survivor of the days of wooden ships and iron men. The newspapers reported that as Dewey's ships entered the harbor and the guns were pointed, a stentorian voice shouted: "Remember the Maine!" That was Purdy's. "Remember the Maine" was the slogan of the war. The attack on Manila had been set for May 3, but Purdy, who was captain of the hold, an old-timer and a privileged character, said to Dewey: "Commodore, don't let's wait till the 3d of May; the last fight I was in on that date the side I was on got licked." He alluded to the battle at Chancellorsville, Va., in 1863, when the Confederates won but lost their leader, Stonewall Jackson. At the Manila fight Purdy dropped also another remark that was to be historic. Dewey's ships had made their first evolution in the attack on the Spaniards and were retiring to overhaul their ammunition, which had been reported short. The Spanish commander took occasion to cable Madrid that the fire of his forts had been so fierce and fatal that the Yankee pigs were hauling off to bury their dead. (Dewey lost but one man, and he a noncombatant.) Gossip got forward that the fighting would be suspended that the men might eat their breakfast, the war right along having been conducted somewhat like a social function, with reporters present to take down notable remarks and to reduce deeds of heroism on the part of the officers to imperishable print. The New York Herald had a representative aboard the Olympia. He shared the delusion as to the cause of suspended hostilities, and had made a note highly complimenting Dewey on his thoughtfulness for the inner men behind the guns. As the newspaperman edged along (probably to windward) toward the forward deck to get a snapshot of the Commodore on the bridge, he encountered Purdy and craved his opinion of the maneuver. Said Mr. Purdy: "To hell with breakfast! Let's finish the fight." The reporter sent the answer to his paper, where it furnished forth a good headline.

Purdy was widely read of books, and so good at talking that navy men called him "The Chaplain," the sobriquet "Holy Joe" being reserved for the individual appointed chaplain by the President. His reputation as a doubter inspired a yarn which appeared in the Evening Post of Charleston, S. C., October 6, 1899. The story ran that while his ship was passing through the Red Sea "Chaplain" Purdy was observed to be very busy with his spyglass, although nothing was in sight. His solemn study of the scene attracted the attention of his shipmates, one of whom went up to him and asked: "What are you looking at?" And Purdy replied: "Why, I am trying to find the place where Moses and the children of Israel forded this pond, and I be damned if can see a thing of it." The account of the South

Carolina paper added that there was "much laughter," which reached the ears of Admiral Dewey, and he sent an orderly to ascertain the cause of the tumult. On being told, the admiral, "going to his cabin, immediately sent for Purdy, and, after chatting pleasantly with him, gave him a good drink."

When Mr. Purdy came to The Truth Seeker office to renew the acquaintance begun in San Francisco in the '80s, he told me of the incidents of the Manila fight; but as to the story in the Charleston Post, he said that editors who rushed that sort of thing into print for solid fact were a queer lot, as he was not a drinking man. (Wooden Ships and Iron Men*.)

Purdy liked the Commodore, which was Dewey's rank before the war, but not the praying Captain Philip of the Oregon, whom he called a murderer for his harsh treatment of his men. He had collided with Philip himself. As a student of religious phenomena he had procured from The Truth Seeker office a copy of the Book of Mormon, which he found exceedingly dull reading. One day as he conned its pages, his literary sense was so offended by the repetitious "And it came to pass" with which

---

* The picture, according to the superscription placed up-it by Mr. Purdy, was "photo'd aboard U. S. S. Mohican in July, 1888, by Dr. Whitecar; appeared in Frank Leslie's Christmas Number of '88. Mohican on passage from Honolulu to San Francisco." Mr. Purdy brought the original to The Truth Seeker office at the close of the Spanish-American war, autographed it, and wrote in the names of his mates on the Mohican. Army and navy papers have printed it as a relic of the days of wooden ships and iron men.

Dave Ireland   G. H. Purdy

Old Griff   John Thing

so many of the verses began, that he expressed aloud his opinion of such writings. A Roman Catholic overhearing him ran to Philip and had him called up for making fun of his religion, and Philip threatened Purdy with the brig and stopped his liberty. This Captain Philip was a truly religious man, who fell upon his knees whenever a gun went off. As soon as the fighting was over at the Santiago engagement he called his men to prayers, and when ashore preached to church congregations from the pulpit.

President McKinley, who ought to have been an ecclesiastic instead of a politician, went to excess in playing the religious game; and his intercessions with the invisibles were so diasastrous that in December The Truth Seeker besought him to issue no more proclamations. "If," said the editor, "there is any connection between President McKinley's thanksgiving proclamations and the events which follow them, our chief executive will do his countrymen a good turn by not issuing any more. Readers will remember his call to prayers dated shortly after the American victories at Santiago; and also that from that time onward all possible disasters overtook our troops. They were not defeated by the enemy, to be sure, for the enemy had been annihilated; but disease then began its deadly work. Up to that time, unassisted by official prayers, our casualties had not exceeded five hundred, though all the battles had been fought and the fortunes of war decided. Since then the deaths have reached two thousand. Such was the effect of a proclamation regarding the war. And a Thanksgiving proclamation issued in accordance with 'immemorial custom,' or on general principles, had a no less deplorable result. Thanksgiving day in New York was signalized by a blizzard, resulting in unspeakable suffering, to say nothing of incomputable pecuniary loss, to thousands. The whole Atlantic coast was torn up. Within three days, a steamer between Boston and Portland, having one hundred and sixty souls on board, went down in a storm and every person perished. For a week we heard nothing but tales of disaster on sea and land. More than two hundred vessels, large and small, were lost; and all this immediately following the observance of a day officially set apart to thank God for his tender mercies, and especially for his mild seasons!"

In addition to McKinley's extra thanksgiving day, a great " peace jubilee" was called in Chicago to express the general gratitude to God that the war which he permitted to begin he had now permitted to end. The crowds that gathered for the jubilee were as thoroughly soaked by a sudden and tempestuous rain as was the great priestly procession at the Eucharistic Congress in 1926. Regarding McKinley's prayer day, Colonel Ingersoll, speaking a little later in New York, uttered words that shocked the then religious Dr. A. Wakefield Slaten. Said the Colonel: "Suppose somebody had done something for which you were grateful, and you went to thank him. What would you think of such a person if he turned the hose on you?"

Liberal lecturers announcing themselves in the field and open to engagements in 1898 were James

F. Morton, Jr., of Boston, who had recently been graduated from Harvard with the highest literary honors; Mrs. M. Florence Johnson, Franklin Steiner, and of course Colonel Ingersoll.

Two additional organizations held meetings—the Dallas, Texas, Freethinkers' Association, O. Paget, president, and the People's Church of Spring Valley, Minn., Dr. P. M. Harmon, minister.

Mrs. Elizabeth Cady Stanton published her reminiscences (1815-1897) "Eighty Years and More."

March 18 Mahatma Virchand Raghavji Gandhi, B.A., M.R.A.S., J.S., of Bombay, India, addressed the Manhattan Liberal Club on the subject of philosophy and religion. Twenty years later Dr. Gandhi made trouble for the British rulers in India.

The Truth Seeker issued its Quarter-Centenary number the first week in September, 1898. Colonel Ingersoll contributed the principal article. We published the names of eight subscribers who had begun with the first number.

The American Secular Union and Freethought Federation held its well-attended twenty-first annual congress in Washington Hall, Chicago, November 18-20. Remsburg as president had delivered a hundred lectures, held many debates, distributed quantities of literature, organized several societies, and increased the circulation of the liberal papers. He was reelected president; E. C. Reichwald, secretary, Otto Wettstein, treasurer.

L. K. Washburn, after a period in the lecture field, resumed in January his editorial connection with the Boston Investigator, "which like all other

Freethought papers—as well as about all of any kind—is feeling the bad effects of the hard times" (Ed. T. S.). Notwithstanding the ability of Mr. Washburn as editor and R. W. Chainey as business manager, the hoped-for restoration of prosperity to The Investigator came not.

Ephraim E. Hitchcock, the virtual owner of The Truth Seeker since 1883 and president of the Company, died at his home in New York, Jan. 13. His name had not appeared in the paper. His frequent contributions to Liberal work were anonymous. He had paid Mrs. Bennett $10,000 for the business, and dying bequeathed his interest to E. M. Macdonald. He was born in Westfield, Vt., Sept. 2, 1822. For many years he was head of Hitchcock, Dermody & Co., manufacturers of hatters' fur, New York.

The founder of the first Freethought society in Philadelphia, and a charter member of the National Liberal League, 1876, died during January in San Francisco 79 years old. His name, Thomas Curtis, has appeared in these records.

Poet, engraver and author, William James Linton, born in London, 1812, died at the close of 1897 in New Haven, Conn. He was said to be the last of the great wood engravers. Mr. Linton as "Editor of The National," wrote a Life of Thomas Paine.

On March 18 Matilda Joslyn Gage, author of "Woman, Church and State," died in Chicago, aged 72. She belonged to the group of Freethought woman suffragists which included Elizabeth Cady Staton, Susan B. Anthony, Lucretia Mott, Ernestine L. Rose, and Lucy N. Colman.

Edward F. Underhill, who had been for thirty years official stenographer in the Surrogate's Court, New York, and still longer an associate of the Liberals of New York, died in June, at 68.

When Parker Pillsbury closed his days at Concord, N. H., July 7, his contemporary, Lucy Colman, wrote to The Truth Seeker: "Mr. Pillsbury, I think, was one of the very last of the old-time reformers. There might be surviving one or two who sometimes spoke for freedom, but Mr. Pillsbury gave his whole time to it." Ralph Waldo Emerson declared him to be the strongest man intellectually of the early Abolitionists, abler than Garrison, Phillips, or Foster. Popularly he was known as the Abolitionists' sledgehammer. James Russell Lowell wrote:

> "Beyond, a crater in each eye,
>   Sways brown, broad-shouldered Pillsbury,
>   Who tears up words, like trees, by roots—
>   A Theseus in stout cowhide boots."

Mr. Pillsbury was 89 years old. I had heard him at the New York Liberal Club in other days and handled his communications to The Truth Seeker.

The death of Mrs. Mary Wicks Bennett, widow of the founder of The Truth Seeker, took place at the home of the editor in Glen Ridge, N. J., July 31, in her 76th year. It was she who gave The Truth Seeker its name.

Reporting a funeral for The Truth Seeker of August 6, 1898, Cyrus Coolridge wrote: " 'The Old Guard,' who with courage and hope planned and fought the battles of Liberalism a quarter century ago, are a thin and straggling few now, as they press on to their final rest under the weight of years, sor-

rows and cares; but none will be more kindly remembered than the one who for years made Science
Hall the home of the Liberal Club and The Truth
Seeker." That was Hugh Byron Brown, whose
dust was on that day, July 14, 1898, laid to rest in
a cemetery near his home at Bay Shore, Long Island.

Mr. Brown came early into these memoirs as the
partner of G. L. Henderson in the establishment of
Science Hall at 141 Eighth street in 1875-6, and as
one of the first contributors to the defense fund of
D. M. Bennett. Mr. Coolridge in an aside said that
"Henderson sits on the shores of the Pacific at Chula
Vista, in the extreme southern part of California,
watching his lemon grove and feeling the rising
pulse of the great world, while his own pulse is
gradually growing less and less."

The San Francisco part of my story tells that I
accepted the privilege of reviewing Judge James G.
Maguire's pamphlet, "Ireland and the Pope," from
the press of James H. Barry, editor of The Star. In
1898 the friends of the author and the publisher
placed them in nomination for office, Maguire for
governor of California and Barry for member of
the fifty-fifth Congress. "Ireland and the Pope"
proved the undoing of both candidates. The Rev.
Peter C. Yorke, Roman Catholic chancellor of the
archdiocese of San Francisco and editor of the San
Francisco Monitor, the recognized newspaper organ
of the Roman Catholic church in California, took
the stump against Judge Maguire, and with "malice,
envy, spite and lies," proceeded to desecrate his
name. The judge estimated that the Catholic op-

position cost him 10,000 votes, and Barry was his fellow sufferer. Both men were of Catholic antecedents. Barry had indulged in a great deal of praise of his "spiritual" mother, her convents and sisterhoods, and of the Rev. Father Yorke, at the same time attacking the "A.P.A." in a manner violent and virulent. And Maguire in Congress had voted for a bill to give the Catholic church ground for a chapel at West Point. But there was "Ireland and the Pope" against them, and Yorke was out, like those organized boycotters, the Catholic Truth Society, to show everybody that it does not pay "to insult the Catholic church." Times have changed a little. The priest in politics has given way to the Protestant parson.

CHAPTER X.

THE TRUTH SEEKER of January 28, being a Paine number, contained much of interest to Paine students. This was the year the Painites discovered Roosevelt's characterization of Paine, by way of his Life of Gouverneur Morris, in the "American Statesman" series, as a "filthy little Atheist." Had all who said something snatched a hair from Roosevelt's scalp, he would have died baldheaded. Moncure D. Conway wrote as follows in the New York Times: "In his unique collection of blunders described as a 'Life of Gouverneur Morris,' Governor Roosevelt says: 'So the filthy little Atheist had to stay in prison, "where he amused himself by publishing a pamphlet against Jesus Christ." ' This sentence, long ago denounced by myself and others without eliciting any retraction, must now remain as a salient survival of the vulgar Paine mythology, and as the most ingenious combination of mistakes ever committed in so small a space in any work professing to be historical."

Through The Century Magazine Paul Leicester Ford, as detected by Dr. J. J. Shirley, then of Washington, D. C., gave his mite to the collected misinformation regarding Paine. When writing on "The

Many-Sided Franklin," Ford told The Century's readers that the "Age of Reason" had been written in 1786 and submitted to Franklin, who suggested changes in it and advised against its publication!

Had Roosevelt looked at the "Age of Reason" he would have known that Paine was a deist, and in that work wrote only respectfully of Jesus Christ. Had Ford ever seen the book, he would have known that Paine began it in France, "under the shadow of the guillotine," 1793, three years after Franklin's death. And Franklin's opinion of Christianity was substantially that of Paine. William Cobbett wrote in May, 1796: "A person to whom the parties were well known has assured me that poor Paine imbibed his first principles of Deism from Dr. Franklin."

The Truth Seeker for June 3, 1899, is another number valuable to Paine students. It contains a history of the Paine monument at New Rochelle down to the day it was surmounted by the "colossal bronze bust" executed by Wilson Macdonald. One of the "Finest," that is to say, Mr. Victor White, a New York police officer, called at The Truth Seeker office in November "to display a portrait of Thomas Paine which he had picked up in his rounds and caused to be nicely framed." Of a *facsimile* of the portrait in the Presentation Edition of the "Age of Reason" George Jacob Holyoake said: "That . . . is the only engraving Paine is known to have seen and approved. I have the one he gave to Clio Rickman. It bears an inscription in Paine's handwriting: 'Thomas Paine to his friend Clio Rickman.'" The member of the Finest, now retired, who discovered

this authentic print, is still a visitor to The Truth
Seeker office.

Ingersoll occupies much of the 1899 record. His
health, apparently, did not warrant him in making
numerous lecture engagements. Early in the year
he gave an interview for publication in which, reviewing a century's progress, he said: "The laurel
of the nineteenth century is on Darwin's brow."
It did not escape notice that the Rev. Archibald D.
Bradshaw, chaplain of the Seventy-first New York,
in eulogizing the regiment's dead, lifted without
credit and adapted without scruple the language of
Ingersoll at his brother's grave; also that President
Guggenheimer of the New York City council, in
welcoming the men of the cruiser Raleigh at a
smoker, assured them that the American people had
"tears for the dead and cheers for the living."
Neither of the plagiaries mentioned Ingersoll or
quoted him correctly. From the card index I have
kept for nearly a third of a century I might quote
scores of such instances, one of the offenders being
Theodore Roosevelt.

For the benefit of the Paine bust fund he spoke on
May 14 at the Academy of Music, to what "was
perhaps the largest gathering of Freethinkers that
ever assembled in New York city." On June 2 he
gave an address entitled "What Is Religion?" before
the thirty-second annual convention of the Free Religious Association in the Hollis Street Theater,
Boston. That was his last public address. At his
summer home, Dobbs Ferry on the Hudson River
highlands, at noon on Friday, July 21, death came

to him with hardly a moment's warning. The immediate cause was angina pectoris. Three men—Prof. John Clark Ridpath, the historian, Major Orlando J. Smith, and Dr. John L. Elliot of the Society for Ethical Culture—conducted the services, July 25. Mr. Ridpath read the poem, "Declaration of the Free," which Ingersoll had contributed to The Truth Seeker on June 3. The closing stanza was as follows:

> "Is there beyond the silent night
> An endless day?
> Is death a door that leads to light?
> We cannot say.
> The tongueless secret, locked in fate,
> We do not know. We hope and wait."

Major Smith read from Ingersoll's writings, "My Religion":

"To love justice, to long for the right, to love mercy, to pity the suffering, to assist the weak, to forget wrongs and remember benefits—to love the truth, to be sincere, to utter honest words, to love liberty, to wage relentless warfare against slavery in all its forms, to love wife and child and friend, to make a happy home, to love the beautiful in art, in nature, to cultivate the mind, to be familiar with the mighty thoughts that genius has expressed, the noble deeds of all the world; to cultivate courage and cheerfulness, to make others happy, to fill life with the splendor of generous acts, the warmth of loving words; to discard error, to destroy prejudice, to receive new truths with gladness, to cultivate hope, to see the calm beyond the storm, the dawn beyond the night; to do the best that can be done, and then be resigned—this is the religion of reason, the creed of science. This satisfies the brain and heart."

The service, which did not occupy more than twenty minutes, was concluded with the reading, by

Dr. Elliot, of the words spoken by Ingersoll at his brother's bier.

The body was cremated July 27, at Fresh Pond, Long Island, and the ashes gathered into an urn of bronze and porphyry with the inscription: "L'Urne Guarde la Poussiere; le Coeur le Souvenir" —the urn guards the ashes; the heart, the memory.

To imitate one of Ingersoll's own figures, if all the tributes to his worth had been blossoms, he would have had a monument of flowers. The secular press was fair; the pulpit could not afford to be. As to the malignant ministers, The Sun made them the best answer. Said the editor of that New York paper, probably Mr. Edward P. Mitchell:

"We observe that some clergymen have been assuming to exercise a divine function by passing sentence of eternal condemnation on the dead orator. That is an awful assumption of omnipotent authority by a human being. No man conscious of his own powerlessness before the Almighty would dare thus to arrogate to himself the judgment that belongs to God alone. Let men rather dwell on the virtues of Robert Ingersoll—his superb courage, his beautiful family life, his justice, his loving kindness. Death silenced in him a voice whose eloquence was sweet as music and a heart filled with humanity—with that sentiment which the founder of Christianity himself has extolled as the chief of virtues; which the believer, seeing in him, the Infidel, may be the more impelled to imitate as he proceeds to work out his own salvation with fear and trembling."

There was, however, in places, a "tolerant pulpit," which The Truth Seeker was able to quote to the extent of a dozen or more charitable opinions.

Ingersoll's detractors disagreed. Prof. Harry Peck endeavored to prove him heartless by saying:

"Ingersoll knew that the vast majority of enlightened men and women cherished the very faith that he attacked." Dr. Lyman Abbott would have belittled him by averring: "The principles that Ingersoll inveighed against have long since ceased to be held by any except the most rude and crude intellects."

Where groups of Freethinkers existed, here or abroad, memorial meetings were held and resolutions of sorrow and respect were adopted.

Far back in this record I quoted the story of the astronomer, the Infidel, and the globe. It was a plain Sunday school lesson. In the fall of 1899 the narrative flowed from the lips of the Rev. Dr. Parkhurst in the following version:

"The late Robert Ingersoll, while in Mr. Beecher's study at one time, saw a large globe standing on his table—a globe that showed in elegant outlines the contour of the earth's continents and seas.

"'That is a fine globe you have there, Mr. Beecher. Who made it?' was Mr. Ingersoll's inquiry.

"'Oh, nobody,' answered Mr. Beecher."

Ingersoll's daughter Maud wrote to the Rev. Mr. Parkhurst: "Will you have the goodness to inform me of your authority for the inclosed?" referring to the anecdote, which she had clipped from The Journal. "My father never visited Mr. Beecher, and no such conversation ever took place." Dr. Parkhurst made the feeble plea that when the matter was brought to him he judged it to be amply authenticated. Of course! And no doubt the story is older than Parkhurst, and was quoted for the first Atheist.

ROBERT G. INGERSOLL (1833-1899).

The Catholic figure in the politics of 1899 was Archbishop Ireland of St. Paul. In a cartoon by Heston, January 14, Ireland on the seat of the government wagon pushes Uncle Sam to one side, and, with McKinley as a small boy seated beside him, takes the reins. The wagon is loaded with the pope's baggage. The President named Ireland as delegate to the czar's peace congress at The Hague, on which one of the approving papers said: "Ever since his induction into office the President has been anxious to testify his appreciation of Archbishop Ireland's Republicanism, which took the form of strong interviews and speeches made during the campaign of 1896." February 4 The Truth Seeker inquired: "Is there anything else within the gift of this administration that Archbishop Ireland would accept? By the decision of the Interior Department the title to twenty thousand acres of land in Minnesota is to be taken from the settlers and given to him. This ecclesiastic has only to express a wish and the government, executive or judiciary, does the rest." A history of the West Point chapel steal occupies page 292 of the 1899 volume of The Truth Seeker. In October the Marquette Club of Chicago held a banquet at which Ireland and McKinley were the guests of honor. Ireland sat at McKinley's right hand, the juxtaposition being so arranged to impress upon the minds of Catholics the fact that the President was carrying out the policies of the church. By fall the heading "Ireland Sees McKinley" had appeared in the newspapers above thirty times, and immediately after each "seeing," the church received some favor from the government, or some Catholic ecclesiastic government preferment. The hook-up of church and government ran over into the administrations of Roosevelt and Taft.

In the '90s the legislature of the State of New York passed a bill absurdly entitled the "Freedom of Worship" act, providing that at their cwn expense the priests of the Roman Catholic church might enter and conduct religious services in certain public and penal institutions for the benefit of Catholic convicts. The bill provided that "nothing herein contained shall be construed to authorize any additional expenditure on the part of the state." The framers and advocates of the measure staked their word, which was about as trustworthy as that of Messrs. Barbee and Smith of the Methodist Steal South, that the people of the state should not be asked to pay for the religious services held in the reformatory or punitive institutions. Nevertheless in October, 1899, the state comptroller, W. J. Morgan, made public the fact that a Roman Catholic chaplain of the State Industrial School, holding that position under the provisions of the Freedom of Worship act, was collecting $1,200 a year for his services, and that sisters of charity, number not stated, were drawing $5 a month each for carfare when visiting the same institution. It is safe to assume that the graft has not diminished in the years that have since passed.

March 6, 1899, saw the departure from orthodoxy of the Rev. S. Parkes Cadman. He was the principal speaker at a meeting of Methodist ministers in New York, where he advanced the proposition that "the inerrancy and the infallibility of the Bible are no longer possible of belief among reasoning men." The newspapers which uniformly quoted him as saying "inherency," not inerrancy, said also that "he was applauded by the other ministers, who voted him an extension of time in order that he might fully develop his thought." The Old Testament stories designated as those which he held open to doubt or total disbelief numbered eighteen.

Charles Watts, the English Freethought lecturer, paid America a short visit in the early part of the year. He suffered a nervous breakdown, and returned to England in April.

Isadora Duncan, billed to appear at the Lyceum Theater, New York, March 14, sent tickets to The Truth Seeker office. The editor chose myself to cover the assignment. The ticket read: "Verses from the Rubaiyat done into dance by Isadora Duncan." Miss Duncan, my report said, might pose for Omar's "cypress slender" maid, being tall and lissome. Her dress, much like the exiguous apparel of the average girl of today, just a short frock or smock in which she danced modestly, evoked criticism in that decade when women wore a semi-train on the street. The newspaper reporter who said next day that the dance did more to illustrate the lines of Miss Duncan than the lines of the poet could not have had his mind on the poetry. When I heard of Miss Duncan's tragic death in 1927 and then read the story of her life, I was glad that she had sent us the tickets to her dance.

"But still a Ruby kindles in the Vine,"
Sang Khayyam, as with cup in hand he sat;

Poured down the sparkling jewel of the wine—
And that's where Omar got his Ruby at.
—G. E. M. in Puck, 1899.

I penned occasional verses and jokes, at this time, and tried them on other papers than The Truth Seeker. Puck nor Judge ever sent anything back. By seeing them reproduced in The Times I first learned that Puck had accepted the foregoing lines, which had quite a circulation in those Omar days.

A court in Lexington, Kentucky, convicted Charles C. Moore, editor of The Blue Grass Blade, of sending Freelove thoughts through the mails. There is nothing indecent in what he wrote. Walter Hurt, editor of The Gatling Gun, Cincinnati, went to jail on the charge of circulating obscene literature. In Montreal, Canada, Norman Murray was put under bonds not to repeat a similar offense. Secular Thought, J. Spencer Ellis, editor, was suppressed for printing a blasphemous Christmas poem, but later released on probation.

The American Secular Union accepted the invitation of the Boston Liberals to hold its '99 congress in Paine Hall, Friday, Nov. 17. The necessary time was given to the business of the Union, and the old board of officers reelected—Remsburg president, Reichwald secretary, Wettstein treasurer—and the rest was a memorial to Ingersoll. The Spiritualists sent a delegation.

Si Slokum, who had written for The Truth Seeker ten years earlier, was in '99 committed to the workhouse at his own request. Once a rival of Ned Buntline, Buffalo Bill, and Old Sleuth, he had outlived his vogue. Why, being a veteran of the Civil War, and having served in the Second Massachusetts Battery, he chose the workhouse to a soldiers' home, remains unexplained. The name under which they committed him to the workhouse was H. P. Cheever.

Dr. R. B. Westbrook, who had been three times elected president of the American Secular Union (1888, '89, '90), died at his summer home, Pacoag, R. I., August 21, 1899, aged 80 years. He was a man of much learning, had been a clergyman and a judge, and was of irreproachable character. Something of his life was told at the date of his election as president of the Secular Union.

The Hon. A. B. Bradford of Enon Valley, Pa., who wrote the article upon which Anthony Comstock based his first arrest of D. M. Bennett, died at an advanced age in 1899. He was a graduate at Princeton in 1830 and was for many years a frequent contributor to The Truth Seeker.

The aged reformer, Edward Truelove, died April 21, in London, aged 90 years. His eulogist, G. W. Foote, said: "He belonged to the past—the past of storm and peril, when the soldiers of Freedom rose almost every week to meet a fresh difficulty or a new danger. He lived right through the heroic age of English liberty. He had seen William Cobbett; he knew Richard Owen; he stood beside Watson, Southwell, Hetherington, and the rest, in their fight for a free press; he loved the unsubduable Richard Carlile; he had some intimacy with John Stuart Mill; he was a friend of George Jacob Hol-

yoake in his fighting days; Karl Marx held meetings
at his house; the Positivists were indebted to him
for hospitality, and he was a staunch supporter of
the great Charles Bradlaugh." He had been prosecuted for his publications. Mr. Truelove might
have written Seventy Years of Freethought.

Dr. Ludvig Büchner, famous author of "Force
and Matter" (born March 28, 1824), died on May
1 of this year.

In the '70s of the past century a man named John
H. Keyser mingled with the New York radicals and
reformers. I saw him many times and was informed
that he had been a member of the Tammany Hall
Tweed Ring; that is to say, he was a manufacturer
of stoves and furnaces and got the city contracts.
But Keyser was a philanthropist. What he took in
as "honest graft" he gave back to the needy of New
York. According to his obituary notice when he
died in East Norwalk, Conn., in 1899, at an advanced age, he must have devoted something like a
quarter of a million in free relief for the destitute.
He looked like a benevolent old chap when I saw
him. It was said that he had given all his money
away and was poor. Those acquainted with his
past overlooked his connection with Tammany Hall
in view of his philanthropies, a list of which the interested may find in The Truth Seeker of September 2, 1899. He was the only Tammany grafter of
the Tweed regime with whom I ever came in contact, and I observed him with much curiosity.

In September Mr. Thaddeus B. Wakeman having resolved to begin life anew as president of the

Liberal University of Oregon and editor of its paper, The Torch of Reason, was on the evening of
the 15th of that month banqueted at the Marlborough Hotel by the Liberal friends to whom he and
his family were saying good-by.

Pearl Geer of Silverton, Oregon, the seat of the
university where Mr. Wakeman proposed to teach,
came east to raise funds for the support of the institution. While he visited at East Orange, N. J.,
with his cousin, Homer Davenport, the cartoonist,
Thomas A. Edison of the same town sent word that
he would like to see him. Geer found Edison
seated before a long table with many jars of chemicals before him. When the wizard had shaken
hands with the young man, he remarked, with reference to his chemicals, "Well, I'm reading my Bible."
Geer replied: "The Bible of nature is a splendid
book if one understands how to read it."

"The best damn Bible in the world," said Edison
with enthusiasm. "Its laws are perfect, and grand,
and all the prayers in the world can't change them.
There is intelligence and law in this world, and there
may be supreme intelligence and law; but so far as
the religion of the day is concerned, it is all a
damned fake."

CHAPTER XI.

A T THE end of the nineteenth century Truth Seeker controvertists were gravely and judicially considering the motion before Congress to deprive of his seat, on account of the polygamous nature of his domestic life, Brigham H. Roberts, a duly elected gentleman from Utah. Mr. Roberts, who had theretofore enjoyed the religious privilege of having three wives, abjured two when Utah was admitted to the Union. But the law which enjoined the putting away of plural wives provided that the man who had herded them to the altar must continue caring for them and the question was publicly debated whether "caring for" meant sleeping with them.

Meanwhile the right of Roberts to his seat was strongly defended by Liberals, including Moncure D. Conway, who wrote us from Paris:

"Impossible as it is for me at present, and at this distance, to engage in any polemics in America, I feel it my duty to warn Freethinkers who are trying to deprive polygamists of political rights that they are hounding on a mob of pious lynchers; also that it is precisely the same mob that is already virtually lynching Freethought. Polygamy is odious to Freethinkers, but Freethought is equally odious to the orthodox millions. . . . Some of us remember that the appointment of Ingersoll by President

189

Hayes to a foreign ministry excited a hue and cry as loud as that concerning Roberts. Ingersoll was generous enough to relieve the President by declining. It was none the less a virtual exclusion from national office, and it was but the continuation of an ostracism long going on. Had Ingersoll been orthodox he would have been President."

Said Dr. Conway: "A man's liberty can be justly forfeited only by crime, not by immorality. A man has as much right to his morality as to his religion, or his irreligion. The law against bigamy was not based on its immorality but upon the criminality of deceiving the second wife. The laws concerning rape, adultery, and seduction were based on injuries to the unconsenting woman, the husband, the father; but there is no law against immorality *per se* in states of social civilization. In these I do not include those in which there are Levitical survivals."

A vote of 268 to 50, January 25, ejected Roberts from his seat and deprived Utah of a representative.

The family of Ingersoll found among his papers an unpublished manuscript of seventy pages bearing the title, "A Few Reasons for Doubting the Inspiration of the Bible," and tendered it to The Truth Seeker for publication. It came out June 30 and July 7, and then as a pamphlet. Ingersoll had quoted eighty-odd passages from the Bible, without reference to chapter and verse. I spent many hours searching the Concordance for these, and when found appended them as footnotes. This perchance brought me the commission to prepare Contents and Index to the twelve-volume Dresden

edition of Ingersoll's Works, then on the press of
Peter Eckler. That was no drowsy pastime for a
summer's day. The work occupied many summer
nights.

INGERSOLL.

Your stream of life majestic flowed,
        Ingersoll, brave Ingersoll;
Your genius with pure lustre glowed,
        Ingersoll, brave Ingersoll.
Your thoughts in words of light impearled,
Or in the tones of thunder hurled,
Have stirred the pulses of the world,
        Ingersoll, brave Ingersoll.

The hand of want, the lips of pain,
        Ingersoll, brave Ingersoll,
To you could not appeal in vain,
        Ingersoll, brave Ingersoll.
Quick to relieve, strong to defend,
In sun and storm the loyal friend,
That e'en in death could comfort lend,
        Ingersoll, brave Ingersoll.

The warmest clasp hand ever knew;
        Ingersoll, brave Ingersoll;
The kindliest voice that e'er rang true,
        Ingersoll, brave Ingersoll.
To you the cup of love we drain,
To you we raise our song again,
And linger on that fond refrain,
        Ingersoll, our Ingersoll.

These verses, written about this time as a hymn with words set to the tune of "Maryland," have been sung, I hear, on many Ingersoll occasions. Once on invitation I attended a Unitarian church in New York. The tune was emanating from the organ as I entered, and the congregation sang "In-gersoll, Our Ingersoll."

The Truth Seeker took Col. T. W. Higginson to task for implying, in his work entitled "Con-temporaries," when paying a deserved tribute to Charles Bradlaugh, that Ingersoll sought "mere sensationalism or the pursuit of antagonism for its own sake." Colonel Higginson was a member of the Free Religious Society of Boston, at whose convention in June, 1899—the year Higginson published his "Contemporaries"—Ingersoll gave by invitation his last public address on "What Is Re-ligion?" The address, which in behalf of women advocated birth control, was too advanced for the Free Religionists, and, according to The Truth Seeker, they greeted the speaker "much as he might have expected to be received by an assemblage of backwoods preachers." The offending words of Ingersoll were: "Science must make woman the owner, the mistress of herself. Science, the only possible savior of mankind, must put it in the power of woman to decide for herself whether she will or will not become a mother."

Dr. St. George Mivart, the English zoologist (1827-1900), an opponent of Darwin and Huxley as regards the doctrine of natural selection, and a professed creative or "directive" evolutionist, whose writings on "Happiness and Hell" the pope had put on the Index, was excommunicated by Cardinal Vaughan in January, 1900, after refusing to make such a retraction as the church had extorted from Galileo centuries earlier. He continued his attacks on the church and its doctrines. Concerning the Virgin Birth, which he questioned, Dr. Mivart made the curious observation that the deity, if he chose, could incarnate himself in an onion. In one of the articles that brought him under the ban he testified that he enjoyed the acquaintance of many pious Catholics who denied the perpetual virginity of the mother of God; that these believed Joseph to have been the natural father of Christ, and that they went to the Brompton Oratory merely to worship the Madonna as the only available representative of Venus! Mivart died on April 1, 1900, a heretic. The church refused to take part in the funeral of England's only Catholic scientist of note, or to allow him to be buried in consecrated ground.

The Presbyterians of America got set for a heresy trial this year, the defendant being one of their most learned ministers, the Rev. Arthur C. McGiffert, who rested under charges because he had denied the full inspiration of the scriptures, the sacramental nature of the Lord's supper, and some other things no duly informed person could believe. He "cheated the sheriff" by resigning from the Presbyterian church.

The Truth Seeker for October 13, 1900, had none of my work. There is reason for suspecting that the busy editor called upon Mr. E. C. Walker for contributions. Walker with less effort produced articles twice as long as those which I was in the habit of writing. And my hand is not visible in the next number, either. Was I "in a journey" as Elijah asked about Baal when that god was not on hand to start a fire? On the third week a letter gives the clue. I was by the sea waves watching and waiting for the death or recovery of a very sick wife. She got over it but we never came back to the city to live. Since our return from the West in '93 we had kept house in rooms over the printing-office, an ideal arrangement for a proof-reader who would have his wife for a copy-holder; and also favorable to long hours, none of them wasted in travel by rail or street car. Now we took a house, which I christened Skeetside, in the south end of Montclair, N. J., and thus I became one with the children of nature known as commuters. She was, I guess, the first woman with bobbed hair in this town. Pernicious malaria had begun the work of stealing her long tresses, and I completed it with the shears.

The adventure into illness at a summer resort out of season, when a hotel must be kept in commission on account of a single guest, was expensive. The Hon. W. S. Andrews, with whose wife the patient (her sister) was visiting when stricken, satisfied the landlady. The doctor lightly penned a bill for $412, and there were incidentals. But C. P. Farrell, Ingersoll's publisher, paid me generously for my work on the volumes, and for mak-

SKEETSIDE
119 Willowdale
Avenue,
Montclair, N. J.
Family
Residence,
1900 to 1919
The
Mark Twain
Fellowship
met here in 1919

ing the Index, which I regret to say went into print during my absence, without my seeing the proofs. My old friend, Capt. Silas Latham, of Noank, Conn., who had taken me on fishing voyages, made the blunder, as he feared, of inquiring whether a loan of $150 would suit me better than a kick in the britches and no breakfast (that was his way of covering the timely proffer), and Mrs. Flora Burtis, of Michigan, chose the same time for sending me and my brother also, a bit of money that was earning her nothing (thus she excused the gift). Hence instead of being long sunk in debt I found myself in a condition of financial buoyancy. A small sum was enough then to make a first payment on a house, and I bought the New Jersey one we were living in, which I had named Skeetside.

On July 27 a propagandist by deed named Angelo Bresci shot and killed King Humbert of Italy at a summer resort near Milan. While the assassin professed to be a liberator and tyrannicide, The Truth Seeker denounced him as a "homicidal fool."

As I then wrote:

"The propaganda by deed—where it includes the removal of any living person—is plain murder, made neither more nor less criminal or abhorrent by giving it another name. And the killing of heads of governments to be immediately replaced by other heads, sure to be used as an excuse for more tyrannical laws, is a stupid crime against liberty.

"Ideal anarchy—meaning the decay of government by reason of every individual's so controlling himself that government will have no excuse for existing—is the most attractive of all unimaginable things; but the anarchy of the Bresci brand is the one imaginable thing that is worse than any known form of despotism. For while it is true that the business of the best and worst governments is to filch, one after another, the citizen's liberties, and to multiply restrictions as they grow older and stronger, they at least leave him his life so long as he does not forfeit it by killing somebody else. But Bresci anarchy, which elevates manslaughter to a political principle, inaugurates itself with an assassination. That is the only function of government it knows.

"The monarchical or republican state arrests, prosecutes, imprisons, and in the end inflicts the death penalty. Propaganda by deed begins with the execution. The anarchist of this variety announces himself a murderer by conviction, and he proves the sincerity of his professions with considerable frequency. In view of the facts, he could not in consistency complain at being hanged in advance of any overt act he may or may not have it in mind to commit.

"Men called kings feel as much concern for their own lives, and possess the same instinct of self-preservation, as other men; and that they have the same right to life, liberty, and the pursuit of happiness as their fellows seems to be perfectly clear. And I know of no authority by which anarchists can establish an exclusive claim to the method of propaganda by deed. Whence it appears to follow, since the king and the anarchist look each upon the other as an enemy of mankind, that it is as legitimate for the man on the throne to strangle his adversary offhand with a rope as for the latter to shatter the monarch to bits with a bomb."

A district-attorney at Louisville, Kentucky, charged that C. C. Moore, editor of The Blue Grass Blade, under suspended sentence for advocating social freedom in 1899, had violated his parole by printing more objectionable matter. Moore was presented to the federal court, which late in the year dismissed the case. The matter complained of had been contributed to The Blade by M. Grier Kidder, a writer of sententious paragraphs. He proffered similar matter to The Truth Seeker, and then complained that his articles had been cut. The editor was a better judge than he of what could be mailed without inviting prosecution.

The United States had trouble on its hands, with war and insurrection threatened in three places over missionaries and on religious grounds. In Turkey and China the missionaries were demanding indemnity for lost lives and goods; in the Philippines the question was that of expelling the licentious friars and restoring the friar lands to the people. Russia and Germany talked of invading China. Turkey denied responsibility and laid Armenian massacres to the Kurds. In China demonstrations occurred known as the Boxer uprising.

F. D. Cummings of Portland, Maine, author of a Rationalistic work, "Religion and the Bible," took the platform against the teaching of religion in the schools of his city. He not only appeared

before the school board and common council, but
hired a hall and addressed his fellow citizens. He
then had his speech printed and circulated. Years
later Mr. Cummings, being elected to the legislature, continued with good effect his work for the
separation of church and state.

The school board of Piermont, near Nyack, N.
Y., expelled Catholic children for refusing to participate in Protestant religious services conducted
in the school. The attention of State Superintendent Charles E. Skinner having been called to
the case, that official said:

"It is a violation of the school law to compel children
to attend religious services after the hour of school opening, and the reading of the Bible in the public schools is
also prohibited."

This prohibition caused recourse to the bootlegging of religion into the schools.

In Nebraska Daniel Freeman of Beatrice instituted a mandamus suit to compel the school board
to stop the holding of religious services in the
schools.

The school committee of Holyoke, Mass., at the
demand of a Catholic priest, dismissed from the
high school faculty Miss Anna B. Hasbrouck, history teacher, for informing her pupils that Jesus
Christ was one of a numerous family of children.
The texts on this subject are Matt. xiii, 56, and
Mark vi, 3.

The Liberal Club made the mistake of electing
as president a half-liberal, Henry Nichols, who was
out of touch with Freethought. The club permitted him to resign, electing E. C. Walker as his

successor. The members held summer meetings at the residence of Dr. E. B. Foote.

The Mail of Kirksville, Mo., published a report that the Rev. George Gibson, pastor of a San Francisco church, the scene of the murder of two girls, for which Theodore Durrant paid the penalty of being hanged, had lately died after confessing himself the criminal. A Truth Seeker reader in San Francisco looked up the facts and found the Rev. Mr. Gibson alive and preaching in the same place.

Boston saw the strange spectacle of a former prize-fighter turned Freethought evangelist and making speeches on the Common. He was known as Billy Frazier. The police suppressed him.

The Marquis of Queensbury, it appeared on his death in London, January 31, was an Agnostic—a supporter of "Saladin" (W. Stewart Ross) and his Agnostic Journal. In his will, probated in Edinburgh, directing that his body be cremated, the marquis wrote: "I particularly request that no Christian mummeries or tomfooleries be performed at the grave, but that I be buried as an Agnostic. If it should be a comfort to anyone, there is a plenty of friends who would come to say a few words of common sense over the spot where my ashes may lie." He is said to have been a high-minded and courageous gentleman.

The will of the Rev. "Father" Charles Pascal Chiniquy—author of another sort of "Fifty Years"—was filed in Illinois in January. It contained a blast at the church of Rome, which he renounced "more than ever." Chiniquy was an excommunicated Canadian priest, born in 1809, who turned Presbyterian. He died in 1899.

William McDonnell, author of "Exeter Hall" and other works, died June 20 at Lindsay, Ont., 87 years old. He was honored by the community and at his funeral eulogized by J. Spencer Ellis, editor of Secular Thought. Stephen R. Thorne, the life-long "Painite," died in New York, June 26. He took pride in the fact that he was born in the year of Paine's death, 1809. A photograph of the Paine monument at New Rochelle, published by The Truth Seeker Jan. 29, 1898, showed Mr. Thorne inside the inclosure. John Clark Ridpath, the historian, died July 31, at the age of 59. His religious sympathies were unknown to the public until he officiated at the funeral of Ingersoll. The philosopher Friederich Wilhelm Nietzsche, having attained the age of 56, died in Weimar, Germany, August 25. His attacks on the Christian system were of unparalleled ferocity.

J. B. Beattie in January communicated to The Truth Seeker from Chicago that the Freethinkers had got together again and organized the Liberal Society; Harry Stannard president, Frederick Mains secretary. Apparently it was a belated an-nouncement, for in September Dr. Thomas B. Gregory, mentioned as the organizer, gave notice that the thriving society would celebrate its first anniversary on October 7.

The New Hampshire Freethinkers held their an-nual meeting in Manchester on August 11, the sixty-seventh Ingersoll anniversary. Mrs. Marilla

M. Ricker, one of the first woman lawyers admitted
to practice in the United States Supreme Court,
was among the speakers. Mrs. Ricker, a remarkably forceful writer, soon got into touch with The
Truth Seeker and contributed freely to its columns.
When the Dresden Edition of Ingersoll's Works
came out, she offered a set to any library in New
Hampshire that would accept them.

Since the discovery a few years previous of
Roosevelt's reference to Paine, in his Life of Morris, as a "filthy little Atheist," those three words
had tailed themselves on to scores of allusions to
"Teddy." October 13, The Truth Seeker said:
"Of late there have been so many inquiries as to
the exact nature of Mr. Roosevelt's offense, when
and where committed, that we have deemed it advisable to publish a resumé of the discussion."
Six and a half columns of history follow, every line
strengthening the charge that Roosevelt had written in ignorance and bad faith. I believe that
W. M. van der Weyde, president of the Thomas
Paine National Historical Association, had in his
possession a letter signed by Roosevelt shortly before his death in which he admitted: "Of course,
Paine was a Deist." But the "filthy little Atheist"
stood in the last edition of the Morris Life, printed
after the truth had come into the author's possession. "Of course," a believer in God could not
gracefully say "the filthy little Deist."

CHAPTER XII.

THE war* in China, provoked by missionaries who were taking to the natives the message of the Prince of Peace, was all over but the looting, and the missionaries had more than shared the plunder. They organized and exploited it to the glory of God. Earl Li Hung Chang, the Chinese viceroy, said that the heads of the American Missionary Board and of the Presbyterian Society "have vast quantities of loot in the shape of silver, valuable furs, jade, etc., and have held frequent auction sales here in Pekin and realized enormous sums of money from the sales." That was after the capture of Pekin by the invading Christian armies.

Said the Hong Kong Daily Mail: "The private looting that took place was most successfully exploited by the missionaries. They took possession of big Chinese houses, where they carried on sales of everything they could seize, engaging their converts to bring in fresh articles stolen from private houses as purchases depleted their stock."

That is, the missionaries had their converts do the stealing, while they acted as fences and dis-

---

*Boxer uprising.

posed of the goods. The Congregational missionaries moved into a prince's palace and sold off his
"pieces of red lacquer, porcelain, and silks and fur-
lined robes." Mark Twain published in The North
American Review an article on the conduct of the
Christian nations which at the behest of the missionaries, having reduced the people of China to
starvation and plundered them of their property,
had levied an indemnity in order to extort the expenses of the robbery. Speaking of the Rev. Mr.
Ament, the most successful of the looting missionaries, who demanded an indemnity in addition to
his loot, Mark Twain wrote:

"By happy luck we get all these glad tidings on Christmas
eve—just in time to enable us to celebrate the day with
proper gayety and enthusiasm. Our spirits soar, and we
find we can even make jokes: Taels I win; heads you
lose."

The guilty ministers straightway charged Twain
to retract and apologize; he did not, but, having
accumulated additional facts and arguments, returned to the pages of The Review with an answer
more blistering than his attack. Major Edwin H.
Conger, U. S., minister to China, coming to the
defense of the missionaries, declared that they
looted no more than some others. Mark Twain
overlooked not a single thought or implication in
the missionaries' plea that in helping to loot Pekin
they merely followed local custom, nor in Conger's
that there were some laymen who equaled the missionaries as looters if not in the hypocritical and
"blasphemous" excuse that the plunder of the
heathen would be "used for the propagation of
the gospel." He asked whether the missionaries

had left at home the civilization and the Christian morality they were supposed to be taking to the heathen.

The French bishop of Pekin, one Favier, "stole goods to the value of about one million dollars." In the Central Synod of the Dutch Reformed church at New Brunswick, N. J., the Rev. Edward P. Johnson, instituted a comparison between Mark Twain and the devil, and decided that "the latter deserved the most honor." Moncure D. Conway teamed up with Twain and did his share in exposing the shameful history of Christian invasion and conquest of the Orient. For half of the year 1901 newspaper correspondents were sending home reports confirming the worst that had preceded them.

The Truth Seeker and its constituency were preoccupied throughout half the year with measures it was hoped would induce the directors of the Pan-American Exposition at Buffalo, N. Y., to open the gates on Sunday. That seemed to be a good year for promoting fairs. There was this all-American one at Buffalo; St. Louis was also getting ready for a blowout in 1903 to celebrate the Louisiana Purchase, and Charleston, S. C., was looking forward to big things in December. As a preliminary in each case the promoters went to Congress for an appropriation—$5,000,000 for St. Louis; $250,000 for Charleston; and Senators Teller of Colorado and Tillman of South Carolina, moved and instigated thereto by the clergy, introduced identical resolutions providing that a condition precedent to the paying of the money should be the closing of the gates to visitors on Sundays "during the whole duration of the Fair." The framing, wording, and offering of the resolutions gives to us and to posterity the measure of those two senatorial humbugs. Liberals concentrated on the Buffalo exposition. The Truth Seeker circulated petitions, and obtained from the Board of Directors a hearing for Moncure D. Conway and Clarence Darrow, which was had during the last week in April, in favor of the Sunday opening. The New York Journal prematurely reported: "The managers of the Buffalo Fair have decided that the Pan-American Exposition shall remain open on Sundays. We congratulate John N. Scatcherd, John Milburn, and the other directing minds on their sound common sense." The addresses of Conway and Darrow were printed in The Truth Seeker of May 4, 1901. Then the Board of Directors, having agreed to open on Sundays, revised their decision in part and closed the amusement places. A Sabbatarian citizen of Buffalo took action against the police commissioner for neglect of duty in not shutting the gates entirely. His suit was dismissed by the courts. Thereafter the Protestant clergy organized a boycott and the Catholic priests, for a wonder, sided with them. In this way the clergy at home looted the people of their liberty and of their rights as citizens and taxpayers in the Pan-American exposition, even as their brethren abroad had looted the heathen of their property "for the propagation of the gospel."

Sunday opening or Sunday observance arguments were tossed back and forth between the Liberals and the Sabbatarians. Senator McMillan of Michigan, with the approval of Herbert Putnam, librarian, offered a measure to admit people to the Library of Congress from 2 to 10 o'clock Sunday afternoon and evening. The labor unions were persecuting non-union barbers for working the first day of the week, and butchers for selling meat. At Walla Walla, in the state of Washington, certain Seventh-day Adventists having been prosecuted for Sunday labor, Judge Brent (July 31, 1901) declared the Sunday closing law unconstitutional. "Business," said the court, "cannot be stopped for the purpose of enforcing religious views."

The Liberal University at Silverton, Oregon, passed from the direction of J. E. Hosmer, who had been the leader in establishing it. He lacked the breadth of mind necessary to the president of a Liberal institution.

The Liberal University opened September 30, 1901.

Helen Gardener lost her husband in the death, January 11, of Col. C. Selden Smart, a native of Ohio and a lifelong Agnostic—"a genial whole-souled gentleman, an outspoken Freethinker, a good friend and a bad foe, big in body and heart, and a worshiper of his wife." Colonel Smart was a native of Ohio, many years his wife's senior, and had sunk considerable money as publisher of The Arena magazine, which for a time Helen Gardener edited. Richard C. Burtis, dying at Watrousville,

Mich., January 17, aged 77, assigned ten shares of bank stock, value not specified, to The Truth Seeker company. Mr. Burtis and his wife Flora were generous donors to the cause. Mrs. Burtis survived him several years, remembering The Truth Seeker in the disposition of her estate. Another of the helpers, John C. Loomiller, died near Hazleton, Indiana, from being shot through the head, probably for purposes of robbery, February 12. He was about 50 years old, and had been blind since the age of 14, notwithstanding which infirmity he accumulated a considerable fortune. The death of Ephraim Hitchcock, president of The Truth Seeker Company, having left the company with liabilities of $1,500, Mr. Loomiller settled the debt. He was survived by a wife wholly devoted to him and sharing his views. The "Ungodly Woman of the Nineteenth Century," Ella E. Gibson, author of "Godly Women of the Bible," died on March 5 at Barre, Mass., having lived nearly eighty years. She had been school teacher, lecturer and preacher, and army chaplain, her appointment being approved by President Lincoln, November 10, 1864. She served without the formality of being mustered in, and did not recover her salary until 1876, when, as D. M. Bennett revealed in his "World's Sages," "a considerable portion of the money which she obtained from the government for her services in the war she generously placed in the hands of the writer of these pages to aid him in his purpose." John S. Hittell, the old newspaperman and writer of California, died March 8, aged 76. His works were "Evidences

Against Christianity," "A Code of Morals," and a "History of Morals." His son Theodore H. is the author of a standard History of California. Mrs. M. A. Freeman, for twelve years identified with the Chicago Secular Union, and for two terms corresponding secretary of the national organization, died in Chicago September 7. In December John Swinton, newspaperman and for years (beginning in 1883) publisher of John Swinton's paper (Labor), a Scotsman 71 years old, died at his home in Brooklyn. Also there died in 1901, if anybody is interested, Judge Charles L. Benedict, 76, before whom Comstock never lost a case and who sentenced D. M. Bennett; and, in a lunatic asylum, Joseph, Joe, or Jo Cook, who as a Christian minister matched Benedict as a Christian judge.

The Chicago Liberals organized around the name of Ingersoll. Said a notice in The Truth Seeker of June 29, 1901:

"A meeting of the Ingersoll Memorial Association will be held at Parlor L 38, Great Northern Hotel, Chicago, on July 6, at 8 o'clock P. M., for a public presentation of the plans and purposes of the organization. Hon. Charles B. Waite, Hon. Thos. Cratty, H. L. Green, William H. Maple, E. C. Reichwald, Patrick J. O'Shea, and R. N. Reeves are expected to deliver short addresses. All admirers of Colonel Ingersoll are invited to be present.— Frederick Mains, General Secretary."

Except for the address of Judge Waite delivered at the meeting, when he was elected president, the activities of the Association were not further reported to The Truth Seeker in 1901. Mr. W. H.

Maple, a member, issued a small periodical named The Ingersoll Beacon.

John E. Remsburg, having declined reelection to the presidency of the American Secular Union, reëntered the lecture field, with engagements in Kansas and Oklahoma and Indian Territories.

In June the New York University dedicated its Hall of Fame, a present from Helen Gould. The press was quick to notice that among the twenty-nine names thought worthy of a place, a disproportionate number were borne by Unitarians or non-church members. The same is to be said of those that have since been added thereto.

The Madrid organ of the Freethinkers, Las Dominicales, suppressed in 1900 by the clerical politicians and its editor jailed, resumed publication early in 1901, the editor having served out his sentence.

Mrs. Etta Semple continued her publication, The Ideal, in Kansas; The Progressive Thinker (Liberal Spiritualist) appeared in Chicago; Charles F. Eldredge began in Kansas City the publication of The Philosopher, a monthly. Mr. Eldredge had furnished The Truth Seeker with stenographic reports of the lectures of Dr. J. E. Roberts. J. D. Shaw of Waco, Texas, had changed the name of his Independent Pulpit to The Searchlight.

The orthodox church of Russia pronounced sentence of excommunication on Count Leo Tolstoy for rebelling "against God and his Christ" by denying the church's authority to tell him what he ought to believe. But Tolstoy was no Infidel. He retained superstitions enough to save him.

The former secretary of the American Secular Union, Miss Ida C. Craddock, who had now turned instructress on the finer points of married life, distributed documents at the capital setting forth her ideas. Judge Scott, before whom the lady was arraigned, expressed the opinion that the contents of her letters dealt with matters that should be discussed only in private if at all. He released Miss Craddock on condition that she should leave Washington. That was the beginning of a persecution by the unwholesome Anthony Comstock that drove this estimable woman to suicide.

Far in the past one of the Presidents of the United States inaugurated the custom of making a grand tour of the country with considerable pomp and circumstance. His progress was called "swinging around the circle." The swing of President McKinley, so planned as to land him at the Pan-American Exposition in Buffalo about the first of September, aroused the resentment of The Evening Times, Cumberland, Md., whose acting editor, Daniel Webster Snyder, a local preacher, said:

"This Republic is not a kingdom or an empire. God will not be mocked. There is no demand or need of a travelling menagerie from the Capitol, and, as I said, *someone will have to die to check this foolishness.* Mark this."

I find that quoted in The Truth Seeker, and the next mention of McKinley is the following:

"President McKinley was shot twice by an assassin as he stood in the Temple of Music at the Pan-American Exposition in Buffalo, N. Y., at 4 o'clock on the afternoon of September 6. The assassin was immediately seized. He had concealed a pistol in a handkerchief, and approached Mr. McKinley under the pretense of shaking hands. He is alleged to have made a confession in which he says his name is Leon F. Czolgosz, that he is an anarchist, and that in shooting the President he did his duty. . . The assassin is reported as saying that the speeches and writings of Emma Goldman moved him to commit the deed."

President McKinley, who was elected in 1896 and reëlected in 1900, died on September 14. A number of arrests, which did not include that of the Cumberland minister, immediately followed the shooting. The first victims were Abe Isaacs and several persons associated with him in publishing Free Society, Chicago, a communist-anarchist periodical. Emma Goldman, in Chicago at the time, was likewise held. The police of New York grabbed John Most, communist-anarchist, for an article written fifty years before by Carl Heinzen of Boston, but brought up to date and stuck into his paper by Most without credit, and as an editorial.

As stated, the minister who a short time previously had said someone would have to die to check McKinley's foolishness, escaped notice by the police; yet Morrison I. Swift of California, who in 1899 had written a book censuring McKinley, now found himself in jail on the charge of "slandering the memory" of the deceased.

While the authorities were in a mood for arresting everybody to whom the word "anarchist" might or might not stick as a term of reproach, they grabbed three members of the Home Colony, in the State of Washington, charging misuse of the mails by circulating obscene literature in the colony's paper, edited by James F. Morton. The report of the arrests in the New York dailies contained the statement: "It is known that the action is taken with the object of breaking up the Home Colony." That paper, Discontent, came regularly to The Truth Seeker office. In content it was wholly inoffensive; its "anarchy" was of the kind described by Huxley, and some of its contributors were nonresistants.

The motive of Czolgosz in assassinating President McKinley never came to light. On the day of his sentence, the district-attorney of Buffalo took his record, or so-called "pedigree," which was as follows:

"Age—Twenty-eight years. Nativity—Detroit. Residence—Broadway, Nowaks, Buffalo. Occupation—Laborer. Married or single—Single. Degree of education—Common school and parochial. Religious instruction—Catholic. Parents, living or dead—Father living, mother dead. Temperate or intemperate—Temperate. Former conviction of crime—None."

The word "common" should be *German*, according to some of the Buffalo reporters who heard and reported his answers placed in the record. He attended German parochial schools, not common schools. Without waiting for the facts to emerge, the priests had been declaring that not only must Anarchy be fought to the death, but our godless public schools must be turned into moral engines by combining religious with secular instruction. Of these false alarms the New York Times of September 28 said:

"Those hasty clergymen, of more than one denomination, who made the crime of the man Czolgosz the basis for vehement denunciation of public schools and the whole system of unsectarian education, may be moved to mitigate the violence of their remarks if their attention is called to certain facts which were called out by the questions put to Czolgosz just before he was sentenced."

Dr. J. B. Wilson, who had been elected president of the American Secular Union in 1900, resigned from that office after holding it about six months. Dr. Wilson found himself, he said, unable to work harmoniously with the other officers. His resignation made a president of Mrs. Josephine K. Henry, first vice-president, of Versailles, Kentucky; but as Mrs. Henry deemed herself unequal to the duties of the office, she declined it. The position was filled by E. M. Macdonald, whom the coming Congress in Buffalo, N. Y., October 4-6, elected president, with E. C. Reichwald as secretary

CHAPTER XIII.

HERBERT SPENCER put forth a book understood to be the closing volume of his life. It had the non-portentous title of "Facts and Comments" and contained thirty-nine articles or essays, but the number was fortuitous and privileged no one to infer that Mr. Spencer, now 82, had formulated a creed in imitation of the Church of England. The aged philosopher could grant no more to the Christian religion as a moral force than The Truth Seeker does. "It needs but to glance over the world and to contemplate the doings of Christians everywhere," he said, "to be amazed at the ineffectiveness of current theology. Or it needs only to look back over past centuries and the iniquities alike of populace, nobles, kings, and popes, to perceive an almost incomprehensible futility of the beliefs everywhere held and perpetually insisted upon." Religion was not now a deterrent to iniquity, and in the opinion of Mr. Spencer, never had been. The verdict of his intellect he rendered in a paragraph which is so strong and ample a warrant for Freethought advocacy that I have quoted it forty times and am reluctant to send a number of The Truth Seeker to press without it. I quote it again:

215

"Whoever hesitates to utter that which he thinks the highest truth, lest it should be too much in advance of the time, may reassure himself by looking at his acts from an impersonal point of view. . . . It is not for nothing that he has in him these sympathies with some principles and repugnance to others. He, with all his capacities, and aspirations, and beliefs, is not an accident, but a product of the time. He must remember that while he is a descendant of the past, he is a parent of the future; and that his thoughts are as children born to him, which he may not carelessly let die. . . . Not adventitious therefore will the wise man regard the faith that is in him. The highest truth he sees he will fearlessly utter; knowing that, let what may come of it, he is thus playing his right part in the world—knowing that if he can effect the change he aims at—well: if not—well also; though not *so* well."

"The highest truth he sees he will fearlessly utter." There is no better or sounder sentiment. Suppose it was written forty years in advance of the "prospect of heaven" passage, its substance was reaffirmed by its author in his autobiography which he left to be published after his death. "If it is asked," he said, "why, thinking thus, I have persisted in setting forth views at variance with current creeds, my reply is the one elsewhere made. It is for each to utter that which he sincerely believes to be true, and, adding his unit of influence to all other units, leave the results to work themselves out."

A postoffice inspector ordered the holding up of the newspaper, Discontent, published by the Home Colonists in the State of Washington. The paper contained nothing to warrant that action; the complaint against the publication was dismissed, and

at once the Department at Washington resorted to
executive action and by a high-handed outrage upon
justice abolished the Home postoffice. And then
Anthony Comstock pursued the gentle Ida Craddock to her death. Mrs. Craddock's coeducational
hobby was the purification of the marriage relation,
which, being something of a mystic, she regarded
as a communion with God. She was tried the 14th
of March and on the 17th sent to the Work House
on Blackwell's Island. The defense was a difficult
one, as in order properly to present her thought to
the intelligent reader, it would be necessary to reproduce what Mrs. Craddock said, and that would
again stir up that mass of muck known as Anthony Comstock. However, the following statements passed the censor:

"Three judges have lately stamped as filthy a piece of
writing which they know to be as clean as anything ever
written. I say they know the writing is clean because I
know it to be so, and I do not assume to be wiser than
the judges. They brand it as blasphemous, but at the
same time they are aware that it is not. Obscenity and
blasphemy in this case are legal fictions. The judges condemned the writer for the same reason that thousands
silently acquiesce in their verdict, because they are too
pusillanimous to vindicate the truth by declaring for an
acquittal. Men of the world, including judges, are likely
to look with disfavor upon such teaching as that of Mrs.
Craddock for the reason that they are condemned by it."

Mrs. Craddock served her three months' term at
the work house, whose inmates found her a "min-
istering angel," and then exposed in writing the
horrible conditions she discovered there. Continuing the distribution of her educative writings, she
fell into Comstock's filthy hands again. He ar-

rested her on the 10th of October; she was admitted to bail, and on the 16th she committed suicide by cutting the veins of her wrists and turning on the gas in her room. By placing her in a position to which death was preferable, her judges had committed a murder. In her last letter to her mother she wrote: "I maintain my right to die as I have lived, a free woman, not cowed into silence by any other human being."

Personally Mrs. Craddock was a surprisingly lovely woman. She and Comstock were the Beauty and the Beast. After her Blackwell's Island experience I had a short conversation with her at The Truth Seeker office, and asked her if she did not regard herself as eligible to the veteran corps. Speaking jocosely, I told her I regretted to see youth and beauty sacrificed to the vice-hunting ogre. She replied that, although she enjoyed living, she would that her life might be turned to water and poured out for cleansing the lives of others. She was every inch a martyr.

If the millions did not rise up to thank her, that was not her fault, but her judges'. She gave her life and her message—and the swine got to them first.

An announcement conceived as follows appeared under the editorial card of The Truth Seeker of March 22, 1902:

"Our readers have, regretfully we know, missed Observations' from these columns for some time. Mr. George Macdonald, who compiles these interesting remarks, has been immured in a secluded spot in the wilderness for more than forty days writing the text around the pictures

for our forthcoming work, 'New Testament Stories Comically Illustrated.' "

Writing the text around the pictures for the
Illustrated New Testament took me through the
Gospels, Acts, and Epistles more carefully than I
had traveled the ground before. This "New Testament Comically Illustrated" (now scarce if not
rare as a separate volume) contains, as the owner
of one will observe, above one hundred and sixty
chapters. The editor found the 400-word limit irksome, and so wrote along until he had done about
forty of the two hundred pages which were to be
written. It was at this point that I took the pictures and other material and retired to Skeetside,
where I pursued my aim at the rate of a half-
dozen pages a day.

There was current talk of putting the "Passion
Play" on the stage in New York, and the Presbyterian ministers were protesting against the piece as
"sacrilegious in the sight of God." Where they got
the assurance that God so viewed the production
they didn't say. But mulling over the story to pick
out material for a page of matter where I could find
it, I couldn't have missed the drama if I had been
looking for something else, or if the Rt. Hon. John
M. Robertson had never pointed it out.

As the prelude to the "betrayal," the curtain was
to be seen by the mind's eye going up on Jesus
and his twelve disciples sitting around the dish that
held their supper. You observe them reaching for
food. As the dish goes down he tells the company, "One of you shall betray me." This shows
he has a way of knowing things. The scene is pro-

tracted by giving them each a line. "Is it I?" they ask, one after another. To Judas, when his turn comes, the leading man of the play (who is Jesus) answers, "Thou hast said." In real life some one would have asked Jesus to explain himself; but this was a mystery. The serious charge against one of their number apparently is accepted as part of the program; they sing a hymn, giving the quartet opportunity to introduce song specialties. They walk off, and when they come on again it is the Garden of Gethsemane. The disciples sleep. As they have taken no precaution to prevent Judas from carrying out his design, he steals away unperceived by all except the audience. Although there is no one awake to make a historical note of the circumstance, we are told that Jesus withdraws and offers up a prayer. Only the dramatist and the fictionist are licensed to state incidents that have no witnesses.

The praying of Washington at Valley Forge, out in the woods away from his staff (a legend perpetuated in 1928 by the issue of the Washington postage stamp that The Truth Seeker named "the Valley Forgery") was undoubtedly suggested to the pious mind of its original narrator by the fictionist who wrote that Jesus "was withdrawn from them about a stone's cast, and kneeled down, and prayed."

In May, 1902, the population of the Island of Martinique, one of the Lesser Antilles, was wiped out by an explosion of the volcanic Mt. Pelée, which utterly destroyed St. Pierre, the island's largest city, and the shipping in the harbor. Forty thousand persons lost their lives when overwhelmed by the fall of hot ashes and lava blown into the air. The population of Martinique was Catholic. Deploring the extinction of life, The Truth Seeker said: "The death of 30,000 good Catholics is not taken as proof that Providence was neglectful, but the finding of a wafer unconsumed in the ruins of the Cathedral demonstrates to the mind of faith that God was at his old trick of working worthless miracles." Reports said that when the explosion came three thousand had gathered into the Cathedral to worship, and none survived. I quote an observation:

"The eruption whereby Mt. Pelée benevolently assimilated the inhabitants of St. Pierre, in the Island of Martinique, left but one man to tell about it; *and he was in jail!* He regards his escape as Providential. About the same thing happened when the cities of the plain were destroyed, a good while ago, for although Lot, the gentleman who escaped, was not an inmate of the jail, he certainly ought to have been. A report from the scene of the late disaster mentions the death of three thousand who had gathered in a cathedral to worship. Was there not in that devout bunch some individual as worthy to be saved as the fellow in the cooler? The event forces the melancholy conclusion that there was not. 'True and righteous,' it has been remarked, 'are thy judgments, Lord God Almighty,' and who am I that I should review the decision?"

The holocaust visited the island on the religious holiday called the Feast of the Ascension. "The interior of the cathedral," wrote a correspondent just after the visitation, "spelled destruction more eloquently than any other part of St. Pierre. At one end the facade, and the great bell, with the gnarled, distorted framework of the bell tower; at the other the shattered marble and the scorched

discolorful fittings of the altar. At one's feet lay
pictured biblical carvings, the beautiful doors of the
sanctuary wrested from their hinges, and the candel-
abra broken like pipestems. The walls and roof
buried all these in an immense mass of debris. The
great Christ that had stood midway between the
towers, seeming from the sea against the background of green as if the statue were erected high
up on the hills, was nowhere to be seen." The de-
vastation was more complete than in the temple of
the Philistine god Dagon, for Dagon, though pros-
trate, was still to be seen.

Herr Johann Most, with his cry of "Nieder mit
der Tyrannei," exhausted the resources of the law
which he contemned, and getting no relief, went to
the penitentiary for a year. William McQueen,
editor of an anarchist paper in New York called
Liberty, using the language made famous in 1912
by the Rev. Father Phelan of St. Louis, served a
term in a New Jersey prison for saying: "To hell
with government." Other sufferers from the censorship were Lois Waisbrooker and Mattie Pen-
hallow. The two innocent old ladies were indicted
in Tacoma, Washington, for an article printed in
Mrs. Waisbrooker's paper "Clothed with the Sun."
The jury acquitted Mattie, while Lois was convicted
and fined $100. It was a penalty on opinion, the
language used being above reproach. Truth Seeker
readers contributed the funds for her defense and
fine.

Two cases growing out of religious exercises in
the public schools were pending in 1902. A son

of Mr. J. B. Billard of North Topeka, Kansas, was expelled for refusing to participate, and Mr. Billard appealed to the courts. In Beatrice, Nebraska, Daniel Freeman advised his son Ray to absent himself during the offering of prayer, singing of hymns, and reading of the Bible. The American Secular Union engaged counsel and fought the case out. Commissioner Ames rendered the opinion that observance in the public schools of customs and usages of sectarian churches or religious organizations was forbidden by the constitution of the state.

RYAN WALKER.

Ryan Walker, the cartoonist, coming to New York from the West early in the year, began to illustrate The Truth Seeker. He had no other engagements and, working rapidly, filled columns and pages with his pictures, w h i c h were good ones.

Theodore Roosevelt, being President, and the Philppines troubles (which were religious ones) not having been adjusted, he sent William Howard Taft to Rome for a confab with the pope. The expelling of the friars and the opening up of the islands to Protestant missionaries were offenses against the holy see that only a money payment could atone for. Ryan Walker caricatured the situation with a picture of Uncle Sam kissing the pope's toe and apologizing for his awkwardness, since this was the first time he had lowered himself to the performance of that act. In the war of this country with Spain the pope had sided with the Catholic country, as had also the German kaiser whom his holiness regarded as a "son"; and for that reason such deference to the Vatican as the mission of Taft denoted was adversely commented upon by non-Catholics. The Truth Seeker announced that Uncle Sam had gone to Canossa.

The editor in a paragraph as of April 26 applauds Mr. Roosevelt. "It gives us all the more pleasure," the piece reads, "to record an instance where Mr. Roosevelt has shown independence and fairness of mind towards an Agnostic. He recently appointed to office a man of national reputation who for twenty years has been a subscriber to The Truth Seeker and a Freethinker who has done what he could to show the fallacy of Christianity." The appointee is not named. It was Mr. Pat Garrett of Texas, who held the post of collector of customs at El Paso until he committed the social error of introducing to the President, and perhaps to Mrs. Roosevelt and Alice, his friend Tom Powers. When Roosevelt learned that Mr. Powers was a noted gambler, the story went, he made an end of Billy the Kid's captor as collector of customs.

A number of ministers in Denver tried without success to banish Mark Twain's "Huckleberry Finn" from the public library on the score of immorality. Mark, in a letter to the Denver Post, expressed the fear that God had dealt unkindly with the ministers in the matter of wisdom. "There is nobody for me to attack in this matter," he wrote, "even with soft and gentle ridicule— and I should not think of using a grown-up weapon in this kind of a nursery. Above all, I couldn't venture to attack the clergymen whom you mention, for I have their habits and live in the same glass house which they are occupying. I am always reading immoral books on the sly and then selfishly trying to prevent other people from having the same wicked good time."

In the way of a social event, Helen Gardener married Lieut. Seldon Allen Day of the United States Army and went to reside in Washington.

A few members of the American Secular Union who withdrew in 1901 when J. B. Wilson resigned the presidency met in convention at Cincinnati under the name of the National Liberal Party.

A Swedish Freethought fortnightly paper, "Forskaren" (The Investigator), flourished in Minneapolis. The "Philosopher," published in Kansas City by C. F. Eldredge, and carrying the name of Dr. J. E. Roberts as one of the editors, ended its career by merging with The Truth Seeker at the end of 1902. The Boston Investigator, L. K. Washburn, proprietor, was not prospering. Mr. Washburn said that he allowed himself a salary of ninety-seven cents per day, and often rashly drew half of it.

Liberal societies met regularly in Boston (J. P. Bland resident speaker), Cincinnati, Washington,

THESE WERE TOGETHER ONCE.

This gem of a picture, as I regard it, is a belated discovery, more timely now, however, than hereafter, for it
dates back almost to what The Times, reviewing "Fifty
Years," Vol. I, called "the late lamented century."

The place is the entrance to the Long Island Business
College, South Eighth street, between Bedford and Driggs
avenues, where the Brooklyn Philosophical Association
held its meetings; the occasion, a congress of the American Secular Union in 1902.   More faces than names
come to mind.   At the upper left-hand corner is Mr.
Winham, who grew old as secretary of the B. P. A.   A
few faces to the reader's right are the author of these
memoirs and his better element; next, in the background,
probably, George Gillen, with Mrs. Gillen in front of him
a step down and forward.   Over near the lady in the um-

brella hat, who might be Mrs. Loomiller, we suspect the presence of M. Goldsmith, who long sat at the door of the Manhattan Liberal Club. From the left again, that might be Mr. Slensby in the hard hat. The adjacent lady next was known to all who went to Liberal meetings forty years ago; Mrs. Robinson, I think. The central figure is either E. C. Reichwald or Henry Rowley, whose pictures resemble each other; then Mrs. Gillen, as aforesaid, and over beneath the outer brim of the Gainsborough hat, Susan H. Wixon, editor of our Children's Corner. The bald man of the triangle is Joseph Warwick. Florence Johnson's young daughters, Bertha and Pearl, are partly concealed by the couple in front (who will doubtless say I ought to remember them). Pearl always captured our boy Putnam, when present, so that would be the future Gob at her elbow. Back of him, Eugene, sometime captain Eleventh Engineers, A. E. F. And so we come to Libby Culbertson Macdonald, not wearing a large birthday cake, frosted on top and down the sides, for a lid, but a hat of the period. The female wearer of the black hat nearby, with a white center, might pass for Miss Levin, the Broadway photographer, whose name in that era was on the pictures of so many of the Liberals and "radicals." Diagonally across the picture from Mr. Winham, E. M. Macdonald, for twenty-six years editor of The Truth Seeker, is standing. Beside him Charles Watts completes the group, which would have been incomplete without him Other figures, unknown to me, are in the original photograph, to the right and left of those included.

D. C., Los Angeles, Philadelphia, New York, and Brooklyn; and Hugh O. Pentecost spoke every Sunday morning at Mott Memorial Hall, New York.

The American Secular Union held its twenty-sixth annual Congress in the Long Island Business College Hall, Brooklyn, November 15 and 16. The announced speakers were Edwin C. Walker,

Charles Watts, Susan H. Wixon, Moncure D. Conway, Herbert N. Casson, Hugh O. Pentecost, and Henry Rowley. The Congress elected E. M. Macdonald president, E. C. Reichwald secretary, and Dr. Foote treasurer. The attendance was good, and the quality of the addresses is guaranteed by the names of the speakers who gave them. That of Charles Watts was the last he ever delivered in America.

Able writers contributed to The Truth Seeker in 1902. The more widely known were Dr. J. E. Roberts of Kansas City, John E. Remsburg of Atchison (Kan.), Judge C. B. White of Chicago, Dr. W. A. Croffut, William Henry Burr, Gen. William Birney, David Eccles of Washington (D. C.), Hugh O. Pentecost and Bolton Hall of New York, Mrs. Elizabeth M. Evans of Munich (Bavaria), Ida Craddock of Philadelphia, and Marilla M. Ricker of Dover (N. H.).

Besides Ida Craddock, the necrology for this year includes Capt. Robert C. Adams, president of the Montreal Freethought Club, and past president of the Canadian Secular Union, who was born in Boston December 11, 1839, and died in Sedgwick, Maine, 1902. A comprehensive sketch of his useful and eventful life is given in Putnam's "Four Hundred Years."

CHAPTER XIV.

THROUGH an oversight on the part of my friends, relatives, and the public, I had never been the guest of a birthday party until the year 1903; so it was a novelty if not a surprise that on the 11th day of April a considerable company assembled at Skeetside in time to greet me with a series of pleasantries which they must have thought of in advance, when I came home from my day's work at the office. My clearest recollection of the occasion is that none of the visitors treated the affair seriously, but thought it best to recall my past with joke and jest.

The ministers of Montclair, N. J., where I have lived since 1900, issued in 1903 an appeal for better observance of Sunday. "We, the undersigned," they said, "have viewed with anxiety many signs of a growing laxity in regard to Sunday observance." The editor of The Truth Seeker, living in Glenridge, was at a loss to know what could be doing at the commuters' paradise so to excite the parsons. I supplied the information, which, having appeared in The Truth Seeker, was copied into a paper circulated in Montclair:

"People living near Skeetside, which is within the limits of

229

Montclair—southeast corner, next to the woods—could give the editor information on that subject, or he could have got it first-hand by dropping around there on the Sunday that the appeal was read in the churches. A busy scene, of an agricultural nature, was then presented to view. A horse that once galloped before the hosecart of the volunteer fire department, but had now got over his hurry, drew a plow through the soil of my garden and chewed stolen mouthfuls of grapevine. A neighbor, who owns the horse, followed the plow and chewed tobacco. At one side stood the neighbor's wife holding a baby, which chewed its thumb. Strung on the wire fence were a number of small children, chewing the last pieces of their breakfast, Soon, not far away, God's hired men would stand in their pulpits, chewing the rag of Sabbatarian controversy.

"It was a clear case of Sunday law violation, and a constable happening along would have caught the gang with the goods on. But I had my defense prepared. The work was one of necessity and charity: the garden needed plowing, and the man who plowed it needed the money. I doubt if the ministers could have put up as strong an argument as that for plowing the atmosphere with their voices."

The case for Sunday observance in Montclair is hopeless. The law might as easily stop automobiling as the work which householders from necessity must do about their premises on the first day of the week.

Under the provisions of a law passed in the craze for exterminating "anarchists" that followed the assassination of McKinley (although the complicity of any anarchist in the crime was never established), Secretary Cortelyou of the Department of Commerce and Labor caused the arrest of John Turner, at English labor agitator and organizer. Cortelyou said that Turner would be deported. In the interest of free speech The Truth Seeker took up Turner's defense, being joined therein by Manhattan Liberal Club members and the Free Speech League. Immediate action followed by Hugh O. Pentecost as attorney, with habeas corpus proceedings. It appeared from the arguments made before Judge Lacombe on a motion to dismiss the writ of habeas corpus that the demand for Turner's expulsion was based on the theory that labor unions are a menace to the republic. Bail was refused. The Defense Committee met at the residence of Dr. E. B. Foote, head of the Free Speech League, which was the predecessor of the present Civil Liberties Union. The League appointed a mass meeting at Cooper Union, to be addressed by Ernest Crosby, John DeWitt Warner, Henry Frank, and Congressman Robert Baker. John S. Crosby, the Single Tax leader, presided. In the list of vice-presidents there were, among others, Dr. Felix Adler, Henry George, Jr., Franklin H. Giddings (the Columbia University professor), and Oswald Garrison Villard, now editor of The Nation. William Lloyd Garrison wrote a letter.

This Turner case ran over into the next year, and the more it was discussed the more absurd it appeared. Turner was in a sense an Anarchist; that is, an idealist. He admitted that he disbelieved in organized government, but he was not one of the kind contemplated by the statute who advocated the overturning of government by force and the removal of heads of government by assassination. He just didn't believe in organized government, and even the conservative newspapers saw the humor of prosecuting or deporting anybody for what he did not believe in.

It was a queer feature of this Turner case that the bondsmen did not have to produce him or forfeit the bond, and he was under no compulsion to remain within the jurisdiction of the court. He had committted no offense in the United States for which he could be held. His crime was thinking the way he did before he came here, and for that he could only be chased back. If he chose to chase himself, the court was agreeable. And that is what he did. When he had stayed here as long as he wanted to, he went home to England. A decision in his favor would have done him no good. It was The Truth Seeker and the Free Speech League that wanted the favorable decision.

Miss Voltairine de Cleyre, an accomplished writer in poetry and prose, and also an eloquent speaker on radical topics, drew a pistol shot from a fellow named Helcher, which severely wounded her; but Miss de Cleyre declined to prosecute him at law for the assault, or even to identify him in court as her assailant. The Truth Seeker said of Miss de Cleyre's refusal to prosecute: "It is left to an Atheist to exemplify in this century the forbearance which his followers say Jesus taught two thousand years ago."

The Curtis Library of Meriden, Conn., accepted the offer made by Mr. Franklin T. Ives of a thousand-dollar gift on condition that the works of Voltaire and Paine should be placed on the library shelves for general use.

Judge Hazen of the Shawnee county court at Topeka, Kan., decided, Jan. 12, that compulsory attendance on prayers and Bible reading in the public schools does not violate constitutional rights. This was adverse to the plaintiff, J. B. Billard of North Topeka, whose son Philip had been expelled from school for not giving his attention to the religious instruction that preceded school exercises, and who sought the boy's reinstatement by the court. Mr. Billard took the case to the supreme court of the state to have the opinion confirmed.

When former Mayor Abram S. Hewitt died, Jan. 18, it was recalled that he was the only recent mayor of New York who "had the independence to refuse to raise a foreign flag on the City Hall"—to wit, the Irish flag on St. Patrick's day.

United Societies of Illinois in Favor of Taxing Church Property held conventions in Chicago. Secretary E. C. Reichwald of the American Secular Union was an officer. The united societies were Turnerbunds and workmen's unions. A deputation carried lists of untaxed property to the capital, consulted with the legislators, and reported to The Truth Seeker of March 14, 1903. The year following Mr. Reichwald wrote that "a large amount of property which previously had been exempted was added to the assessment roll."

The Bible having been excluded from the schools of Chicago, the ministers and pious women's organizations tried to get it back in the form of "selections." The American Secular Union, which had been instrumental in banishing the Bible, successfully opposed the readings, and they were rejected by the school trustees.

An independent party invited Clarence S. Darrow, then a member of the Illinois legislature, to be a candidate for mayor of Chicago. Mr. Darrow before accepting warned his proponents that if elected he would be unable to fulfill their expectations. However, he appears to have placed himself in the hands of his friends. Mr. Darrow was not elected mayor of Chicago. On the other hand, he took to wife Miss Ruby Hammerstein of Galesburg, Ill., a newspaper contributor of the pen name of Ruby Stanleigh. Of this The Truth Seeker approved.

The new "religious associations" laws of France were being put into operation. They required the associations to register and give a list of their inmates and property, while the religious schools were brought under supervision. Orders and schools not complying with the law were suppressed. Many of them went to other countries, one at least to take refuge in New York, but conditions existing prior to the adoption of the law have since returned through politics following the World War.

The German kaiser visited in state the Pope at Rome with the hope to assume the protectorate over Catholics theretofore exercised by France. The pope not being ready to offend France denied the Kaiser's application. The Church is still hopeful of bringing her eldest daughter to repentance.

Were I writing a work on special providences, I should include the following newspaper dispatch: "Reynolds's Bridge, Conn., June 23. — During a

thunderstorm George Norton's house was struck.
The bolt seriously damaged an old Bible, but dodged
a copy of Paine's 'Age of Reason'."

The Doukhobors (Spirit Wrestlers), called also
Tolstoy Quakers, made an unusual religious demonstration in Manitoba when they removed their
clothing and took to the road as a protest against
the breaking up of a pilgrimage they had previously inaugurated. It is one of the mysteries of religion why some women in their practice of it
should wear the all-concealing garb of a nun, while
others wear none at all.

Societies meeting were the Boston Freethought
Society, the Washington Secular League, the Lib-
eral Club, the Progressive Club, and Free Speech
League of Los Angeles, the Friendship Liberal
League in Philadelphia, the Manhattan Liberal
Club, and the Brooklyn Philosophical Association.
Pentecost lectured every week at Lyric Hall and
Henry Frank at the Carnegie Lyceum. Newark,
N. J. had a Truth Seeker Club, meeting at 17 Park
Street. Jewish Freethinkers in New York organ-
ized the Liberal Arts Society in the image of the
Manhattan Liberal Club. In November The Truth
Seeker reported: "The Liberal meetings in New
York these days are crowded." The American
Secular Union held no congress in 1903.

Stuart Robson, the actor, a friend of Ingersoll's
and a Freethinker, as his son told me, assigned to
himself the part of challenger of the clergy when
any of them alleged the morals of stage people to
be low. In order to answer in kind Mr. Robson
compiled a scrapbook, which in time grew to the

size of the largest dictionary, composed entirely of pieces clipped from newspapers, on the crimes and misdemeanors of the ministers. With this material ready to be quoted, he offered to prove to the incautious preacher that he had libeled a profession producing fewer criminals than his own. Mr. Robson died in May, 1903.

When Eliza Boardman Burnz, for seventeen years teacher of phonography in Cooper Union, went from Walters Park, Pa., June 9, 1903, to where the good Freethinking women go, the editor of The Truth Seeker paid his tribute of admiration to her "as a defender of the right and a zealous advocate of reform." Her advocacy ran along with that of this paper in its adhesion to freedom of the press, and her reform was the simplified spelling she induced D. M. Bennett to adopt. When she began teaching in New York, there were not half a dozen woman stenographers in the city. She introduced girls to the profession and "earned the proud title of Mother of the Young Woman Stenographer." She lived 80 years.

For many years New Hampshire's best known Freethinker was William C. Sturoc of Sunapee, who about 1900, being of sound and disposing mind and getting old, sent me a set of the poems of Peter Pindar (John Wolcott, 1738-1819), and the bound volumes of "Porcupine's Works" (Cobbett). Mr. Sturoc, Scotch by birth, practiced law in New Hampshire and served in the state legislature. His writings for The Truth Seeker were scholarly and precise. He died May 31, 1903, at the age of 80 years.

Mrs. Ingersoll's mother, Harriet E. Parker, died July 27 at Walston, Dobbs Ferry, New York. Mrs. Parker, née Lyon, Newton Lower Falls, Mass. in 1816, and her husband, Benjamin Weld Parker of Boston, were both of Bunker Hill ancestry. They moved west to Tazewell county, Illinois, where they raised Eva, whom Ingersoll married. They were a family of Agnostics, and Mrs. Parker could name Abraham Lincoln as one of the guests at her home.

One day in September, Capt. Silas Latham of the fishing schooner Ester and Anita, lying at anchor at Five Fathom Banks off Atlantic City, came on deck in oilskins and jackboots, to take the wheel while the men made sail, when a wall of water, mast-high, swept over the starboard bow, carrying away the foremast on which sail had been hoisted, and clearing the deck of everything movable, including the boats. The men forward, who had seen the wave coming and made themselves fast, climbed into the rigging and looked astern. The captain and two sailors were far away making a brave fight for life by swimming. Another great wave went over them and they were seen no more. Captain Latham, master and owner, was one of the most successful men in the fishing fleet that went out of New York. During the war he was a pilot of Union vessels in the South. On the subscription list of The Truth Seeker he was marked "Forever," and put his name down on all subscriptions. Once every season, in vacation time, he gave me a week afloat in his schooner. The fatal storm was a hurricane that wrecked many craft and drowned many men.

The founder of the New York State Freethinkers' Association in the early days of The Truth Seeker, H. L. Green, publisher of the Freethinkers' Magazine, died October 30 in Chicago. In his 75 years, begun at Virgil, N. Y., 1828, he had been farmer, log rafter, school teacher, lawyer, office holder, justice of the peace, and anti-slavery speaker. At his death T. B. Wakeman and Pearl Geer combined the magazine with their Torch of Reason and called the result The Liberal Review. Under that name it passed to Mr. M. M. Mangasarian and became an independent religious periodical, not long-lived.

An address on "The Life and Work of Herbert Spencer," before the Liberal Club, by Franklin H. Giddings, professor of sociology at Columbia, appeared in two sections in The Truth Seeker of November 7 and 14, 1903. Professor Giddings said: "Mr. Spencer rather than Mr. Darwin had given to the world the complete philosophy of evolution, of development. Mr. Darwin showed the evolutionary process of one particular sphere of natural phenomena, that of living beings, and he showed the working of one particular process in this mighty change, the process of natural selection, as it is called. Mr. Spencer has shown that the process of evolution is universal; that it pertains to the great starry systems of the skies from the nebula of gaseous matter; that it pertains to the long, slow development of the crust of the earth through geologic time; that it pertains also to the rise of social institutions and the development of man's mind, his laws, his customs, his governments, his morality, and his art."

Mr. Spencer died at Brighton, England, on the morning of December 5, 1903, in his eighty-fourth year.

The Liberal University of Silverton, Oregon, moved the first of the year 1903 to Kansas City, Mo., where it planned to reopen in October. The Northwest Business and Normal College of Salem took over the Silverton buildings and land. These facts, with the additional one that The Torch of Reason would thereafter be published in Kansas City, were communicated to The Truth Seeker by Mr. T. J. Tanner, then and now (1929) a Kansas City resident. At the same time Mr. D. Priestly of Newburg, Ore., wrote disparagingly of the institution, saying the Liberal University never had been so much as a good high school since the Hosmers were displaced, Mr. T. B. Wakeman now being the whole thing; and it sounded funny to Mr. Priestly, he averred, to call one man a University. Mr. Priestly resented Mr. Wakeman's circulating a petition against the seating of Reed Smoot, the Mormon senator from Utah. He was for years a continuous correspondent of The Truth Seeker, and when his letters ceased coming the editor wrote him to ask why. He replied that he was getting along in years, and had lapsed into silence with the idea that it was as well for a man to be forgotten for a little while before death as immediately afterwards.

My final Observation for the year appears to be the following: "At this season the public school teachers take upon themselves without extra pay the burden of familiarizing young minds with the story of the babe in the manger, illustrated by cuts. In a school near Skeetside, which is in New Jersey, the teacher showed a small boy an idealized picture of the holy infant, with the accessories of radiant star and effulgent nimbus. The boy looked at the display, and then asked if the child was really born on Christmas Day. The surprised instructress replied yes, of course, and inquired the reason for so strange a question. "Because," said the boy, "with an eye on the coruscating symbols, "I thought from the fireworks they are setting off he must have been born on the Fourth of July."

The desultory religious education given to the boys I have brought up left them free to form unbiased conclusions.

CHAPTER XV.

OFTEN The Truth Seeker has been admonished that its influence would be enhanced and its circulation widened if it would broaden its field. Naturally the admonition comes from persons who want it to broaden in the direction of the particular advocacy in which they are most interested; but since the paper does not so expand itself by thinning the original mixture, they remain cold. Should the broadening take place in some other way than theirs, they would denounce the editor for not sticking to his subject.

Long since the editor of The Truth Seeker discovered that he must carefully watch his step; that while he might not give his adhesion to all of the reforms proposed by radicals, he at the same time could slight none of them without hurting the feelings of a subscriber. Trial and error taught him that this principle held good as regards, for example, vegetarianism, prohibition, anti-vivisection, anti-vaccination, dress reform, woman suffrage. One section of his readers he might offend by writing down Socialism, another by aiming at Anarchism or the Single Tax. Expressed incredulity as regards the facts of Spiritualism invariably brings a rebuke conceived more in pity than in anger. The same of Buddhism. Finding that all reforms are at one against orthodoxy and conservatism, the editor arrived at his generalization—"the oneness of heterodoxies and the pervasiveness of Freethought in all reforms." They are all one, and Freethought is the constant factor.

Early in life Herbert Spencer went so far in reform as to take up vegetarianism—then regarded as a subtle form of Atheism—and although he later abandoned the error, which he held responsible for failing mental vigor, it had implanted the seeds of disbelief, and he died an Atheist to the gods of his generation.

Some one will correct me if I am wrong, but I think that every species of reform or fad, political or social, industrial or religious, has on one occasion or another swum into The Truth Seeker's ken and been remarked upon—unless it be medical reform which ought to be fortified with something more than opinion. Whether the editor's theory of the "oneness of reform" be verified or not, it still accounts for the wide circle of Freethought interests, of which those I have mentioned are in no wise a complete list. The circle includes many branches of science, evolution, eugenics, marriage and divorce, dietetics, family limitation, feminism, and so on.

The Truth Seeker had been prohibited in Canada since 1895, when in January, 1904, Postmaster Van Cott of New York, having thrice held up our Canadian mail, replied to the Editor's inquiry by saying that since the paper was undeliverable in

Canada, he could accept for transmission no copies addressed to that country. When the editor rejoined that the exclusion from Canada was based on religious grounds not recognized in the United States, Mr. Van Cott wrote that the matter would be referred to the Hon. First Assistant Postmaster-General at Washington· for an opinion. The functionary named, being R. J. Wynne, a Roman Catholic, and the excluding officials of Canada being Catholics likewise, the Editor's hopes fell. "Fat chance for favorable action there," he said. But Mr. Wynne promised he would refer the correspondence to N. M. Brooks, general superintendent of the foreign mail service. That he so referred it is doubtful, since in a short time Postmaster Van Cott of New York wrote again: "I beg to inform you that the Hon. First Assistant Postmaster-General (Wynne) directs this office to advise you that *the appeal made in your letter has been determined in your favor.* Copies may be presented for mailing as second-class matter at your convenience"! And Wynne a Roman Catholic!

The Editor learned that the appeal never left the office of Mr. Wynne, and that the Hon. First Assistant himself took the responsibility of making the favorable determination.

The Canadian prohibition has never been rescinded, but Mr. Wynne's successors have shown themselves poorer Americans than he was by consenting to it and ordering copies of The Truth Seeker bearing Canadian addresses to be stopped at the New York postoffice.

Herbert Spencer was recently dead, and between the powers of light and darkness there went on a struggle for the possession of his soul. The ministers paid Spencer posthumous honors as a near-Christian. But I quote from my Observation column:

"The struggle of the theologians to demonstrate that Herbert Spencer was really a promoter of religious faith is the most ineffectual form of pious endeavor that I have noted. The doctors of divinity have seldom started on any course where it was so easy to head them off. The Synthetic Philosophy is no religion. Any belief that is enough like religion to warrant passing the contribution box in its behalf must have a deity or a god who hears and understands when he is addressed in language. There has to be a god between whom and the worshiper it is possible that some sort of intelligible relations can be set up. Spencer claims no knowledge of anything like that. I doubt that there is the least excuse for thinking of religion when Spencer's philosophy is under notice, except to note that the philosophy contradicts religion, or for speaking of gods when his 'unknowable' is mentioned, farther than to remark that it is no deity. The Unknowable is not a He but an It, which cannot be worshiped or even blasphemed. John Fiske believed, or said he did, that Spencer was a friend of religion; but he was so only to the extent that one may do another a friendly act by showing him that he is a liar. Not long ago Mr. Goldwin Smith maintained, in a discussion with Dr. Moncure D. Conway, that Spencer was a religious man because he believed that veneration and gratitude are due to 'the ultimate essence of things.' Dr. Conway denied that Spencer ever expressed such a belief, but he bowed to the memory of Mr. Smith, who asserted that he recalled reading it in Spencer's writings. Nevertheless Dr. Conway was right. What Mr. Smith evidently had in mind was a passage in Spencer's discussion with Frederic Harrison, the Positivist. Harrison urged that veneration and gratitude are due the

Great Being, Humanity. Spencer acknowledged no such debt as owing in any direction, but said the obvious answer was that '*if* veneration and gratitude are due at all, they are due to the Ultimate Cause from which Humanity, individually and as a whole, in common with all other things, has proceeded.' Mr. Smith, thinking that religion needed the indorsement of Mr. Spencer, ignored the subjunctiveness of the clause and forgave him the 'if.' Harrison did the same thing, but Spencer protested: 'I have nowhere "proposed" any "object of religion." I have nowhere suggested that anyone should "worship the Unknowable." No line of mine gives grounds for inquiring how the Unknowable is to be sought "in a devout way," or for asking what are "the religious exercises"; nor have I suggested that anyone may find "consolation therein." '

"What the friends of Spencer, who are also friends of religion, should do is to dilate on the philosopher's service to the truth, and then, in a subsquent discourse, they may adduce proof, if any exists, that religion and truth are ei.her identical or bear any relation to each other. And they will find that the thing is not so simple as it looks."

One reason why Spencer apparently quit trying to correct men's erroneous beliefs about religion was that he realized it would be effort wasted. "In my earlier days," he said, "I constantly made the foolish assumption that conclusive proofs would change beliefs, but experience has long since dissipated my faith in men's rationality." Again: "If it be asked why, thinking thus, I have persevered in setting forth views at variance with current creeds, my reply is the one elsewhere made: It is better for each to utter that which he sincerely believes to be true, and, adding his unit of influence to all other units, leave the results to work themselves out."

One of Philadelphia's most prominent educators told a representative of the Philadelphia North American, May 2, 1904: "Andrew Carnegie is an Infidel."

"I don't believe in God," said Carnegie to a man who went to see him seeking financial aid for "God's work." But the ironmaster's disbelief, like Mark Twain's, took the form of irreverence. He perpetrated in that year 1904 a practical joke on Dickinson College, Carlisle, Pa., a Methodist institution. The college had lately lost one of its buildings by fire, and the mind of its president, Dr. George E. Reed, turned to Carnegie as the possible source of a contribution to erect a new one. Dickinson chanced to be the institution that in 1852 had bestowed the prefix reverend on Carnegie's admired friend, Moncure D. Conway; and so, notwithstanding Dr. Conway had dropped the ministerial title, turned Infidel, and was at the time in Rome as a delegate to the International Freethought Congress, Mr. Carnegie told the man who solicited his money in behalf of the Methodist seat of learning that he would subscribe fifty thousand dollars toward a new building if they would call it Conway Hall. The trustees consenting, the hall was built and named accordingly. The Truth Seeker chortled with unholy joy to see an institution founded in Calvinism in 1783 by John Dickinson, and taken over by the Methodists one hundred and twenty years later, pay this distinguished honor to a living Freethinker.

During 1904 Steven T. Byington, a scholar who

is now writing occasionally to the New York Nation, but then best known as a contributor to Benjamin R. Tucker's Liberty (being in general agreement with the opinions therein expressed), sent to
The Truth Seeker, in a letter of considerable length,
"A Challenge to Freethinkers." In the first part
of it he made the declaration: *"I suppose it to be
a fact that irreligious children of irreligious parents are likely not to be worth much"; and "I do
not seem to remember any case where one of irreligious parentage and education has amounted to
enough to be a credit to his opinions."* Mr. Byington named Pownall, Vermont, as an irreligious
town, or one where no church had ever thrived,
nor had intelligence or education developed much,
while it had been the scene of two whitecappings
within a short time. He evinced the purpose of
holding Freethought responsible for the low status of Pownall. Now not a soul in the town was
known to The Truth Seeker subscription list, nor
as a correspondent or purchaser of books; and
Pownall had no liberal society. There was no
Freethought community concerned here. Pownall
was to The Truth Seeker as Nineveh and Tyre.
But as to the offspring of Freethinkers, well, I
begged Mr. Byington to accept of one who
amounted to a plenty. To quote:

"There was a person once who challenged Colonel
Ingersoll to name an inventor of the last century who
was not a professor of the Christian faith. Ingersoll
might have mentioned more, but contended himself with
one—that profound Agnostic, as he called him, John
Ericsson, who thought out the Monitor and invented a
hundred patentable devices while building her.

"Now Mr. Byington craves the name of an irreligious man of irreligious parentage who amounts to anything. I shall follow the example of Colonel Ingersoll and offer him but one—CHARLES DARWIN. Darwin's father, Dr. R. W. Darwin, F. R. S. was a Freethinker, and Charles, a man of the first rank, an Agnostic, virtually an Atheist, who bestowed his name upon the century in which he lived—The Century of Darwin.

CHARLES DARWIN.

"For personal cause," so my Observation ran, "I speak upon this topic with modesty and reserve, for my mother, the parent I take after, is totally irreligious, and if my father had religious convictions, which I doubt, his opportunity to impart them to me was spoiled by the Civil War, which took him when I was an infant. And irreligious parents reared the angelic Being who condescended to marry me, so I and mine are in a position to be observed, if not counted."

Mr. Byington acknowledged that the parentage of my brother and myself tended to invalidate his theory, but that was all; he wouldn't have it that Darwin was the son of an irreligious man. Thus he compelled me to cite the bald facts. The truth behind my cataloging of Darwin as the offspring of a Freethinker was that in the year 1872 Mr. Francis Galton addressed a number of questions to scientific men on their nurture and nature. The questions related also to the nurture of the fathers of the persons addressed. In replying, Mr. Darwin described his father as a *"Freethinker in religious matters."* Those were the words Mr. Darwin chose. Question and answer are on page 357 of Vol. II, "Life and Letters of Charles Darwin."

And Darwin, himself a Freethinker, reared two sons, distinguished but showing no signs of sprouting any wings.

Mr. Byington forgot perhaps the daughters of Ingersoll. And then let him consider the Huxleys. Thomas Henry and his son Leonard and grandson Aldous, are the same class of evidence against the Byington theory. So is my contemporary Charles A. Watts, son of Charles. For that matter I can put two sons of my own on the stand. They bring no discredit to the opinions of their parents, and they are paying taxes that are doubtless split to salary the courts that put the products of religious education into our penal institutions. If religion-teaching parents would stock the earth for a generation or two with such men, then might be realized Mr. Byington's Tolstoyan ideal of the stateless life. He is, by the way, the only philosophical Anarchist I know of who retains faith in the Christian religion. The great body of Christians are archistic and are persuaded that in order that they may have eternal life, they must be their brother's jailer.

When this discussion arose, Clarence Darrow had not published his book of boyhood reminiscences, "Farmington." In that book Darrow revealed that he had inherited his religious views from his father; and his father, a subscriber to The Truth Seeker, was the village Infidel. So I brought Darrow forward for Mr. Byington to contemplate, and while on the subject gave him also Arthur Brisbane, whose father, Albert, was a radical, a close friend of Theron C. Leland, and their children playmates. Extending the inquiry, I found that the irreligious John Stuart Mill was the son of an irreligious father. Dr. Conway fortified me further, as below I wrote:

"I have now a new name, that of Francis William Newman, who was eminent enough to be classical leader in Bristol College and Latin professor at London University. He gave up Christianity in 1850, and wrote numerous anti-Christian books to explain why. One of these was 'Religion not History,' published when I was a youth by The Truth Seeker. Professor Newman inherited his unbelief, as is now for the first time made known to the world by Dr. Conway in his 'Autobiography, Memories, and Experiences,' which is a very valuable work on account of the extent to which it exposes the heresies of the great. In a letter to Conway, Newman said: 'I learned at last, as I came to be about seventeen, that my father was an entire Freethinker, as much as I am now.' The elder Newman was in fact an old follower of Thomas Paine."

On The Truth Seeker list are the names of worthy descendants of men who took the paper in their day and generation.

American Freethinkers had observed the birthday of Thomas Paine for more than half a century when the English Freethinkers held their first Paine celebration in 1904. A representative gathering met at Lewes in Sussex, June 8, to commemorate the 167th anniversary of his birth and the 95th of his death. (Lewes was Paine's place of residence from 1768 to 1774, when he came to America.) George Jacob Holyoake, Charles Watts, and Dr. Clair J. Grece were there to speak.

The 1904 International Congress held in Rome September 20-22 drew a large and distinguished attendance. America sent Dr. Moncure D. Conway as a delegate. Haeckel represented Germany; Lombroso, Italy; Berthelot, France; Maudsley, England; Hector Denis, Belgium; Bjornson, Norway; Novikov, Russia; Salmeron (ex-president), Spain. Haeckel and several of the others named were present; all were appointed honorary vice-presidents. More than five thousand delegates attended. The pope pronounced the congress "satanic" and shut up the Vatican while it was in session.   He also decreed a "solemn function of atonement for the outrage to Divine Majesty and for the vindication of the honor and good name of the city."

William Heaford and Joseph McCabe reported the event for The Literary Guide; Dr. Conway for The Truth Seeker. Prof. Ernst Haeckel communicated to the congress a plan for a universal Freethinkers' Alliance.

George William Foote, president of the National Secular Society of Great Britain, and editor of The Freethinker, returned to London to report that the gathering was a magnificent affair; yet it was not a Congress; it was a Demonstration.

The condition of the Freethought papers in 1904 showed a falling away. The Boston Investigator, established in 1831 by Abner Kneeland, and now being issued at a loss by L. K. Washburn, suspended publication on July 30 and turned over its subscription list to The Truth Seeker, Mr. Washburn signing up as contributing editor. Secular Thought, Toronto, Canada, hitherto for twenty years a weekly, now issued as a monthly, J. Spencer Ellis, successor to Charles Watts, continuing the editorship. The postoffice authorities revoked the second-class mailing privilege of Lucifer, the radical paper conducted by Mrs. Lillian Harman in Chicago, and ordered stamps on every copy; but the discrimination was short-lived. Joseph Symes, for two decades publisher of The Liberator, Melbourne, Australia, was compelled to discontinue. He gave as the reason, lack of support, the result

of bad times brought on by "mad legislation, whole-
sale sport, gambling, and Socialism in its most insane form." The Searchlight, successor to The
Independent Pulpit, survived at Waco, Texas, J.
D. Shaw publisher. Free Society, anarchist-communist, Chicago, announced its permanent suspension. On August 13 The Truth Seeker abandoned
the use of movable type, except for advertisements,
and shortly went "on the machines" of the Lecouver Press, where it has remained ever since.

Citizen George Francis Train, in whom the elements were so mixed as to make him an eccentric genius, died the 19th of January in his 75th
year. Mr. Train, who was a non-Christian, spoke
many times from the Liberal Club platform and
had spells of writing for The Truth Seeker. On
the irrational side, he believed himself destined to
immortality of the flesh, and fancied he possessed
a force which he called "psycho" whereby he could
control the actions of others and exercise powers
over life and death. As a promoter of great
schemes in railways and shipping, he made a fortune and lost it.

The distinguished English Agnostic, Sir Leslie
Stephen, an associate of the Rationalist Press, died
in London, February 22, at 72.

Since Senator George F. Hoar of Massachusetts had contributed occasional articles to The
Truth Seeker, he may be mentioned as one of its
correspondents lost by death. He passed away
September 30, in his 79th year. He was one of
the great senators of his generation.

The American Secular Union and Freethought Federation called the 27th congress of the society to meet at St. Louis, October 18, in connection with the International Freethought Congress, for a five days' session. Of this gathering The Truth Seeker says editorially:

"The International Congress for Progressive and Liberal Thought, in conjunction with the annual congress of the American Secular Union and Freethought Federation, held in St. Louis, Mo., from October 15 to October 20, was not, as was the Rome congress to some extent, rendered unwieldy by its size, nor hampered in its deliberations by confusion of tongues. Although, as was to be expected of an international congress, especially one held under the auspices of the Freie Gemeinde, there were present many to whom English is not native, all the proceedings were had in that language. The business and deliberative sessions were held in the pleasant Freie Gemeinde Hall. The 'propaganda mass meeting' took place in the Olympic Theater. The attendance was large and representative, the deliberations were wise, the addresses able, the speakers eloquent, the hearers enthusiastic.

"The event of the Congress was, of course, the receipt of Professor Haeckel's proposal for a Monistic Alliance, which he had caused to be rendered into English for presentation before the St. Louis gathering. It will be found on the second and third pages of this number of The Truth Seeker" (Oct. 29, 1904).

The allies of the Secular Union at this meeting were of German antecedents, as their names indicated. The Committee on Organization was composed of Leopold Saltiel, Ad. Falbisaner, Prof. Geo. Kral; on credentials; George Fritz, Selmar Pabst, Henry Heider.

The Congress elected as officers for the ensuing year: E. M. Macdonald, president; E. C. Reichwald, secretary; E. B. Foote, treasurer. The editor said: "The Congress was a success as regards attendance, enthusiasm, and those other features which have made previous congresses successful. Professor Haeckel's contribution has made it memorable."

The proposition of Haeckel related to a Universal Monistic Alliance—that is, an alliance of all freethinking societies as Monists. "The Philosopher of Jena, the Darwin of Germany, is the most eminent man," remarked the editor, "who has ever offered 'a thesis of organization' for the guidance of Freethinkers."

The fundamental principle of Monism, based on experience, reason, and science, is the unity of the world. It contradicts the theory of two worlds, the material world or nature, and a spiritual or supernatural world, as inconsistent with modern science. The body and soul (psyche) have the same origin and are the products of evolution as we know them. The opposite theory is founded on defective knowledge of reality, confused thinking, and mystical tradition. Organization on this thesis was mainly confined to Germany, where it became a considerable cult, with the adhesion of many educators and men of science.

For the first time in history, a Sunday ball game between professionals was played in New York on April 17. Freethinkers hailed the event as promising, being "the widest breach yet made in the sabbatarian walls." The Sundayites hastened to close it, and succeeded, with the aid of timid politicians, in reducing the breach to the playing of games to which no admission fee was charged.

In The Truth Seeker of May 28, 1904, first appears the name of Edward Tuck as a contributor to the paper's sustaining fund. He is credited with $100. Mr. Tuck is still giving.

Within a week of the time I am writing this, the public has been disturbed by a great marine disaster, the sinking of the steamship Vestris with the loss of upwards of one hundred lives. One day in June, 1904, the excursion steamer General Slocum burned in the East River above Hell Gate and more than a thousand perished. "Where man is powerless, heaven cannot save." That was an appropriate quotation regarding the tragedy, because this was a Sunday-school picnic under the auspices of St. Mark's Lutheran church in Sixth street, Manhattan. About fifteen hundred persons went aboard; the bodies recovered, mostly of women and children, with those that were missing, numbered 1,040.

The following Observation from The Truth Seeker of October 15, 1904, has historical interest because it concerns a man who later became a good Freethinker:

"I am invited by the Rev. J. R. Slattery of Baltimore, Md., to send him the names of my departed relatives and friends, inclosing twenty-five cents, and in return for the same, as I grasp the proposition, he undertakes that two 'novenas of masses' shall be said or done for the repose of their souls. As a kind of feeler he forwards a small envelope containing five thin aluminum 'medals' which, as I learn from the printing outside, are 'blessed.'

John R. Slattery was at that time a priest at the

head of a Catholic institution in Baltimore. A few years later he began reading The Truth Seeker, and in 1910 was a contributor. Slattery as a priest was an amateur; that is, he played the game because he liked it, supposing it to be square. An educated woman lent him Herbert Spencer; he read "Ecclesiastical Institutions," saw that the church was a system for exploiting everybody but the higher clergy, and not being dependent on the church for a living he got out of it—all as simple, he said, as taking off the clerical collar. He turned Rationalist, not an anti-clerical, who is often only an inverted Catholic. He knew the church from the inside—was familiar with the system, knew some of the bishops' mistresses; knew the habits of the priests, and allowed them to be neither better nor worse than other men with their limitations and opportunities. He thought many of them would jump the job if they could better themselves. It was like going into politics. The priests were as good as the politicians, he supposed, and the calling of one was as "sacred" as the other. To regard the nunneries as "brothels" he held was absurd. The women who went into them had generally "missed their man" because they were unattractive—had no lure and maybe no desire. The boss women among them might have their favorite priests; but priests had the run of the parish; the good-looking ones enjoyed themselves, and perhaps needed more address to avoid intrigues than to get one going. Lively ladies made a lark of their confessions and put ideas into the head of their confessor.

CHAPTER XVI.

FREETHOUGHT to an important extent takes the form of protest against various sorts of stealing and of dishonesty practiced in the name of religion. I have told of the "Methodist Steal South"—a huge appropriation procured from Congress, by false pretenses and plain lying, for the Methodist Book Concern in Tennessee. The Truth Seeker of 1905 chronicles a Catholic Steal West. It was during the Roosevelt administration, when before the Senate Committee on Indian Affairs, January 31, Senator Bard of California disclosed that, by direction of the President, funds appropriated by Congress for Indian schools had been diverted to Catholic and other sectarian institutions in violation of the law. The sum involved was upwards of one hundred thousand dollars. Roosevelt at once denied that he "directed" the misappropriation, though admitting he approved it. That the proceeding was in violation of the law, as Senator Bard declared, no one took the trouble to deny. The Catholic church then had in Washington an agent, or lobbyist, one Dr. E. L. Scharf. The senator from California stated that he had been approached by Dr. Scharf with the proposal that if the Republicans would agree to bring about the

legislation permitting the diversion of Indian trust
funds to the Catholic schools on reservations, the
Catholics would see that twenty congressional districts in which the Republicans were weak were
carried for the party. Senator Bard would not assent to the deal, but it caught Roosevelt and was
passed to his credit as a politician. The United
States attorney-general had pronounced the appropriation illegal. Roosevelt was obliged to explain
his approval of the steal, which robbed the Indians
of their funds and gave them to the church. His
explanations did not explain. The law against the
misappropriation was unmistakable, but the church
kept the money. It soon became apparent that
Roosevelt had adopted the policy of patronizing
the Catholics. A list of his appointments of them
to government positions would fill a page. A two-
column article in The Truth Seeker for August 19,
1905, sets forth the facts, then publicly known, now
ancient history, which were dwelt upon in later issues as further evidences of Roosevelt's truck-
ling to the Catholic element accumulated. The press
paid no attention to the religious complexion of the
appointees, but in many instances exposed their incompetency.

The worst sufferer from press censorship in 1905
was, as usual, Moses Harman. Exclusion from the
Canadian mails came first, and then arrest on a
charge of depositing prohibited matter in the mails
of the United States. The Free Speech League of
New York took up the defense. Lucifer printed essays on sex reform, which the editor of The Truth
Seeker said were "mostly tommyrot and hogwash,"

but had no obscene words in them. The articles were
"physiologically puerile and sociologically impossible," yet powerless to injure the morals of anybody. It was an infamous injustice, the editor declared, to "imprison a man like Moses Harman for
printing some foolish stuff from writers who mean
well even if they do not know much." A grand
jury indicted Harman and at the same time found a
true bill against Dr. Alice B. Stockham, a public
speaker, a writer on medical themes, and author of
"Tokology," "Karezza," and other works on the
marriage relation. The courts convicted in both
cases, and both appealed. Meanwhile Lucifer was
suppressed or censored. The Truth Seeker printed
the judge's charge in the Stockham case as "interesting in its moral stupidity." Clarence Darrow
appeared for the defendants, who were fined $500.

George Bernard Shaw came out nobly in Harman's defense, condemning comstockery in America and priding himself that he lived in "a comparatively free country." That was Mr. Shaw's delusion, for every instance of triumphant moralism
in America can be paralleled in England. London
had just suppressed Maeterlinck's latest play, destroyed an edition of Balzac, and sent a translator of
Zola to jail. The tragedy of Ida Craddock in
America was duplicated by that of Miss Allonby in
England. That country had prosecuted the sellers
of Havelock Ellis's works and so set a precedent for
banning them in the United States. The magazine
called The Adult suffered over there the same as
Lucifer here. England once prohibited Paine's

works, and a century later sent G. W. Foote to jail
for blasphemy. And there have been later instances,
so that on the whole England and the United States
are about equally afflicted with church-bred moral·
ism.

We probably got one lap ahead of England when,
in 1905, the New York police forced Arnold Daly
to withdraw Shaw's play, "Mrs. Warren's Profession," from the boards of the Garrick Theater as
"socialistic," and the public library put all of
Shaw's books on the restricted list. Dr. Felix Adler
of the Society for Ethical Culture, arguing that there
is much going on that we can afford not to know,
approved the stopping of the Shaw plays. Dr.
Adler always was nervous in a moral crisis.

Mrs. Helen Wilmans Post, the "mental science"
practitioner of Sea Breeze, Fla., convicted of using the mails for fraudulent purposes in the conduct
of her business as a long distance healer, was sentenced to a year and a day in prison, but appealed
her case and won out in a higher court. Mrs. Wilmans deemed it an instance of religious persecution,
she being a known Agnostic and her prosecutors
orthodox Christians.

The Free Speech League had in Washington a
scout, Dr. Pfeiffer, who reported occasionally to
The Truth Seeker. The Freethinkers were backing
E. C. Reichwald, secretary of the American Secular Union, in suits he had brought to enjoin the use
of school buildings as places of worship and of
school children for congregations.

The foregoing show what I mean when I say
that the job of Freethought forces is mostly oppos-

ing various sorts of thefts and similar practices in
the name of religion.

In Los Angeles a serious attempt made by Singleton W. Davis to establish a magazine of Rationalism resulted in The Humanitarian Review, begun
in May, 1904. Mr. Davis was his own editor and
compositor. He conducted The Humanitarian Review for about eight years, until overtaken by the
infirmities of age and obliged to suspend. But that
was not a prosperous era for journals of opinion.
The Banner of Light, aforetime Liberal Spiritualist,
had turned more or less rel'gious.

Three lectureships were announced in New York
at the beginning of 1905. Hugh O. Pentecost spoke
every morning in Lyric Hall (now, I believe, called
Bryant Hall) and Henry Frank at Berkeley Lyceum.
On Tuesday evenings, James F. Morton, Jr., lectured at Clinton Hall. Pentecost's lectures were
regularly reported for The Truth Seeker. Dr. E. A.
Wood of Syracuse reported the organization of a
local Secular Society with fifty members. In August
Mrs. Marilla M. Ricker, one of the first woman
lawyers to be admitted to practice in the United
States Supreme Court, called a convention of the
New Hampshire Secular Union to meet in Dover,
the city of her residence, for an Ingersoll's birthday
anniversary celebration. Another lawyer, Anson
G. Osgood of Manchester, president of the society.
Lemuel K. Washburn of The Truth Seeker, Carl
Burell, noted botanist, Frank W. Coburn of New
Durham, and Mrs. Ricker were the speakers. The
International Freethought Congress was held this

year in Paris, September 4-7. Very largely attended
—for three thousand delegates from nearly every
country in Europe were there—it resembled the congress of the previous year at Rome in being badly
managed and thrown into disorder by the quarrels
which socialists and anarchists had brought there to
be settled. One feature of the meeting was a great
success. That was the organization of a parade past
the statue of Chevalier de la Barre, a young man of
19 who was brutally tortured and k:lled in the days
of Voltaire for not saluting a religious procession.
There were one hundred thousand persons in this
parade. America sent no delegate. The reports of
Bradlaugh's daughter Hypatia and Editor G. W.
Foote of the London Freethinker were copied in
The Truth Seeker of October 7. In this, the fifth
season of M. M. Mangasarian's Independent Religious Society of Chicago, his congregations had outgrown the Grand Opera House and necessitated removal to the new Theodore Thomas Orchestra Hall,
with a capacity of 2,500 persons.

The Truth Seeker for 1905 contains, I think, the
first contributions by John D. Bradley—a column of
Sunday Enforcement News. I understood from the
editor that these reports were compiled for the
Seventh-Day Adventist press and exchanged with
The Truth Seker for certain books. It is also
understood that these books so obtained by Mr.
Bradley had something to do with his ceasing to be
a Seventh-Day Adventist. John G. Palmer of
Pennsylvania wrote that he was recently turned
down and refused a school, as teacher, because his

views were not orthodox. Mr. Palmer, nearly a quarter of a century later, st'll occasionally writes to The Truth Seeker. You cannot keep a good man down. He holds a judicial office. There is a letter, September 23, from Chas. C. DeRudio, Major U. S. Army, retired. Major DeRudio, a constant reader for years, had a career as thrilling as that of any soldier of fortune. The Saturday Evening Post published it a few years ago.

An Ohio man named Cyrus Sears communicated with the paper a long time before we found out he was a Civil War hero, cited and promoted for valor.

On May 1, 1905, the office of The Truth Seeker, ending 18 years' tenancy of 28 Lafayette Place, removed to 62 Vesey street, up one flight, and so within a few doors of the Lecouver Press at No. 51, where the paper already was printed. The floor at No. 62 had lately been occupied as a pool room and prepared with "refrigerator" doors in expectancy of raids by the police. The reputation of the loft was revealed when the editor made application for a telephone. That must aforetime have been a sporting locality. Our office was discovered by Christopher Morley of the Evening Post (No. 20 Vesey street), who commented facetiously on the truth being so accessible—only one fl'ght up. The rent, begun at $50 per month, kept climbing until it reached $150, when it was cheaper to move.

Morgan Robertson, the nautical story writer whose literary career began with the Log of Noah's Ark in The Truth Seeker, invented in 1905 a device that he called an "invisible searchlight." This was the periscope used on submarines. The Holland Submarine Boat Company took up the invention. Robertson applied for a patent, seeing a fortune ahead, and bade farewell to literature. But the patent never came out, the office in Washington having discovered that Jules Verne had mentioned some contraption whereby the crew of a submerged vessel were able to look about them above water. It was ridiculous that another story teller, who invented nothing but tales of impossible voyages, should have dashed the fortunes of a real inventor, but the wise men of the Patent Office allowed it to happen, and Robertson, disappointed, returned to the spinning of yarns.

There occurred this year a wordy discussion of the sex of angels. The Episcopals building their Cathedral of St. John the Divine on Morningside Heights employed sculptor Gutzon Borglum to create some angels for the Belmont memorial chapel, and he produced two beings which the Episcopal building committee declared to be females and as such unauthorized by holy writ. One of the beings had been conceived to represent the Angel of the Annunciation, commonly called Gabriel. In defense of his non-masculine piece of work, Mr. Borglum said he could scarce imagine that a male person who was not a family doctor would be sent to tell Mary of her condition and to discuss how it had happened; hence he had omitted sexual characters, whiskers and so on, as far as possible. He also left out the female curves. Yet they detected femininity in the plaster cast and said it would never do. Mr. Borglum yielded and smashed the models, but maintained that the idea that God sent a man to tell Mary she should bear Jesus was too gross for him, and anyway he was astounded, absolutely, that any clergyman could stand in the presence of images of a purely religious and spiritual character and see nothing in them but sex. Perhaps he had not done much work for ministers.

The ministers were scripturally sound. Biblical angels are men antagonist c to race suicide. It might be "gross," as Mr. Borglum said, to send a man on so delicate a mission as that of the Angel Gabriel to Mary. Yet such was the custom. One came to notify Sarah, mother of Isaac, and likewise to her who was to bear Samson, one of the predecessors of Jesus as a messiah. Those doubtless were angels who were called sons of God in the sixth of Genesis; they had the angelic habit of seeing the daughters of men. Following their appearance, units were added to the population of Judea. I wrote a three-column article on angels, evidencing a knowledge of the subject which I do not now possess.

The climax of all Paine celebrations that had been held since the beginning marked Saturday, October 14, 1905. That was the occasion of the rededication and assignment to the care and custody of New Rochelle of the Thomas Paine Monument on North street, erected in 1839 by Gilbert Vale and other Freethinkers and since kept in repair and supplied with a bronze bust of Paine by the liberals of New York and the country at large. For upwards of sixty years the monument had stood in a small inclosure at the southeast corner of North street and

the lane that led therefrom to the Paine residence
or farmhouse, a little way back.

The art of sculptor Wilson MacDonald had supplied a fine bronze bust of Paine to surmount the
shaft. Now the town of New Rochelle had brought
the monument out of its obscurity and placed it almost on the curb of the main avenue (North street)
and rounded the corners of the lane so as to make
a small "park" with roads on three sides of it. To
quote from a description written at the time: "The
monument itself is much better situated than formerly. In the middle of Paine avenue (for so the
lane is called), it is on more elevated ground, has
a raised and curbed walk about it, and is immediately surrounded by a yet more elevated base and
an iron fence." The city council of New Rochelle
which had prepared the new site, expressed a readiness to take title to the monument and care for it
in the future. The Freethinkers organized a Society with Moncure D. Conway as president to hand
it over. There were present at this day of celebration representatives of the Army and the National
Guard and the Sons of the American Revolution.
The army post at Ft. Slocum sent a band and a bat-
talion; the National Guard a battery of five guns,
which unlimbered in an adjacent field and roared a
salute. The town turned out, and a parade led by
Minute Men and Continentals, and including the
school children, came up North avenue between
residences displaying the American flag on staffs or
at their windows. Then music by the band, singing
by the school children, a speech by the Mayor, and
addresses by the chairman, Dr. E. B. Foote, Theo-

dore Schroeder, and T. B. Wakeman. I quote another paragraph: "The addresses had been interspersed with music by the Fort Slocum Band. The children had sung 'America,' 'Columbia the Gem of the Ocean,' and had begun the last number but one on the program, which was 'The Star Spangled Banner.' Hats were off now, and before they could be got on again, one of the cannon over in the field spoke its word for Paine and the hills were reverberating. It was a salute of thirteen guns, one for each of the original states."

That was a great occasion, like a Fourth of July new risen or Independence Day.

The Rev. Wilbur F. Crafts, who for long had canvassed the country as a promoter of blue Sunday laws, established in Washington, D. C., an International Reform Bureau, otherwise known as "The First Christian Lobby." His tools in Congress were Senator Gallinger of New Hampshire and Representative Gillett of Massachusetts who let him use their franking privilege to mail his literature of Reform. The Washington correspondent of the New York Herald (July 17, 1905) smoked out the scheme and exposed the scandal of it. The correspondent estimated that Mr. Crafts' business by mail had amounted to thirty-five tons of matter, transported at a public cost of $6,300, the reverend reformer being that much to the good through the use of the congressional frank. It was not so bad as that, according to letters that Crafts sent to The Truth Seeker, but the fact remained that he had been working both the Government Printing Office and free mailing privileges to distribute his documents.

*The New Ro-
chelle Memorial
to Thomas
Paine.*

The exposure did the First Christian Lobby serious harm. Since the death of Crafts the Methodist Board of Temperance, Prohibition, and Public Morals has functioned in his place.

In the fall the Rev. Dr. Algernon S. Crapsey, an Episcopalian minister of Rochester, N. Y., having gone beyond the requirements of his ordination vow by telling the truth about the Bible, was accused by a brother clergyman of preaching "erroneous and strange doctrines contrary to God's word." Thus began a famous heresy case which ended in the conviction of Dr. Crapsey.

The bill for the separation of church and state in France, passed by the Chamber of Deputies in July, was adopted in the French Senate on December 6 and became a law. It did away with a concordat which for more than a century had regulated the relations of the civil power to religion in France and reduced the public worship budget by about eight million dollars.

The French law so seriously curtailed the privileges of the church that there was a considerable exodus of the sisterhoods, many of them establishing themselves in the United States, where their surviving members exercise the franchise.

The death list of well-known American Liberals in 1905 contains the name of Watson Heston, who, beginning in 1886, made pictures for The Truth Seeker, with a short interruption, for twelve years. He was a native of Ohio, and 59 years old when he died in Carthage, Mo., Jan. 17, 1905.

There was no congress of the American Secular Union in 1905.

CHAPTER XVII.

THE TRUTH SEEKER in 1906 published weekly a column of lecture and meeting announcements. Five or six of the meetings held were in New York. Elbert Hubbard was touring in season, discoursing on such mordacious themes as "Respectability: Its Rise and Remedy," and running a list of his engagements in the column. Jack London also was speaking. The advocacy carried on by the "social science" and "liberator" groups, who supplied the paper with their notices, had little to do with Freethought and Secularism. In a national way, organized Freethought was quiescent; the American Secular Union not functioning beyond the publication of the "Report of the International Congress for Progressive Thought and of the Twenty-seventh Annual Congress of the America Secular Union and Freethought Federation" (1904). This work contained Haeckel's Letter to the Congress; his Theses for Organization; addresses by John E. Remsburg, Judge C. B. Waite, Moncure D. Conway and others.

Freethought organization was marking time. Of such work as the American Secular Union had done under the presidency of Putnam and with E. A. Stevens for secretary, there was nothing to report. Nevertheless Volume XXXIII of The Truth Seeker preserves some of the most interesting history in our annals. There was a notable heresy trial. The standing committee of the Diocese of Western New York brought formal charges against the Rev. Dr. Algernon Sidney Crapsey, alleging that Dr. Crapsey denied and impugned the doctrine that Jesus Christ is God; or was begotten by a ghost or born of a virgin who knew not a man, or rose from the dead after suffering death by capital punishment and then being buried. The trial came off at Batavia before an ecclesiastical court that followed the procedure of Judge Benedict in Comstock cases, ruling out the testimony of experts prepared to testify that Crapsey's opinions were not heretical as compared with those they held themselves. Convicted and suspended, Dr. Crapsey appealed to the Court of Review, and that tribunal, sitting at the Clergy House across Lafayette place from The Truth Seeker office, confirmed the verdict and gave the doctor thirty days to repent.

To gain the distinction of a convicted heretic this was the worst that Crapsey could say:

"Jesus did not succeed because he was born of a virgin or because he was reported to have risen bodily from the dead. These legends concerning him are the result, not the cause, of the marvelous success of the man. These stories were told of him only because the simple folk could in no other way adequately express their conception of the greatness of Jesus. Only a virgin-born could be as pure as Jesus. Only a life more powerful than death could have the strength of Jesus. The creeds of Christendom are of value not as historical statements, for primitive and medieval Christians had no historical sense

Looking for another heresy action, the Baptists made public demand for the dismissal of Prof. George B. Foster, an instructor in Chicago University, who had written a book on "The Finality of the Christian Religion." The trustees failed to act in the matter and Dr. Foster carried on.

The law for the separation of church and state in France now going into effect, the pope cried "persecution." The law provided that the clergy and the members of a given parish might organize themselves into an "association" and lease from government the property belonging thereto. Such a transaction required that an inventory be made, which the church refused to permit. The priests, charging the faithful that it would be sacrilege to "number" church property, rallied the strong-arms, the toughs, the fanatics, and the enemies of the republic who called themselves royalists, to resist the officers of the state. They said: "Who is going to put a renting price on the host and the sacraments?" Catholics have a quick conscience when asked to carry out a civil law or any order at the expense of things consecrated. At about that time there was in Chicago an organization of the building trades that detailed members to dynamite structures erected with "scab" labor. The McNamara brothers belonged to this union, and it fell to one of them to blow up a Catholic church that had employed non-union hands. But the McNamaras were Catholics. The delegate insisted on knowing first whether the church had been consecrated, and when he found that mummery had

been performed he asked to be excused. Consciences like that defeated the Associations law
in France, as they have made the separation laws
of Mexico hard to enforce.

Moses Harman, editor of Lucifer, Chicago, went
to Joliet, March 1, to begin serving a year's sentence for printing something unorthodox in his paper. A long petition for his pardon went to President Roosevelt, who by denying it missed his chance
to say: "That which I am about to do is a better
thing than I have ever done." He missed the
chance to dignify a life that on the whole was a
footless splurge, with one generous act for the future to applaud.

The Christian Advocate published a letter
ascribed to Benjamin Franklin, as written "To
Thomas Paine." The Truth Seeker showed why
the letter couldn't be anything of the kind; that it
might not have been written by Franklin and certainly not meant for Paine. Thereupon Editor
Buckley of The Christian Advocate dispatched a
"commission" to Washington to examine the original manuscript on file in the Department of State.
What the commission reported added no strength to
the contention that Franklin wrote the letter to the
author of the "Age of Reason." In the controversy that ensued, Dr. Moncure D. Conway took
part; and that all readers might judge for themselves whether the letter justified the "To Thomas
Paine" title, reproduced it as it was alleged to have
come from Franklin's hand:

"Phila., July, 1786.[1]
"Dear Sir: I have read your Manuscript with some

Attention. By the Arguments it contains against the Doctrine of a particular Providence, tho' you allow a general Providence, you strike at the Foundation of all Religion: For without the Belief of a Providence[2] that takes cognizance of, guards and guides & may favour particular Persons, there is no Motive to Worship a Deity, to fear its Displeasure, or to pray for its Protection. I will not enter into any Discussion of your Principles, tho' you seem to desire it; At present I shall only give my Opinion, that tho' your Reasonings are subtle, and may prevail with some Readers, you will not succeed so as to change the general Sentiments of Mankind on that Subject, and the Consequences of printing this Piece will be a great deal of Odium drawn upon yourself, mischief to you, & no Benefit to others. He that spits against the wind, spits in his own Face. But were you to succeed, do you imagine any Good would be done by it? You yourself may find it easy to live a virtuous Life without the Assistance afforded by Religion, you having a clear Perception of the Advantages of Virtue & the Disadvantages of Vice, and possessing a Strength of Resolution sufficient to enable you to resist common Temptations. But think how great a Proportion of Mankind consists of weak & ignorant Men & Women, and of inexperienced & inconsiderate Youth of both Sexes who have need of the Motives of Religion to restrain them from Vice, to support their Virtue, & retain them in the Practice of it till it becomes habitual, which is the great Point for its security. And perhaps you are indebted to her originally, that is to your Religious Education, for the Habits of Virtue upon which you now justly value yourself. You might easily display your excellent Talents of reason on a less hazardous Subject, and thereby obtain Rank with our most distinguished Authors.[3] For among us, it is not necessary, as among the Hottentots, that a Youth[4] to be received into the Company of Men, should prove his Manhood by beating his Mother. I would advise you therefore not to attempt unchaining the Tyger, but to burn this Piece before it is seen by any other Person,

whereby you will save yourself a great deal of Mortifica-
tion from the Enemies it may raise against you, and perhaps a good deal of Regret & Repentance. If Men are
so wicked as we now see them with Religion,[5] what would
they be without it? I intend this Letter itself as a Proof
of my Friendship & therefore add no Professions of it;
but subscribe simply   Yours,   B. F......."

Notes on the Letter

1. July, 1786.—The date is given on the authority of Henry Stevens of Vermont, an antiquarian,
who collected Franklin papers. It is uncertain,
the writing in the original being obscure. At that
time Paine and Franklin were meeting daily and
were therefore under no necessity to communicate
by letter. In his fourth "Letters to American Citizens" Paine said: "In my publications I follow
the rule I began with in 'Common Sense,' that is,
to consult nobody, nor to let anybody see what I
write till it appears publicly." He began the writing of his "Age of Reason" in Paris, 1793. Franklin had died in 1790, three years earlier.

2. This is poor literary criticism. Paine's arguments are against the Bible and the Christian
system, not Providence, general or particular,
which is not brought up in the "Age of Reason."

3. Already there was not a more distinguished
author in America than Paine. Franklin writing
to Paine might conceivably warn him against risk-
ing the loss of the rank he had won, but he could
not ignore it.

4. Paine was no "youth" in 1786, being 49 years
old.

5. Franklin's religion, if he had one, was not

the Christianity that Paine argued against. The discarding of that Christianity could not be regarded by Franklin as a parting with all religion.

The view persisted in by the Christian miseducators, that Franklin rebuked Paine for writing the "Age of Reason" seven years before Paine began on the work—is contrary to Franklin's own habits of thought, as shown by a bit of biblical criticism in which he indulged. Franklin observed that the commandment "Increase and multiply" was in the Old Testament, and so preceded that other injunction: "Love one another," and he held that the precept which was last in order in the scripture should come first in practice.

During the summer of the year now under review my old Californian friend John Beaumont wrote the editor inquiring: "Where is G. E. M. now?" He had seen no Observations in the paper for quite a while. The editor replied: "G. E. M. at the present moment is hibernating at Skeetside putting the finishing touches on A Short History of the Inquisition, which we are to issue this fall." It was a book of above six hundred pages which the editor had held in mind for some years, and E. C. Walker had made a stack of copy for it. But Mr. Walker had written little about the Inquisition. He had done three hundred pages on Protestant Persecutions, the Warfare of Religion and Science, and the Attitude of the Church Toward Slavery—very valuable matter, but not Inquisition. In the spring of 1906 the Editor suggested that I should get together the necessary "bibliography," express the authorities and reference books to Skeetside, and stay with them until the history was done. I did so, and in the course of the season produced a quantity of manuscript equal to the contribution of Walker, which is to say enough for another three hundred pages.

For imparting information, neither the reading nor studying of history can compare with trying to write it. My "history" of the Inquisition unveiled to the writer, myself, some curious facts and led to unforeseen conclusions. For instance. The school histories teach that the good and pious Queen Isabella of Spain, having hypothecated her personal jewelry, gave Christopher Columbus the proceeds and said to him: "Take this, my all, and go and discover America." It may be rude to give a lady away after she is dead (so I wrote in 1906), but the records of the Inquisition show that while Isabella may have slipped the money to the great navigator, she had previously drawn an order on a Jewish gentleman for the coin. The fact is that when either Isabella or her husband Ferdinand needed funds, they had only to mention the circumstance to a Jew who possessed the amount required, and, as the phrase is, he came through with the mazuma. He knew there was no use in his saying he hadn't got it, nor any idea where to look for so much money, for if he made that excuse their royal majesties would reply: "We will see if the Inquisition cannot help you find it"; and following that the Jew would wake up some morning in the donjon of the nearest Robbers' Castle provided by the inquisitors for the entertainment of their guests.

On the morrow his property would be confiscated and in due time sold to the speculators in real and personal estates, and the money from the sale covered into the royal treasury minus as much as had stuck to the hands of the chief inquisitor and his subordinates, all of whom were thieves. Later on, maybe, he would get some sort of a trial before the Board of Conviction called a tribunal, but the inquisitors attended to the liquidation of his property first. The charge of heresy was enough to warrant the confiscation of his goods. Often their majesties, Ferdinand and Isabella, preferred to deal directly with the wealthy Jewish subject, as they had found there was an appreciable percentage of waste when the estate of a heretic was administered upon by the functionaries of the Holy Office. Luis Santangel, a man of Jewish lineage and antecedents who financed Columbus in the discovery of America got it "coming and going," for after Isabella had borrowed his ducats the Inquisition penanced him and took what he had left.

In 1905 Judge Brewer of the United States Supreme Court published a book to substantiate his dictum in a case brought under the Alien Contract Labor law, that the United States is a Christian country. The judge based his argument on the ground that the discoverers of America were Christians. He did not know, and it would not have affected his conclusion if he had known, that a heretical Jew paid the bills.

In March the English Princess Ena, on the point of marrying the king of Spain, went into the Roman Endowment House at San Sebastian a member of the Church of England and came out a Catholic, having in the process recorded her belief that the other Battenbergs and the rest of the royal family would be damned.

At the marriage of the Princess to Alfonso in Madrid, a crazy Anarchist named Morral threw a bomb into the wedding procession with fatal results, although it missed the newly-weds. The authorities discovered that Morral had once written to Francisco Ferrer asking for a place as librarian in the Modern School that Ferrer, with the aid of a wealthy lady, had established in Spain. There was no other basis for the action of the Spanish authorities, instigated by the church, in arresting Ferrer, closing his Modern Schools, and robbing him of all the funds at his command. Except for protests from scholars and humanitarians the world over, Ferrer would have been courtmartialed and shot. It was only a three years' reprieve. They got him in 1909.

"The long and useful life of George Jacob Holyoake, the Father of Secularism and pioneer in many important political and industrial movements, reached its close at Brighton, England, on January 22. He died at the age of 89 years, full of honors, beloved by thousands, and respected by the world." The "Secularism" which Mr. Holyoake fathered (about 1846) consisted of a system of ethical and social principles not dependent for their sanction or in any other way upon religion. The word "Secular" gives a name to the national society of

GEORGE JACOB HOLYOAKE

Mr. Holyoake was known to his contemporaries as the
Father of Secularism.

Freethinkers in England that Charles Bradlaugh headed a dozen years after Holyoake introduced the idea. At his maturity, Mr. Holyoake, a militant Freethinker in his younger days and a prisoner for Atheism, took up economics in the form of cooperative trade. But The Truth Seeker says that he "died the same radical and agitator that he had been through more than two generations."

Almost as full of years as Holyoake and equally deserving of public honors, Mrs. Lucy N. Colman died at her home in Syracuse, N. Y., on the 18th of January. Her age was 88. Mrs. Colman left the New England church she had been born into, and all other churches, because of their "complicity with slavery," and she was a fellow-worker with the abolitionists. She joined with The Truth Seeker in its endeavors toward the abolition of Anthony Comstock, whom she heartily despised, and kept in touch with the paper for a quarter of a century as a reader and contributor.

Editor Charles C. Moore of the Blue Grass Blade, previously known to these memoirs, departed this life at Lexington, Ky., February 7, in his seventy-second year. Moore had been a Campbellite preacher. He served one term in jail for libeling a church, one for fighting, and one for advocating "free love." He narrowly escaped another for violating the obscenity statutes, and a fifth for blasphemy.

These annals must chronicle the fact that Charles Watts of England, of whom I have said so much of an appreciative nature, died on the

night of the 16th of February, 1906. Having been
born at Bristol on February the 27th, 1836, he was
almost seventy years old. His first lecture, delivered at the age of 14, was entitled "The Curse of
the Nation and Its Remedy." It was an attack on
the demon Rum. At about the same period he
grew to be a favorite amateur actor, and never lost
his interest in histrionics. At that era also he
heard a lecture by George Jacob Holyoake and went
into Secularism for life. There are said to have
been years when he averaged more than a lecture
a day. He was with Bradlaugh on the National
Reformer, with Holyoake and W. Stewart Ross
on The Secular Review, with Foote on the Freethinker more or less, and with J. Spencer Ellis on
Secular Thought in Canada. Although Bradlaugh
preceded him on a visit to the United States, his
mission was political and Watts was the first English Freethinker "to cross the Atlantic and mount
the American Freethought platform."

Mr. Watts was equally fortunate in his son
Charles Albert, with whom also there was "no one
like Dad," and who by founding the Rationalist
Press Association effectively continues his father's
work.

The colaborer and eulogist of Mr. Watts, W.
Stewart Ross, who took the pen name of "Saladin," failed to live out the year, and died November 30. This writer of force and fire was a Scot,
born in Galloway in the year 1844.

"With the death of Miss Susan B. Anthony de-
parts the last of the trio of great women who
brought the woman suffrage cause to the front —

CHARLES WATTS.

Mr. Watts, a great lecturer and debater in his day, was the father of Charles A. Watts, founder of the Rationalist Press Association.

Susan B. Anthony, Elizabeth Cady Stanton, and
Matilda Joslyn Gage." To the mention of this trio
The Truth Seeker of March 24, 1906, adds the reflection: "There are no other women engaged in
the work who at all approach them in ability." Susan's departure took place from Rochester, N. Y.,
March 13. The three able women were Agnostics.

When Peter Eckler, printer of Ingersoll's works,
died in Brooklyn, May 1, in his eighty-fourth year,
he had been associated with New York Freethink
ers for six decades—ever since 1845. He knew
Gilbert Vale, who erected the Paine monument in
New Rochelle about 1840. I have heard that he
published a paper called The Age of Reason.

The pioneer Liberal lecturer of the Pacific coast,
Dr. James L. York, "passed to a higher life," as
his fellow Spiritualists believed, from San Francisco on July 12. He had lived 76 years and devoted at least thirty of them to lecturing. I never
heard him speak. Samos Parsons of San Jose told
me that Dr. York was a Son of Thunder.

As though the necrology list for 1906 were not
long enough already, we must add the death of
Dr. E. B. Foote, the "grand old man" who for a
quarter of a century and more had been sought as
protector of all unchampioned victims of the Comstock censorship. He had lived to be 79 years old,
and might have exceeded that age but for a sun-
stroke suffered while attending a medical meeting
in the West. He had survived nearly all of the
New York Old Guard who worked with him in
the nineteenth century. One—T. B. Wakeman—

was left to give the funeral discourse, but except Lillie Devereux Blake and David Hoyle there was none in the gathering that listened to it. An ample biography of Dr. Foote is in Putnam's "Four Hundred Years of Freethought." His son, "Dr. Ned," printed a Memorial pamphlet, in which I reminisced at some length about his worthy senior. He was fortunate in having a son after his own heart to follow him in the field of free speech. I have already, somewhere, set down the regrettable fact that the name of Foote as borne by the grand old Doctor is extinct; no one living bears it as his descendant. The administrators upon his affairs, and those of Dr. Ned, appear to have regarded me as in some way the repository of his memory, since they sent me his large terra cotta bust to keep it present to my own. My name, I reflect, will share the fate of Dr. Foote's, for the grandchildren are all girls. However, there is no bust to be rolled in mats and consigned to an alien attic.

The Belgian (by birth) Dr. Felix Leopold Oswald, a graduate from the Brussels University in 1865, an author of numerous health books and two Freethought works, "Secret of the East" and "Bible of Nature," stepped by inadvertence in front of a train at Syracuse, N. Y., on September 29, and was killed. He had reached the age of 60 years.

I shall not have so many deaths of the Freethought captains to report in 1907. There are not so many left.

The public library of Brooklyn placed Mark Twain's "Tom Sawyer" and "Huckleberry Finn"

on the restricted list of books accessible only to
"patrons who have attained a certain degree of
maturity." This drew from Mark the well-known
sentiments he held on the Bible. One of the libra-
rians, Don Dickinson, who had voted against the
decree, wrote him soliciting something in favor of
the proscribed books and got the following reply:

"The mind that becomes soiled in youth can never
again be washed clean. I know this by my own experience, and to this day I cherish an unappeasable bitterness
against the unfaithful guardians of my young life, who
not only permitted but compelled me to read an unexpurgated Bible through before I was fifteen years old. None
can do that and ever draw a clean, sweet breath again
this side of the grave.

"Most honestly do I wish that I could say a saving
word or two in defense of Huck's character, since you
wish it, but really in my opinion, it is better than those
of Solomon, David, and the rest of the sacred brotherhood.

"If there is an unexpurgated Bible in the children's
department, won't you please help that young woman
remove Tom and Huck from that questionable companionship?"

The San Francisco earthquake, followed by a
disastrous fire, was an event of 1906. All the Almanacs say the disaster took place on April 15 at
5:14 o'clock in the morning, that three hundred
lives were lost in the city and neighboring towns,
and that this was the worst earthquake shock ever
felt in the United States. Some of the phenomena
were remarkable, as for instance this: that "the
monument to James Lick, Freethinker, in front of
the City Hall, was unscathed by fire or quake, while
all about it was in ruins." Again, the destroying

elements left scarcely a "house of God" standing, while sixty barrels of whiskey belonging to a whole-sale liquor dealer named Hotaling, although in the midst of the burned district, came through without starting a bung. A member of the Bohemian Club perpetuated the miracle in deathless verse:

> "Now if the good Lord spanked the town
>   For being over frisky,
> Why did he knock the churches down
>   And save Hotaling's whiskey?"

The idea of trial marriage had its birth in the year of grace 1906. Mrs. Elsie Clews Parsons, daughter of the banker Henry Clews and wife of Congressman Herbert Parsons, wrote a work on "The Family" with a passage running: "It would therefore seem well, from this point of view, to encourage early trial marriage, the relation to be entered into with a view to permanence, but with the privilege of breaking it if it proved unsuccess-ful," and so on. The bright idea helped to sell an otherwise unstimulating book.

Hugh O. Pentecost, counsel and defender in free speech cases and lecturer for the Unity Society, was his own client when he went one Sunday to Schenectady and, while in the midst of an address on "Our Dangerous Classes," was placed under arrest by a local peeler for doing business on Sun-day. Held in $50 bonds for appearance on the following day, he defended himself in the magis-trate's court so successfully that the judge let him off. At the same time the court fined J. Franz, who had brought Pentecost to Schenectady, $10.

The Rev. Charles T. Russell, founder of the International Bible Students and Russellite sect, in 1906 fixed the date of the millennium, or the second coming, otherwise a new dispensation, as the year 1914, and was drawing large numbers after him, when Mrs. Russell exploded a scandal by suing him for divorce in the courts of Alleghany, Pa. Mrs. Russell named two corespondents, a girl appearing in the record as "Rose" and another as "Emily." Newspapers gave wide currency to a remark attributed to Dr. Russell by his wife. It ran: "I am like a jellyfish; I float around, and touch this one and that one, and if they respond I embrace them." The accused Rev. Russell conducted his defense in Zion's Watch Tower, printing a double number to bring out all the facts. It required considerable space to explain away Rose and Emily, to vindicate himself in the light of 1 Cor. vii, 1, and to show that his actions had been misconstrued.

The same year that other prophet, Alexander Dowie, founder of Voliva's Zion City, Illinois, blundered into similar complications and others. Alas for prophets! Dowie's fate was a girl he picked up somewhere and christened his "Little Lump of Gold."

There was an observant Freethinker in Detroit in 1906 named E. G. Weber, who was alert for news to send The Truth Seeker. One of his best contributions concerned that year's pilgrimage of Detroit Catholics to the historic miracle joint known as the shrine of St. Anne de Beaupre at Quebec, in quest of health. A Detroit priest, the

Rev. Father Van Antwerp, had in past seasons acted as local press agent for the shrine as well as organizer and personal conductor of the pilgrimages. This year also he headed a large party of the faithful who set out hopefully for the joint. But just before they reached Quebec the Rev. Van Antwerp complained of not feeling well, was in fact taken sick with some ailment not specified, and instead of keeping on to the shrine, where the cure to which he was guiding his flock awaited him, he hastily returned to Detroit and placed himself in the hands of a doctor, who was quite likely to have been an Atheist scoffer at the bone of St. Anne.

That genius of the drama, Henry E. Dixey, heard that the Young Men's Christian Association of Pittsburgh, Pa., had refused membership to an actor on the ground that one of the "profession" could not be a moral person. Mr. Dixey thereupon offered to give a thousand dollars to charity if, by showing there were more of them in the penitentiary, it could be proved that actors were less moral than ministers; and he ventured another thousand that there was no state in the Union without its preacher in jail. A newspaper polled the prisons to test Mr. Dixey's judgment. The returns, which indicated that he would have lost had anybody taken him up on his second proposition, were highly unreliable; for while they gave 43 ministers in jail to 13 actors, they revealed "no clergymen" in a number of states where ministers had lately been sent to jail for serious offenses. Still the Pittsburgh Y. M. C. A. never called upon Dixey to deposit the money.

The Rev. Mr. Torrey, an evangelist of some reputation, took on an assistant liar for his spring revival in Philadelphia. Known as the Rev. Dr. K. W. Kumm, F.R.G.S., and professing to have been "formerly a pupil of the great philosopher, Ernst Haeckel," the recruit described a recent call upon Haeckel at his home in Jena, when the aged scientist made confession that about many things he had changed his mind and would have to change many statements in his books. The Rev. Kumm expected Haeckel openly to confess Christ and come to Jesus publicly as he had privately.

Haeckel's exposure of the Kumm person followed at once. From Jena, April 9, he wrote:

"The curious story of my Christian conversion, told by Dr. Karl Kumm, in the meeting of the Torrey-Alexander mission, and quoted in the newspapers the 27th of March, is a pure invention of Dr. Kumm. I do not remember the visit (two years ago), and certainly I never said to him that I had given up my monistic conviction. That has always remained the same since fifty years ago. I am quite convinced that I shall never be converted to Christianity.

"I am not eighty-five but seventy-two years of age, and have today the same monistic philosophy which you know from my books. The false report that I have completely changed my monistic conviction arose from the falsifications of a Jesuit reporter. He telegraphed on the occasion of my first Berlin lecture, April 14, 1905, to London and New York that I recognized the error (instead, the truth) of Darwinism, etc. . . .

"You will find the whole story of my personal development and my scientific activity in the new book, just published by T. Fisher Unwin, London, 1906, 'Haeckel, His Life and Work.'   ERNST HAECKEL."

CHAPTER XVIII.

THE noisiest individual in the United States was President Roosevelt. About June, in Everybody's Magazine, he raised a disturbance over the animal-story writers, the "nature-fakers," as he called them. He mentioned by name Jack London, C. G. D. Roberts, Ernest Thompson Seton, and the Rev. William J. Long. To give their books to children, said he—why, it is an outrage. "If these stories were written as fables, published as fables, and put into the children's hands as fables, all would be well and good. There is no more reason why the children of the country should be taught a false natural history than why they should be taught a false physical geography." He had incorporated an Ananias Club, and London and the rest were elected by acclamation.

Some fellow at the Socialist headquarters in San Francisco quoted: "And I saw a beast rise up out of the sea having seven heads and ten horns," and asked Roosevelt how John the Revelator compared with the Rev. Dr. Long as an expert in natural history. He rejected as ridiculous some author's fancy about a wolf guiding lost children home, and I asked him to consider this: "And

Elijah the Tishbite . . . went and dwelt by the brook Cherith, and the ravens brought him bread and flesh in the morning, and bread and flesh in the evening." Was it any more improbable that children should get out of the woods by following a wolf than that crows should bring meat sandwiches twice a day to a preacher?

On the nature-fakers Colonel Roosevelt never acknowledged enlightenment, but he soon offended the clergy and had to reverse himself. Under his directions the late Augustus St. Gaudens had produced a design for new coins, leaving off the words "In God We Trust." When a specimen appeared from the mint the ministers made a loud clamor, accusing the President of "an unchristian act." He made a long defense on religious grounds. Said he:

"Everybody must remember the innumerable cartoons and articles based on phrases like 'In God We Trust—for the other eight cents,' 'In God We Trust—for the short weight,' 'In God We Trust—for the 37 cents we do not pay,' and so forth and so on. Surely I am well within the bounds when I say that a use of this phrase which invites constant levity of this type is most undesirable."

However, he invited Congress to direct him to replace the motto, which Congress immediately did. A history of the inscription, how it happened to be on the coin in the first place, is given at length in The Truth Seeker of November 30, 1907. Roosevelt's reason for removing the motto was whimsical and could not stand against the opposed whim of the clamant ministers.

Dr. Rufus K. Noyes published a fine large book; there were 800 pages in it, printed on costly paper with gilt edges, entitled "Views of Religion." The views, given in above six thousand quotations, were all liberal ones; it must have taken the doctor years to collect them. L. K. Washburn published it at $5.

On the 17th of February, anniversary of the burning of Giordano Bruno by order of the Inquisition, a procession made up of 10,000 persons marched through the streets of Rome, and halted in the Campo del Fiori to deposit wreaths on the Bruno monument. That was before the days of Mussolini, one of whose first acts was to break up the Giordano Bruno society.

Robert Blatchford, publisher of The Clarion, Socialist, began printing Freethought articles. He knew nothing of Freethought history or traditions, not even, apparently, that it had other advocates than himself. When Mr. Blatchford had withdrawn the support of Freethinkers from their established press, he went over to God and Spiritualism.

Under the head of "A Vindication of Religious Equality," The Truth Seeker reported that by about a three-fifths majority the United States Senate voted, February 20, to retain in his seat Senator Reed Smoot of Utah, whose expulsion had been demanded on the ground that he was a Mormon. The fight against Smoot had lasted since his election in 1903.

One of the yarns that make up the sermons of evangelists came to the hearing of a Mr. C. J. Ferguson, a Freethinker of La Crosse, Wisconsin, by way of W. E. Biederwolf, who conducted a rev:val in that town. The story ran that Infidels once founded a town in Minnesota, providing in the charter that the name of Jesus Christ was not to be mentioned within its limits except in blasphemy or vulgarity. The rest of the story ran:

"The town was burned down. It was rebuilt. It again burned down. It was again rebuilt. Then it suffered from an Indian massacre. It again flourished and was once more destroyed by fire. Then the inhabitants sent in great haste to the East for a missionary to come and preach to them the gospel of Jesus Christ. Today the place is prosperous and happy; the spires of the churches of God point heavenward," etc.

Evangelist Biederwolf bragged that if in La Crosse there was an unbeliever who doubted the truth of what he had related, he would take him to the place, paying his carfare, and prove to him that every word he had said was true. Mr. Ferguson wrote to the evangelist, inquiring the name of the Infidel town and accepting the invitation to visit on the terms stated. Biederwolf delayed his reply until he was ready to leave La Crosse for Chicago. He omitted to name the Infidel town, but being further pressed revealed that it was New Ulm, Minn., settled in 1854 by Freethinkers. However, investigation conducted by Mr. Ferguson showed that it had not been burned down; that there had been an attack by Indians, and afterwards a devastating cyclone. But the name of Jesus had never been excluded, nor had his followers. The people never sent for a missionary. In fact, religious people came early, of their own accord, and erected churches which the cyclone either destroyed or seriously damaged. Biederwolf's account was to all intents and purposes a manufactured lie.

A. M. Roos of Lamberton, Minn., submitted the following facts: in 1881 New Ulm was visited by a cyclone, which destroyed a large part of the town and killed thirteen people. One of the peculiar features of this storm was that it razed every church in the town, while Turner Hall, known as the temple of Freethought, was practically unhurt. Of the thirteen killed, not one was a Freethinker.

"Shortly after the cyclone, a preacher at Grinnell, Iowa, in a sermon, told how New Ulm was destroyed by the wrath of God; how Infidels were killed and their properties destroyed, while the churches and the properties of the faithful were saved. A few years later a cyclone struck the town of Grinnell, when the Congregational church was destroyed and the pastor who made the above statement was killed."

New Ulm is the publication place of Der Freidenker, begun in 1870.

One looking for a record of organized activity in 1907 will find little of it. In April the American Secular Union addressed the Illinois legislature to protest against the tax exemption of clerical residences. Secretary Reichwald and his voluntary co-worker, Mr. E. P. Peacock, had kept up an agitation against the Bible in the schools. A December paper recorded that Reichwald had won, defeating the efforts of the Women's Educational Union, and that "neither the Bible nor any other book of a religious character would be introduced as a text book in the Chicago public schools." Except for a fine large congress of Bohemian Freethinkers held in Chicago the 13th to 15th of June, there was no foregathering of Secularists.

Francisco Ferrer, founder of the Modern School in Spain, who with no scrap of evidence against him had been arrested in 1906 for complicity in the bomb outrage at the king's nuptials, was so ably defended that at his trial the next June three "hand-picked" judges were obliged to acknowledge his innocence, give a verdict in favor of his acquittal, with costs, and recommend the removal of the embargo on his property.

For years a decoration on the wall of The Truth Seeker office was a photograph of Mr. J. F. W. Copenheaver, a Pennsylvania subscriber, with wife and children. There was one wife and sixteen children, all of them born since Mr. Copenheaver began taking The Truth Seeker. An old school teacher, he left that profession for want of the reputation for piety required in Pennsylvania. He became so atheistic as not to believe in vaccination, and rather than subject his children to innoculation he withdrew them from school, organized them in classes, and taught all grades himself. They made a good-sized school for a country place. Not all the rural schools of the day had an attendance of sixteen.

About 1875 a subscriber named John Hart of North Troy, N. Y., began to mention his age when renewing his annual subscription. He loved to

recall that as long ago as 1840 he attended meetings at Broadway and Grand street, New York,
and heard addresses by Benjamin Offen, Ernestine
L. Rose, and Robert Dale Owen. The Freethought
papers of his younger days were The Regenerator,
published by Orson S. Murray; Abner Kneeland's
Investigator; Robert Dale Owen's Free Inquirer;
and Gilbert Vale's Beacon. Men appeared to be
able to live to a great age and defeat race suicide
without embracing the Christian system. The relatives of John Hart did not notify us of his death,
and The Truth Seeker had no record of him aftei
he was 104.

A list of forgotten Liberal papers would include
"Here and Now, a Journal of Freethought," a
monthly begun by Dr. J. E. Roberts at Kansas City.
The following named "magazinelets" came to The
Truth Seeker office: The Papyrus, Michael Mona-
han, editor, East Orange, N. J.; The Swastika,
New Thought, by Dr. Alexander J. McIvor-Tyn-
dall, Denver, Col.; Reason, Spiritualist, B. F. Aus-
tin, Rochester, N. Y.; The Live-Forever Magazine,
Harry Gaze, Boston. To these add The Philistine,
Elbert Hubbard, East Aurora, N. Y., the most
famous of the list.

A religious caricature of George Washington in
the form of a placque and representing the Father
of His Country kneeling in prayer at Valley Forge
was stuck on the front of the Sub-Treasury Building in Wall street through the connivance of the
Y. M. C. A. and Secretary Edwards of the Treasury Department.

The Army and Navy Journal called the thing "a ridiculous fiction in the trappings of a pious fraud." If ridicule could have any effect on enduring bronze, the placque would have been laughed off the front of the Sub-Treasury. But it had stuck there for twenty years when the absurd Post-office Department at Washington transferred an engraving of it to a two-cent postage stamp known while it lasted as the Valley Forgery.

The sort of liberal religious writers and preachers known as Modernists appeared at about the time of which I am writing. The Holy Roman and Universal Inquisition had issued an encyclical giving a syllabus of the truths which were to be anathematized (T. S., August 17, 1907). The progressive Catholic scholars who declined to be committed to the pope's position published a pamphlet entitled "The Program of the Modernists," and his holiness replied with a decree forbidding the faithful to read it and excommunicated its anonymous authors. So the original Modernists were Catholics.

Helen Wilmans Post, who had seen trouble with the postal authorities on account of her absent treatment by mail, discontinued in December the publication of her persecuted magazine devoted to the conquest of death. Mrs. Post held that only those need die who lack the will to live.

The Cooper Union addresses of Prof. Franklin H. Giddings of Columbia University were reported in The Truth Seeker. His last for the year was on "The Jew in America." The professor said it was because of the scientific interest of the Jews that America was opened to the European world. "It is part of the record, it is part of the traditional teaching anent the voyage of Columbus," he stated, "that the first individual of his party actually to land on American soil was a Jew." Tradition gives the name of the particular individual who came first ashore as Luis de Torres.

In Austin Bierbower of Chicago The Truth Seeker had an occasional contributor, the philosophy and humor of whose writings in these days should have brought him a lasting fame which I am afraid he missed.

The Chicago and Zion prophet, John Alexander Dowie, died in 1907 in such circumstances that none was there left to do him reverence or preserve his memory. He had lately made a tour of the world, and while in India had predicted the end of Mohammedanism and of the reign of its prophet, whom he called the prince of impostors. But in Qadian, Gurdaspur, in the Punjab, a successor to Mohammed had arisen known as Mirzah Ghulam Ahmad. This chap, who had a considerable following, as in fact he has to the present day, challenged Dowie to a prayer contest, each to pray for the downfall of the other, and the one who died first should be regarded as the loser. "Pray to God," he said, "that of us two whoever is the liar may perish first," and of Dowie he said: "He shall leave the world before my eyes with great sorrow and torment." When Dowie died, Mirzah triumphantly claimed the decision. He died a few months later.

HUGH O. PENTECOST (1847-1907).

On the death of Ernest Howard Crosby, January 3, a New York woman said: "Ernest Crosby is dead, and there are one hundred and fifty-five thousand two hundred and three preachers left alive!" Ernest was the heretical son of a bigoted Presbyterian preacher and had a record as a radical social reformer. The woman who spoke as above looked to the editor for a comment on this dispensation. He explained that "when it came to picking out the fellows to go, the Lord didn't seem to know his business." Mr. Crosby died at 50 years.

Death came to Hugh O. Pentecost on February 2, when he was 60 years old. Hugh had a brother who was a widely known evangelist, and a New Thought wife, and they gave him a funeral from which his Liberal associates were excluded. The brother, George F. Pentecost, officiated. The mourners sang "Nearer, My God, to Thee." During his brief illness the household sent word to his Lyric (later Bryant) Hall congregation that no visitors or messages would be received, and a rumor gained currency that in the end he had "caught another glimpse of the eternal verities." Nobody believed a word of it. Pentecost's real funeral, attended by a thousand, took place in the hall where his meetings had been held.

Pentecost in his lifetime preached all things to all men, from Calvinism to Atheism, and from Socialism to Anarchy.

As a speaker in Lyric Hall to the congregation gathered by Pentecost, John Russell Coryell continued the meetings. He was as radical as Pentecost, but more of a writer than a speaker. He and W. J. Terwilliger, calling themselves the Corwill Co., issued a weekly that contained his Sunday talks. It was known as "The Wide Way."

M. Marcelin Berthelot, the French scientist and Freethinker; Karl Blind, German republican and Freethinker; Walter Richard Cassels, Englishman, author of "Supernatural Religion"; Gerald Massey of London, poet, archeologist, Freethinker, and political reformer—all these closed lives of honor and usefulness in 1907. And just as the year was going out it took by the hand Lewis G. Reed, an old contributor to The Truth Seeker, and so led him from sight. Mr. Reed was 92. He and his family were people of Surry, N. H. Some of them were the town's benefactors, founding a library there not far from fifty years ago. His granddaughter wrote: "There could not have been a more beautiful end to anyone's life than his. He was perfectly happy and ready to go, and lay there waiting for the end. Although he knew he was dying, he was still the same as he had been all his life. It was a great pleasure to receive from The Truth Seeker a little poem of his which was handed to him on his deathbed." He had written his own funeral song.

When I had finished the necrology of 1906, I said in my haste that the list would not be duplicated, but death has a way of making forecasts and promises vain. On August 14, in Washington, D. C., died Gen. William Birney at the age of 88, and on August 17 all the members of the Washington Secular League, with his fellow Freemasons, representatives of the school board, and his colleagues of the Bar, came to bury him. General Birney was born at Huntsville, Alabama, May 28, 1819. His father, James G. Birney, the abolitionist, was twice the Free Soil nominee for the presidency of the United States (1840 and 1844). William Birney, for many years a member, was more than once president of the Secular League. Dr. J. J. Shirley and Hyland C. Kirk were his funeral eulogists. The general spent years in France, and what he observed there qualified him to write the series of

articles he contributed to The Truth Seeker while
the excitement was on over the abolition of the
concordat with the pope and the separation of
church and state.   During our Civil War, when

MONCURE DANIEL CONWAY (1832-1907).

the government assigned him to the duty of enlisting and organizing colored regiments, and he recruited from the slave pens of Baltimore, Secretary
of War Stanton called him to Washington to explain his activities in setting black men free. Unfortunately the general wrote no autobiography.

The death of Dr. Moncure D. Conway took away
a member of The Truth Seeker family. It befell
him in Paris, November 25, 1907, just after he had
written the editor he was returning to America.
Dr. Conway was 75 years old (born March 17,
1832, in Stafford county, Va.), and the physicians
attributed his death while asleep to the weakness
of old age. Conway was the first Christian minister to preach a laudatory sermon on Thomas Paine
—the result of his attending a Paine anniversary
meeting of Cincinnati Freethinkers about 1860.
Thirty years later he wrote the standard Life of
Paine, and in 1894 edited and published Paine's
Complete Works. I made his personal acquaintance
a few years later by discovering a copy of the "Age
of Reason," of which he said in the London Athe-
næum, August 27, 1898: "If there are or were
other copies it appears unaccountable that none of
Paine's contemporary editors and biographers, such
as his friend Rickman in London and Fellows in
New York, should have known nothing of these additions and facts, and that I myself should never
have discovered the existence of such a work while
searching in the chief libraries and archives of
Paris, London, and America." After I had owned
this unique copy of the "Age of Reason" for some

months, I, one week, being short of material for
the Letters of Friends column, used the unique matter for a filler. Conway saw it in the paper, and
called to see the book and its owner. After that
his connection with The Truth Seeker was close.

Dr. Conway's life is well documented with his
"Earthward Pilgrimage," his "Pilgrimage to the
Wise Men of the East," his "Memories and Experiences," and so on. He was a good observer,
who wrote with a flawless diction.

CHAPTER XIX.

THE religious confidence-people in 1908 made their fight to have restored to the coins of the nation the motto "In God We Trust," which President Roosevelt had removed out of respect for God, because it was a joke. The battle fiercely raged. In their desperation the *pro deos* circulated the report that a conscientious minister in Pennsylvania had spurned a gift of one hundred dollars in gold from his congregation because the coins did not bear the motto. Freethinkers refused to credit the report, alleging that the age of miracles was past—if there ever was an age so miraculous that a preacher would refuse money. The minister himself vindicated their skepticism by denying that his congregation had even offered him the gold. In Congress Representative Morris Sheppard of Texas made a speech that filled three columns of The Congressional Record, mostly a reply to The Truth Seeker's reminder that acknowledging the deity on the coin of commerce was a defiance of the injunction of the savior that "ye cannot serve God and Mammon." Mark Twain ridiculed the pious motto by saying that ever since it was dropped the country had been obliged to de-

pend on J. P. Morgan. Representative Knowlton
of California urged irreverently upon the congressional committee having the matter in charge that
clearing house certificates and notes of hand ought
to be engraved: "I know that my redeemer liv-
eth." Representative Moore of Pennsylvania, sustaining the agitated Sheppard of Texas, read into
the record a piece from The Truth Seeker where
it was said that there are a lot of people who do
not trust God in financial matters; that they know
nobody else does who is sane, and therefore they
do not see why every coin issuing from our mints
should carry forth to the world this official lie.
That was all a year's protest by The Truth Seeker
accomplished—to get a part of one of its editorials
into The Congressional Record; and Representative Moore didn't even have the fairness to name
the paper he was quoting from. Congress passed
the restoration act, the President signed it, and the
incident was closed. God, if such was Christ, had
declared to them in advance that the proceeding
was unlawful, but Congress and the President
didn't trust him.

While things took this turn in the United States,
they went the other way in Italy. I quote from
an article published January 25 to this effect:

If at the beginning of the last quarter of the nineteenth
century somebody had told us that the generation then appearing would live to see an Atheist elected mayor of
Rome, we should have disregarded him and set down his
prediction as an extravagance into which he had been betrayed by his ignorance of history. But he would have
been right. Ernesto Nathan, whom an aldermanic vote

of 60 to 12 has just made mayor of the pope's city, is an Atheist. More than that, while his mother was an Englishwoman, his father was a Jew!

The Catholic press, with a strange want of that tolerance which it recommended as a high virtue in America twenty years later when a Catholic was standing for President of this secular Republic, denounced the election as "absurd, monstrous, anomalous, incredible." The Truth Seeker remarked that times appeared to have changed since the days when Jews from various parts of Europe were making pilgrimages to Rome to beg at the feet of the pope, and to purchase with the remnants of their fortunes a dispensation which they mistakenly supposed would protect them from persecution by Catholics.

Acts of comstockery were committed while the year was yet young. Some Boston perverts, either denied or forsaking natural uses, turned in their lusts toward the agent of Duffield & Co., publishers, and had him indicted for selling Elinor Glyn's "Three Weeks." Then, on the score of sacrilege, Comstock arrested Charles Vanni, newsdealer at 248 West Broadway, for importing anticlerical papers from Italy. The expensive defense made by Vanni to vindicate the principle that the pope should not be allowed to censor literature in America did him no good. Searching his premises, the prosecution discovered a French "comic," upon which it convicted Vanni and fined him $150. The Truth Seeker inquired with heat if we were going to allow the pope to say what literature should b sold in the United States. The prosecution answered the question in the affirmative. Our government cheerfully did the pope's dirty work and does it still for his confederates. This government of the United States will not receive at its postoffice copies of The Truth Seeker addressed to pope-ruled Canada. In 1929 this government, which seems eager to soil its hands with that sort of work, barred the anti-Fascist Il Martello from the mails. To continue the 1908 record: without due process the government had confiscated the published issues of Moses Harman's Journal of Eugenics. Harman went from Chicago to Los Angeles to prospect a new field, hoping to revive the magazine on the coast.

In the City of the Angels, Mrs. Dorothy Johns, wife of an author who was associated with Jack London, observing that the preachers were talking upon the streets, began an open-air advocacy of her views. With three other women she was arrested and made prisoner in the city jail. At the same time the authorities shut up or placed in the chain gang thirty-five men for street speaking. One of these was E. A. Cantrell, then a minister, but later to become a well-known Rationalist. The prisoners refused bail. Such a state of affairs, said The Truth Seeker, involving as it does discrimination against Socialists and in favor of religious howlers, would not long be tolerated. Brought to trial, the prisoners were all acquitted; and Channing Severance wrote: "The Socialists and Freethinkers of Los Angeles have won a notable victory for free speech—that is, the right to speak unmolested on the street—and religious ranters no longer enjoy a monopoly given them by pin-headed officials afflicted with the idea that only believers in the Christian superstition have any rights under a secular government." I believe that the right of Freethinkers, then won, to do open-air speaking is still enjoyed in Los Angeles.

The religion in the school fracas of 1908 was the set-to of Mr. Arthur Watts of River Edge, New Jersey, with the local board. Mr. Watts protested against his children's being held under compulsion while religious exercises were conducted. The Hackensack Liberal Club, F. C. Stevens president, did the fighting for Mr. Watts, and won after a three months' contest. The Department of Education of New Jersey, at Trenton, made a ruling that "the attendance of pupils at religious exercises in public schools must be entirely voluntary."

The Spiritualists reported a fifty per cent decrease in their numbers. President George Warne of the National Association made the announcement when vainly attempting to organize a Spiritualist "church" in Pittsburgh, Pa. Channing Severance wrote that organizing · Spiritualists into churches, with worship conducted by "reverends," had sent the philosophy down the skidway with a rush. C. Fannie Allyn, another this-world Spiritualist, agreed with him. But the "church" tendency was too strong. The lecturers of the cult are now reverends. The public was scandalized in 1908 by the appearance of cigaret-smoking girls at the Sunrise Club. I deprecated the habit as detri-

mental to the charm of the young girl, but my point
was overflowed by James F. Morton's defense of
the equality of the sexes, which I had not denied;
and smoking by girls prevailed.

"The killing of a Roman Catholic priest in Denver by a miserable Sicilian murderer has been the
signal for the discovery of anarchist societies bent
on the total destruction of the Catholic church by
the simple process of killing off all the priests."
When this appeared in The Truth Seeker the Rev.
Father Heinrichs had lately been killed by a Roman Catholic from Sicily. Nothing came out to
connect the killer, whose name was Alia, with any
organization, anarchist, anti-clerical, or Socialist.
When asked if he were an anarchist, he inquired
what that might be. But the feverish politicians
accused all three groups.

Police Commissioner Bingham of New York
asked for an appropriation of $100,000 to "hunt
down anarchists." The board of aldermen, who
probably knew that there was not an anarchist in
the city who could not be found in his home or
at work by any policeman at an hour's notice, rejected the application by a vote of 36 to 12. President Roosevelt, in a message to Congress in April,
declared that "when compared with the suppression of anarchy, every other question sinks into
insignificance"!

The Denver papers reported the imprisoned
Sicilian to be a devout observer of the religious requirements of his church. The Truth Seeker,
quoting the Denver Weekly Post, said: "A good

Catholic will go to his reward when Alia, the slayer of Father Leo Heinrichs, mounts the gallows." The Post described the genuflexions of the prisoner, and said: "This gives strength to the supposition that Alia's sentiments were not anti-Catholic, but anti-clerical; that his grievance was not against the Catholic church, but against her ministers." According to Alia's friends he was "against" this particular minister, who had injured him as a husband or father, and locating him in Denver had gone thither from Chicago and taken a Sicilian's revenge by killing him.

Daniel Henry Chamberlain, a former governor (1874-7) of South Carolina, dying in 1907 at the age of 72, left a paper in which he had set down his conclusions on the subject of religion. They were those of a Freethinker, excluding "the idea of a presiding or controlling Deity who continually watches over the universe, exercising the function either of keeping the machinery of the universe in working order or putting it in order on occasions." Governor Chamberlain rejected "such ideas as sin, redemption, conversion, salvation, atonement, the person, office and the work of Jesus Christ, the Trinity, in a word, the whole circle and array of dogmas and beliefs which make up the Christian religion."

Being "much more than an Atheist," Governor Chamberlain chose a Freethinker as "the truly descriptive phrase" denoting the position at which he had arrived, and said: "I know of no earthly inducement which could lead me to go back to what now seems to me the darkness and unrest of former days and beliefs."

William Jennings Bryan early in the year erected his presidential lightning rod in the hope that it would be hit; began his crusade against the doctrine of evolution, and talked interminably. The reaction of William Howard Taft, his prospective opponent, was deplorable, for Taft also began to preach. "Christianity and the spirit of Christianity," said Mr. Taft, addressing a religious meeting and talking what he knew to be buncombe, "are the hope of the world and the only hope of popular self-government." It was awful. Bryan had been set back amongst the Methodists by a remark of Bishop Fowler, which the death of the bishop in this crisis recalled, that is: "Before I would vote for Bryan I would go to sea in a boat of stone, with sails of lead, oars of iron, the wrath of God for a gale, and hell for a port."

The national election of 1908 in its religious features resembled that of 1928. William Jennings Bryan, twice defeated candidate for president, had put himself up again for the office, and the Democratic convention at Denver ratified the nomination. Justice Gaynor of Brooklyn had been slated for vice-president on the Bryan ticket, and would have got there but for the exposure of the fact that he belonged to the Christian Brothers, a Catholic order, and had withdrawn. The Catholics fought his nomination and the convention dropped him, choosing instead Mr. John Worth Kern of Indiana.

Meanwhile the Republicans nominated William Howard Taft, whom the orthodox Protestants at

once attacked as a denier of Jesus Christ, Taft being a Unitarian; and the tail of the ticket was
James Schoolcraft Sherman, reputed to be of Catholic sympathies and association. As President
Roosevelt chose Mr. Taft he had to champion him,
and did so in a letter addressed to a man who said
he had heard that Taft was an Infidel. It was a
coincidence that before writing the letter Mr.
Roosevelt took counsel of Cardinal Gibbons, as
twenty years later Al Smith consulted Father Duffy
before expressing himself.

The British courts convicted a blasphemer named
Harry Boulter, a street lecturer; notwithstanding
which medieval proceedings, said The Truth
Seeker, "this is the twentieth century of the era
of Christian love, charity, and forgiveness, as may
be verified by reference to the Almanac." The
court withheld sentence, but placed Boulter under
promise thereafter to modify his language, which
had been indicted as impious. Mr. Joseph Mc-
Cabe, then a comparatively new accession to the
ranks of Rationalism, caused a controversy among
the English Freethinkers by contending that the
only liberty denied Boulter was the liberty to express himself in scurrilous language. Having been
educated as a Catholic brother, Mr. McCabe had
not quite grasped the principle of free speech, as
enunciated by George Jacob Holyoake, that a man
has the right to say what he chooses in his own
words; and so, instead of waiting for such light
as Mr. G. W. Foote, Mrs. Hypatia Bradlaugh
Bonner, and Mr. F. J. Gould were prepared to pour

in upon him, he made the mistake of discussing the affair from the point of view of the police and the complaining witnesses.

In June, 1909, Mr. Boulter having again ventured to express his thoughts, was rearrested and sentenced to one month's imprisonment.

If nothing else happens, there are always deaths to set down. Each year I feel a hope that the next list will be lighter; but look at 1908! And the decedents are those of the Old Guard without whom we might once have thought the cause could not go on or the paper be sustained. First went Prof. Henry Martyn Parkhurst of Brooklyn, on January 21, aged 82. Dr. Parkhurst, son of a preacher and cousin to another of that name, had been newspaper man, court stenographer, professor in astronomy. His death left W. H. Burr the last of the pioneer group of stenographers who were Freethinkers, which included Stephen Pearl Andrews, Theron C. Leland, and Edward F. Underhill. And Burr soon followed him. William Henry Burr of Washington died in his 90th year, February 27. After graduation (1838) in Union College he learned stenography, was official reporter in the United States Senate and on the Congressional Globe, now Congressional Record. He compiled "One Hundred and Forty-four Contradictions of the Bible," was the author of "Revelations of Antichrist" and other revelatory writings—was the man whom Ingersoll called the "greatest literary detective." Particulars of his life occupy two columns in The Truth Seeker of March 14. Aunt Elmina

Slenker, the good Quaker lady and industrious worker for Freethought, died just past 80 at her home in Snowville, Va. Aunt Elmina wrote a hand that caused compositors to blaspheme, and could do no public speaking because of a hare-lip. She placed her name on the scroll, however, despite the difficulty of deciphering her signature. Edward Chamberlain, New York lawyer and in-veterate enemy of Comstockism, nearly thirty years a subscriber to The Truth Seeker, laid life aside at 65, in January. His religious family, for his funeral, engaged an Episcopal priest, who con-ducted the services according to the book. One could imagine a smile coming to the face of the man in the coffin when they perfunctorily buried him "in the sure and certain hope." Mr. Cham-berlain was a very serious man, as one must be, perhaps, effectively to contend with folly and fraud. I recall the evening at the Liberal Club when he announced a solemn duty he felt he had to perform in behalf of woman. He then read the vaseline and acid formula for birth-control which had been given circulation by President Colgate of the So-ciety for the Suppression of Vice, and surprised his audience by castigating the author and dis-tributor of such information. Let every woman beware, he warned, of this nefarious cabal. "Why," he exclaimed, "the recipe has no efficacy whatever, and many a poor girl who trusted in its treacher-ous promise has been lost."

The "millionaire lumberman," Delos A. Blod-gett, of Grand Rapids, Michigan, was an Agnostic to the day of his death in November, 1908. He had lived 83 years. Blodgett, a captain of industry, did Liberal work handsomely. Our lecturers were sure of profitable engagements in Grand Rapids, because he made the arrangements and paid the expenses. His charities were large. The Children's Home which he gave to Grand Rapids was building at the time of his death. He impressed me as a great man when I met him on his visits to the coast while I was there.

The ripe ages reached by these Freethinkers are extraordinary. The last time that William Henry Burr was in New York he remarked that a few old fellows like himself, standing one beside the other, could reach back to the beginning of the Christian era and shake hands with Jesus Christ (whom, of course, he regarded as a myth).

Canadian Freethinkers revived the Pioneer Freethought Club of Montreal, and Herald Rosario Holmes reported its meetings. The Toronto Secular Society also manifested new life. The Liberal Club of Hackensack, N. J., under Dr. F. C. Stevens and F. W. Emmer was a live organization. Notice was given that on May 6 it would listen to James F. Morton, Jr., and sing the hymn "America" in honor of his grandfather, the Rev. S. F. Smith, who wrote it. At the Independent Religious Society of Chicago, M. M. Mangasarian debated with the Rev. Dr. A. S. Crapsey, lately deposed for heresy, the proposition: "Resolved, That the Jesus of the New Testament is a historical Personage." Mangasarian took the negative and published the debate. The New York Bohemians, as reported by Jaroslaw V. Nigrin, held a convention to organize a Freethought Educational Federation, April 5. The Friendship Liberal League, Philadelphia, celebrated the twenty-fifth anniversary of George Longford's service as secretary. The Buckeye Secular Union, George O. Roberts president, held a state convention at Canal Dover, Ohio, September 6. The former Rev. J. P. Bland, resident speaker, addressed the Boston Freethought Society every Sunday in Paine Memorial Hall. The Manhattan Liberal Club was meeting in Mott Memorial Hall, 64 Madison Avenue, New York. Familiar names appeared on the program of the Washington Secular League: Prof. Charles W. Paflow, Dr. J. J. Shirley, Prof. David Eccles, Mr. J. A. Hennesy, Mr. J. W. Nigh. Eudorus C. Kenney was treasurer. At a meeting in December the League took up a collection amounting to $20 and on motion of Dr. Shirley sent the money to the Editor of The Truth Seeker, who received it with emotions of great pleasure, and made this response: "The Truth Seeker gratefully accepts this assistance, this sympathy, but our friends must remember that we have only a fount of ink and white paper wherewith to express our thanks; and how can these record the jumps of the heart, the liquefaction about the eyes, and those other reactions to kindness which are felt but must remain unspoken?" Alexander S. Irvine had succeeded John R. Coryell in the attempt to keep the Pentecost society together at Lyric Hall.

The contributors of articles to The Truth Seeker in 1908 were those whose names are familiar to readers of these pages, and some who wrote once and were heard from no more. Others began then and have stood by ever since, among these François Thane, with his Sojourner's Note Book. And look who is here! Woolsey Teller, by all that is good and great! He has just discovered The Truth Seeker and near the beginning of the year and in the kindness of his teens writes to the editor: "Allow me to tender my earnest appreciation of your well conducted journal."

Two stanzas of verse by Walter ("Southpaw") Thornton are to be seen. Walt, when pitching for the Chicago Nationals, read Ingersoll instead of playing poker for a pastime; and subsequently, employing figures recognizably taken from frontier life in Snohomish, wrote this:

TO COL. ROBERT G. INGERSOLL

"You left behind Creed's settlement,
    With rifle true on shoulder thrown,
To follow-through the trail of Truth—
    On frontier peak you stood alone.

As true of you, in praise I'll sing
    Your words when Ebon 'crossed the bar':
    'In night of death Hope sees a star;
Love hears the rustle of a wing.'"

At last accounts, Walt was preaching. but he quoted Ingersoll in his sermons.

June 27 the editor, E. M. Macdonald, in a signed article, released the fact, which he long had been

withholding, that in the previous July he had exhibited symptoms of tuberculosis, confirmed by
medical examination. He wrote that "during the
past year callers at this office have been lucky to
catch me in, and very few subscribers who have
written me have received personal replies." When
the editor spoke thus he had been for three months
living in the town of Liberty, Sullivan County, N.
Y., and was then occupying a tent on the farm of
Cyrus Coolridge, treating himself to a diet of eggs
and milk. He expected with returning strength to
do more writing. Meanwhile his brother George,
he said, would continue as "office editor." I at
that date had been "office editor" for twelve years
or since 1896. My brother wrote from his tent
on the Coolridge farm: "I am on a hill all alone,
away from the road, out in the sun and the wind
all the time. I have eggs right from the nests, milk
just from the cows, strawberries from the garden,
and I cook such simple food as I desire. My appetite is slowly returning." He always reported an
increase of appetite and strength, but the time soon
came when he was unequal to the cooking of the
simple food he desired, and needed a tent-keeper.
My own better element was one of the three who
thus served. In October she submitted to The
Office Editor a letter from Liberty, illustrated with
snapshots that told more of the Editor's condition
than her words.

The editor in due time moved into a house at
32 St. Paul's place, in Liberty, his goods having
arrived from the one on Hillside avenue, Glen
Ridge, which had been his home for some years.

I spent Sunday, October 25, with him, and found him not in as "good flesh" as at our last meeting. Apparently he was under sentence of early death. No change had taken place December 13, when I visited him again.

I returned to the city knowing that I should see the Editor no more alive. He had the cough that kills; I recognized it by its peculiar sound. Some persons cough as a habit in which they are confirmed, and it is more wearing on their hearers than on themselves. The cough goes for a greeting or a good-bye, or is used where profanity would be better. The editor's cough was the sort that thuds and hammers on the lungs, the bruising kind, which is not a habit but a deadly affliction.

CHAPTER XX.

THIS story of The Truth Seeker left its Editor at the end of 1908 in his rented place at Liberty, New York, taking the open air cure for tuberculosis of the lungs and hoping to make favorable reports. The first number of the paper for 1909 was silent. The second one acknowledged in the language of the Office Editor the many New Year's gifts sent to the sick man by subscribers. Then more silence, until the ninth number, dated February 27, brought to donors a brief letter of thanks—the Editor's last communication to the paper, for on the 26th he died. At 5 o'clock of that day a paroxysm of coughing "broke down the wall of some impaired artery, and there was a gush of blood as though a heart had burst." We brought the body home, and held the funeral on March 1, at the Crematory in North Bergen, N. J.

Abbreviated, the formal biographical sketch I prepared for Putnam's "Four Hundred Years of Freethought" will serve here.

Eugene Montague Macdonald was born at Chelsea, Maine, February 4, 1855. He spent his early boyhood on New England farms, attending winter terms of schools, walking two or three miles morn-

E. M. MACDONALD (1855-1909).

He was with The Truth Seeker thirty-five years, and its
Editor for a quarter of a century.

ings and evenings. In 1869 he came to New York and began to learn the printer's trade. In 1870 he returned to New Hampshire and worked in the office of the Cheshire Republican, published in Keene. Later he was employed as a printer on The Sentinel in the same city, and became an expert "jobber." At 18 he came again to New York and set up as a printer, bringing out the fifth number of The Truth Seeker and then selling his outfit to D. M. Bennett, who hired him as foreman. He was probably the most boyish, if not the youngest, foreman in the city. A competent one nevertheless, he held the position until called in later years to the editorial chair. Meanwhile he attempted writing in prose and verse. His first article was accepted by The Boston Investigator, signed with his full name, Eugene Montague Macdonald, which made a fair line in The Investigator's narrow columns. Bennett knew on whose shoulders his mantle would fall; and in this he was not disappointed, for he lived to see The Truth Seeker pass under the management of his young successor. At Mr. Bennett's death in 1882 applicants for the editorial and business control of the paper appeared in such force that Mrs. Bennett concluded to throw upon others the burden of meeting them. In 1883, E. M. Macdonald, Charles P. Somerby, and Ephraim E. Hitchcock purchased the business and formed The Truth Seeker Company. The literary ability of the combination was centered in the Editor, who retained his place, and before many years had passed, the third member of the firm, Mr. Hitchcock, discovered that he also had superior executive capacity.

He became owner and publisher in 1892, having bought out Somerby with funds lent him by Hitchcock. He was a shrewd, judicious, and discreet editor; as a writer direct and vigorous, with occasional touches of ornamentation. That he possessed business sagacity is proved by his success in carrying the paper through times so troublous that none of his Liberal contemporaries survived him. Of our personal relations I wrote:

"His nature was always that of the protector; his attitude ever that of the elder brother and guardian. Who doubts that he knew the approach of the last guest when he wrote, February 16, ten days before he died:

"'DEAR GEORGE: I am sorry the double holiday [Sunday and Washington's birthday] delays your visit. As I told Charles Smith, you are the one on whose shoulder I must lean my head. So I miss your visit, having made up my mind you were coming. But the next will be all the more looked forward to.   GENE.'

"The self-reliant one, the support of others, might lean at last; but the head he would rest upon the shoulder of another was bowed alone by death."

While we were boys together in New Hampshire, from infancy to the ages of 12 and 14, we were inseparable playmates and schoolmates. Amongst other boys, an injury to one of us was an injury to both, and by both repaid. At school he was in the advanced classes, having the age of me by two years. So he also went "out to work" first, and then I knew what it was to be lonesome. In 1867, at 12 years, as the "boy" on the Crehore place in Walpole, two and a half miles from home, he was allowed to come and see me but once in a fortnight, and I was not allowed to go and see him at all; but

on the Sundays between his visits I used to run
away, and by traveling about two miles I could
reach a place in the road from which the Crehore
house was visible. Having bent my gaze on that
for awhile, perhaps catching sight of 'Gene as he
passed from the house to the barn, I would turn
around and run home again. On the Sundays he
came I went with him to the same spot at the end
of the day, and watched him as long as he was in
sight. His death revived these memories, which
took on a renewed value, seeing they were now all
of him that was left to me.

The men with whom he had the larger commercial dealings were first to write to the paper expressing their regrets. They were "Bob" Lecouver,
president of the Lecouver Press Company, printers, and Edwin C. Wood, of Buckley & Wood,
Binding and Mailing. Said Lecouver: "In all my
business relations with him I found our departed
friend to be at all times consistently fair, sound, and
just. I shall always remember him as one who
stood for a 'square deal.' In the broadest sense of
the word he was a manly man. The numerous volumes of The Truth Seeker are his monument."
And said Wood: "For over twenty-five years Eugene and I were more than business associates; we
always esteemed each other as personal friends.
Please accept my deepest sympathy in your bereavement. It is also mine."

We should have had, I doubt not, the same expression of regret at the loss of a friend from Murphy, the man who had supplied the white paper,
only that Mr. Murphy had retired and was out of

TO E. M. MACDONALD

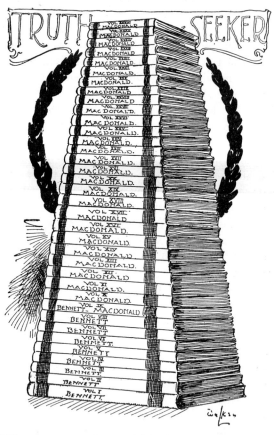

"The numerous volumes of The Truth Seeker are his Monument."

communication with us. Ryan Walker, illustrator
for the International Newspaper Syndicate, took
for a text the words of Lecouver, "The numerous
volumes of The Truth Seeker are his monument,"
and drew the picture herewith. George William
Foote, editor of the London Freethinker, said: "He
was entitled, in his degree, to echo the noble words
of Heine: 'Lay a sword upon my coffin, for I
was a loyal soldier in the war of the liberation of
humanity'."

The centenary of Charles Darwin, falling like
Lincoln's on February 12, 1909, was celebrated by
all the scient'fic societies and by Freethinkers; Lincoln's also by Freethinkers and by patriotic societies. The churches of America, paying little
attention to Darwin, gave out a few new Lincoln
myths for The Truth Seeker to explode. Darwin
and evolution were specifically banned in Russia.

It being the centenary of the death of Thomas
Paine, the Freethinkers began early to plan a Paine
rally at New Rochelle on June 8. Some of the papers reported the proceedings as a "birthday" celebration. The matter spread to the daily press, and
the wide discussion led to a new evaluation of
Paine and a verdict in his favor. The Truth Seeker of June 12 was a Paine number. At the rally
about the New Rochelle monument Thaddeus B.
Wakeman presided. The Rev. Dr. Thomas R.
Slicer, Unitarian m'nister; Dr. David Muzzey of
the Ethical Culture Society (now professor of history at Columbia University), and Elbert Hubbard
were the speakers. That was the first time I had

seen Hubbard, and pronounced him hard to classi-
fy: "he might turn out to be a progressive Quaker
or a poet or a benevolent Pawnee Indian, and he
might offer one a poem or a sermon, or a bottle of
Pawnee Remedy." That was judging from his
appearance, for he was long-haired and broad-
brimmed. He proved to be an entertainer of rare
gifts.

Toward the end of the year, Current Literature
summed up the "conflicting estimates" of Paine
with this result: "The present indications are that
posterity will preserve the favorable rather than
the unfavorable picture of Thomas Paine. His influence is steadily growing. Clergymen participated
in the centenary exercises. New editions of his
important works have been lately published. And
his admirers are at this moment converting the
house he occupied at New Rochelle, New York, into a permanent Museum to be devoted to his honor."
And then the Eden Musée Company in West Twenty-third street placed a fine figure of Paine in its
Historical Chamber and featured it on its billboard
in huge letters. The Paine verdict of 1909 has not
been changed. He came into his own then and retains it still.

Accusing all other than church schools of
"preaching anarchist doctrines against religion and
social order which no government could tolerate,"
the authorities in Barcelona, Spain, decreed the
closing of such schools as were not conducted by
priests. This was an order against the Modern
Schools of Francisco Ferrer. William Heaford

FRANCISCO FERRER.
"He was judicially murdered by church and
state," October 12, 1909.

of Surrey, England, wrote to The Truth Seeker that
Ferrer's life was in peril. His letter appeared October 16. An editorial in the number for October
23, headed "Ferrer and His Assassins," more than
confirmed Heaford. "According to the demand
of the Catholic church which it is sworn to uphold,"
the article said, "the government of Spain has put
to death Prof. Francisco Ferrer, the founder of
a system of modern schools which competed and
interfered with the system of education under the
control of priests."

Ferrer's arrest had been procured previously in
an attempt to connect him with the man who threw
a bomb at the queen's bridal procession. A civil
tribunal acquitted him. Now the accused was relaxed to the military arm, which courtmartialed
him behind closed doors, denied him the right to
testify in his own behalf, and shot him to death
on the morning of October 12. He died with the
words "Long live the modern school" upon his
lips.

The assassination of the educator was so generally condemned in all countries that the pope
thought it best to appear "dejected" over the event.
The indignation spread to all not under Catholic
obedience. Even the conservative American Federation of Labor "adopted resolutions expressive
of organized Labor's protest for the cause of free
speech and free education, which has found in
Francisco Ferrer another martyr." The Catholic
press, however, called upon Master Workman
Samuel Gompers to disavow the Federation.

Joseph McCabe, having reviewed the proceedings against the Spanish educator, concluded that "Ferrer's schools were closed, his property confiscated, and his life ruthlessly taken because he was a Rationalist."

Ferrer's admirers called him the Herbert Spencer of Spain. He thus expressed his philosophy: "Time respects only those institutions which time itself has played its part in building up. That which violence wins for us today another act of violence may wrest from us tomorrow. Those stages of progress are alone enduring which have rooted themselves in the mind and conscience of mankind before receiving the final sanction of legislation. The only means of realizing what is good is to teach it by education and propagate it by example." Ferrer belonged to the Freethinkers.

Twice in 1909 slight quakes of heresy disturbed the orthodox. Harold Bolce contributed to the Cosmopolitan Magazine some articles on "Blasting the Rock of Ages." He showed by the right number of apt quotations that college students were learning unbelief and lax moral sentiments from their professors, including Franklin H. Giddings of Columbia and Lester F. Ward of Brown University. Bishop McFaul of the diocese of Trenton, N. J., at the commencement exercises of the College of St. Francis Xavier in New York, made reference to the "popular colleges like Harvard, Princeton and Yale" as schools "where rascality, immorality, and disrespect of womankind are fostered," and to other large colleges where students do not even learn the ten commandments such as 'Thou shalt not steal,' 'Thou shalt not commit adultery,' and 'Thou shalt not bear false witness against thy neighbor." This shows how the blast that rent the rock of ages shook up the reverend clergy.

Dr. Charles W. Eliot's five-foot shelf of books, one hundred in number, which he held would give any man a liberal education, came into vogue in 1909. Dr. Eliot then was referred to as the former president of Harvard; later as President Emeritus. Few propositions have had the longevity of this five-foot shelf of Dr. Eliot's, which is still mentioned oftener than the five books of Moses.

But the five-foot shelf soon was temporarily obscured by Dr. Eliot's proposed "Religion of the Future." He gave out enough of it from time to time to keep the clergy busy answering him, and then printed it in a book. The Truth Seeker, in answering the inquiry, "What is this new religion?" said: "It is what Christianity is not." Its author was guilty of separating religion from ethics and dispensing with the priesthood.

The Christian ministers agreed that "The religion of the Future" was immoral, blasphemous, and atheistic.

The Public Library of Spokane, Wash., denied the request of Mr. A. E. House of that city to have The Truth Seeker placed on file for the benefit of the reading public.

The 1909 contributors to The Truth Seeker were for the most part veterans, but two youthful ones were welcomed, namely, Louis C. Fraina and E. L. Macdonald. Fraina was out for a literary career and wrote on "Shelley, the Atheist Poet," "Victor Hugo's Religion," and "Historical Materialism." He handled large themes ably. Eugene did some reporting and had a piece headed: "At the Sunrise Dinner—The Guests Discuss an Address by Dr. Juliet H. Severance and Voice the Bitter Cry of the Married." He reported Mrs. Winifred H. Cooley, who spoke before the Brooklyn Philosophical Association on "Woman as a Citizen." Mrs. Cooley, daughter of the suffragist Ida Husted Harper, is organizer of the contemporary dining club known as the Morons. He also gave The Truth Seeker a story of the "High Jinks for Ryan Walker" (who cartooned him) at the Friars Club of New York. His work was good. Fugitive pieces were contributed by Mrs. Eufina C. Tompkins of San Francisco; by Ben Reitman, who was Emma Goldman's partner; by U. Dhammaloka, the Buddhist Monk of Burma and Ceylon; J. M. Gilbert of Texas; W. W. Edwards of Louisiana.

A group of Freethinkers not among The Truth Seeker's constituents held a congress to organize the Rationalist Association of America in Bowman's Hall, St. Louis, Mo., November 14, 1909. They were readers of The Blue Grass Blade, Lexington, Ky.: founder, Charles C. Moore, deceased; present editor, John R. Charlesworth, first secretary of the Freethought Federation of America. This St. Louis convention elected Mr. Charlesworth president; secretary and treasurer, D. W. Sanders, already named as holding those offices in the State Association of Indiana.

The Los Angeles Liberal Club held its Fourth

of July celebration in Central Park, where the president, Charles T. Sprading, addressed an audience of above two thousand. The club published as a monthly The Agnostic Index.

Williar Thurston Brown and J. H. Duren Ward started a magazinelet in Denver in 1909 and called it Up the Divide.

Incidental to the Paine anniversary M. M. Mangasarian journeyed to Washington as a messenger from the Independent Religious Society of Chicago, for the purpose of interviewing President Roosevelt and requesting him to reconsider his offensive mention of Paine as a filthy little Atheist. But the courage, of whatever sort it may have been, that supported Roosevelt when he outfaced the facts of history and emitted that piece of low detraction, deserted him at the approach of the messenger of truth and he declined to receive Mr. Mangasarian. He preferred to shut himself in with the lie for company.

The Liberals of Muncie, Indiana, organized the Humanitarian Society with sixty-seven charter menbers. The treasurer, Dr. J. T. Bowles, and the secretary, H. D. Fair, M.D., were Freethinkers of long standing. Organization of the Indiana Secular Association followed, meeting in convention at Indianapolis in December; Dr. Bowles, president, D. W. Sanders, secretary. Mr. Sanders reported the convention "a brilliant success in every way." Norman Murray started The Church of Aristotle in Montreal.

At my request Thaddeus B. Wakeman, who so far as known was the only survivor of the original founders of the New York Liberal Club, prepared a history of that organization for The Truth Seeker. It appeared in two numbers of the paper.

The Liberal Club had lost its old meeting-place in the German Masonic Hall, East Fifteenth street, and was occupying Berkeley Hall in West Forty-fourth street. The audience failed to follow it to its new home, and the season of 1908-1909 was its last. The Club, having been organized in 1869, had carried on for forty years.

The San Francisco Materialist Association, at the Auditorium Annex, Page and Filmore streets, listened in September to an exposition of "The Darwinian Theory" by David Starr Jordan, president of Stanford University.

Secretary E. C. Reichwald of the American Secular Union kept watch upon attempted bootlegging of the Bible and religion into the public schools. Where schools were threatened in this way he followed the practice of sending some anti-biblical literature, couched in plain language, to the members of the school-boards and promising that the district should be flooded with "more of the same." In this way he discouraged the invaders.

Thirty Sunday bills, some better and some worse than the law in force, were before the New York legislature, and the advocates were heard by a legislative committee. One was a bill to legalize ball playing on Sunday. This The Truth Seeker selected as the most meritorious, and asked James F. Morton, Jr., to make a journey to Albany and appear in its behalf before the committee to whom it might be referred. Mr. Morton did so. When the bill came up he arose as its champion, and while on his feet told the assembled solons that to make Sunday safe for liberty they might as well go the whole distance and repeal the law altogether instead of amending it. One of his opponents, declaring, "No Sunday, no Christ," accused him of crucifying his Lord anew. A guard of reverends appeared to defend their "Sabbath." Probably the mouths of most of them are by this time "stopt with dust," and New York has Sunday baseball.

DEPARTURES.

Under Deaths I include that of Mr. Augustus LePlongeon the explorer, because both he and his wife Alice were Freethinkers and contributors to The Truth Seeker. He evidently preceded other antiquarians by a quarter of a century in unearthing the ancient civilizations of the Mayas and Quiches of Peru and Yucatan. "Messiah" Cyrus R. Teed had gone the way of all flesh December 22, 1908. Teed, or Cyrus, or Koresh, was head of the Koreshan colony at Estero, in Southern Florida. His followers, who accepted him as the second Jesus Christ, expected he would rise again on Christmas, the third day, but this did not occur. For a man of intelligence and sanity Teed entertained many delusions. His magazine, The Flaming Sword, survived him for some years to illustrate his teaching that the earth is concave and that the sun and moon are electrified points. But Teed insisted on having The Truth Seeker all the latter part of his life, which ended when he was 69.

Daniel Freeman of Beatrice, Neb., the mover

many years before in a suit to stop the school teachers of his district conducting religious services during school hours, died December 30, 1908, at the age of 80, after reading The Truth Seeker for a generation. Mr. Freeman had the distinction of being the first "homesteader" in the United States. His land, which became the town of Beatrice, is known as entry No. 1, proof of residence No. 1, patent No. 1, recorded on page 1 of book No. 1 of the General Land Office of the United States at Washington, D. C. When they buried him the little town occupying the site of his homestead had never seen so large a funeral.

The Freethinkers of those days lived long. W. W. Davis of Lincoln, Kan., who died Jan. 18, was 82. Mr. Davis's daughter, an illustrator, married Ryan Walker, the cartoonist. New Rochelle lost a "character" in which it took pride when Capt. George Loyd, who thirty-five years before had constituted himself caretaker of the Paine monument, was removed from that position by death, July, 1909. Loyd was a veteran of two rebellions, Dorr's and the Southern states. James B. Puffer, an ardent Freethinker and well-loved citizen of Binghampton, N. Y., took off for the great adventure on July 4, leaving a wife who asked to have "Mrs." prefixed to the name on The Truth Seeker subscription list, and so it still stands.

Daniel T. Ames, handwriting expert, associate editor of The Freethought Magazine, and presiding officer at the 1907 congress of the American Secular Union, died August 27, near San Francisco, at 70 years.

JUDGE C. B. WAITE (1824-1909).
Mr. Waite was appointed by President Lincoln in
1862 Associate Justice of Utah. He served
several terms as President of the American
Secular Union and was an author of
distinction.

We learned from a resident of Antioch, Cal., that on October 3, Mrs. Lois Waisbrooker had "passed to a higher life," aged 83. In her battling for freedom of the press she had done her part in behalf of a higher life in this world.

When there passed away at Hubbards, Nova Scotia, in h.s 80th year John E. Shatford, a patriarch of Agnosticism and a lifelong resident of that village, the funeral was the largest that ever took place in West Halifax county. And the funeral was notable in another respect, for the orator and eulogist, as reported by A. W. Shatford, was "Marshall J. Govang, a young man of much promise and ability from Moncton, N. B." Thus was Marshall J. Gauvin first introduced to the readers of The Truth Seeker. The printer made out the name to be Govany, but there is no doubt the son of the deceased (Mr. A. W. Shatford) had attempted to English its pronunciation by writing Govang.

And so the aged Freethinkers passed to their rest. With those I have already named also, Sept. 7, the veteran Rationalist Aaron Davis, Park Ridge, Md., 89, who rang his farm bell every year on Paine's birthday; and "Uncle Robert" Trowbridge of Tully, N. Y., July 24, likewise full of years.

The most distinguished of these veterans who died in 1909, Judge Charles B. Waite of Chicago, author of "The Christian Religion to the Year 200," had died in the spring (March 25) aged 85. The Liberals of Chicago used to celebrate his birthday along with Paine's, for it fell on the same day, Jan. 29. He was born in Wayne county, New

York, in 1824. In 1846, being an Abolitionist, he published the anti-slavery Liberty Banner in Rock Island, Illinois. He owed his title of Judge to Abraham Lincoln, who in 1862 appointed him judge of Utah territory and associate justice of the Supreme Court of the United States. He was president of the American Secular Union in the early '90s, and his daughter, Dr. Lucy Waite, has been one of the vice presidents for years. Three pages of Putnam's "Four Hundred Years of Freethought" are occupied with a biographical sketch of Judge Waite.

SPENCER IN THE RECANTATION STORY.

A book that came out in 1909, the author being Henry Murray, brother of David Christie Murray, the English publisher, contained the "recantation" of Herbert Spencer. It followed the usual form of such fabrications:

"Walking up and down the lawn of Buchanan's house in Mansfield Gardens, I told him, in a momentary absence of our host, what a load of personal obligation I felt under to 'First Principles,' and added that I intended to devote the reading hours of the next two or three years to a thorough study of his entire output. 'What have you read of mine?' he asked. I told him . . . 'Then,' said Spencer—and it was the only time I have heard such counsel from the lips of any writer regarding his own work—'I should say that you have read quite enough.' He fell silent for a moment, and then added, 'I have passed my life in beating the air.'"

For more than a hundred years nothing original enough to be copyrighted has been added to the standard version of Infidel recantations. Persons witnessing to the retractation never change the

testimony.   Paine died near the beginning of the
nineteenth century.   Associated with the recantation afterwards prepared for him was a woman
who is purported to have had with the dying man
the following conversation: "Paine asked her if
she had ever read any of his writings, and on being
told that she had read very little of them, he inquired what she thought of them.   She told him
that when very young his 'Age of Reason' was
put in her hands, but that the more she read it the
more dark and distressed she felt, and she threw
the book into the fire.   'I wish all had done as you,'
he replied, 'for if the devil ever had any agency
in any work, he has had it in my writing that
book.'"

The parallels show that the author of Spencer's
retraction depended upon the author of Paine's.
Observe them:

Paine inquired of the woman "if she had read
any of his writings."   Spencer asked Murray:
"What have you read of mine?"   The woman said
she had read the "Age of Reason."   Murray said
he had read "First Principles."   Paine did not advise the woman to read further.   Spencer told
Murray: "You have read quite enough."   Paine
indicated the futility of his writings by wishing
they might be thrown into the fire.   Spencer confessed: "I have passed my life beating the air.'

Investigation of the story of Mary Hinsdale,
the witness to the recantation of Paine, revealed no
evidence that she had ever seen Paine to speak
to him, and educed testimony from her acquaintances that she was an habitual liar.   If the deadly

parallel still held, as it might, what would become of Murray's statement that he talked with Spencer "in the momentary absence of our host?"

The year I am writing of differed from all the twenty-two last preceding ones in the respect that in 1909 I went on a vacation in New Hampshire—revisited the scenes I knew as a boy and have mentioned in Volume I. I see from a letter written at the time that I was able to get away because "James F. Morton, Jr., consented to do my work and E. C. Walker my worrying." The letter here repeats what the reader already knows, that Walker was office editor of the paper in the nineties; that Morton was a Harvard man and that his grandfather Smith wrote the hymn America, although one would sooner expect to find among his ancestors the Anarchist who wrote the Declaration of Independence. Mr. Morton at that period was an Atheist. He wrote that God had grown up in the imaginations of men and had never existed anywhere else. I took with me for a companion on my vacation the son born at the Golden Gate eighteen years previously.

The old house shown in the drawing that embellishes the beginning of this story (vol. i, p. 25) burned down in 1888, when lightning hit the barn.

In the old burying-ground at Surry, South End, the slumberers still waited, as the quaint inscriptions on their gravestones said, "till Christ appears." They had been waiting more than a hundred years, and "as regards the appearance of Christ all things are as they were before the fathers fell asleep."

On the road from Surry village to the Hill where the old farm lies I directed my boy, who complained of thirst, to a clump of bushes beside the way where he would find a spring of water I knew once was there; and while he searched for it I ran my eye along the sandy ruts ahead, which were so like what they always had been that it seemed I ought to see the barefoot prints I made there forty years before. I saw them not.

While in the neighborhood I called upon the old farmer on the Walpole hills whose first hired man I had been when he went into agriculture and matrimony about 1870. He dropped his pitchfork and unhitched his team and took me into his house, where he cranked a fine victrola and gave us entertainment. The record he put on as his favorite piece was from "Rigoletto," sung by Caruso, Sembrich and other artists proficient in the Italian tongue. He had been a singer himself, when his wife was alive to play the little organ in the sitting room, and he observed, regarding this selection, that he couldn't understand a word of it, but liked the tune. He was a devotee of music for its own sake. I never saw him again.

CHAPTER XXI.

NOT far from the year 1920, a subscriber asked me to settle a bet he had made, by telling him whether any minister or religious newspaper had ever asserted that Robert G. Ingersoll recanted on his deathbed. Sometimes a subscriber relies on his memory and commits himself to a proposition he is not prepared to prove, and then refers to me for the facts. This one wanted the name of a religious paper that had published such an assertion by a minister as that Ingersoll died repentant. To save my successor the time spent tracing the report, I will here set down the name of such a paper. It was The Christian Union of Des Moines, Iowa, May 13, 1909, which quoted another religious paper, The Church and School. This marked the original appearance of the noted affidavit attributed by Evangelist D. E. Olson to a certain Archie E. Berry, who affirmed: "I do hereby declare that Robert Ingersoll confessed to my father, Joehiel S. Berry, on his dying bed, that he did not believe the doctrine he preached." For good measure the affidavit went on with the story that the Colonel said to the elder Berry: "I do not believe what I have preached, and only did it for

346

the money there was in it." And to heap up the measure, this was added: "His daughter then asked, 'Whose life shall I live after, yours or mother's?' Mrs. Ingersoll," Berry swore, "was a strict Baptist and a sister to my father."

The affidavit is all lies. Ingersoll had no dying bed. But three persons were in the room at Walston, Dobbs Ferry, N. Y., July 21, 1899, when with a smile he passed from life while seated in a chair. These persons were his wife, Eva A. Ingersoll, and her sister, Sue M. Farrell, both Agnostics, born Parker, and Sue Sharkey, a long-time Catholic member of the household. I will repeat their story:

"During the night of July 20, 1899, he had an attack of acute indigestion and slept very little; but he came to breakfast the next morning and afterwards sat on the piazza, as he was wont to do, reading and talking with his family. At about 10:30 he said he would lie down and rest a little, and would then come down and play pool with his son-in-law. Mrs. Ingersoll accompanied him to their bedroom and remained with him while he slept. At about 11:45 he arose and sat in his chair to put on his shoes. Miss Sue Sharkey came into the room, followed by Mrs. Sue M. Farrell. Mrs. Ingersoll said: 'Do not dress, Papa, until after luncheon; I will eat upstairs with you.' He replied: 'Oh, no; I do not want to trouble you.' Mrs. Farrell then said: 'How absurd, after the hundreds of times you have eaten upstairs with her.' He looked up laughingly at Mrs. Farrell as she turned to leave the room, and then Mrs. Ingersoll said, 'Why, Papa, your tongue is coated; I must give you some medicine.' He looked at her with a smile, and as he did so he closed his eyes and passed away without a struggle, a pang, or even a sigh. No one else was present."

The lies started by the publication of the purported Berry affidavit in these religious newspapers,

The Church and School and The Christian Union,
have not been withdrawn from circulation. In 1929
one heard them at a Salvation Army meeting in
Steubenville, Ohio. And the listener, although a
Truth Seeker reader, was unacquainted with the
circumstances of Ingersoll's death. Ingersoll spoke
in the voice of experience when at the Paine monument in New Rochelle in 1894 he said he knew of
nothing that had the same prospect of longevity
as a good healthy religious lie.

The year 1910 saw numerous Ingersoll memorial
meetings and the announcement of the Ingersoll
Birthday Book arranged by Grace L. Macdonald. It
likewise saw Ingersoll plagiarized by—of all men!
—Theodore Roosevelt. I quote from the Washington Star of December 4:

"Mr. Roosevelt, in one of his addresses in New York's
East Side last month, made a neat epigram. 'The difference between a politician and a statesman is this,' he
said. 'A politician wants the people to do something
for him, and a statesman wants to do something for the
people.'"

Colonel Roosevelt enjoyed for a season the applause evoked by that sentiment, and then the ax
fell. Ingersoll's biographer, Herman E. Kittredge,
wrote to the Washington Star that if the reader
would go to the third volume of the authorized edition of Ingersoll's works, and look on page 130, he
would find in the famous lecture on Abraham Lincoln, published in 1894, the following language:

"Lincoln was a statesman; and there is this difference
between a politician and a statesman. A politician schemes
and works in every way to make the people do something

for him.   A statesman wishes to do something for the people."

In his Gouverneur Morris book Roosevelt likens the words of Ingersoll to the contents of "a bladder of dirty water"; and here we find him taking them into his own mouth.

The good will toward Paine engendered by the observance of the one hundredth anniversary of his death was kept alive throughout the following year. Celebrations of Paine's birthday were numerous and largely attended, and a new element predominated. That is, so far as New York was concerned, the old Paineites were succeeded by a constituency that could be called nothing more than liberal. At the close of the meeting held by the Paine Association and addressed by Mr. George Haven Putnam on Paine as the "Pioneer in International Copyright," and by others on topics equally safe, I jotted down the following for an editorial comment:

"Our New York Paine celebration differed in one particular from previous occasions of the kind. No mention was made of Paine's religious heresies; all the critics and calumniators, clerical and other, escaped censure; and except for certain passages in the address of the Rev. Marie Jenney Howe, nothing irreverent was said."

The religious denomination served as minister by the Rev. Mrs. Howe was not disclosed. She was the wife of Frederic C. Howe, afterward Commissioner of Immigration of the Port of New York.

The Thomas Paine National Historical Association, organized and incorporated September 11, 1906, with Moncure D. Conway for its first president, this year took a new lease of life. The officers elected at its annual meeting were Leonard D. Abbott, president; Wm. M. van der Weyde, secretary; Dr. E. B. Foote, treasurer. On May 30 (Memorial Day) the association dedicated and opened to the public The Thomas Paine National Museum in the historic old Paine house at New Rochelle.

Supervisor Henry Payot of San Francisco proposed the name of Paine for one of the city's avenues, but when two local Catholic priests came before the board and represented Paine as an Infidel who did not believe in the deity, the motion was lost.

Abbott and Van der Weyde were two of a committee of four to call a meeting in the hall of the Harlem Liberal Alliance, 100 West 116th street, New York, June 3, with a view to organizing a Francisco Ferrer association in honor of the murdered schoolmaster of Spain. The organizers elected them president and secretary respectively, and Dr. Foote treasurer. The religious presswriters created a Ferrer myth which represented the educator as a monster of blood and bombs—an anarchist and nothing else. The Emma Goldman group of radicals accepted him as one of them, and in his name labored for the founding of a Modern School in New York. The Ferrer colony at Stelton, N. J., was the outcome. Ferrer had quite plainly repudiated the doctrine of destructive anarchism. "So far as we know," The Truth Seeker of November 12 said, "the nearest he came to allying himself with any group was when he stood with a company of Freethinkers to be photographed at an International Freethought Congress."

A "True Story of the Martyrdom of Francisco
Ferrer" was written by Joseph McCabe in a book
of 94 pages. Against the protests of "fifteen million Catholics" in America, McClure's Magazine
commissioned William Archer, the English critic
and Rationalist, to tell the story of Ferrer, which
was done (McClure's for November and December,
1910), and one of the literary events of the following year was the "Life, Trial, and Death of Francisco Ferrer" by the same author.

January numbers of the local paper of Moncton,
N. B., reported lectures by Marshall J. Gauvin, still
known as Govang. In November Mr. Gauvin wrote
The Truth Seeker that, owing to prejudice, he could
no longer secure a hall in Moncton, and that he contemplated going to western Canada. His first published lecture appeared December 24.

Mrs. Marilla M. Ricker, the New Hampshire
lawyer and Freethought speaker and writer, who
had offered every library in the state a set of Ingersoll's works, early announced her candidacy for
governor on a woman's rights platform. In her behalf one of the Concord papers related that Mrs.
Ricker was a publicist, litterateur, platform orator,
and thoroughly equipped for public office. I doubt
that The Truth Seeker exaggerated in terming her
"the intellectual equal of any man ever elected to
the office of governor of New Hampshire." She
had been admitted with honors to the bar of the
Supreme Court of the District of Columbia in
1882, and to the bar of the United States Supreme
Court in 1891. In opposition to the opinion of

former United States Senator William E. Chandler, the New Hampshire attorney-general ruled that being of the sex she was, Mrs. Ricker could not lawfully be named on the ballot.

The International Congress of Freethinkers at Brussels in August compared favorably with its predecessors, according to Chapman Cohen, who, as delegate of the National Secular Society, reported it for the London Freethinker, and Ernest Pack of the British Secular League, who wrote tne story for The Truth Seeker (Sept. 24).

At the thirty-fourth annual congress of the American Secular Union, held in the Grand Pacific Hotel, Chicago, November 25-27, John E. Remsburg presided, but declining reelection as president, the members elected E. P. Peacock, formerly a vice-president and a good worker. Reichwald was reelected secretary. James F. Morton, Jr., represented The Truth Seeker and reported the proceedings (T. S. Dec. 3 and 10). He stated that the congress was much better than his report.

At St. Ansgar, Iowa, Prof. A. J. Clausen is seen to have organized a local Secular Union and to be holding Bible classes for the young.

Bruce Calvert, editor of The Open Road (Griffith, Ind.), and Elbert Hubbard, editor of The Philistine (East Aurora, N. Y.), were speakers at the second convention of the Indiana Rationalist Association, at Indianapolis, November 4-7. Dr. T. J. Bowles of Muncie and D. W. Sanders of Covington were respectively president and secretary of this state organization.

The South African Rationalist Press Association

functioned actively in Johannesburg under the presidency of Mr. John Latham.

Topeka, Kansas, elected a good man for mayor that year, almost wholly on a religious issue so far as the opposition could make it one. Mr. J. B. Billard, a sturdy Freethinker of the Old Guard who had carried on a fight to exclude religious teaching from the public school attended by his children, stood for the office and was elected. The religious people called him an Atheist, who for that reason should not be chosen to rule over a Christian town. The Atchison Globe said: "There is no contention that he is otherwise unfit for the office. In fact, it appears that nothing else can be said against him. No one denies, even among his strongest orthodox opponents, that he would, in all probability, make a most excellent mayor." Paying tribute to Mr. Billard as a man of clean and upright life, who had amassed a comfortable fortune without making enemies of those with whom he dealt, and considering the opposition to his election on the grounds of his unbelief, The Globe declared: "There is nothing in the boast of religious liberty in this country." Mr. Billard was reelected the following year.

The people of Portugal in the fall of 1910 chucked their king in an orderly and bloodless revolution, and set up a republic with Theophilo Braga as provisional president. Senhor Braga was a Positivist and had been a member of the International Freethought Federation and an attendant at its congresses for twenty years. The separation of church and state, a feature of the new government, caused the priests all over the world to predict that it would be short-lived. The next president, Dom Manoel Arriaga, was an Atheist, and the government at Lisbon still lives.

A congress of the International Freethought Federation at Lisbon was opened by Dr. Braga, October 13, called Ferrer Day and dedicated to the memory of the Spanish Freethought martyr.

The bitter cry when Prof. Arthur Drews of Berlin propounded and answered in the negative the question, "Did Jesus ever live?" was an affair of 1910. The professor appeared under the auspices of the League of Monists, the disciples of Ernst Haeckel, before a large concourse of people. at the Zoological Gardens, and defended his theory that there never was such a person as Jesus of Nazareth. So many present wished to confute Professor Drews that the discussion of the historic·ty of Jesus lasted until 3 o'clock the next morning, and continued in the press for many months. Dr. Drews soon published a book embodying his theory. His name is pronounced Drevs.

The reappearance of Halley's comet in 1910 was the subject of a learned editorial article in The Truth Seeker of May 28, by the able James F. Morton, Jr., who, failed not to animadvert upon the superstitious belief once held that comets were messengers bearing divine warning, or else satanic visitants. In the Middle Ages (1456) Pope Calixtus III went to the trouble of issuing a bull against this comet that since 1680 has borne the name of the astronomer Halley.

The friendly relations heretofore subsisting between our public men, especially the Presidency, and his holiness the pope, were in 1910 subjected to a strain. When Pius X celebrated the golden jubilee of his ordination, President Taft sent no congratulatory message; instead, he preached in the Mormon Temple at Salt Lake City. That fighting organ of the church, The Catholic Observer of Pittsburgh, demanded of Mr. Taft his reason and an apology for this discourtesy and neglect. Taft kept mum.

While in Egypt, on a world tour, Roosevelt received from Rome, relayed by the American ambassador, Leishman, a message which read: "The Holy Father will be delighted to grant audience to Mr. Roosevelt on April 5, and hopes nothing will arise to prevent it, such as the much-regretted incident which made the reception of Mr. Fairbanks impossible." In reply, the Colonel said to Mr Leishman that the pope could receive him or not as he chose; but, "on the other hand," he added, with no doubt a rising inflection as he thought of the cheek of this foreigner telling the hero of San Juan Hill where he got off at—"on the other hand, I in my turn must decline to make any stipulations or submit to any cond'tions which in any way limit my freedom of conduct."

The pope wouldn't budge, and Leishman so informed Mr. Roosevelt. "Proposed presentation is, of course, now impossible," said the Colonel, making it snappy; and that closed the incident.

Judge William J. Gaynor, mayor of New York, said at a meeting of the Sinking Fund commissioners that he saw no reason for exempting the churches from local assessments. Mayor Gaynor was already disliked by the Catholics because he was an ex-member of their church; he now fell under the criticism of Protestants also. Undeterred by the censure he brought upon himself from these sources, he made a publ'c address condemning censors and vice agents. Said he: "When I meet a man whose chief passion is to arrest somebody, I know I have met a man with a criminal heart. He may try to hide it, but at heart he is vicious."

When Judge Gaynor was a candidate for mayor, a Catholic priest, the Rev. W. J. Dougherty, denounced him from the altar of the Church of St. Athanasius, in the Bronx. "There is one candidate who seeks our votes," the priest said, "who is utterly unworthy. This man has denied h's God. He is an Atheist." In August, 1910, a Catholic named Gallagher shot and dangerously wounded Mayor Gaynor as he was about to sail for Europe on a vacation. A strange feature of the case was that three months later Gallagher had not been brought to trial. I recall how a Socialist speaker named Patrick L. Quinlan almost lost his reputation among the readers of The Call (Socialist) by wr'ting to The Truth Seeker about this mystery and then mentioning it while speaking from a Socialist platform. Some one accused Mr. Quinlan of being an "anarchist" and promoting violence. In replying to his accuser he named Gallagher, "The Roman Catholic Knight of Columbus and Tammany man, who attempted the assassination of Mayor Gaynor"; and then Mr. Quinlan went on to inquire why Gallagher had not been tried. The Call's correspondents protested that attacking the Catholic church was no legitimate part of the Socialist propaganda, and they desired to hear no more of it.

The procrastination in the trial of the egregious Gallagher was no doubt due to the forbearance of the "Atheist" Gaynor. The mayor tended to be pagan and stoic, and quoted the moral maxims of Epictetus until the habit became a joke. He was a good mayor, but the men whose chief passion is to arrest somebody, the men vicious at heart, survive and succeed him. He opposed the censorship of pictures and plays, and he refused to suppress on complaint of the Federation of Catholic Societies, Sara Bernhardt's play "La Samaritaine," with a presentation of Jesus Christ, who had a speaking part. In 1911 the Legislature of New York added to the Penal Law paragraph 2074, "preventing presentation of living characters representing the Divine Person."

The Supreme Court of Illinois, the opinion being handed down by Judge Dunn, decided in 1910 that the reading of the Bible, the singing of religious hymns, and the repetition of the verses of scripture known as the Lord's Prayer in the public schools was in violation of the constitution of the state. Holding that religious exercises in schools at which attendance was compulsory made religious worship obligatory, Justice Dunn said: "The free enjoyment of religious worship includes the freedom not to worship."

Bernarr Macfadden, "a victim of Comstock-promoted eroticism," found himself amerced in a fine of $2,000. President Taft approved a recommendation that Macfadden, instead of going to jail, should be allowed to pay his fine in installments. I believe this is the only instance of executive clemency where conviction has been had under the United States statute against sending obscene literature through the mails.

Secretary N. Levy of the Secular Society of Edinburgh, Scotland, published for a while a lively little penny monthly named The Universal Reformer. The Liberal League of Los Angeles issued The Agnostic Index, C. Severance principal contributor, to announce and report its meetings. Mr. Y. Oyama, becoming a Freethinker through reading The Truth Seeker while in Oakland, Cal., returned to his native land and started a monthly of his own, Junri (The Rationalist) in Yokohama. The Searchlight, Waco, Texas, J. D. Shaw editor, suspended publication.

Early in 1909 the White Star liner Republic was rammed by the Italian steamer Florida in a collision sixty-five miles off Nantucket. Those were the early days of wireless telegraphy. The Republic had on board as operator a young man named Binns, who won world-wide applause for his courage in standing by and sending out distress calls until other vessels came and took the four hundred and fifty passengers off the ship, which shortly went down. The Truth Seeker congratulated the materialistic scientist Marconi, who invented the wireless, for the triumph of his system, and asked what the believers in prayer had to say about it. Said an editorial paragraph: "The Rev. Father William Walsh, a Jesuit, preaching in the Roman Catholic church of St. Paul the Apostle, New York, told his congregation that the wireless telegraph illustrates the harmony between science and religion and shows how communications by prayer pass from men to God. But the Rev. Walsh's theory lacks demonstration, for even if it were admitted that men in their distress might communicate with God by wireless, it has yet to be shown there ever was a response from the receiver such as came to the Republic from the vessels that got its messages. In the matter of the answer, or the want of it, the parallel drawn between wireless and prayer must fail."

In its argument The Truth Seeker did not avail itself of the fact that another fatal unlikeness could be seen in the sender of the message, who was not by any means a praying person. It failed to mention the wireless operator, Jack Binns. But Mr. Binns later came in and revealed himself as a Freethinker, a purchaser of Freethought literature, who in 1910 submitted an article destructive of religious belief, which was printed with his picture on the front page.

Mr. Binns became the radio expert editing "Picked Out of the Air" in Collier's.

Commander Robert E. Peary, the arctic explorer, who returned from a voyage with the North Pole for a bowsprit, as some one said, reported the discovery of a tribe of Eskimos who were good without God. In the February number of Hampton's Magazine he wrote:

"Without religion and having no idea of God, they will share their last meal with any one who is hungry, while the aged and helpless among them are taken care of as a matter of course. They are healthy and pure blooded; they have no vices, no intoxicants, no bad habits—not even gambling. Altogether, they are a people unique upon the face of the earth. A friend of mine calls them philosophic Anarchists of the North."

For The Truth Seeker of December 24 I had to write a eulogistic editorial, illustrated with his picture, on Edward Tuck, Dartmouth's favorite son, who had just made that educational institution a gift of $400,000, completing a million. Mr. Tuck had been for several years, was then, and is now, a supporting subscriber of this magazine for Freethinkers. If I have not said before, I will say now, that the Dartmouth College Class Book, 1862, contained the biographies of two Freethinkers, Edward Tuck and Samuel P. Putnam, and that their lives furnished more material for the biographer than any of the other members of that class.

Such members of the Fourth New York Liberal League as survived were notified in January of the death of their former hostess, Mrs. Emma L. Fernandez, a woman quite distinguished in her way, who "twenty-eight or thirty years ago had a house in Second avenue, this city, and opened its parlors to this local Liberal organization, which held there a number of entertaining meetings."

In the same month the Washington Secular League mourned the loss and honored the memory of Capt. F. W. Crosby, who had just died at 86. Captain Crosby, by profession a geologist and mining engineer, founded the large collection of geological specimens which bears his name, in the National Museum.

January 20 Samuel Toomey of Canal Dover, Ohio, pioneer in thought and industry and a strong support of Freethought in state and country, ended a life remarkable in many ways, in his 80th year.

Editor Moses Harman of Eugenics, formerly Lucifer the Lightbearer, baffled further pursuit by Anthony Comstock and other hounds of that breed by quietly dying in Los Angeles, January 30, near the close of his eighth decade.

When Spiritualism doubled in Freethought, in the '80s, John R. Francis, an old newspaper man, established in Chicago The Progressive Thinker, which soon became the most widely circulated Spiritualist paper in the world. He died on the second of March, aged 78. The Progressive Thinker survives.

Returning in December from his annual trip to Bermuda, Mark Twain (Samuel Langhorne Clemens) announced that he had written his last book, if not finished it. In feeble health he survived a few months and died at Stormfield, his country home in Redding, Conn., April 22, 1910, being 74 years and almost six months old. He was a most irreverent writer and speaker, although he sometimes said he was not so irreverent as he sounded. He did not to my knowledge call himself a Free-

MARK TWAIN (GERHARDT'S BUST).

The Truth Seeker called him its most irreverent subscriber, but he said he was not so irreverent as he sounded.

thinker, and yet for years he took The Truth Seeker
and had just renewed his subscription. Wm. Dean
Howells, Mark Twain's close and intimate friend,
wrote of his belief, in Harper's Monthly:

"He greatly admired Robert Ingersoll, whom he called an
angelic orator, and regarded as an evangel of a new gospel,
the gospel of Freethought. He took the warmest interest
in the newspaper controversy raging at the time as to the
existence of a hell; when the noes carried the day, I suppose that no enemy of perdition was more pleased. He
still loved his old friend and pastor, Mr. Twichell, but he
no longer went to hear him preach his sane and beautiful
sermons, and was, I think, thereby the greater loser. Long
before that, I had asked him if he went regularly to church,
and he groaned out: 'Oh, yes, I go. It 'most kills me, but
I go,' and he went because his wife wished it. He did tell
me, after they both ceased to go, that it had finally come
to her saying, 'Well, if you are to be lost, I want to be
lost with you.' He could accept that willingness for supreme sacrifice, and exult in it, because of the supreme
truth as he saw it. After they had both ceased to be
formal Christians, she was still grieved by his denial of
immortality, so grieved that he resolved upon one of those
heroic lies, which for love's sake he held above even the
truth, and he went to her, saying that he had been thinking
the whole matter over, and now he was convinced that the
soul did live after death. It was too late. Her keen vision pierced through his ruse, as it did when he brought
the doctor who had diagnosticated her case as organic disease of the heart, and after making him go over the facts
of it again with her, made him declare it merely functional.

"To make an end of these records as to Clemens's beliefs,
so far as I knew them, I should say that he never went
back to anything like faith in the Christian theology, or
in the notion of life after death, or in a conscious divinity.
It is best to be honest in this matter; he would have hated
anything else, and I do not believe that the truth in it can
hurt any one. At one period he argued that there must

have been a cause, a conscious source of things; that the universe could not have come by chance. I have heard, also that in his last hours or moments he said, or his dearest ones hoped he had said, something about meeting again. But the expression, of which they could not be certain, was of the vaguest, and it was perhaps addressed to their tenderness out of his tenderness. All his expressions to me were of a courageous renunciation of any hope of living again, or elsewhere seeing those he had lost."

Norway's distinguished poet, dramatist, and Freethinker, Björnstjerne Björnson, died in Paris, April 25, seventy-eight years old. A member of the International Freethought Federation, a translator of the writings of Ingersoll, a defender of the prosecuted Viktor Lennstrand, there was no doubting where he stood on the religious question.

From The Truth Seeker of June 18:

"The death of Prof. Goldwin Smith removes one of the most important and striking figures among the representatives of advanced thought. The more notable leaders in the direction of mental emancipation are rapidly passing from us. Mark Twain, Bjornson, Goldwin Smith, have followed in rapid succession, hard upon the all-too fresh losses of Conway, Swinburne, Meredith. Perhaps Georg Brandes, the magnificent champion of progressive thought, is the most towering figure among the surviving pioneers of the stupendous intellectual advances of the past generation."

Goldwin Smith was not one of the Freethinkers of his day, but was to be honored by them because he defended their right to be heard. A resident of Toronto and editor of The Week, he condemned the exclusion of The Truth Seker from Canada. In religion he was a Modernist. He left an unpublished address in which the following good advice is found: "Frankly let us accept what is really proved, however unwelcome. Frankly let us give up what has been clearly disproved, however dear. Of what we give up let us not try to fill the place with figments."

It was related of Joseph L. Buxton, partriarch of Milford, Mass., who died April 26, aged 74, that he would "stop on the street to comfort a crying child," or "pick a stone out of the street to save a horse from stumbling"; that he once paid the fine of an employee who had robbed him; that he was never too busy to stop and mend a child's broken top; and that he would rather be known as one who loved "the flowers, the birds, and the babies"—all things both great and small—than be the richest man in Milford. The Milford Daily News stated that the creed of Mr. Buxton was "in brief the plat-form on which the founder of the faith established his ministry to human kind," and that his disposi-tion was "as closely allied to the spirit of Christ as the flower is related to the sunshine." This shows that a man's belief is not to be inferred from his disposition and his acts, for Mr. Buxton, a read-er of The Truth Seeker, was an Atheist, a philo-sophical Anarchist, a social radical or Freelover, and unorthodox withal.

There is quite a historical romance in the life of Major Charles C. DeRudio, U. S. A., retired, Italian by birth, who closed his 78 years of exciting exis-tence on Nov. 1, 1910, at Los Angeles. He had a two-column obituary in The Truth Seeker and more than that in the newspapers.

CHAPTER XXII.

FOR its first number in 1911 The Columbian Magazine accepted an interview with Thomas A. Edison by Edward D. Marshall, a correspondent crippled in the service of his newspaper, according to my recollection, in the Spanish-American War, and incapacitated for active reporting. Edison had already let the public understand that he had no belief in Christianity; this interview was an expression of his opinions on religion extended to the length of a magazine article. He re pudiated theology as a structure of inaccuracies, asserted by the theologians without study, investigation, or attempt at proof. He said he did not believe in immortality, in heaven or in hell, and that while he saw intimations of the existence of a supreme intelligence, he in no wise related this intelligence to the deities of the prevailing religions.

The Freethinkers of the United States having been invited to participate in a Monistic congress at Hamburg, Germany, September 8-11, 1911, The Truth Seeker asked them to name delegates. Dr. E. B. Foote, Jr., president of the Thomas Paine Historical Association, authorized Thaddeus Burr Wakeman, who was just Haeckel's age, to repre-

THOMAS A. EDISON, 1910.

He harrassed the clergy by rejection of heaven, hell, immortality, and the deities of the current religions.

sent that society. The American Secular Union appointed James F. Morton, Jr.

Haeckel at this period was under fire from two church societies, the Catholic Thomists, named after Thomas Aquinas, and the Keplerbund, composed of Protestant Fundamentalists, who "misused the name of the great astronomer Johann Kepler to veil their true aim," the discrediting of evolution by an attack on the integrity of its leading exponent in Germany. Haeckel, long a reader of The Truth Seeker, forwarded his "Answer to the Jesuits," Catholics and Protestants, and we printed it.

Haeckel also sent to The Truth Seeker his article on the Kernfragen, or kernel questions, of Philosophy, published as "What Monism Really Is," preceded by "My Church Departure," stating the reasons for his late withdrawal from the state Evangelical church. These articles kept up the interest,

On August 12 came the announcement: "The amount needed for the expenses of the delegates to the Monist Congress, together with the cost of collecting it, has now been received." The "cost of collecting" included solicitations to subscribe sent by mail to all the Liberals we could reach, and the return of a receipt in the form of a handsome Souvenir that looked like a gold bond. Morton got away the 5th of August. Wakeman departed on the 24th of the same month, bearing with him the greetings of American Freethinkers to Haeckel, to be delivered at the Haeckel home in Jena. On his arrival at Hamburg he had a letter to "Dear G. E. M." as he addressed me, ready to mail. Morton wrote on a postcard that the distractions of the trip had prevented him from writing. No distraction ever stopped Wakeman. He commuted from Cos Cob, Connecticut, to New York, and wrote articles on the way. From Hamburg he sent word regarding the prospective excursion of one hundred and fifty delegates to Jena: "The presentation of our address will be the great feature of the occasion." That address, composed by Mr. Wakeman and left to be printed at the proper date, greeted Haeckel as "Rightly Honored and Worshipful Sir" (for Wakeman held that worship was only another way of spelling worthship), and recounted his services in working out human emancipation and salvation through the sciences. In view of these, it said, "we become sensible of a profound feeling of indebtedness and gratitude toward you too great for us either to express or measure."

Mr. Wakeman reported the proceedings of the Monist Congress, and then went to Jena to present the address to Haeckel. He is in all the pictures, and he summed up his story in "An Hour with Haeckel." Mr. Morton also gave some of the details. The secretary of the Congress, Mr. C. Reiss, furnished The Truth Seeker with digests of the addresses made by the Europeans, who had prepared them in advance. They were translated by the former Rev. Mr. A. Kampmeier of Iowa and printed with portraits.

This photograph shows the last grouping of the foreign delegates and visitors to the Hamburg Congress as they were about to leave the house of Professor Haeckel at

Jena on the morning of September 13, 1911. The distinguished features of Haeckel appear at the centre of the group near the door. In front, at the reader's left, sits Prof. Lester F. Ward, the eminent author and sociologist of Brown University, Providence, R. I. At his left will be recognized the features of Prof. T. B. Wakeman, our senior delegate. The picture is a souvenir of the large meeting at the above place and date by the said delegates, visitors and friends from abroad, to interview, address, and take leave of Professor Haeckel. On this occasion the address from the twelve hundred contributors to the American Delegate Fund raised by The Truth Seeker was read and presented by Delegate Wakeman. The address was afterwards appropriately engrossed, enrolled with the names and residences of the contributors, and forwarded to Professor Haeckel.

Haeckel's fine response to the greetings of American Freethinkers appeared December 2. "So much more precious and gladdening to me," he said, "was the visit of the comrades from Hamburg to Jena, and especially the circumstance that the American delegates, headed by Prof. Thaddeus Burr Wakeman and Prof. Lester Ward, shared in the visit, and gratified me by their lovable presence, while honoring me by their thoughtful addresses."

On complaint of two Christian missionaries in Moulmein, one hundred and seventy-five miles from Rangoon, Burma, the local authorities brought to trial for blasphemy the Buddhist monk U. Dhammaloka, who, besides defending Buddhism, organized the Burma Freethought Association and made an aggressive fight against Christianity and the Bible. The court held him under substantial bonds "to keep the peace" or for "good behavior."

Harry Franck, on a "Vagabond's Journey

Around the World," 1903-4, interviewed this Bud-
dhist monk and quoted him as saying that "Jaysus
Christ was the biggest faker the world ever saw
or didn't see," or words to that effect. For U.
Dhammaloka was an Irishman and his name was
O'Rourke.

India's only Freethought journal, edited by Dev
Ratan, came from Parbatashram, Solan district,
Simla, under the name of Vigyan Mulak Dharma
(Science Grounded Religion).

In Austria, which, as William Heaford wrote,
had "become the last refuge of the papal owner,"
the public prosecutor at Prague began an action
against sixteen members of a section of the International Freethought Federation for having formed
a Freethought society without the authorization of
the magistrates. The motive of the prosecution was
first the suppression of Rationalism, and second to
defeat the proposed congress and demonstration of
the five hundredth anniversary of John Hus in 1915.
The secretary of the society dissolved by the government, Dr. Bartosek, edited for many years Volna
Myslenka (Freethought) and issued other Rationalist publications. The prosecuted Freethinkers
were subjected to fines of 410 kroner (about $100)
each.

The Polish Freethinker and writer, Niemojewski,
was sent to a Russian prison for blasphemy. He
had criticised the catechism.

At Leeds, England, J. W. Gott and T. W. Stewart were summoned for blasphemy.

In the State of Washington, U. S. A., Mr. Jay
Fox, editor of The Agitator, Home Colony paper

at Lake Bay, was put under $1,000 bonds on a charge of "publishing matter tending to encourage disrespect for the law and the courts."

For playing tennis on Sunday, Upton Sinclair and ten other members of the Single Tax colony at Arden, Delaware, spent eighteen hours in the New Castle county workhouse, seven hours of the time breaking rocks on the stone pile. Mr. Sinclair expressed great indignation and said it made him feel "like blowing up someone with a bomb."

In Little Rock, Arkansas, a court declared Mr. E. W. Perrin, then a resident of that city, incompetent as a witness for refusing to affirm his belief in the existence of a god.

The Rev. John H. Dietrich, pastor of St. Mark's Memorial Reformed church in Pittsburgh, Pa., chose this season for the preaching of certain heretical sermons. In one, entitled "The Kind of Salvation the World Needs," he affirmed that "above all else we need to be saved from that scheme of things which starts from the fall, with an atonement wrought by a dying God midway, and an eternal hell at the end." His congregation which liked him grew wonderfully, and "stood by the pastor to a man"; but the Alleghany classis impeached him of heresy and he resigned. Mr. Dietrich answered a call to the Unitarian church in Spokane, Washington, and has been a minister of that denomination ever since. He is now (1929) minister of a flourishing humanistic Unitarian society in Minneapolis, Minn., of which Lemuel K. Washburn was "pastor" not far from fifty years ago.

James W. Stillman, lawyer, author, and Free-thinker, made a formal application to United States District Attorney French, in Boston, to know whether the Bible, with its grist of passages that would have a tendency, when read, to corrupt the morals of those open to such influences, was a mail-able book under the law against the circulation of obscene literature. Mr. Stillman left a copy of the Bible with the district attorney for his exam-ination. Mr. French, having looked into it, de-cided that passages referred to, in their place and context, could never tend to affect deleteriously even "the most prurient and lascivious mind." Here then, is a "phenomenon," for how a rational mind can call anything at all indecent, and yet give the Bible a certificate for purity, is one of the most impenetrable mysteries that ever baffled human in-quiry.

On account of 1911 being the tercentenary of the King James version of the Bible, the book re-ceived many eloquently conceived testimonials in public speeches by politicians who had not parted its covers since they went to Sunday school.

The Union Theological Seminary educated Nor-man Thomas to be a Calvinist minister, but at the last moment something went wrong, for ten mem-bers of the New York Presbytery in solemn con-clave pronounced him unorthodox and opposed his application for a license to preach.

Paul F. Berdanier illustrated the paper in 1911, usually with antipapal pictures. He was an artist of remarkable skill. His decorative work is to be seen in the Ingersoll Birthday Book.

Mrs. L. S. Carter of Kansas, a Truth Seeker reader, added to the long list of Freethought charities by founding, in her eighty-third year, the Carter Home for Babies at Wichita, Kansas.

Singleton W. Davis, Los Angeles, gave up the publication of his Humanitarian Review on account of his age, which was 70.

Marshall J. Gauvin, still known as "Govang," claimed the front page with a lecture and a picture May 13. The picture is reproduced on page 597.

A Sunday rest bill for the District of Columbia got into the Senate, and Heyburn of Idaho argued that if the fourth commandment was to be enforced its provisions should be taken up in their order, the first being "Six days shalt thou labor." The bill did not pass.

George Oliver Roberts and J. Atwood Culbertson were president and secretary of the Buckeye Secular Union, which held a convention in Dayton, Sept. 3. Mr. Culbertson and Bruce Calvert, editor of The Open Road, two of the speakers, are still with us in 1929.

John T. Craps and twenty-five others, assembled in Federation Hall at Columbia, organized in May the Rationalist Society of South Carolina, S. Revelise, secretary and treasurer.

The young sculptor, Fritz Triebel, a Peorian born and reared, executed a bronze statue of Ingersoll to be placed at the Grand entrance of Glen Oak Park, Peoria, Illinois. It was unveiled October 28, in the presence of a splendid gathering, by Ingersoll's grandson, Robert Ingersoll Brown. Eugene F.

INGERSOLL'S FAMILY AT HIS STATUE.

The picture was taken Sunday, October 29, 1911. The persons appearing in it are from left to right: Mrs. Wallston H. Brown (Eva Ingersoll), Maud Ingersoll, Mrs. Ingersoll, Robert G. Ingersoll Brown, Eva Ingersoll Brown.

Baldwin, president of the Ingersoll Monument Association and editor of the Peoria Star, made the first address, and one would need to attend many memorial meetings to hear a better one. The speakers following were Charles Francis Adams, the Hon. John J. Lentz, the Rev. B. G. Carpenter, Clark E. Carr, and Judge French. Dr. Carpenter read letters from Andrew Carnegie, Ernst Haeckel, Andrew D. White, Thaddeus B. Wakeman, and Bolton Hall.

The Truth Seeker Company published in 1911 the Ingersoll Birthday Book, which was the work

of many years by the Lady opposite me in family life, with a Preface by Eva Ingersoll Brown, granddaughter to the author of the contents of the book. The accompanying picture is that of Miss Brown, who was an occasional contributor to The Truth Seeker in r e v i e w s, biographical sketches, and verse. Her first appearance pictorially was in the familiar photograph of Ingersoll "with daughters' babes upon his knees."

Secretary Reichwald of the American Secular Union was obliged to bring an injunction suit against the Cook County Commissioners to restrain them from allowing a Catholic church to be erected on county land. Reichwald was applauded for his courage in grappling with so large a proposition

as Catholic graft in Chicago. He took issue with
the authorities also on the right of Freethought
speakers to hold open air meetings, religious speakers talking undisturbed. A young man named Bertrand L. Weber, making anti-Christian speeches,
was several times arrested. After a number of
appearances in court, Weber, backed by Mr. Reichwald, won his point. "The splendid success of our
friends in Chicago," said The Truth Seeker, "is

He was
President
of the
New York
Liberal Club
and
Presided
while a
Candidate
for the
Presidency
of the
United States.

simply one of the results of the American Secular Union."

Meeting notices filled a column of the paper every week, but the Manhattan Liberal Club was no longer among them, so that members could not be gathered to celebrate the one hundredth anniversary, February 3, of its ancient president, Horace Greeley.

The former mayor of Racine, Wisconsin, M. M. Secor, 65 years old, died Jan. 5, and his body was laid to rest beneath a marble shaft on which he had caused to be inscribed the question: "Why did a good God create a bad Devil?" The ministers, said the press report, "raised a great uproar and by every means tried to have the inscription removed." The report added: "Secor was known here as honest, sincere, and charitable, and an outspoken Freethinker." He had taken The Truth Seeker for fifteen years.

We had for many years as a contributor C. L. James of Eau Claire, Wis., author of an excellent, perhaps the best of its size, "History of the French Revolution." He died June 3 at an advanced age.

Editor-in-Chief Charles Eric Borglund of the Swedish Freethought paper Forskaren, published in Minneapolis, was said to be the best informed man, scientifically, writing in Scandinavian in the Northwest. He died the 20th of July, aged 62.

In February a notice of the book by Baroness von Zedtwitz, "The Double Doctrine of the Church of Rome," mentioned the maiden name of the author, who had recently died, Mary Elizabeth Caldwell, and of her sister, Mary Gwendolen Caldwell.

These women as the daughters and heirs of William Shakespeare Caldwell had given respectively $300,000 and $50,000 to the Catholic church. Two former Catholic priests told me that a bishop wheedled the money out of the sister who put up the most of it by making her his mistress, and that his subsequent desertion of her for another was the cause of their abjuring the errors of Romanism.

ASENATH CHASE MACDONALD.

"The Close of a Useful Life." So was entitled an article from my pen in The Truth Seeker for March 18, 1911. The life which had been closed was that of my mother, Mrs. A. C. Macdonald, who died in Westmoreland, N. H., March 10, in her eighty-first year, and the story of most of it has been related early in these pages. After living in New York for some thirty-five years, mother went West and made her home at my house in Snohomish. When I came back to The Truth Seeker she went to Seattle, and thence to the Socialist colony in Burley, where she was appointed to the office of Superintendent of Domestic Economy, the duties of which proved to be washing dishes for the group. Though an efficient, energetic, and willing worker, she soon perceived that this was not the solution of the domestic problem; and, withdrawing from Burley (which retained as much of her membership fee as had been paid), she cast her lot with the individualist-communists at Home, in the same state. Among these kindly idealists, where none was expected to "cooperate" by doing other people's work, she would probably have ended her days, except for a desire to see her boys again, which brought her back to the vicinity of New York in 1907, to find at last a "home" in New Hampshire suitable to the condition as regards bodily and mental health to which she had become reduced by age.

Her life was remarkably full and complete. There were in it no gaps of idleness or frivolity. Her duties as wife and mother were not neglected. A war widow who raised and educated two sons to the best of her ability has done her part. She could do a woman's work in the house, or a man's work out of doors if it came to that, and take pride in it. She could have knocked a habitation together with a hammer, and then sat inside it and done lacework. She had a philosophical mind which might have produced a critique on Kant as abstruse as Kant's critique on reason. She was at ease in all society, unfluttered by the presence of the distinguished, the great or the learned, nor uncomfortable if the company was poor and ignorant so long as it was honest. Her views were broad within limits, and she was always a Freethinker. At the funeral one of her oldest acquaintances, Thaddeus Burr Wakeman, spoke in the chapel of the crematory at North Bergen. In an address feelingly delivered, he eulogized this spiritual descendant of Thomas Paine—for like Paine she was reared a Quaker—and the example she had set, by her multiplied activities, to guide those women of arrested development who stop satisfied with only one look in the direction of progress.

The account of my childhood days, following the

Civil War, relates how my mother came to be one
of the first trained nurses. From "references"
which she obtained, and which in some mysterious
way have been preserved, it appears that prior to
being graduated as a professional from the school
of Dr. Dio Lewis she combined housekeeping with
nursing. In an undated envelope upon which she
had written "Testimonials" I discover a reference
signed by the Rev. Nath'l Allen, Principal W. N.
(West Newton, Mass.) English & Classical School,
Sept. 16, 1867, which bears testimony that Mrs. A.
C. Macdonald "has been in our family as Nurse
and Acting Housekeeper for our family of thirty."
The family must have taken boarders, and seeing
that there were thirty whom she served as Nurse
and Acting Housekeeper, those whom it might concern would not be surprised at her reverend employer's next remark: "She is a woman of more
than common ability and executive talent." She
needed to be. He adds—and one Carrie B. Allen
approves by appending her signature: "I consider
her a woman of high-toned and irreproachable moral character." The same year the Rev. William O.
White, "for 16 years pastor of 'Keene Unit'n Cong.
Soc.'," wrote: "I find that the opinion respecting
her trustworthiness and her excellent traits as a
nurse, which I feel warranted in expressing, is
shared by those who have known her still longer
than myself."

As Judge Joseph Wheless instanced in his review of Volume I of this History, I am of high
moral and religious antecedents. I append a fac
simile testimonial strengthening the impression

made by the two I have quoted by adding definite "Christian principle" to the lineage:

Cambridge, Mass. Sept. 9. 1867.

Mrs. A. C. McDonald was a member of my family in Scattboro Mass, for nearly three years, 1863-1866. She is of the most respectable New England connections, of great intelligence and energy of character, and one who, in my judgment, can be wholly trusted in any situation which she may undertake & may be found competent to fill.

(Rev.) J. H. Allen.
Editor of Christian Examiner.

This witness, besides being a minister, was a religious editor. There is doubt in my mind that mother would have passed a close examination, even then, on her orthodoxy, for she was reading The Banner of Light, the Spiritualist weekly published in Boston. Spiritualists, with their new revelation, looked upon orthodox Bible Christians as "benighted."

Regarding death, I never knew a woman who had so little apprehension about it as this mother of mine. From her long experience with last moments, she reached the conclusion that no one who is sick enough to die is afraid, or takes any thought at all about the future state. Cremation was her choice, on which she remarked that she would prefer to pass to her final rest in the light of her own views. I felt exceedingly grateful to my friend James P. Morton that in an appreciative paragraph of the "Certain Comments" he was writing weekly for the paper he should have quoted this from Henley:

"To her Death came—the great Deliverer came!—
As equal comes to equal, throne to throne.
She was a mother of men.

. . . .

Between the river and the stars,
O royal and radiant soul,
Thou dost return, thine influences return
Upon thy children as in life, and death
Turns stingless! What is Death
But Life in act? How should the Unteeming Grave
Be victor over thee,
Mother, a mother of men?

Mr. Morton said, in the words of the poet, that she was the mother of men. To her being the mother of two is due the survival of the Truth Seeker from the death of its founder in 1882 until the present time.

CHAPTER XXIII.

THE first editorial article in Volume XXXIX of The Truth Seeker was a census of the men then living who had been active in Freethought work in the paper's first decade. They were few in number: Israel Betz of Pennsylvania, Dr. W. A. Croffut and David Eccles of Washington, W. F. Jamieson of Michigan, B. F. Underwood and Dr. Juliet H. Severance of Illinois, John E. Remsburg of Kansas, David Hoyle, T. B. Wakeman and E. C. Walker of New York, and Joseph Warwick and Mr. Slensby of Brooklyn. Walker, Czar of the Sunrise Club, is the lone survivor now (July, 1930).

To fill a want long felt, George E. Macdonald, James A. Conway, and James F. Morton organized and incorporated the Freethought Tract Society, electing themselves respectively president, treasurer, and secretary. Generous gifts provided for the publication of tracts, and one hundred thousand were printed. The venture revealed that the printing of tracts was no problem compared with getting them distributed. Perhaps that end was not handled with sufficient zeal. We ought to have engaged a man to give his whole time to it. The Truth Seeker and its works have, in fact, never profited by the services of a skilled circulator. The field is too limited to pay one. I doubt that a success could have been made of such a venture just then, for the World War was coming on, the cost of production doubled and trebled, and owing to these and the difficulties of operation the Tract Society ceased to be active, although it was never dissolved and still pays an annual corporation tax.

In April, on her maiden voyage, the White Star passenger steamer Titanic, newest and largest of the ocean liners, struck an iceberg five hundred miles from Halifax, N. S.; and in this, the worst marine disaster in the history of ocean traffic, some fifteen hundred persons lost their lives.

All unusual events are myth-breeders. A maudlin one went drifting abroad from the wreck of the Titanic to the effect that as the ship went down its heroic band played "Nearer, My God, to Thee" until the musicians were swept from her deck by the angry waves. In the fall Col. Archibald Gracie, an eye-witness and one of the survivors—by the favor of the angels, as he believed—making a speech before the University Club of Washington, D. C., exploded the myth. Colonel Gracie denied that the band showed such bad taste as to play the hymn mentioned, or any other, and the musicians were not quite crazy enough to sit there blowing out psalms till the water flooded their instruments. They played "rag-time," and laid aside their instruments half an hour before the ship went under.

The record of the ministers of the country in

1912 was scandalously bad. It began with the confession of the Rev. Clarence V. T. Richeson of Hyannis, Mass., who had murdered his fiancée Avis Linnell. Undoubtedly this was the meanest murderer known to history, the most pious, and the most treacherous since the Lord raised up Ehud to dispose of King Eglon.

The Rev. Richeson promised to marry two girls. He had no intention of marrying the Linnell girl, who was in trouble by him. He aimed to marry another, who was wealthy and could not be had without marriage. He procured poison and instructed Avis to drink it while immersing her feet in hot water, which she did and died. He hung.

One case plumbed the depth of tragedy. The president of a university in New Orleans, a noted Baptist preacher, writer and educator, sixty-five years old, being in Philadelphia, visited a house of prostitution and died there from an attack of heart disease. And his funeral and burial were conducted in the presence of his wife and daughters. How could they find in their religion or elsewhere alleviation for the mental agony they must have endured? I hope, but doubt, that in their grief and humiliation they found among their fellow-Christians in New Orleans as much commiseration per capita as I felt for them and do now.

The Rev. Jeremiah J. Crowley, for some years a priest in Chicago under the jurisdiction of Archbishop Quigley, exhibited in The Truth Seeker office the photographs of Chicago premises which he averred were, as they appeared to be, devoted to immoral purposes; and he said that they belonged to Archbishop Quigley, who collected the rent.

To continue the subject of ministerial morals in 1912, it was a coincidence that two clerical delegates attending the general conference of the Methodist church in Milwaukee should have been detected in the same offense, that of unlawful cohabitation; which proceedings caused Chicago, through its press, to felicitate itself that among all persons arrested there during the previous year only 17 were clergymen! It was a high percentage as compared with total population and general arrests, but gratifyingly small, the Chicago boomers thought.

A Long Island parson named Jere Knode Cooke, leaving the society of his lawful spouse, did turn in his infatuation to Miss Florence Whaley, a young and sentimental girl, who accepted him as her husband "before God." It was a celebrated case. Next, in the not large town of Kokomo, Indiana, four ministerial scandals came in a row. The situation got no end of publicity in the press. It drew to its consideration the highest efforts of some of our finest minds, and moved the poetess Ella Wheeler Wilcox to devote her best thought to a solution of the problem why in this manner men and women go astray. Mrs. Wilcox advanced the hypothesis, which she held might be established as a tenable theory, that there were present in the human system, possibly to be isolated with the progress of science, what she named as "love microbes," of two kinds, the benign and the pernicious. The latter sort, she concluded, caused the mischief.

Now this gave me an opportunity to bring forth another theory having the sanction of time and papal infallibility. As one may read in Draper, shortly after the return of Columbus and his crew to Europe, the reigning pope, who found himself and many of his priests disabled by a malady of mysterious origin, laid the infection to "a certain malignity in the constitution of the air." Draper proposed as an alternative explanation "a certain infirmity in the constitution of man"; but Draper was neither pope nor poet. Speaking of current conditions, I concluded that the atmosphere of Kokomo, Indiana, was especially malign and contraindicated for ministers, and alleged in behalf of the Rev. Mr. Cooke of Long Island that he had probably taken one of the Wilcox microbes into his system, with the result that he was found out.

The incendiary language of the Rev. Father John A. Belford of the Catholic Church of the Nativity in Brooklyn caused a stir among the Socialists, who demanded action upon it as an incitement to murder. The priest in his April bulletin, The Nativity Mentor, spoke as follows:

"The Socialist is busy. He flaunts his red flag and openly preaches his doctrines. His great point of attack is religion. His power is an actual menace in our city. There seems to be no law to suppress or control him. He is more dangerous than cholera and smallpox—yes, he is the mad dog of society and SHOULD BE SILENCED if need be BY A BULLET."

Brooklyn Socialists applying to the Gates Avenue Court to have a warrant issued for the arrest of the reverend inciter to murder, were repulsed. Belford's advocacy of the bullet for Socialists who attack religion stood approved by the secular authorities.

The scenes from clerical life for 1912 seem less interesting as I have been obliged to reduce space in order to bring them into the picture. But they will not get even this space again.

The largest of all Paine dinners ever held in New York commemorated the 175th anniversary. More than three hundred persons were there.

It was a Sunrise Club dinner, under the auspices of the Thomas Paine National Historical Association, whose president, T. B. Wakeman, had the opening speech. As the years go by, I remarked in my report, Mr. Wakeman becomes more and more a devotee of Paine, and finds in his writings a perennial fount of philosophy as well as of political and sociological science. He was now prepared to say that no one who has not studied Paine is fitted to be a teacher of sociology or can have true knowledge of the principles of republicanism.

Prof. Lester F. Ward, who was then delivering nine sociological lectures every week to the students of Brown University, sat beside Mr. Wakeman. Mr. Ward looked like Huxley, and at this remark of Wakeman there was such a twinkle in his eye as might have come to the optic of Huxley if told that his neglect of Paine's works unfitted him to speak as an authority in biology.

A new truth seeker came to the front at this meeting in the person of the Rev. Edgar Swann Weirs, minister of Unity church, Montclair, N. J.

Present also as a speaker was Mr. David Saville

Muzzey, who by a coincidence had been a classmate of Mr. Weirs in the Union Theological Seminary where Presbyterian ministers are manufactured. He is now (1929) called Dr. Muzzey, being history professor in Columbia University. Professor Ward sent me a dollar for Truth Seekers containing the report of his address. I covered a dollar bill into the treasury of the company ,and retained his check as a keepsake.

Very truly yours
Lester F. Ward

I may as well go on from this beginning to make up the story of Freethought in 1912 by the events. George William Foote was elected president of the National Secular Society (England) for the twenty-third consecutive term. Thomas Jackson, an English Freethinker, served a fourteen days' term in jail at Leeds for blasphemy. Stephen Edward Bullock underwent prosecution at the Leeds Assizes for the same offense. Ernest G. Whitney of Kansas City, Kansas, incurred a fine of $300 for displaying on a sack in which he carried radical literature for sale certain sentiments approving materialism as better than religion, and predicting: "The world will finally discard religion altogether." The court remitted the fine on condition that Mr. Whitney discontinue his display.

A large and representative attendance, embracing all European countries, made the International Con-

gress at Munich, Bavaria, Aug. 31-Sept. 3, "an un-
qualified success."

The Indianapolis Rationalist Association held its
annual congress in Indianapolis in November, and
"enters upon the new year with hope, vigor, and a
comfortable balance in the treasury."

Mr. F. J. Gould, Ethical leader and Positivist,
who contributed occasionally to The Truth Seeker
then, and often since, went to India at the request
of the Bombay government to lecture on the Rational Basis of Morals.

To oppose the holding of a religious revival in a
non-sectarian school, twenty-five students of the
Ohio State University at Columbus organized the
Young Men's Infidel Association. Freethinking
students of Cornell, Ithaca, N. Y., associated themselves "to study, investigate, and criticize existing
religions," as the Robert Ingersoll Club.

What I regarded as a wonder took place in Boston in March, when a Roman Catholic organization
there, the Charitable Irish Society, bade President
Taft to its banquet in the Hotel Somerset on March
18—a summons to which the executive unquestion-
ingly responded; and when at his right was seated
Cardinal O'Connell, with Governor Foss assigned
to third place at the table and put third also on
the list of speakers, the wonder occurred. This was
it. Governor Foss, having in his keeping the dignity of the state, declined to sit below "the representative of any foreign or ecclesiastical body." It
was the opinion of Mr. Foss that the governor of a
sovereign state, to the exclusion of all petticoated
man-milliners appointed by the pope, should in his

own bailiwick sit at the right hand of the President of the Union, and he had the courage to manifest his preference for that position by declining an inferior one.

Herman E. Kittredge·of Washington published this year his Appreciation of Ingersoll, which is the standard Ingersoll biography. Alfred H. and Woolsey Teller brought out a fine pamphlet entitled "Gems of Biblical Literature." Dr. William Hirsch's "Religion and Civilization: The Conclusions of a Psychiatrist" appeared under The Truth Seeker Company's imprint. It was a tremendous work of six hundred pages; its main contention is that the patriarchs and prophets, the messiahs and the apostles, including Jesus and his disciples, were mentally unsound—in short, paranoiacs.

Stuart Robson, the eminent actor (died 1903), was a Freethinker in his day and generation who believed thoroughly in the mission of the stage and entertained the heartiest contempt for its clerical defamers. When the clergy attacked the morality of the stage people, Mr. Robson answered them. To make his reply effective he kept a scrap-book in which he collected all published accounts of "ministerial conduct," and this famous book had attained the dimensions of a dictionary unabridged. At his death the volume disappeared. Mr. Robson's son, Stuart Robson, Jr., an actor like his distinguished father, was like him also in being a Freethinker— and he had a notebook. Young Mr. Robson, as bright as a new dollar and earnest withal, liked to draw his notebook on a preacher and ask the man of God to clear up for him some difficulties met in his perusal of the Bible. He came to The Truth Seeker office to report his collisions with the ministers and street evangelists.

In 1910 Prof. Ernst Haeckel had taken his departure from the state church and given his reasons. His example was followed by thousands. "Two modern Brotherhoods of Jesuit societies," as Haeckel called them, "the Evangelical Keplerbund and the Catholic Thomasbund," rivaled each other in concocting slanders about the head of the Secularist movement and Rationalist organization called Monists. On Haeckel's side, among others, was Prof. Wilhelm Ostwald, the chemist and Nobel prize winner. In 1912 the news reached the Secu-

A cartoon in the German newspaper Lustige Blaetter, showing Haeckel and Ostwald widening the church doors to let out the seceders, while the state, represented by the officer, helplessly looks on. The word over the door is deciphered to be "Ausgang" (Exit).

lar press of America from Berlin that "a great falling away from the State church is taking place all
over Germany."

The British Association for the Advancement of
Science held its annual meeting at Dundee, Scotland, and Prof. A. E. Schafer made the presidential
address. His theme was the artificial production of
life, and his thought ran along with that of Prof.
Jacques Loeb's address at the Hamburg Monist
congress in 1911. Professor Schafer stated that
"nothing stands between chemical elements and the
phenomenon called life but the knowledge of exactly how to combine the elements." This knowledge,
he did not doubt, can be obtained. He went further
and "curtly dismissed the idea that there was direct
supernatural intervention in the first production of
life as a theory devoid of scientific foundation,"
which was the same as saying he did not believe
the theory had anything in it. It was Atheism so
far as creation is concerned. A cablegram from
Dundee predicted "torrents of criticism from orthodox pulpits and press." I don't remember, but
leaving aside the aid of memory I'll stake my reputation for veracity that the president of the British
Association never apologized to a Catholic cardinal,
as the president (Osborn) of the American Association apologized to Cardinal Hayes for heresies
uttered at the meeting in New York in 1929.

A Western judge, advising the young to attend
Sunday school, stated that among all the juvenile
delinquents brought before him, none had been a
Sunday school attendant. We thought his experi-

ence exceptional if he had told the truth. The
proof:

"The facts as to church girls come out glaringly
in a paragraph that occurs in the American Year
Book, 1912, published by the Appletons, where it
is related that a church society named the Mission
of Help last year undertook a 'study' of church
girls who had 'gone wrong.' From correctional institutions the society obtained the records of 300
fallen girls—'vagrants,' 'disorderlies,' and 'common prostitutes.' Of the three hundred no less
than 229 were 'church girls,' that is, they had been
'closely connected with some church.' Moreover,
'nearly half of these girls had been communicants,'
and the report frankly describes them as 'the discovered failures of the church.' If the church fails
to that extent with girls, does anybody believe that
the records of any court will show it has uniformly
succeeded with boys?"

The people of Beaver Falls, in Pennsylvania, en-
thusiastically praised the Memorial Day oration of
the Rev. W. A. Sunday, evangelist, and the editor
of the Beaver Falls Times, who printed the address in full, disclosed that the winged words of the
orator were "tipped with fire from heaven." But
the words were Ingersoll's. Evangelist Sunday had
appropriated them without credit.

Mr. Thomas S. Vanasek wrote to the Editor: "I
have an important question to ask you. Will you
please tell me what becomes of the soul after death?
Inclosed find stamp for a reply." He was answered
with another question: "If The Truth Seeker
should die, what would become of Mr. Vanasek's

subscription?"   When Mr. Vanasek died, fifteen years later, he left The Truth Seeker a bequest of five hundred dollars.

The Truth Seeker volume for 1912 carries a history in many chapters of the development of the sectarian Indian school system in this country, by Robert G. Valentine, former United States commissioner of Indian affairs.   As showing how the United States treasury had been burglarized by the sects who maintained, at government expense, schools for teaching Indians their religion, it is worth notice.

I am treating of the year when Theodore Roosevelt organized the Progressive or Bull Moose party, adopted "Onward, Christian Soldiers" as his campaign slogan, and defeated the party that had put him in the White House.   The Catholics failed to deliver to the Republican candidate, William Howard Taft, the support he had paid for out of the country's funds.   While in Milwaukee, in October, a Roman Catholic crank named Schrank, who pretended to have a message from the spirit of former President McKinley, directing him to kill the third-term candidate, shot at Roosevelt and wounded him in the chest.   In the election Roosevelt took second place, Mr. Taft being third, and Woodrow Wilson first.   Taft attended Catholic mass in Washington on Thanksgiving day.   After the election Mr. Wilson seemed to look good to the clericals, who had opposed him in the campaign.   During the Democratic convention in Baltimore, the following passed over the wires:

DR. EDWARD BOND FOOTE (1854-1912).
He was a noble character, compact of all the heresies—
medical, social, political and theological.

"To the Rev. Father Gordon: Have Polish leaders and politicians wire Roger Sullivan to stand by Clark, as the Polish vote will be cast solidly against Wilson on account of his religion, anti-foreign, and prohibition sentiments. Wire any other delegates you know immediately.

"W. J. STONE."

Roger Sullivan was a delegate to the convention; the author of the telegram was William Joel Stone, otherwise "Gumshoe Bill," United States senator from Missouri; the Rev. Father Gordon, pastor of a Polish congregation. In printing the telegram, not found in any of the other papers, for it was a scoop, I suppressed dates and places to conceal the source of the "leak," the telegrapher who handled Senator Stone's message. The "Clark" mentioned was Champ Clark of Missouri, Wilson's rival for the nomination. The incident shows how the Sacred Cow horns-in at political conventions.

The first obituary for 1912 was that of Judge Parrish B. Ladd of Alameda, California, who had written a number of acceptable Freethought books.

John Helm of Port Hope, Canada, was the next —a lifetime subscriber to The Truth Seeker whose subscription had yet four years to run. His local paper, the Port Hope Guide, said: "His lifelong philanthropy won universal respect, and few men leave behind them such universal regret. His loss to the community will be irreparable." Mr. Helm had organized and was president of the Port Hope Benevolent Society, and he would have been 100 years old if he had lived until his subscription to The Truth Seeker expired. And that was the age of his contemporary, another who always took The

Truth Seeker, Dr. H. S. Borrette of Susanville, California. He died in March at 100 years 9 days.

In the year 1883 I wrote a note introducing Miss Susan H. Wixon to the readers of The Truth Seeker as editor of the Children's Corner. She had otherwise contributed to the paper for several years. In 1912 I must record her death, August 28, at her home in Fall River, Mass. Miss Wixon was the first woman to lecture in Paine Hall, "the first to break ground with a Freethought lecture in Fall River," where she held a place on the school board for twenty-one years, and had other honors conferred upon her by her town and state. She was descended from a long line of sea captains who sailed out of Dennis Port, Cape Cod. I do not know her age, which she never told, but probably she could be credited with 65 years.

I have been recording the deaths, mostly, of the elders in the Freethought communion; now it is one of my contemporaries, Dr. E. B. Foote, Junior, called Dr. Ned to distinguish him from his father. After being for many months a shut-in from a trouble that began in what he called "neuritis" but was probably due to blood poisoning contracted when he was a medical student, Dr. Ned died of paralysis the 12th of October, 1912. The last letter he dictated, a few days before that, was addressed to The Truth Seeker.

At the close of the year Maud R. Ingersoll, elder daughter of Robert G. Ingersoll, was married to Wallace McLean Probasco in the home of her mother at 117 East Twenty-first street. Dr. John Lovejoy Eliot officiated.

CHAPTER XXIV.

A LTHOUGH I had recorded in 1912 a resolution to waste no more space on scenes from clerical life, yet in June, 1913, I was compelled by the force of circumstances, as well as a sense of duty, to write an editorial article on "Waywardness of the Clergy," citing instances. This became all the more appropriate, necessary and imperative because a Catholic clergyman, taking exception to the way he had been characterized by my assistant Mr. Morton, and professing to act as "protector of the good name of the priesthood," summoned me to appear in court and answer a charge of criminal libel.

I go now to the instances, which provide a background, as it were, for the account of my prosecution, that year, by one of the cloth:

In Tennessee a minister had had his brother's wife and been put into the chain gang; another in the same state had carried intimacy too far with a lady member of his church, who confessed it; a third was clapped into jail, to stay three months, for selling whiskey; a fourth was serving a fifteen years' sentence for rape. The Federal authorities arrested a Catholic priest in Illinois for using the

mails to defraud; a New Jersey priest married a
woman and deserted her; a Protestant minister
of that state betrayed a girl of 19, and another,
inspired by religious enthusiasm, as reports said,
gave his wife grounds for divorce by taking up
with a woman missionary.

The offenses of a certain parson in Westfield,
N. J., disclosed peculiar features. There were twin
girls of 18 in his congregation, and one of them
he seduced. Accused to his face, he in his confusion made damaging admissions, but his mind
cleared and he saw a way out. Appealing to anatomical science, he obtained the testimony of a
physician to the virginity of the girl. At the trial
the prosecution put the other twin in evidence, and
the doctor testified that this was the one her pastor
had paid him $50 to certify. So the minister was
found guilty. With the remark that here was a
good plot for a medical novel, I regretfully resumed.

A Denver preacher abandoned the girl who was
the mother of his infant and married another. One
Indiana Sunday school teacher and theological student committed forgery; one bootlegged. An Illinois clergyman enticed his young organist to elope
with him; one invaded a home and committed a
crime against childhood, and so on. The priests
and ministers went on about like that throughout
the year, making a record as bad in all respects—
worse in some—as that of 1912.

The wayward ministers were orthodox to a man,
except a brace of Unitarians who sued each other
at law; and yet that special month was thought by
Archbishop Ireland of St. Paul to be the accepted

time for the delivery of a homily on "the decay of religious education and in necessary sequence the decay of morals"; and while the newspapers syndicated these Irelandics a Roman Catholic priest in New York, who had no other education than a religious one, cut up the body of a girl he had corrupted and murdered, and sank torso and limbs in the North River. That was the Rev. Hans Schmidt, officiant at the altar and confessional of St. Joseph's church, 405 West 125th street. The archbishop had affirmed a relation between morals and religion. The facts I had summarized showed the relation was bad for morals. The priest Schmidt involved the Bible and the Catholic religion in his crime by asserting that St. Elizabeth appeared to him and directed him to make a bloody sacrifice, "as the Bible says God did Abraham."

As counsel at his trial, Schmidt was represented by one Alphonse G. Koelble, a hyphenated German Catholic, who gave out that funds had been contributed for the defense. I was told the Knights of Columbus, with other Catholic orders and societies, raised $50,000 for "high-priced legal talent."

Curious facts came to light at the trial. The testimony of the first witness, Miss Anna Hirt, who held at the parish house of St. Boniface a situation like that of Miss Aumuller in the parish house of St. Joseph's, brought to view the queer conditions in clerical establishments. The young woman told the court she had known of the relations between the priest and the maid for at least four months before the murder. Although a Catholic and brought up to believe in the chaste and austere character of the religious, Miss Hirt told her story collectedly, not appearing to be unduly shocked by the immorality of Schmidt. Obviously she regarded the conditions as normal, and not having occasion to mention the affair, never troubled her superiors by communicating the matter to them. It was not news.

I have gone into the case of the Rev. Hans Schmidt, who ultimately went to the electric chair, because I think that a connecting ligament may be followed therefrom to the outcome of a prosecution of myself begun by the Rev. James B. Curry, pastor of St. James's Catholic church, New York, East Side. A summons, issued October 7, brought me on the 9th to the magistrate's court in Center street, with Gilbert E. Roe as counsel. The Rev. Father Curry impeached me of criminal libel, and his attorney, a Jewish lawyer, prayed the court would lock me up for safekeeping. The court, personified in Magistrate Schulz, said the commitment would be deferred until the matter could be looked into to see whether the complaint was well founded. The features of the Rev. Mr. Curry, a man apparently of 65, who sat within the rail, surrounded by younger priests, wore a look of extreme indignation.

The next day we read in the New York Tribune these words:

"What would have happened, father, if some one had said the things of which you complain while in your parish, instead of publishing them?" was asked as he [the priest] left the court room.

"There would have been a call for an ambulance, I am sure," was the reply.

He was "sure," not *afraid,* that some person would have been attacked and beaten. And he expressed to the newspaper man no intention of taking measures or issuing counsel to his parishioners that would avert the violent and unlawful acts that he was certain they were capable of committing.

The alleged libel consisted of certain critical remarks on the plaintiff by James F. Morton in our issue for October 4. Morton, on and about the date of the alleged libelous utterance, was keen for woman suffrage. He worked for The Truth Seeker then, and when he went forth to luncheon he was likely to stop somewhere around the City Hall and make a speech on woman's just claim to the ballot. While so propagandizing on one occasion a gang rushed him and cleaned out his pockets, which embittered Mr. Morton against the foes of suffrage. Therefore when the Rev. Father Curry, in a letter to The Tribune, asserted that all suffragists were doing their best "to lower the standard of womanhood," and that "the woman good and true" did not desire the ballot, Mr. Morton hurled the accusation that the priest, "moved apparently by no cause but the innate impulse of a congenial blackguard," had placed himself, "beyond the pale of decent manhood."

The "common mind" was thus crudely expressed, in both instances by Catholics:

"Bill the Plumber, who sends his children to the parochial school, inquires: 'If a priest can't be a Christian and forgive his enemies, why don't he be a good sport and take his medicine?'

"The man on the street observes: 'These people who

are always calling the rest of us names make the loudest holler when we hand it back to them.'"

Publicity brought to me from Catholic women, or women reared as Catholics, proffers of testimony to the corrupted morality of the priesthood.

Appropriate to the Schmidt case, a girl who had her own grievance against a recreant priest-lover, informed me that the priests were on the watch for immigrant girls not knowing English, to bring them to the parsonage as "assistant housekeepers," but in fact as "mistresses."

A maternity ward in a Catholic hospital in New York, so says a nurse who was employed there, is occupied entirely by girls sent there by priests. But all this was to me much like the Schmidt-Aumuller "intrigue" to Anna Hirt of St. Boniface parish house. It wasn't news, nor available as a defense, though kindly volunteered.

Jacob Riis, the distinguished author and discriminating settlement worker, remarked concerning the residents of the plaintiff's parish: "The poor of the tenement districts have many hardships to endure, but the greatest hardship is to have a man like Father Curry for a pastor."

Whenever my case came up, bringing the Rev. Father Curry to the Center street Court, he said a few words to representatives of the press. Resenting the imputation that he was out for personal revenge, he assured a Tribune reporter that he had been attacked solely because he was a Catholic priest; that through him every Catholic clergyman in the country had been assailed, and the single purpose of his suit was to protect them from further "insult." When he talked as protector of the good name of the priesthood, I cited the Rev. Father Hans Schmidt as one who must feel specially in need of the protection which the East Side father and friend of Tom Foley aimed to give an innocent and persecuted priest.

But I discerned a reason why, after all, Father Curry should not feel so almighty friendly toward Father Schmidt. Away back at the beginning of the suit, my counsel, Gilbert Roe, had moved to have the case continued under the summons until the grand jury could act; and the magistrate, Judge Corrigan, seconded the motion. "If this is a case for the grand jury," said the judge, "why not take it to the grand jury instead of occupying the time of this court?" At that point occurred an incident of the trial that has given me a happy moment every time I have thought of it since; for the assertive little Israel'tish lawyer for the priest uprose and vociferated:

"Because the grand jury has got everything else blocked, and can't be reached for weeks on account of getting an indictment of Hans Schmidt."

The months declined and the year set, and nothing came out of the grand jury room. Meanwhile, as emanating from the prosecut'on, three proposals reached me: (1) that the suit would be withdrawn if I would pay the costs; (2) that it would be withdrawn if I would retract and apologize; (3) that it would be forgotten if I would stop writing about Curry. I accepted the third of the overtures, and the name of the Rev. Father Curry has not appeared in The Truth Seeker for sixteen years, although St. James was the parish of the Hon. A. E. Smith.

Comstockery flourished in 1913 to a limited extent. Before Judge Hazen in the United States District Court at Buffalo, N. Y., appeared Elbert Hubbard of the Philistine, East Aurora, N. Y., and pleaded guilty to circulating through the mails "certain prints of an obscene character." He had not done so, but it was more economical to pay a fine of $100 than to put up a fight for free mails. Thomas Watson, publishing Watson's Magazine in Georgia, suffered an indictment on the same charge. The matter consisted of questions Catholic priests are authorized to put to woman penitents at the confessional. Watson had braced himself for a free press fight when the federal judge, Rufus E. Foster, sustained a motion to quash the indictment.

The New York Freethought Society began holding meetings January 5, in Bryant Hall, 725 Sixth avenue, with William Thurston Brown as speaker. The ex-Rev. Mr. Brown had long since lost his pulpit, as these pages elsewhere have said, for preaching economic heresies. Without complete success he had tried to establish a Modern School after the plan of Francisco Ferrer. As speaker for the Freethought Society he was on firmer ground. Mr. Brown's socialistic ideas not being regular, when he took up Freethought speaking his party dropped him and he drew few Socialists. The lectureship lasted till the end of April.

The Society resumed its meetings at the same hall in November with James F. Morton as lecturer. Meanwhile an International Freethought Congress had been held in Lisbon, Portugal, October 6-8, which Mr. Morton attended as the American *consulato*. The delegates were received with a welcoming speech by President Manoel Arriaga of the Portuguese republic and Senator Magelhaes Lima.

The Indiana Rationalist Association held a memorable Congress at Indianapolis November 8 and 9.

In December Charles T. Sprading, president of the Los Angeles Liberal Club and national lecturer for the Rationalist Association, came to New York and called a meeting at Bryant Hall with the announced intention of waking up the Liberals of the metropolis. He drew an unexpectedly large audience, and gave a stirring address. There had lately been exhibited throughout the country a "miracle painting" entitled "The Shadow of the Cross." The exhibitors represented that the artist had painted on the canvas only a portrait of Jesus, and that the cross which appeared when a spectator looked at the picture just right was the result of divine intervention—a miracle. Mr. Sprading brought with him a duplicate of this miracle picture, which he presented to his audiences, showing only the portrait of Christ, and while one gazed the cross appeared, exactly as in the other faked-up picture that had gulled thousands.

When in 1928 all Catholic women, including unidentifiable nuns, were seen going to the polls to vote for a Catholic candidate who was trying to "crash the presidency," memories that ran back for fifteen years recalled that the prelates of the Catholic church were then making a mean fight against female suffrage. Cardinal Gibbons sent to

a meeting of woman antis in Baltimore a letter expressing the opinion that anything like public life
spoils woman. The sent'ment "evoked hearty applause" when read to the ladies. At the same
date was published, from the diary of Abdul
Hamid, the deposed sultan of Turkey, the sentiment that anything like public life spoils woman.
So the minds of the Turk and Catholic ran along
together. The maintenance of either polygamy or
celibacy—the harem or the convent—necessitates
a subordinate pos'tion for woman.

In The Truth Seeker of November 22, 1913, is
found an editorial article on the subject of "Nuns
and Votaries." The original "nun" was a votary,
a woman of the temple, who devoted part of her
income by prostitution to keeping up the house of
the Lord. The statutes of the Jews prohibited
the practice, and they have no nunneries.

In the spring of 1913 the State of Ohio suffered
great loss of life and property from one of the
worst floods in its history. Out of the wreck and
ruin came a piece of irony unintentional on the
part of its author. The Cleveland Plain Dealer,
describ'ng the fall of a big chimney through the
roof of an apartment house to the cellar bottom,
leaving ruin in its wake, said:

"But the worst wrecked of all the rooms in that cara-
vansary was the dining room of one of the cozy suites
of apartments. The floor was gone, the furnishings
were gone. The first to enter the apartment found only
one thing left—a scriptural text, framed, and still hanging
pathetically on a patch of miraculously preserved wall
space. The placard read:

THE LORD
HATH BEEN
REMINDFUL
OF US."

So human beings capable of suffering, and lives that could not be replaced, were swept away to death and destruction, and an old scriptural lie was "miraculously preserved."

The proprietors of Oddfellows' Temple in Cleveland, Ohio, expelled the Cleveland Freethought Society because the attitude of Henry Frank, its lecturer, toward religion was "objectionable to the interests owning and leasing the building."

The Jewish author and encyclopedist, Isidore Singer, took from The Truth Seeker certain arguments advanced by Hyland C. Kirk of the Washington Secular League to show that Christopher Columbus, discoverer of America, was a Jew. The fruit of the inquiry had a bitter taste in the mouths of the Knights of Columbus.

The old Freethinker and abolitionist with a record dating from antislavery days, G. W. Brown of Rockford, Illinois, was honored in 1913 by the State of Kansas, where some of his best work had been done, by the hanging of his portrait in the capitol at Topeka. Dr. Brown attended a meeting of Freethinkers at Bismarck Grove with John E. Remsburg and David Eccles in the days when our "Fifty Years" was just beginning.

On Thanksgiving day President Wilson, following the precedent set by Roosevelt and imitated by Taft, paraded to mass at St. Patrick's Catholic church with his cabinet and a military escort.

This year being the fortieth anniversary of The Truth Seeker, a review of the four decades seemed to be appropriate, and Mr. E. C. Walker was commissioned to write it. The review began the 20th of September (the paper's birth month) and ran through seven numbers.

During the summer a young Englishwoman named Margaret L. Galois favored The Truth Seeker with her photograph and an article which was so amusing and also so informing that I thought of making it into a tract. Miss Galois, now a Rationalist, had once been missionary for a Scotch Presbyterian Society, which sent her to Vuna-Taviuni, one of the Fiji group of cannibal islands in the South Pacific ocean, exactly at the 180th meridian, where every new day and every new year begins and also ends. The article was interesting throughout as a description of life in the Fijis. The part I quote furnishes the information and amusement:

"The government of the island was largely in the hands of the missionaries, and, curiously enough, both the devout Roman Catholics and our own equally devout company of Presbyterians buried our differences and joined forces to control the natives and put some restraint on the traders. Both the Catholics and the Presbyterians were strong Sabbatarians; among other restrictions, a law was passed making it a criminal offense to sell alcoholic drinks on the Sabbath day. The converts were about equally divided between the Catholics and the Protestants. I noticed, shortly

after the passing of the Sabbath Day law, a row
of shanties being erected exactly on the line of the

The decorative Miss Galois, when a Christian missionary, called on Sir Hiram Maxim to collect funds.   Sir
Hiram pointed out the defects of the missionary system,
after which she became his secretary and a contributor
to The Truth Seeker.

one hundred and eightieth meridian. At first I did not understand the object of this arrangement, but I soon learned. Suppose, for example, that it was Sunday morning on the west side of the meridian line, Sunday would commence to travel westward, and would take twenty-four hours to get completely around the earth and arrive at the east side of the same meridian, then again, the very instant that Sunday arrived, Monday morning would start on the west side, therefore, while it was Monday on the west side of the meridian it was Sunday on the east side, and this peculiar state of affairs was taken advantage of, not only by the natives, but also by the traders. When a bar room was exactly on the line, it was only necessary to move the bottles from one side to the other to enable the dealers to sell rum every day in the year without infringing the Sunday law.

"I was much amused at the ingenuity displayed in the arrangement of one restaurant with a bar room attached. It was a light wooden structure about twenty feet wide and sixty feet long, mounted on wheels in such a manner that the whole building could be moved from one side of the line to the other. By this ingenious arrangement, not only could the bar be opened every day in the year, but the restaurant was very convenient for the Catholics, as it enabled them to eat meat every day in the week without ever eating it on Friday.

"Another great advantage to the island was the fact that no matter what religious party one belonged to, one could catch fish every day in the year without fishing on Sunday, for while it was

Sunday on one side of the island, it was either
Monday or Saturday on the other side. It was absolutely impossible for it to be Sunday on both sides
at the same t me. This was much appreciated by
the beachcombers and natives who depended very
largely upon fish for their food. Moreover, men
with large families were able to work every day
in the year without working on Sundays.

"It was thus that I learned definitely where the
new year commences, and, for that matter, where
every day in the week commences, but, curiously
enough, this small island, with its few thousand
inhabitants, is the only land, except in the frozen
arctic regions, where such a state of affairs
prevails."

DEPARTURES.

The deaths the announcement of which in 1913
brought to Freethinkers regrets, mourning, and lessons of submission to the inevitable began with
that of William S. Andrews, son of Stephen Pearl,
aged 72. In the course of a career of great activity, Mr. Andrews had been actor, soldier, legislator, lecturer, and newspaper man. He had been
commissioner of records for sixteen years at the
time of his death.

A paragraph April 5 pays tribute to M. Florence
Johnson, a daughter of Moses Hull and mother of
Bertha, Pearl and Olive Johnson. She died March
24 in her 57th year. Her last literary work was done
for the Children's Corner of The Truth Seeker.

William Fosket, a wealthy man of Chicago, died
as a result of injuries received in a railroad wreck.

Mr. Fosket's ideal was a Home for Aged Free-
th nkers, to which he proposed to leave his money.
E. C. Reichwald was working for the organizing
of such a home when Mr. Fosket's life was prematurely closed. His death took place March 25,
and his funeral was conducted by Freethinkers.

Prof. Lester F. Ward, having reached the age
of Thomas Paine, of whom he was an early reader,
succumbed to illness at the Kensington Apartments
at Washington, D. C., April 18. He had spent his
72 years usefully and with distinct on. He was

PROF. LESTER F. WARD (1841-1913)
Professor Ward and other Liberals organized in Washington, D. C., in 1869 the National Liberal Reform League
(now the Washington Secular League). Our picture is
a detail from the group shown at the home of Ernst
Haeckel in The Truth Seeker July 13.

among the founders of the Washington Secular League; made many contributions to sociology and science, and was president of Brown University (Rhode Island).

Thaddeus Burr Wakeman deserves here the many columns of tribute that appeared in The Truth Seeker of May 3 and in following numbers. My own began like this:

"At Jena, Germany, in September, 1911, three old and distinguished men met for the first time.

THADDEUS BURR WAKEMAN (1834-1913)

When they shook hands at parting they knew they would not meet again. They were Ernst Haeckel, Lester F. Ward, and Thaddeus B. Wakeman. Two of them have already passed to silence. Mr. Wakeman died in his home at Cos Cob, Connecticut, not far from New York, on the night of Tuesday, April 22, in the 79th year of his age. He had not been ill. Had been busy during the day in his garden; at bedtime he lay down for the usual night's sleep, and did not wake."

Between these paragraphs runs a sketch of Wakeman's life. He was born December 23, 1834, at Greenfield Hill, Fairfield county, Connecticut, of old and honored New England stock. Putnam's "Four Hundred Years of Freethought" has his biography. During his last twenty years his was the voice heard at the last rites of Freethinkers in the vicinity. He was speaker at the funerals of two editors of The Truth Seeker, D. M. Bennett and E. M. Macdonald, and of my mother. He buried Theron C. Leland, Stephen Pearl Andrews, Courtlandt Palmer, Hugh Byron Brown, and Dr. E. B. Foote, Sr. His own funeral discourse was delivered by William Thurston Brown, lecturer for the New York Freethought Society.

E. P. Peacock of Chicago, who was elected president of the American Secular Union in 1910, and acted as assistant to Secretary Reichwald in preparing the Union's literature, died in September at 76. He was a native of England; a good soldier of Freethought.

CHAPTER XXV.

IN THE Freethought field, during most of 1914, there was enough activity so that one would notice it.

The Indiana State Rationalist Association had voted at its last convention to be a national organization, with Libby Culbertson Macdonald as president and Charles T. Sprading lecturer. Meetings on the coast were not only well attended but thronged from San Francisco to Portland. In Chicago, at their respective places of meeting, Dr. J. E. Roberts, M. M. Mangasarian, and H. Percy Ward drew large audiences. Street speaking went on there under the surveillance of the police and the protection of the American Secular Union.

Franklin Steiner had gathered and published this year his statistics of prisons, showing the religious preferences of criminals. Joseph E. Hosmer, formerly promoter of the Liberal University at Silverton, Oregon, was now publisher of the Silverton Journal and had been convicted of libeling the nuns of the Benedictine convent at Mount Angel by publishing in a pamphlet the story of an escaped nun, one Mary Lasenan, told to a local Protestant minister. He was fined $200 with the alternative of going to jail. He chose the jail, and from its confines sent out defiant messages. The escaped nun disappeared, and evaded summons as a witness.

The "Lectures and Meetings" column was filled and turned over. We had the New York Secular Society in The Bronx, Thomas Wright speaker. Walker ran the Sunrise Club; Wm. A. Winham as secretary advertised the Brooklyn Philosophical Association; the Ferrer School held lectures and discussions; Hubert Harrison, colored, conducted the Radical Forum.

Mrs. Margaret Sanger figured as defendant in one of the free press cases in 1914. On the morning of the 4th of July a little group of anarchists were engaged, as the account ran and as is perhaps the fact, in the manufacture of an explosive bomb for use at Tarrytown, where the I. W. W. was having trouble with John D. Rockefeller, and some men had been imprisoned for street speaking. The bomb exploded prematurely and four of the persons in the flat occupied by the group were killed, among them a man named Arthur Caron, said to be an inoffensive Frenchman. Mrs. Sanger at the time published a paper called The Woman Rebel, with the motto, "No god, no master," which was not far behind Emma Goldman's Mother Earth in voicing discontent with things as they were. It occurred to Mrs. Sanger or to a contributor to her paper that these men who were making a bomb to use in abolishing the ills of society were quite heroic persons, and it was so stated. Issues of The Woman Rebel were arbitrarily suppressed by the postoffice authorities and Mrs. Sanger indicted.

The burden of the year 1914 was naturally the opening of the World War among the Christian nations of Europe, while the heathen scoffed, or were represented as so doing.   The delayed blast, for which material long had been accumulating, seems to have been touched off by an act of the papal authorities at Rome, backed by officially Catholic Austria, in coercing the kingdom of Serbia, a Greek Catholic country, into the signing of a concordat June 24, whereby Roman Catholicism acquired an official standing in the Balkan state.   Serbians resented the imposition, and four days later Archduke Francis Ferdinand of Austria was assassinated in Sarajevo, Bosnia, by a Serbian youth, while making a tour of the Balkans.   So after sending to Serbia an unacceptable ultimatum, Austria, which was allied triply with Germany and Italy, declared war on Serbia, while the Kaiser's army began a march through neutralized Belgium as the nearest way to Paris.

Then the religious circus began.   The ministers of America in their pulpits prayed for peace, to no effect.   President Wilson appointed a day of prayer for peace, which was duly observed.   It failed, and Great Britain made the same experiment with like results.   There was no peace.

The Hon. Joseph Cannon of Illinois, for many years member of Congress and at this time speaker of the House, grew weary of the pretentious and insincere exhibitions of piety.   Said he: "During the Civil war the ministers of the Southern churches prayed for the preservation of slavery. In the North the preachers all prayed for the freeing of the slaves. . . . I have yet to hear of a case where the deity has intervened in human affairs in response to prayers."

Pope Pius X was reported as feeling slighted because governments were appealing to God direct instead of through him as God's representative. England recognized him by appointing a minister to the Vatican. He died August 20, grief-stricken that the nations should be fighting without his consent, and that the papacy had lost the power it once possessed to make them lay down their arms. American Catholics were so violently pro-German that when Ernst Haeckel and Rudolph Eucken addressed patriotic letters to the universities of America, the Catholics, to whom he had previously been anathema, praised Haeckel as an eminent and learned man. The Catholic press doped out what was going to happen. Germany would whip England and then, to "spank" Italy for not coming into the war on the right side, the Kaiser would restore the temporal sovereignty of the pope and present him with a small strip of the Italian seashore.

The Kaiser developed gifts as a preacher that seemed to place him ahead of our own William J. Bryan, secretary of state and supposed to be responsible for the prayer day we had observed.

Americans were supposed to be neutral as between the allies (that is, the triple entente, Great Britain, France and Russia) and the Central Powers (Germany, Austria, and so on), but were not. The Irish and other Catholics were for Germany, as against England, and so were descendants of immigrants from the Fatherland. Persons of English descent or stock favored Great Britain and

France. The former division of the population hoped the war would go on until England was humbled; for they had utter faith in Germany's ability to do that trick. The sympathizers with Britain and France were for peace.

The peace principles of Socialists and Anarchists held no better than those of Christians, but gave way to the war spirit. Emma Goldman in her magazine Mother Earth "mournfully conceded" that "Anarchists no less than Socialists and 'intellectuals' were found wanting when the crisis burst." Kropotkin, the exiled Russian prince, turned patriot and championed the cause of the czar, and all of the French Anarchists were either dumb or shouting for France. The German reds prayed for the kaiser. Mother Earth had "good reasons for believing that nothing can remove the stain cast on the Anarchist and allied movements by recent events." Hardly could the blowing up of a policeman with a bomb atone for this military alliance with capitalism! The Call (Socialist) declared that in enlisting the Social Democrats the Prussian-German regime had won a victory over an inner foe "well worth all the wasted blood of the German people."

It was the year of the Zapatista constitutional insurrection in Mexico. Catholic representatives appealed to our department of state to intervene and enforce respect for religion and put an end to atrocities perpetrated against the Catholics of Mexico. The list of atrocities reads much like what the Germans were charged with doing against the Belgians, who were as Catholic as the Mexican sufferers, and yet American Catholics did not protest the acts of the Kaiser. A complaint against Villa's men lodged by the committee of the American Federation of Catholic Societies appointed to induce this government to take up the cause of the church in Mexico (not in Belgium) laid stress upon the desecration of churches and the "violation of sisters." Former President Roosevelt wrote an article for a newspaper syndicate charging the Wilson administration with being "partially (and guiltily) responsible for some of the worst acts ever committed even in the civil wars of Mexico." He stated that nuns had been outraged by Zapata's soldiery. Later advices made it plain that the charge should have been changed to "enticed." The Mexican bandit or revolutionist has the custom of taking his women with him to do the cooking, or to "rustle the grub," and for other purposes. It was true that Zapata's men opened the doors of nunneries, but they did not sack them nor constuprate the nuns. The girls in the convents preferred going with the soldiers to remaining cooped up where they were. Readers who are not too young will remember the thorough investigation made by President Wilson, in which he employed every representative of this government then in Mexico; and he issued a statement over the signature of his Catholic secretary Tumulty that not one single instance of violence offered to nuns by the Constitutionalists had been proved, not a charge substantiated.

Three New York societies celebrated Paine's

177th birthday anniversary: the Freethought Society, the Thomas Paine National Historical Association, and the Sunrise Club, where the dinner was a memorial to Paine, Bruno, and Ferrer. Speakers were James F. Morton, Henry Rowley, Joseph Rinn, and Mr. Nicholas Aleinikoff, "who looks as if he might be an escaped Russian professor." To these Sunrise speakers are to be added Miss Clara Wakeman, who took the place of her father, the late T. B. Wakeman, at the first celebration he had missed, and spoke on Bruno; and also the Hon. Charles H. Betts, editor of the Lyons, N. Y., Republican, who crowned Paine with fresh laurels as the originator of our representative system and proposer of the Constitution of the United States. I drew this picture of the speaker, who perchance may not appear again in this story. "Mr. Betts wore dinner clothes, and in respect of dress was not one second behind the clock. Earnestness and seriousness were in his spectacled glance, in his demeanor, and in his voice, which carried to his hearers with force and distinctness a speech replete with statement, argument and demonstration as clear and penetrating as itself. The gesture, the emphatic nod of the head, the flourish of the right hand and the position of the left that slightly lifted the skirt of the coat, were reminiscent of the old school and the polished speakers—Phillips, Garrison, Albert Brisbane—of forty years ago."

Shelby Moore Cullom of Illinois, for many terms a United States senator and man of influence in the country's affairs, published in 1912 a book of reminiscences in which he confessed that the evidence of a future life did not command his belief, that he had no faith in the dogma of immortality, and that if he had his life to live again he would not join any church, but would nourish his mind with the writings of the great skeptics.

Another Atheist and damned soul was discovered and advertised by Cole Blease, governor of South Carolina. Blease asserted that Thomas E. Clemson, the philanthropist for whom the State Agricultural College is named, was an Atheist. The statement occurred in the governor's message to the legislature on February 6, and was inspired by Blease's wish to have the name of the college changed, so that "Northern millionaires" may make "large gifts" to the institution. He would have the Clemson Agricultural College renamed the Calhoun University. There had been a great fall from Calhoun to Blease. When Calhoun spoke for South Carolina the president of the state's university was Dr. Thomas Cooper, Freethinker and Materialist. If the benefactor of the Agricultural College was an Atheist, there is added another name to the list of Freethinking philanthropists.

Good contributors have not been a want of The Truth Seeker for many years. A. S. Garretson, author of "Primitive Christianity and Early Criticism," a very valuable work, gave us a number of articles in 1914. Frederick J. Gould of London was writing. Mrs. Brigham Leatherbee wrote "Christian Mythology," published serially and reprinted in a book. The name of William Smith Bryan appeared this year.

Dr. Homer Wakefield's "Myth of the Civil War" was among the memorable articles. It gave the facts with regard to the "Miraculous Spring" of Andersonville prison for Union captives in Western Georgia. Said Dr. Wakefield:

"I wish to submit the version of it of Mr. A. Theodore Ives, president of the Illinois Association of Union Ex-Prisoners of War, who was more closely associated with this spring than any other man, and was probably the first to discover and drink from it.

"Mr. Ives, who is now hale and hearty at seventy years of age, and whose reputation for truth and veracity is the very highest, gives the following version:

"A short time before the advent of the spring, Mr. Ives and some other prisoners from an Illinois regiment, like other prison groups, undertook to tunnel under the stockade as a means of escape. From a well dug under their shelter, they tunneled toward the exterior, but in going under the stockade, its great weight caused a cave-in which exposed the project to the Confederates. In the sinking of the well at the entrance of the tunnel, they, like many others, struck a vein of water, thus showing a subterranean vein at this point. When the Confederate keeper of the pen discovered this and perhaps other tunnels caving in under the north wall of the stockade, he had a trench dug along the inner side of it, five feet deep, intermediate between it and the inner fence or rail called the Dead Line. This deep trench running parallel with the stockade, and intended to unearth all tunnels crossing this twenty-foot intermediate space, extended east and west down a steep slope. Shortly after this, an unusually heavy downpour of rain caused torrents of water to flow down the hill in this trench, which washed it out still deeper, and undoubtedly opened up the veins of water which had been struck in the well so close by, for the next morning, the flow was found to have come to the surface a little farther down the hill. Such is the spring from perfectly natural causes, which is ascribed to supernatural and providential origin."

Notwithstanding this well-known and perfectly natural explanation of the appearance of water, the name of "Providence Spring" has been attached to it, and pious persons have erected there a monument bearing the imbecile inscription:

"The prisoners' cry of thirst went up to heaven; God heard, and with his thunders cleft the earth and poured his sweetest waters gushing here."

The religious mind does not consider it worth while to record any event as it really happened when the supernatural may be introduced in a few words of pious lying.

Professor Langdon of Oxford, translating some Babylonian tablets in the archeological collection of the University of Pennsylvania, found a flood story that he decided was "clearly the original of that preserved in the book of Genesis." The ministers made the most of the discovery as proving the historical correctness of the scriptures. But it proved too much when the people saw that "Moses," without credit, had lifted the material for his scenario.

Friends and pupils of Ernst Haeckel, the Darwin of Germany, celebrated his 80th birthday, February 16, by "telling how they became acquainted with his ideas, what effect those ideas had in moulding their view of the world, and in general what they owed to Ernst Hæckel."

When at the age of 19 I took up the reading of Haeckel and, as a compositor, set weekly installments of his "History of Creation" for The Truth Seeker, I was not looking forward to the correspondence I was to have with the distinguished author in the next century.

The Washington Secular League in May expressed formally its approval of the act of the Italian government in appointing as commissioner to the Panama-Pacific International Exposition in San Francisco the distinguished Italian Freethinker, Signor Ernesto Nathan, former mayor of Rome. Nathan, a Freemason, was openly hostile to the church. How American Catholics felt about his choice as commissioner will be discerned "between the lines" in this heading quoted from The Western Catholic, Quincy, Illinois.

"Eighteen Million American Citizens Resent Insult Given by the Italian Government—The Ignorant, Blasphemous and Anti-Christian Nathan, Ex-Mayor of Rome, Could Hurl His Vile Insults at the Venerable Prisoner of the Vatican, but He Will Not Insult with Impunity Eighteen Million American Citizens—Which Shall it Be? Nathan's Recall? or Dead Exposition?—Nathan Must Not Be a Delegate—He Is Absolutely Odious to America—He Is Fit for the Slums of London or the Rat-Holes of Rome, but Not for Free America—Recall Nathan or the Exposition Will Be a Joke for the Nations."

That "bedizzened old harridan," as Professor Huxley called Mother Church, is a sly sister of the oldest profession. She is not preserving for future reference the record of this exhibition of her malevolence; and when again one of the progeny conceived in her system attempts the highest office in the land, with a view to making her the mistress of the White House, she will sham one of her attacks of hysteria, and scream bigotry and prejudice if somebody objects on suspicion of his tainted and infected blood.

The Catholic Directory gave the United States

sixteen million adherents of the church, counting the babies. The church paper said that eighteen million of these were "insulted." The church was then, as now, very thin-skinned. Nobody ever was insulted so often as Mother Church except the daughter of the street who frequently warns the crowd, all and sundry, not to get too fresh with a lady. Throughout the season Catholic gatherings and functions adopted resolutions condemning the Panama-Pacific Exposition for not rejecting the pope's adversary as a commissioner from Italy.

The address of Nathan that so stirred the rednecks was printed in The Truth Seeker of June 20. The signor was Jovian; his words were thunderbolts, and he had the distinction of being the one statesman of his day honest and courageous enough to answer and defy the attacks of the Catholic church on modern life and thought.

By a fluke the State of New York, at the date I am writing about, had a governor who, while a professed Catholic, talked like a secularist. The former Lieutenant-Governor Martin Glynn became Governor through the impeachment of Sulzer. Questioned by a "Guardian of Liberty" he answered as though he had the Nine Demands of Liberalism before him. He did not consult Father Duffy, and lost the Catholic vote. The Truth Seeker of October 31 printed his letter, which was used against him as a candidate for reelection.

In the year 1914 the stars and stripes could not be carried into a Catholic church. They tried it in Huntington, Pa., where members of the Grand Army of the Republic, having draped the coffin of

an aged veteran with the national colors, learned
upon reaching the church that a coffin so decorated
must be left outside. The church was the only
institution having precincts too sacred for the admission of the country's flag. (T. S., xli, 485).

M. M. Mangasarian visited Geneva, Switzerland,
in July and brought home the photograph of a
monument the "sons of Calvin" had erected to
Michael Servetus in expiation of the "error" into
which their spiritual ancestor fell when he burned
the Unitarian doctor at the stake. The inscription
on the monument mentions this inadvertent slip of
Calvin's in imprisoning, torturing, and committing
deliberate and premeditated murder on a man
whose views were more enlightened than his own,
as not his fault but that of his age." But Calvin's
crimes no better fitted that century than the murder
of Ferrer fitted the first decade of the twentieth.
They were merely some of its worst features, as
Calvin was one of its worst men. They were characteristic of him, not of his contemporaries save
other leading exponents of Christianity. To the
extent that the age was brutal the church had made
it so.

"President Wilson set aside a precedent established by his two predecessors, Roosevelt and Taft,
and did not attend the Thanksgiving mass at St.
Patrick's church in Washington on November 26.
While Secretary Bryan, cabinet members, and representatives of the diplomatic corps were there and
stayed to luncheon, the President went somewhere
else." (Truth Seeker, Dec. 5, 1914).

If any President since has picked up the practice dropped by Wilson, I do not recall the circumstance. It was a detestable custom, in which the author of the Thanksgiving proclamation played the people false by not "assembling" in his usual place of worship as he had the cheek to advise free Americans to do.

But Mr. Wilson had, alas! the common habit of breaking from the restraining hold of fact when on religious subjects. Speaking unreflectingly at the dedication of the American University in Washington in June, he in one sentence said:

"This is the reason why scholarship has usually been fruitful when associated with religion, and scholarship has never, so far as I can at the moment recall, been associated with any religion except the religion of Jesus Christ."

A Chinese laundryman or a Greek banana circulator could have exposed that statement as false. A Jew took the liberty to do so. Mr. Wilson replied that it was "one of the risks and penalties of extemporaneous speaking that you do not stop to consider the whole field, but address yourself merely to the matter in hand."

Reading in this review of The Truth Seeker, week after week and year after year, the countless lies that the great man, in common with the gutter evangelist, has not been ashamed to tell that the truth of God might more abound, I have become convinced that should Christianity lose the support it gets from lying it could not stand for a minute.

The name of George Seibel became familiar to readers of The Truth Seeker during the latter half

of the year 1914. The war in Europe brought
forth trenchant partisans on each side. Seibel engaged in valiant debate with David Eccles, Herbert

GEORGE SEIBEL, author of "The Religion of Shakespeare" and other Rationalist Books, who first wrote for
The Truth Seeker in 1887.

Cutner, and other adversaries, with whom a few years later he was on the friendliest terms.

George Seibel, however, had been a Truth Seeker reader and contributor since his fourteenth year. In 1887 he won a prize offered by Susan H. Wixon in her Young Folks page for the best essay on "Why I Am a Liberal." A little later he contributed a poem on "Our Flag," which was praised by Voltairine de Cleyre. For the fiftieth anniversary number he wrote an article giving memories of Charles Watts, Felix L. Oswald, and other great Freethinkers he has known. He is dramatic and literary critic of the Pittsburgh Sun Telegraph; has written a book on "The Religion of Shakespeare," published by the R. P. A.; is the author of "The Leper" and other dramas, and national president of the American association founded by German Rationalists who came to America in 1849.

Siebel's conversion to Freethought was a curious bit of irony. A certain Father Lambert had written a volume of "Notes on Ingersoll," answering the "Mistakes of Moses." By accident a volume of Lambert got into the hands of the 14-year-old boy, who had never heard of Ingersoll before. He read it, and saw clearly that the book did not answer Ingersoll at all. That started him on the road to reason.

DEPARTURES.

The Truth Seeker of April 4, 1914, said:

"In times past the names of R. C. and Flora A. Burtis, always appearing together as contributors to the cause of Freethought, have been familiar ones to the readers of this paper. They lived in Wayne, Mich., and were among

the most respected citizens of that town. Mr. Burtis died
in 1901, not forgetting the interests of Freethought in the
disposition of the competence he had acquired. Mrs. Burtis
was left with sufficient means of maintenance and a surplus
for the benevolences which both had practiced. Years ago,
having estimated her probable length of life and computed
the outlay, she wrote to E. M. Macdonald that she had
set aside the sum of $5,000 as a bequest to the cause.
Afterwards, knowing what Christian courts and Christian
executors have done with such bequests, she began making donations, until it is likely that more than one-half
of the contemplated bequest had been bestowed. But her
calculations on her length of life proved to be mistaken.
Living until the age of eighty-two, blind for several years,
and wholly dependent upon relatives and medical service
for comfort, she lived until February 27 of the present
year, and came so near to the end of her resources that
The Truth Seeker was called upon to discharge a portion
of the expense of her funeral. Mrs. Burtis was a woman
of education and refinement, of broad and liberal mind,
without fear and without superstition."

The Evening Herald of Ottawa, Kansas, in recording the death of Etta Semple on April 11,
speaks of her as the "Samaritan" and "one of the
greatest benefactors for humanity Ottawa has ever
had." Mrs. Semple was a Freethinker, a native of
Quincy, Illinois, where she was born on September
21, in 1855. In the '90s she edited a little paper
named the Freethought Ideal.

John Peck of Naples, N. Y., died April 29, 1914,
in his 95th year. He contributed articles to The
Truth Seeker for some four decades. Mr. Peck's
standing in his home town was so good that the
Naples Record published an obituary which, reprinted in The Truth Seeker, covered nearly a
page.

CHAPTER XXVI.

THE heading of the "Happy New Year" leader for 1915 needed a question mark after it, for the war in Europe made a sarcasm of the compliments of the season.

All war making powers have looked to religion for sanction. What is the church for? The state has it subsidized and expects the ministers to justify the rulers before God for their crimes, if any.

So the German pastors quoted scripture that warranted the Kaiser in invading Belgium. They found the matter in the second of Deuteronomy, where Moses wanted Sihon, King of Heshbon, to let him go through, but the Lord hardened Sihon's heart, forcing Moses to destroy him.

The pope appointed prayers for peace. England appointed an envoy, Sir Henry Howard, to the Vatican, to keep watch on the envoys of Austria and Germany, for the Vatican was a nest of Austrian spies. The Germans, on seizing the Belgian capital, removed the statue of Francisco Ferrer. The Freethought societies and press in Germany were suppressed or censored. In America, where the Catholic-Irish were partisans of Germany, the Clan-na-Gael lodges were hymning the Kaiser and asking when he would set Ireland free.

On May 7 a German submarine torpedoed the Cunard liner Lusitania off the Irish coast with the loss of one hundred and fourteen American lives. This nation was then ready for a fight, waiting only for the keynote from President Wilson. Mr. Wilson, speaking in Philadelphia on May 10, said: "There is such a thing as a man being too proud to fight. There is such a thing as a nation being so right that it does not need to convince others by force that it is right." The belligerent Roosevelt declared: "We earn as a nation measureless scorn and contempt if we follow the lead of those who exalt peace above righteousness." The words of Wilson seemed the saner to The Truth Seeker.

Owing to his inability to approve a note to Germany by Wilson, Bryan resigned as secretary of state and returned to private life babbling of the "Prince of Peace." The Seventh Day Adventists at their yearly meeting in Texas dated the second coming of Christ and the end of the world on the day the Allies should capture Constantinople.

The countries involved in the war held midsummer prayers for victory. The French cardinals ordered the appointing of a prayer day by the bishops; the Germans held thanksgiving over the capture of a Russian fortress. The whole British empire united on August 4 in prayers to this God who had helped the Kaiser; the Czar proclaimed to his subjects that God was with them; and Italy, too, was fervent in its supplication to the deity. The London Freethinker reported that worship was compulsory in the British army. Colonel Roose-

velt, agitating preparedness, wrote a magazine article quoting Ezekiel xxxiii, 2-6, the lesson of which
is that if a man, "hear the sound of the trumpet
and take not warning, his blood shall be upon him."
President Wilson, in November, being then a preparedness convert, wrote a letter to Mayor Seth
Low of New York citing the same passage in Ezekiel. But both Roosevelt and Wilson were copiers,
for immediately after the sinking of the Lusitania,
a German Reformed pastor in Cleveland, Ohio,
had quoted Ezekiel xxxiii, 2-6, to show that the
American passengers on the doomed ship, "were
guilty of their own blood."

Bryan rebuked Wilson for going to the Old Testament instead of the New for his scripture. Jesus,
Mr. Bryan intimated, sounded no note for preparedness. I quoted him this one: "What king,
going to make war against another king, sitteth not
down first, and consulteth whether he be able with
ten thousand to meet him that cometh against him
with twenty thousand?" That seemed to be good
authority for recruiting the army. I collected these
theological expressions by warring moguls:

"With God on our side we shall, with our good German
sword, conquer our enemies."—Emperor William.

"The dear God who has fought with my armies so faithfully."—The Emperor of Austria-Hungary.

"Remember, my soldiers, when you are in battle that God
is always beside you."—The Czar of Russia.

"If my efforts were crowned with success it is due to
God's gracious guidance."—Field Marshal von Hindenburg.

The activity of the Red Cross in Europe brought
out a bit of history, published in the censored
Freidenker, Munich, Germany:

Conflicting
Prayers.
From a
Cartoon by
Ryan Walker.

"To the beneficent deeds in the direction of love for an enemy belongs the work of the Freethinker Henri Dunant, a Swiss, who felt most deeply on the battlefield of Solferino how pitilessly the wounded were at that time still abandoned to suffering and death. By his appeal to mankind, Dunant founded the Red Cross. It is a humanitarian institution, not a clerical one. Dunant was a Freethinker, and chose the cross as an emblem because it is an emblem of Switzerland." [The Swiss flag is a white cross on a red field. Dunant reversed it.]

The Confederated Catholic Societies in February published for the guidance of the postoffice officials a list of papers and magazines deserving to be excluded from the mails as 'journalistic reptiles, bitterly anti-Catholic in tendency," that forced a "defensive" battle on the Catholics of the country. The list occupied some pages in a magazinelet called The Catholic Mind, which was published monthly as an annex to the Jesuit weekly America, and had The Truth Seeker in it. The other condemned publications, eighteen in all, were Protestant, denominational, or anticlerical. A hearing on bills to carry out the Catholic purpose was had before the House Committee on Postoffices at Washington in February. One bill provided for the exclusion of "any publications which are, or which are represented to be, a reflection on any form of religious worship practiced or held sacred by any citizens of the United States."

The bills, sponsored by Roman Catholic representatives from New York and Massachusetts, failed of passage. But those bills were educative. They

JOHN D. BRADLEY.
The President of the Washington Secular League appeared before the Congressional Committee to oppose the press-muzzling bills and reported the proceedings in The Truth Seeker.

let the country see what would happen to a Freethought or non-Catholic press with a Catholic majority in Congress. They exposed the Catholic mind. The Church being what she is cannot have the instincts of a gentleman.

This was the year of the killing of William Black,

the anticlerical lecturer, at Marshall, Texas, by delegates from the local Knights of Columbus. Richard Potts, newspaper man of Dallas, investigated and reported to The Truth Seeker (March 20).

Rupert Hughes has observed that man by himself is capable of being bad enough, but working with God he is a thousand times worse. In 1915 men having a god to serve were responsible for the repeated arrests of Freethinkers and other idealists for exercising the common right of free speech and press. The Chicago police arrested D. F. Sweetland for selling The Truth Seeker. This for the love of God only, since the courts discharged Sweetland. The Rev. Irwin St. John Tucker and twenty-one others, including Mrs. Lucy Parsons, were pinched for meeting near where the Haymarket tragedy took place thirty years earlier. The Comstock Society gathered in William Sanger, husband of Margaret, for selling a pamphlet on "Family Limitation." The Supreme Court upheld the conviction of Jay Fox, editor of The Agitator, Home, Wash., for speaking disrespectfully of the law. Henry M. Tichenor of The Melting Pot, and his partner, were indicted for printing a Billy Sunday cartoon, and fined $200 and costs. The authorities of Paterson, N. J., closed the town to Freethought speakers, and Patrick Quinlan and Elizabeth Gurley Flynn were jailed for writing and talking. A New York man named A. Stone, speaking in Madison Square under the auspices of the Secular Society, and Thomas Wright, lecturer, were repeatedly arrested on complaint of a deacon, and either discharged or let go with light fines. Thomas E. Watson of Georgia was before the federal court at Atlanta for printing quotations from books on the Roman Catholic religion. The University of Pennsylvania fired Scott Nearing, teacher in the Wharton School, who had expressed his mind on Billy Sunday and the people who backed the revival in Philadelphia.

The eugenists organized the Birth Control League, Clara Gruening Stillman, secretary, and began an agitation for the repeal of the part of the Comstock law that prohibits information on methods of limiting births. In Portland, Oregon, Judge W. N. Gatens, reversing a lower court that had assessed a fine of $100 on distributors of Mrs. Sanger's pamphlet, showed that he had penetrated the mask of the moral hypocrites, by saying:

"It seems to me that the trouble with our people today is that there is too much prudery. Ignorance and prudery are the millstones about the necks of progress. We are all shocked by many things publicly stated that we know privately ourselves, but haven't got the nerve to get up and admit it, and when some person brings to our attention something we already know, we feign modesty, and we feel that the public has been outraged and decency has been shocked when as a matter of fact we know all these things ourselves."

The state attorney-general of Minnesota rendered an opinion that Bible reading in schools was unlawful, but the scofflaw advocates of such reading persisted in forcing the practice on teachers and pupils.

On June 1, the Constitutional Amendment Committee at Albany, N. Y., heard arguments on an amendment offered by James L. Nixon of Buffalo, abol'shing the exemption of church property from taxation. The Truth Seeker sent James F. Morton, Jr., to represent Secularists.

At this constitutional convention of which I write, the Hon. Alfred E. Smith, being a member, manu- factured ammunition for his adversaries of 1928 by moving the repeal of the section of the state constitution forbidding the distribution of publ'c money to sectarian schools.

The Congress of the National Rationalist Asso- ciation, Libby Culbertson Macdonald, president, held August 1-4, in Scottish Rite Temple, San Fran- cisco, was a large event, whose sessions derived en- hanced interest for being held during the Panama- Pacific Exposition, and on the other side of the street from a Billy Sunday revival.

On the establishment of the Portuguese repub- lic in 1910, the philosophic Freethinker, Dom Theo- ph'lo Braga, was chosen provisional president. Braga was pronounced a dreamer, and the early dissolu- tion of the republic predicted. Other men suc- ceeded him in office, but the republic seemed to be receding from the principles on which it had been founded. In May, 1915, there occurred a revolu- tion, and at its close the Nat'onal Assembly elected Dom Theophilo Braga president by a vote of 98 to 1. President Braga, seventy years old, had long held the chair of professor of sociology in the Lis- bon University.

The fifth centenary of the martyrdom of John Huss, Bohemian reformer, fell in 1915. Huss was

the Francisco Ferrer of his day, being the head of
a school.   The higher clergy sitting in council at
Constance condemned him as a heretic, sentenced
him to the stake on July 6, 1415, and immediately
sent him to the place of execution.

This Ingersoll myth of 1915 and earlier reap-
pears unto this day:

"Twenty-five years ago the American Agnostic, R. G.
Ingersoll, predicted that 'in ten years the Bible will not be
read.'"

A version of 1925 dated Ingersoll's prediction
"one hundred years ago"—before he was born. Ingersoll could not have said it consistently, for Ingersoll declared that he knew of nothing that could
equal in longevity a good healthy religious lie.

Somebody with plenty of it at his disposal should
search the files of time and count the Ingersoll
myths; also the plagiarisms of public speakers.
Vice-President Thomas Marshall, in the spring of
1915, spoke at the University of California, praising the home, and declaring: "I will never shoulder
a musket in defense of a boarding-house." Marshall
was extraordinarily pious. The name of Ingersoll
could not pass his lips except accompanied by
words of detraction, but he could steal from him.
Ingersoll, in "About Farming in Illinois" (1877),
had said: "Few men have been patriotic enough to
shoulder a musket in defense of a boarding-house."

DEPARTURES.

Having lived 94 years and done much fruitful
work, Dr. George Washington Brown died February 4 at Rockford, Ill., a resident there for half a
century.   The press, describing Dr. Brown as "a

heroic figure in spreading the gospel of freedom in
the days of 'bleeding Kansas' and a pioneer in
Americanism," devoted a column to the account of
his life, but ignored his connection with Freethought. About 1890 he published his "Researches
in Oriental History," dealing with the sources of
the Christian religion and resolving the Christian
messiah into a myth.

D. M. Boye of Mills, California, dying at eighty,
left his estate, worth $10,000, as a scholarship fund
for graduates of the Kinney School, near Mills, to
obtain an agricultural education. Judge Daniel K.
Tenney of Madison, Wisconsin, "philanthrop'st,
successful lawyer, descendant of an old English
family, and citizen of high standing, is dead," reported the Madison Democrat. He had died February 10, in his eighty-first year. Judge Tenney,
says the paper, "gave money generously towards
the establishment of Tenney Park, which was
named in his honor, contributed liberally to hospitals and to charitable organizations, and gave considerable aid to many worthy causes of which the
outside world knew nothing."

The Truth Seeker of April 3 admitted this was
a week of obituaries. David Hoyle, Charles P.
Somerby and Morgan Robertson had departed.
Mr. Hoyle, who died March 23, aged eighty-four,
was a Freethinker before my time. I found him
one of the Old Guard when I came to New York,
and he held on for forty years thereafter. He
loved this life, lived it worthily, and, like Thomas
Paine, died looking for another. He was of English birth. Mr. Somerby also was here when I

came, and had a Freethought bookstore at 139 Eighth street. For about eight years following the death of D. M. Bennett he was a business partner in The Truth Seeker. Philosophically, he belonged with Positivists, the disciples of Auguste Comte. I suppose he was seventy years old when he died, March 24. Morgan Robertson died the same day, at Atlantic City. His first literary work appeared in The Truth Seeker and his career has been rather closely followed in my pages. He had lived only fifty-four years.

The years of Joseph Warwick, born the other side of the Atlantic and in his youth a campaigner with Charles Bradlaugh, were eighty-four when he died in Brooklyn, July 23. The readers of The Truth Seeker had helped place him in a home for aged men, where he ended his days in comfort after a strenuous life that had seen privation. Warwick was a charter member of the Brooklyn Philosophical Association, honorary vice-president of the Paine Association, first vice-president of the American Secular Union, and became president, on the death of E. M. Macdonald, in 1909.

A rare character passed away through the death of W. A. Croffut in Washington, D. C., July 31. His life could not be summed short of many pages. The book I am now writing makes allusions to his work and services; some to his influence on the formation of my youthful mind. Born in 1830, he was eighty-five when he died. Redding, Conn., was his native place; his first job, that of reporter on the New Haven Palladium. Later his journalistic work, mainly editorial, was done on the Rochester

GEORGE WILLIAM FOOTE (1850-1915).

Democrat, St. Paul Times, Minneapolis Tribune, and the New York Tribune, Graphic, and World. Numerous books came from his pen, and he wrote the opening ode for the World's Columbian Exhibition in 1893.

On July 3 The Truth Seeker reprinted from the London Freethinker an article by the editor of that paper, George William Foote, entitled "Death the Democrat." Lines under the picture of Mr. Foote accompanying the article said:

"He survives a serious and protracted illness, complicated with German bombs dropped in the vicinity of his residence; and resumes the editing of the London Freethinker with force and philosophic calm."

On October 30 the picture appeared again and lines under it read: "George William Foote: January 11, 1850-October 18, 1915." So he had gone to be the companion of Death the Democrat.

Anthony Comstock did better than he had ever done before when at the end of the summer he died.

The close of this 1915 installment completes forty years of my association with the Freethought movement. Using my Uncle Clem's "retrospective cognizance," as I "prolong the vision backward" to the time I began, I perceive that in these four decades I have composed, compiled and combined more of such matter as The Truth Seeker prints than anyone else has done.

CHAPTER XXVII.

THAT pestilent breed, the arresters, which we have always with us, just as we do the poor, from whom they so differ that we may not add when mentioning them "but honest," figured with the war and the infantile paralysis as the misfortunes of 1916. The first Truth Seeker for the year reports the trial of Daniel F. Sweetland of Chicago for "peddling" this paper on the street without a license. Sweetland did not peddle the paper; he did not sell it on the street, although he had a legal right to do so, and for the sale of newspapers in Chicago no license was required. He occupied with the owner's consent the vestibule of a building in Monroe street. Against Sweetland the arresters had no case, and when he had lain six weeks under bonds furnished by E. C. Reichwald, who likewise provided counsel for him, the court ordered the prosecution withdrawn.

To New York Mrs. Margaret Sanger, who had written a pamphlet on "Family Limitation," as birth control was then called, returned after a year abroad to stand trial under indictments found against her. William Sanger, her husband, had served a term in jail for giving a copy of the pamphlet to a Comstock spy. The indictments were

451

quashed by Justice Dayton, February 18. The police arrested Emma Goldman to prevent her giving a lecture on Atheism. They charged that she was going to talk about birth control, and the judge sent her to the workhouse. Dr. Ben Reitman, her coadjutor, landed behind the bars on a like count, and Bolton Hall, who took up the defense, was put under arrest. In the fall the charge against Mr. Hall failed, for he had not circulated any birth control literature by mail. The arresters, cheated of this victim, again took into custody Miss Goldman, who had served her term and came forward as a witness. In Boston, where the Catholics instigated the prosecution of Van K. Allison, aged 22, for handling birth control literature, a Roman Catholic judge sentenced the accused to three years in the penitentiary. Thomas E. Watson of Thomson, Ga., and four men connected with the anticlerical Menace, Aurora, Mo., were prosecuted early in the year for reprinting the penetralia of Catholic moral theology, but got the "break" and were acquitted. Watson was arrested and acquitted again in the fall.

The Christers with beast instincts pursued the street speakers for the new York Secular Society continually. Irving Meirowitz was arrested at the instance of a priest who had got drunk and created a disturbance in the crowd. I attended one trial of Meirowitz when the charge was "disorderly conduct." The arresting officer admitted that not the speaker but individuals in his audience were the disorderly persons. But Meirowitz was convicted and finger-printed.

The speakers for the New York Secular Society whose names I recover were Mitchuly, Stone, Meirowitz, Kosby, Sonnenschein, Murlin, Thomas Wright, and Hubert Harrison.

Meetings were held every Sunday at Harlem Masonic Temple. Edward Henn made a model presiding officer who kept the speakers to the subject before the house, which was Freethought. All the persons named have passed from view except Henn and Wright.

In September the State of Connecticut staged a genuine blasphemy trial. Michael X. Mockus, a lecturer from Detroit, delivered an address on religion in Waterbury, in that state, before the Lithuanian Freethought Society. As charged in the indictment Mockus said to his audience: "Dievas yra melagis. Dievas yra paleistuvis. Dievas kaip gelezine varle." Theodore Schroeder appeared for the defense and made the case a great issue for free speech. Mr. Schroeder was secretary of the Free Speech Defense League, one of the organizations among Freethinkers, like the National Defense Association, that grew out of the prosecution of Dr. E. B. Foote and D. M. Bennett by Anthony Comstock, and were the forerunners and progenitors of the American Civil Liberties Union. A police court found Mockus guilty and imposed a sentence of ten days in jail and a bond of $1,000 for good behavior. On Schroeder's appeal the court released the defendant, who gave $500 bond. Mockus might have pleaded guilty and gone free under a suspended sentence, but elected to stand on the merits of his cause.

The lurking beast with the arresting instinct saw photographers keeping their places open on Sunday and appealed to the police. The picture shooters, compelled to close up on their best business day of the week, were ruined and closed permanently in many instances. A statement in The American Sentinel covers the case and others of the kind:

"There is a law-book—'The Law of Sunday'—written by a lawyer, and only as a law-book.

"In it nearly a thousand Sunday law cases in the United States are examined.

"And from all, the author's sober conclusion is this: *"Nearly every prosecution* under our Sunday laws, is the result of *petty spite, meanness and malice."*

With regard to the war in Europe the editor observed an attitude of neutrality, for Freethinkers were divided in sentiment, and, like God and Jesus Christ, the boys who had been brought up to read The Truth Seeker were on both fronts. Readers gave their views till government suppressed debate.

The Rev. Dr. Ott, one of the Kaiser's chaplains, reported to the Vossiche Zeitung a speech or sermon by Wilhelm II before a squad of chaplains he was sending to the west front. Transmitted to The Truth Seeker by Bolton Hall, the preachment appeared in the August 5 number. It was a come-to-Jesus exhortation. When later the theologians among the allies attributed all the monstrosities of the Kaiser to his reliance on his pagan deity, the old German God, to the exclusion and neglect of the "personality" and teachings of Our Lord the Christ, it gave me satisfaction to requote that speech, and to point out that so far from not seek-

ing the guidance of unsers Herrn und Heilandes
Jesu Christi, the Kaiser was the only head of a
government who had said anything about him.
Statements of the cause of the war by two New
York clergymen are quoted on one page. The
Rockefeller pastor, Dr. Woelfkin, affirmed in so
many words that "Darwin caused the war," while
the Rev. Dr. Eaton laid it to survival of the fittest,
a jungle law, he said, that had no place among human beings. The ministers supposed that Darwin
had invented evolution and the survival of the fittest, and imposed them on mankind; that Germany,
assuming itself to be the fittest, had started the
war to exterminate the unfit, and so Darwin was
to blame for the war.

These are fair specimens of clerical hebetude
brought out by the necessity they were under of
explaining why Christian nations were fighting one
another beneath the banner of Christ.

Dr. J. Rudis-Jicinski, Bohemian physician, Freethinker, and journalist of Chicago, returned there
after a year of campaigning against disease in
Serbia. He had sent his story to be printed in The
Truth Seeker of March 11, 1916. Dr. Jicinski discovered that the Slavs, especially the Bohemians,
Slovaks, and Croatians, had a poor stomach for
fighting in the armies of their ruler, Emperor Franz
Joseph of Austria, who was of the Hapsburgs, the
historic oppressors of their people. They particularly resented the officiousness of the Austrian
chaplains, so the doctor wrote, who exhorted them
to go forward and meet the death of victors for

the love of their emperor. They replied to one of
these that since he was more sure of heaven than
they were, instead of hunting a safe spot behind a
big tree he ought to lead them. For vividness of
description, the letters of Dr. Jicinski surpassed
those of any newspaper correspondent. He was
in the field working among the sick and wounded.

The Lady Hope myth of the deathbed conversion of Darwin, which had been exploded in 1915,
enjoyed only four months of prosperity in The
Watchman-Examiner, the newspaper that first gave
it being. The religious periodical announced itself
convinced by the testimony of Darwin's family
that Lady Hope never visited the head of that
household. The fraud is treated at length in The
Truth Seeker of January 8, 1916. In the same
number is quoted a minister who fabricated that before George William Foote, editor of the London
Freethinker, passed away he "publicly abandoned
his occupation, announced his belief in spiritual
truth," and wrote: "I believe in God and in the
immortality of the soul of man." Also in the same
issue of the paper one sees a letter by Mr. Leonard Huxley refuting a tale set afloat by the Rockefeller pastor, Woelfkin, involving Prof. Thomas
H. Huxley in a confession of unspeakable regret
caused by his inability to accept Jesus as his personal savior. The yarn said that Huxley, "greatly
agitated and deeply impressed," having listened to
a Christer, "arose and walking up and down the
verandah declared in a voice filled with emotion:
'I would give my right arm if I was able to believe

as you do'." Mr. Leonard Huxley pronounced it
piffle.

The Liberals of St. Paul, after listening for two
seasons to Edward Adams Cantrell, organized the
Rationalist Society. The Rationalist Association of
Chattanooga, Tenn., held two meetings a month
in Oddfellows Hall. James Carl reported an ex-
periment at organizing in Toledo, Ohio. Secretary
L. Rall wrote of a new society in San Diego, Cal.
The Michigan Rationalist Society, which Edmund
Marshall had organized and addressed many times
in Detroit, was advertising for a Sunday evening
speaker. In Chicago, January 29-30, the American
Secular Union held its first congress since 1911,
electing John E. Remsburg president, E. C. Reichwald secretary and treasurer; reported in The
Truth Seeker of February 19, but previously in The
Progressive Thinker of Chicago, the Spiritualist
paper, which was strongly represented, as were other Chicago groups. The Rationalist Association of
North America appeared to be in poor standing,
and did not participate. Libby Culbertson Macdonald, who was its organizer, formally resigned in
April. M. M. Mangasarian was here heard for the
first time at a Secular Union congress.

Dr. M. S. Holt of Weston, West Virginia, proposed early in the year a state-wide Rationalist
Society and called for a meeting at Clarksburg to
organize.

Leonard D. Abbott communicated in July the information that on Sunday, June 25, in a barn at
Stelton, New Jersey, near what used to be the

Tewes farm-house and what is now the Children's
Day School founded in memory of Francisco Ferrer, a new organization, "The Modern School Association of North America, came into existence.

The Truth Seeker was glad to welcome a Freethought contemporary:

"The Crucible, 'a red-hot Agnostic newspaper,' published
monthly at Seattle, Washington, at 25 cents per annum,
with Hattie A. Raymer as editor, and a considerable list
of well-known Rationalists as associate editors, has reached
its fourth number and ventures to print the picture of its
business manager Charles D. Raymer, who is also president of the Seattle Rationalist Society and proprietor of
Raymer's Old Book Store. It is a readable paper of excellent appearance. In number 4 the editor is brought under
criticism in a letter from Alexander Berkman for advocating Prohibition, and in another from J. A. Wilson for
recommending compulsory education, but she replies with
spirit."

On page 793, Vol. XLII of The Truth Seeker
(1915), I had to report that James F. Morton, Jr.,
was leaving us. Mr. Morton was competent and
trustworthy. His copy needed no censoring for the
elimination of ideas he might have cherished personally but that were alien to the policy of the paper.
He was conscientious about that; he showed judgment in selecting and preparing matter for the
paper, and he knew how to make up the pages and
see them through the press. In his signed contributions he inclined to invective.

When we had been parted from Mr. Morton and
his vocabulary for a season, there came George
William Bowne, a former Episcopal minister, to
take the vacant place of assistant. He had already
contributed in prose and verse articles signed and

1916] FIFTY YEARS OF FREETHOUGHT 459

unsigned. The signed ones were under the pen name of Richard Ellsworth.

The last position the professor held before coming to The Truth Seeker office was that of language teacher in the Jesuit College of St. Ignatius Loyola at Park avenue and Eighty-third street, New York. He gave me to understand he had declined reappointment there to devote himself to Rationalist writing and lecturing. I doubted whether the cause of his leaving the school, even the pulpit, was not his being rather hard to get along with. I have mentioned Osborne Ward's summary of the defects in the constitution of man, to wit, "intemperance, concupiscence, and irascibility." Of the first two the Professor can be acquitted, but he was irascible "to a degree," or "in the extreme," to borrow a pair of his favorite locutions. He certainly was a learned man, familiar with the Hebrew, the Greek, the German, and the Latin languages.

I suppose that the professor had studied abroad, for he had the Oxford manner of speaking and dismissed as pointless the following, to wit, which I excerpted from a communication to The Nation by Lucian Price of Amherst:

A noted divine had the misfortune to read Scripture at the college church in Anglican accents. Whereupon, as often as one of the fraternity brethren swerves up to the dormitory terrace resplendent in a Ford car, or appears in a new suit, you hear:

" 'Who is this king of gleaury?' "

And an antiphonal voice will chant:

" 'The leaurd of heausts. *He* is the king of gleaury!' "

The trial of Professor Otto of Wisconsin University for teaching Agnostic ethics aroused the combative instincts of Theodore Schroeder of the Free Speech League, who notified the trustees of the University that if the charges against the professor were pressed he was prepared to take up his residence in Madison and propagate the principles of Freethought and academic freedom so long as he could obtain listeners; and he would debate the subject with any representative the churches might elect.

The American Secular Union, the Rationalist Society of Milwaukee, and other liberal forces took up the agitation. The case against Professor Otto faded off the calendar and never reached a decision.

The fight of Mayor John Purroy Mitchel for an accounting, by the church, for the five million annually appropriated by the municipality for the support of city wards, lasted throughout the year, and resulted in the trial of some of the priests for obstructing the administration of justice, and for conspiracy to commit crime.

Father J. J. Crowley told enough about his fellow Catholic clergymen to put him in jail for life if it had been false, or to send a lot of them there if true. He wasted it all on the empty air so far as they were concerned, for while he was mobbed once or twice and attacked with violence when lecturing on the subject, they never took him into court. Among the other scandals he brought to light was the interesting one that Chicago women who were the mistresses of priests got the choicer and more desired positions as teachers in the public schools.

THEODORE SCHROEDER.

Mr. Schroeder's work for Freethought began in the days of the old National Liberal League, before that organization became the American Secular Union. He subscribed himself A. Theodore Schroeder, and his communications to The Truth Seeker came from Salt Lake City, Utah, where he practiced law ten years. From his study of Mormonism, which was thorough, have come many essays supporting the erotogenetic interpretation of religions. He is the founder of the Free Speech League.

Ten thousand rioters at Haverhill, Mass., attempted to lynch Thomas F. Leyden, who advertised an anti-Catholic lecture in the Haverhill town hall. They attacked the houses and smashed the windows of Protestant ministers in sympathy with the speaker. That was a historic incident. The Boston Transcript of April 4 pronounced the affair "a disgrace to Massachusetts," though suppressing the fact that the riot was a religious one and that the assailants of Leyden were Roman Catholics.

"We shall have to place our Idaho friend and subscriber, Mr. G. H. Holbrook, in the calendar of Freethought philanthropists. Lately it entered the mind of Mr. Holbrook that having a comfortable accumulation of property, he would make The Truth Seeker what he has the modesty to describe as 'a little present,' and in carrying out that generous intent he transferred to the Truth Seeker Company, principal and interest, a mortgage he held on some real estate in his community." (Truth Seeker, May 20, 1916.) The mortgage was for $2,500. Mr. Holbrook sent with his gift a sketch of his life from which he omitted dates except his birth, 1838. He was an Idaho pioneer and twice crossed the plains.

Under the head of "Science and Eternity—World-War Thoughts on Life and Death, Religion, and the Theory of Evolution," The Truth Seeker began in March to publish copious translations from Prof. Ernst Haeckel's work entitled "Eternity" (Ewigkeit). Haeckel had forwarded the book under his own inscription to The Truth Seeker. Be-

fore the end of the year we printed the work complete. It is a fine summary of Haeckel's views on
the subjects indicated, and it was hardly off the
press before Canada shut it out.

On the chance that the question of this country's
swapping diplomatic representatives with the pope
will be discussed in Washington, I quote from a
review of Johnson's history of "American Foreign
Relations," appearing in 1916:

"Was Franklin aware of the momentous consequences
that were to spring from the decision made by the Congress upon a document which he laid before it in 1783--
the request of the apostolic nuncio at Paris for American
ratification of a newly appointed apostolic vicar for the
United States? Franklin was directed to reply to the nuncio that, 'the subject of his application being purely spiritual, it is without the jurisdiction and power of Congress,
who have no authority to permit or refuse it.'"

The Congress, by terming the application "purely spiritual," withheld recognition of the pope as
a temporal sovereign.

Mark Twain's "Mysterious Stranger" appeared
in the fall. The story deals with the criminal follies and inhumanities that human beings are led
into by their religious beliefs. The God idea is so
monstrous that Satan wonders why mankind has
not perceived that the whole universe and its contents must be a hideous dream. Developing this
thought, he says:

"Strange, because they are so frankly and hysterically
insane—like all dreams: a God who could make good
children as easily as bad, yet preferred to make bad ones;
who could have made every one of them happy, yet never
made a single happy one; who made them prize their bitter
life, yet stingily cut it short; who gave his angels eternal

happiness unearned, yet required his other children to
earn it; who gave his angels painless lives, yet cursed
mind and body; who mouths justice and invented hell—
mouths mercy and invented hell — mouths Golden Rules,
and forgiveness multiplied by seventy times seven and
invented hell; who mouths morals to other people and has
none himself; who frowns upon crimes, yet commits them
all; who created man without invitation, then tries to shuffle
the responsibility for man's acts upon man, instead of
honorably placing it where it belongs, upon himself; and
finally, with altogether Divine obtuseness, invites this poor,
abused slave to worship him!"

DEPARTURES.

"The death of N. F. Griswold of Meriden,
Conn.," wrote L. K. Washburn, January 29, "takes
the last, I believe, of the old guard of Freethinkers
that stood behind me and Freethought in New
England thirty years ago. Mr. Griswold was
nearly 92 years old." He was a wealthy business
man of Meriden who contributed considerable sums
of money to the support of the good cause. Washburn said: "I received personal aid from his open
hand more than once, and the wisdom of his charity has contributed materially to the comfort of my
old age."

The Washington Secular League reported the
death of an honored member, William D. Mackenzie, a veteran employee in the quartermaster-gener-
al's office of the War Department.

Of the passing of Sir Hiram Maxim The Truth
Seeker said:

"We must record this week the death of a friend and
Freethinker, Sir Hiram Maxim, who for some three years
before the breaking out of the war was a frequent contributor to The Truth Seeker. Sir Hiram was born at

Sangersville, Maine, February 5, 1840. He died in London on Friday, October 24, and was therefore 76 years of age. He began inventing more than forty years ago, and after having achieved distinction in electrical works, he invented the automatic firearm known as the Maxim gun. In consideration of his valuable scientific and mechanical achievements he was created a knight in 1901.''

We lost also, through death this same year, the old subscriber Joseph A. Kimble of Vestal, N. Y., who had been with us from the beginning and left the editor a small legacy.

Elizabeth M. F. Denton, widow of William Denton, the geologist and explorer (1823-1883), died April 2 at Wellesley, Mass., in her ninetieth year. Unlike her distinguished husband, who inclined to belief in Spiritualism, Mrs. Denton, also distinguished in her own right, was a Materialist and upheld that philosophy with voice and pen.

Dr. Titus Voelkel died in November. Born in Prussian Poland in 1841, he acquired a superior education, was teacher in the higher schools of Germany until 1880, and then became "sprecher" for a number of Freethought associations and editor of a German Freethought paper. He was prosecuted for blasphemy and served two years in one of the prisons of the Fatherland. I first met him about 1894, when he said that he had just completed his sentence and had come to America to enjoy freedom of speech.

CHAPTER XXVIII.

EARLY in 1917 was discovered the melancholy fact that free speech in behalf of anything but religion and war had gone. The suppression made miserable the lives of the street speakers of the New York Secular Society. Except that the churches, the Salvation Army, the patrioteers, and the hyphenated Catholic-Americans, all of them privileged parties, were making outdoor propaganda and needed the highways for their purposes, an amendment of the federal Constitution prohibiting street speaking altogether would have been favorably received by the authorities that closed the mouths of the Secular orators. The courts without scruple imposed fines and imprisonment regardless of law or evidence, found the accused guilty as charged when the charges had been disproved or withdrawn, and policemen without intelligence censored the speaking.

Freethinkers did not provide the courts with quite all the opportunities the magistrates were capable of using to make manifest their incapacity. The littleness and meanness of the tribunals was fed on cases enumerated in a Truth Seeker Note at Large near the beginning of the year

There prevailed an epidemic of "law-enforcement," not on criminals, for that never happens; the courts dealt with the propagandists and idealists; and the snoopers were as elated as the proverbial fice with a mile and a half of hitching-posts ahead.

The Socialists of Waukegan, Illinois, engaged Michael Mockus for a lecture, which he delivered in the face of threats of prosecution. Arrest and trial for "blasphemy" followed on a charge of "disorderly conduct." Lawyer Frederick Mains, the Chicago Freethinker formerly associated with W. H. Maples as publisher of The Freethought Beacon, defended the case and secured an acquittal.

The young men who were talking Rationalism on the streets of New York suffered arrest so frequently on flimsy charges that the Secular Society talked of retaining permanent counsel.

Some of the acts of appointed or volunteer government agents against eccentric pacifists were silly; others were brutal. "Uncle Jenk," as he called himself when addressing his young people, or the Rev. Jenkin Lloyd Jones, editor of Chicago Unity, as the world knew him, when encamped at Clear Lake, near Janesville, Wis., raised his flag with a white border around it to symbolize peace. The United States district-attorney, having heard of this trivial act, gave orders to the local sheriff that the flag must be hauled down. Mr. Jones struck his colors. The successor of Mr. Jones as editor of Unity, the Rev. John Haynes Holmes, announced that he was not going to pray for the triumph of our arms. There were murmurs and threats, but what difference could it make whether he prayed for the country or not?

England, preoccupied as she was with the war and the prosecution of traitors and conscientious objectors, tried and convicted two "blasphemers," J. W. Gott and J. J. Riley. Neither the National Secular Society nor the Rationalist Press Association would take up the defense. They held a case to be without merit when the language complained of was such as would result in a prosecution if used in discussing any subject whatever.

The Masses, Max Eastman editor, which seemed to be near pro-German in sentiment, had its August and September numbers excluded from the mails by the New York Postmaster. Employing Gilbert E. Roe as attorney, Mr. Eastman brought an injunction action. Postmaster General Burleson communicated to the Senate a denunciation of The Masses, and named Tom Watson's Jeffersonian in the same class. Eastman lost his mailing privileges, but in the end recovered them with $11,000 compensation. And then his associate, the man who wrote "The Socialization of Wealth," stole the money and got away.

The American Library Association began a drive for a million to buy and forward books for the soldiers in the cantonments, designating the New York Public Library as one of twelve to receive books and funds. To find out whether Freethought books would be forwarded one of our subscribers called at the Library and interviewed the man in charge of the department. The man doubted that literature of a controversial nature would be forwarded. For example, volunteered he, "We could not send The Truth Seeker." The inquirer came away persuaded that neither would they send Freethought books. He advised concentrating on The Truth Seeker sent direct to enlisted men as individuals. With a contribution of $5, and more added from time to time, he started a Soldiers' and Sailors' Truth Seeker fund, which grew to goodly proportions, the readers supplying names of men in army or navy. So our warriors overseas got their paper.

Newspapers ran patriotic sentiments in conspicuous type at the head of the editorial columns—the best ones being selected from Paine and Ingersoll. This of Ingersoll's flew at the masthead of many a journal. *"Let us proudly remember that in our time the greatest, the grandest, the noblest army of the world fought—not to enslave, but to free; not to destroy, but to save; not simply for themselves, but for others; not for conquest, but for conscience; not only for us, but for every land and every race."*

Paine was a great favorite:

"The cause of America is in a great measure the cause of all mankind. Many circumstances have arisen and will arise which are not local but universal, and through which the principles of all lovers of mankind are affected, and in the event of which their affections are interested. The laying of a country desolate with fire and sword, declaring war against the natural rights of mankind, and extirpating the defenders thereof from the face of the earth, is the concern of every man to whom nature hath given the power of feeling."

They all quoted with emphasis:

"These are the times that try men's souls. The summer

soldier and the sunshine patriot will at this crisis shrink from the service of their country, but he that stands it now deserves the love and thanks of man and woman."

The severing of diplomatic relations with Germany took place by act of President Wilson the 3d day of February. At the proclamation of war The Truth Seeker announced "The Lost Fight for Peace" and urged all, including the pacifists, loyally to accept the situation. Some did and some did not. There were a great many objectors, conscientious and conscienceless. Some imagining themselves conscientiously opposed to war defended the Kaiser for starting one. The loyal Mr. Robert Lanyon of Chicago sprang on them a quotation from Paine: "If ye really preach from conscience, convince the world thereof by proclaiming your doctrine to our enemies, for they likewise bear arms."

When Congress passed a bill creating twenty new army chaplains to represent the Jews, the Christian Scientists, Unitarians and other as yet unrecognized denominations, the Secularists were quite over-looked. "Does not Congress see," I inquired (proposing a few Infidel appointments), "that it would be an intellectual stimulus to the soldiers if secular chaplains were provided and posts and camps enlivened with debate?"

The poets of America, headed by Robert Underwood Johnson, then our minister to Italy, organized an ambulance service for the Italians, each ambulance honoring an American poet. Mr. F. F. Ayer, a New York Agnostic, invited to name his poet and to subscribe, gave $2,000 for an ambulance with the inscription:

To the Memory of
ROBERT G. INGERSOLL

On the same date the Pittsburgh Chronicle Telegraph blundered into saying that it would be interesting if unbelievers could be included in the record
of altruistic service in connection with the war!

On behalf of unbelievers I pointed out that, unlike professional Christians, Freethinkers worked
not through organizations exempted from the burdens of the state and employing agents exempted
from military duty; that Freethinkers pay taxes on
their property and serve in the ranks rather than at
lemonade stands back of the front, and that their
activities on behalf of our fighting men are conducted, without newspaper advertisement, through
secular and non-religious channels, such as the Red
Cross and the mail agencies. Their work was personal rather than organized, I informed the editorial
writer on the Pittsburgh paper. Therefore com-
parisons would be personal; and I signified my willingness to compare what the editor of The Truth
Seeker had done with the service rendered by the
editor of The Chronicle Telegraph. No response.

My sons, Eugene Leland and Putnam Foote,
though "Put" was under the military age, enlisted
and went across—Eugene with the Eleventh Engineers, Putnam with the "gobs" who sailed in the
Leviathan. Readers made kindly inquiries after
the fortunes of the lads. From the initials, the following appears to be a Letter Box reply to Mrs.
Hazel Sauve of Iron River, Wisconsin, who read
The Truth Seeker when she was a girl:

"Yes, the Boy Gene left for the war nearly a month ago, arrived in England in safety, and paraded before the king that day (Aug. 15) when the lid was lifted in London. We take it he has been boosted out of the ranks, as in a censored letter he speaks of having another parchment to hang with his S. B. diploma. The Boy Putnam has been received into the Navy. He relates that by reason of his excess in height above six feet, the surgeon who passed him climbed a step ladder to look at his teeth. There were questions of a personal nature: Do you smoke or chew? No. Drink beer or whiskey? No, nor coffee or tea. What religion? None. Marked 'No vices'."

Eugene's "parchment," to be hung with his Bachelor of Science degree from the Massachusetts Institute of Technology, consisted of a second lieutenant's commission, followed almost immediately by a "first," and on the heels of that a captaincy. "Bobbie" Brown, the Ingersoll grandson, repaired to Plattsburg as a candidate for aviation.

The sons of many Freethinkers volunteered, as mine did. Those of military age visited The Truth Seeker office on the way to the front. Among the callers was J. Danforth Taylor, M.D., of Boston, going over as army doctor. The son of the hopelessly unregenerate W. S. Bryan was the second or third American soldier to cross the bridge into Germany. A reader in South Africa, John Latham, who had headed the Rationalist movement in the Transvaal, was sent back from the front three times, wounded in action. He was promoted to a captaincy for valor. A blackguardly American priest, conducting an open-air mass, told the multitude: "Atheists will be the first to be shot in the back when forced to go to war by conscription." It was none of my business how many Irish Catholic

MALES OF THE FAMILY IN 1917.

The boys volunteered in order to choose the preferred branch of the service. Eugene (right) was a soldier; Putnam (left) a sailor.

subjects of Great Britain were skedaddling; yet I asked: "And those Irish slackers who have reached America from England by the boatload since the war began—are they all Atheists?" Canada was as loyal and sacrificing as Britain herself—all but Catholic Quebec. The Catholics there were of French antecedents, and they were British subjects, but, advised by their priests, they refused to join the armies of either France or England.

The promoters of the Bible Society in America urged the purchase of Testaments for the soldiers. President Wilson in a thoughtless moment gave them a pious sentiment for the flyleaf, and the front would have been littered with the gospel if the shipmasters with limited transportation facilities and holds bursting with war supplies had not protested against loading their vessels with junk. Stories came back of soldiers saved from death by bullets and fragments of shells that penetrated their pocket Testaments as far as some passage applicable to the situation and there stopped. An atheistic British soldier returned to his father pages of the London Freethinker that on separate occasions had gone with him safely over the top. The soldier wrote: "Some people will tell you that before going over, the biggest Atheist will send up a prayer. Don't you believe it. I suppose this last time I had as narrow an escape as ever I could wish for, but even at that terrible moment I trusted to a clear head and sane thinking." Thoughts of God or the church did not enter his mind.

An American soldier belonging to the Coast Defense Command wrote to The Truth Seeker that his company had been paraded and sent to church on Sunday by order of Colonel Skerrett. The correspondent, obliged to listen to the preaching, reported: "The same old god, devil, and hell were spouted by a long-eared pulpiteer."

Taking a letterhead of the New York Secular Society, and writing as an officer thereof to Secretary of War Baker and others in authority, I inquired:

"Is there anything in the Rules and Regulations of the War Department that denies to an enlisted man—whether soldier or sailor—the constitutional right to religious freedom? If not, why does the War Department permit a certain brand of religion to be forced down the throats of unwilling enlisted men?"

The Secretary of War passed the inquiry to Adjutant-General R. K. Kravans, who replied at length and with the proper circumlocution, quoting a letter from the War Department signed by Adjutant W. A. Simpson:

"Returned. The Department Commander does not approve of the action of the Coast Defense Commander in requiring compulsory attendance at divine service of persons under his command. Necessary action will be taken accordingly.

So far as this decision came to the attention of commanders and was made known to the men, no soldier who preferred to spend the church hour reading, writing, or resting need suffer more from the spouting of the "long-eared pulpiteers."

When the country went into war I had misgivings

as to where the Philosophicals, remnant of the Tucker group of Libertarians, would be found. E. C. Walker at times had gone through short periods of melancholy because the Freethinkers of the United States formed no organization like the Rationalist Peace Society of Great Britain; but at the click of the first trigger Walker flung Old Glory to the breeze and took his place under it. James F. Morton joined him. Word came from France that Benjamin R. Tucker sided with the Allies and looked upon America's participation in the war as a necessity. And William Thurston Brown, whom I had viewed as irretrievably committed to the works of Emma Goldman and Alexander Berkman, contributed to The Truth Seeker from Ferrer Colony, Stelton, N. J., as "A Libertarian's View of the War" a perfectly reasoned defense of conscription as a necessity of present civilization and of an enduring society. These men of old American stock must have heard the voices of their ancestors. Brown, the schoolmaster at Ferrer Colony, endured the reproach of his associates; but when he and his fellow colonists fell under the suspicion of disloyalty, that article from The Truth Seeker held like an anchor to windward.

Joseph McCabe, the English Rationalist who had done "twelve years in a monastery," and wrote a book so entitled, was a guest in America in this year (1917). Then and for some time thereafter I had difficulty in adjusting Mr. McCabe's personality to his huge and heavy literary product. Somebody, probably Ed. Henn, came in the next day

after Mr. McCabe's call upon the editor and asked
how the distinguished man sized up when seen;
and I answered offhand that he was a 135-pound
Irishman below the medium height. Mr. McCabe
belongs to the order of Little Giants, being less
than middle-sized but mighty. While his pen travels
at speed, its trail is as legible as print and softer
on the eyes. For him, translating goes as smoothly
and rapidly as copying. He is that combination of
attributes and aptitudes that makes the prolific
writer; and given learning besides, here is the almost perfect machine for the making of textbooks
on Rationalism.

Freethought Societies holding meetings at the
close of 1917, named in the order their notices appeared in The Truth Seeker, were as follows: The
Brooklyn Philosophical Association, Wm. A. Winham, secretary; The Ferrer Association, New
York; the Paterson (N. J.) Philosophical Society,
Frank Bamford, secretary; the Boston Freethought
Society, J. P. Bland, resident speaker; the Pittsburgh Rationalist Society, Marshall J. Gauvin, lecturer; the Rationalist Society of Toledo (Ohio);
the Chicago Freethought Society, H. Percy Ward,
lecturer; the Columbus (Ohio) Rationalist Association, Olin J. Ross, secretary; the Twin City Ra-
tionalist Society, Edward Cantrell, lecturer; the
Cedar Rapids (Iowa) Freethought Congregation,
Jos. J. Hajek, speaker; the Michigan Rationalist
and Freethought Association (Detroit), Arthur A.
Senger, secretary; the Friendship Liberal League,
Philadelphia, F. Garfield Bowers, secretary; the
Milwaukee Rationalist Society, Joel Moody, presi-

dent; the Washington Secular League, John D. Bradley, president; the Los Angeles Liberal Club, Charles T. Sprading, lecturer; the Church of This World (Kansas City, Mo.), J. E. Roberts, lecturer; the Seattle Rationalist Society, J. E. Wheeler, president. In June George Lowe, secretary, reported the organization in Buffalo, N. Y., for Promoting Rational Ethics, Gus H. Lang, president. The Clarksburg (W. Va.) Rationalist Society opened in February and heard an address by Hugh M. Martin; G. A. Miller, secretary. The Rationalist Society of North America, organized in San Francisco in 1914, held but one congress, that of 1915, when reorganization took place. After that most of the leaders dropped out and there was no other congress. Martin L. Bunge, editor of the Freidenker, Milwaukee, became acting president and lectured on the Pacific coast. An unsigned article, marked "contributed," in the July 21 number of The Truth Seeker, probably by Charles T. Sprading, attributed the passing of the association to "war and other difficulties."

In the lecture field, Stanley J. Clark debated with the clergy of Texas, as Dwight Spencer of Coalgate, Oklahoma, reported. William F. McGee, an ex-priest, spoke from Percy Ward's platform in Chicago. Bishop William Montgomery Brown of Galion, Ohio, later to become a notable heretic, numbered the churches to ascertain their attitude on war, and found them 3 to 1 in favor of it.

Mr. Jesse W. Weik of Greencastle, Indiana, co-author with W. H. Herndon of Herndon and Weik's Life of Lincoln, sought the advice and cooperation of John E. Remsburg with regard to erecting a suitable granite marker for the grave of Herndon in Springfield, Illinois. Mr. Remsburg communicated with The Truth Seeker in an approving article, from which I quote the last paragraph:

"Judge Weik's proposal is a worthy and a timely one, and merits the approval of Rationalists everywhere. His call for help will, I am sure, be answered by a generous response. I suggest that those who wish to contribute to the work send their contributions to The Truth Seeker to be forwarded to Judge Weik. The American Secular Union will give $10, and more if needed. The cost of the marker need not be confined to $100. If more is raised a larger stone can be erected."

Herndon, for twenty years the law partner of Lincoln, is the chief witness to Lincoln's anti-Christian beliefs, and Judge Weik rightly apprehended that the Freethinkers would be most interested in honoring his memory. The publication of his appeal, with the endorsement of Remsburg, proved it. The amount was oversubscribed. Relying upon recollection of the circumstances, I must add that the judge published elsewhere a report of his success in raising the money for the Herndon gravestone, without saying that the Freethinkers contributed most of it.

A religious census taker, the same being a young woman, came to our house in 1917 and inquired the denomination of the family. I replied that we were Freethinkers. Said she: "Freethinkers? What's that?" To aid her understanding I asked: "Did you ever hear of Inger-

soll?" The light broke on her mind as she an-
ewered, "Oh, yes, but how do you spell Freethinker?" After that I understood why religious
census takers report so few Freethinkers. They
cannot spell the word.

The Rev. E. H. Reeman brought out a theological work with the title, "Do We Need a New
Conception of God?" The author, after stating
the old conception, pioposed in its place a conception based on modern knowledge. Nothing
happened. A dozen years later, at a meeting of
the American Association for the Advancement
of Science in New York, Prof. Harry Elmer
Barnes, the sociologist and historian, propounded
the same question. The Catholic Cardinal Hayes
discovered in the inquiry a declaration of war by
science on the church, and set up defenses in a
sermon at St. Patrick's cathedral. President
Henry Fairfield Osborn made haste to repudiat
Dr. Barnes on behalf of the Association. The
incident seemed to show that the courage of science was on the ebb.

The increased cost of production forced The
Truth Seeker to raise its subscription price in
November from $3 a year to $3.50.

The marriage of Eva Ingersoll Brown, daugh-
ter of Mr. and Mrs. Walston Hill Brown and
granddaughter of Robert G. Ingersoll, and Lieut.
McNeal Swasey of the Officers' Reserve Corps,
United States Army, took place on October 6 at
Walston, Dobbs-Ferry-on-the-Hudson. Lieuten-

ant Swasey was in the aviation branch of the
service with Eva's brother.

DEPARTURES.

William Wood of Toronto, Canada, whom we
knew only as a subscriber of some years' standing, died in October, leaving five hundred dollars
to The Truth Seeker—one hundred of it for the
services of a Freethought speaker at his funeral.
Prof. G. W. Bowne, then associate editor, answered the call. Mr. Wood had been a substantial supporter of the Toronto Secular Society.

In the will of John H. Ludwig the Thomas
Paine National Historical Association was named
to receive a specific bequest of $25,000 for the
erection and maintenance of a home for needy
members. Mr. Ludwig was not known to be
among the Freethinkers until after his death.

The Truth Seeker of June 9 gave a biography,
written by Franklin Steiner, of Col. E. A. Stevens, former secretary of the American Secular
Union. June 23 appeared the correction from the
subject that while not commissioned during the
war, he had about fifteen commissions since en-
titling him to wear the colonel's silver eagle.
September 14, 1917, he died at his home in Chicago at the age of 74, and the funeral services
were conducted on the 16th by M. M. Mangasarian.

Col. Edward A. Stevens was born in Mirfield, Yorkshire,
England, June 8, 1844. When a youth he ran away from
home to join a detachment of Garibaldi's army called
"Garibaldi's Englishmen," commanded by Colonel Peard.

He saw some severe hand-to-hand fighting. The officers of the company sent him home to England, much to his chagrin.

Heretical ideas on the subject of religion took root in his mind even in youth. His education was derived chiefly

COL. E. A. STEVENS (1844-1917).
This "soldier, author, editor, poet, orator, and always the courtly, knightly gentleman," was secretary of the American Secular Union 1886-1889.

from travel, observation and experience. He came to
America,, went to Buffalo, N. Y., and enlisted in the
187th New York Volunteers. He served in the first division, second brigade of the Fifth Army Corps. That division
was selected by General Grant to "receive" the surrender
of Lee's army at Appomattox.

When the war was over Colonel Stevens returned to
his trade, that of a printer. He expanded himself into a
a writer, an editor and a publisher, in all of which he was
successful. Becoming interested in labor questions, in 1876
he joined the Knights of Labor, and on his refusal to
take the oath prescribed was received on his honor. He
also held a number of important offices in the Typographical Union. In 1881, when in Chicago, he organized a
branch of the National Liberal League. In 1886, when
the League's name was changed to the American Secular
Union, Colonel Stevens was elected national secretary, a
position to which he was re-elected in 1887 and 1888. He
brought the Secular Union to its highest point of efficiency
and made it a power that the church felt. One of his
activities as secretary was the suit against the Roman
Catholic archbishop of Chicago for receiving public funds
for sectarian institutions, in which he was sustained by the
Appellate Court, costing the Roman Catholic church $60,-
000 in the three years it operated. Stevens had a census
made of all church property in the city of Chicago which
was published in The Truth Seeker at that time. He raised
in less than three weeks the $1,500 pledged for the Bruno
monument in Rome. He resigned in 1889, to the regret of
all supporters of the Union. His salary as secretary was
small, and while holding the position he had been obliged
to draw upon his own private resources.

CHAPTER XXIX

WITH the guns going and the American Expeditionary Forces getting into action all 1918 conversation tended to be war talk. Business had to be transacted, however, and magazines, books, and newspapers must be brought out by those engaged in that trade. Hence affairs went on as usual; themes that before had interested the reading public, or any part of it, continued to be written upon; but meanwhile the big war was the unfinished business before the house the world over. As for The Truth Seeker, there might have been some editorial moralizing on the conduct of the war, but not much, if the preachers, the Kaiser included, had only left God and religion where they belonged instead of elevating God to the high command and proclaiming the preservation of Christianity to be the thing at stake in this conflict. But when the Kaiser opened the new year with the tidings that "God's hand is seen to prevail," while President Wilson in America and Premier Lloyd-George in England gave out the news they were trusting in heaven, the Freethinkers let it be known frankly that they viewed the situation as too serious for pious persiflage, which ought therefore to be chased hence.

The spurious coinage was uttered and taken at its face value by the veteran newspaper man, Henry Watterson of the Louisville Courier-Journal, that "the Kaiser never appeals to Christ." Now that might truthfully be said of George Washington or of Abraham Lincoln, but of Wilhelm II, never. While Wilson satisfied the bibliolaters with a piety paragraph on the flyleaf of the gospels distributed to the American Expeditionary Forces, the Kaiser slept with a New Testament on the lightstand by his bed; and he told the first gathering of chaplains despatched to the front: "We must make him [Christ] the ideal of our practical life." And Elsie, the fair daughter of Field Marshal von Hindenburg, sent to the soldiers fighting under her father this favor for their Christmas:

> "Christ Jesus gave his life for me;
> From every debt I now am free.
> He to the bayonet thrust gives vigor,
> The joy to aim, to pull the trigger."

We, the people, with President Wilson's approval, were trading with the Bible Society for four hundred thousand Testaments and shipping them to the soldiers. And while the government sent the Testament to citizens abroad, the courts sent citizens at home to jail for quoting it. In Los Angeles the Rev. Floyd Hardin, the Rev. Robert Whitaker, and Harold Storey, a Quaker theological student, were sentenced each to six months in the county jail and $1,200 fine. Storey had said it was "difficult for many Christians to conceive of the carpenter of Nazareth thrusting a bayonet into the breast of a brother." The prosecuting attorney fiercely quoted: "But these mine enemies, bring hither and slay them before me." A stupid court charged Whitaker with degrading religion by using it as a cloak for disloyalty. The judge couldn't see the million clerics, parsons, priests, and theologs, who were using their religion to escape military duty.

My associate editor, Dr. Bowne, took issue with Governor Lowden of Illinois that the God of the Kaiser and the God of Joshua were different and opposed deities. In an article (April 13, 1918) headed "The Clergy Arraigned," the professor wrote this paragraph:

"We have carefully compared the reputed offenses of the German emperor with the hideous doings of God as related in the Bible, and there seems to be but one conclusion to draw from the comparison, and it is this: The former received his inspiration from a careful study of the performance of the latter. Indeed, it is well known that the Prussian generals who published books explanatory of the German idea of war, based their notions directly upon the lessons they had learned from a very painstaking study of the Holy Scriptures. And it is also well to note that not one of these German works has been answered from the biblical standpoint which forms the groundwork for their authority."

The professor inclined to the use of many words, yet in his statement there was the kernel of truth. He repeated only what the Kaiser's own theologians had already said. He touched not at all on America's own way of conducting the war; and when our New York postmaster, the Hon. Mr. Patten, dropped us a note saying that the Solicitor of the Postoffice Department, the Hon. W. H. Lamar of Washington, had pronounced The Truth Seeker of April 13, 1918, unmailable under the Espionage Act, it did not occur to me that this paragraph of Dr. Bowne's had an incendiary content, and nearly six weeks of inquiry passed before that information could be elicited from the office of Mr. Lamar. During this time I had held correspondence with the Hon. Solicitor, who showed no reluctance to answer my letters. He was prompt though reticent; he would not divulge wherein The Truth Seeker had offended. I told him I thought the matter should be acted upon, for if I had been guilty of disloyalty I doubtless ought to be hanged.

The Hon. Solicitor replied that in view of what I had said, there would be no proceedings, and while it was not the general practice of his office to indicate to publishers particular matter appearing in an issue of a publication regarded as non-mailable by the Department under this act, he would advise me that *the paragraph* (which I have italicized) *from the Professor's article formed the basis of the ruling of the Department!*

I turned, then, to criticism and exposure of the

graft of the churches and religious organizations, which had procured exemption for the whole body of the clergy, including theological students; they imposed upon the nation an army of chaplains, fifteen thousand strong, with the rank and pay of commissioned officers; they obtained protection from criticism under the Espionage Act, and on the railroads taken over by the government the whole profession, Salvation Army and all—anything religious, priest or nun—rode on half-rate tickets, while soldiers and sailors in uniform paid full fare.

Early in the war, the New York Sun collected from voluntary contributors a fund to supply the soldiers with tobacco. The goods so provided, labeled for identification, were to be given, not sold, to the men overseas. Well, I contributed $5 to that fund—unselfishly, for neither of my boys used tobacco. The Y. M. C. A. acquired free the tobacco my V paid for, and *sold* it to the soldiers. A soldier reader brought with him to the office a bunkie who had something to show me. He had bought at a Y. M. C. A. hut a package of tobacco, and upon examining it found it marked as a free contribution with the compliments of the New York Sun's tobacco fund!

The gouging propensities of the Y. M. C. A. gave rise to the story brought home by my boy in the navy. A "Y" secretary fell overboard and yelled to a gob leaning on the rail to give him a line. The gob continued to lean on the rail as he replied: "I can't give you a line, but I will sell you one." An order was issued requiring enlisted men to salute "Y" secretaries as officers. It was not obeyed.

The Salvation Army wangled a reputation for distributing coffee and doughnuts to the men in the trenches. A few actual instances created the legend that such was the common performance with the Army. After the war, Raymond Fosdick, head of the Welfare missions, stated that the Salvation Army often was higher priced than the "Y." In a copy of the War Cry with news from France I saw a picture of a file of Engineers, each raising to his face a Salvation Army pie, which he appeared to be wolfing, and sent the paper to my son in the Fighting Eleventh, remarking that he should avoid luxurious living in a strange country. He replied that the picture was taken at Fort Totten where the Engineers were encamped before they went across, and that he had seen nothing like it in France.

After the postoffice detained The Truth Seeker of April 13 our columns bore no more attempted identifications of the Kaiser's God with Joshua's. Nevertheless the officials exacted an advance copy every week to be censored. The paper therefore reached its subscribers late if at all. When another number, August 31, had been pronounced unmailable, I resorted to the postoffice for information. The assistant postmaster would vouchsafe none, and the Hon. Solicitor W. H. Lamar at Washington also kept mum, despite the receipt of so many inquiries and protests from readers that he was obliged to print a form letter of reply. In September he took from his files and mailed to me, requesting its return, as he had no other copy, some matter relating to the offense of a pro-German in Wisconsin, who, besides expressing the opinion that the welfare societies, including the Red Cross, were a "bunch of grafters," had attacked the government. "Who is the government?" this disloyal person inquired. "Who is running this war? A bunch of capitalists composed of the steel trust and munition makers."

How did this apply to The Truth Seeker? I had never mentioned the Red Cross except to designate it as the one legitimate form of welfare work, and this talk about capitalists and trusts being responsible for the war I had pronounced "the canned product of demagogues." But I had overlooked something. The district judge, by *obiter dictum,* in this obscure Wisconsin case, had included the "Y" in the "armed forces of the United States," and to disparage our armed forces was espionage. Moreover, Congress had amended the Espionage Act in accordance with this decision of the "courts," as the Hon. Solicitor termed the district judge in Wisconsin, and had included chaplains as commissioned officers not subject to criticism.

Here was occasion for gloom. The postoffice took our money and destroyed whole editions of the paper, and since we could not deliver the goods, receipts fell off. As at this time an edition of The Nation had been held up, and then released through some action taken by the proprietor, Mr. Oswald Garrison Villard, I called at the

Nation office to learn how he did it. Mr. Villard
had consulted a lawyer and then gone personally
to Washington. He gave me the name of the
attorney with the warning that this man of law
was expensive. I determined to see the lawyer,
nevertheless, and let Mr. John R. Slattery take
a trip to the capital in our behalf. I heard that
Mr. Villard saw the President, but Mr. Slattery
got no farther than the Hon. Solicitor, Mr. Lamar, who, he reported, looked and talked like a
cross-roads justice of the peace. Meanwhile, I
consulted Mr. Villard's attorney, whose expen-
siveness the editor of The Nation had not over-
stated. He kept me waiting an hour and gave me
ten minutes, while he walked the floor, agitating
his mind and extemporizing. His oral expressions
contained the advice that I should criticise the
solicitor in such a way as to make it appear that
he had personal motives in putting the paper out
of circulation.

The Hon. Solicitor had written to Olin J. Ross
of Columbus, Ohio, and to others that—

*"The Postoffice Department has taken no action
against The Truth Seeker because of its being an
Agnostic paper or because of any views expressed
in it on any religious questions, nor has any action
been taken against this publication as such."*

To show that in this letter to Mr. Ross the
Hon. Solicitor had departed from the facts, I
quoted his letter to myself in which he cited the
paragraph from Dr. Bowne's article on God and
the Kaiser, and advised me it was the language
that formed the basis of the action of the Depart-

ment in declaring the issue of the paper containing it to be unmailable.

With his written signature reproduced and attached, attesting the genuineness of both, the two letters of Solicitor Lamar—the one to me quoting Bowne's polemic as the cause of the action, and the one to Mr. Ross denying it as such cause—were printed on pages facing each other, in facsimile, so that their contradictory statements fell under the eye at the same time. And then, in an accompanying article, I maintained that even shifting the accusation from that of aspersing the God of the Bible by associating him with the Kaiser, to that of criticising a parasitic religious organization attaching itself to the state, the *question was still a religious one;* and The Truth Seeker, a loyal newspaper, had been repeatedly suppressed for the advocacy of Secularism, the separation of the civil from the ecclesiastical.

No further numbers of The Truth Seeker were rejected by the postoffice.

I have always believed that somebody at Washington cherished an intent to "get" The Truth Seeker on its religious views.

From the pacifist platform it was only a step to the penitentiary. I counseled all to watch that step. Dr. William J. Robinson of The Critic and Guide, who strenuously objected to war with Germany, used so little vigilance in this regard that the arresters got him put under $10,000 bonds. Fortunately for the doctor, his views were not too strongly held to admit of his changing them. At an early date, then, he perceived the error of his ways and pledged fealty to the good old U.S.A. until German junkerdom should be no more. The followers of Dr. Charles T. Russell got in quite bad by circulating the plainly unpatriotic book called "The Finished Mystery." Judge Joseph Rutherford, Russell's successor, was convicted of conspiracy, and sentenced with six of his followers to twenty years in the Atlanta penitentiary. The Postoffice Department pronounced the June number of The Masses unmailable, and editor Max Eastman changed its name to The Liberator while he went to law for the restoration of his rights. A New England preacher, the Rev. Clarence Waldron, was jailed for obstructive pacifism; in Kansas City Mrs. Rose Pastor Stokes, who had committed herself to whatever her deluders meant by the phrase "This is a rich man's war," went behind bars. In New York Scott Nearing landed in durance because he had got the habit of saying the same thing and couldn't make the pass to something else. The Public (Single Tax), which had accomplished the about-face from non-militant to militant, lost a number in the postoffice discard by advising the administration to do something different. Walter Hurt's paper, The Paladin, St. Louis, came out twice, but its first number, published in behalf of the "Friends of Freedom," died in the postoffice. In Chicago Cassius V. Cook, once associated with Rationalism, started a League of Humanity and was held under federal charges for anti-draft activities. The Chicago agent of The

Menace (anti-clerical) was beaten up by Catholic thugs. The arrest of Eugene V. Debs, four times Socialist candidate for President, took place in Cleveland, where he said something construed as violative of the Espionage Act. The Weekly People, once conducted by Daniel DeLeon, Columbia professor, deceased, lost its second-class mailing privilege. The case against Dreiser's "Genius," by Sumner of the Comstock Society, was thrown out of court. Mrs. Margaret Sanger lost in the higher courts of New York on the constitutionality of the law which designates birth control information as obscene. The liberal Justice Brandeis granted her an appeal to the United States Supreme Court, where of course she lost, for that high tribunal never interferes in behalf of liberty. While the editor of the New York Nation was preparing a strong article condemning the exclusion of The Truth Seker from the mails, the New York postoffice withheld his own paper from dispatch.

The terrorism exercised by the enemies of free speech and free press was in the main confined, during the war, to America and the Central Powers. As it existed here and in Austria-Germany, it was comparatively unknown in England, France, Italy, Canada, and Australia. The Socialist Ramsay MacDonald was the Eugene V. Debs of England, but he went to Parliament and was later made Prime Minister, while we sent his American mate to a federal penitentiary. A Freethought paper in

London might freely impeach the usefulness of the black army of chaplains.

The voices of Emma Goldman and Alexander Berkman ceased to be heard in the land when after trial they were in January sent to Jefferson prison for a minimum of two years. They had said that government was imperfect.

Our subscriber, Mrs. George Alexander Wheelock, "chief yeoman and champion recruiter of the world," who in 1917 went to Albany to speak in support of a bill to abolish church exemption, was the first of her sex to wear the insignia of a lieutenant in the navy. She earned her commission by recruiting 17,000 men for Uncle Sam's ships. The Freethought street speakers in New York registered for the service, and Mitchuly and Meirowitz were called. Meirowitz related that when he went to the camp library for a book, and signed a card supposing it to be a receipt, he found it bore Y. M. C. A. stuff that pledged him to be loyal to King Jesus.

Our talented contributor Mary Monico betook herself to the camps and sang for soldiers. J. A. Hennesy's son Hugh, who made the picture that is now on The Truth Seeker's cover page, did cartoons for Barbed Wire, the Madison Barracks, N. Y., camp paper. Edward Tuck, in Paris, held a directorship of the University Center, where Americans foregathered. Mrs. Tuck founded the officers' rest camp at Nice.

In 1918 Mrs. Walston Hill Brown, Ingersoll's younger daughter, with the approval of the government, organized the Soldiers' Families of America, Commodore Wadhams of the navy, director. Amelia Schachtel, for many years treasurer of the Manhattan Liberal Club, labored in behalf of the American Women's Hospitals for War Service. The author known to literature as Madeline Bridges, and to our circle as Mary Devere, wrote a poem entitled "Ready," which, recited by the actor Edwin Brandt (of "Daddy Longlegs") at the noon hour in Wanamaker's department store, to stimulate the sale of bonds, or at the moving picture theaters and in the schools to promote war savings-stamps, was always cheered on its own merits and its repetition demanded, while the listeners bought every time. The press described the effect as "tremendous."

There were many disbelievers in military measures who would subscribe for a peaceful fight, and there was peace enough in Madeline's martial song to make a Quaker subscribe to a war fund. The best verse the world war inspired had no religion in it. "In Flanders Fields" by Lieut. Col. John McCrae of the Canadian Expeditionary Forces, who fell in battle on the ground he celebrates, seemed plainly to echo Ingersoll: "And then I vowed to grasp the torch that they had held, and hold it high, that light might conquer darkness still."

A Catholic-American auditor tried to vex a Freethought street speaker by asking: "Where is your registration card?" The speaker replied: "It is in my pocket; where is yours?" The interrupter had none. "Come on, then," said the speaker, "I'll go with you to the nearest recruiting station and enlist." After this speaker had been called to the colors, a Common Cause (hyphenate) orator, holding forth against the unbelievers, shouted: "What has become of the Atheists you used to hear spouting their blasphemies on the street corners?" A voice in his audience replied: "They are at the front defending the country for slackers like you!"

Good memories will recall the fanatic efforts of some of the Catholic editors to claw back after slipping their moorings and drifting off in the wake of the Socialist Morris Hillquit, who as candidate for mayor of New York drew a following of pacifists and pro-Germans. Those of the doubly hyphenated Catholic-Irish-American papers, the Freeman's Journal, Gaelic American, and Irish World, temporarily lost their mailing privileges for "giving aid and comfort to the enemy."

A fire-eating anti-hyphenist at my elbow says: "You ought to have a line in saying that the Irish and Germans fell into each other's arms; and that Irish papers in this country from 1914 onwards flourished like the green bay-tree, moribund ones reviving and new ones being started. Bernstorff was the Santa Claus."

The following intimation appeared in the paper for March 23:

"Mark Twain, in his 'Pudd'nhead Wilson,' mentions a Freethought Society of which a local jurist was president and Pudd'nhead Wilson secretary. The society held regular meetings attended by the president and secretary, but there were no members. The Mark Twain Fellowship of

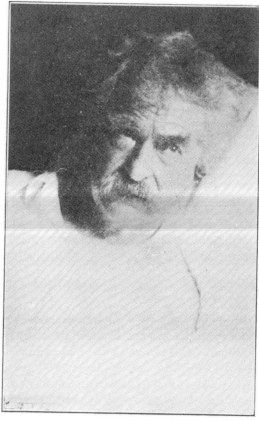

MARK TWAIN at the age of 70 (1905) lived at
21 Fifth avenue, New York; and there William
M. van der Weyde, later president of the Thomas
Paine National Historical Association, was summoned to his room to take his picture. Van der
Weyde, writing in 1921, said that no matter what
time of day he called, his subject was always in
bed, wherein he did much of his writing.

Montclair, N. J., is not so well off for officers, as president and secretary is combined in one person, who is the editor of The Truth Seeker, but it has members. The fellowship was formed on March 10 by residents of Montclair, a town of 35,000 population, none of whom is, as was Mark Twain, a subscriber to The Truth Seeker. It was 'The Mysterious Stranger' and 'What Is Man?' that separated these few from their faith; hence the name of the society. Proceedings at meetings, to be held at present in the editor's house, will consist of readings embracing the philosophy and heresies of Mark Twain. The secretary invites correspondence addressed to him at Skeetside, Montclair, N. J."

The meetings, social and informal in character, were continued as long as the members who had organized the fellowship cared to attend. I reported the discussion to the town paper, and so made many residents acquainted with Mark Twain's opinions.

When the war was over, Premier Lloyd-George of England said: "Let us thank God." Editor Chapman Cohen of The Freethinker asked bluntly: "In the name of man, for what?" There was no reply. In America we had an equally irrelevant Thanksgiving day. They did things better in France, where the government and the generals thanked the soldiers. Marshall Foch's message to the men on their victory was a model:

"Officers, non-commissioned officers, and soldiers of the Allied Armies: After having resolutely stopped the enemy, you have for months fought him with faith and indefatigable energy, without respite. You have won the greatest battle in history and saved the most sacred cause—the liberty of the world. Be proud. You have adorned your flags with immortal glory. Posterity preserves for you its recognition."

Credit for keeping the New York Secular Society alive when its active members were off to the wars belongs to David Rubin, who accepted the presidency and took the chair at the meetings at 131 West 125th street. Wm. B. Fleck, former Catholic priest, addressed open-air meetings and suffered persecution. A Catholic friend pointed to the fate of John Purroy Mitchel, former mayor of New York who had antagonized the church in the matter of charity grants, and had caused the reverend clergy to be prosecuted for a conspiracy to defeat the ends of justice. Mitchel met death July 6, 1918, at a government flying field, having enlisted in the aviation corps; and the counselor of Fleck professed to know that Catholics under instruction of their superiors had tampered with his plane and caused the accident that killed him.

On Memorial Day, 1918, in Oak Ridge cemetery, Springfield, Illinois, the monument of William H. Herndon, law partner and biographer of Abraham Lincoln, was dedicated. Mr. Harry W. Meltzer of Chicago wrote: "The amount was put up by forty-two contributors," and "not by Freethinkers," as he had hoped might be the fact. The participation of the Freethinkers, it seemed, had been concealed.

In answering the congratulations of his friends on his 84th birthday, February 16, the venerable Ernst Haeckel addressed to them a circular letter bidding all a last farewell, as owing to accumulating infirmities he had no hope of living out the year.

VICTORY.

"The world war ended, as officially announced in Washington, at 6 o'clock on the morning of November 11 (11 o'clock Paris time) by the signing of an armistice by the German representatives meeting Marshal Foch in the field. The terms of the armistice are dictated by the Allies. It is a surrender on the part of Germany. Ex-Emperor William II, his heir and staff, are fugitives in Holland."

The American press imitated the pulpit in ascribing the result to the fulfilment of the "divine purpose." The pope advertised that his prayers had been answered, which The Truth Seeker denied. "The pope did not pray for that which we celebrate—the triumph of the Allies and the United States and the cause of civilization. Let us remember that."

For the right word we have to turn again to France. The Paris Municipal Council caused the walls of the city thus to be placarded:

"Citizens, victory is here—triumphant victory. The vanquished enemy lays down his arms. Blood ceases to flow. Let Paris emerge from her ordered reserve. Let us give free course to our joy and enthusiasm and hold back our tears. Let us testify our infinite gratitude to our grand soldiers and their incomparable chiefs by festooning our houses in the colors of France and our allies. Our dead can sleep in peace. The sublime sacrifice they have made for the future of their race and the salvation of their country will not be in vain. The day of glory has come. Long live the republic! Long live immortal France." ,

For a sentiment worthy of America we turn again to Paine: "The times that tried men's souls are over, and the greatest and completest revolution the world ever knew gloriously and happily accomplished."

In order fully to enter into the spirit of those words we are obliged to forget the crimes of the Espionage law enactors and enforcers that smirch what might have been America's record unsullied.

DEPARTURES IN 1918.

The Philadelphia Public Ledger of January 7 recorded the death at York, Pa., on the day preceding, of Dr. Israel H. Betz, local historian and one of the oldest practicing physicians in York county. Dr. Betz, best known to Truth Seeker readers through his articles written under the name of "Historicus," began his subscription with the first number, published at Paris, Illinois, in 1873. He was 77 years old.

Dr. Henry Maudsley, at the age of 82 years, died in London Jan. 23. Dr. Maudsley, Materialist, regarded Christianity as a system made up of "incredible dogmas and fables." In his "Pathology of Mind" he seemed to regard religion as a form and cause of dementia. Contrary to the religious opinion that Infidels give nothing to charity, he contributed the sum of £30,000 ($150,000) to the Asylum Committee of the London County Council for the furtherance of treatment of mental disorders.

The death of Henry Rowley on August 2 closed a rather remarkable life. He was a self-made and self-educated man. He was diligent in business and held high places in large commercial concerns. He was studious and well-informed. As an orator he was brilliant and solid, eloquent and witty. He seemed to gather knowledge at sight, as nothing else could account for his mastery of learning and languages. He gave numberless lectures and addresses on Freethought occasions and was in demand as a speaker in literary, educational and social circles. He had the presence, the personality to impress an audience, the informing ideas to instruct, and the flexibility to adapt, interest and amuse. Physically he was rather magnificent —tall, broad-shouldered, deep-chested, erect and imposing. Mr. Rowley was born in Leicester, England, in 1854 and came to America at about the age of thirty-five, uniting himself with the Brooklyn Philosophical Association, as member, president and speaker.

Dr. Andrew Dickson White (died in Ithaca, N. Y., November 4, at the age of 86 years) most served his generation and those to come after him by his historical writings on the warfare of science with theology. His great book, "A History of the Warfare of Science with Theology in Christendom," growing out of his experience as an educator, made him known to all Rationalists.

CHAPTER XXX

SCARCITY of paper hampered the press of England, as in the United States, and labor in 1919 exacted wages so high that the editor of the London Freethinker offered to exchange his week's pay for the printer's—for the artisan sat on the top of the world. But to material and labor difficulties in England there appear not to have been added the malicious interferences of such meddlers as held office at the time in the United States.

To prevent the more enlightening publications of the North from penetrating the Bible belt below the Mason-Dixon line, a southern Congressman procured the passage, supposedly a war measure, of a postal law establishing "zones," and charging postage according to distance (although distance has little to do with the expense of mail distribution), and penalizing advertisements by charging extra postage when less than 80 per cent of a publication is reading matter. The first guess, that the religious press would be exempt from the provisions of the law and received by the postoffice at special rates regardless of content or zones, was the right one. That the regulations would be applied to The Truth Seeker with a severe rigidity that amounted to discrimination was also a safe inference.

A church might issue a weekly bulletin, made up entirely of advertising and propaganda matter, and enter it for distribution at pound rates.

Penalties imposed for statement of fact or expression of opinion are inexpugnable prime elements in the history of religious and political freedom. The sentencing of a half dozen "Russellites" to twenty years in a federal prison for circulating their crazy book, "The Finished Mystery," gave these comparatively harmless fanatics undue importance and a thin article of justice. The United States Circuit Court of Appeals reversed the conviction.

An issue of The Public, a Single Tax paper, long edited by Louis F. Post, was "suspended," August 17, 1918, and released the following March. The publishers never were informed of the reason for the course chosen by the government on either date.'

The Irish World, hyphenate, denounced President Wilson as "the silver-tongued traitor of trustful democracy," and the flag of the Irish Republic, pro-German, was raised on the city hall in Newark, N. J., and elsewhere displayed. The flag of Socialism was "damned," and when Eugene V. Debs indulged in some mild criticism of the government he with some of the comrades was put into jail for ten years. The Socialists must have been puzzled to know how the Hibernians were able so far to exceed them in disloyalty and to get away with it.

The imprisonment of Debs more than stains, it defiles the record of the United States.

Albeit they had been more or less honorably discharged as a subdivision of the "armed forces of the United States," all of the sects—Catholic, Protestant, Salvation Army and Jewish—continued their money demands on the public. Expert managers of "drives" instituted by the government for selling bonds found employment between times with the religious organizations, and blackmailed the public for millions. Even the courts were so corrupted that in some instances they compelled delinquents to push money into the stocking of the State's kept woman, the Church.

The war being over and the enforcement of the Espionage law relaxed in a measure, the story of how the "Y" profiteered on the soldiers could be told. "It became known today," said a Paris dispatch to the New York Sun, dated January 14, "that three Y. M. C. A. workers are under arrest in Paris charged with defalcation of funds by the Association." One of the defaulters was a minister; the amount involved, $38,940. In September, Garland Pollard, head of the Disciplinary Board of the "Y," revealed the fact that since January 1 seventy-two Y. M. C. A. workers had been tried on various charges. It looked probable that in proportion to the total personnel, the "Y" contingent contained more crooks than the army they went over to uplift.

Flubdub about "who won the war" appeared in varied versions. Where Yankees and Britons met, the king's soldiers answered: "England won the war"; and the Yanks responded: "A. E. F.—After England Failed." But Elsie Janis, the actress who entertained the boys with songs and stories, made the best return when General Pershing, commander of all the American forces, paid her the compliment, too ridiculous to be sincere: "I have said that other subdivisions of our forces were worth regiments; you are worth a whole division." Elsie replied: "Well, General, you know your army best." In soldiers' quarters the inquiry was popular: "Who won the war?" The response came in unison from all within hearing: "The Y. M. C. A. won the war." In its valedictory The Stars and Stripes, which was the doughboy newspaper of the American Expeditionary Forces in France, took to itself the distinction of being "the only subdivision of the A. E. F. that does not claim to have won the war single-handed." This, the editor inferred, could be explained by the fact that "we have no personnel recruited from the Y. M. C. A." The "Y" was proclaiming through its press agents that it not only won the war but "kept the soldiers *fit to come home*"—more than can be said of some of its own secretaries, who landed in the penitentiary instead of the arms of their countrymen.

The last trick of the "Y" was maybe the worst. Buying material with its "welfare" money, it embarked in various building projects in France, and the government allowed the outfit to keep American soldiers there to do the menial labor at a dollar a day, when they were anxious to come home.

One member of the 59th Pioneer Infantry who had been kept abroad for this slave labor and had seen the major part of his regiment leave without him wrote:

"Most of us have been two years in the service and we surely feel grateful that now when everyone else is going home we must remain here to carry out a project of the Y. M. C. A. We feel sure that the people back in the States will be glad to learn that their money *instead of being used to benefit the men is a means of keeping them away from home.*

"Just another word before I bring this to a close. Can anyone explain why it is necessary for enlisted men of our company to work in Y. M. C. A. canteens, washing dishes and performing other such tasks, when there are so many 'Y' secretaries in Paris with apparently nothing to do but promenade on the boulevards?"

Before the Truth Seeker could adjust itself completely to the hundred and fifty per cent rise in postal charges, with a parallel reduction of one hundred per cent in the amount of advertising it was permitted to carry on the new terms, and to the doubling of the costs of production, all the union printers in the city struck, or took a vacation, except those employed on the daily papers. To cut our garment according to the cloth, we had already printed two 8- instead of 16-page editions, but we were doing the 16 a week when the strike came. Immediately upon the settlement of the "strike," near the end of November, we received notice from the employing printer of 33 1-3 per cent. advance. This final raise rather more than trebled the cost of issuing the paper as of 1913, and raising the subscription to $5 a year amounted only to a gesture toward covering the difference. If the thoughtful H. P. Burbage of South Carolina had not taken time by the forelock and started a Sustaining Fund, the end of 1919 might have been the end of The Truth Seeker, which in suspending would have had the company or the precedent of some two hundred other publications.

Under restrictions imposed by the New York police department on street speakers, the vanishing freedom and equality existing before the war had nearly reached extinction. A speaker for the Secular Society assumed the soapbox at the risk of being mobbed by Catholics. The police officers found it easier or more in line with their prejudices to take the speaker to court than to disperse the gang. The courts held with one I have already quoted, that where a speaker says anything which creates disorder among his hearers, why, he is a disorderly person. He sometimes found when he reached the court that his pockets had been picked and his overcoat stolen. He had no redress.

The arrival home of a few "veterans" from overseas in January put it into somebody's head to ask if my boys were expected soon, and brought out this paragraph in the Letter Box:

"Yes, we are looking for the boys to arrive any time now, though it may be weeks or months, as many are kept on duty over there. In the year 1863 a small boy in a New England town used, through the long summer days, to keep an eye lifted for all the men who came through his street, scrutinizing them carefully in the hope of identifying one at last as the returning father whose death the previous year at Bull Run he was too young to understand. He is an old fellow now, and when he sees approaching a sailor in blue or a soldier in cap and khaki, or hears a footstep at the door or the bell rung in the night, there arises in his mind the hope of a returning son."

That was in January, but winter and spring had passed and it was near fall when the boys got home. The sailor, after the influenza at Brest and bad food afloat, spent most of the season in naval hospitals, and came home with a variety of disabilities fastened upon him—tuberculous, nephritic, and aural. Being too near the muzzle of a big gun when it went off took away his hearing on that side. Homesickness was probably one of the complications, for he began to mend as soon as he joined his family.

In August, Mr. J. E. Ismay, who had boys of his own "over there," inquired about mine. Another paragraph in the Letter Box answered:

"Yes, both boys are home. The seaman got an honorable discharge by reason of incapacities incurred in the line of duty, which was serving as a hand on a supply ship between Cardiff and the Brest. Seeing that in its service he was reduced from a condition 100 per cent. fit to 80 per cent. unfit, a grateful and generous government allows him a 'compensation' of 20 cents per day during good behavior and bad health. The Captain of Engineers, U. S. A., returns in good order, with two new languages, a thirty days' leave of absence and an abiding admiration for the American 'buck private,' the one buck ($) a day man. He drops the remark that having now finished with the war that was anybody's, he will start one more personal to himself, from which we infer matrimonial intentions and measures not covered by the League of Nations. We therefore are still wearing the service pin."

W. S. Bryan, then an occasional contributor, in an article on "Sin, Salvation, and Soldiers," February 17, placed this paragraph:

"I have a fondness for The Truth Seeker Editor. Any way, he and I have a common bond that I cannot forget. He had two fine boys in the war fought for liberty and humanity, and now they are coming home to him alive and well. I too have a son 'over there,' my only boy, who enlisted as a private the day after war was declared, and who has filled every place except corporal up to first lieutenant, and is now on the regimental staff of the 138th Infantry as intelligence officer. He has had two citations for bravery under fire, and was promoted from second to first lieutenant in acknowledgment of the first citation. He was wounded the third day of the battle of the Argonne, but the piece of shrapnel which might otherwise have killed him struck his pistol scabbard and did nothing more than temporarily paralyze his leg. Now if that pistol scabbard had been a Bible the incident might have been published as a miracle!"

["The picture of 'Germans Welcoming American Troops Entering Germany,' on page 15 of The Literary Digest, January 18, shows our correspondent's soldier son in the van. He is the young officer on the right of the column (the reader's left), behind the right hand of the tall officer who is his captain.—Ed. T. S."]

I will now finish what I began to say about my boys, who will then for the time pass out of the picture. The older one, Eugene, having attained a captaincy, went with a company into the occupied territory across the Rhine and took charge of the public service in a small German city—the delivery of water, light and fuel. By reason of an extraordinary load on the municipal electric power plant, he was one evening, so he tells me, obliged to refuse the request of a preacher for light whereby to conduct a prayer meeting. It was war, and hardships must be shared. When Eugene returned he announced that he purposed to marry immediately.

Prohibition, which threatened the country, drew the fire of the Catholic clergy. The Rev. Father Belford of Brooklyn declared that "no one should have the least scruple" about evading, breaking, or defying the liquor law. "Smaller things than this," he said, "have brought on revolutions." Cardinal Gibbons, in a set argument issued early in the year, reflected: "To me it is very strange that after two thousand years men should pass legislation that strikes at the very fundamentals of the Christian religion."

The war being over, the government launched the Victory Liberty Loan of $4,500,000,000, the call to subscribers being in the old form, somewhat after the idea of Vice-President Marshall, who understood that the war had been fought to wipe out the Darwinian doctrine and bring the world back to Christ.

John Sharp Williams, a man who seemed to share Marshall's ignorance of the facts, circulated on Senate stationery, under his frank as a United States senator from Mississippi, a begging letter in behalf of the Fundamentalist University of the South (Sewanee, Tenn.). Senator Williams asked for a million dollars to combat the "scientific civilization, godless and Christless," which produced the war!

This paragraph requires no comment, but a profane expletive might relieve the reader's heart:

"Senator Curtis of Kansas," says a recent Washington

dispatch, "was notified today that it would be contrary to established policies to grant reduced rates to harvest hands." The Kansas City Times thinks "it might occur to the average layman that the thing to do, then, was to disestablish the policy rather than the harvest hands." The fact is that the government has exhausted its reduced tax rates for civilians by granting them all to priests, ministers, nuns, Salvation Army agents and the like, and there are none left for the productive worker.

At the suggestion of a reader, the names of ministers who had turned "state's evidence" or advocates of Freethought, were published October 18 and December 13. They numbered twenty-three—eighteen Protestants and five Catholics. They all have been named in this history, and all but the first one—Abner Kneeland—have written for The Truth Seeker.

The sickle of the Harvester was keen and active. There fell before it in 1919, Ernst Haeckel, John E. Remsburg, E. C. Reichwald, J. P. Bland, and others of the Freethought circle.

And now that my work is so near its end I may say that the writing of all these death records depresses me. They are of men and women I have known, with whom I have corresponded, whose manuscripts I have handled, whose hands I have taken. Their departure, one after another, leaves with the survivor, as though they were of his own family, a sense of bereavement. As our young novelist Wetjen says in his "Way for a Sailor": "You learn to love men, and then the gray water takes them."

On February 5, in a Chicago hospital, death came suddenly to E. C. Reichwald, secretary of the American Secular Union. Mr. Reichwald was probably about 70 years of age. He was born in Milwaukee, Wisconsin, came to Chicago in 1865, and helped to establish the firm of fruit and vegetable dealers of which he was the surviving member. He was member of the Produce Exchange and by his long term in business gained the name of the Dean of Water Street, that being the street in Chicago where the produce business is centered. He was married until the death of his wife about 1909. He had been an officer of the American Secular Union for more than a quarter of a century—treasurer and then secretary.

H. H. Burwell, long associated with the Washington Secular League, died March 6. He had prepared a Valedictory which he requested the president of the League to read at his funeral and to send to The Truth Seeker for publication, but his religious family had so little regard for his wishes that they gave him a religious funeral. However, his Valedictory was printed.

Ernst Haeckel died at his home in Jena, Germany, August 9. Because of the war and the view that he had taken of it as a patriotic German, he was generally so unfairly treated by the American and English press that an editorial paragraph in The Bulletin of San Francisco shines out like a bright star in a black night. Said The Bulletin:

"A light of the modern world has gone out, and yet the rays which came from it will continue to shine even as the light from stars long since extinguished. When the clouds of war broke over Europe the international glow of the Haeckel genius became obscured. World benefactor though he had been he was thought of as a German, as an enemy, and for the time being he became more the patriot than the scientist. But he lived to see the light of peace, and with its coming his fame was restored. The world will remember him only as the great scientist born in Germany, but belonging to all mankind, to the international republic of progressive thought."

Haeckel had a middle name, Heinrich, which does not appear in his works. He was born August 9, 1834, within two days of a year after Ingersoll, his native place being Potsdam, Germany, and his father a lawyer. After studying at Würtzburg to be a doctor, he did a year's hospital work in Vienna. At 21 a Christian defending his belief in dis· cussions with Freethinkers, by the time his medical studies were completed he had abandoned the notion of a wise providence in the struggle for existence. When he read Darwin's "Origin of Species," he exclaimed: "I might have written much of this book myself." It expressed clearly what had existed in his mind as vague thoughts and ideas.

Andrew Carnegie, who died in August, aged 84, had offered a million dollars for convincing proofs of a future life. As no one earned the million, the fact was brought home to minds open to such impressions, that a future life, the preaching of which has been so profitable to the ministers and so expensive to everybody else, is without vital statistics.

The Boston papers announced the death on September 3 of "the Rev. John P. Bland of Cambridge." But John Pindar Bland has long since ceased to be known as a "reverend." For eighteen years he was the regular lecturer on Sunday afternoons at Paine Hall, Boston. He was born in Halifax, Eng., March 27, 1842, and came to this country at the age of 18. He worked his way through college and went to the Harvard Divinity School, where he finished his course in a single year. Immediately after his graduation he became minister of the Lee Street Unitarian church in Cambridge, where he remained for thirteen years. He went to Sheffield, Eng., and was for five years minister of Upper Chapel. He then returned to this country, living in Cambridge, and conducting his Sunday Freethought meetings. He died at the ripe age of 77 years, closing a progressive career, respected and honored.

The life of John E. Remsburg, who died at his home in Porterville, Cal., September 23, in his 72d year, was known to Freethinkers, in his writings. The biographical part is brief. He was born near the village of Fremont, Ohio, in 1848; was a poor boy and almost self-educated; was perhaps the youngest soldier to carry a musket in the Union Army. When twenty years old he went to Kansas, and at twenty-four was superintendent of public instruction for Atchison county.

His first writings appear to have been a series of small tracts called The Image Breaker. They were on "The De-

JOHN E. REMSBURG (1848-1919).

cline of Faith," "Protestant Intolerance," "Washington an Unbeliever," "Jefferson an Unbeliever," "Paine and Wesley," and the "Christian Sabbath." The pioneer in the research tending to show that unbelief prevailed among the Revolutionary fathers was probably Gilbert Vale. Remsburg continued the work and wrote "The Fathers of Our Republic"—Washington, Jefferson, Franklin and Adams, all heretics. In 1880 was published his "Paine: The Apostle of Liberty."

At this date he took the Freethought lecture platform, and before he retired, twenty years later, had delivered more than three thousand lectures, speaking in fifty-two states, territories and provinces, and in twelve hundred and fifty cities and towns, including every large city in the United States and Canada. In the performance of this work he traveled three hundred and sixty thousand miles. That was a marvelous achievement.

During his platform activity, covering many years, Remsburg's home was in Atchison, Kansas. About 1907 he removed to Potter, Kansas, and became editor and proprietor of The Kansan, a weekly newspaper. He removed to Porterville, Cal., in 1917.

Dr. Juliet H. Severance, in her 87th year, wrote a letter to The Truth Seeker reporting a meeting she had attended and addressed. She opined that what she had said on the subject of marriage as a civil contract dissoluble at will would cause the audience to reflect. In this comforting thought she died a few days later, Sept. 2, 1919. The doctor was born at DeRuyter, N. Y., July 1, 1833; studied medicine; was graduated from a medical college, practiced at Whitewater, Wisconsin; advocated woman suffrage; was the first woman to deliver a Fourth of July oration (Sterling, Illinois); was first vice-president of the National Liberal League and acting president under Hon. Elizur Wright in the early days of the organization; was master workman of the Knights of Labor, and president of the Milwaukee Liberal Club. She died in New York, where for some years she had ministered free to unfortunate girls, to her honor as physician and humanitarian.

CHAPTER XXXI.

THE oneness of religion in all times and places is the first principle of philosophy. Observing, long since, that the game of the medicine man—who as Spencer said could not be differentiated from the modern ecclesiastic—must have been identical with that of his successors, the priest and parson in the twentieth century of Christian grace, I have often recalled a conversation had in my boyhood with Uncle Eliphaz Field, who is in the first volume of this history (page 60). It was in the spring of 1871, doubtless, that Uncle Eliphaz wanted to know of me whether the suckers were running yet in the river (the Ashuelot) that bordered his meadows. The sucker was a fish of dull intellect that had the habit of lying in the more quiet places of the stream, leisurely moving a tail-fin to maintain his position against what little current there might be, and through a circular orifice that was his mouth drawing in water that escaped at the gills. The sucker was to be caught by dropping a baited hook in front of his nose. He did not seize the bait; he did not "bite," but just sucked in the hook. Uncle Eliphaz, being then past the middle of his ninth decade, could have gone fishing for suckers, as a boy, before Thomas Jefferson was President. I asked him how he used to catch 'em then, and he said in the same way I have described. Said he: *"You don't ever have to change the bait to catch suckers."* If the first medicine man who pretended to have influence over the invisibles— which influence he would exercise for the benefit of less favored individuals, provided they would make him gifts—could come back and see how his successors play the same old tricks on the believing public of today, as they have done ever since his time, he would remark in language like that of Uncle Eliphaz Field that you don't ever have to change the bait to catch suckers.

The successor of John E. Remsburg, deceased, as president of the American Secular Union was J. W. Whicker, an attorney, of Attica, Indiana. Secretary Reichwald having died, Mr. Whicker called a meeting of the Union for the election of officers to be held February 28, 29, 1920, in Masonic Temple, State and Randolph streets, Chicago. At this meeting (reported in The Truth Seeker March 20) the management was placed in the hands of a board of directors and new by-laws adopted. The old organization known as the American Secular Union and Freethought Federation passed out of existence and was replaced by one with the Freethought Federation omitted from its title. On adjournment of the meeting the chosen directors elected officers —Marshall J. Gauvin for president, W. L. Maclaskey for secretary, Edward Morgan for treasurer; as official organ, The Truth Seeker. Mr. Gauvin made an ideal keynote speech and took the field as lecturer, communicating with The Truth Seeker weekly. As secretary, Mr. Maclaskey also conducted a department. That year we reported contributions of $5,000 to keep Mr. Gauvin in the field as president of the national organization. Owing to the high cost of travel and of hall rent, the amount proved insufficient and he discontinued his itinerary. It was Gauvin's year nevertheless. His lectures delivered at many places were of the first quality and his weekly letters were literature.

One keeping a journal of events related to free speech, free press and civil rights would record that at the beginning of 1920 seats were denied to five persons elected members of the legislature of the State of New York because they belonged to the Socialist party; and that when Dr. William J. Robinson, editor of The Critic and Guide, spoke with severity of this treacherous and poisonous act of the majority, the grand jury indicted him for criminal libel. The doctor had called members of the assembly "drunken harlots" and affirmed that "the blackest souled crook in state prison was a saint in comparison with Speaker Sweet." That was the Dr. Robinson who a few years before had made the objection to Secularist propaganda in Hyde Park, London, that the speakers employed impolite language!

The annalist would set down the fact that in Chicago 85 members of the Communist party, including Mrs. Rose Pastor Stokes, were indicted on general principles; that in Boston Alfred Nettle was assaulted by an Irish Ulsterman because, as reported in The Herald, "the word Rationalist was misunderstood as 'Nationalist' "; that a grand inquest "for the State of New Jersey and for the body of the County of Warren," indicted Mnason Hountzman, otherwise Paul Blandin Mnason, for pretending that he was "Christ and God," the defendant being found guilty and sentenced to six months in jail and a fine of one hundred dollars. In the Sydney Domain, at the antipodes, a Rationalist speaker named O'Donell paid a fine of three pounds three shillings for saying there were four gods in Victoria—God the father, God the son, God the Holy Ghost, and God Blimey" (God blame me). The courts of Melbourne, Australia, convicted and fined two Seventh-day Adventists for doing "certain worldly labor or work at their ordinary calling" on Sunday. The law in the case was so old that it provided for putting the culprits in the "stocks" if they failed to pay their fines; and Australia had no stocks though their contemporary, the Sunday law, still lived.

Eugene V. Debs lay in jail for some observation he had let fall, and the Socialists nominated the prisoner for President. Wilson wasn't the sport to pardon him out and let him make the best fight he could. Debs from his prison said: "It is not I but Woodrow Wilson who needs a pardon, and if I had it in my power I would set him free."

The New York Call, a Socialist paper long excluded from the mails, won a decision in the Supreme Court of the District of Columbia. The court decided that a newspaper could not be excluded from the mails on the assumption that it was about to print something unmailable.

Colrado in these days was represented at Washington by a Rationalist, Senator Charles Thomas. The senator spoke against the recognition of "God" in the League of Nations covenant; he made a speech against the resolution of Senator Myers of Montana calling on the President to proclaim a minute of daily prayer, preceded by the ringing of church bells, called the angelus; and in the course of the debate declared: "I have never made any pretensions toward Christianity." Mr. Thomas retired from the Senate in 1921.

The Soviet government of Russia came into being amidst the cheers of political liberals and enemies of despotism. Of the new stuff I observed: "Bolshevism, communism, soviets, socialistic commonwealths imply the same as monarchy, republicanism, autocracy—in short, government. They imply nothing better for the insurgent, because every form of government is ruthless in measures for self-defense." There is nothing to modify, and nothing to add but Fascism.

While the public remained in the giving mood induced by war drives for religious societies, the most ambitious drive of all was launched under the the name of the Interchurch World Movement.

This combination aimed at the gigantic graft of one billion three hundred million dollars ($1,300,-000,000). The campaigners planned to take a religious census of the country, to list the name, according to religion, of every man, woman and child in it; and then to establish week-day and vacation schools, and "give a religious education to very child." The funds from munitions profiteers came in so gratifyingly fast that Fred B. Smith chairman of the Commission on Interchurch Federation, "almost came to the conclusion," as he stated, that "for the good of Christianity" there "should be a war every five years."

The war welfare societies stuck like barnacles to the ship of state, and only with great difficulty were to be pried loose. The "Y" embarked on a drive in the spring and made a big haul without changing the bait.

The successor and imitator of the drive, and its natural offspring, was the post-war public hold-up man, with methods direct and crude, and with the pretense left out. The gunman took more risk for less profit. He saw the easy money and went after it in his own way. When caught he is put in jail if he has no political friends. Like Lecky's eternal priestess of humanity, he is blasted for the sins of the people.

Ever and anon Freethinkers lift their voices in protest against insulting the country's flag by hoisting the church pennant above the Stars and Stripes. Here on page 217 of The Truth Seeker, vol. lxvii, a thought is recorded:

"If Senator Truman H. Newberry of Michigan had not been found guilty of corrupting an election and sentenced to a $10,000 fine and two years in a federal penitentiary, his name might have been preserved as that of one of the church's idols, a man of upright life and a consistent Christian; for it was he who, when he was secretary of the navy, put the church above the state by decreeing that the church flag should be hoisted over the Stars and Stripes—not a new practice but hitherto without official approval. It is our opinion that an official who will order an act of that sort is equal to any other kind of rascality; the history of religious rogues justifies that conclusion, and Mr. Newberry's conviction is no surprise."

Miss Lovisa Brunzell of San Francisco prepared a Questionnaire to be addressed to men of science for the purpose of collecting their views negative to the truth of Christianity. It seemed to Miss Brunzell that the discoveries of science made nonsense of the Bible from Genesis to Revelation and of the Christian religion from its first mistake to its last dogma, and that the testimony to that effect, cheerfully supplied by the scientists, along with their photographs, and both published in a book, would be the death warrant of a great lying church which too long had deceived a world of credulous mankind. It may be told at this early point in her endeavor that the result did not exceed the hope of Miss Brunzell, or even come up to it. She applied herself perseveringly for several years to the task of questioning the eleven thousand members of the American Association for the Advancement of Science, the replies being summarized and digested to start in The Truth Seeker's Jubilee number, September 1, 1923. But Luther Burbank, the plant wizard of Santa Rosa, Cal., answered promptly and his reply, which showed him to be the "Infidel" he afterwards announced himself, appeared August 7, 1920.

In several numbers of the paper from April on the centenary of Herbert Spencer (1820-1903) was observed. Being interested in the Synthetic

Philosopher as a Freethinker, I quoted at some length from the place in his "First Principles" where he expresses his astonishment that the God a conception of whom is to be derived from the Bible, could be identified with the Cause from which have arisen twenty million suns, and so on. The excerpt closed with the words: "These and other difficulties, some of which are often discussed but never disposed of, must force men hereafter to drop the higher anthropomorphic character given to the First Cause, as they have long since dropped the lower." Grant Allen wrote the memorable tribute containing the lines:

"But he who builds for time
Must look to time for wage."

Spencer in my judgment has not yet drawn all the wages coming to him. His native land made a partial payment by excluding his remains from that temple of fame, Westminster. Better for it to be asked why one should not be there than why he is.

With the name of Herbert Spencer Freethinkers of the past associated that of John Tyndall (1820-1893). In him they recognized a scientific Materialist, who said that if he were looking for an honest man he should expect to find him among the Atheists with whom he was acquainted. Like his successor, Schafer, as president of the British Association for the Advancement of Science, he left the ghosts out of his philosophy; and he saw in what we call matter the possibilities of all forms of life. He gave the thinking world something to bite on.

The International Freethought Federation held its 1920 congress at Prague, in the new Republic of Czechoslovakia (formerly Bohemia), September 5 to 9. Owing to unsettled traveling conditions, the American societies sent no delegates.

The newspapers reported a notable debate, held before the Advertising Men's club of Los Angeles, between Will Rogers, then known as a cowboy actor, and a local stunt preacher, the Rev. J. L. Brougher, on the proposition: "Resolved, That cowboys have contributed more to civilization than preachers." Rogers proposed that the debate be confined to statements of facts, as otherwise his opponent would have the advantage of him, since lying was the preacher's profession. The newspaper decision gave Rogers the most points, but the referees chosen by the Advertising Club pronounced the question irrelevant, irrational, and absurd, since neither preachers nor cowboys had ever done anything for civilization.

DEPARTURES IN 1920.

"He has 'joined the choir invisible of those immortal dead who live again in minds made better by their presence'," wrote Frederick Mains of his friend William Henry Maple, who died Jan. 31, 1920. Mr. Maple, a native of Peoria county, Ill., was 79 years old, and long before his death at Lombard had provided for an appropriate obituary notice in The Truth Seeker. He had been country editor, county school superintendent in Iowa, and lawyer and realtor in Chicago. Also in Chicago he wrote his book "No Beginning" and published the Ingersoll Beacon, afterwards The Freethought Beacon, for ten years following its first number in 1904. He had been a soldier in the Civil War and the flag of his country draped his casket as he was borne by military pall-bearers to his grave in the cemetery at Elmhurst, Ill.

George W. Moorehouse, who died in Chicago on March 20, was in his eightieth year; he suffered constantly from a gunshot wound received in the Civil War fifty-eight years ago, so that pain added its burden to his years, and death came as a friend. None the less his going left sad relatives and friends, and a poorer world. Mr. Moorehouse was a competent writer in science, especially on astronomy, his favorite subject, as his "Wilderness of Worlds" bears testimony. His last writing was done for The Truth Seeker, in which he was deeply interested. He was a pioneer in scientific thought and a fearless supporter of truth regardless of consequences.

Edward Morgan, treasurer of the American Secular Union, and assistant principal of the Nicholas Senn High School, Chicago, Ill., died July 7, 1920, in the 47th year of his age.

The Daily Times of Chattanooga, Tenn., September 11, reported the death at 91 years of M. M. Murray, the county's "best-known truck-grower and philosopher." Mr. Murray was a native of Vermont. His father, Orson Murray, a radical of the abolition days, was the only delegate from Vermont at the formation of the American Anti-salvery Society, Philadelphia, 1833.

On September 16, Ralph Chainey, aged 47, fell on the steps of Paine Hall. Boston, and was found dead on the morning of the 17th.   Mr. Chainey

MARILLA M. RICKER (1840-1920).

had for some time been the largest owner of the stock of the Paine Hall Corporation, and was manager and treasurer. He was part owner of The Investigator after the retiring of Ernest Mendum.

The extended notice of the death and life of Marilla Ricker here given is deserved and more:

"The death of Marilla M. Ricker, which took place on November 12, ends the career of one of the most remarkable of women, and brings rest to one of the strongest intellects of this day. For the past ten years, nearly, her name has made frequent appearances in The Truth Seeker, and her picture is familiar. Her writings were characterized by great strength and force of expression. A sketch which gives as much of her life as we have ever known was printed in the Sunday Tribune, November 13," and reproduced.

Mrs. Ricker's heroes were Freethinkers—Paine and Ingersoll; her aversions were Jonathan Edwards and Theodore Roosevelt. She disliked Edwards for his savage theology, and Roosevelt, first, for his slander of Paine, and second for what she thought was his political recreancy. When she entitled one of her books "I'm Not Afraid—Are You?" she uttered truth. She was not afraid, either of this life or any other. She uniformly paid her tax with a protest against the exemption of the churches, and she distributed more copies of The Truth Seeker, perhaps, than any other person. She had a great deal of legal and historical knowledge. She knew how to state her case and was a good speaker. B. New Durham, N. H., 1840.

CHAPTER XXXII.

ONDITIONS in 1921 compelled The Truth Seeker to change quarters. It was a year noted for real-estate transactions in conveyances and leasings, all speculative. The agency for the renting of 62 Vesey street had passed from our friend of the Missionary Department ("Atwood Manville") into the possession of a man who was asking three times as much rent as we paid to Atwood when we came in sixteen years previously thereto.

Our occupancy of No. 62 had become a part of the literature of the day. In his book "Pipefuls," Christopher Morley quoted our sign "THE TRUTH SEEKER, ONE FLIGHT UP," and remarked that truth is generally found a flight or two higher up than the observer or searcher.

"It now looks," says our announcement of an early removal, "as though The Truth Seeker might be two flights up on the 1st of May, for the rent has already taken four flights." I saw the new landlord and implored him to have, as the saying was then, a heart. He may have had one, but I did not touch it. That real-estater wanted as much for the rent of our floor for the period of one year as I had paid not far in the past for a deed to the house I lived in at Skeetside, Montclair.

The Truth Seeker moved May 1 to 49 Vesey street, two flights up.

The itinerary of Marshall Gauvin, national lecturer, terminated in Minneapolis, Minn. His first reports for 1921 concern successful and well-attended lectures in Columbus, Ohio, the local press taking notice. In the State Journal a resident bewailed the fact that "a man can come into our city and make a success of a lecture on evolution." Bryan had been there lately and, attacking "Darwinism" as Infidel, atheistic, and paralyzing in its influence on Christianity, declared: "There is not a single fact in God's universe that establishes a single part of his theory—not one." Some of the earnest Christians in the community thought that Bryan should meet Gauvin and withstand him face to face. Bryan was wiser. He would not meet Gauvin in debate.

There had been in Minneapolis a Twin City Rationalist Society, meeting in the Shubert Theatre, with Edward Adams Cantrell as lecturer. Mr. Cantrell went Socialist—perhaps in an endeavor to widen the scope of his work. Those who had been with him then, now asked Mr. Gauvin to "locate" and build up a strong Rationalist association. He was lecturing as president of the American Secular Union and sending something "From the Lecture Field" twice a month. Soon his contributions became transcripts of his lectures in place of reports from the field. In the fall a paragraph says: "President Gauvin of the American Secular Union is speaking in Minneapolis for the Twin City Rationalist Society." So he had "located," and the Twin City Rationalist Society renewed its notices in the Lectures and Meetings department. I quote the Letter Box, September 10: "Mr. and Mrs. Marshall J. Gauvin announce the birth of Madeleine Suzanne Gauvin on Saturday, August 20, 1921."

The affairs of the American Secular Union were weekly reported upon by the secretary, W. L. Maclaskey, 137 No. Dearborn street, Chicago. The directors met in the secretary's office on February 28, 1921, and elected officers for the following year: President, Marshall Gauvin; vice-presidents, Libby C. Macdonald, Geo. E. Macdonald, Mrs. Eva A. Ingersoll, J. W. Whicker, Bennett Larson, Richard J. Cooney, Dr. Lucy Waite; treasurer, Ethel M. Maclaskey; secretary, W. L. Maclaskey. Mr. Maclaskey continued his weekly notes and observations. Attention was called to a decision of the Supreme Court of Pennsylvania enjoining further grants of state money to sectarian institutions. This meant only that the legislators must obey the constitution, against the plain terms of which, in the thirty years from 1891 to 1921, Catholics, Protestants and Jews, gathered into their hands by legislative appropriations of state funds annually, the sum of ten millions four hundred and thirty-seven thousand and two hundred and thirty-nine dollars: Catholics, eight millions; Protestants, one million, and Jews a million.

The strictly orthodox Philadelphia Public Ledger

admitted that these appropriations were the source of "gross evils" and "political abuses." Representative Charles Brenner of Cleveland, Ohio, introduced in the legislature of the state a bill to tax all property used for public worship. Leaders of the Presbyterian church gave notice to the country that the Supreme Court of the United States would be asked to decide whether the Bible can lawfully be excluded from the public schools in any of the states. Evidently the Presbyterians supposed that the U. S. Supreme Court had jurisdiction over state schools. In Los Angeles J. E. Dill, a Freethinker, filed his annual protest against paying taxes while religious persons and properties were exempt.

Bishop William Montgomery Brown's book, "Communism and Christianism," started by its appearance the first of the year the dispute that was to end in the deposition of the author from the episcopacy. The Rt. Rev. Mr. Brown had been bishop of the diocese of Arkansas. Now with the slogan "Banish Gods from skies and Capitalism from earth," he proclaimed himself "Episcopos in partibus Bolshevikium et infidelium"—that is, Bishop of Bolshevik and Infidel countries.

There were two blasphemy cases. In England J. W. Gott, publisher of The Rib Tickler, faced trial in Birmingham for his irreverent jests, and got six months and costs. In America, to wit in the state of Maine, Michael X. Mockus, a Lithuanian, who in 1920, in a lecture at Rumford, treated the doctrine of the incarnation disrespectfully, was condemned to jail for two years.

Two Ingersoll myths were brought forth—one

of them by an editorial writer on the New York
Herald. It ran:

"The writer of this remembers being sent by Mr. Dana
about the middle of the seventies, to observe an auction
sale of heathen idols. The whimsicality of the advertised
collection of miscellaneous deities tickled Dana's sense of
the curious and unusual. The sale was in Broadway somewhere near Great Jones street. The room was crowded
and the bidding lively. Behind the reporter sat a bald-
headed gentleman of cherubic countenance and animated
demeanor who was invincible in his determination to acquire every particularly grotesque god that went under
the hammer.

"The more ridiculous the object exhibited by the auctioneer the more eager the bidding by this amateur of
ugly divinity. He let nothing desirable escape him, however active the competition, but the lower the price fetched
by any crude clay or bronze or brass or wooden effigy
that had actually been worshiped by human beings somewhere on the face of the globe, the broader the smile of
satisfaction on the buyer's face. At the end of the sale
this mysterious purchaser had accumulated a huge armful
of gods of all sorts and sizes, gathered from the heathen
of Africa and Asia and the isles of Oceanica. A question
to an attendant solved the mystery of the proceeding:
'That's Bob Ingersoll; he's always in the market for cheap
idols.' A year or two later the Colonel's ironic treatise
entitled 'The Gods' was published in Washington.'

In the "middle of the seventies" Ingersoll lived
in Peoria. His "treatise entitled 'The Gods'" was
published in 1872 and contained nothing likely to
have been suggested by "an armful of gods of all
sorts." Ingersoll never had such a collection. In
a letter to Dr. Theo. Wolf of New York, March
18, 1887, he wrote: "Somebody had the kindness
to publish a statement that I had purchased a large

number of gods—all kinds. The fact is I never had but a few genuine gods, and I think all of them have been given away, with one exception."

The second Ingersoll myth followed a proposal by the Illinois superintendent of registration to restore an inscription on the cornerstone of the State House at Springfield. The cornerstone once bore the name, with others, of Robert G. Ingersoll. Tradition said that a local religious fanatic came there by night, and in his zeal to obliterate the name of Ingersoll mutilated the entire list of state officials under whom the State House was erected.

Mrs. Eva Ingersoll Brown sent a telegram to State Architect Edgar Martin, asking for the facts. In reply Mrs. Brown received both a telegram and a letter from Architect Martin, who, as might be expected, was unable to trace· the reports to anything but "idle gossip."

The people of Dresden, New York, invited the county to make a public holiday of August 11, 1921, and to join them in dedicating as a memorial the house standing in that town where Ingersoll was born. Dresden is in Yates county and some four hundred miles northwest of the City of New York. The house, which was the parsonage when Ingersoll's father preached in Dresden, had been bought and put in repair by Walston Hill Brown, Ingersoll's son-in-law, and presented to Mrs. Brown.

On August 4 William L. Sharp, president of the Village of Dresden, issued a proclamation in due form announcing the coming event and bespeaking

hospitality for visitors. Accordingly the resources
of the town were placed at the disposal of the
guests. The ladies of the Methodist church furnished forth a dinner for one hundred. Mr. John
H. Johnson of Penn Yan, the county seat, came to

THE INGERSOLL BIRTHPLACE AT DRESDEN, N. Y.

preside, and brought with him the Penn Yan Band. The Lotus Club of New York was represented by two members, E. R. Johnstone and Charles W. Price; the Ethical Society by Dr. John L. Elliott; the stage by Augustus Thomas; the Paine Society by William Cable of Pennsylvania; Mark Twain, in a way, by his biographer, Albert Bigelow Paine. United States Senator Charles Thomas of Colorado, Oscar S. Straus of New York, Gen. Nelson A. Miles of Washington, Thomas A. Edison of New Jersey, sent letters and messages; Edgar Lee Masters, a poem. Col. Isaac H. Elliott of the 16th Illinois spoke on Ingersoll as a Soldier. The gathering listened also to the Penn Yan Band, to Mr. Price of the Lotus Club, to Mr. Paine, to the Hon. Calvin J. Huson, to Dr. Elliott, to Thomas Mott Osborne, and to Mr. Thomas. It was the greatest day Dresden had ever known. The report of the dedication is in The Truth Seeker of August 20; the letters and addresses appeared later.

At this season The Truth Seeker published "Letters by Robert G. Ingersoll" occupying two pages in each number for seven weeks. I never read so interesting a series of letters as these were. To one of them I have frequently appealed when some mistaken friend of the Colonel would praise him as one too wise not to believe in God:

"New York, Nov. 11, 1887.

"To the Rev. Henry M. Field, D.D., Stockbridge, Mass.

"My Dear Mr. Field—I have no objection to anything in your Answer to me. If you really think my reply was coarse, or rude, you are at perfect liberty to say so.

"The allusion you make to my father is certainly not objectionable.

"I am exceedingly gratified that you and I have demonstrated that it is possible for a Presbyterian and an Atheist to discuss theological questions without exhibiting a theological temper.—Yours always,   R. G. INGERSOLL."

The beliefs of two men here are indicated—the person to whom the letter is addressed and the writer—one a Presbyterian, the other an Atheist. We are aware that Ingersoll was not the Presbyterian.

Henry Ford published the Dearborn Independent with a mission to destroy the Jews. He accused the Jews as being responsible for Bolshevism and other evils. Against their insidious influence we must protect the Christian Sabbath and Bible reading in schools, so Mr. Ford's paper said.

As religious sectarians the Jews, of course, are no worse and no better than Christians, Catholic or Protestant, or Mormons or Mohammedans. They will, if they can, compel non-Jews to conform to Jewish practice. As evidence, they have forced civil recognition of their sabbath by refusing to sit as jurors on Saturday; they have asked to have night schools called off on Friday evening because their holy day begins at Friday sundown; they defeated the holding of a primary election on Saturday; Jewish school teachers insist on drawing full pay though absent on Jewish holidays, thus requiring the public to reward them for practicing their own religion. A Christian evangelist preaching in the Jewish quarter when Gaynor was mayor of New York was mobbed exactly as an anti-clerical speaker would be mobbed in a Catholic quarter. The Jews disinherit their children for change of belief, or for

"mixed" marriage. They are as bigoted as Christians, and it goes without saying that if they could
turn a public school into a synagogue, as Christians
turn it into a church, they would not scruple to
do so.

Exactly like the Christians, whom the Jews infected with so many of their beliefs, they complain
of persecution when they are its victims and not because they object to it on principle. Baxter, whom
DeQuincy quotes, called religious toleration "soul
murder," and if you reminded him that this want
of toleration was his own grievance, he replied:
"Ah, but the cases are different, for I am right."
The Catholics tried to stop the anticlerical press
by closing the mails; the Jews were strong enough
in some places to prevent the sale of Ford's paper,
and asked libraries to shut it out. They introduced
in the Michigan legislature a bill providing penalties of fines up to $1,000, or a year's imprisonment,
"for the circulation of statements intended to hold
up to public ridicule any religion or its adherents."

Except for finding it in the record, I should not
venture to say that the pope's great battle with women's clothes began so long as ten years ago, if not
earlier. All my news and views about female duds
in the last decade have come from reading after
the pope. In 1921 he raised skirts, with dancing,
to be the theme of an encyclical—a circular letter
to the higher clergy. But the pope cannot perform
with an encyclical the miracles he can with a dogma.
Compare the case of Mary, espoused to Joseph.
She was a prospective mother when she came to
her husband. Yet with a dogma the pope not only

rendered Mary immaculate, but obliterated facts of experience and restored to her the innocence of virgin childhood, which he made perpetual. An encyclical worked no wonders in social regions. The dances he condemned as sources of sin went out of use by the natural process that works the doom of things no longer interesting; so did the clothes, displaced by some that reveal more of the wearers. The pope ought to be thankful for what it has been given him to behold in his day and generation, and omitting further remarks retire and give posterity a chance, without obscuring the scenery.

More favored still than the pope in being clothed with infallibility and sitting at the receipt of revelation, in 1921, was Heber J. Grant, president of the Church of Latter Day Saints, or Mormons. At the Mormon conference in the Temple at Salt Lake City, President Grant flung this defiance to the Pope of Rome and his children who have visions and revelations: "Any man, woman, or child who claims that he or she or any person except Heber J. Grant has received such revelation is either a plain liar or has been deceived by the powers of evil."

With regard to the proper length of a dress-skirt, a clergyman who met Clarence Darrow in debate liberated an illuminating thought when decrying the prolixity of sermons. "A sermon as to length," he said, "should be like a lady's dress. It should be long enough to cover the subject, but short enough to sustain interest."

All of the inspired, the infallible and the revelators are experts in women's clothes, and are competent by virtue of their holy office to tell them what not to leave off.

In California, Mr. James M. O'Hare of Sacramento, a member of the Typographical Union, issued an anti-Sunday tract effectively worded and widely circulated, which with a strong resolution by the Sacramento Federated Trades was sent to the California representatives in Washington, D. C., as a protest against a District Sunday law. The best anti-blue law that history records is the one introduced at Albany by Assemblyman Frederick L. Hackenburg of New York. Mr. Hackenburg's bill proposed that nothing legitimate on a week day should be unlawful; it prohibited all future legislation aimed at Sunday restrictions, and imposed a penalty on the uplifters demanding legal or judicial interference with the free spirit of happiness. For malignity, as expressed in Sunday laws, Christians have not changed from the first. The early ones were condemned, says the reputed Annals of Tacitus, not so much for the crime with which they were charged, the burning of Rome, as for "their hatred of mankind." Love of mankind never conceived a Sabbath law.

An open platform and unedited discussion of topics alien to Freethought have been of no help to Liberal organization. Rather they have proved the bane of Freethought, the society offering its opponents a free platform. Economic radicalism deracinated our oldest metropolitan Freethought organizations—the Manhattan Liberal Club and the Brooklyn Philosophical Association—caused the

expulsion of the one from German Masonic Temple
and the other from the hall of the Long Island
Business College, where these societies had taken
root.

"A Sojourner's Notebook" is seen as the heading
of a contribution to The Truth Seeker in 1921. The
contributor, "François Thane," is identified with
the author of a "Dictionary of Grammar," published by Funk & Wagnalls. (Francois Thane was
James A. Hennesy, long a government employee
in Washington, and he was still a contributor
when he died in 1930, aged 68 years.)

The theocrats of 1921 made a serious bid for a
law to make Bible reading compulsory in the public
schools of Ohio. Mr. J. A. Culbertson of Cincinnati prepared an able brief against the motion,
which was lost. The theocrats have attempted the
same measure at least twice since that date, with
diminishing prospects of success.

The mayor of Kansas City appointed Dr. John
Emerson Roberts, lecturer for the Church of This
World, a delegate to the meeting of the American
Academy of Social and Political Science in Phila-
delphia, May 13 and 14.

"In what way," a Truth Seeker correspondent
inquired, "do you answer persons like the late Goldwin Smith, who could see no purpose in life nor
any incentive to good deeds unless there is a hereafter in which they are rewarded?" This is a good
question, but I think the following the answer:

An anecdote under the head of "In Best of Humor"
relates that a small boy was instructed to go and wash his
face in the event of expected visitors arriving. "But," said

the unwilling boy, "suppose I go and wash up and then the company doesn't come!" He had not yet discovered that a clean face is a good thing in itself; and so these persons who see no incentive to right conduct and high thinking unless there is another life to reward them, forget, if they ever knew, that a good life has its advantages, and a bad one its penalties, in this world, irrespective of any other.

On the Fourth of July, in New York, the Irish-Americans marked the hymn "America" off the program of every band that marched in their parade, as the New York Herald reported. A New Jersey priest already had started the exclusion by directing his congregation to hiss "My Country, 'Tis of Thee," whenever they heard it, as a puritan hymn.

Joseph McCabe's Biographical Dictionary of Modern Rationalists, a work attesting the great industry of its compiler, appeared at this period. It preserved the names collected by J. M. Wheeler in his Dictionary of Freethinkers, and added many to the list, especially of Europeans. Some were "Freethinkers, but—"; that is to say, their sentiments were correct at times, but they did not act with Rationalists. With sentiments and acts reversed, these Rationalists are also "Christians, but—"; they do not believe in Christian doctrines, but act as if they did.

Walcott, Iowa, enjoyed brief renown as a town fifty years old, prosperous and orderly, that never had a church or a Sunday school within its limits. "It once had a jail," said the New York Evening Mail, "but, like its only church, established sixty-five years ago and which existed for a few years, it was put in the discard."

New Hampshire had once a considerable corps of Freethinkers, with good correspondents amongst them. In 1921 a late accession, Mrs. Ellen P. Sanders of Claremont, wrote of the religious situation in that town. Claremont is distinctly in the Bible belt and its Christian residents ready to respond to any sort of revivalism whether by Holy Rollers, Y. M. C. A. secretaries, or the local clergy. "The revival boom is always on," wrote Mrs. Sanders.

A Sunday evening in November, 1921, was the time, and Town Hall, New York, the scene of the first raid by a police mob on a mass meeting called to hear a discussion of family limitation by means of birth control. Distinguished speakers, particularly Mr. Harold Cox, the scholarly editor of the Edinburgh Review, would have addressed the meeting if allowed, but the police mob dispersed those present and turned everybody out before speeches could be made. For the lawless action the press blamed Mayor Hylan and Police Commissioner Enright. They appeared not to be responsible. Motion to suppress the meeting originated with Archbishop Hayes, now cardinal, who gave his orders to the captain of the precinct. To save the archbishop's face as a law-abiding citizen the uninformed Catholic press denied his instigation of the police mobbing; but the prelate himself continued on the offensive, and published a statement that the silencing of speakers was a public duty because the subject was unfit for public discussion. He then discussed it publicly and at length.

JOHN BURROUGHS (1838-1921).
Any God there might be, he said, must be conceived
of in terms of universal nature; and he admitted that in
the light of the old theology this was no God at all.

DEPARTURES IN 1921.

John Burroughs, naturalist, was almost 84 years old
when he died March 29, 1921. His birthday was April 3.
Orthodox Christians being the judges, Burroughs was
in after life a Materialist and Atheist. He believed in the
immortality of nature, but not of man. "My consciousness ceases as a flame ceases," he said. "Man invented
God and acts of creation." He professed to conceive of

God in terms of universal nature, but added: "In the light of the old theology this is no God as all." No believer in God ever spoke in those terms, nor in these: "How surely is God on both sides in all struggles, all causes, all wars, righteous and unrighteous! We behold warring nations praying to the same God for victory, . . . now apparently favoring one side, now the other." This is Atheism, with the argument by which Atheism is demonstrated.

Once he thought the Bible to be a repository of ethics. The year before his death, however, he wrote: "We seek more and more a scientific or naturalistic basis for our rules of conduct, for our altruism, for our charitable organizations, *for our whole ethical system*." He no longer found this in the Bible; his thought would have been Infidelity fifty years ago. His books, "The Light of Day" and "Accepting the Universe" are agreeable reading for Freethinkers. The Atheist Otto Wettstein quoted Burroughs as saying: "When I gaze upon the starry heavens at night, and reflect upon what I really see, I am constrained to say: There is no God."

In past chapters of this writing Mrs. Mattie P. Krekel has figured as a Liberal lecturer. She died October 13, aged 81 years. Mrs. Krekel was the widow of Judge Arnold Krekel, the first judge of the United States District Court for the western district of Missouri, who died in 1888. She had done work on the Liberal platform from her fifteenth year, when in 1900 she retired. She married T. W. Parry in 1862. Up to the beginning of the present century there were few names more familiar to readers of The Truth Seeker than Mattie Parry Krekel.

F. H. Hesse of Los Angeles, California, a materialistic philosopher, who wrote a score of articles for The Truth Seeker, died in November at 80. He served in Co. E, 3d Missouri Volunteers, 1861-64, and was buried by his comrades in arms.

A mortuary card received in December announced that "William F. Gable died at the residence in Altoona, Pennsylvania, Monday morning, November twenty-eighth, nineteen hundred and twenty-one." Mr. Gable was a man considerably advanced in years, one of the Old Guard of Freethinkers. He was the proprietor of a large mercantile establishment in Altoona and evinced his interest in Freethought by subscribing for many years for three copies of The Truth Seeker and by his generous support of the Thomas Paine Historical Association. Mr. Gable was of such good repute in his home city that all business houses were closed during the hour of his funeral, traffic was momentarily suspended, and members of clubs to which he belonged "stood silent for one minute as a tribute to his memory." He was leading merchant, first citizen, and famed philanthropist.

One of our centenarians, Elias Livesey of Baltimore, some months past 102, passed away on Nov. 4. He had been with The Truth Seeker from its beginning and made large contributions to the Freethought cause.

Overcome by the high cost of publishing, the San Francisco Star, in its January number, spoke the last word for itself, said its own obsequies, and pronounced its own eulogy. I suppose that the editor, James H. Barry, has by this time been gathered to his associate editors, Perkins and Cridge. They are all named in the first volume. The Star lasted from 1884 to 1921, when it was slain by the demands of labor for big wages—and Barry thought he was Labor's friend.

CHAPTER XXXIII.

THE hot debate on evolution in 1922 acquainted us incidentally with the reason why scientific truth makes slow headway against religion. It was that the exponents of truth never could depend upon the scientists to rally around and battle for the right interpretation of facts. From the first of my Freethought reading I had learned that science traversed every article of faith held by the Christian world. The light of science, the writers of fifty years ago finely said, had dissolved the mists of superstition, or were destined to do so at an early date. And Evolution —why, evolution didn't leave religion a peg to hang its millinery on. But they hoped against experience. Science didn't dissolve the mists; the mists befogged science.

There is that old Science of Astronomy, with all its facts. that in the days of Galileo and Copernicus created a new heaven and a new earth wholly incompatible with Bible geography, aeronautics and ascensions. The Bible had residents in heaven and on earth swapping visits and returning calls; and belief in that sort of thing—this ascension of persons from the pages of the Bible into heaven—has survived the clearly demonstrated truth that there is nowhere for such persons to go. The belief is still so common that it is only the unusual man or woman who will openly express doubt that Jesus was received bodily into heaven wearing his Sunday clothes. There is prospect that before my book is out, the pope, yielding to tradition and the request of many heads of religious societies, will promulgate the dogma—and see it accepted next day by the newspapers—of the "assumption" of the virgin; that is, that the mother of Jesus was snatched alive, with all her disabilities, into the presence of her son, seated just to the right of his father in heaven. Copernicus handed that foolishness a fatal blow; yet one may now examine orthodox faith closely and not find a dent made in it by astronomical fact.

That other great science, Geology, by which it is certified that the six thousand year period since Genesis is less than sixty seconds on the clock of the world, disturbs the faith of no one who really wants to be a child of God and accept Jesus as his personal savior. This notwithstanding that no man having such endowments of horse sense that he knows a contradiction when he sees one can believe in modern astronomy and geology and in Christianity at the same time.

Still it is hard to give up the belief, taught some of us at our mothers' knees, as it were, that knowledge shall yet dissolve the morning mists of superstition like fog before the rising sun.

In 1922 Miss Lovisa Brunzell of San Francisco,

who had been brought into Rationalism by the 1915 Freethought Congress in that city, thought to hang Christianity higher than Haman by taking the depositions of all the men of science in America and publishing them in a book for general circulation. Hence her famous Questionnaire, which before she completed her part of the work had been sent to all of the eleven thousand men and women who were members of the American Association for the Advancement of Science. Luther Burbank, the Darwinian plant "wizard" of Santa Rosa, California, answered promptly and favorably on one of the first forms distributed, and returned the questions with the answers here appended:

Q. Do you believe in the divinity and miraculous conception of Christ?

B. I do not; there is no proof of it, either natural or otherwise.

Q. Is it your opinion that prayer is answered by an intelligent being from without?

B. I do not believe that prayer has been or ever will be answered by any intelligent being from without. There is absolutely no proof whatever of this, though it may be very comforting to some to believe this myth.

Q. Do you think that the sole value of prayer consists in its effect on the person praying?

B. Mostly. Sometimes it might prove of value to others.

Q. Has science taught you that heaven and hell do not exist?

B. The common orthodox heaven and hell do not exist. They could not exist if there were an all-powerful and just ruler. No criminal could be as cruel as the God who would consign human beings to a hell.

Q. What is your opinion of the Bible? Is it the work of God or of man?

B. Without the shadow of a doubt the work of man, being a history of the lives of ancient tribes reaching up toward civilization, and constructed mostly unconsciously by men both good and bad.

Q. Do you assume that the soul of man ceases to functionate at death?

B. In other spheres, I do. Its influence will live in humanity—will live for good or bad for all time. We actually live in the lives of others.

Q. Do you agree with Büchner that "the brain is the seat of the soul"?

B. A very difficult question to answer in a few words. The brain, if we include the whole nervous system, is the soul. Millions of souls functionate, through heredity, through our own personal ones.

Q. Would you say that matter and force govern the universe rather than a supreme being?

B. Matter, which in its last analysis is force, governs what we know of the universe.

Q. Can you harmonize the Christian faith with the laws of nature?

B. In part, though this requires more than a "Yes" or "No." It is a faith grown up in our heredity, and has been an important factor, even though it does not harmonize with the laws of nature.

Q. Can you say with Darwin that "Agnostic would be the more correct description of my state of mind"?

B. Yes, with reservations.

Q. Have your labors in the field of science and research caused you to alter your earlier opinions on religion?

B. All my work in the field of science and research has come through a change in my earlier opinions on religion. Growth is the law of life. Orthodoxy is the death of scientific effort.

Q. What facts of nature substantiate your views?

B. The evolution and development of man and his civilization through his own efforts, and only these.

Q. Is life after death proved or disproved by science?

B. It has never been proved or disproved, but it is rapidly, in my opinion, being disproved and so accepted by intelligent people.

Q. What, in your opinion, has given rise to religious beliefs?

B. Probably two things: First, the desire to extend our present life; and second, the desire of its teachers to be supported by those who labor.

Q. Is religion of any value in the conduct of human affairs?

B. There is no possible doubt that it has been and, like police force, will be in the future to those who are not able to govern themselves, especially in their relations toward others.

Further remarks: The thousands of religions which exist and have existed are stepping-stones to a better adaptation to environment, and are one by one being replaced by the clear light of science and knowledge—in other words, as the fables of childhood are being supplanted by a better understanding of the facts of life.

Faithfully yours, LUTHER BURBANK.

Miss Brunzell printed the answers of Burbank on a separate sheet and inclosed them with future copies of the Questionnaire, in the trust they would "encourage to frankness some of our scientific men who might otherwise feel that they would be too much alone in expressing heretical opinions," supposing they held them.

Hudson Maxim, the inventor, junked the Christian religion and threw it into the scrapheap. He said that the story of Joshua holding up the sun and moon, the incident of Jonah and the whale, the gossip about a miraculous conception, the fable of the Holy Trinity, and a hundred other stupid inventions were absurd myths that Christian fanatics had for two thousand years tried to compel mankind to believe, using the tortures of the Inquisition for that purpose.

A professor in the university at Tucson, Arizona, for the first time in his life yielding to the temptation to write an anonymous letter, argued that if all men of science should express their views for publication, it would bring the conflict between science and religion to an issue in which the adherents of science would be squelched unless they took shelter in the church.

Candid replies were submitted by a score who withheld their names from publication; but so many more made inconsequent answers that, as I read their responses, I concluded that we had overestimated the importance of the opinions of the scientists about religion.

I am at a loss to know with what word of distinction to characterize 1922; yet it deserves to be celebrated somehow, for it was the year that saw

the birth of Fundamentalism. And the birth of
Fundamentalism was "on this wise." The Baptists
moved on the works of Dartmouth College (Han-
over, N. H.) to capture and make it a denominational institution. Raising the clamor that the college employed instructors who were unorthodox,
they protested that "no teacher should be permitted
to continue in any one of our schools without the
clearest expression of faith in and acceptance of
our Baptist fundamentals."

Now, Baptist "fundamentals" are the dogmas in
dispute between the orthodox and the liberal. They
affirm Adam and Eve, Jonah and the whale, the
virgin birth, the early return of Christ, and worse.
"It is the duty of the Baptist communities throughout the country," these Fundamentalists went on,
"to displace from the schools men who impugn
the authority of the scriptures as the word of God
and who deny the deity of our Lord." They put
this issue up to the Dartmouth president, Dr. E.
M. Hopkins. I wonder if President Hopkins had
in mind Edward Tuck, Dartmouth's favorite son
and principal benefactor. Perhaps not, but something prompted him nevertheless to make the right
answer. He said No; emphatically, No. "I believe," he stated, "that the honest agnosticism or
doubt of any mind has the right to full play, and
that only out of such freedom of speculation can
a genuine and strongly founded belief of any po-
tentiality be acquired."

The engagement which ensued was for the Baptists and their allies the Battle of the Marne—which
they lost. It was the breaking of the doctrinal

storm that has not yet cleared off. Those foes of "honest agnosticism" were from that time forward called Fundamentalists. The word with a capital initial is seen in The Truth Seeker but a few weeks after the Dartmouth incident. "Modernists," originally a term of reproach, now also came into vogue to distinguish the non-Fundamentalists. The pope had broadcast it in his encyclical of 1907 against Abbe Loisy and other "heretical exegetes, defilers of the flesh and corrupters of morals." These were Modernists, the pope said. It is likely that the Fundamentalists took it from him, and denominated Modernists those ministers who in the days of Briggs and McGiffert must have been branded as heretics because there was no other name for them.

Not being able to coerce the college faculties otherwise, the Baptists, joined with other lower orders of Christians, resorted to legislation with a view to crystallizing Fundamentalism into law. They tried Kentucky first with this bill:

"It shall be unlawful in any school or college or institution of learning maintained in whole or in part, in this state, by funds raised by taxation, for any one to teach any theory of evolution that derives man from the brute, or any other form of life, or that eliminates God as the creator of man by direct creative act."

This, the first of the "monkey" bills, came close to passing the Kentucky House. The vote taken March 9 stood 41 to 41, when a member named Bruce Cuniff, viewing anti-evolution as "an infringement on personal liberty," voted against and so defeated the bill.

College presidents and professors, accused by William Jennings Bryan of evolutionism and therefore Atheism, made but a feeble resistance. President E. A. Birge of the University of Wisconsin produced a certificate of membership in the Congregational church. Bryan asked him to say whether or not he believed in "the virgin birth as reported in Luke," but he declined to answer. Certainly it was impudent in Bryan to put the question, and yet who would not gladly know whether this college president could reconcile evolution, or biology, or science, or anything else he taught his pupils as fact, with Luke's report that the mother of Jesus gave birth to a son without antecedent organic union with a male of her species. Bryan congratulated himself on "tying the tongues" of the professors. He addressed to Dr. R. C. Spangler, biology professor in West Virginia University, who refused to repudiate the simian ancestry of man, the inquiry: "From what ape did you descend?" The professor frankly traced his ancestry according to Haeckel, and to Bryan said: "I assure you that your embryological development was the same as that of other men, except that I do not know whether your tail degenerated before your birth or was amputated afterward."

The Fundamentalists were saying that the evolutionists dispensed with the deity, denied the inspiration of the Bible, made a myth of the story of creation, robbed Jesus Christ of his divinity and his mother of her reputation, and set aside the second coming as a delusive expectation. That was the opportunity for the men of science, disdaining compromise and evasion, to reply: "We admit it. We concede that all we have added to our knowledge by research and study, all the facts we have discovered and demonstrated, are contradictory of what has been taught as religion; that evolution does to your fundamentals exactly as you say. And this being so, what are you going to do about it?"

Fundamentalist slaps at seats of learning hit Hamilton College (Clinton, N. Y.), whose president, Frederick Carlos Ferry, had said that "college students no longer pray or give account of their religious experience vocally anywhere." Maintaining his position, President Ferry later added that parallel with the subsidence of religious expression by college men there had come about "an improved sense of honor."

It had passed into theological fiction, disseminated industriously by the anti-evolutionists, that religon, which the colleges were destroying or neglecting, was "the only basis of morals." But Dr. Frank L. Christian, superintendent of reformatories in the State of New York, in investigating the personal histories of 22,000 inmates of penal institutions, "found but four college graduates in the lot." No report on the number of Fundamentalist preachers in the round-up was made by Dr. Christian.

During 1922 there were scenes in clerical life which could not be ignored. The Rev. Dr. J. Roach Straton preached against the theatre as demoralizing in its influence on actors. William A. Brady, theatrical producer, asked for a few minutes' occupancy of the clergyman's pulpit for the purpose of saying to Mr. Straton and his congregation that church people committed more crimes than stage people and that more preachers than actors were in jail. Following the Herald's impartial report of the meeting (that is, February 14), Joseph F. Fishman, for fourteen years inspector of prisons for the United States government, said: "Taking at random four annual reports of the United States Penitentiary in Atlanta, I find there were during the entire period covered by the reports a total of 15 actors and a total of 43 preachers in confinement." This, the prison inspector averred, was "fairly typical of conditions in both federal and state penitentiaries." A tabulated statement by Inspector Fishman showed that in four years the number of actors in the Atlanta institution had increased from 3 to 4; of ministers, from 8 to 20; so there were 5 preachers to 1 actor.

Two blasphemy cases were tried, one in England, with the irrepressible Gott as victim (nine months' imprisonment); and one in Germany, where the court gave Karl Einstein, a writer, the alternative of paying 10,000 marks or going to jail for six weeks, and imposed half that penalty on his publisher.

Boston's district attorney, Joseph C. Pelletier, a Roman Catholic decorated by the Pope and internationally known as Supreme Advocate of the Knights of Columbus, went on trial before the Supreme Judicial Court of Massachusetts charged with misfeasance, malfeasance and nonfeasance. He was found guilty of blackmail, extortion, and conspiracy, and removed from office.

Against the protests of Jews and Secularists the New Jersey legislature, instigated thereto by the Junior order of American Mechanics, wrote a law on the statute books providing for the reading of passages of the Old Testament as well as the New in the public schools. The Jews thought that only the Old Testament, accepted by both Christians and Jews, should be read. In California the Supreme Court ruled that the King James translation of the Bible "is the accepted Protestant version" and that therefore its purchase by schools is a direct violation of the state law prohibiting the acquisition of sectarian books by the public schools.

The American Secular Union directors held their annual meeting in the secretary's office, 127 North Dearborn street, Chicago, February 28 (reported in The Truth Seeker of March 25), and re-elected officers—Marshall J. Gauvin, president; W. L. Maclaskey, secretary; Ethel M. Maclaskey, treasurer. Without complete success the secretary tried to organize "get-together meetings" among Chicago Liberals, and a few were held.

The thirty-fifth annual congress of the National (Belgian) Freethought Congress took place at Brussels, the last of July. Libby Culberson Macdonald, then at Nice, France, supplied The Truth Seeker with the story.

Oregon voters at the general election in November confirmed an initiative measure known for a time as The Oregon Law—or the Compulsory School Bill—requiring all children to be sent to the public schools from 8 to 16 years of age. As, according to its intent, it would have emptied

parochial schools of their pupils, the Catholics contested its constitutionality. They carried it to the
Supreme Court of the United States—and got the
decision. The Truth Seeker had not approved the
law, which raised the question of religious freedom in education. The appellants pleaded that
point, no doubt, and the court dodged it. The court
said, or had said, that the people could not look
to the federal government or courts for protection
of their religious rights. Had the Supreme Court
pronounced the Oregon law unconstitutional on the
ground that it violated the first amendment, that
would have established a precedent for the application of the secular clause to the curbing of state
theocracies. The court therefore ignored the first
amendment and its provisions, and took up a provision in the fifth that a person could not be deprived of property without due process of law.
Property, not liberty, peeled the bark in that court;
but why the fifth amendment more than the first
reached the situation in Oregon, one must ask the
judges to learn. The Catholic appellants represented to the court that running a parochial school
was a remunerative business, which the law would
make less profitable, besides depreciating the value
of the real estate. So the court called the Oregon
law unconstitutional.

Attorney-General Daugherty of President Harding's cabinet also registered a remarkable opinion.
A custodian of alien property had seized a church
belonging to an enemy country. Mr. Daugherty
decided that churches being houses of God, in the
last analysis the title to church property was vested

in God. Said he, then: "If it is held by the Deity, it would be sacrilegious to hold there is an enemy interest." The malodorous decision made a good blend with the reputation of its author, which was no violets.

Freethought societies and workers kept something doing. Martin Bunge, former editor of the German-language Freidenker, in Milwaukee, took Southern California for his field and tried to rally and organize the Los Angeles Freethinkers "scattered by the war and the after-effects of the war." John McLoud of Arondale, Okla., busied himself forming an Oklahoma Rationalist Society. The New York Secular Society requested that Central Park should either be thrown open to Freethinkers or closed to the bands of fanatics who blocked the entrances. A girl of 12 years in Inglewood, California, Queen Silver by name, answered Bryan on Darwinism and evolution. Miss Silver had read Darwin, and when conservative evolutionists protested that "neither Darwin nor any other competent biologist ever said that the human race descended from apes," she quoted chapter and page in the "Descent of Man" where Darwin had recorded that, in his opinion, the human race had precisely that ancestry. (Truth Seeker, September 16, 1922.) The astonished editors in Los Angeles discussed Queen as a "prodigy." Her mother, Mrs. Grace Verne Silver, attributed the unusual mental maturity of her daughter to rational education, or education in Rationalism.

William Plotts of Whittier, Cal., brought injunction proceedings to restrain the county super-visers of Los Angeles from spending $20,000 of public money to stage a religious spectacle called the Pilgrimage Play. Upton Sinclair offered W. J. Bryan $200 to debate evolution with President Birge of Wisconsin University. Bryan must have sniffed at the amount and deemed Sinclair a "pik-er," for Mr. Plotts had dangled $5,000 before him as a temptation to meet Edward Adams Cantrell.

To raise The Truth Seeker's Sustaining Fund in 1922, Mr. W. L. Klein, "An Alabama Friend," pro-posed that a reader in every state contribute a hun-dred dollars, as he was doing and has done several times since.

After thirty-five years at the calling, Henry Frank was still delivering liberal lectures, his 1922 station being the People's Church in Los Angeles. A Rationalist Society met Sundays at Long Beach.

Stanley J. Clark, sometimes heard in debate with ministers, spent his 1922 Christmas in Leaven-worth, a political prisoner since 1918, under a sen-tence of 10 years and $30,000 fine. Comrade Clark, as Socialist, Atheist, and advocate of fair treatment for workers, lost his liberty at a time when it was dangerous to question the actions of anyone functioning as part of the government—the copper men, for example, who were producing the metal at a cost of nine cents a pound, charging the government twenty-nine cents, and paying the min-ers low wages. How things stood even in 1922 can be judged from the arrest of William Allen White, widely known editor of the Emporia Gazette, for saying when a railroad strike was on that he thought the men were half right. Arthur Ross of San Pedro, California, distributed copies of The Truth Seeker. The police seized the papers as "of a seditious nature," and took Ross into custody. Acts like these, taken with the fact that our government still stands, warrant us in claiming to have a foolproof system.

The year was favorable to a large crop of religious heretics besides Bishop Brown. They "disfellowshiped" the Rev. Fred W. Hagan, minister of the First Congregational church in Huntington, West Virginia, who spoke up saying: "If my church forced me to believe in the infallibility of the Bible, the second coming of Jesus in person, the bodily resurrection, the damnation of those who refuse to believe in a certain creed, the hell-fire theory and the virgin birth, I would choose to be numbered among the Atheists, Infidels and Agnostics."

The Rev. J. D. M. Buckner, pastor of the Methodist church at Aurora, in Nebraska, lost his pulpit and his license to preach by trying to make out that God is not so bad as the Bible paints him. Edwin Anders, high school teacher in Sacramento, California, remarked that "Protestant ministers often marry and have families, while Catholic priests do not marry but sometimes have families." Fired. Dr. Samuel D. McConnell, once rector of Holy Trinity church, published his "Confessions of an Old Priest." He had ceased to believe in Christianity or its moral influence. William Jewell College, Liberty, Mo., dismissed Dr. A. Wakefield Slaten, head of the Department of Biblical Literature and Religious Education, for unswallowing the scriptures.

A Chicago newspaper offered a daily prize of $5 for the best motto. Julius Rosenwald, head of the Sears-Roebuck mail-order business, took the money one day with the sentiment: "I had rather be a beggar and spend my last dollar like a king, than a king and spend my money like a beggar." (I have corrected the wording according to Ingersoll.) The press carried Rosenwald's motto all over the country and abroad. Only The Truth Seeker remarked that it had been picked out of Ingersoll's "Liberty of Man, Woman and Child." The rest of it is: "If you have but a dollar in the world, and you have got to spend it, spend it like a king; spend it as though it were a dry leaf and you the owner of unbounded forests." A man named Charles T. Lambert wrote to the Peoria Star that he had heard Ingersoll deliver a "withered leaves" speech at the Illinois state fair in 1877, and it was so sharply criticized that he omitted it from his published works. A pure myth! But Mr. Lambert's myth was harmless. A certain H. H. Kohlsaat, writing his memoirs for the Saturday Evening Post, invented a malicious one. Kohlsaat, who being a kind of newspaper man ought to have abjured lying, stated that at the national Republican convention in Chicago in 1888, Colonel Ingersoll so exasperated the delegates in a speech assailing the Christian religion that with one impulse they left the hall.

Olaus Jeldness of Spokane, Washington, a reader

of Ingersoll from the beginning, had preserved a June, 1888, copy of the Portland Oregonian that reported the convention and Ingersoll's speech. It showed that Ingersoll said nothing whatever about the Christian religion; that his address elicited "great applause, the Illinois delegation standing on chairs and cheering loudly"; that no one left the hall, but that "friend and foe were held captive by oratory never excelled." If Kohlsaat's falsification has been printed in a book, here is the correction.

A Western paper gave to Kermit, in West Virginia, the distinction of being the only town without a church. To the contrary the files of The Truth Seeker showed that in 1914 the borough of East Washington, Pennsylvania, had been called a Utopia with no church within its borders, and but one arrest in a population of 1,500. In 1915 Carlstadt, New Jersey, had been referred to as "the only officially irreligious town in the United States." The founders of Carlstadt put into its charter the provision that no church should ever be permitted to exist within the town limits. In 1917 the press reported that not a town in King county, Texas, supported a ministry, nor a saloon, and that the jail had been vacant for eighteen months; and in 1921 columns of newspaper space were given to the fact that Wolcott, Iowa, had no church or Sunday school, being good without God, and wealthy and orderly unaided by religion. A resident of Staples, Louisiana, asked to have his town listed as church-less.

And peoples or tribes without God, they too were marvels. As late as the time when Dr. Johnson wrote "Rasselas," the dogma went undisputed that belief in God and immortality were inherent in all men. The doctrine got its hold before any investigation had been made to determine whether it was true or not. Later explorers came upon numerous tribes of primitive people who had neither God nor religion. Spencer mentioned them; they were found by Peary and Stefansson; Curator Hornaday of the Bronx Zoological Park met them in Borneo; the Christian missionary M. R. Hilford, who spent years among the black people of the Mandingo country, West Africa, told of millions without any religious belief and "immune to the gospel." The American Indians have no such "Great Spirit" as has been bestowed upon them by pious romance. That was the gift of the missionaries, who supposed that belief in God was innate, and the Indians having none, they thought it necessary to invent one. Warren G. Van Slyke, a New York lawyer, who made a hunting trip to Indo-China in 1922, found a tribe in the jungle which had no gods nor any trace of religion. Van Slyke called this tribe the Moys. "Neither," he said, "did I see any indications of superstitions among them, and superstitions are the most primitive form of religion."

The last month of 1922 produced the inquiry: "Where are the ideals of yesteryear?" I quoted a paragraph written in 1890 by Prof. Thomas H. Huxley in an essay on government, where he said:

"Anarchy, as a term of political philosophy, must

be taken only in its proper sense, WHICH HAS
NOTHING TO DO WITH DISORDER OR
WITH CRIME; but denotes a state of society in
which the rule of each individual by himself is the
only government the legitimacy of which is recog-
nized. In this sense, STRICT ANARCHY MAY
BE THE HIGHEST CONCEIVABLE GRADE
OF PERFECTION OF SOCIAL EXISTENCE;
for, if all men spontaneously did justice and loved
mercy, IT IS PLAIN THAT ALL SWORDS
MIGHT BE ADVANTAGEOUSLY TURNED
INTO PLOWSHARES, AND THAT THE OC-
CUPATION OF JUDGES AND POLICE
WOULD BE GONE."

When those words were written there were in
both England and America groups of bright men
who held to the political philosophy they so well
define. One over there was Huxley's friend Au-
beron Herbert. Among the adherents here were
Benjamin R. Tucker (who founded the "school"
that The Truth Seeker named Philosophical Anarchists), John Beverley Robinson, Steven T. Byington, Victor Yarros, Samuel P. Putnam, Hugh
O. Pentecost, James F. Morton, Jr., George Gillen,
Edwin C. Walker, and enough more to give Mr.
Tucker a corps of contributors to his magazine
Liberty and constituents enough to establish a circulation.

This "highest conceivable grade of perfection of
social existence," as Huxley so generously admitted, although he had not himself received the promise, will be found feebly explicated in my earlier
attempts at writing. I reproduce the words at this

late date as still embodying the ideal of social existence. Of any notion that society will ever approach this ideal I have long been disillusioned; but disillusionment is the penalty exacted for outliving hopes based upon the narrow chance that all men may sometime be quaint enough spontaneously to do justice and love mercy, and abolish the censor, which would come near in many cases to abolishing themselves. While we can do little toward realizing our ideals, it seems like treachery toward a past full of high and earnest aspirations if we abandon them now.

DEPARTURES, 1922.

"He lived in a house by the side of the road, and has been a friend to man," said a January obituary notice in the Plymouth Register, Yarmouth, Mass., recording the death of Joshua Crowell of East Dennis. That was one way of saying that Mr. Crowell was not a Christian. More commonly, they say that his religion was the Golden Rule. Mr. Crowell died full of honors, at the age of 78, having read The Investigator and The Truth Seeker for half a century.

Judge W. W. Edwards of Louisiana, born at Charlton, N. Y., in 1826, died at Abbeville, La., March 10, 1921. Judge Edwards long had taken The Truth Seeker, and when he died his family allowed it to continue in his name. He was fortunate in that respect, that immediately on his death no member of his family ordered the paper discontinued. It goes to the same family now. In 1922, page 155 of The Truth Seeker, an article entitled "A Rationalist," tells the story of his mental evolution.

Arthur M. Lewis, who was born in England and was the author of several books of merit, had lectured for sixteen years for the Workers' University Society in Chicago, when death came to him suddenly in August, 1922, in his 49th year.

The death of Thomas E. Watson, which occurred this year, though I do not find the month and day, was commemorated in an appreciative article by Professor Bowne (Oct. 21, 1922), and a sonnet by Robert F. Hester. While Mr. Watson was not a professed Freethinker, he was one of the characters whose insurgency brought his name into many of the chapters of this History.

England's last prisoner for blasphemy, John W. Gott, ended a sentence of nine months at hard labor, his fourth term, in August and died November 4. He was sick when sentenced, in a lower state of health when liberated, and could not recover.

CHAPTER XXXIV.

THE New Year's greeting of The Truth Seeker to its readers, January 6, 1923 (this being the extraordinary occasion of striking out "Vol. 49" in the main heading and inserting "Vol. 50," the half-century mark), predicted that the year we are now entering would see the rival contenders, science and religion, coming to grips, with more vivacity on the part of science, it was hoped, than previously had been displayed. The outlook was good, seeing that the Council of the American Association for the Advancement of Science, lately meeting at the Massachusetts Institute of Technology, in Boston, had adopted resolutions that were nothing less, in significance, than a vote of confidence in Evolution, which was Atheism to the godly. The council took fearless cognizance of the fact that W. J. Bryan had challengingly declared Evolution to be nothing but a "Mere Guess." On behalf of their Association, with its membership of 11,000, the scientific gentlemen accepted the wager of battle. "This council," they resolved with great fortitude, "affirms that the evidences in favor of the evolution of man are sufficient to convince every scientist of note in the world." To this they added the heresy of deeper dye that "evolution is one of the most potent of the great influences for good that have thus far entered into human existence."

Some philosophers have counseled care in the propagation of scientific conclusions averse to current religious belief for fear of removing somebody's consolations. A Boston Traveler reporter talked about this with Dr. Burton E. Livingstone of Johns Hopkins University during the meeting of the scientists. He asked: "But now won't the theologian argue that you would take all the beauty away from the saintly little woman who worships at her religious shrine?" Dr. Livingstone replied: "Science doesn't take away anything. If she does not come to hear the result of science she loses nothing that she now possesses, and if she does come she receives something that will take its place. She would lose nothing."

Charles Proteus Steinmetz (1865-1923), Materialist, Atheist, and the greatest of electrical experts, had said, a little while before, talking to a Unitarian congregation in Schenectady, New York, that as regards science and religion, the two were not necessarily incompatible being "different and unrelated activities of the human mind." Between the lines of Dr. Steinmetz's address could be read his meaning that science dealt only with facts, and that as religion hadn't any facts, science did not enter religion's field. The address involved Steinmetz in controversy with a minister who disputed the right of men of science to express an opinion about re-

ligion and warned them to stay in their own backyard; to which the professor replied that if ministers would take their own advice and reserve their
opinion on scientific questions, they would appear
at less disadvantage. The minister urged the incompetence of science to account, as religion did,
for the origin of life; and Steinmetz, conceding the
difficulty of originating living mater, replied that
neither was it possible artificially to produce a piece
of granite; and yet granite was doubtless a result
of the processes of nature.

On this and the incendiary resolutions adopted
at the M. I. T. meeting of the Association's Council, The Truth Seeker grounded the remark that
"science, like John Paul Jones, has just commenced
fighting." I regret now to record that this opti-
mistic view was unsupported by events that followed, for science never fought at all—that is, the
Association didn't. Religion did all the leading,
and science hardly put up its hands to protect its
face. It is true, of course, that two representative
men, Prof. Henry Fairfield Osborn, president of
the American Museum of Natural History, and
Prof. Edwin C. Conklin, Princeton biologist, prepared answers to Bryan; but when Prof. R. A.
Millikan of the Laboratory of Physics, Pasadena,
Cal., got out his statement, assigning to the clergy
a more important place in human affairs than that
of science, both Osborn and Conklin attached their
names to it. The articles of surrender that Millikan had prepared were circulated in Washington,
D. C., and obtained the signatures of forty persons
in business, politcal, and scientific pursuits:

"We, the undersigned, deeply regret that in recent controversies there has been a tendency to present science and religion as irreconcilable and antagonistic domains of thought, for, in fact, they meet distinct human needs, and in the rounding out of human life they supplement rather than displace or oppose each other.

"The purpose of science is to develop, without prejudice or pre-conception of any kind, a knowledge of the facts, the laws and the processes of nature. The even more important task of religion, on the other hand, is to develop the consciences, the ideals, and the aspirations of mankind. Each of these two activities represents a deep and vital function of the soul of man, and both are necessary for the life, the progress and the happiness of the human race.

"It is a sublime conception of God which is furnished by science, and one wholly consonant with the highest ideals of religion, when it represents him as revealing himself through countless ages in the development of the earth as an abode for man and in the age-long inbreathing of life into its constitutent matter, culminating in man with his spiritual nature and all his Godlike powers."

No known Roman Catholic, orthodox Jew, or Fundamentalist was among the signatories to the Millikan-water proclamation.

The battle against evolution went on in the Bible belt. At Fort Sumner, New Mexico, F. E. Dean, superintendent of schools, lost his job by teaching it. His superiors maintained that no man distinguished for scholarship believed in it, but Dean produced the following letter written by a former President of the United States to Prof. C. W. Curtis of the University of Missouri, where Dean had been graduated:

"WASHINGTON, D. C., 29 August, 1922.

"MY DEAR PROFESSOR CURTIS: May it not suffice for me to say, in reply to your letter of August 25, that of course

like every other man of intelligence and education I do believe in organic evolution. It surprises me that at this late date such questions should be raised. Sincerely yours,
"WOODROW WILSON."

For two years the anti-evolutionists had quoted Prof. William Bateson's address at Toronto (December, 1921) as witness to the downfall of Darwinism. Bateson had said that "though no one doubts the truth of evolution, we have as yet no satisfactory account of that particular part of the theory which is concerned with the origin of *species* in the strict sense." He knew he should be misrepresented by the anti-evolutionists (he used the word "Obscurantists") and therefore added:

"I have put before you very frankly the considerations which have made us Agnostic as to the actual mode and processes of evolution. When such confessions are made the enemies of science see their chance. If we cannot declare here and now how species arose, they will obligingly offer us the solutions with which obscurantism is satisfied. *Let us then proclaim in precise and unmistakable language that our faith in evolution is unshaken.* Every available line of argument converges on this inevitable conclusion. The obscurantist has nothing to suggest which is worth a moment's attention. The difficulties which weigh upon the professional biologist need not trouble the layman. Our doubts are not as to the reality or truth of evolution, but as to the origin of *species,* a technical, almost domestic, problem. Any day that mystery may be solved. The discoveries of the last twenty-five years enable us for the first time to discuss these questions intelligently and on a basis of fact. That synthesis will follow on analysis, we do not and cannot doubt."

A notable group of Fundamentalists held a meeting in Calvary Baptist church, New York, in December, to "reaffirm the historic Baptist belief in the divine inspiration and authority of the Bible," with the rest of the orthodox program, including the virgin birth. Here appeared that pillar of Fundamentalism, E. C. Miller, a wealthy New York merchant, to say that without the virgin birth "our Lord is made a bastard," and without his atoning death "he immediately becomes a liar and a cheat." W. J. Bryan came also to argue that unless the Bible was infallible the Atheists were right and there was no God. Will there ever live another godist with the candor to affirm, as Bryan did at this meeting—

"The question of the infallibility of the Bible as the word of God is the fundamental question and greatest issue in the country today. It is a question of whether there is a God. Since we get from the Bible our conception and opinion of God, and since it is the only source of knowledge of God, *if the Bible is not the truth, then there is no God.*"

The Committee on State Affairs of the Texas House of Representatives reported unfavorably on a bill, introduced by Representative Stroder, prohibiting the teaching of Darwinian or theistic evolution in the public schools of the state. A similar anti-evolution measure in Florida won the approval of some of the state press, as when the Havana (Fla.) Star (supposing it dealt with a living character) condemned Mr. Darwin editorially as a seeker after "cheap notoriety," and called on him to explain certain features of his theory. Mr. Darwin, the editor charged, "is using thousands of unsuspecting people as a stepping-stone to fame."

The Freethinkers in 1923 paid the usual honors to Thomas Paine. The National Association celebrated the 186th birthday at the Fifth Avenue Hotel, with Carl Van Doren, literary editor of The Century, as principal speaker. Chicago celebrants listened to Arthur M. Lewis. The Rationalists of Columbus, Ohio, presented a long list of good speakers. The discovery was communicated to The Truth Seeker by Mr. James B. Elliott, the veteran Painite of Philadelphia, that the first birthday celebration took place in 1825. Quoting a certain Edward Thompson of Philadelphia, the narrative says:

"In America it appears that the first effort to celebrate Paine's birthday after his death, as far as my researches have disclosed, was in New York city by a few zealous individuals in Harmony Hall in 1825. This was a secondrate tavern, but later the more renowned Tammany Hall was the annual meeting-place."

Mr. Thompson himself introduced the Paine birthday celebration in Philadelphia in 1834 with a meeting at Military Hall.

At the 1923 celebration at New Rochelle Memorial Day, there appeared for the first time among the celebrants the Hon. Sidney Vale Lowell of Brooklyn, who was the grandson of Gilbert Vale, author of the earliest authentic life of Paine published in America and for many years editor of The Beacon, a Freethought journal, in the first half of the nineteenth century.

On June 9 the Greenwich Village Historical Society dedicated a memorial tablet to Paine. The tablet was affixed to the house, No. 59 Grove Street, occupying the site of the one Paine died in (1809). The proceedings were not quite worthy of the occasion, and it was only a half-and-half celebration. The speakers were apologetic. Paine's praises were sung in the key of the first sentence of President Harding's letter, reading: "There always will be many among us to differ keenly from some of the views of Thomas Paine."

President Harding, in his letter, having made it clear that he did not indorse all the views of Paine, wrote: "But surely there cannot be many to doubt the value and splendid sincerity of his patriotic service to the cause of liberty in his own country and elsewhere, which have richly deserved the commemoration you are planning."

The Grove street tablet, which is about 18x24 inches in size, has a map of the United States at the too, a map of France in the lower left-hand corner, with one of England to the right of it. The center is occupied by a medalion portrait of Paine, beneath which are the words:

THOMAS PAINE
BORN 1737
DIED 1809
ON THIS SITE

Above the map of the United States is the quotation, "The World is My Country"; at the left of the portrait, from top to bottom, "All Mankind are My Brethren"; at the foot, "I believe in one God and No More." There is also the legend: "This Tablet was placed on June 9, 1923, by the Greenwich Village Historical Society." The tablet was designed by Samilla Jameson Heinzmann.

Said The Truth Seeker in July: "The name of Paine is going to be familiar hereafter to the residents of Doylestown, in Pennsylvania. Mr. Frank Hart of that munic'pality has lately developed a ten-acre tract formerly the grounds of an English and classical seminary which is now no more. Mr. Hart bought the tract in 1891. In 1915 he began extending streets through it. This spring he broke ground for the construction of a new street, 500 feet long, which he intends shall bear the name of the author-hero of the Revolution, Thomas Paine. Neighboring streets are Washington, Jefferson, Franklin, and Lafayette, so that Paine street will be in the company of great contemporaries. There will be three Paine thoroughfares when this one is opened. In New Rochelle, New York, is Paine avenue. In Irvington, New Jersey, where George Gillen and his family reside and have property and influence, is another Paine avenue. And now Paine street, Doylestown, Pa."

In The Truth Seeker office the issuing of a Golden Jubilee number, September 1, ranked as the event of the year. Inside this sixty-four page edition the eight-page initial number, dated September, 1873, photographically reproduced, was printed and bound. The Lecouver Press Company contributed the line in bronze over the first-page heading: "1873 —GOLDEN JUBILEE NUMBER—1923," and beyond doubt that was the largest and finest specimen of a Freethought paper ever attempted. In it was begun a summary of the answers of men of science to the questionnaire sent to eleven thousand by Miss Lovisa Brunzell.

The reproduced copy of The Truth Seeker Vol. I, No. 1. 1873, contained the advertisements of six

Liberal papers then issuing, and perhaps it was not a complete list of those then in existence. None of them outlived the century.

Discussion of the dismissal of Dr. A. Wakefield Slaten from William Jewell College, Liberty, Mo., for heresy, had not died down when the Presbyterians took up the case of the Rev. Harry Emerson Fosdick, special preacher in the First New York Presbyterian church, who characterized the virgin birth as a "biological miracle" exceeding belief. Fosdick was a Baptist, and one Presbytery after another "presented" him and demanded that he conform to the Confession of Faith or stop preaching in a Presbyterian church and cease eating on Presbyterian money.

The Rev. Percy Stickney Grant of the Episcopal Church of the Ascension preached his celebrated "Bunk" sermon in 1923. Pointing out some of the absurdities and superstitions of orthodoxy, he said to the fathers and mothers in his congregation:

"When your son comes back from college, and you say to him: 'Come to church this morning,' do you want him to reply: 'Father, no; don't ask me to listen to such bunk as that.'?"

Grant's ecclesiastical superior, Bishop William T. Manning of the Episcopal diocese of New York, admonished and reprimanded him, but he was impenitent. He withdrew from the ministry for social reasons and died in 1927.

The game of kissing the pope's toe had a one-performance revival when King Alfonso and Queen Victoria of Spain, being received by Pope Pius XI

on their visit to Rome, observed that ancient ceremony. On first reports of the mummery, a Catholic editor denied in violent language that it ever
was done, but the National Catholic News Service
confirmed the worst. The Catholic Citizen of Milwaukee stated: "American Catholics feel uncomfortable about such news." They had reason to be
sore after contending that stories of toe-kissing
were an invention of the enemies of God to injure
his church.

For The Truth Seeker of April 7 I accepted an
article by a certain Charles Smith on "Materialism or Idealism." Smith's next was on the subject
of "Selling Freethought in Forty-second Street,"
for he had turned newsman and specialized on The
Truth Seeker. Assisted by Mr. John Kewish, who
lectured at Columbus Circle, and Mr. Walter Merchant, who sold on the street, he ran the weekly
street sales up to above 800. All three of these
workers wrote for the paper, Walter Merchant being especially industrious with his pen. Crying and
selling the paper invited insult and abuse; arrest
occasionally and getting chased off the street quite
frequently.

The directors of the American Secular Union,
at the 1923 meeting, Chicago, February 28, elected
me president. Conscious of my unfitness for the
office and my inability to discharge its duties, I
was obliged to decline.

By the will of John Bryan, a Freethinker, who
died in Cincinnati, 1918, there were bequeathed to
the State of Ohio five hundred acres of forest and

meadow lands for a natural history preserve. But the will specified that there should never be any church or religious exercises on the grounds, and for that reason three governors—Davis, Cox and Donahey—successively vetoed acts of the state legislature accepting the gift. On May 2, 1923, the legislature repassed the bill over the veto of Governor Donahey. Mr. Bryan, who made this magnificent gift to the state of Ohio, was described as "typical of the poor boy become rich through work and thrift." His religion was hospitality, "he was intolerant of nothing but intolerance," and he was known for the open-door policy of his home.

Vesey street on its south side, for some two hundred feet west of Broadway, runs along the burying-ground of St. Paul's church. The absence of any business or traffic on that side of Vesey street made it a favorable spot for speaking if the orator could find vacant space between the parked automobiles. Evangelists pervaded the spot in 1923. Mr. John T. Kewish, Freethinker, also held forth there at the noon hour. Passersby and loiterers in the proportion of about two to one, preferred his talks to the exhortations of the evangelists, who were poor specimens of their kind.

The preachers, beaten at the game, prepared a letter to the mayor of the city charging Kewish with blasphemous discourse and with "scattering" a paper, The Truth Seeker, containing blasphemous printed matter. There was no action.

President Warren G. Harding died August 2, and left us Coolidge. An earthquake in Japan at the end of the month took a toll of 225,000 killed and 450,000 injured. Coolidge, who joined the church after Harding's death, called on the people of the United States, in his Thanksgiving proclamation, to assemble and thank God. The New York Times perceived and mentioned the delight of Mr. Coolidge "that God, having determined to smite somebody, passed over us and selected the friendly people of Japan."

I notice that in 1923 the Rt. Rev. Bishop Manning organized himself to purify the stage, for the cry had come up to him that, in some of the theatres, actresses were appearing nightly "not entirely surrounded by clothes." And then, before he could act, he read in the newspapers that in one of his own churches, dances in illustration and interpretation of certain joyous forms of pagan worship were being performed by barefooted girls. Investigating at once, Bishop Manning "learned that not only were the girls bare as to feet, but their costumes were so looped and windowed as to bring to the view of spectators and worshipers considerable expanses of hip and thigh." This at the old church of St. Mark's in the Bouwerie, and the innovations were the work of the Rev. William Norman Guthrie, pastor. It took Bishop Manning a year or more to effect the return of Guthrie to godliness and sobriety, for he fell into the company also of heretics and Infidels like Bishop William Montgomery Brown of Ohio, who was under charges.

DEPARTURES, 1923

In the 83d year of her age, Mrs. Eva A. Ingersoll, "a woman without superstition," to whom her husband, Robert G. Ingersoll dedicated his first published volume, "The Gods," died at her home, 117 East Twenty-first street, New York, Friday morning, February 2.

Mrs. Ingersoll, whose maiden name was Eva A. Parker, was born in Illinois in 1841. She was a descendant of the old Parker family of Massachusetts and came of a line of Freethinkers. She was married to Robert G. Ingersoll in February, 1862, when he was 28 years old and on the eve of joining the Union army. She was at that time and remained until death a Freethinker.

Eugene Hins, Belgian born, founder of *La Pensee,* dying at 84 years of age, was buried with distinguished honors at Ixelles, Belgium, Feb. 11. He had served long as secretary-general of the Federated Freethought Societies, and was honorary president at the time of his death.

The death of Herbert Tullson, of Grand Haven, Mich., in his 47th year, was a loss to Freethought, and a discouragement. Tullson was a student of science, a good writer, a Freethinker. He contributed more than fifty valuable articles to The Truth Seeker. His wife, Juna Tullson, had written four. A meteorologist of the U. S. Weather Bureau, he had spent most of his life in the service of the government. I paid tribute to him by saying that he would have made a good editor.

Over in Brooklyn died, May 12, a woman of about

EVA A. INGERSOLL, 1841-1923

"There is no home in America, into which Robert Ingersoll's words in behalf of women and children and the home life have penetrated, that does not owe her a debt of gratitude. No other life could bless her as she has blessed this. She has not gone to her reward. She had it in the fruits of her life here."—Dr. John Lovejoy Elliott.

75 years who never got aged and was still called by her first name by young and old. This was Mrs. Marie Andrews, wife of Charles, the son of Stephen Pearl, and her death took place on the fifty-third anniversary of their marriage. Said the notice in The Truth Seeker: "We have to place her with the Old Guard of Liberals, although she was one of the younger set, whose acquaintance The Truth Seeker made when it came to New York in 1874. Her house was the place where the young people of Liberal connections foregathered for their 'parties' forty years ago, and many of these, now grayheads themselves, never forgetting her nor by her forgotten, feel her death as a personal bereavement."

Emil Seidel, former mayor of Milwaukee, delivered the eulogy, May 15, at the funeral of Capt. James Larsen, one of those sturdy seafarers who come out of Denmark and strengthen our American citizenry. The Wisconsin legislature adopted resolutions or respect, and his nephew, Bennett Larson, praised him in the obituary notice we printed.

Other deaths of the year were those of J. C. Hannon, one of the founders of the Philadelphia Liberal League; Charles Proteus Steinmetz, Materialist, the leading genius of the electrical world, at Schenectady, N. Y., Oct. 26; and James A. MacKnight, Atlanta, Ga., Nov. 21, who had written much for the paper under the name of "Diogenes II."

This year died also the distinguished Rationalist, Rt. Hon. John Morley, Viscount of Blackburn,

Sept. 22, aged 85 years. A religious service was held over his body, and the London Freethinker said: "Nothing could be more disgusting than a clergyman mouthing a religious service over a man who believed in neither God nor a soul, who held that the whole of the Christian religion could be explained out of existence, and who looked forward to the race being one day civilized enough to replace the worship of God with the service of humanity."

The myth, previously connected with Huxley, is to be found in a late Life of Morley, saying that he once declared to a religious woman that he would give his right arm to be a believer in Christianity.

CHAPTER XXXV.

W RITING of a time so recent as 1924, it is fit that I begin with the after-dinner speaker's precaution: "Stop me if you have heard this one." But the events of 1924 will in a little while be ancient history, and the English I record them in may seem quaint for want of style, as Paine's was to his contemporaries because it contained no classic allusions. And the year was notable in some respects. You remember the Bishop Brown heresy trial—the papers were full of it. Rupert Hughes wrote his "Why I Quit Going to Church," accepted by the Cosmopolitan Magazine and then published by The Truth Seeker Company in a book. The American Rationalist Association came into existence, and so did the Science League of America. It was the tercentenary of New Amsterdam, which is to say New York, when Alfred E. Smith, Catholic governor of the state, was obliged to issue a proclamation in celebration of a great Protestant event. Mark Twain's Autobiography appeared. The Ku Klux Klan was at high tide and almost swamped the national Democratic convention. The Leopold-Loeb trial with Darrow for the defense still echoes. The Rev. Wil-

liam N. Guthrie, of St. Mark's, aggravated his previous offenses. One of his sermons later found its
way into The Truth Seeker, and he harbored the
heretic Bishop Brown. Bishop Manning took away
Guthrie's candlestick, excluded him from the ministrations of the church, contributions fell off, and
his efforts to instruct and amuse ended in failure
and surrender.

It must have embarrassed Mary, the wife of
Joseph, had she been living, to hear all the 1924
discussion over the paternity of her first child.
She would have asked: "Can't they let a poor girl
alone? Doesn't it often happen this way with the
first one?" The virgin-birth took the place of
Jonah and the whale as the test of orthodoxy.
Candidates for ordination were withholding assent
to the ghost-theory, and the New York Presbytery
was turning them down. I thought the candidates
too finicky on that point, for the virgin birth is as
easy to believe as anything else religious. "We are
persuaded," I wrote in an editorial paragraph,
"that the present denial of the virgin birth by certain
liberal theologians is a modern fad, like Dr. Guthrie's bare-legged and bare-hipped symbolical danc-
ers. Some have adopted the fad and some have
not. It is as unimportant as the question disputed
by Calvin and Servetus, whether Christ was the
eternal son of God or son of the eternal God. An
earnest believer should not feel bothered to yield
assent to either or both."

The heresy charges against Bishop William M.
Brown were made to stick, the trial being set for

May 27 in the Trinity Episcopal cathedral, Cleveland, Ohio. The defendant bishop said it would be the first trial in his church for heresy since the Reformation. His case differed from that of the English Bishop Colenso, whose book on "The Pentateuch" (1862) was condemned by the House of Convocation and its author deposed by the metropolitan. Colenso had no trial.

The report of the Bishop Brown trial is printed in The Truth Seeker of June 14; reviewed at length by Theodore Schroeder July 12. The case has a big literature—books and books, and newspaper articles numberless.

The Truth Seeker and the writings of its contributors were the efficient causes of Dr. Brown's loss of faith.

There were and are Freethinkers, David Eccles having been one, who distinguish between religion and that which passes current for it. The Truth Seeker, then, must define its position. The editor asked readers to understand that when this paper said religion it meant the thing that the Constitution forbade Congress to legislate about.

Years after 1924, the advocates of religious instruction in schools and other places still cite two youths named Leopold and Loeb as horrible examples of the output of a college where the theory of evolution is permitted to come to the notice of students. These two youths, of respectable Chicago families, kidnapped and killed a boy named Franks, and in excuse of their act averred they sought a "thrill."

Deducing Atheism from the education the boys had received in school, the godhoppers called Leopold and Loeb Atheists and laid their crime to unbelief and want of religious training. Yet as the sons of religious parents they had not missed such conventional religious training as that of the average youth. They were good students, advanced in heir studies, which fac' also was imputed to their alleged Atheism, used against them, and considered as further evidence that they were great monsters. But the reports that came from the boys in prison pictured them as turning their minds to philosophical disquisition, pointing to the skeptic only. They show the originator of them has had religious instruction.

The notoriety attending the crime, the trial and its principals, was due to elements injected by the ingenious Clarence Darrow, easily the most famous lawyer in the United States; and he an Infidel. Since the clergy have chosen to retain these young men as examples of the lack, as is pretended, of religious teaching and the inculcation of Modernist ideas, I see it is the duty of somebody to set off against this single recorded instance of atrocious crime committed by Atheist youths (such Atheists as they were), a few specimen crimes of religious persons—crimes, some of them, even actuated by religious belief. Two typical ones occurred that year in Florida, where a young man believing that he had in some manner sinned against the Holy Ghost. sacrificed first his young sisters by burning them up, and later expiated his offense against the Ghost. as he confessed, by killing his father and mother. A

Florida woman, having attended the meetings of a
faith-healing evangelist—one Richie, patronized by
the wife of William Jennings Bryan—"had her ail-
ing husband killed by her daughter because she was
not satisfied with the way he reacted to the healer's
ministrations." In the State of Illinois, town of Ina,
the Rev. L. M. Hight, a Methodist minister, supplied poison to the woman he desired, with which
she killed her husband, Wilford Sweeten, and murdered his own wife in the same way. He then had
the cynicism to preach the funeral sermon of the
slain man and to boast that it was he who had led to
Christ him they were now burying. These murders
by Hight, the clergyman, received some notice from
the press—not, however, to the prejudice of religion
or the clerical profession, but were cited, rather, as
proof *how rarely capital crimes were committed by
ministers!* A contributor to the New York World
named Rowland Thomas found "only four ministers involved in major crimes in a decade." As a
matter of fact, there were nearer forty—ten of
them in the two years then just passed.

In that two-year period the Rev. George Blocker
of Nevada got life imprisonment for killing his
wife; the Catholic priest Dillon of Kalamazoo,
Mich., received the same sentence for killing another priest; the Rev. J. J. Grady of Pittsburgh, Pa.,
a third priest, was "involved" in a murder charge;
a preacher named Lee of Milwaukee, Wis., was doing a life sentence for murder; the Catholic priest
(No. 4) John J. Mullin of Chicago, killed a man and
was charged with murder; the Rev. Basil Stetsuk,
Greek Catholic, Chicago (priest No. 5), was killed

592 FIFTY YEARS OF FREETHOUGHT [1924

in a fight with another priest; at Hiawatha, Kan.,
the Rev. T. P. Stewart killed his wife; the Rev.
A. C. Pennington, Natchitoches, La., murdered a
man with a shotgun, and the Rev. A. Q. Burns of
Mexico, Mo., was so involved in a shooting that he
was held in $5,000 bail. Add Hight of Illinois, and
there were ten in two years. To see how past
years averaged with '22-'24, I scanned the volume
"Crimes of Preachers," and found that in forty
years ministers had done 167 murders, an average
of more than four a year.

The Christian religion has no valid excuse to be,
unless the account of the fall of man in the book
of Genesis is historical; and then not in this life or
on this earth except as the time and place to round
up the victims. The glorious Eve broke the first
command laid upon Adam—she wasn't there herself when the command was delivered—and so was
divinely permitted to plaster future generations
with that reprobation which her act of self-expres-
sion caused us all to fall under. The Christian religion began right there. Through another woman
not so glorious, a second Adam was born to take
the curse off; and unless Christianity can turn that
trick of taking off the curse, then Christianity is a
false alarm. I discover no grounds for denying the
affirmation of the son: "He that believeth not shall
be damned," or for doubting that by belief the situation may be reversed. The idea is too idiotic for
words. I merely contend that religion isn't good for
anything else. For religion is not morality, it is not
virtue, nor honesty, nor education. No virgin ever

conceived and bore a son to exemplify any ethical principles, which one may have and hold from his youth up while free from any taint of religion whatsoever. Hence the exasperation induced when persons gifted with voices but no discrimination talk of religion and morality as though they were hatched out of the same egg. Religion is not the moral code but is viewed as a substitute; the churches inject religion and never were known to teach pure morals.

There is a chance that when these muddlers force the morality card on the bystander they do so with a purpose. Assigning morality to religion provides an excuse for tolerating that which of itself has no merit unless, as I have said, believing in religion really makes the difference between being saved and being damned, which is a fundamental of Christianity; and when an informed and intelligent person says that he accepts this and the other fundamentals of Christianity as true and all its childish, vicious, or monstrous fables as factual, I take the liberty of doubting his word. I think he is lying. As Huxley framed the proposition, he "has the opportunity to know, and therefore is bound to know," that the Christian religion spreads falsities both ways from the middle—from the fabulous birth of Jesus backward and forward.

One scanning the volume for 1924 checks upon the margin of the pages a few of the incidents more or less notable. The November, 1923, number of the organ of Rationalism in Australia, conducted by R. S. Ross and called "Ross's," had announced its suspension after eight years.

The Rationalist Forum, Charles Calhoun, editor, Los Angeles, Cal., began with the year. This little magazine is still issued in 1930. Editor Calhoun is more than one hundred years old.

The answer of George Santayana, a man of science and professor of philosophy, to the Questionnaire, appeared February 2. Dr. Santayana observed that religion, so far as it professed to be an account of matters of fact, was "entirely fabulous."

A gathering in Chicago, February 3, launched the American Rationalist Association; Percy Ward, president; Franklin Steiner, secretary. The list of officers included Judge L. A. Stebbins, Bessie Novak and Harry Wirth Meltzer. Judge Stebbins and Mr. Meltzer, with the sturdy Steiner as secretary and F. W. Coleman as treasurer, are still on the board. The president in 1929-30 was the Hon. Spencer M. DeGolier, mayor of Bradford, Pa.

From Sendai, Japan, Yoshiro Oyama reported that some time previously he had organized a native Rationalist and Freethought Association and started a small paper entitled "Junri" as the organ of the movement. Oyama went abroad looking for support, and in his absence the earthquake of Sept. 1, 1923, demolished his house and library.

The Libertarian League at Los Angeles, headed by Charles T. Sprading, and with a distinguished list of contributors, published a few numbers of its magazine, The Libertarian, "devoted to the principle of equal liberty for all."

The Board of Directors of the American Secular Union held a meeting on May 1.

From the year 1922 Mr. William Plotts of Los

Angeles county, California, fought an appropriation of $20,000 voted by the county supervisors for the production of a religious play or pageant. He failed to get the court decisions in his favor but caused the payment of the money to be held up until the occasion for spending it had passed.

Meetings of the Brooklyn Philosophical Society, one of our oldest Freethought organizations, were suspended. The society had taken root at the hall of the Long Island Business College, but having an open platform it was unable to control the utterances of propagandists with no stake either in the country or in Freethought, and had been forced on that account to change its quarters.

The reviewers of Mark Twain's Autobiography, published in two volumes by the Harpers, passed unmentioned the author's irreverences and profanities. These "outstanding" features of the work The Truth Seeker alone quoted. Clemens dissipated the halo of piety thrown about Grant by Parson Newman, and performed other similar services for the general's memory. He was a born unbeliever, like his daughter Susie, who stopped saying her prayers, and to her mother explained: "Well, mama, the Indians believed they knew, but now we know they were wrong. By and by it can turn out that we are wrong. So now I only pray that there may be a God and a heaven—*or something better.*"

A letter by William Herndon to B. F. Underwood, the Freethought lecturer, turned up in an auction room and sold for $345. Nobody concerned knew who Underwood was until Van der Weyde of the Paine Association referred the inquirers to The

Truth Seeker office. The letter stated that "Mr. Lincoln was an Infidel in the very best sense of that abused word. . . . Lincoln was an Infidel and so died." In the 1880s Herndon was a contributor to The Truth Seeker, his subject being Lincoln. If that Underwood letter was worth $345, his Truth Seeker manuscript, had I possessed the sense to preserve it, would in 1924 have fetched a fortune.

In the fall Superintendent Preston Harding of the Perry County, Indiana, Public Schools invited Marshall Gauvin to deliver five lectures before the Teachers' Institute at Tell City, the series to close with an illustrated lecture on Evolution. The local clergy, with a rising temperature, allowed Gauvin to speak four times, and then successfully joined forces to prevent the fifth lecture. Gauvin yielded so far as to change the subject, but announced a lecture on another theme and invited all the ministers to attend. Mrs. Gauvin transcribed his words and The Truth Seeker had them for October 18. That speech—which got the clerical hide and nailed it to the barn door—ranks among the great ones. A man who had made one as good could afford to have it printed in a book and trust it to vindicate forever his reputation as an orator.

California Fundamentalists agitated for the exclusion from the schools of some fifty textbooks that recognized Evolution. Maynard Shipley of San Francisco appealed through The Truth Seeker for assistance in forming a nucleus to fight Fundamentalism. The nucleus became the Science League of America.

MARSHALL J. GAUVIN.

Bennett Larson, the Milwaukee attorney, who was born into The Truth Seeker family and named after its founder, addressed a large meeting in opposition to a resolution before the local school board "designed to place the pupils in charge of religious teachers." It was another of those speeches on which a man's reputation for ability might rest. I do not know of any cause that has abler expositors than the one known as "the best of all," that is, Freethought.

The advocates of religion in school are persistent. Not a juvenile criminal is apprehended but they lay his delinquency to want of religious training and blame secular schools; and this when the offenders have had the best of parochial or Sunday-school training. I would suggest, as an experiment, allowing these advocates a few schools, and then charging all the crimes their pupils ever commit to the religious training they have received there. If secular schools, or schools where evolution is taught, are to be held as the cause of all the offenses their pupils may sometime be guilty of, then it cannot be otherwise than just to fasten upon religion the guilt of all criminals who have had religious training.

These Bible bawds and invaders of the schools with their synthetic religious instruction, regardless of law, were first called "religion bootleggers" by Charles Smith in The Truth Seeker.

It was not a very good year for arrests. Charles Smith's numbered three, for selling The Truth Seeker, and he was once fined. John T. Kewish, addressing a Labor Day outdoor meeting, had a brief session with a magistrate on complaint of a man too ignorant to know the meaning of the terms he used. The court ridiculed the charge, reprimanded the complainant, and dismissed the case.

The Ingersoll house at 117 Gramercy Park (or East Twenty-first street), once occupied by Courtlandt Palmer and the famous Nineteenth Century Club, and the home of the Ingersolls since 1894, fell into the hands of the wreckers in December. Mrs. Ingersoll had owned the house, and dying there, willed it to her daughter Maud (Mrs. Probasco). Offered a sum that could not reasonably be refused, Maud disposed of the premises and bought at 72 Irving Place, which shelters the remaining members of the Ingersoll family.

The Thomas Paine National Historical Association celebrated the 187th birthday at the Fifth Avenue restaurant, with Norman Thomas for the best eulogist. Mr. Thomas, 1928 Socialist candidate for President and for mayor of New York in 1929, accepted Paine as a potential economic reformer of the Socialist school. I recalled the instance, many years before, when a speaker was assigned to talk at one of our celebrations, on "Paine as a Socialist," while young Dr. Foote was to discuss him as a Humorist. The doctor made out fairly well, but the other was obliged to default. He said he had read Paine through without discovering a trace of Socialism.

A reorganization of the Thomas Paine Monument Association of Chicago, forty years old, was reported. As a testimony to the faithfulness of the original trustees the following record should be preserved:

Early in the year 1880 Colonel Ingersoll gave the proceeds of lecture, amounting to $1,300, to this cause. An association to take charge of the fund and carry out its

object was formed. The members were I. N. Stiles, Hervey
W. Booth, Van Buren Denslow, Christian Wahl, Gerhard
C. Paoli, George A. Shufeldt, Christian S. Engle, L.
Marshall Beck, George F. Westover, Burton Sewell, Her-
bert Darlington, H. D. Garrison, Christopher Hotz, Bronson
C. Keeler, and Ernest Prussing—all Freethinkers and most
of them known to Truth Seeker readers in their day.
Two of them, Denslow and Keeler, were authors. Forty-
four years later, that is, in February, 1924, the following
despatch appeared in the New York Tribune:

"Chicago, Feb. 9.—Fourteen directors who had charge
of a fund of $1,300 raised in 1880 from Robert G. Ingersoll's
lecture to start a fund for a monument to Thomas Paine
have died since the Paine Monument Association was
formed on March 3, 1880. The fund has grown to $4,300
and the Circuit Court, on petition today of the surviving
director, Harrison Darlington, appointed fourteen more to
fill up the list and 'cooperate with Darlington to carry into
effect the purpose for which the organization was char-
tered.' "

One of the New York papers, publishing a symposium of religion, nominated the editor of The
Truth Seeker to "sketch briefly from a Freethought
point of view the difference between the Fundamentalists and Modernists." While I was concentrating on the theme a Vermont subscriber submitted the following, which I understood him to vouch
for as authentic, to wit: An officer in the navy
was lecturing to a body of sailors. "Perhaps," he
said, "you men, not having been on land for some
time, have not heard about the Fundamentalists
and the Modernists in religion and their differences
of opinion. I will illustrate. Take the matter of
the finding of Moses by Pharaoh's daughter. The
Fundamentalist says: 'That is a fact. She found

the child among the flags, just as scripture asserts.'
The Modernist says: 'That was the lady's story.'"

I wrote for the newspaper symposium the matter requested, and the publisher paid me ten dollars for about twenty lines (for I never was pro-
lix till I began writing these Memoirs). The voluntary contribution of the Vermont subscriber was
worth much more.

President James Wood of the American Bible
Society worked off this howler on Henry Ford's
Dearborn Independent:

"Queen Victoria struck at the heart of the whole matter
forty years ago when Li Hung Chang, Chinese ambassador
of the old Manchu dynasty, came to her saying:

"'Your Majesty, the Emperor of China has sent me to
inquire of you what has made your nation so great?'

"And the Queen replied, laying her hand on the Bible,
'This Book.'"

Regarding this piety tale, Mr. George H. Townsend of Dundas, Canada, wrote early in 1925 that
he knew it to be "an unmitigated lie made out of
whole cloth. This knowledge came to me," said
Mr. Townsend, "by way of a Montreal daily paper.
It was in the late '90's, I think, that I noticed two
letters in this Montreal paper. The first was to the
late Queen Victoria. It recounted the story and
asked for verification. The second was the answer from Sir Henry Ponsonby, then private secretary to the Queen. He stated that the matter
had been referred to her Majesty and that he was
instructed to reply that her Majesty had informed
him that the story had no foundation in fact and
that the incident had not occurred."

Politics boiled with religious heat. The politicians fought shy of taking sides: the religious editors, Catholics especially, did not. They called for an anti-Ku-Klux-Klan plank in the Democratic platform. They urged the nomination of Alfred E. Smith for President, and Mr. Smith placed himself in the hands of his friends. The nominee John W. Davis, a Presbyterian, was credited with quoting from Jean Paul Richter, this:

"There will come a time when it shall be light; and when man shall awaken from his lofty dreams and find his dreams still true, and that nothing had gone save his sleep."

What use has the country for a President literary enough to quote that high-brow stuff that was caviar to the general and "a lot of boloney" to Al Smith, who never read a book? The nation rejected Judge Davis on election day.

THE DEPARTURES OF 1924.

B. C. Murray, a newspaper man of Denison, Texas, lived to be 87. He had published the Denison News, begun in 1872, and ten years later the Denison Gazetteer, the latter being as much a Freethought as a local paper. He was the wise man of the town. His funeral eulogist, Judge W. S. Pearson, remarked that the "deceased was a man free from the blight of superstition, antique fables, and mythological fictions."

Prof. G. W. Bowne, almost ten years a contributor to The Truth Seeker, and for eight years an associate editor, suffered a stroke of apoplexy on March 23, and lived only until the next day. He was about 70 years old. He came of an ancient family, for an ancestor was a former mayor of New York, and one of the city streets bears his name. G. W. Bowne had been Episcopal minister, a convert to Catholicism, and an instructor in a Jesuit college; but his change to Rationalism was complete, and he died an Atheistic Materialist.

A nationally known Freethinker departed the company of his fellow unbelievers when Dr. T. J. Bowles of Muncie, Indiana, accepted the inevitable, April 19. Dr. Bowles was 87 years old. He had been a Freethinker, a contributor to the Freethought press, a lecturer and officer of Freethought societies, for so many years that few can remember when he was not prominent in those activities. He was the oldest practicing physician in Indiana, the state in which he was born, July 24, 1836. In the year of his death, knowing he was too ill to recover, Dr. Bowles dictated his "last words to The Truth Seeker," reaffirming the views he had stated for a generation through its pages. He was a Boanerges on the platform, and almost a son of thunder with his pen. Those who knew him personally testified that he was the gentlest of physicians and friends.

Walter Merchant, born in Mississippi in 1875, reared in Texas and Oklahoma in the Methodist communion, by turn farmhand, grocer's clerk, jockey, came out of Methodism into the "anarchism" of the Emma Goldman school, not really finding himself until he found The Truth Seeker, which he began selling on the street when Charles Smith set the fashion. That was his final work, and the record says that "in speaking for the last time he mentioned The Truth Seeker." He wrote well and industriously. His life never got off to a good start, but he made it count in the end.

I have given space to John Russell Coryell—so far back in this work that he must have passed from the reader's memory, as he had from mine, when he died in July, 1924. Coryell apparently had receded from the radicalism of his younger days, when he held the state no higher than the church, and called the church a reactionary conservator of old ignorance. The Nick Carter stories and Bertha M. Clay novels that he wrote had gone out of fashion, and he was editing magazines for Bernarr Macfadden at the end, when he was 76.

A native of Germany, born there in 1859; forty years later one of America's most distinguished and original scientists; the friend of Ernst Haeckel; Monist, Freethinker and Materialist; an attendant at the Hamburg congress in 1911, sending his address there to The Truth Seeker; sometimes in 1913-14 coming to meetings of the Freethought Society in Bryant Hall; one who applied the scientific principle of animal automatism to unreflecting human beings, and so accounted for mass delusion —that, and more, was Jacques Loeb, who died in Hamilton, Bermuda, the 11th of February. His eulogist, Paul de Kruif, observed that it was "not surprising to find he was not religious in the ordinary sense." He was not religious in any sense that I could detect.

CHAPTER XXXVI
(1925)

THE date at the head of the chapter is the latest one regularly included in these Memoirs; for, besides being the year of American Independence the one hundred and forty-ninth, this is the fiftieth year of my mustering-in. And Fifty Years are all that is nominated in the bond. A half century is all that the title of the debenture calls for; and could that year's predictions of the Christers have been believed, it is all the time there was to be; for the date of the end of the world had been set, on good Second-Advent authority, as early in 1925 as the sixth day of the second month—February.

The believers made preparations for meeting the Lord in the air on two sides of the globe—at Sydney, Australia, and then again at Patchogue, Long Island, N. Y. In Sydney they built a pavilion and sold seats; and purchasers, they promised, would see Christ "walking on the water from Southead towards Balmoral across the entrance of the harbor."

News of the near end came to New York from Los Angeles, where a prophetess of doom arose who bore the name of Rowen. The Patchogue disciple, one Reidt, warned New York by driving up Broadway in a Ford car, exposing a large sign which plainly read: "Prepare to meet thy God."

The first second coming known to Christian annals is predicted at Matthew xvi, 28, where "Christ" says that "some standing here" —persons within the sound of his voice—should witness his return. At 2 Peter iii, 4, the scribe quotes the sarcastic inquiry of a scoffer: "Where is the promise of his coming? for since the fathers fell asleep all things continue as they were from the beginning of the creation."

Throughout the Christian ages, anyone who wanted to catch suckers on this end-of-the-world proposition has had a good season's fishing. They never have had to change the bait.

The astronomers contributed somewhat to the mental disturbance of persons suffering with a belief in Christ's return, by predicting an eclipse of the sun, to occur two weeks before the prophets had dated the second coming.

No one could complain that the astronomers did not put on a perfectly successful show and present all the features they had promised. After the reliability of prediction had been demonstrated by the eclipse, anything might happen. A man who employed a Catholic stenographer told me the girl grew nervous as the 6th of February and the last days came nigh. He assured her no one could possibly tell when the end of the world would happen; but, said she: "They told when the eclipse would happen, and it did."

The heresy trial of Bishop Brown of Galion,

Ohio, went on to a finish. The Episcopal Court of Review, sitting in Cleveland, rendered the verdict January 15: "It is the judgment of this court that you, William Montgomery Brown, should be deposed from the sacred ministry." The Bishop was 70 years old. At 28 he had been a deacon, and a priest of the Episcopal church two years later; and he was rector at Galion till 1891. About that time they consecrated him bishop coadjutor of Arkansas. He resigned from that office on account of bad health in 1912. As regards his religious heresies, which shortly developed, they ran about like this:

"There is no rational doubt about the fictitious character of the divine Jesus."

"Jehovah is the sun-myth rewritten to fit in with the ideals and hopes of the owning master class of the Christians."

"The birth, death, descension, resurrection and ascension of all the savior-gods, not excepting Jesus, are versions of the sun-myth."

"Both the Old and New Testaments are utterly worthless as history."

In the fall of 1925 Bishop Brown got his case before the House of Bishops at New Orleans, and was then definitely deposed.

Concerning the Oregon school law of 1922 which was adjudicated upon this year (1925), Governor Pierce of that state laid down the proposition, which appears to be arguable, that "if a state cannot compel certain children to attend public schools, it cannot compel any children to do so."

The United States Supreme Court held otherwise in its decision of June 1. Having granted an injunction to keep the law from going into effect, the Court pronounced the Oregon school law invalid on the ground, so far as I can make out, that its provisions interfered with the Catholic sisters' remunerative business of conducting religious schools.

COUNSEL IN THE SCOPES TRIAL
Mr. Darrow was retained by the defense

The Court, as we see illustrated in its approval of a number of meddlesome statutes, may go into the states to attack and destroy liberty, religious or personal, but not to shield.

Tennessee's illustrious anti-evolution statute, since known as the Monkey Law, came into being in 1925. Following is its caption and text:

"Public Act, Chapter 37, 1925. An act prohibiting the teaching of the evolution theory in all the universities, normals, and all the public schools of Tennessee which are supported in whole or in part by the public school funds of the State, and to prescribe penalties for the violation thereof.

"Section 1. Be it enacted by the General Assembly of the State of Tennessee, That it shall be unlawful for any teacher in any of the universities, normal and all other public schools in the State, which are supported in whole or in part by the public school funds of the State, to teach any theory that denies the story of the divine creation of man as taught in the Bible, and to teach instead that man has descended from a lower order of animals.

"Section 2. Be it further enacted, That any teacher found guilty of the violation of this act shall be guilty of a misdemeanor and upon conviction shall be fined not less than $100 and not more than $500 for each offense.

"Section 3. Be it further enacted, That this act take effect from and after its passage, the public welfare requiring it."

The governor of the state of Tennessee, Peay by name, was reported to have said when he signed the Act that no prosecutions would take place under it. He no doubt understood the purpose of the Fundamentalist forces which had procured its enactment. That purpose was to make use of the law in weeding out candidates for teachers' jobs—

hiring only those pledged not to teach evolution. That would give the Fundamentalists complete control of the Tennessee schools. The arrest in May of John T. Scopes, science teacher in the Rhea County High School, on complaint of the opponents of the law, was for a test of its constitutionality. George W. Rappelyea, a chemical engineer and advocate of evolution, who had the warrant issued, stated that the American Civil Liberties Union would furnish financial backing to defend the case and appeal it. Scopes retained a former dean of the University of Tennessee Law School, Judge Randolph Neal, who had felt impelled to resign when six professors of as many sciences were displaced because one had ordered for his class a consignment of James Harvey Robinson's "Mind in the Making." The Civil Liberties Union retained Clarence Darrow, while William Jennings Bryan, who had once been a lawyer, consented to represent the World's Christian Fundamental Association as chief religious prosecutor.

Some of the newspapers reported the Scopes trial as a comedy, others as a tragedy. One called it a "comical tragedy." In the presiding judge, John T. Raulston, when the case opened at Dayton, July 10, they had a man accustomed to exhort at revivals. He opened court by reading the Bible, while clergymen present were invited to offer prayer. Clarence Darrow (Chicago), John R. Neal (Knoxville, Tenn.), and Dudley Field Malone and Arthur Garfield Hays (New York) stood for the defense.

William Smith Bryan, who reported the proceedings for The Truth Seeker, predicted in his first communication that Scopes would be convicted. It was no trial, but an inquisition; and of William Jennings Bryan, who looked on, he wrote: "His frozen smile, his beak of a nose, the narrow slit across the face which serves the purpose of a mouth, his deepset glittering eyes, his high, narrow forehead, and that tremendous chin which clamps like the jaws of a steel trap, unite in revealing him as the reincarnation of an ancient inquisitor. All that is wanting to complete the picture is the chained victim and the glare of the lighted fagots." The testimony of scientists was not allowed to go before the jury.

William Jennings Bryan consented to be examined by Darrow as a witness, July 20. The questions and answers, which filled six wide columns of

THE ANTI-EVOLU-
TION FACE OF
WILLIAM
JENNINGS BRYAN.
PICTURE TAKEN
AT THE SCOPES
TRIAL

The Truth Seeker in the smaller type (August 5), were on the Bible. Darrow years before had invited Bryan to answer a series of questions on the Bible; now he had an opportunity to put them and insist upon answers. As a result of his inability to cope with superior knowledge and a keener intellect, the witness Bryan suffered humiliation and loss of respect. And he died there in Dayton, of "heart disease," July 27.

They found Scopes guilty and fined him $100. Appeals were futile. While England poked fun at America, a London correspondent of the New York Times discovered something like the Scopes case in the English town of Bootle, where the town council disciplined a local teacher who had suggested that the Adam and Eve story might be mythical. The London Literary Guide described a case much like ours that took place in 1907, in which a reference to "the Darwinian theory of evolution" constituted the offense of a school mistress "engaged in a small village in the West Riding of Yorkshire." Mr. Cohen of The Freethinker saw many parallels in the past, and supposed the reason why English school teachers were not disciplined for the offense of Scopes was because they did not commit it by teaching evolution in a way to "deny the story of the divine creation of man as taught in the Bible."

The District of Columbia, it soon transpired, had a law, passed by both houses of Congress, whereby any school "superintendent, assistant superintendent, director of intermediate instruction, or supervising principal who permits the teaching of disrespect of the Holy Bible" can be penalized by withholding his pay; none of the appropriation for the support of the schools is available for the payment of salaries of such offenders.

A government employee in Washington named Witner, learning that evolution was taught in the District schools, attempted by instituting a suit to stop the pay of the school officials. The courts decided Witner hadn't sufficient interest as a taxpayer. Moreover, he was an Atheist; it turned out he had not taken the required oath when appointed, and might be removed.

April 15 a tree was planted with appropriate ceremonies, at Riverside Park, near the Grant tomb, to the memory of Ingersoll; John L. Elliott of the Ethical Culture Society making the address and reading Ingersoll's "Vision of the Future." A more elaborate ceremony is reported in The Truth Seeker of November 21.

An upper floor of the lofty new hotel at 52 Gramercy Park, North, in this city, contains rooms that duplicate one of the floors in the house, 117 East Twenty-first street, that was the old home of Robert G. Ingersoll. The site of the new hotel covers the ground upon which the Ingersoll house stood, and conspicuously upon its front there is now this tablet in bronze:

On This Site Was the Home of
ROBERT G. INGERSOLL
"He knew no fear except the fear of doing wrong."
Born August 11, 1833.   Died July 21, 1899.

On the afternoon of Monday, November 9, the tablet was unveiled. The date was the 125th anniversary of the birth of Ingersoll's mother, Mary Livingston Ingersoll. Dr. Elliott presiding, paid tribute to the beautiful home life and domestic virtues of the Agnostic. Former Senator Charles S. Thomas of Colorado, who in 1899 delivered a noble speech on Ingersoll's death, was again his eulogist.

Paine Memorial Day proceedings took place at New Rochelle, the scene being a plot of ground, formerly belonging to the Paine farm, which the Thomas Paine National Historical Society had acquired for a Memorial Building; and the feature of the gathering of about a thousand persons was the breaking of ground for this building by Thomas A. Edison. Mr. Edison made no address,

IN HONOR OF PAINE.

The persons in the front row are, left to right (standing) President van der Weyde; (seated) Dr. Muzzey, Edison, and Mr. Thomas.

his sentiments being expressed in a letter he had
written, read there by President van der Weyde. A
piece of sod had been loosened and a small American flag planted beside it.   To this Mr. Edison,
spade in hand, moved with sprightly step.   In
his handling of the shovel there was revealed no
want of skill, and the sod was turned with a motion that showed the hand is quicker than the eye.
The speakers that day were Harry Scott, mayor
of New Rochelle; the Quaker Dr. John Franklin
Brown, a professor of philosophy; David Saville
Muzzey, Columbia history professor, and Norman
Thomas, who was to be candidate for president in
1928, and for mayor of New York in 1929.

Joseph Wheless of New York, one of the few
in "Who's Who" describing themselves as a Freethinker, wrote in 1925 his antibiblical book: "Is
It God's Word?" to be followed, after five years
added research, by "Forgery in Christianity." This
author, who is a member of the law staff of one
of our biggest utility corporations, is a Ten-
nesseean by birth (1868), and ranked as major
and judge advocate, on duty at Chicago, during the
World War.

Rupert Hughes, novelist, playwright and historian, living in Hollywood, California, contributed
articles to The Truth Seeker in 1925.   We had
published his book, "Why I Quit Going to Church,"
a perfect twentieth century "Age of Reason,"
which drew the fire of people who resented criticism of their faith.   His articles in The Truth
Seeker were his replies to them.

Through Laurence B. Stein, a taxpayer, Joseph

Lewis, president of the Freethinkers' Society, brought suit to enjoin the board of Mt. Vernon, N. Y., from dismissing public school children to attend religious instructions forty-five minutes each

JOSEPH WHELESS.

He has written "Is It God's Word?" and "Forgery in Christianity."

week. Mr. Stein set forth that this proceeding and the participation of the teachers in it constituted an illegal diversion and waste of public funds. The Teachers' Union of New York passed resolutions declaring that the injection of religion into public school administration would "paralyze the trunk nerve of education." The week-day church school, promoted by the clergy, was wanted by neither pupils nor teachers.

The Mt. Vernon battle, contested before Justice Albert F. Seeger of the Supreme Court of Westchester county, went to the Freethinkers. In his decision, June 22, Justice Seeger said:

"The Education law, Section 620, describes the instructions required in public schools. Religious instruction is not one of them. Consequently it is UNLAWFUL AND UNAUTHORIZED for a Board of Education to substitute religious instruction in the schools in place of the instruction required.

"If it is necessary or advisable that such instruction be given on school days, each day is long enough for such instruction without encroaching on school hours."

The court granted Mr. Stein the prayed for injunction, applicable to all the schools of the county. This was during vacation. Litigation went on until the case for secular education was lost in the state courts at Albany.

Three governors of Ohio vetoed a legislative measure that accepted from the Freethinker John Bryan, deceased, $50,000 worth of land near Yellow Springs for a Natural History Reserve with the stipulation that no public religious service should ever be held on it. Judge Scarlett of Franklin county validated the will. The last of the vetoing governors, Donahey, argued that the state was a "community temple" that would be desecrated by a spot where God could not be worshiped publicly. "Let us see," he exhorted, "that it reaches our children unprofaned." It shows a mystery that following shortly after this expression, Governor Donahey's own son, eighteen years of age, committed a misdemeanor and spent three days in jail.

Any father whose sons go wrong and are a disgrace to him has my sympathy, even if he is a religious hypocrite, or a canting Fundamentalist minister. The sons of Freethinking parents grow up under the scrutiny of religious communities. The heathen in the Far East would hear of it if one of these were to commit a crime. In 1925, in the town where I have lived since 1900, two boys of good families scandalized the community by giving liquor to a girl of 18 and deflowering her. Were they the boys whom I had raised with no knowledge of religion except what they might get from parents who had none? They were not. *They were sons of orthodox ministers.*

Dr. A. Wakefield Slaten, dismissed in 1922 as a heretic from William Jewell College, in Missouri, spoke in April, 1925, as president of the Pacific Coast Conference of Unitarian Churches, in favor of fraternal relations between Unitarians and Rationalists. In October he succeeded the Rev. Charles Francis Potter as pastor of the West Side Unitarian church in New York. Dr. Potter was leaving the pulpit, as he said, because of the futility of preaching. The church under Dr. Slaten retained its denominational title, to which was added "Humanist." His ministry, though radical to members not prepared to accept The Truth Seeker along with his discourses printed in it, was a four years' success. Then something untoward happened which caused his resignation, and farewells were said.

Events allowed to pass with small comment, as they were things to be expected with the rotation of the earth, were: The meeting of the American Secular Union in January and the re-election of Marshall Gauvin. Georg Brandes, Denmark's great man, published his "Legend of Jesus," placing the Christian savior in the category of myths with William Tell, and Lovisa Brunzell translated a digest of the work for The Truth Seeker (June 13). From Germany came the announcement that Prof. Hubert Grimm of Munster had deciphered certain tablets long since discovered by the English scholar, Flinders Petrie, in the Sinai peninsula, and identified them as the original of the ten commandments, supposed to be those named in Exodus xxxi, 18—"tablets of stone, written with the finger of God"; but no one got excited over the thought that the world now had specimens of God's handwriting. Henry L. Harris, Jr., first lieutenant U. S. Army, retired, of Pacific Grove, California, wrote excellent articles as a Truth Seeker contributor.

B. E. Leavens, Toronto, reported lectures by E. V. Sterry. The Freethinkers of the Canadian city organized a Rationalist Society. Sterry began publishing a small paper on Christian evidences, and later was imprisoned for blasphemy. M. Canova, member of the Swiss National Council, was convicted of blasphemy and fined two hundred francs at Coire for saying God is a "scoundrel." A bill, noble in motive, was introduced in the California legislature by Assemblyman S. V. Wright to tax all churches employed for political purposes. A week-day church school bill (religious education) was defeated in Indiana. The Hon. F. D. Cummings, in the Maine House of Representatives, discussing an amendment leading to the use of public funds for sectarian purposes, made an eloquent and argumentative address on "Separation of Church and State" (published in The Truth Seeker April 18 and 25).

The International Freethought Congress was to have met in Rome, in 1925, but as reported in The Journal of Charleroi, a Belgian daily, "the regime of Fascist terror would not permit," and the International Committee chose Paris, where the event came off in August. Libby Culbertson Macdonald, as delegate, represented American societies. A note of November 7:

"M. M. Mangasarian, for many years the successful lecturer for the Independent Religious Society of Chicago, has retired from the platform and taken up his residence in Piedmont, Cal."

Charles Smith, Freeman Hopwood and Woolsey Teller organized the American Association for the Advancement of Atheism, giving its aims, supported by argument, "as purely destructive." A justice named Mitchell denied the association a certificate of incorporation on account of its purpose. The incorporators took their application elsewhere, and before Justice John Ford of the Supreme Court (November 16) were successful. Mr. Smith left the employ of The Truth Seeker for the presidency of the new organization. He is a man with no sense that enables him to detect defeat. He has lectured and been hissed, debated and lost the decision, taken the aggressive and been repulsed, agitated and landed in jail, talked Atheism and been convicted of blasphemy, attempted the enlightenment of a prophet of God and been fined for his pains. And he thinks the Four-A will win the world.

"Scurrilous and blasphemous reference to the Queen of Heaven and her Divine Son" set the Catholic press going against the Curtis publications. These were the publications, including the Public Ledger of Philadelphia and the Evening Post of New York, both dailies, issued by Cyrus H. K. Curtis, and they printed passages from a book on the Philippines, "The Isles of Fear," by Katherine Mayo. According to Miss Mayo, family relations among Filipino Catholics were complex. On the testimony of a physician, "the children of girls of 12 or 14 not seldom belong to their own brothers, fathers or uncles." Miss Mayo stated that such moral breaches were by no means approved by the church, which still resented criticism. One priest, for instance, said in palliation: "When the Queen of Heaven, according to official count, has three synchronous spouses, one of whom is her own Son, why should the spirit of mortal be proud and assume a stricter virtue? If things stand that way ın heaven, why should mortals try to improve upon them?"

The relations of Jesus, Jehovah and the Virgin Mary are admittedly a Question. Jesus said that **he** and his father were one, that is, he was God; **and** God being the common father of mankind, and hence the father of Mary, he was grandfather to Jesus; and Jesus, as God, was Mary's father as well as her son; and being one also with the Holy Ghost, by whom he was begotten, he was his own father, besides being consort of his mother. Moreover, as Mary is queen of heaven and God the **king**, the relation of husband and wife is implied; **and** Jesus and the Holy Ghost each being God, she would have three husbands after a manner of speaking.

In order that a Christian may be saved it is essential that he believe that each of the persons of the Trinity is God. Mary is the Queen of Heaven; God is the King, and Jesus and the Holy Ghost are God. What is true of God is true of them. If he is now her spouse, which it is not unorthodox to affirm, how are they anything else?

The son of Mary rose from the grave and ascended to the father in the flesh. The assumption of Mary herself, according to Catholic belief which is soon likely to be confirmed by a papal dogma, means that she attained heaven with the same personality that distinguished her as the mother of Jesus and husband of Joseph. How did the unlettered Filipino priest, taught that Cain married his sister and that the patriarch who begot offspring by his daughters was "delivered" by God and called "just Lot," know what kind of relations were dispensed with in heaven?

When The Truth Seeker tried so to untangle the relations of the heavenly family as to make Miss Mayo's offense look less like "an appalling sacrilege against the supreme sanctities of the Catholic faith," a Romanist contemporary quoted my demonstration and shouted:

"Here is the first and ONLY word ever uttered by any publication on earth in extenuation of the Curtis-Mayo-Ledger offense to religious decency. . . .   Surely Cyrus H. K. Curtis, Katherine Mayo, and The Public Ledger ought to be proud of their one, single, and ONLY defender—THE TRUTH SEEKER. All the rest of the world stands aghast at their infamy."

Miss Mayo apologized.   Perhaps Mr. Curtis appeased the raging editors with a present; and for a time he was so cautious about stirring up the Catholics with sacrilege against their sanctities that he forbade his reporters to call the St. Louis ball team (who may be so named because its members illustrate the seven deadly virtues) the Cardinals.

Mr. Archibald C. Weeks, having deciphered some seventeenth century records of the town of Brookhaven, Long Island, submitted the following pointer as to how the boys and girls were carrying themselves two hundred and fifty years ago as compared with their activities in this loose age:

"2 whereas It haue bene two coman in this towne for young men and maieds to be out of ther fathers and masters house at vnssessonable tiemes of niete It is therefore ordered that whoesoever of the younger sort shall be out of there fathers or masters house past niene of the clock at niet shall be somonsed in to the next court and ther to pay cort charges with what punishment the cort shall se cause to lay vpon them ecksept thay can giue suffissiant Reson of there being out late."

Richard Blanck, a young man in Baltimore who read The Truth Seeker, sat at eve on the steps of

THIS IS THE VISION that Meyer Kanin, the youthful cartoonist, professes to see when the author of these Memoirs looks him in the eye. (In the background, the former editors of The Truth Seeker, D. M. Bennett and E. M. Macdonald.)

his boarding-house, with his landlady's little girl beside him, looking at the stars and imparting to the inquiring child some idea of their magnitude and distance. The landlady, overhearing him, came and snatched her daughter away. Said the mother: "There are not going to be any female Bob Ingersolls raised in this family if I know it."

DEPARTURES

The conventional local eulogy of the dead Freethinker states that "his religion was the Golden Rule." When the obituary notice contains those words, it is known that the deceased was an Infidel.

The first departure from the ranks of 1925 was that of Dr. William J. Cruikshank, the distinguished Brooklyn physician and writer (March 3). A tragical one was that of Maude Helena Walker, daughter of our old subscriber, W. W. Davis of Kansas and Missouri, and wife of the cartoonist, Ryan Walker. She lived at Great Notch, N. J., with Ryan, and was killed on the morning of August 15 on the Erie train by which I regularly came to the city in the morning. She wrote for the Children's Corner when a girl. The death of Jonas Myers of San Diego, Cal., in 1924, came to our knowledge in 1925 through a bequest of $500 to the editor of The Truth Seeker.

Helen H. Gardener, a young woman of enviable person and talent who in 1884 won public notice as an advocate of Freethought, would count as one of the Old Guard had she continued in the Cause until the end, July 26, 1925. Her lectures were published by The Truth Seeker Company in 1885 as "Men, Women, and Gods."

She willed her brain to Cornell University for the purpose of a physical demonstration of her theory that the brain is immune from sex—that woman's is the same as man's. The test seemed to substantiate that thought.

THERE may be compensating virtue in things of bad repute. For instance, procrastination. By delaying the completion of this story until five years after the close of the period it attempts to cover I am able to refer to a work supremely worthy to be spread upon the records. This is the Rt. Hon. J. M. Robertson's stately "History of Freethought in the Nineteenth Century," which indeed shows how high the Freethinking spirit has risen, especially abroad, for in the United States the author finds material for a scant two score pages out of his more than six hundred.

A dozen years before the close of the nineteenth century I was "among those present" at a meeting of the Chicago Secular Society and heard a young fellow of my own age offer remarks from the floor. That was Clarence Darrow, who had appeared in The Truth Seeker ten years earlier. Today Darrow, the outstanding Freethought defender, who to be identified does not really need the seldom omitted description, "famous Chicago lawyer," is almost as well known in the United States as the prime minister is in Great Britain. When a work is restricted to the nineteenth century, men who have made their greater reputation in the twentieth do not belong. However, from the vantagepoint of 1929, Mr. Robertson makes some contemporary observations, such

as the deserved notice he gives on page 604 to
Harry Elmer Barnes, who shook up the American
Association for the Advancement of Science at its
1928 meeting with a suggestion in line with George
Jacob Holyoake's that God should be retired on
half pay. The name of Darrow as the protagonist
of Freethought would not inappropriately occur in
the note on the later and less aggressive Barnes.

At the point where my own History leaves off I
have the consciousness, as authors always admit, of
faults in the report on fifty years of Freethought.
Some of these faults have been pointedly referred
to by readers as the story was told through The
Truth Seeker. But the accident I should most regret
has not happened. While reporting on the days and
works of scores of my fellow Freethinkers in whose
good company, if so be, I am content to share
oblivion, I do not recall that anyone has rebuked
me for shortening the roll by omitting names belonging to my time and to the Story of The Truth
Seeker. In enlarging the list to take in the Old
Guard whose immediate descendants may feel like
resenting, or at least not advertising their inclusion,
I believe I am doing their future ones a good turn.
The day will come when these, if they are worth
anything, will be proud to call themselves sons and
daughters of men and women bright and brave
enough to be Freethinkers, and they may search the
pages of this work to establish their descent and
justify their pride.

CONCLUSION

THE satisfaction of ending the last chapter of this work is not so keen as I thought it was going to be when, three years ago, I began the first one. The writing of it even then had been put off from one year to another—for this History had been proposed when The Truth Seeker celebrated its "golden jubilee" in 1923—and then reluctantly begun. However, the reader is more likely to be reconciled to the deferred beginning than to the belated close, while I am as reluctant to stop as I was to start, for events continue though the story stops. I planned an Autobiography, but lost of myself in the company. There was good reason for lowering the percentage of biography and raising that of history. Life in New England, where the earlier scenes of Volume I were laid, had been full of incident; New York supplied novelty for a time, and San Francisco and Snohomish days were varied; but existence in this humdrum metropolis and its environs after 1893 was without adventure or change. I had signed on as a family man out west in 1888, and the usual uneventful life of most of us became mine—the life, most strenuously, of the worker, and, in a more relaxed way, that of him who would "make a happy fireside clime to weans and wife." Somewhere else, if not in the present work, I have shown how far I am an example and a light to young men who would be authors. I wrote in 1879 an essay that became the booklet entitled "New England and the People Up There." Twenty-five years later I did another, "Thumbscrew and Rack." And in 1930, I am producing the two-volume work. The example

THE FAMILY IN 1925
These nine bear my name, inherited or acquired

is plainly presented. Let the young writer begin
with a pamphlet at twenty-two, and by industry and
application he may print his book at seventy-four
and see his name on the list of authors gathered
in "Who's Who." It won't be long.

Goethe said that for the good life a man must
plant a tree, build a house, and beget a child. In
fulfilling the conditions I missed the order here
named, for I had a child two years old to move
into the house when I built one, and another century
arrived before I had planted a tree. We built our
house on Avenue C, in Snohomish, Washington,
and the building was not much more like a real
house than my "New England" was like a book.
Still it was a dwelling, and I long had wanted one
of my own, if only a shack. The fireside clime
was there.

In another year I was domiciled in New York.
Then the earth, making a few more revolutions,
deposited me in Montclair, New Jersey. I trace
my New Jersey home to a New York malaria germ
that caused the illness, when she was in Asbury
Park, N. J., of the wife Grace, who wouldn't come
back to the city, the habitat of the germ. We rented
and afterwards bought for a humiliating sum of
money, as the realtor viewed it, the residence called
"Skeetside." That name for an "estate" fetched
a grin to the face of the creator of "Chimmy Fad-
den," Mr. Edward W. Townsend, who was our
postmaster. We kept Skeetside and the bridge
hard by for nineteen years—long enough to determine which Montclair neighborhoods are choice and
which untenable. This was the latter, and we in-

THE HOP OFF

The Farm is in Upper Montclair, New Jersey, adjacent to the railway station designated as Montclair Heights, and is numbered 600 Upper Mountain avenue. It has a 104 foot front, open all the way to Freethinkers living near or far off, and the latchstring is out. There are restful retreats in summer under trees that make fuel for a cheerful blaze in chilly weather.

vited someone else to take the "estate." Not a
soul in a white skin would make a bid, for a colored
invasion gave Skeetside and adjacent property a
black eye in a racial sense. We "rented colored."
Whilst it had been our residence a kind old lady
in Michigan with no one about her whom she
wanted to trust as executor of her will and testament transferred to me some negotiable securities
intended, specifically, to discharge the Skeetside
mortgage and give us an unencumbered home. They
did that and more.

I am thinking now of the year 1919, when no
real estate investor professed to know whether
prices would go up the ladder or come down. The
experts predicted a descent. None the less we had
to move. In Upper Montclair, the whole length of
the town from Skeetside, and at a considerable
elevation, a young mining engineer (at this date a
lecturer at Columbia University) whom the government called to its Washington Bureau of Mines, advertised his home for sale. Homeseekers bit not.
Grace looked the property over and inveigled me
by reporting it was "a little farm" where I might
work myself out and die an agricultural death if
that was my choice—for I had uttered the wish
to end as I began, a farmer. We swapped the
remainder of the securities for the property, called
it The Hop Off, and hopped to it. Since then I
have been told that we didn't *buy* the place—we
stole it. Thus, as aforesaid, I shine again as a
home-buyer. I say to the young: Buy a home,
pay interest on mortgages, and instalments on principals, from 1892 to 1930. It won't seem long—

MRS. GRACE LELAND MACDONALD (continued from Volume I, page 453). A life acquaintance, writing recently to a sister twenty years abroad, said: "Grace has not changed since you saw her, except to grow more beautiful." If in the letter there was a reference to myself, it has not been quoted to me.

afterwards. Another "parcel" of land has grown up with us. When we lived on the Pacific coast prior to 1893 Grace remitted to a New Jersey tax collector the $10 assessed annually against five acres in Bergen County—a gift from her mother. She owns the land now, and the tax for 1930 was $220.48. A habitable building, previously vacant for years, has rented since the war for more than the tax. Skeetside, being "sold colored," brought three times its purchase price twenty years before.

In the space of a half century devoted to the pen, with forty-odd years of it given to home-seeking, I have book and house of my own. To make the account run according to romance, this later period should be called one's "declining years, spent among his books and flowers at his suburban retreat." All but the decline and the retreat. He is still a minion of the clock, and looking about him from his station somewhere near the front, the elderly one sees other things declining, but not his own years. For an example, the covers have "declined" off the books in his reference library, which are falling to pieces. Dictionaries have disintegrated from much use. Encyclopedias, Concordances, and Bibles more than anything else, have been retired and replaced. A minister might preach a lifetime from Bibles and not wear out so many copies as this editor has used up verifying quotations. Pages of volumes struck from type that he set more than fifty years ago are yellowed deep. Printed things that he pigeonholed for reference when the world was young, and never referred to since, are as crumbly as P. B. Hayward's crackers, such as he ate sitting on the rail around the common in Keene, N. H., just after the Civil war. Old letters and photographs are faded. Chairs long accustomed to his weight are fallen apart, desks become unglued at the joints. Bracket lamps, associated with joyous overtime work done half a century since, have disappeared from the walls and show up again as parlor ornaments with electric illumination and high prices attached; the flickering gas and its fixtures are outdated; things antiquated are junked, all but himself, and their places taken by something else. Benevolence has proposed some kindly disposal of ineffective age, but nothing has come of it.

Sometimes rejuvenation is discussed. I doubt I should have the courage to accept youth as a gift. Not long ago I asked the wife if she would care to try life over again. She thought not. The joy was in exploration and encountering the unexpected. We might miss some of the fun the next time. Better to keep on toward the evening; and she brought out her scrapbook that holds my rhymes, and read:

> "The sunset lends to close of day
>   Unequaled glories, all its own;
> They are not seen by noon, and they
>   To fairest morn were never known,
> So may life's evening hour be blest
> And days to come hold all the best."

Youth having passed, there is nothing to lose but memory. Cherishing the past without regrets and viewing the future without misgivings, we wait, then, for the nightfall, when one may rest and call it a life.

INDEX

Abbot, Francis Ellingwood, i, 18i.

Abbott, Leonard D., ii, 457.

Abbott, Rev. Lyman, on Jonah and whale, ii, 138; 179.

Abraham, a modern, i, 257.

Actors, number in prison in proportion to preachers, ii, 558.

Adams, Robert C., ii, 159, 228.

Addis, Henry, ii, 144.

Adler, Felix, i, 189.

Adonis, Byron, i, 256.

Adventists, prosecution of, ii, 109.

Age of Consent, symposium, ii, 105.

Age of Reason, unique edition, ii, 157, 235, 305.

Alexander, J. B., ii, 75.

Alfonso, King, kisses pope's toe, ii, 579.

Algie, William, Freethought hall, i, 368, 411, 413.

Allen, Ethan, on his death-bed, i, 81; myth about, ii, 128.

Allyn, C. Fannie, ii, 311.

Alphaism, i, 276.

Altgeld, Gov. J. P., ii, 76.

Amberley, Viscount, his Analysis of Religious Belief, i, 187.

Ambulance, the Ingersoll, ii, 470.

"America" (hymn) discarded by Catholics, i, 543.

American Rationalist Ass'n, organized, ii, 594.

American Secular Union, i, 390, 413, 432, 466, 491; ii, 64, 85; joins Freethought Federation, ii, 107, 146,

170, 185; see yearly mention.

Ames, Daniel T., ii, 146, 339.

Anarchists, Chicago, i, 382, 409, 419; ii, 76, 196, 312.

Anarchy, Huxley on, ii, 566; disciples, 567.

Anderson, Jim, of Returning Board, i, 272.

Andersonville, myth of, ii, 428.

Andrews, Emerson and family, i, 78.

Andrews, Marie, ii, 585.

Andrews, S. P., on Guiteau, i, 181, 306, 307, 308; on Mormon church, 363, 404-408.

Andrews, William S., ii, 416.

Angels, sex of, ii, 265.

Anthony, Susan B., ii, 110, 283.

Anti-Catholic papers, bills to exclude from mails, ii, 441.

Anti-evolution bills, ii, 555, 575; Tennessee, 609.

Anti-Poverty Society, i, 420.

Anti-Slavery agitators, in Liberal ranks, i, 267.

Arresters, ii, 443, 451, 452, 466, 520, 598.

Atheism, American Ass'n for the Advancement of, ii, 620.

Atheists, in the war, ii, 474.

Australia, Liberator suspends, ii, 252.

Aveling, Dr. E., in America, i, 403.

Ayer, F. F., Ingersoll ambulance, ii, 470.

Badgepin, Freethought, i, 327.

Ballou, Addie, i, 511.

Ballou, Evangeline, i, 537.

Bankruptcy of Science, ii, 111.

Barnes, Harry Elmer, ii, 480.

Barrett, Judge G. C., i, 433, 460.

Barry, J. H., i, 458, 529.

Barter, H. L., a Comstock victim, i, 281.

Baseball, Sunday, in New York, ii, 256, 337.

Bateson, Prof. Wm., ii, 574.

Beal, C., Pres. Or. Sec. Union, i, 521.

Beard, Dr. George M., i, 348.

Beecher, H. W., on loss of Arctic, i, 38; sermon on hell, 194; introduces Ingersoll at meeting, 290; adopts evolution, 327; refutes resurrection story, 365; and Cleveland, 370; d. 418.

Beeny, Col. H., ii, 75.

Belford, Rev. J., incendiary language of, ii, 390.

Belgian Freethought Congress, ii, 559.

Bell, W. S., i, 179, 229, 498.

Bellamy, Edward, his Looking Backward, i, 447, 533.

Benedict, Judge C. L., i, 180, 244.

Bennett, C. R., Comstock agent, i, 458 523.

Bennett, D. M., i, 140 (1875) to 326 (1882). Liberal League, i, 351. Monument, i, 365. -Teed discussion, i, 194.

Bennett, Mary Wicks, i, 141, 349; ii, 172.

Berthelot, M. Marcelin, ii, 302.

Besant, Annie, Socialist, i, 433; theosophist, 532.

Betts, C. H., ii, 426.

Betz, Israel H., ii, 502.

Bible reading in schools, i, 512; ii, 119, 357, 559; exclusion of Bible from mails proposed; ii, 335; prophecy attributed to Ingersoll, 446.

Bible, polychrome, ii, 129.

Bible obscene, See Wise, J. B., ii, 119.

Bierck, Adolph, ii, 103.

Bierstadt, A., i, 22.

Billard, J. B., mayor of Topeka, Kan., ii, 223, 233, 256, 353.

Billings, Col. M. E., i, 533.

Bierbower, Austin, ii, 300.

Binns, Jack, ii, 359.

Birney, William, ii, 303.

Birth control, Colgate style, i, 225; Ingersoll on, ii, 192; an arrest, 443; B. C. League, 444; meeting raided, 544.

Black, William, killed, ii, 443.

Blaine, James G., Burcharded, i, 369.

Blair Education bill, i, 511.

Blake, Lillie D., ii, 286.

Blanck, Richard, ii, 625.

Bland, J. P., ii, 513.

Blasphemy prosecutions: Rosentranch, i, 313; G. W. Foote, 350; Reynolds, 414; Niemojewski, 373; Lennstrand, 493; Voelkel, ii, 75; Moore, 80; Hanele (a play), 84; Boulter, 315; Dhammaloka, 372; Bullock, 392; Jackson, 392; Mockus, 453, 467; Riley, 468; Gott,

468, 533, 569; Einstein, 548; street speakers accused, 581; Canova, 620.

Blatchford, Robert, ii, 294.

Bliss, Porter C., i, 284, 383.

Blodget, Delos A., ii, 317.

Bohemians in San Francisco, i, 499; ii, 319.

Borglum, Gutzon, sculptor of Angels, ii, 265.

Borglund, C. E., ii, 380.

Borrette, H. S., ii, 401.

Bowles, Dr. T. J., ii, 603.

Bowne, G. W., assistant editor, ii, 458, 602.

Boye, D. M., ii, 447.

Boyle, A. F., i, 384.

Braden, Clark, i, 268, 456.

Bradford, A. B., i, 190; ii, 186.

Bradford, Gov. Wm., i, 115, 128.

Bradlaugh, Charles, i, 171, 326, 493, 535; ii, 87.

Bradley, John D., ii, 265, 442.

Braga, Theophilo, president Portuguese republic, ii, 70, 353.

Brandes, Georg, ii, 619.

Brann, W. C., editor Iconoclast, ii, 104, 141.

Breckinridge, W. C. P., i, 393; ii, 81.

Brenner, Chas., ii, 533.

Brenner, Wm., (ii), xiii.

Brewer, George David, ii, 279.

Briggs, Rev. C. A., suspended from ministry, ii, 75, 81. ,

Brisbane, Albert, i, 208, 502.

Bristol, Augusta Cooper, i, 287.

Brooklyn Philosophical Association, ii, 70, 595.

Brooks, Mrs. Anna, meets Ingersoll, ii, 122.

Broun, Heywood, i, 180.

Brown, Eva I., marriage of, ii, 480.

Brown, G. W., i, 266; ii, 412, 446, 486.

Brown, Hugh Byron, i, 173; ii, 173.

Brown, John, a Presbyterian, i, 267.

Brown, Dr. T. L., i, 194, 387, 432.

Brown, Bishop W. M., ii, 478, 533, 588, 606.

Brown, Wm. Thurston, ii, 120, 409, 476, 606ff.

Browne, Frank L., i, 445.

Brunetiere, F., on bankruptcy of science, ii, 111.

Bruno, Giordano, i, 371-5, 475, 501; ii, 295.

Brunzell, Lovisa, author of questionnaire, ii, 524.

Bryan, John, his gift to Ohio, ii, 581, 617.

Bryan, William J., ii, 22, 128, 314, 556; challenged, 562, 575, 612.

Bryan, W. S. ii, 427, 510, 610.

Buchanan, Dr. Joseph Rodes, i, 517.

Buchner, Dr. Ludwig, i, 348; ii, 187.

Buckner, Rev. J. D. M., loses pulpit, ii, 563.

Bullock, S. E., prosecuted for blasphemy, ii, 392.

Bundling, i, 92.

Burbank, Luther, i, 413; answers to questionnaire, ii, 550-552.

Burdick, L. S., i, 287.

Burnham, A. H., i, 287.

Burns, John, in America, ii, 91.

Burnz, Eliza Boardman, i, 190; ii, 236.

Burr, William Henry, i, 368; ii, 316.

Burroughs, John, ii, 545.

Burtis, Flora A., ii, 435.

Burtis, Richard C., ii, 207.

Burton, James, sheriff, ii, 26.

Burwell, H. H., ii, 514.

Butland, R. B., i, 387, 411.

Butler, B. F., candidate for president, i, 369; counsel for anarchists, 409.

Butts, Asa K., editor "Man," i, 269.

Buxton, Joseph L., ii, 365.

Byington, Steven, ii, 246.

Cadman, Rev. S. Parkes, departure from orthodoxy, ii, 183.

Cæsar's Column," by Ignatius Donnelly, i, 513.

Caldwell girls, ii, 380.

Calhoun, Charles, ii, 594.

California State Liberal Union, i, 470; ii, 65.

Calvert, Bruce, ii, 352.

Calvin, John, his crimes, ii, 432.

Canada: Freethought Ass'n of, i, 368; O. T. Stories banned in, ii, 67; Secular Union, 70; Truth Seeker prohibited in, ii, 99-110; allowed to be mailed to, 243; Pioneer Freethought Club, 318.

Cannon, "Uncle Joe," on prayer in war time, ii, 422.

Cantrell, E. A., ii, 310, 457, 531.

Carnegie, Andrew, i, 433; contributed to Conway Hall, ii, 246.

Caron, Sir Adolphe, prohibits Truth Seeker, ii, 101; his night out, 157.

Carter, Mrs. L. S., founds home for babies, ii, 376.

Carus, Paul, i, 366, 433.

Cassels, Walter Richard, ii, 302.

Catholic church steal, ii, 140, 258.

Catholic girls, morals of, i, 209.

Catholic women, their testimony against priesthood, ii, 407.

Censorship ii, 222, 309.

Censustaker, Freethinkers unknown to, ii, 479.

Chainey, George, i, 287, 294, 330.

Chainey, Ralph, ii, 528.

Chamberlain, Gov. Daniel Henry, of So. Carolina, a Freethinker, ii, 313.

Chamberlain, E.. W., i, 426; ii, 317.

Chanfrau, Frank, i, 158.

Chaplain, vetoed by Gov. Bradley of Kentucky, ii, 143.

Charleston, cruiser launched, i, 518.

Charlesworth, John R., i, 465; ii, 64.

Chase, Dr. Sarah B., i, 187.

Chautauqua, Freethinkers' Convention, i, 267.

Chicago Liberal League, i, 396, 437; ii, 59, 70.

Chickering, A., on Ingersoll, i, 88.

Childs, Judge Francis, i, 422.

Chilstrom, P. O., i, 472.

China, missionaries in, ii, 204.

Chinese printing office, i, 514.

Choate, Rufus, i, 384.

Choynski, Joe, i, 486.

Chiniquy, C. P., ii, 200.

Christ, law prohibiting presentation of, ii, 85.

Christian Amendment perished, ii, 115, 803.

Christian Statesman, would suppress T. S., ii, 99.

Christianity, its sole excuse for being, ii, 592.

Christmas, not kept by Puritans, i, 126; Carlyle on, 127.

Church, Elizabeth H., i, 512.

Church attendance for service men, ii, 475.

Church-government scandals, ii, 153.

Church property exemption, bill to abolish, i, 257; ii, 79, 445; Alfred E. Smith's proposal, 445; decision regarding alien, 560; see Grant, U. S.

Clark, James G., ii, 149.

Clark, Stanley J., ii, 478, 562.

Clemens, S. L., see Mark Twain.

Clemson, Thomas E., atheist philanthropist, ii, 427.

Cleveland, Grover, Sabbath breaker, ii, 116.

Cobbett, W., ii, 176.

Codman, C. A., i, 171.

Cohen, Chapman, ii, 142.

Colby, Mrs. A. H., i, 287.

Colby, W. L., i, 146; ii, 77.

College men, discarding of religion by and scarcity of in penal institutions, ii, 557.

Collins, Hon. John A., i, 478, 502.

Collins, May, ii, 132.

Colman, Lucy, i, 229, 430; ii, 110, 281.

Columbus, C., was he a Jew? ii, 412.

Comet, Halley's, ii, 354.

Companionate Marriage, instance of, ii, 66.

Comstock, Anthony, i, 179, 209; repeal of law opposed by Ingersoll, 281; ii, 309, 450.

Congress Liberal League, i, 303. See National Liberal League.

Congress of Universal Federation, i, 280. See International Congress.

Conklin, Roscoe, memorial, i, 465.

Connelly, W., (ii), xi.

Convent, Visitation, many keys, i, 523.

Conway Hall, ii, 246.

Conway, Moncure D., i, 175, 450; ii, 65, 146, 175, 206, 251, 267, 305.

Cook, Joseph, i, 256, 317; ii, 209.

Coolridge, Cyrus W., ii, 125.

Cooper, Peter, i, 173, 347.

Copenheaver, J. F. W., ii, 297.

Cornell Ingersoll Club, ii, 393.

Corrigan, Archbishop, ii, 162.

Coryell, John Russell, ii, 302, 604.

Coudert, F. R., debate with Ingersoll, i, 350, 493.

Craddock, Ida C., persecution of. i, 491, 519; ii, 211, 217.

Crafts, Rev. Wilbur F., i, 492; ii, 268.

Craig, D. W., i, 190.

Crapsey, Algernon S., ii, 270, 272, 318.

Cremation, i, 368.

Cridge, Alfred Denton, i, 446.

Crimes and religions, ii, 590, 591.

Croffut, W. A., i, 211; ii, 118, 448.
Croly, David G., and J. J., i, 211.
Crosby, Ernest Howard, ii, 301.
Crosby, F. W., ii, 361.
Crowell, Joshua, ii, 568.
Crowley, J. J., ii, 460.
Crucifixion, a drama, ii, 219.
Culbertson, J. A., ii, 542.
Cullom, Shelby M., ii, 426.
Cummings, F. D., ii, 198, 620.
Curry, Rev. J. B., his libel suit, ii, 405, 408.
Curtin, Andrew G., ii, 88.
Curtis, Thomas, i, 317, 501, 537; ii, 171.
Czologosz, Leon O, ii, 212ff.

Dana, Chas. A., ii, 100, 147.
Darrow, Clarence, i, 287, 437; ii, 206, 234, 250, 260, 610, 612; viii.
Darwin, Chas., i, 326; son of a Freethinker, ii, 248; Lady Hope myth, 456; opinion of Florida editor, 574.
Davidson, T., on Bruno, i, 373.
Davis, Owen Thomas, ii, 78.
Davis, Aaron, ii, 341.
Davis, Singleton W., ii, 262.
Davis, W. W., ii, 339.
Day, where begun, ii, 414.
Debs, E. V., ii, 505, 521. •
Deland, Margaret, i, 513.
DeCleyre, Voltairine, ii, 242.
DeGolier, S. M., ii, 594.
Delaware, Ingersoll, excluded from, i, 299.
Delescluze, Mme. Henri, i, 378.
Denslow, VanBuren, i, 287.
Denton, M. F., ii, 465.
Denton, William, i, 350.
Denver, priest killed ii, 312.

Depew, C. M., i, 400.
DeRudio, C. C., ii, 264, 365.
DeVoe, W. F., ii, 95.
Dewey, Geo., takes Manila, ii, 163.
Dhammaloka, U., ii, 372.
Diaz, Porfirio, ii, 70.
Dickinson College, ii, 246.
Dickinson, Don M., defense of Sabbath breaker, i, 531,
Dist. of Col. Bible law, ii, 612.
"Divine Person" law, ii, 85.
Dixon, Rev. A. C., ii, 66.
Dixey, Henry E., ii, 290.
Doane, T. W., i, 383.
Dobson, Edward, i, 184.
Donnelly, I., i, 513.
Doukhobors, ii, 235.
Dowie, J. A., i, 458, 502; ii, 289, 300.
Draper, J. W., i, 326.
Dresden, Ingersoll birthplace, ii, 355, 535.
Dress, reform, i, 257, 276.
Drews, Arthur, ii, 354.
Dunant, Red Cross founder, ii, 441.
Duncan, Isadora, ii, 184.
Dunn, Judge, ii, 357.
Duryea, Sam'l B., i, 414.
Eastman, W. H., i, 496.
Eccles, David, i, 267; (ii), xi.
Eccles, R. G., i, 267.
Eckler, Peter, publishing Co. i, 262, 428; ii, 285.
Economics, discussion of adverse to Freethought organizations, ii, 541.
Edison, Thomas A., i, 234; ii, 188, 367, 614.
Edwards, T. C., i, 234.
Edwards, W. W., ii, 568.
Egoism, i, 503, 505.
Einstein, Karl, ii, 558.
Elliot, J. L., ii, 178, 583, 613.
Ellis, Henry T., i, 61.

Ellis, J. Spencer, i, 429; ii, 185, 252.
End of World, ii, 605.
Equinoctial storm, i, 38.
Era of man, i, 371.
Ericsson, John, ii, 247.
Eskimos, godless, ii, 359.
Ethical Culture Soc., i, 190.
Evans, J. Ick, i, 387.
Evarts, W. M., i, 327.
Everett, city of, ii, 31.
Evolution and the Fundamentalist, ii, 548, 553, 573 ff, 590.
Exemption of church property, petition against, i, 257; bill to abolish in N. Y., i, 414.
Eye, newspaper, ii, 1.

Ferdinand, assassinated, ii, 422.
Ferguson, C. J., ii, 294.
Ferguson, E. C., ii, 45.
Fernandez, Emma L., i, 279; ii, 360.
Ferrer colony, ii, 357.
Ferrer, Francisco, ii, 280, 297, 332, 350.
Ferrer, executed, ii, 332.
Ferry, F. C., ii, 557.
Field, Eliphaz, i, 60 ff.
Firebrand, The, ii, 144.
First Secular church, ii, 114.
Fiske, John, i, 327; in debate, i, 400.
Fiske, Photius, i, 512.
Fitzhugh, Percy, ii, 145.
Flag, Am. excluded from Catholic church, ii, 431; church flag placed above American, ii, 523.
Flag pole incident, ii, 23, 26.
Flood in Ohio, motto left by, ii, 412.
Flood, original story, ii, 429.
Foote, E. B., i, 179, 192, 231, 426; ii, 82, 285.
Foote, E. B. Jr., i, 208; ii, 65, 401.

Foote, G. W., i, 350, 365, 493; ii, 126, 135, 450.
Ford, Henry, ii, 538.
Ford, James L., i, 202.
Ford, Paul L., ii, 175.
Fosdick, H. E., ii, 579.
Fosket, Wm., ii, 416.
Foss, E. N., gov., ii, 393.
Foster, G. B., ii, 273.
Foster, Warren, ii, 160.
Four Hundred Years of Freethought, ii, 77.
Francis, J. R., ii, 361.
Fraina, Louis C., ii, 334.
France, religious laws, ii, 234, 270, 273.
Frank, Henry, i, 516; ii, 61, 562.
Franklin, B., his alleged letter to Paine, ii, 274, 277.
Franklin, Emerson, i, 134.
Frazier, Billy, ii, 200.
Free Lance Soc., ii, 145.
Free speech denied, ii, 443, 520, 563, etc.
Freedom of worship bill, ii, 66, 183.
Freelovers, i, 388.
Freeman, child sacrifice, i, 257.
Freeman D., first homesteader in U. S., ii, 223, 338.
Freeman, Mrs. M. A., ii, 63, 209.
Freeman, W. J., ii, 149.
Freemasons, excommunicated, ii, 93.
Free Religionists, ii, 192.
Free Speech League, ii, 231.
Freethinkers' Ass'n, i, 194, 411.
Freethinkers' Soc., New York, ii, 216.
Freethinkers, creditable children of, ii, 247, 250; in the war, ii, 471, 495; sons in, 510.

Freethought Federation, ii, 64, 73, 85, 107.

Freethought journals, i, 180; forgotten, ii, 296.

Freethought lecturers, ii, 478.

Freethought, weekly, i, 444, 543.

Freethought press in 1904, ii, 252, 298.

Freethought Tract Soc., ii, 386.

Friday in year 1886, i, 410.

Frothingham, O. B., i, 194, 246; ii, 121.

Fundamentalism, birth of, ii, 554.

Gable, Wm. F., ii, 546.

Gage, Matilda Joslyn, ii, 76, 110, 171, 285.

Galois, Margaret, ii, 414.

Gandhi, V. R., at Liberal Club, ii, 170.

Gardener, Helen, i, 364; ii, 105, 225.

Garfield, James A., assassinated, i, 300; no religious consolations, 301.

Garrett, Pat, Sheriff, i, 302; ii, 224.

Garrison, William Lloyd, i, 384; ii, 110.

Gauvin, Marshall, ii, 341 351, 519, 531, 596.

Gaynor, W. J., mayor, against exemption of churches, ii, 355; shot by Gallagher, 356.

Geer, Pearl, ii, 114; visit with Edison, 188.

George, Henry, i, 297, 397, 418, 420, 422; ii, 148.

Gerry, E. T., ii, 84.

Gibbons, Card., agt. votes for women, ii, 410.

Gibson, Ella E., i, 177, 234; ii, 208.

Giddings, Franklin H., ii, 238, 299.

Gillen, Kate, i, 413.

Gilmore's Garden, i, 159.

Gilroy, T. J., ii, 85.

Girard, Stephen, i, 234, 491; ii, 141.

Girls, church, morals of, i, 209; ii, 397.

Globe, Ingersoll myth, i, 428; ii, 180.

Glynn, Martin, ii, 431.

God, new conception of proposed, ii, 480.

God-in-constitution amendment, ii, 83, 115.

Godless tribes, peoples, towns, ii, 359, 566.

Godly women, i, 177.

Goethe, his suggestion, ii, 103.

Goodell, N. D., ii, 114.

Gorsuch, W. J., i, 381-2.

Gott, J. W., ii, 468, 533, 569.

Gould, F. J., i, 279; ii, 393.

Grannis, Eliz., ii, 102.

Grant, Rev. P. S., heresy and death of, ii, 579.

Grant, U. S., church taxation message, i, 180; d., 383.

Graphic, The Daily, i, 211.

Graves, Kersey, i, 287, 348.

Greek vs. Roman church, i, 459.

Greeley, Horace, i, 389; ii, 90, 379.

Green, H. L., i, 194, 348; ii, 238.

Greenbackism, i, 173.

Greenwich Village, tablet to Paine, ii, 577.

Gregory, Rev. Thomas B., ii, 104; (ii), xi.

Griffith, J. I., ii, 32, 35.

Griswold, N. F., ii, 464.

Guiteau, C. J., assassin of Garfield, i, 300, 308-9.

Gunther, Robert, i, 476.
Guthrie, Rev. W. N., ii, 582.

Hacker, Jeremiah, ii, 113.
Haeckel, Ernst, i, 180; ii, 254, 291, 372, 395, 429, 462, 513.
Hackenburg, F. L., his proposed anti-blue law, ii, 541.
Hagan, Rev. F. W., disfellowshiped, ii, 563.
Hannon, J. C., ii, 585.
Hardie, Keir, in America, ii, 91..
Harding, President W. G., on Paine, ii, 577; d., 581.
Hardy, Thos., quoted, i, 327.
Hardman Hall, ii, 108.
Harland, H., i, 260, 262.
Harman, Lillian, i, 402, 424.
Harman, Moses, i, 302; arrest of, i, 424, 530; ii, 68, 75, 110, 259, 274, 310, 361.
Harris, H. L. Jr., ii, 619.
Harrison, Benj., ii, 265.
Harrison-Spencer, debate, i, 368.
Hart, Frank, ii, 573.
Hart, John, i, 268.
Hart, John, ii, 297.
Hatch, Junius L., i, 474.
Harte, Bret, i, 443.
Hartman, Leo., i, 394.
Haupt, Prof. Paul, ii, 129.
Haverhill, Mass., Catholic riot in, ii, 462.
Hawaii, few inhabitants converted, ii, 32.
Hawes, Gilbert R., i, 414.
Hayes, Archbishop, ii, 544.
Hayes, R. B., denies Bennett pardon, i, 269.
Hayes-Tilden, campaign, i, 189.
Haymarket riot, i, 396; ii, 76.
Helm, John, ii, 400.

Henderson, G. L., i, 173, 179; ii, 173.
Henn, Edward, ii, 453.
Hennesy, J. A., ii, 542; xi.
Herald of Freedom, i, 266.
Heresy, Bishop Brown's, ii, 587.
Herndon, W. H., i, 313, 493; ii, 479, 500, 595.
Heston, Watson, i, 393; ii, 145, 270.
Hewitt, Abram S., i, 399; ii, 233.
Heywood, Angela, i, 57.
Heywood, Ezra H., i, 190, 228, 231, 244, 321, 530; ii, 65, 74.
Higginson, T. W., ii, 192.
Hindenberg, Elsie, ii, 485.
Hins, Eugene, ii, 583.
Hinton, W. M., i, 443ff.
Hitchcock, Ephraim E., i, 349; ii, 171, 208.
Hittell, John S., i, 474, 475; ii, 208.
Hoadley, G. H., i, 348, 390.
Hoar, G. F., ii, 74, 253.
Hoboken Ministers and Ingersoll, ii, 96.
Holbrook, G. H., ii, 462.
Holman, J. R., i, 39.
Holmes, Sarah E., i, 165.
Hollow globe theory, i, 150.
Holt, Dr. M. S., ii, 457.
Holyoake, Geo. Jacob, i, 267, 301; ii, 280.
Home Colony, ii, 203.
Hope, Lady, her Darwin myth, ii, 456.
Hopkins, Dr. E. M., his stand against Fundamentalism, ii, 554.
Hopwood, Freeman, ii, 620.
Hosmer, Joseph, ii, 420.
House, A. E., ii, 334.
Howland, Marie, i, 481.
Hoyle, David, i, 200; ii, 447.
Hubbard, Elbert, ii, 330, 409.

646 INDEX

Hughes, Rupert, i, 113; ii, 443, 587, 615.
Hugo, Victor, i, 383.
Hull, Moses, i, 145.
Humanity, Society of, i, 417.
Humanitarian Review, ii, 262.
Hurt, Walter, ii, 185, 493.
Huss, John, ii, 445.
Huxley, T. H., Chickering Hall lectures, i, 175; ii, 112; myth about, 456; xi.

Iconoclast, The, ii, 103.
Index, Boston, i, 412.
Indian burial customs, ii, 40.
Indiana Ass'n, ii, 420.
Indians, sectarian schools among, ii, 398.
Infallibility, papal, i, 82.
Infidels and achievement, i, 516.
Infidel town (New Ulm), ii, 294.
Ingalls, Olive H., ii, 110.
Ingersoll, C. H., ii, 62.
Ingersoll, Ebon Clark, i, 274.
Ingersoll, Eva, i, 390.
Ingersoll, Eva A., ii, 583.
Ingersoll, Maud R. (marriage), ii, 401.
Ingersoll, Robert G., i, 103, 152, 174, 264, 266, 281, 282, 283, 290, 413, 423, 465, 516; ii, 65, 87, 95, 96, 116, 122, 144; death, 177; 209, 264, 290, 347, 393, 446, 469, 535; an Atheist, 537; 599.
As He Is, ii, 116.
Birthday book, ii, 378.
Cathedral, ii, 96.
Cornell Club, ii, 393.
House in New York sold, ii, 599.
Lay Sermon, i, 413.
Memorial Ass'n, ii, 209.
Mountain, ii, 95.
Thanksgiving Sermon, ii, 60.
Secular Society, ii, 70.

Ingersoll (con.)
Tree, ii, 613; tablet in Gramercy Park, 613.
In God We Trust motto, ii, 293, 307-8.
Inquisition, Short History of, ii, 277.
Interchurch movement, ii, 522.
International Congress, London, i, 293; Paris, 263, 492; Madrid, ii, 69; Chicago, 73; Rome, 251; St. Louis, 254; Amsterdam, 348; Lisbon, 410; Prague, 526; Paris, 620.
Investigator, Boston, suspended, ii, 252.
Ireland and the Pope, i, 458.
Ireland, Archbishop, in politics, ii, 140, 182.
Ironclad Age, i, 350; ii, 114.
Irvine, Alexander, ii, 319.
Irving, Henry, ii, 87.
Ismay, J. E., i, 276; ii, 510.
Ives, Franklin T., ii, 232.

Jackson, T., ii, 392.
James, C. L., i, 327; ii, 380.
James, Frank, i, 311.
Jameson, D. (ii), xiv.
Japan, Rationalist Ass'n in, ii, 594.
Jesse, W. W., ii, 114.
Jews, their demands on the state, ii, 538.
Johnson, M. Florence, ii, 416.
Johnson, Robert U., 470.
Jones, George, ii, 27.
Jones, J. Lloyd, ii, 467.
Jones, Thomas, i, 447.
Joseph, Immanuel, ii, 7.
Jordan, David Starr, on revival drunkenness, ii, 143, 337.
Julian, G. W., i, 266.
Junius Letters, i, 297.
Junri, Japanese paper, ii, 594.
Jeldness, Olaus, ii, 564.

Kaiser, German, and pope, ii, **234**; his piety, 454.
Kansas Freethought Ass'n, ii, 111.
Kant, Immanuel, i, 157.
Kaweah colony, i, 533.
Kehm, Katie, i, 521.
Kellogg, burlesque spirit phenomena, i, 510.
Kelso, J. R., i, 287, 301, 538.
Kentucky antievolution bill, ii, 555.
Keyser, John H., ii, 187.
Kimball, E. P. i, 33.
Kimball, Horatio, i, 34.
Kimble, Jos. A., ii, 465.
Kirk, Hyland C., ii, 412.
Kittredge, H. E., ii, 394.
Kline, W. L., ii, 562.
Kneeland, Abner, i, 487.
Knights of Columbus, Supreme advocate convicted, ii, 558.
Knights of Pythias, excommunicated, ii, 93.
Krekel, Arnold, i, 462.
Krekel, Mattie P., i, 287; ii, 546.

Ladd, Parrish B., ii, 400.
Lafayette Place, i, 430.
Lake, Mrs. H. S., i, 287.
Lambert, "Notes on Ingersoll," i, 378.
Lamar, solicitor, ii, 287-492.
Lamaster. W. H., i, 302.
Land Reformers, i, 222.
Language, New England, i, 121.
Lant, John A., i, 179.
Lanyon, Robert, ii, 470.
Larsen, Bennett, ii, 597.
Lassalle, F., relict of, i, 410.
Latham, John, ii, 353.
Latham, Silas, ii, 196, 237.
Lawrence, D. H., i, 243.
Leader Fair, i, 410.
League of Nations, ii, 522.
Lecky, W. H., i, 121.

Lecouver Press, ii, 252.
Lecturers, 1878, i, 236; 1885, 389.
Legitimation League, ii, 159.
Leibnitz, G. W., i, 373.
Leland, Grace, i, 451-455
Leland, Lillian, i, 451, 506.
Leland, Mary A., i, 450, 537.
Leland, T. C., i, 208, 231, 303, 383-5.
Lemme, E., S., i, 471, 496.
Lennstrand, Victor E., i, 493; ii, 114.
Leonard, Cynthia, i, 151, 224, 374.
Leopold-Loeb case, ii, 587.
LePlongeon, ii, 338.
Leubuscher, A., i, 272; ii, 75.
Lewis, A. M., ii, 569.
Lewis, Dio, i, 21, 340.
Lewis, J. Hamilton, ii, 41.
Lewis, Joseph, suit agt. Mt. Vernon school board, ii, 616.
Liberal, town of, i, 297, 401, 431, 464.
Liberal Club, New York, i, 143, 152. 171, 173, 193, 319, 337, 389.
Liberal League, National, i, 231 (and year by year).
Liberal League, 4th N. Y. i, 257.
Liberal leagues, auxiliaries, i, 364.
Liberal lecturers, i, 189, 236, 532.
Liberal organizations and societies, ii, 145. 225, 227, 318, 336, 457, 477. etc.
Liberal papers, i, 189, 465; forgotten ones, ii, 298, 578.
Liberal party, organized, i, 264.
Liberal university, ii, 126, 207, 239.
Libertarian League, ii, 594.
Liberty "licked" i, 453.

Library, free secular, i, 413; Spokane excludes Truth Seeker, ii, 334.

Lick, James, i, 183; Freethinkers excluded from his hall, 472; academy of science, i, 474; dilatory trustees, 486; raised Paine picture over procession, 511.

Liebknecht, W., i, 404.

Lies, their longevity, i, 516.

Life, artificial production of, ii, 396.

Lincoln, A., ii, 596.

Linton, W. J., ii, 171.

Livingstone, B. E., ii, 571.

Livesey, Elias, ii, 547.

Locke, J. N., names Mt. Ingersoll, ii, 95.

Loeb, Jacques, ii, 604.

Longevity of Freethinkers, ii, 298, 318, 339.

Longfellow poem censored, i, 518.

Longford, G., (ii), xii.

Long Island early law, ii, 623.

Loomiller, J. C., ii, 208.

Los Angeles, free speech won in, ii, 310.

Lowell, J. R., misquoted, ii, 89.

Lowell, Sidney Vale, ii, 576.

Loyd, Geo., caretaker, Paine monument, ii, 339.

Lucifer, ii, 252.

Ludwig, John H., ii, 481

Lusitania, sinking of, ii, 438.

McCabe, Joseph, in America, ii, 476.

Macdonald, Asenath C., i, 19, 302; ii, 381-5.

Macdonald, E. L., i, 520; ii, 334.

Macdonald, E. M., i, 46ff, 172, 221, 248, 293, 349, 460; ii, 214, 320, 328.

Macdonald, G. E., birth and boyhood, i, 11-140; Soldier's Son, 17; first verse and "lecture," 258-9; interview with Ingersoll, 390-1; in San Francisco, 443-543; married, 455; observations on government, 500; in Snohomish, ii, 1-58; return to Truth Seeker, ii, 77; address at annual congress, 108; editor Truth Seeker, from year 1909.

Macdonald, Grace L., Ingersoll Birthday Book edited by, ii, 378.

Macdonald, Henry, i, 11ff.

Macdonald, Wilson, ii,, 176.

McDonnell, Wm., i, 368; ii, 201.

Macfadden, Bernarr, ii, 358.

McGiffert, Arthur C., ii, 193.

McGlynn, Rev. Edward, i, 399, 420, 421, 491; ii, 75.

Maguire, James G., i, 458; ii, 173.

Mackenzie, Wm., ii, 464.

McKinley, William, ii, 140, 168, 169, 211.

MacKnight, James A., ii, 585.

Maclaskey, W. L., ii, 519.

Maine, warship, ii, 162.

Maltsbarger, J. I., ii, 117.

Man, Era of, i, 371.

"Man," Liberal League organ, i, 369.

Mangasarian, Rev. M.M., i, 391; ii, 263, 432, 620.

Manhattan Liberal Club, ii, 70; 25th an., 90; 145, 319; end of, 337; see Liberal Club.

Manning, Bishop, ii, 582.

Maple, Wm. H., ii, 526.

Mark Twain, ii, 204, 224, 287, 361-3, 463, 498, 595.

Mark Twain Fellowship, ii, 498.

Marriage, companionate, i, 366; ii, 66; Catholic and Protestant, i, 464; trial, ii, 288.

Marshall, Edm. (ii), xiii.

Marshall, Thos., lifts from Ingersoll, ii, 446, 512.

Martin, J. S., ii, 3.

Martinique, island of destroyed, ii, 220-222.

Mary, virgin, relations of with the Trinity, ii, 622.

Mass, presidents assist at, ii, 432.

Masses, monthly, ii, 468.

Massey, Gerald, ii, 302.

Maudsley, Henry, ii, 502.

Mayo, Katherine, ii, 621.

Maxim, Hiram, ii, 464.

Maxim, Hudson, ii, 553

Mead, Thomas, ii, 87.

Mendum, J. P., i, 319, 535.

Merchant, Walter, ii, 603.

Meridian, 180th, ii, 415.

Methodist steal South, ii, 153-5.

Mexico, Zapata rebellion, ii, 424-5; no nuns hurt, 425.

Miller, Herbert, i, 472.

Miller, Joaquin, i, 206-7.

Miller, Jos. Dana, ii, 125.

Miller, Leo, i, 383.

Millikan, R. A., his irenicon, ii, 572.

Mills College, i, 508.

Miln, Geo. C., i, 312.

Ministers who became Freethinkers, ii, 513.

Missionaries, looting by in China, ii, 203-5.

Mitchell, E. P., ii, 179.

Mitchell, J. P., conflict with church, ii, 460.

Mivart, St. George, excommunication, death, ii, 192-193.

Mockus, M. X., ii, 453, 467.

Modernism, rise and vogue of, ii, 555, 600; originally Catholic, ii, 299.

Modern Times, i, 451.

Monico, Mary, ii, 495.

Monism defined, ii, 255.

Monistic Alliance Congress, ii, 254, 366, 369.

"Monkey Bills," ii, 555.

Monroe, Dr. J. R., i, 427, 540; ii, 114.

Montclair, N. J., ii, 630.

Moody and Sankey, i, 178.

Moore, Charles C., ii, 80, 147, 185, 198, 281.

Moore, H. H., i, 286.

Moral instruction in schools, i, 491; A. S. U. book of, 534.

Morals, new for old, i, 119.

Morehouse, Geo. W., ii, 527.

Morgan, Edward, ii, 527.

Morley, Chris., ii, 264.

Morley, John, recantation myth, ii, 585.

Mormonism, rise of, i, 363.

Mormons, i, 394; property of confiscated, 431; as Freethinkers, ii, 78, 189; president infallible, 540; in Congress, see Roberts and Smoot.

Morton, D. A., i, 264.

Morton, James F., ii, 170, 212, 402, 409, 458.

Most, Johann, i, 381, 396; ii, 222.

Mount Ingersoll, ii, 95.

Mount Macdonald, ii, 96.

Mulford, Prentice, i, 169, 178, 210, 212.

Munro, H. (ii), xii.

Munsen, James E., i, 202.

Murray, B. C., ii, 602.

Murray, M. M., ii, 527.

Murray, Norman, ii, 185.

Murray, W. H. H. i, 133.

Museums, New York, open Sunday, i, 492.

Nathan, Ernesto, ii, 308, 430.
Nation, The, ii, 490.
National Defense Ass'n, i, 426; ii, 65, 82, 84.
National Liberal League, i, 179, 181, 194, 231, 281, 314, 348, 361; name of American Secular Union adopted, 362.
Nationalism, i, 478ff.
Neal, Randolph, ii, 610.
National Reformer, ii, 76.
New Amsterdam, tercentenary, ii, 587.
Newark Liberal League, ii, 70.
"New England and the People up There," i, 258.
New Hampshire Secular Society, ii, 262.
New Rochelle, Ingersoll at, ii, 87; Paine monument presented to, 266.
New Testament, Comically Illustrated, ii, 219.
New Ulm, myth, ii, 295-6.
New York State Convention, i, 389.
Niemojewski, ii, 373.
Nietzsche, F. W., ii, 201.
Nineteenth Century Club, i, 350, 433.
North, J. W., i, 471, 502.
Noyes, J. H., i, 223, 411.
Noyes, Rufus K., ii, 293.
Nun, escaped, ii, 420.
Nuns as voters and votaries, ii, 410-11; none hurt in Mexico, 425.

Oath, right to register without making, i, 460; lecture on the, ii, 108.
Oddfellows, excommunicated, ii, 93.
O'Hare, Jas. M., ii, 541.

Ohio Liberal Society, ii, 70.
Olcott, H. S., i, 317.
Old Baldy, renamed, ii, 96.
Olds, Nettie M., ii, 114, 124.
Olson, D. E., ii, 346.
Omar Khayyam, ii, 84.
Oneida Community, i, 136, 222, 411.
Open Court, i, 433.
Oregon School law, ii, 559, 607.
Oregon Secular Union, i, 521; Liberal convention, 533; ii, 114.
Ormsby, W. L., i, 389.
Osborn, H. F., ii, 396.
Osgood, Anson G., ii, 262.
Oswald, Felix, i, 430; ii, 286.
Otto, Professor, ii, 459.
Overton, C. M., i, 431.

Packard, C. H., ii, 1ff.
Paine, Thomas, i, 176; Memorial Hall, 183; farm sold, 193, 297; history of monument cited, ii, 176; first celebration in England, 251; monument moved, 266; new evaluation, 329; quoted during World War, 469; Historical Ass'n, 349, 549; first celebration, 576; Greenwich Village tablet, 577; memorial building, 614.
Palmer, Courtlandt, i, 327, 347, 414, 433, 461.
Palmer, John G., ii, 263.
Papal sovereignty, and Congress, ii, 463.
Papers, anticlerical, Catholic list, ii, 441.
Parker, Harriet E., ii, 237.
Parker, Judge, in Moore case, ii, 80.
Parkhurst, Rev. C. H., ii, 68, 180.

Parkhurst, Henry M., ii, 316.
Parsons, Mrs. E. C., of trial marriage, ii, 288.
Parsons, Lucy, i, 518.
Parsons, Samos, ii, 75.
Parton, James, i, 189, 283, 389, 539.
Passion, Christ's examined, ii, 219.
Peabody, Philip G., i, 368.
Peace jubilee, McKinley's, ii, 169.
Peacock, E. P., ii, 419.
Pearv, R. E., godless Eskimos found by, ii, 359.
Peck, John, i, 234; ii, 436.
Peck, Harry T., ii, 179.
Pelletier, J. C., K. of C. advocate, ii, 538.
Pentecost, Hugh O., i, 423, 465, 517; ii, 82, 302.
People's Party and Freethinkers, ii, 82.
Pepper, Wm., i, 413.
Perectionism, i, 223.
Perkins, F. B., i, 446, 473, 498.
Perrin, E. W., ii, 374.
Peterson, Col. R., i, 180.
Philadelphia Liberal League, ii, 70.
Philippines, ii, 223; Katherine Mayo on, 621.
Phillips, Wendell, i, 365.
Pillsbury, Parker, ii, 110, 172.
Pinney, Lucian V., i, 431.
Plagiarising Ingersoll, ii, 177.
Play, Hannele, "blasphemous," ii, 84.
Plotts, Wm., i, 178; ii. 595.
Pocasset tragedy, i, 257.
Political Convention, (Freethinkers), i, 264.
Polygamists, political rights of, ii, 161, 189.

Polygamy, prohibition of, ii, 13.
Pope, Abner J., ii, 144.
Pope, U. S. Congress refused to approve nuncio from, ii, 463.
Pope, Leo XIII, encyclical by, ii, 94.
Pope toe kissed by Spanish royalty, ii, 579; against women's clothes, ii, 539.
Populism, ii, 15, 47; piety in, 83-4.
Portuguese Republic, ii, 70, 353, 445.
Positivism, i, 173.
Post, Amy, i, 493; ii, 110.
Post, Helen Wilmans, ii, 261, 299.
Post, Louis F., ii, 284, 330, 422, 505.
Postal laws of 1876, i, 177; rates advance, ii, 504.
Post office, New York, refuses The Truth Seeker, ii, 242.
Power, Lulie M., ii, 114.
Prayer in Wartime, Joseph Cannon on, ii, 422.
Preachers and actors, in prisons, ii, 558.
President McKinley's pious gestures, ii, 168; comments by Ingersoll, 169.
Press, the Liberal, i, 431.
Preston, S. H., i, 181, 186.
Prevention of conception, i, 225.
Pringle, Allen, ii, 131.
Private reading, ii, 159.
Proctor, R. A., i, 175, 462.
Prophecies, i, 517.
Purcell, Archbishop, i, 411.
Puffer, James B., ii, 339.
Pugilist, Freethinker, ii, 200.
Purdy, G. H., his remarks, ii, 163, 164.
Puritans, Rupert Hughes on, i, 113.

652 INDEX

Putnam, G. H., ii, 349.
Putnam, Samuel Porter, i,
234, 256-7, 294-5, 339, 341,
360, 388, 390, 432, 436, 455,
471, 485, 516, 541; ii, 10,
72, 104, 132, 134-137.
Putnam's Butte, ii, 95.

Queen of Heaven, her con-
sorts, ii, 622.
Queensbury, Marquis of, ii,
200.
Questionnaire, ii, 524.
Quigley, Abp., his Chicago
property, ii, 388.

Radical Review, i, 348.
Railroads, free to religious,
ii, 513.
Rapelyea, G. W., ii, 610.
Rarey, horse handler, i, 134
Rationalist, Auckland, N. Z.,
i, 389.
Rationalist Ass'n of Amer-
ica, ii, 335.
Rationalist Forum, ii, 594.
Raulston, J. T., ii, 610.
Ravlin, N. F., ii, 145.
Rawson, A. L., i, 181, 194,
281.
Raymer, C. D., ii, 458.
Red Cross, founder, ii, 441.
Reforms, oneness of, ii, 241.
Reed, Lewis G., ii, 303.
Reed, Milton, i, 148.
Reeman, Rev. E. H., ii, 480.
Reichwald, E. C., ii, 73, 378,
513.
Religion and morality, in
girls, ii, 397, 592-3.
Religion, defined, ii 589.
Religion in schools, ii, 199.
Religion of Humanity, i, 73.
Religion vs. science, ii, 571-
572.
Remsburg, John E., i, 266,
287, 364, 378, 389; ii, 93,
210, 513.
Replogle, Georgia, i, 505.

Replogle, Henry, i, 388, 401,
503.
Revivalism, Sunderland on
hysteria of, i, 327; Jordan
on drunkenness of, ii, 143.
Reynolds, Charles B., i, 364,
387, 414, 442; ii, 2, 130-1.
Reynolds, Mrs. F. C., i, 411.
Ricker, Marilla M., ii, 202,
351, 529.
Rickman, Clio, ii, 176.
Ridpath, John C., ii, 178,
201.
Riis, Jacob, ii, 407.
Riley, J. J., ii, 468.
Rinn, Joseph, ii, 426.
Risser, J. A., i, 411.
Robert Ingersoll Club at
Cornell, ii, 393.
Roberts, Brigham H., ii, 161,
189.
Roberts, John Emerson, ii,
119, 542, 544.
Robertson, Geo. L., ii, 64.
Robertson, John M., editor
National Reformer, ii, 76;
his "History of Free-
thought," 626.
Robertson, Morgan, i, 40n;
ii, 87, 129, 264, 447.
Robinet, John, i, 467.
Robinson, Gov. Chas., of
Kansas, i, 266; ii, 92.
Robinson, W. J., ii, 492, 520.
Robson, Stuart, ii, 235-6.
Robson, Stuart, Jr., ii, 394.
Rock of Ages, ii, 333.
Roe, Gilbert E., ii, 405.
Rogers, Will, ii, 526.
Rome, international cong-
ress, ii, 251; Atheist
Mayor, 308.
Roosevelt, Theodore, i, 399;
his allusion to Thomas
Paine, ii, 175, 202; re-
moves inscription on
coins, 293; on nature fak-
ers, 293, 315; plagiarizes

Ingersoll, 348; refuses to see pope, 355.
Roscoe, Hon. Christopher T., ii, 45, 53.
Rose, Ernestine L., ii, 70.
Rosenwald, Julius, wins prize with Ingersoll motto, ii, 564.
Ross, Stuart W., ii, 283.
Rossa, O'Donovan, i, 380.
Ross's, Australian Rationalist paper, ii, 593.
Rowe, William, i, 411.
Rowley, Henry, ii, 502.
Roy, A. L., i, 375, 377, 394.
Rudis-Jicinski, J., ii, 455.
Ruedebusch, E. F., ii, 159.
Russell, Bertrand, i, 187.
Russell, C. T., ii, 289, 493.
Russian Soviet, ii, 522.
Ryan, Daniel E., i, 234.

Sabbath breaking case of, i, 531.
St. Ann's church, verse on, i, 355.
St. Louis, Congress, ii, 254.
Salter, William, i, 437.
Salt Lake Liberals, ii, 145.
Salvation Army, war graft, ii, 489.
Samoa, shipping disaster, survivor of, i, 483-5.
Sampson, G. W., i, 405.
Sanders, Ellen P., ii, 544.
San Francisco, experiences in, i, 443, 543; Freethought Society, 472; strange results of earthquake, ii, 287; mediums, 479; materialist ass'n, ii, 337.
Sanger, Margaret L., her Woman Rebel," ii, 421, 451.
Sanger, Wm., ii, 443, 451.
Sanger, W. M., ii, 20.
Sanger, W. W., i, 209.
Santayana, George, ii, 594.

Sauve, Hazel, ii, 471.
Sawyer, Mattie, i, 151.
Schafer, A. E., pres. Brit. Ass'n, ii, 396.
Schmidt, Rev. Hans, murderer, ii, 404.
Schou, A. H., i, 457, 497.
Schreiner, Olive, i, 513.
Schroeder, J. H., i, 533.
Schroeder, Theodore, ii, 461.
Schuenemann-Pott, F., i, 471.
Schumm, George, i, 348.
Schurz, Carl, i, 327.
Science Hall, i, 173, 179.
Science in place of religion, ii, 550, 571; men of and Bryan, 572, 573.
Science League of Am., ii, 596; Am. Ass'n, ii, 396.
Scopes, J. T., ii, 610, 612.
Scott, Irving M., i, 474.
Scott-Browne, D. L., i, 337.
Searchlight, The, ii, 358.
Sears, Cyrus, ii, 264.
Seaver, Horace, i, 319, 494.
Secor, M. M., ii, 380.
Secular Thought, i, 429; suppressed, ii, 185.
Seeger, Justice A. F., his decision in Mt. Vernon school case, ii, 617.
Seibel, George, ii, 433-5.
Semple, Etta, ii, 111, 144, 436.
Servetus monument, ii, 432.
Serviss, G. P., ii, 62, 63; xi.
Severance, C., i, 470; (ii) xi.
Severance, Juliet, i, 287, 403, 517.
Seward, J. L., i, 12, 148.
Shatford, John E., ii, 341.
Shaw, George Bernard, i, 270; ii, 160, 260.
Shay, William B., ii, 46-7.
Shelley, Jonathan, i, 75ff.
Sherman, Henry H., i, 202, 277, 521.
Shevitch, M., i, 410.

Shipton, prophecy, i, 295.

Shinburn, Max, i, 30.

Shorthand pioneers, ii, 316.

Shrine Anecdote, ii, 289.

Silver, Queen, ii, 561.

Sinaloa colony, i, 481.

Sinclair, Upton, ii, 374.

Siwash Indians, Puget Sound, ii, 12; burial customs, 40.

"Sixteen Crucified Saviors," i, 287.

Skeetside, ii, 194, 630.

Slaten, Dr. A. Wakefield, i, 516; ii, 563, 579, 618.

Slattery, J. R., ii, 257, 346.

Slenker, Elmina D., i, 276, 425; ii, 316.

Slocum, The General, loss of, ii, 256.

Slokum, Si, i, 394; ii, 185.

Smart, C. Selden, ii, 207.

Smith, Alfred E., ii, 445.

Smith, Charles, T. S. contributor and salesman, organizer Four-A, ii, 580; 598, 620.

Smith, Goldwin, ii, 100, 364.

Smith, John Brown, i, 257.

Smith, Katie Kehm, ii, 76, 113.

Smith, Olive K., i, 287.

Smith, Orlando J., ii, 178.

Smoot, Reed, ii, 294.

Snohomish, Wash., life in, ii, 1-58.

Socialists denied seats in N. Y. legislature, ii, 520.

Society of Humanity, i, 194.

Somerby, Charles P., i, 180, 289, 349; ii, 68, 447.

Somerset, Lady, ii, 92.

Sons of Temperance, ii, 93.

Sons of Veterans, ii, 23-26; farewell reception, ii, 52.

Sotheran, Chas. i, 265.

South African Ass'n, ii, 352.

Sovereigns of Industry, i, 151, 172.

Soviet government ii, 522.

Spain, Freethinkers dispersed, ii, 69; war with, 162ff.

Spangler, Dr., reply to Bryan, ii, 550.

Spelling reform in T. S., i, 289.

Spencer, Herbert, in America, i, 327; debate with Harrison, 368; closing volume, ii, 215, 216, 230, 238, 242, 244; in recantation story, 342, 524.

Spinoza, Benedict, i, 373.

Spiritualism, work and break with Liberalism, i, 361, 386.

Spiritualist Lyceum, i, 151.

Spiritualist papers, i, 431, 465.

Sprading, C. T., "miracle" painting, ii, 410.

Stanton, Elizabeth Cady, ii, 70, 107, 110, 170.

Steiner, Franklin, ii, 69, 93, 420, 594.

Steinmetz, Chas. P., ii, 571, 585.

Stenographers, pioneers, ii, 316.

Stephen, Leslie, ii, 253.

Stephenson, Charles, i, 180.

Sterilization, ii, 102.

Stevens, E. A., i, 348, 432; ii, 481.

Stillman, James W., i, 337; proposed exclusion of Bible from mails, ii, 375.

Stockham, Alice B., ii, 260.

Stokes, Rose P., ii, 493, 520.

Stone, Henry A., i, 279.

Straton, Rev. J. R., ii, 557-558.

Straus, Oscar, eulogist of Paine, i, 365.

Street-speaking, arrests for in Los Angeles, ii, 310; in New York, 453, 509.

Strike of printers, ii, 508.

Sturoc, William C., ii, 236.

Suffrage, woman, identical views of Cardinal Gibbons and Abdul Hamid, ii, 411.

Sun, The, Tribute to Ingersoll, ii, 179.

Sunday, bill defeated in California, i, 524; history of Sunday fraud, no relation to resurrection of Jesus, ii, 71, 72; imprisonment for working on, 73, 374; law declared unconstitutional in California, 124; for what purpose enforced, 454.

Sunday, W. A., his theft from Ingersoll, ii, 397.

Sunderland, LaRoy, i, 327, 383.

Sunrise Club, ii, 311.

Surry, town of, i, 27ff.

Sutro, Adolph, i, 516.

Swartz, Clarence, ii, 75.

Sweetland, D. F., arrest of for selling The Truth Seeker, ii, 443.

Swift, Morrison I., ii, 212.

Swinton, John, i, 207, 377; ii, 209.

Symes, Joseph, ii, 252.

Taber, Henry M., ii, 149.

Tacoma Secular Union, ii, 70.

Taft, W. H., controversy about the religion of, ii, 315; no congratulations to Pope, 355.

Talmage, Rev. T. DeWitt, i, 309.

Teed, Cyrus R., i, 194; ii, 338.

Teller, Woolsey, first letter, ii, 320, 394, 620.

Temporal sovereignty, Congress denied pope's, ii, 463.

Tennessee, anti - evolution law, ii, 609.

Tenney, Daniel K., ii, 447.

Thane, F., ii, 320, 542.

Thanksgiving mass, presidents attend, 432.

Thomas, Sen. Charles, against God in League of Nations, ii, 522.

Thomas, Henry J., i, 248, 521.

Thomas, Norman, ii, 375; at Paine Anniversary, 599.

Thomas, Rev. H. W., i, 301.

Thompson, Denman, i, 100.

Thorne, Stephen R., ii, 201.

Thornton, Walter, ii, 20, 320.

Tillotson, Mary E., dress reformer i, 257, 375, 404, 404.

Tilton, Josephine, i, 228.

Titanic, loss of, ii, 387.

Tolstoy, his "Kreutzer Sonata" non-mailable, i, 513; excommunicated, ii, 210.

Toomey, Samuel, ii, 361.

Toronto Secular Soc., ii, 70.

Topolobampo and Sinaloa colony, i, 481.

Towns without churches, ii, 543, 565.

Townsend, E. W., ii, 630.

Train, G. F., i, 259; ii, 253.

Traubel, Horace, i, 194.

Tribes and peoples, godless, ii, 359, 566.

Treibel, Fritz, ii, 376.

Trinity church, pastor imported by, ii, 67.

Trowbridge, Robert, ii, 341.

Truelove, Edward, ii, 186.

Truth Seeker Annual, i, 364.

Truth Seeker, The, i, 138, to end; exchanges, 328; Truth Seeker Company, i, 332; prohibited in Canada, ii, 99; moves headquarters, 264; bills to exclude from mails, 441; denied distribution by Postoffice, ii, 487-492; comes to Vesey St., 530; Jubilee Number, 578; selling on street, 580.

Tuck, Edward, ii, 256; gifts to Dartmouth, 360; xiii.

Tucker, Benjamin R., i, 189, 270, 403, 501; on courting prosecution, i, 531; ii, 75, 92, 476.

Tullson, Herbert, ii, 583.

Turner, John, ii, 230-2.

Twentieth Century, weekly, ii, 62.

Tyndall, John, ii, 78, 113, 585; rejected by Canada, 113.

Underhill, Edw. F., i, 207; ii, 172.

Underwood, B. F., i, 179, 268, 330.

United States statute, ii, 156.

Valley Forge prayer, ii, 220.

Vanasek, Thomas S., ii, 397.

Vanbrugh, play cited, i, 91.

Van der Weyde, W. M., ii, 350; xi.

Van Deusen, Alonzo, i, 477.

Van Doren, Carl, ii, 576.

Vanni, Charles, ii, 309.

Vatican: U. S. Congress refused to approve papal nuncio, ii, 463; British envoy to, 437.

Verity, J. S., i, 383.

Verse, Old Man's Choice, i, 412.

Villard, Oswald G., ii, 490.

Virgin birth, rejected by Fosdick, ii, 579.

Visitation Convent, i, 523.

Voelkel, Titus, ii, 75, 465.

Vosburgh, Mrs., a virgin, i, 375.

Waisbrooker, Lois, ii, 68, 222, 341.

Waite, Judge C. B., ii, 63, 73, 341.

Waite, Lucy, ii, 342.

Wakefield, Homer, explodes a civil war myth, ii, 428.

Wakeman, Clara, ii, 426.

Wakeman, Thaddeus B., i, 194, 228, 303, 327, 388, 400, 411; ii, 82, 110, 187, 366ff, 418.

Walker, Edwin C., i, 280, 312, 402, 424-5; ii, 72, 79, 121, 277, 413, 476; xi.

Walker, Dr. Mary, i, 375, 404.

Walker, Ryan, ii, 223.

Walker, Thomas, i, 431.

Walser, G. H., founder of Liberal, Mo., i, 297, 330, 388, 401.

Wanamaker, John, as postmaster-general, i, 490, 513.

War, Spanish-American, ii, 162ff; world war, how begun, 422ff; prayers for victory, 438; where God was, 439; welfare societies, ii, 506, 523.

Ward, Mrs. Humphry, i, 513.

Ward, Lester F., ii, 372, 417.

Ward, Osborne, i, 150.

Wardwell, Burnham, i, 412.

Warren, Josiah, i, 450.

Warwick, Joseph, ii, 448.

Washburn, Lemuel K., i, 193, 304; ii, 93, 374; x.

Washington, D. C., sale of Sunday papers prohibited; action by Secular League, ii, 143.

Washington, George, Sabbath breaker, ii, 117; the Wall street placque, 298.

Washington Secular League, ii, 319.

Watkins Convention, i, 228.

Watson, Thomas A., ii, 409, 569.

Watts, Arthur, ii, 311.

Watts, Charles, in U. S., i, 327, 413, 464; ii, 87, 126, 135, 184, 226, 281-3.

Weeks, Archibald, ii, 623.

Weik, Jesse W., proposes marker for Herndon, ii, 478.

Weirs, Edgar Swann, ii, 391.

West Point Catholic steal, ii, 140, 155.

Westbrook, R. B., i, 466, 491, 519; ii, 186.

Wettstein, O t t o, designs badgepin, i, 327, 374, 387.

Weyman, Elliott, i, 98.

Wheeler, George B., i, 276.

Wheeler, J. M., ii, 70.

Wheelock, Mrs. G. A., ii, 495.

Wheless, Joseph, ii, 615.

White, Andrew D., ii, 503.

White, Victor, ii, 176.

White, Rev. W. O., i, 148.

Whitehead, Celia, i, 276.

Whitman, Walt, i, 194, 313.

Whist Club, Omega, ii, 47.

Who's Who, Liberal, of 1878, 236.

William II, his piety, ii, 454.

Williams, Sen. G. E., i, 257.

Williams, John Sharp, ii, 512.

Williams, Roger, i, 114.

Wilmans, Helen, ii, 142.

Wilson, Dr. J. B., ii, 214.

Wilson, Woodrow, parades to mass, ii, 412, 432-3; on evolution, 574.

Wingate, Gen. G., i, 22.

Wise, J. B., prosecuted for mailing Bible verse, ii, 82, 103, 124, 142.

Witches, surviving belief in, i, 112.

Wixon, Susan H., i, 351; ii, 401.

Woman Suffrage, ii, 107.

Woman's Bible, ii, 107.

Wood, Edwin, i, 417.

Wood, William, ii, 481.

Woodhull, Victoria, i, 172, 178.

Woodford, Stewart L., i, 350, 493.

Woodrow, Dr., removed from seminary faculty, i, 371.

World's Fair, C h i c a g o, closed on Sunday by padded petitions, ii, 60.

Wright, Elizur, i, 202, 232, 277, 281, 385.

Wu Tingfang, i, 70.

Wynne, postmaster-general, ii, 243.

York, J. L., i, 179; ii, 285.

Young Men's C h r i s t i a n Ass'n, its war profiteering, ii, 488, 490, 506-8.

Young Men's Infidel Ass'n, ii, 395.

Youmans, Edw. L., i, 327, 429.

Zedtwitz, Baroness, author "Double Doctrine of the Church," ii, 380.

THE ATHEIST VIEWPOINT

AN ARNO PRESS / NEW YORK TIMES COLLECTION

Amberley, [John Russell], Viscount. **An Analysis of Religious Belief.** 1877.

Atheist Magazines: A Sampling, 1927–1970. New Introduction by Madalyn Murray O'Hair. 1972.

Besant, Annie. **The Freethinker's Text-Book:** Part II—Christianity. n.d.

[Burr, William Henry.] **Revelations of Antichrist.** 1879.

Cardiff, Ira D. **What Great Men Think of Religion.** 1945.

Champion of Liberty: Charles Bradlaugh. 1934.

Cohen, Chapman. **Primitive Survivals in Modern Thought.** 1935.

Drews, Arthur. **The Witnesses to the Historicity of Jesus.** Translated by Joseph McCabe. 1912.

Ferrer [y Guardia], Francisco. **The Origins and Ideals of the Modern School.** Translated by Joseph McCabe. 1913.

Foote, G. W. and W. P. Ball, editors. **The Bible Handbook.** 1961.

Gibbon, Edward. **History of Christianity.** 1883.

Holyoake, George Jacob. **The History of the Last Trial by Jury for Atheism in England.** 1851.

Komroff, Manuel, editor. **The Apocrypha or Non-Canonical Books of the Bible:** The King James Version. 1936.

Lewis, Joseph. **Atheism and Other Addresses.** 1960.

McCarthy, William. **Bible, Church and God.** 1946.

Macdonald, George E. **Fifty Years of Freethought.** 1929, 1931. Two volumes in one.

Manhattan, Avro. **Catholic Imperialism and World Freedom.** 1952.

Meslier, Jean. **Superstition in All Ages.** Translated from the French original by Anna Knoop. 1890.

Nietzsche, Friedrich. **The Antichrist.** 1930.

O'Hair, Madalyn Murray. **What on Earth Is an Atheist!** 1969.

Robertson, J. M. **A Short History of Freethought.** 1957.

Russell, Bertrand. **Atheism: Collected Essays, 1943–1949.** 1972.

Shelley, Percy Bysshe. **Selected Essays on Atheism.** (n.d.) 1972.

Teller, Woolsey. **The Atheism of Astronomy.** 1938.

Wells, H. G. **Crux Ansata:** An Indictment of the Roman Catholic Church. 1944.